ORACLE Performance Tuning

ORACLE Performance Tuning

Peter Corrigan and Mark Gurry

O'Reilly & Associates, Inc.
103 Morris Street, Suite A
Sebastopol, CA 95472

ORACLE Performance Tuning

by Peter Corrigan and Mark Gurry

Copyright © 1993 O'Reilly & Associates, Inc. All rights reserved.
Printed in the United States of America.

Editor: Deborah Russell

Production Editor: Leslie Chalmers

Printing History:

October 1993:	First Edition.
December 1993:	Minor Corrections.
June 1994:	Minor Corrections.

This book is printed on acid-free paper with 50% recycled content, 10-15% post-consumer waste. O'Reilly & Associates is committed to using paper with the highest recycled content available consistent with high quality.

ISBN: 1-56592-048-1

Foreword

Because ORACLE performance tuning is my specialty, it was a real pleasure to be asked to write the foreword to *ORACLE Performance Tuning* by Peter Corrigan and Mark Gurry. In October of 1989 at International ORACLE Users' Week in Dallas, I gave my first lecture on performance tuning with Dr. Rick Stahlhut; we called that lecture "It's Not in the Manuals." Since that time, I have traveled all over the world presenting tips and techniques on how to tune an ORACLE application and database.

In my years of working with ORACLE, I've seen the system, the requirements for performance tuning, and the documentation increase in complexity. With Version 4 of ORACLE, the first version I used, there were only three manuals describing everything I needed to know about the system. Now there are three manuals just for the database administrator. ORACLE's multiplicity of manuals and huge array of choices is a double-edged sword: What I like most about ORACLE is that I have all this information and all these choices; what I dislike most about ORACLE is that I have all this information and all these choices!

Nowhere is the need for good and easy-to-find documentation more apparent than in the area of performance tuning. When I gave my first lecture on performance, it was based on ORACLE Version 5, a far simpler database than the one we work with today. The database changed dramatically with the onset of Version 6, largely because ORACLE listened carefully to its customers and started to supply the information those customers needed. The problem with Version 6 was that, although ORACLE provided many tools, they didn't always give us the know-how to be able to use them to best advantage. With Version 7, it's all coming together.

As the complexity of the ORACLE database has increased, so has the complexity—and the importance—of performance tuning. It's a problem shared by all ORACLE shops. I keep a full-time staff of consultants busy helping clients solve performance problems.

(We call this service Team OPTIMAL [ORACLE Performance Tuning of I/O Memory Applications and Lock Contention]). For years I have felt that the ORACLE market has needed a good book on performance tuning. In fact, I had planned to write one myself! But, between managing my own company and handling my commitments as President of the International ORACLE Users Group, I have not been able to find the time to write this book. Luckily for all of us, Peter and Mark did. *ORACLE Performance Tuning* will give you the information you need to solve your ORACLE performance problems. No matter what your skill level, this book has something to offer you. Enjoy reading it!

Michael J. Corey
President International ORACLE Users Group
Principal, Database Technologies, Inc.

Table of Contents

List of Figures

List of Tables

Preface

The ORACLE relational database management system (RDBMS) is the most popular database management system in use today. Organizations ranging from government agencies to small businesses, from large financial institutions to universities, use ORACLE to make sense of their data. Running on computers as diverse as mainframes, minicomputers, workstations, PCs, and Macintoshes, ORACLE provides virtually identical functions across machine boundaries.

ORACLE offers tremendous power and flexibility, but at some cost. It is a large and complex data processing environment, including dozens of software components, hundreds of statements, commands, and utilities, and about 50 volumes of documentation. Although in theory ORACLE could be administered by a single user, in practice its administration and use are most commonly shared by many people performing a number of specific design, administration, and programming roles.

With this multiplicity of functions and users comes the potential for diffusion—and confusion—when things go wrong. Because ORACLE is a thoroughly tested and well-functioning system, what goes wrong isn't basic operation, but performance. With any large piece of software operating in the real world, the number of users increases as time goes on and organizational needs grow. More and more data needs to be managed. More complex queries need to be processed. More reports need to be produced. Groups within the organization need new capabilities. As new operating system releases and networking features are added to the environment, programmers develop more demanding applications. The load on the system grows, and performance suffers. And people in the organization start to ask questions:

"I've been waiting 30 minutes for a response to my query—what's going on?"

"My system administrator says our system is I/O-bound—what can I do?"

"Our application ran fine in testing, but the response is terrible now that we're in production—help!"

"Our backups take too long—how can we speed them up?"

"Our database is fully normalized, but response time is bad—why?"

How do you respond to these questions? Some organizations buy more powerful and expensive computers. Some hire expert consultants. Although you may eventually find that adding computing power is necessary, there is a lot you can do to increase the performance of the system you already have. That's why we wrote this book: to share what we've learned—sometimes at great expense to our patience and hairlines—during our 15 years of tuning ORACLE systems. Every ORACLE manager, designer, programmer, database administrator, and system administrator has a bottom drawer crammed full of helpful tips, tricks, traps, articles, and e-mail messages that help them run their ORACLE systems more efficiently. What we've tried to do in this book is to collect the contents of these bottom drawers and organize them into a comprehensive collection of performance tuning suggestions for ORACLE.

This book is the result of our own experiences with a number of different ORACLE systems. We've used at least ten different platforms at a dozen different sites—ranging from government to manufacturing to finance, and from mainframe to minicomputer to personal computers and workstations. The book reflects our own experiences, and those of many other ORACLE users and administrators throughout the world. In this book, we pull together our real-life experiences in the hope that we can save you the headaches we've all suffered while trying to get a little better response, to use a little less memory, and to get that report out a little bit faster.

This book is aimed especially at people who use ORACLE, of course. But what it has to say about database performance and tuning has meaning beyond the confines of an ORACLE system. Sites running any large database system—Informix, Sybase, Progress, Ingres, even non-relational systems using a hierarchical or network model—share common performance problems and can benefit from the tune-ups we suggest in this book. We try to answer general questions that go beyond the specifics of the ORACLE products:

- How important is tuning—what does it buy you?

- How can you tune at each stage of the system development life cycle?

- How can you coordinate your tuning efforts with those of other people at your site so there are no weak links in the great tuning extravaganza? Will too many cooks spoil the broth?

- How can you use your site's own unique configuration of memory, disk, CPU, and networking connections to best advantage?

- How can you examine and understand your site's own workload, turnaround requirements, and response times?

- How can you be proactive—not reactive—so you can nip tuning problems in the bud, or keep them from occurring in the first place?

This book takes a thorough look at database performance problems, but it does not attempt to teach you how to use the ORACLE products and features it describes. We assume in this book that you are familiar with SQL and the other ORACLE tools, statements, and concepts we mention. We are not attempting to teach you how to use any of these ORACLE products, but to tune them so they work more efficiently in your own particular environment. (Remember, you have 50 volumes of documentation!) Rather than a coordinated tutorial, this book is a collection of tips and tricks in many different areas. Start with the sections of most concern to you, and use them in conjunction with ORACLE's own product and performance manuals.

This book cannot cover all the details of tuning specific operating systems. ORACLE runs on so many hardware and software platforms that we can't address all of the machine- and operating system-specific performance issues that may arise. You'll have to look carefully at your own system and system documentation for help in this area.

As we've mentioned, in most ORACLE shops, responsibility for system operation and use is distributed among a number of types of administrators and users. Depending on who you are and what your responsibilities are, you may be more interested in some parts of the book than in others. Most readers will read Part I, the parts of the book pertaining to their own job roles, and the summary of Version 7 in Appendix A. However, don't forget that your role overlaps others, and that the tuning and performance decisions that others make will affect your own ability to improve system efficiency. Reading, or at least skimming, the other sections of this book should help you to coordinate your job with others in your organization.

This book is divided into seven parts.

Part I, Overview. Chapters 1 and 2 introduce performance and tuning issues, and describe overall system tuning operations and common performance problems with different phases of development and different system resources (memory, disk, CPU, network).

Part II, Tuning for Planners and Managers. Chapters 3 and 4 describe how the equipment and configuration decisions you make during the planning stage will affect system performance for years to come. These chapters focus on management checkpoints that affect performance, the standards you need to establish for ORACLE database and application design and development, and the decisions you'll need to make about response times and workload at your site.

Part III, Tuning for Designers and Analysts. Chapters 5 and 6 describe how to design for performance without sacrificing functionality. If you don't design for performance, the chances that your application will perform successfully are slim, regardless of the tuning magic of the database administrators (DBAs), programmers, and system administrators at your site. The tuning advice in these chapters focuses on normalizing and denormalizing your database and defining indexes.

Part IV, Tuning for Programmers. Chapters 7 through 10 describe how to get the best performance out of your programs. The tuning advice in these chapters focuses on SQL, PL/SQL, and SQL*Forms, and on how to select a table- or row-locking strategy that results in the best performance.

Part V, Tuning for Database Administrators. Chapters 11 through 14 describe how to structure, monitor, and tune your database and its data dictionary so it uses memory and disk efficiently. These chapters show you how to tune a new database, how to monitor and tune an existing one to remedy performance problems, and how to use a variety of ORACLE diagnostic and tuning tools.

Part VI, Tuning for System Administrators. Chapters 15 through 18 describe how to tune long-running jobs so they don't degrade overall system performance, how to tune in a client-server environment, how to perform capacity planning, and how to do certain kinds of system-specific tuning.

Part VII, Appendices. Appendices A through D contain summary material. Appendix A is a summary of the new features in ORACLE Version 7 that affect performance or allow you to tune your system in new ways. Appendix B lists the common questions we hear about performance, their answers, and references to sections of the book where you can learn more. Appendix C contains a summary of how you can tune the ORACLE Financials product. Appendix D contains a list of dynamic performance tables you can monitor.

Which ORACLE Release?

In general, the suggestions in this book apply to ORACLE systems running on all platforms, from mainframes to PCs, from VSE to VMS to UNIX to DOS. In a few cases, our comments apply to one particular hardware platform or operating system. In these cases, we'll clearly note this limitation.

Many ORACLE shops are now running Version 7 (ORACLE7), the latest and greatest ORACLE release. Many more are still running Version 6 or even Version 5. We've tried to share our experiences with Version 7 by focusing on the special features and peculiarities of that release, and we've included an appendix that summarizes those features. But most of the tips and tricks described in this book are of equal use in Version 6 (and earlier) systems. Where a tuning suggestion is applicable only to Version 7, we'll note that in the text. Because Version 7 is still new, we expect to evolve this book over time as more and more users gain familiarity with Version 7 and its performance implications.

Chapter 9, *Tuning SQL*Forms*, focuses on SQL*Forms Version 3. Chapter 16, *Tuning in the Client-server Environment*, discusses SQL*Net Version 1 and Version 2.

We'd Like to Hear From You

A note about the advice in this book: we try to give you the benefit of our experience tuning many databases, and we've tried to standardize our experiences as best we can. The fact is, though, standard advice isn't always enough for non-standard situations. In very large and complex organizations—and there are many ORACLE sites that run 25 hours a day (or so it seems), servicing 25,000 or more online users—you'll find that there is no substitute for your experience and your ability to be flexible and adaptive. With such applications, you'll need to experiment, compromise, take risks, and take precautions; in short, you'll need to cope with whatever is thrown at you! We'd appreciate it if you'd share your experiences with us so we can include advice in future editions of this book that may help others take advantage of what you've learned.

We have tested and verified all of the information in this book to the best of our ability, but you may find that features have changed slightly (or even that we have made mistakes!). Please let us know about any errors you find, as well as your suggestions for future editions, by writing:

O'Reilly & Associates, Inc.
103 Morris Street, Suite A
Sebastopol, CA 95472
1-800-998-9938 (in US or Canada)
1-707-829-0515 (international/local)
1-707-829-0104 (FAX)

You can also send us messages electronically. To be put on the mailing list or request a catalog, send e-mail to:

nuts@ora.com   (via the Internet)
uunet!ora!nuts (via UUCP)

To ask technical questions or comment on the book, send e-mail to:

bookquestions@ora.com   (via the Internet)

Conventions

The following typographic conventions are used in this book:

Italic	is used for filenames, utility names, and command names in systems such as UNIX and VMS. It is also used to highlight comments in command examples.
Bold	is used in examples for emphasis, to show the feature being described in the section containing the example.
`Constant Width`	is used in examples to show the SQL, PL/SQL, SQL*Forms, or SQL*DBA input that you enter, it is also used to show the output from commands or programs.
`Constant Bold`	is used in examples to show prompts displayed by SQL*DBA and other products.
`Constant italic`	is used in examples to show variables for which a context-specific substitution should be made. The variable *`filename`*, for example, would be replaced by some actual filename.
. . .	stands for text in an example of code or output that has been omitted for clarity or to save space.

Examples

The examples in this book are available electronically in a number of ways: by FTP, FTPMAIL, BITFTP, and UUCP. The cheapest, fastest, and easiest ways are listed first. If you read from the top down, the first one that works for you is probably the best. Use FTP if you are directly on the Internet. Use FTPMAIL if you are not on the Internet but can send electronic mail to Internet sites and receive it from these sites (this includes CompuServe users). Use BITFTP if you send electronic mail via BITNET. Use UUCP if none of the above works.

NOTE: The examples were prepared using a UNIX system. If you are running UNIX, you can use them without modification. If you are running on another platform, you may need to modify these examples slightly. For example, whereas under UNIX every line ends with a line feed character (the carriage return is implicit), under DOS every line must end with explicit line feed and carriage return characters. Depending upon your own configuration and transfer method, you may need to append carriage returns. See the README file accompanying the examples for additional information.

FTP

To use FTP, you need a machine with direct access to the Internet. A sample session is shown below. For clarity, we deviate from our typeface conventions in this session by showing the input you enter in boldface.

```
% ftp ftp.uu.net
Connected to ftp.uu.net.
220 ftp.UU.NET FTP server (Version 6.34 Thu Oct 22 14:32:01 EDT 1992) ready.
Name (ftp.uu.net:janet): anonymous
331 Guest login ok, send e-mail address as password.
Password: janetv@xyz.com          Use your user name and host here
230 Guest login ok, access restrictions apply.
ftp> cd /published/oreilly/nutshell/oracle
250 CWD command successful.
ftp> get README
200 PORT command successful.
150 Opening ASCII mode data connection for README (xxxx bytes).
226 Transfer complete.
local: README remote: README
xxxx bytes received in xxx seconds (xxx Kbytes/s)
ftp> get orcs93
200 PORT command successful.
150 Opening ASCII mode data connection for orcs93 (xxxx bytes).
226 Transfer complete. local: orcs93 remote: orcs93
xxxx bytes received in xxx seconds (xxx Kbytes/s)
ftp> quit
221 Goodbye.
%
```

The **orcs93** file contains the major examples from the book. Follow the instructions at the beginning of the **orcs93** file to create the individual example files. The **README** file contains additional instructions for how to use **orcs93** and suggestions for how to modify this file for your own system.

FTPMAIL

FTPMAIL is a mail server available to anyone who can send electronic mail to and receive it from Internet sites. This includes any company or service provider that allows email connections to the Internet. Here's how you do it..

You send mail to *ftpmail@online.ora.com*. In the message body, give the FTP commands you want to run. The server will run anonymous FTP for you and mail the files back to you. To get a complete help file, send a message with no subject and the single word "help" in the body. The following is an example mail session that should get you the examples. This command sends you a listing of the files in the selected directory, and the requested example files. The listing is useful if there's a later version of the examples you're interested in.

```
% mail ftpmail@online.ora.com
Subject:
reply janetv@xyz.com            Where you want files mailed
open
cd /published/oreilly/nutshell/oracle
dir
get README
mode binary
uuencode
get orcs93
quit
```

A signature at the end of the message is acceptable as long as it appears after "quit."

BITFTP

BITFTP is a mail server for BITNET users. You send it electronic mail messages requesting files, and it sends you back the files by electronic mail. BITFTP currently serves only users who send it mail from nodes that are directly on BITNET, EARN, or NetNorth. BITFTP is a public service of Princeton University. Here's how it works.

To use BITFTP, send mail containing your FTP commands to *BITFTP@PUCC*. For a complete help file, send HELP as the message body.

The following is the message body you should send to BITFTP:

```
FTP   ftp.uu.net   NETDATA
USER  anonymous
PASS  your Internet e-mail address (not your BITNET address)
CD    /published/oreilly/nutshell/oracle
DIR
GET README
GET orcs93
QUIT
```

Questions about BITFTP can be directed to *MAINT@PUCC* on BITNET.

UUCP

UUCP is standard on virtually all UNIX systems, and is available for IBM-compatible PCs and Apple Macintoshes. The examples are available by UUCP via modem from UUNET; UUNET's connect-time charges apply. You can get the examples from UUNET whether you have an account or not. If you or your company has an account with UUNET, you will have a system with a direct UUCP connection to UUNET. Find that system, and type:

```
uucp uunet\!~/published/oreilly/nutshell/oracle/README yourhost\!~/yourname/
uucp uunet\!~/published/oreilly/nutshell/oracle/orcs93 yourhost\!~/yourname/
```

The backslashes can be omitted if you use the Bourne shell (*sh*) instead of *csh*. The example file should appear some time later (up to a day or more) in the directory */usr/spool/uucppublic/yourname*. If you don't have an account but would like one so that you can get electronic mail, then contact UUNET at 703-204-8000.

If you don't have a UUNET account, you can set up a UUCP connection to UUNET using the phone number 1-900-468-7727. As of this writing, the cost is 50 cents per minute. The charges will appear on your next telephone bill. The login name is "uucp" with no password. For example, an *L.sys/Systems* entry might look like:

```
uunet Any ACU 19200 1-900-468-7727 ogin:--ogin: uucp
```

Your entry may vary depending on your UUCP configuration. If you have a PEP-capable modem, make sure `s50=255s111=30` is set before calling.

GOPHER

If you are on the Internet, you can use the *gopher* facility to learn about online access to examples through the O'Reilly Online Information Resource. Access *gopher.ora.com* as appropriate from your site.

Acknowledgments

We owe a debt to many people who have helped us get to this point. We both started our computing careers back in the days when computer resources were expensive and hard to find. Code had to run efficiently—or it wouldn't run at all. As hardware prices have come down, too many people have forgotten the art of tuning. We are grateful, though, that we learned the early discipline of coding right from the start with performance in mind.

The idea of this book first came to us when Mark was asked by a customer to determine whether it would be feasible to use client-server computing at a large site in Australia where client machines were located as much as 2000 miles away from the server. The team had eight days to bring response times down from as much as 22 seconds to under 2.5 seconds. Making this deadline required a lot of tuning research and a little magic. After the dust had settled, Mark started working with Peter and with Shane Hocking (a Telecom ORACLE DBA and senior technical support) on the idea of a book on performance tuning. In a series of meetings at the RedSox Hamburger shop in Melbourne, we discussed our respective bottom drawers of performance tips over burgers and fries. After some time, Shane decided to withdraw from the project, but with the help of some experts like Andrew McPherson (an ORACLE DBA and senior technical support) and

Stuart Worthington (an ORACLE consultant currently specializing in ORACLE Financials administration and tuning in Germany), we continued to meet, to argue over contents and structure, and to scribble ideas. We are grateful to Andrew for suggesting that we structure the book into parts aimed at the different types of ORACLE users. Our goal was to have a book in time for the Asian Pacific ORACLE User Group Conference to raise money for our user group, and with a good many long nights we had one.

That early book draft has changed almost beyond recognition in the past year. Bill Johnson (the marketing director of MARKADD and a former newspaper editor and author), and Chris Jones and John Darragh (and John's staff) from ORACLE Australia helped us a great deal by covering our draft with red ink and good ideas. People started to ask for the book in Australia and elsewhere, and we found ourselves spending far too much time printing copies and waiting in line at the Australian Post. We decided to take the next step and see if we could find an international publisher who would be interested in the book.

We had long admired O'Reilly & Associates and the Nutshell guides. *System Performance Tuning* by Mike Loukides was a particular favorite. We took a chance and sent the book off to Tim O'Reilly. To our surprise, Tim himself called one day to say he might be interested. (Being ORA fans, having Tim on the phone to us was like having Prince Charles or Lady Di call a royalist!) Tim recommended that we contact acquisitions editor Deborah Russell in the Cambridge office because she had an interest in database books. We sent e-mail back and forth, arguing about possible new material and restructurings, and we were delighted to finally get the go-ahead. Working with Debby, who was so clearly a professional editor, has been terrific. We have been very happy with the editorial guidance (i.e., her insisting again and again that we needed to write clearly and explain completely), as well as the speed with which our sometimes rough text was transformed into readable prose as our little book mushroomed to almost three times its original size. We were all determined to have a book in print in time for the International ORACLE User's Group (IOUG) conference in the Autumn of 1993, and doing so took many nights and weekends on all our parts.

Writing, editing, and producing this book was a feat made possible by advances in computing and connectivity. We wrote the book in Richmond, Australia on our separate personal computers (Peter on a PC, Mark on a Mac), then sent our Microsoft Word files to Debby in Cambridge, Massachusetts—some on Mac disks and others via e-mail. Because of the 14-hour time difference, we communicated throughout the hectic cycle of editing and rewriting almost exclusively by e-mail (with a little help from Federal Express, FAX machines, and occasional phone calls at odd hours). The three of us wrote and rewrote these Mac files until that final moment when the book was converted to O'Reilly's own FrameMaker format for final production. Along with our other acknowledgments, a hearty thank-you goes to the Internet for making possible almost instantaneous communication across continents, time zones, and hardware platforms.

We have so many other people to thank. In addition to Shane Hocking, Andrew McPherson, Chris Jones, John Darragh, and Stuart Worthington for their early contributions (and a special thanks to Stuart for writing Appendix C, *Tuning ORACLE Financials*), we would like to thank those who reviewed the revised version of the book on a very tight schedule; they come from all over the world, from the United States to Australia to Germany; this is appropriate since ORACLE is very much an international product. Thanks to Michael Corey, IOUG president and tuning expert who reviewed the book and contributed the Foreword; Martin Picard, president of Patrol Software and former Director of Networking Products at ORACLE; Ian McGregor from the Stanford Linear Accelerator Center; Bob Fees, a senior information technology management consultant; Lurline Archay, director of Park Lane in Australia, president of the Australia and New Zealand ORACLE user group, and IOUG vice-president; analyst/programmers Frank Magliozzi, Colin Trevaskis, and Ross Young; Paul Kendall, project leader of ECPLAN, a large Telecom ORACLE application; and Joyce Chan, an analyst/designer who formerly worked for ORACLE in Canada. We are very grateful for these review comments and have made every effort to integrate them into the book. Thanks as well to all of the people we've worked with, too many to be named, at ORACLE sties through the years and around the world. Many of your suggestions, warnings, tips, and caveats have made their way into this book.

Please note that, although a number of people who work for ORACLE read this manuscript and made suggestions for improvements, they did so in an informal way. Their help is not to be construed as an official endorsement of this book by ORACLE Corporation.

A big thank-you to all of the people at O'Reilly & Associates who brought this book into being. In addition to thanking Debby Russell, who made it all happen, we're grateful to Leslie Chalmers, who managed the production, and Lar Kaufman, Mike Sierra, Clairemarie Fisher O'Leary, and Stephen Spainhour, who formatted the final text under a very tight deadline; to Gigi Estabrook, who worked against the clock to get the text out for technical review; to Edie Freedman and Jennifer Niederst who designed the cover and the internal format; to Chris Reilley and Michelle Willey who created the figures; and to Ellie Cutler who helped with the index.

A final thank you to our wives, Mary Corrigan and Juliana Gurry, for those many months of listening to us say, "We're almost finished." Finally, we are!

I

Overview

Part I introduces the process of performance tuning in the ORACLE system: what does your organization get out of tuning, who takes responsibility for tuning, when do they tune, and when do they stop tuning? It takes a look at the tools ORACLE provides to help in the tuning process and at the special tuning requirements for the latest version of the ORACLE RDBMS, Version 7. It also looks at the most common sources of performance problems in ORACLE.

1

Introduction to ORACLE Performance Tuning

In the ORACLE Relational Database Management System (RDBMS), as in any large and complicated system, performance is a key issue. It's an issue that you need to deal with on an ongoing basis, through all the stages of your system's life cycle: from planning to design to programming to testing to production. Your responsibility for performance never stops. Even after a system is in production, you'll need to keep monitoring and tuning and improving it as time and circumstances change.

Performance tuning was a simpler process in the old days of a mainframe computer, a centralized database, and batch jobs. Technology has changed, and requirements for tuning have changed along with it. Several major developments in computing have had a dramatic impact on performance issues for ORACLE products:

Downsizing. In recent years, there has been increasing pressure on organizations to downsize their hardware configurations. Inevitably, though, when an organization makes the decision to save hardware dollars by replacing its mainframe with a system costing one-tenth as much, the organization doesn't downsize its throughput needs and response time expectations. Its users, who are accustomed to mainframe response times, continue to expect the same performance from the downsized system. If anything, an organization expects more, not less, when it moves to a new system. It's not impossible to get equivalent or better responsiveness, when you move from a mainframe to a smaller system, but it's going to take some work. Performance tuning is vital.

Client-server and distributed databases. New technologies demand new types of tuning. With client-server (which we'll discuss later in this chapter and in detail in Chapter 16, *Tuning in the Client-server Environment*) and distributed databases, your user processes may now communicate with the RDBMS over a network instead of within a single processor. As your system grows to encompass new platforms, new operating systems, and new network models, you'll find that you'll need to know more about the overall computing environment to get decent performance out of your system.

Graphical user interfaces (GUIs) have added a new dimension to databases and database access, but the new interfaces require special kinds of tuning to avoid dragging down the performance of a system. Because GUIs make systems more usable and more friendly, GUIs may also open doors to more users in your system.

An increase in users and processes. As time goes on more users, administrators, and managers within your organization become familiar with the ORACLE RDBMS and its associated products. Managers find that they can get quick results from the system, so they make more queries. The organization grows and diversifies, so more data is added to the database. As users, data, and capabilities grow, you'll need to tune your system so it absorbs the increased load and continues to give you the performance you need.

Fortunately, ORACLE is a highly tunable system which provides many automatic tools for monitoring operations and diagnosing slowdowns and bottlenecks. Although tuning is a time-consuming and demanding process, you'll find that ORACLE gives you the necessary tools and support for this task. You'll also find that the time, money, and energy you spend tuning your system pays you back by saving your organization money and making your users happy. By tuning your system in the right way, you'll often find that you can turn a slow and nearly unusable system into a usable one, and a usable system into a real powerhouse.

Why Tuning?

What does your organization get out of performance tuning? Tuning benefits the bottom line and also the people in your organization and your customer base.

Financial Benefits of Tuning

Tuning saves your organization money in several different ways:

- If you thoroughly tune the system you have you can often avoid buying additional equipment.

- You can downsize your configuration and reap huge savings. By tuning this downsized system, you can often get the same performance or even better performance than you got from your larger, more expensive configuration.

- If you have less, and cheaper, hardware, you'll also pay less for maintenance and both hardware and software upgrades.

- Saving on computing equipment and support frees up money that can be spent on other resources (e.g., market research or advertising) or lets you cut your product costs. In these ways, tuning can potentially give your organization a market advantage over your competitors.

- A high-performance, well-tuned system produces faster response times and better throughput within your own organization. This makes your users more productive.

"Downsizing" is the buzz word you hear in database circles, as you do everywhere in the computing world today. Downsizing means spending less on computing hardware to achieve the same, or even better, results. This trend is made possible because of the emergence of client-server models and because you get increased computing resources per dollar at the low end of the market (PCs and LANs, in particular).

Although the old unitary model, in which one mainframe serves all of your computing needs, is still viable in many organizations, many other organizations are finding that they can save a large amount of money by adopting a client-server model. With a client-server model, ORACLE runs across several computers, rather than running on a single, considerably more expensive mainframe computer. One computer (the server) coordinates access to the ORACLE database, and the other computer (the client) serves the application programs and users. There are usually many clients in the configuration. Client-server computing, in contrast to traditional unitary computing, shares the computing load across machine boundaries, with each machine performing specialized functions. There are many viable types of client-server configurations. Some sites use a minicomputer as the server, and they provide all of their staff with PCs or workstations. Others use PCs exclusively. (Chapter 16 discusses the general issues of client-server configurations.)

The cost savings you can achieve by going to a client-server configuration can be significant, regardless of exactly how you achieve it. The initial purchase, the hardware upgrades, and the annual maintenance are all factors. We have consulted to organizations that were spending tens, or even hundreds, of millions of dollars unnecessarily on supporting a mainframe configuration. A lot of this expense is in ongoing upgrades and support. The numbers are mind-boggling: A mainframe might cost $30 million to buy. A simple upgrade to add computing power might cost another $10 million a few years down the road. Annual maintenance, usually a percentage of the initial purchase, can be extraordinarily expensive. (15% of $30 million is $4.5 million yearly!)

NOTE

All dollar figures, here and elsewhere in this book, are Australian (as we are). At the time we went to press, $1.00 Australian was equivalent to $.67 U.S.

Although converting to a client-server configuration often requires a good deal of effort, and corresponding expense, the payoff is substantial. One organization we helped downsize and tune several years ago spent about 14 months and $1.2 million converting from a mainframe system to a client-server configuration. Because of the dramatic savings in equipment and support, all expenses were recouped within seven months after the launch of the system. Annual maintenance expenses dropped from $2.5 million to $31,000. (For a rundown of how costs were cut in this system, see Chapter 16.)

Moving to client-server is not a one-sided or trivial decision. The decision will impose new demands on everyone in your organization. In a client-server environment, it is vitally important that your ORACLE system be tuned to achieve performance that rivals mainframe performance. Client-server also introduces new tuning issues. For example, in a client-server environment, passing packets of data over a network (as opposed to within a single mainframe computer) slows down processing considerably. To make performance as good as it can be, you'll need to minimize network traffic by performing as much work as possible at either end of the network link and reducing necessary data transfers.

Human Benefits of Tuning

In addition to the financial benefits of performance tuning, there are human benefits to consider. Nothing can be more frustrating for an employee who is trying to be productive than having to wait for computing resources or finding response time painfully slow. You can dramatically improve response time by tuning your ORACLE system.

Some organizations we've worked at have instituted "tuning service agreements" between the computing staff and the users. These agreements specify, among other things, what "acceptable" response time is within the organization. How do you define acceptable? Each organization needs to make its own assessment. In general, "acceptable" is what a user requires to get the day's work through the computer system, or to provide adequate response times to customers. Some organizations include tuning agreements in their contracts for system development and maintenance. A client need not accept a system until response times are below or equal to those specified by the agreement. Once the system is in production, that organization may suffer payment penalties if response times exceed expectations. (For a discussion of assessing response times and tuning agreements, see Chapter 3, *Planning and Managing the Tuning Process.*)

In addition to increasing the productivity and morale of your own users, a well-tuned system benefits your organization's customers. If your ORACLE system does online transaction processing, or otherwise serves customers who expect speedy, real-time responses to queries, poor response time can cause a lot of unhappiness and lose business. A customer who telephones to inquire about the activity in his or her bank account expects quick response and does not expect to hear an excuse about the slowness of the Account Inquiry Screen.

Who Tunes?

Tuning is not the sole responsibility of the system administrator, or any single individual. It's a broad activity that has an impact on many different types of people in your organization. As mentioned in the Preface, we have organized this book in separate parts aimed at distinct types of readers, each of whom performs a specific role in your system. Although there is a considerable amount of overlap in the topics, and, in some organizations, in the roles, this presentation focuses attention on the particular activities that are most likely to be of concern to particular types of people.

The system planner/manager. This person oversees the entire tuning process, from planning to production and ongoing monitoring. The section below called "Planning the System" contains an overview of the decisions made during the planning process that have an impact on performance. Chapter 3 describes this process in greater detail.

The designer/analyst. This person or staff of people designs the data model for the database, as well as the overall application, for performance. The section below, called "Designing and Analyzing the Application" contains an overview of the decisions made during the design process that have an impact on performance. Part III describes this process in detail.

The programmer. This person or staff of people develops the application and tunes all programs for performance. The section called "Developing the Application" contains an overview of the decisions made during the development process that have an impact on performance, and "Testing and Assuring Quality in the System" describes the testing of the application and the database. Part IV describes this process in detail.

The database administrator (DBA). This person is usually involved in the design of the database and takes responsibility for tuning the database for performance as well as ongoing database tuning once the system is in production. The section below called "Monitoring Performance During Production" describes the type of monitoring the DBA performs. Part V describes DBA functions in detail.

The system administrator. In addition to the overall operating system maintenance performed by the system administrator, this person monitors ORACLE performance by juggling the system resources needed by both ORACLE applications and the other systems within the organization. The section "Monitoring Performance During Production" describes the type of monitoring the system administrator performs. Part VI describes the system administrator functions relevant to ORACLE performance tuning.

When Do You Tune?

Too many people think of tuning as an add-on, a tinkering you do when the engine starts faltering and people start complaining. Wrong! Performance is a design goal, something you build into the system from the beginning, not something you fiddle with only when things go wrong and time is short. But, performance is also something you never finish and forget about. It's something to be concerned about through the entire life cycle of your ORACLE system.

In this section, we talk about increasing performance during various stages of system development: planning, analyzing and designing the data model and programs, developing the application, testing and "QA"-ing the application, and monitoring the system after it goes into production.

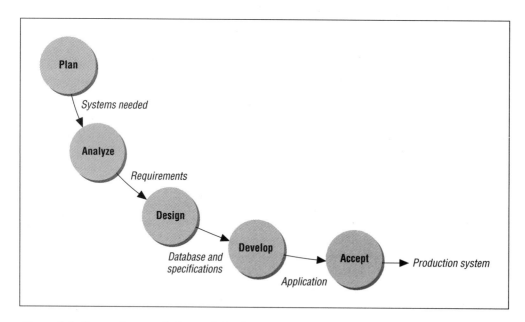

Figure 1-1: Stages of system design and development

Planning the System

If you make bad performance decisions during the first stage of the system development cycle, you'll regret them forever. Here is a brief list of what needs to be done before you even start designing your ORACLE database and developing your programs. Although many of these activities and decisions are typically performed by "management," they impact all of the people in an organization and everybody should have an opportunity to share information and opinions during this stage. Certain activities, for example, looking at hardware/software resources and choices, should obviously be coordinated with the system administrator.

1. Describe all the systems and applications required by your organization. Performance will be far better down the road if you can think globally during this phase. Make sure that you define all your applications in an integrated way, so all of the data required by different applications is stored in a single, coordinated database. This is a major performance boost because it means you won't need to exchange data between applications—a task that consumes a lot of system resources.

2. Select your organization's hardware and software configurations. As you investigate different products that you might incorporate into your configuration, be sure to assess their performance implications, not just the functions they offer. Do your homework by asking people at other sites how their performance has been affected—for better or worse—by the products you're considering.

    Here are some of the questions to ask during this stage:

    Hardware/software resources

    *   Should we use a client-server or unitary model?
    *   What should the line speeds be?
    *   Where should we put the physical hardware?
    *   What size and speed do we need from our hardware?
    *   Will we be able to upgrade whatever we buy?

    Database resources

    *   What are the ORACLE database requirements (memory, etc.)?
    *   What are the backup and recovery expectations?
    *   What is the likely transaction mix? Mainly transactions? Mainly reporting?

    User resources

    *   What is the expected number of users?
    *   What are the user resource requirements (GUI workstations, etc.)?

3. Be sure to project for future growth in your hardware/software selection. The number of users may dramatically increase, for example, depending on your own organizational needs and budgets. Chapter 17, *Capacity Planning*, describes in detail how you can examine your system requirements and plan for the future. Typically, the system administrator will conduct the capacity planning study, but you'll need to track results closely.

4. Plan for scheduling delays. You may need to wait a long time for equipment to be delivered. Try to project your hardware/software configuration needs as much as 18 to 24 months in advance. Place your orders at least three to six months in advance to avoid problems with vendors' long lead times.

5. Set standards for system design and development. Chapter 4, *Defining System Standards*, describes software selection, version control, and other areas you'll need to be concerned about.

6. Determine what acceptable response times will be for the system. Chapter 3 describes how to establish and monitor response times for your site.

Designing and Analyzing the Application

The design stage is crucial to ensuring good performance later on. All the tuning wisdom of your site's programmers, DBAs, and system administrators can't make up for the slowdowns that will result from bad design decisions during this analysis/design stage.

Here is a brief list of the tuning activities you'll have to perform during this stage:

1. Design the data model for performance. Sound design is a combination of doing it by the book and using your head. Doing it by the book means doing a classic relational analysis of the data: what are the entities, relationships, and attributes of the data? The goal of relational database design is to normalize the data as best you can. But on top of that classic database design, you'll need to apply a good dose of common sense. Where should you denormalize the data? Where should you introduce redundancy in the data in order to increase performance? There are a lot of real-world decisions only you can make regarding what design is best for your data and for what your users are actually going to be doing with it.

2. Design your programs for performance. Make sure you design your programs in a modular way that permits later change and tuning. For example, if several programs need to perform a common function, such as updating account details, design your application so the update code exists as a small, separate module that each program can call as needed. Adding logic to this update program, or tinkering with it to increase performance, need be done only once, with all the calling programs reaping the benefits.

    Modularization produces other benefits. Small programs typically require less memory than large ones, so your overall memory requirements are reduced. Modularization also simplifies maintenance, because any changes to the module are made only once, rather than separately for each program that includes the code.

3. Decide when to use indexes on tables. Learning to design indexes effectively should be a priority for any designer. Retrieval of data using indexes is usually much faster than retrieval by scanning tables from start to finish. Typically, an indexed retrieval takes no more than a few physical reads from disk to retrieve the necessary rows from the table, whereas an unindexed retrieval may take several thousand reads. The problem is compounded when tables are being accessed as a group, or joined, without being able to use indexes. Chapter 6, *Defining Indexes*, gives you pointers for when to use indexes and when you'll do better not to use them. Because developers sometimes find later on that indexes can improve the performance of their programs, you'll have to coordinate index design with your development staff.

4. When you design your data model, accommodate your interfaces. GUIs are becoming more and more popular in ORACLE configurations, especially in client-server environments. GUI products offer a new dimension in user friendliness and quality of presentation, but they also present design problems. During the design stage, you need to figure out how the GUIs will address the data in your ORACLE database. If you design incorrectly, a user may run into major performance problems later on. For example, suppose a user enters a complex, multi-row query that requires joining many tables. The user will need to specify how the tables are to be joined through a complex data model, which will be annoying for the user and have a potentially large impact on response time—the user's and that of others in the system. You might want to consider the alternative of presenting data to the GUI user in the form of a spreadsheet with many indexes. To improve overall system performance, the system could create the spreadsheet overnight (if the data from last night is current enough) or could build it from redundant tables maintained in the database. You'll have to consider a trade-off here: Does the convenience of GUI users' being able to get timely responses justify the additional cost of maintaining redundant tables?

For details about design trade-offs, see Chapter 5, *Designing Your Data Model for Performance*, and Chapter 11, *Tuning a New Database*.

Developing the Application

During the development stage, you'll create the actual tables, indexes, and programs needed by the application. Here's what you'll have to do during this stage:

1. Choose the optimizer you will use. The ORACLE optimizer is a part of your system that examines each SQL statement and chooses the optimal execution plan, or retrieval path, for the statement. The execution plan is the sequence of physical steps the RDMBS must perform to do the database retrieval you've requested. With Version 7, you have a choice between the traditional rule-based optimizer and the

more intelligent new cost-based optimizer. The choice becomes a particularly important one if you are migrating from ORACLE Version 6 to Version 7. Chapter 7, *Tuning SQL*, describes how the optimizers work and explains how you can complement or override their efforts to achieve better performance.

2. Tune your SQL, PL/SQL, and SQL*Forms statements. There are many ways of accomplishing the same results with alternative statements. With the help of the ORACLE optimizer and your own knowledge of your system, you can get the best possible performance out of your statements.

3. Decide which locking strategy is best for your application. With Versions 6 and 7 you have a choice of table locking or row locking. Chapter 10, *Selecting a Locking Strategy*, describes the issues.

Testing and Assuring Quality in the System

During this stage, you test the system before it is moved into production. In addition to performing functional testing on all individual program modules, make sure that all of the modules work well together, and that performance is acceptable for both individual modules and the system as a whole. Here is a brief list of the tuning activities you'll have to perform during this stage:

1. Make sure the volume of data you are using for testing is large enough. If you have too little data in the database, performance problems often won't surface. (They'll wait until production!)

2. Make sure you run on the same type of configuration that will be used for production. If production users will be running client-server, make sure your testing staff does too.

3. Make sure to test on a configuration that runs the same, or slower, than the one that will be delivered to production users. Although it sounds obvious, many testers forget to take the speed differential into account, and may test on a faster configuration. Response times that are adequate on the test system may be too slow when you finally go to production. If you're able to test the database on a configuration that's slower than the production configuration, all the better. Then, when you move to production, and a faster system, you'll have a little extra performance up your sleeve!

4. Make sure you aren't sharing the machine with production users. The QA staff will be testing new versions of programs. If QA and production are sharing a machine, you may find that faulty programs cause performance problems that affect the response times of the production users.

5. Inform your DBA of what you learn about performance problems. Although your job doesn't ordinarily involve performance testing, you'll learn a lot while you test for functionality. During QA, the DBA has a final chance to fine-tune the database to provide better performance. It's much harder to do a redesign once the system is in production. If you can give good information to the DBA during this stage, he or she will be able to use your input to tune the database for performance before production begins.

Monitoring Performance During Production

Tuning is a job that's never done. Throughout the life of your ORACLE system, you'll need to keep monitoring performance, considering the needs of your system's users, and tinkering with the tools that let you tune the system effectively.

Ideally, the database and programs that are delivered for production are already well-oiled machines that are raring to go. When production users start using the database in a serious way, they'll hardly be starting from scratch. But, inevitably, using a database in a production environment adds new stresses and strains that can't always be detected during testing. And, as time goes on, and more users and more data are added to the configuration, increasing demands are placed on the database.

Throughout the life of the ORACLE system the DBA and the system administrator, in conjunction with the project manager, share responsibility for monitoring the system and the data, trying to make sure that ORACLE makes effective use of all of the system's resources: memory, disk I/O, CPU, and the network. Chapter 2, *What Causes Performance Problems?*, outlines performance issues for each of these resources.

Special monitoring responsibilities of the DBA include:

1. Be proactive in tracking performance problems. You can't just wait for complaints and react to them. Many users don't report response problems at all. Other users report problems at the slightest opportunity and may tend to overreact to them. You'll have to figure out, in conjunction with your project manager, what's really going on in your system. See the section called "Managing the Problem of Response Time" for a discussion of assessing complaints about response time.

2. Be sure to monitor all ORACLE performance screens and exercise all tools on a regular basis. Chapter 12, *Diagnostic and Tuning Tools*, describes the tools you can use to identify bottlenecks and optimize performance in your system.

3. From time to time, run procedures against the production database, just as users would. Record response times at discrete intervals throughout the day using the same forms that production users most commonly use. (See Chapter 3 for details.)

Special monitoring responsibilities of the system administrator include:

1. Make sure the speed of the hardware and the network are acceptable for the amount and type of processing that is going on.

2. Apply all system fixes and operating system improvements to ensure that users will be able to use the latest releases from ORACLE and other vendors.

3. Monitor performance by checking on free memory, paging and swapping activity, and CPU, disk, and network activity.

4. Coordinate all ORACLE tuning with overall operating system tuning. The system administrator is usually also responsible for administering office automation, system software, and other resources in the system. Make sure that these applications coexist with ORACLE and do not negatively affect ORACLE RDBMS performance (and vice versa).

The DBA and the system administrator need to coordinate all tuning and monitoring activities. Together, they will decide whether there is a need to reorganize the database, provide contiguous space on disk for new files, and perform various other tuning tasks.

A Look at ORACLE7

When ORACLE Version 6 was introduced, users found that the new version offered tremendous improvements in performance. ORACLE7 offers better performance, as well as many tools that allow you to tune your system still further. Version 6 put a lot of tuning responsibility in the hands of the programmer; ORACLE7 extends the ability of the DBA to tune the database for performance.

In most cases, you will simply be able to transfer your entire application from Version 6 to ORACLE7 without difficulty, and reap the benefits. However, in some cases, you will have to rework your database and applications to take advantage of the new Version 7 features, There have been a very few complaints that, in some special circumstances, ORACLE7 actually creates some performance problems, but overall, the performance improvements are noticeable and easy to use.

The most remarkable improvements in ORACLE7 performance are at sites where programmers did not know how to optimize their programs for performance. This is because the cost-based optimizer available in ORACLE7 relieves much of the burden on the programmer to figure out how SQL statements can best access the database.

ORACLE7 also greatly improves performance in client-server environments. When combined with SQL*Net Version 2, ORACLE7 substantially reduces the number of packets that need to be transferred across the network, which results in a corresponding increase in performance.

Here is a summary of the major new ORACLE7 features that have an impact on performance. For more information about these and other features, see Appendix A, *Planning for ORACLE7*.

Cost-based optimizer. In Version 6, a rule-based optimizer applies a predefined set of rules, precedence operations, and indexes to figure out the most efficient execution plan, or retrieval path. This path is the set of physical steps needed to access the database for a retrieval or update. In ORACLE7, a more sophisticated and intelligent optimizer looks at statistics collected about the characteristics of your actual data, and makes a decision based on the comparative costs of alternative access paths. As we mentioned above, use of the cost-based optimizer significantly improves performance, especially for untuned SQL statements. As discussed in Chapter 7, you may still need to do some manual tuning of complex statements.

Shared SQL area. In Version 6, all individual user processes have individual areas. In ORACLE7, there is a SQL area that can be shared by users. In addition to using less memory, the shared SQL area may use less CPU because statements need to be parsed only once if they remain in the shared area.

Multi-threaded server. This server lessens the burden each user process places on the ORACLE system. The server creates less system overhead, increases the maximum user connections possible for a given configuration, and automates load balancing.

Hash clusters. Up until now, hash clusters have been available only to high-performance hierarchical databases. They provide very fast access to data by performing a computation on the key field(s) of a table to obtain an address to access the desired location in the database directly.

Rollback segment size adjustment. Rollback size can now be adjusted without having to shut down the database. By allowing larger rollback segments to be created for overnight processing, this feature has the effect of speeding up large update operations. An optimal SIZE clause allows a rollback segment to shrink back to its original size, enabling the DBA to control more closely the space in the database.

TRUNCATE command. This command allows all rows to be deleted from a table significantly faster than with the Version 6 DELETE command. The command is equivalent to dropping and recreating a table.

Database integrity constraints. These constraints can now be stored in the database. Because integrity checking code no longer needs to be included in programs, this reduces the size of programs and the amount of memory required per program. It also reduces network traffic. Because all checks are stored within the database and can be performed within one database visit, fewer packets need to be transferred between the client and the server machine. Integrity checks are also optimized because they are performed only when the column is modified.

Stored procedures, functions, packages, and triggers. These are simply a collection of PL/SQL and SQL statements that are stored as a single compiled unit within the actual database. Having them available in the database means fewer database calls across the network. All procedures and functions are stored in a parsed form and are shared among users, thus reducing the size of the programs and their memory requirements. The SQL is shared, regardless of which interface package is being used to access it.

Resource profile limits. These limits prevent user processes from running away with system resources and inhibiting the response times of other users. The major limitations that can be applied are concurrent sessions per user, maximum CPU per session, maximum CPU per SQL call, maximum continuous connect time per session, maximum idle time before a user is disconnected, maximum database blocks read per session and per database call, and maximum size of the private part of the System Global Area.

Distributed database. Version 6 provides a distributed query feature that allows you to retrieve data that is distributed on various machines. In Version 7, you can update that data as well, via a two-phase commit function. This facility can bolster performance when the majority of local data is required locally and there is a need to reduce network traffic.

Table replication or snapshots. These allow read-only copies of single tables, subsets of tables, or complex query joins. The copies have the potential to provide a source for GUI and ad hoc reporting users. Snapshots can improve performance by reducing the amount of network traffic because they maintain these tables at the database end for all changes made.

How Much Tuning is Enough?

A perfectly tuned system is a movable target. When do you know that you've tuned enough? In our years at the front, we've found that many sites tune too little, but that some actually do tune too much.

Some sites are downright paranoid about performance monitoring. They instruct their DBAs and system administrators to stare into monitor screens all day waiting for poor response to occur—kind of like air traffic controllers, waiting to avert a disaster. Complete vigilance is unrealistic. Some perverse law states that poor response times occur only at the moment that the unwitting DBA takes a short break. Most organizations are far better off implementing a way to report performance exceptions automatically.

Some DBAs are always tinkering with INIT.ORA parameters and other system settings. You can certainly make major performance improvements by doing this; we explain in Chapter 11 the settings we recommend. Be sure not to make too many changes at once, however, or you won't know which changes actually cause improvements in performance. There also comes a point when the system is in balance and it's better not to fiddle around with these settings trying to achieve infinitesimally small performance improvements. It's the law of diminishing returns. At some point, your time is better spent elsewhere.

Another problem with changing parameters is that sometimes improving performance in one area of the system may degrade performance in another. For example, adding an index to a table may improve performance for certain programs, but may actually hurt the performance of others. You'll have to be careful and sensitive about making changes once your system is in production. For best results, always monitor performance in the QA environment before you make a change in the production system.

Another way you need to balance your tuning efforts is to make sure that tuning remains a team effort. If a developer tests every possible SQL statement alternative before completing a program, the program will never get written. If the system administrator spends many hours a day tuning the ORACLE system, that effort will be at the expense of other important work, like backing up and recovering files, installing new hardware and software, and so on. You'll need to work together at your own site to find the right balance for your own system and staff. If you have a tuning service agreement (described in detail in Chapter 3), the requirements of that agreement are the bottom line for how much tuning you must do. You must tune until you reach the agreed-upon response times. Beyond that, monitor on an ongoing basis to make sure the response times are maintained. Any other tuning is a matter of debate and agreement among the people in your own organization.

2

What Causes Performance Problems?

There are many reasons for poor performance in an ORACLE system, ranging from poor database design to specific programming problems to human factors. This chapter briefly outlines the areas where things can go wrong. Subsequent chapters describe performance problems in much more detail, and describe how you can tune the different aspects of the system for better performance.

Problems with Design and Development

After tuning quite a few ORACLE sites, we have observed a pattern where performance problems slow down processing. Figure 2-1 shows our observations of (a) where the problems occur and, (b) comparatively, how hard it is to fix them.

Design   Design problems are typically caused by analysts and designers who have not:

- Considered performance when setting up the data model
- Designed programs that are appropriate for a relational database
- Designed programs that are appropriate for the hardware configuration being used

Programs   Program problems are typically caused by programmers whose SQL statements don't make efficient use of the optimizer.

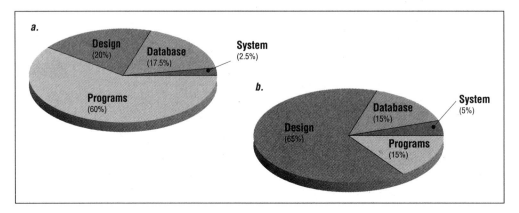

Figure 2-1: (a) Causes of poor response times (b) Effort required to fix problems

Database   Database problems are typically caused by DBAs who have not:

- Used the machine's resources effectively

- Structured the database to spread disk I/O appropriately (including choice of tablespaces, placement of data files, correct sizing of tables and indexes, etc.)

- Set INIT.ORA parameters to avoid contention for redo logs and other objects

As a consequence, any of the following might occur:

- Excessive disk I/O

- Disk I/O that is badly balanced across disks

- A database that is fragmented

- A database that is not effectively indexed

Systems   Systems problems occur as a result of:

- Other (non-ORACLE) systems adversely affecting ORACLE

- An untuned operating system

- A machine size or configuration that is inadequate to support ORACLE

The best way to fix performance in your system is to keep performance problems from occurring in the first place. Obviously, this isn't always possible, or even likely (why else would you have bought this book?) As Figure 2-1 shows, though, fixing problems that result from poor design of your data model and programs isn't as simple as resetting a parameter or running a diagnostic. The only way to contend with poor design is to reorganize and recode.

Do your best to make your design as sound as it can be the first time around. However skilled your programmers may be, if they are writing programs against improperly tuned database tables, their chances of producing code that results in adequate response time is minimal. Similarly, however skilled the DBA's monitoring and tuning of the database, if programmers have coded programs that pay no attention to performance, the overall chances of good performance are bleak.

Problems with System Resources

To get the best performance out of your system, you must be aware of how the four basic components of your machine environment interact and affect system performance:

Memory. Memory bottlenecks occur when there isn't enough memory to accommodate the needs of the site. When this happens, excessive paging (moving portions of processes to disk) and swapping (transferring whole processors from memory to disk to free memory) occur.

Disk I/O. Disk bottlenecks occur when one or more disks exceed their recommended I/O rate.

CPU. CPU bottlenecks occur when either the operating system or the user programs are making too many demands on the CPU. This is often caused by excessive paging and swapping.

Network. Network bottlenecks occur when the amount of traffic on the network is too great or when network collisions occur.

Remember that memory, disk I/O, CPU, and network problems don't exist in a vacuum. Each of these problems affects the other resources as well. At the same time, an improvement in one resource may cause better performance of the others. For example:

- If your organization buys more memory, the CPU needs to spend less time handling paging and swapping operations that occur because memory is scarce. This helps avoid CPU bottlenecks as well.

- If you have a disk I/O bottleneck, you might be able to use memory to store more data, thus avoiding having to read the data from disk a second time.

- If you have a network traffic problem in a client-server environment, you might be able to improve things by using more memory, disk I/O, and CPU on either the client or the server side to avoid having to transfer data across the network.

Remember, in tuning your resources, the goal is to use all resources as fully as possible, without running them dry. Some people seem to believe that a site is performing well when memory is plentiful, CPU and disk I/O are close to ideal, and network traffic is low. This sounds a lot like a well-equipped hospital with no patients in it! Your system is meant to be fully utilized.

What constitutes an ideally tuned system? It's a matter of debate. We say that you should tune in such a way that:

- As close as possible to 100% of your memory is used.

- Your disk load is spread evenly across devices, and all of your disks are operating marginally within their recommended maximum I/O rates.

- As close as possible to 100% of your CPU is used during peak periods, with no user programs waiting for the CPU.

- Network traffic is only marginally below the maximum recommended, with no collisions.

- There is an insignificant amount of paging and swapping going on.

- User throughput and response times meet the standards established for your organization. (See the discussion in Chapter 3, *Planning and Managing the Tuning Process*).

The key is to get all of these resources to work together. In Figure 2-2, we show an untuned system. In such a system, one component degrades before all the others. In this particular case, when you attempt to achieve more throughput, you are stopped by a memory bottleneck (that is, all of the memory has been used, and paging and swapping have become excessive, as we will describe in later sections). In this example, if you add more memory, the CPU will be the next item to cause a performance bottleneck, followed by disk I/O and the network.

In a perfectly tuned system, on the other hand, all factors degrade simultaneously. As illustrated in Figure 2-3, up until the point where performance finally starts to degrade, all system resources are in balance, and throughput is optional. Note, though, that if the throughput required at your site is substantially less than the point at which your components begin to degrade (even after allowing for planned expansion to your application), this may indicate that you have bought more hardware than you really needed.

Memory Problems and Tuning

In general, the more memory available to your system, your applications, and the individual data structures within the applications, the faster your programs will run. How much memory is enough memory? A good rule of thumb is to use as much as possible, but never to let the free memory in your system drop below 5%. If free memory drops below 5%, you run the risk that when the next user logs on, your system will not have enough memory to service that user.

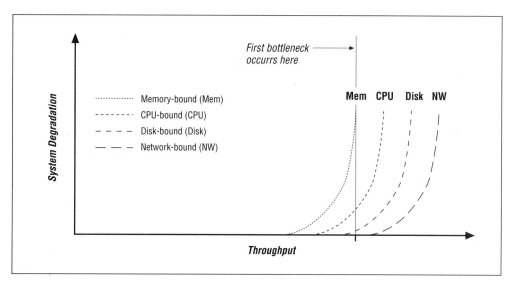

Figure 2-2: An untuned system

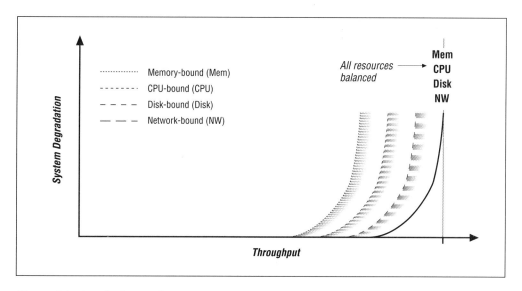

Figure 2-3: A perfectly tuned system

If there isn't enough memory to handle the demands upon it, the operating system will react by paging, and may eventually resort to swapping entire processes from memory to disk to free up memory. Then, the next time a swapped process is needed, the system will have to copy the entire memory image for that process from disk back into memory. Because disk access is so much slower than memory access (sometimes tens or even hundreds of thousands of times slower!), performance suffers whenever the system needs to go to the disk in this way.

Paging and swapping affect the CPU as well. When demands are placed on the operating system to provide memory for additional processes, CPU performance also suffers. The bulk of the machine's CPU is consumed by paging and swapping activities. Instead of servicing user requests, memory and CPU are occupied shuffling data back and forth.

It's also possible to leave too much memory free. Although conserving memory is an admirable performance goal, remember that it's not efficient to have memory sitting unused on your computer instead of using it to store data. If you have more than 10% free memory, then you're not using memory effectively.

Don't assume that you need to buy more memory just because your memory usage is close to 100%. There are many ways to reduce demands on memory by proper tuning and careful management. One important way is to control the number of users and processes in the system.

Every user who logs onto an ORACLE system uses memory. User patterns vary a lot. Some users might limit themselves to running Pro*C, which needs about 300K of memory. Others may log on four times each, with each login requiring three megabytes of memory. The amount of memory used depends upon a number of variables:

- The program the user is running
- The product or language in which the program is written
- Various ORACLE and operating system parameters
- The operating system that is being used
- The number of times a user is logged on

At some sites we've worked at, we've found users logged onto a machine as many as six times. Each user who runs SQL*Forms uses as much as three megabytes of memory. If you get into a situation where each user is actually using 18 megabytes (because of being logged on six times), forcing your system to be short of memory, no amount of tuning will result in good performance. Usually, your system administrator is responsible for specifying who can log onto the system and how many times.

Even when a user isn't doing any work on the system, memory may be used. For example, some users log on, look at one or two screens, and then stay logged on the rest of the day. Others remain logged on when they go to lunch. Logged-on users are still using memory, even though no active work is being performed. Such users can affect the response times of other users if memory is scarce, and paging and swapping become excessive. Sophisticated operating systems are able to identify dormant processes, such as those where a user may not have performed any activity for 15 minutes (although this function requires CPU usage, which may also be a scarce resource). In other systems, you can write your own scripts to do the same thing. If you can manage it, try to set up a policy that forces users to log off the system under such circumstances. This policy will improve performance *and* security.

Several parameters in your site's INIT.ORA file can be reset to improve memory performance. One important parameter is SORT_AREA_SIZE, which the DBA can reset to allow ORACLE to sort a larger amount in memory. Another one, DB_BLOCK_BUFFERS, sets the size of the buffer cache. Sometimes, the DBA will choose to set certain parameters on a per-user basis, rather than for the entire system. For a complete discussion of memory tuning parameters, see Chapter 11, *Tuning a New Database*, and Chapter 13, *Monitoring and Tuning an Existing Database*. Remember that these parameters will not tell the whole story; you'll also need to consider factors like the number of times a user can log on, the non-ORACLE software on your machine, and other such factors.

The time required to access data that is in your computer's memory is much faster than the time required to access it from disk. ORACLE provides a number of ways to store both user data and its own data dictionary data in memory (e.g., the users who are allowed to use the system, the table definitions, the access rights users have on the various tables, etc.). Figure 2-4 shows how ORACLE structures different components in memory, and who at your site typically takes responsibility for tuning these components.

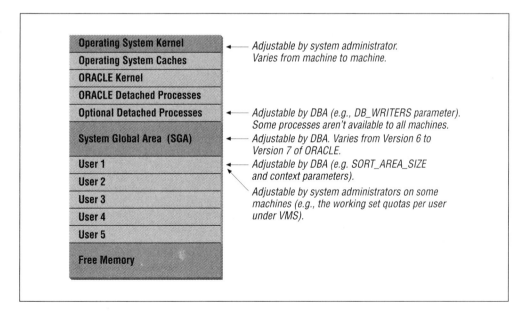

Figure 2-4: Tuning of memory components

Disk I/O Problems and Tuning

With ORACLE, as with any large database system, there is a lot of disk activity. Physical memory is never large enough to handle all of a system's program and data needs, so data must be brought in from disk as needed. Access to even the fastest disk is orders of magnitude slower than memory access. With the enormous amounts of data stored and processed by the typical RDBMS, disk I/O can become a major performance problem. As we mentioned in the previous section, memory problems can also impact disk activity when memory limitations cause excessive paging and swapping.

The way in which you organize data on disk can have a major impact on your overall disk performance. Most ORACLE systems have a number of disks that share the system's data load. Try to spread the disk workload as evenly as possible across drives to reduce the likelihood of performance problems occurring from disk overloading.

There are a number of specific ways you can reduce performance problems that arise from poor disk management. The simplified configuration shown in Figure 2-5 illustrates the basic principles of disk load sharing. As shown here, it normally pays to separate the operating system disk (used for paging and swapping files) from the disk containing ORACLE database files. It is also advisable to put tables on one disk and their indexes on another disk, because these are accessed in unison. (The index locates the data, which is then read from the table using that address.) The redo logs should usually be on their own disk because they are written to as data is changed (which can be often).

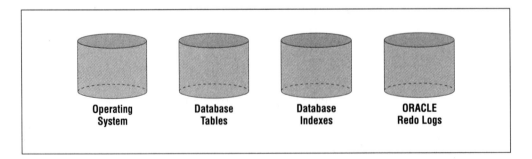

Figure 2-5: A typical disk configuration

When tables, indexes, and rollback segments are created, they are assigned an initial storage allocation. If that allocation is exceeded, ORACLE must assign additional extents in a process called dynamic extension. Access to data is most efficient if extents are contiguous. When a table's extents are discontiguous (potentially scattered all around the disk), access is much slower because the system needs to scan these discontiguous areas. This problem of disk fragmentation, illustrated in Figure 2-6, is a common cause of disk bottlenecks. In this example, data from the ACCOUNTS table is spread across the database. The disadvantage of storing data in this way is the excessive head movement required to retrieve groups of ACCOUNTS data. If tables and indexes are sized correctly so one contiguous area on disk (extent) contains all of the data, the time required to retrieve data is considerably less.

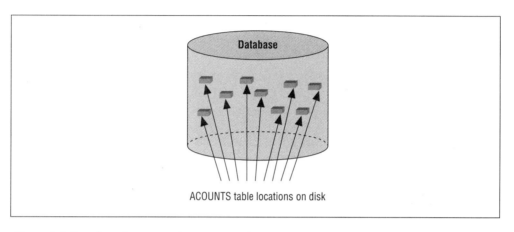

Figure 2-6: Database fragmentation

Disk chaining, illustrated in Figure 2-7, is another possible cause of disk problems. When a row in a table is updated and the amount of memory available in the current data block is not large enough to store the row data, ORACLE has to assign another block. The single row is then spread across several discontiguous locations on disk. This situation can be avoided by correctly sizing the table, as we will describe later in this book.

The goal of tuning an ORACLE program is to reduce the number of times that the program needs to access the database on disk. There are a number of ways to reduce database accesses. One important way is indexing, discussed in Chapter 6, *Defining Indexes.* Severe disk problems can occur either because indexes were specified incorrectly during system design or because the indexes were mistakenly dropped.

Several INIT.ORA parameters can be reset to improve disk I/O performance. Two particularly important ones are LOG_CHECKPOINT_BUFFER, which specifies how often to write to the database, and LOG_BUFFER, which controls the size of what's written and the frequency of the writes. For a complete discussion of disk I/O tuning parameters, see Chapters 11 and 13.

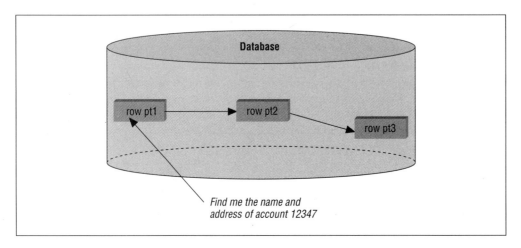

Figure 2-7: Disk chaining

CPU Problems and Tuning

The CPU controls the activities of the other resources in your system, and it executes user processes. While all computer hardware costs have dropped in recent years, CPU continues to be more expensive than memory and disk. Although there are occasional situations in which a CPU is genuinely not fast enough to cope with the workload at a site, these situations are rare. Before buying an expensive new CPU, make sure that your CPU problems are not being caused by any of the following:

- Untuned applications

- Users being logged on multiple times

- Long-running batch jobs running during prime production hours

- Other types of memory or disk I/O bottlenecks

CPU problems frequently occur when several processes are trying to use the CPU at the same time. We've talked about the stresses paging and swapping put on your system. In the worst case, paging and swapping turn into thrashing, a dire situation in which the whole CPU is dedicated to simply moving processes from memory to disk and back again. To avoid this worst case, don't let your system run out of memory!

Because CPU services the operating system and user programs, usually correcting the disk and memory bottlenecks in your system will also help alleviate CPU bottlenecks. Memory bottlenecks have a more severe effect on CPU than do disk I/O bottlenecks. Excessive paging and swapping, if they occur, make continual demands on CPU, whereas disk I/O demands CPU only after data is returned from disk—a slower process than returning data from memory. Although your system administrator can often transfer the more damaging memory bottleneck to disk, and thus ease the pressure on the CPU, this is usually a temporary measure. You may eventually need more memory.

The major way in which you can keep CPU problems from occurring is to avoid running long jobs during times of peak usage in online transaction processing (OLTP) systems. Although sites need to decide on standards that make sense for them, our own personal bias is to move long jobs either to a different machine (using a backup database) or to off-peak hours. We define long-running jobs in a very strict way: anything that takes longer than 45 seconds to run! (See the discussion of managing such jobs in the section in Chapter 3 called "Managing the Problem of Long-running Jobs," and of tuning such jobs in Chapter 15, *Tuning Long-running Jobs.*)

On some computers you can tune CPU use by assigning priorities to some of the processes in your system. If priority setting is available on your machine, you have two alternatives. You can try setting the priorities of long-running jobs lower than those of the interactive processes to make sure that they don't interfere with the processes being run by online users. Alternatively, you can set the priorities of certain long-running jobs higher than those of the interactive processes, at certain times of day, to make sure they run as quickly as possible and then get out of the way.

Remember, work being performed by the long-running jobs may also be performed by the ORACLE detached processes DBWR (database writer) and LGWR (log writer). Be sure you never change the priorities of these processes.

Many long-running jobs tend to be I/O-bound rather than CPU-bound, so although they do consume a large amount of CPU, they consume even more I/O. This problem is especially serious if the long-running jobs need to access the same disks accessed by the interactive users. To improve performance, avoid having users run long-running jobs on the same system used for online transaction processing during times of prime online usage.

Network Problems and Tuning

Network bottlenecks occur when the amount of data that needs to be transferred across the network exceeds the network capacity. In client-server configurations particularly, data distributed on different machines must often be transferred over the network. By tuning your programs to reduce the need for database access, and by carefully distributing data on your machines and disks, you can often greatly reduce the volume of data that needs to be sent.

Here are some suggestions that might help. For detailed information, see Chapter 16, *Tuning in the Client-server Environment.*

- If you are running client-server, try to keep all long-running jobs at the database server end if possible.

- If you are propagating data across applications, send only what is needed. Figuring out the exact data requirements may take longer, in the short-term, but could help network traffic significantly in the long-term.

- Before transferring data across the network, make sure you use any data compression utilities available in your operating system (e.g., *compress* and *uuencode* for UNIX).

- If the users at your site frequently download report files to their personal computers for use with their packages, consider producing nightly extract files and placing them on file servers to reduce network traffic.

II

Tuning for Managers and Planners

Part II describes what managers, planners, and project leaders of ORACLE systems need to know about tuning. What response times are acceptable in your system? How can you manage the workload to produce better response times? Do you need a larger computer? It outlines the critical management checkpoints that affect performance in your system, and it describes briefly the design and development standards that you need to formulate during the planning stage.

3

Planning and Managing the Tuning Process

Earlier chapters introduce the ORACLE tuning process and explain why tuning is so necessary in the ORACLE environment. This chapter focuses on the questions you'll need to ask, and the decisions you'll need to make, about system performance and tuning from a planning and management point of view:

What response times are acceptable in your system?

- How can you manage the workload at your system to produce better response times?

- Can your system perform effectively with the system resources you have, or do you need a larger machine, more memory, or other resources?

- What are the crucial management checkpoints for tuning at your site?

Chapter 4, *Defining System Standards*, discusses another management function: the standards that need to be set for system design and development to improve the chances that a system will perform well. The rest of this book describes the specific choice of database design approaches, the use of SQL and related statements in programs, and the selection of appropriate diagnostic and tuning tools.

Managing the Problem of Response Time

In most systems, the bottom line for performance is response time. Users don't care whether the system slows down because of a problem with memory, disk, CPU, networking, or a workload that's too large for the available system resources. The net effect is the same: users can't get their queries and reports run as fast as they need to.

Face the facts. Users will never thank you for making response time fast. Users will always want faster response times, even when performance is already blazing. Particularly when a site has downsized from a mainframe to a smaller machine, users will continue to expect mainframe response times and are likely to be disappointed, at least until tuning brings the speed up.

You may not be able to please all of the users all of the time, but there are some very important things you can do to minimize complaints and maximize user satisfaction.

First, you need to formulate a policy for how to deal with response time problems. To whom do users complain? Who investigates and acts on the reported problems?

Second, you need to assess the truth of the situation. Managers often say to us, "My production users keep complaining that response times are poor. The support staff denies the claim. How can I figure out the truth of what's going on?"

Third, you need to improve response times if the complaints are, in fact, warranted.

Planning for Complaints About Response Time

Here are some suggestions for formulating a policy to handle response time complaints and reporting.

1. Make sure users know who to complain to. When response time problems occur, users must know how to report the details to the appropriate person or group. If correct reporting channels are not in place, users probably won't try to figure out how to report their concerns. Instead, they'll complain to their co-workers, and this informal discussion may be very damaging to the credibility of the system and its administrators. It's helpful to set up a chain of communication for all response time complaints, just so all the people who need to know about the problem are, in fact, notified. Here's a typical chain:

    Production users report the problem to a production support team.

    The production support team then reports the problem to the development team, the DBA, or the system administrator.

    The development team reports the problem to the DBA.

The DBA and system administrator report the problem to each other or to the development team, where applicable.

2. Make sure the DBA and the system administrator are geared up to respond quickly to response time problems.

3. Check what else is going on in the system. Be sure to find out about the user's CPU usage and disk I/O, as well as internal locking information from the ORACLE monitor screens. Here's what you should record:

    User's name

    User's phone number

    User's login ID

    Machine user is logged onto

    Application user is running

    Program (and version of the program) user is running

    Date and time the problem occurred

    Description of what was being done with any key field values being entered

    Response time (total, or amount up to the present, if the function is still running)

    Any additional information that you think might be useful in solving the response time problem

Remember to take complaints about response time seriously even when those complaints come from people on your own staff. Complaints about response time are legitimate, even if they come from developers, DBAs, system administrators, or QA staff. Any user of a computer system can experience poor response times, and any user's productivity can be damaged when he or she can't get the throughput needed on a certain day.

Investigating Complaints About Response Time

How do you decide if your users' complaints about response times warrant making changes? The problem is, you usually have a maze of conflicting information. Your staff may provide you with a lot of information about how well individual SQL statements perform against the database and how long it takes the network to process a particular request. That doesn't necessarily tell you what the individual user is experiencing.

Here are some suggested steps to follow:

1. Make sure the problem really is one of response time. Sometimes, another problem may actually cause the slowness in response. We've known users whose terminals were unplugged, and others who didn't know how to activate a response from an

application wait for a response that the application had not yet received. When users are trained in how to use the system, they must also receive training in how to detect poor response time and what to do to be sure the problem really is at the system end. That's why collecting all of the information we've listed in the previous section is a good idea.

2. Check the complaint against the standard and against other users' experiences. Sometimes, although users complain about response times, those times may not be too far off the mark; for example, the standard may be 2.5 seconds, and the response comes back in 2.6 seconds. When a user reports a response problem, it's good practice to check the response times of other users who are running the same function.

3. To investigate particular complaints, run procedures against the production database, just as users would. Record response times at different times throughout the day. Try to use the same forms that production users most commonly use. (It's a good idea to do this monitoring on a regular basis, even when you aren't investigating complaints.)

SQL*Forms provides a function that allows you to automate this process by recording the keystrokes a user would type to a typical database query. Typically, you record the time of day just before running the recorded procedure, then run various forms using the recorded keystrokes, and then record the time of day once again after exiting the procedure.

Make sure you mimic the user environment as closely as you can. If the user is running client-server, make sure you do too. Make sure that the distribution of data on different machines is the same as it is in the user's environment. If you are running in client-server mode, make sure you have the same script running on all of the client machines. Otherwise, you may not take into account the fact that certain machines produce different response times.

Considering Tuning Service Agreements

How do you define "acceptable response time?" Acceptability is a somewhat amorphous concept. What's acceptable to one user may be totally unacceptable to another. It's a good idea to establish a standard for acceptable response time—a standard that makes sense for your organization and the work your users need to perform. Then, you'll have a yardstick you can use to measure actual system operations and to resolve user complaints about performance. You and your users won't continually be arguing about whether system performance is good or bad.

More and more organizations are adopting the notion of tuning service agreements. These agreements, made between the computing staff and their clients, provide an effective way to ensure that optimal response times are achieved, and continue to be achieved. If such agreements are in force for a system developed for a client, the client may not accept a system until response times are below or equal to those specified by the agreement. Once the system is in production, you may be subject to payment penalties if the response times are exceeded.

Tuning agreements are a good idea within your own organization as well. You also have a responsibility to your own developers to provide a system that offers them decent response times.

Expectations for response time must be realistic. Sub-half-second response times, for example, are ridiculous for a system that supports many users on a small minicomputer. A reasonable standard, and one that's specified for online interactive queries by many tuning agreements, is the following:

- Ninety-five percent of the functions must be performed in 2.5 seconds or less.

- Certain complex functions may realistically not be able to be performed this quickly. But, there should be no more than two functions per application that exceed 2.5-second response time.

- No response time may exceed 10 seconds (if it does, it should be run in batch).

In addition to specifying acceptable response time, service agreements should also specify up-time for a system and should include a plan for disaster recovery.

Tuning service agreements do more than just protect system users. They also place more pressure on the designer and the DBA to design for performance, and on the development team to code for performance.

Managing the Problem of Long-running Jobs

Sometimes organizations pay a lot of attention to tuning interactive jobs and not nearly enough to tuning or scheduling long-running jobs. Carefully pruning your response time from 3 seconds down to 2.5 seconds for your interactive jobs won't make much difference if the long-running jobs hog the system for many minutes or even hours.

Every organization has a set of reporting or accounting functions that take a long time to run, some for many hours. Too often, sites try to run long-running jobs at the same time that interactive users are demanding speedy responses to their queries. The long-running jobs can get a stranglehold on system resources, making the system unworkable and many hundreds of users very unhappy. And often, there is no reason to run long-running jobs during times of peak usage in the system. A little common sense in scheduling such jobs will help your overall performance a lot.

Often, a site will put a lot of effort into tuning its interactive jobs and will ignore the tuning of long-running, resource-intensive jobs. Although it's true that all the tuning in the world won't make these jobs complete in seconds, or even minutes, it is neverthe-less possible to improve their performance quite a bit. Remember, improving interactive performance by reducing a query's response time from four seconds to two seconds (a 50% performance improvement) yields a savings of two seconds. But improving a ten-hour-long batch job by the same 50% yields a saving of five hours!

Just as you impose required response times on interactive jobs, consider imposing similar standards on batch jobs. These jobs might be moved to overnight or otherwise non-peak processing. If it is possible to have these jobs run on machines other than those used for heavy transaction processing, that will also improve performance. You also need to impose tuning agreements on long-running jobs, just as you do on interac-tive jobs. The specifics of the tuning agreement for long-running jobs will have to be worked out within your organization; sites differ greatly in what they need to produce. A general rule of thumb many sites follow is to run, during off-peak hours, any job that takes more than three minutes. As we mention in Chapter 2, *What Causes Performance Problems?*, we take a stricter approach than this; the cutoff we recommend is 45 seconds. In other words, if you are running in an OLTP system, any job that takes more than 45 seconds should be run on a different machine (against a backup database) or moved to off-peak hours. For complete information about keeping long-running jobs from impacting your system's performance, see Chapter 15, *Tuning Long-running Jobs.*

Managing the Workload in Your System

To speak of "tuning users" has a nasty, computer-centric sound to it. But, in fact, your human users may be able to cooperate in ways that will have an enormous effect on system performance without hindering their own productivity at all. To tune your system effectively, you need to understand the people behind the system. How many people are using the system? What are they doing? What are their expectations? What are their priorities? In short, what is the expected workload?

In most ORACLE systems, the workload isn't constant from one week or day or hour to the next. For example, over the course of a single day, you'll typically find that peak interactive usage occurs for about six hours a day, between 9:30 a.m. and 12:00 p.m., and between 1:30 p.m. and 5:00 p.m. Over the course of a year, you're likely to find that the height of system activity occurs just before the end of a financial year, as users are finalizing the year's accounts and developing budgets for the next financial year. Over the course of your system's lifetime, you'll probably find that the workload grows gradu-ally, but significantly, as the number of users logging onto the system increases. This steady increase is known as workload creep. Don't let it creep up on you, catching you without adequate resources to operate effectively.

Although you may not have the power to change your users' daily or yearly activities to even out performance, you can at least be aware of these peaks and valleys in system use, and you can use this information to improve overall system performance. Be sure to ask your users what they really need; maybe their requirements are flexible, and you can shift scheduling to improve overall performance in the system:

- Does a particular report need to be run immediately, or is tomorrow morning soon enough?

- Will the jobs scheduled for overnight processing actually be completed overnight, or do they have the potential for continuing into the next day?

- For batch jobs, when do they need to run? One particular night of the week, or any night? Once every two weeks? Quarterly? Annually? Make sure you know what the schedules are for these batch jobs well in advance, so you can factor them into the overall schedule while keeping performance high.

- For sets of reports, do they need to be run in any particular order?

The most difficult kind of system to administer and plan for is one in which users request many resource-intensive, ad hoc reports in an unpredictable fashion. Unfortunately for your ability to sleep nights, as GUIs gain popularity and the number of PC users increases, this unpredictable use of the system is likely to grow significantly. If you plan carefully, though, you'll be able to accommodate such users without adversely affecting your other users and your overall system performance.

Once you have a handle on what the workload tends to be in your system, remember to plan for unanticipated emergencies. If an unexpectedly large workload appears one day, you don't want to plunge the entire organization into chaos.

At some sites, staggered hours help system performance a good deal. For example, some people in the organization may begin work at 7:00 a.m. and go home at 3:00 p.m. Others may come in at 3:00 p.m. and leave at 11:00 p.m. Other organizations may offer flextime in which employees can arrive and leave within a three-hour spread. Whenever work is staggered in this way, you'll notice better performance, even when you don't explicitly change any of your procedures. When you tune specifically to take advantage of this scheduling, you'll get even better results.

You'll have to be particularly careful about scheduling long-running jobs when your organization is an international one. For example, when it is 4:00 p.m. in San Francisco, it's 9:00 a.m. the next day in Melbourne, Australia. Such international spread can be advantageous in distributing the workload in systems offering 24-hour online help systems, for example. But, in such staggered environments, it may also be hard to know when to run long-running, resource-intensive batch jobs and backups. Such jobs have the potential for severely disrupting online response time.

If you stay flexible and creative, you'll find a way to make workload scheduling work to the advantage of system performance. Consider the case in which users from Boston and New York share a computer system. When it's 6:00 p.m in Boston, it's also 6:00 p.m. in New York. When online users go home, the long-running overnight reports begin running. But, because there are comparatively few users logged on at this time, there is no serious impact on interactive user response times. Now, suppose that users from Los Angeles join the system. When it is 6:00 p.m. in Boston and New York, it's only 3:00 p.m. in Los Angeles, prime working time. Continuing to run overnight reports at this time would have a serious impact on the new users' response times. The obvious move is to adjust the overnight processing so reports are run after most of the Los Angeles users have logged off, a three-hour difference. (Although this seems to be a very obvious adjustment, we're constantly amazed at how resistent people are to changing their schedules and procedures; we've had to fight this battle many times!)

Remember that normal system administration is a part of the mix of jobs at your site. At one site we visited, users complained that their response time was poor in the morning but fine in the afternoon. None of the application's long-running jobs was being run during the day. But the system administrator ran a backup job first thing every morning, and this job had a serious impact on application performance. When we recommended that backup be run late at night or earlier in the morning, we were told that the computing staff was not allowed to work outside normal business hours. Not a very enlightened policy: this decision cost the company productivity, throughput, and ultimately revenue.

Making the Decision to Buy More Equipment

As we've mentioned in Chapter 1, *Introduction to ORACLE Performance Tuning*, by tuning your system effectively you are often able to avoid the need to buy a larger computer or more memory or disk resources. Before you spend any money on equipment, ask these questions—of yourself and your computing staff:

Has your application been completely tuned in single-user mode? Is every response time within the standard specified in your service agreement? There can be no exceptions to the rule. Do not proceed past this point until your application is totally tuned!

What is your average amount of memory per user, the expected disk I/Os per user, and the average CPU MIPS per user in the current configuration? You must know what you are using now before you can assess statistics for any new equipment or applications you'll be considering.

What is the expected growth rate in users at your site? You'll usually need to plan for growth, but in some organizations the number of users will actually be expected to drop over time. Make sure you have correct projections for your own organization.

What resources are causing the most performance problems in your system? Is the machine short of memory? Is it experiencing CPU wait times? Is it I/O bound? Is it experiencing network bottlenecks? Make sure you get solid answers from your DBA and system administrator.

Chapter 2 introduces the specific memory, disk, CPU, and network bottlenecks that may occur, and suggests some basic ways to deal with them. Later chapters provide much more detail on how you can tune these resources to the best advantage.

If you've tuned your system as effectively as you can, and you're still experiencing major problems in resource availability and response time, you'll probably have to face the decision to buy more equipment. You may need a new computer, or you may need to upgrade only certain components (e.g., more memory, additional disks). Don't just blindly add to the configuration you already have. This is an opportunity to ask whether it's time to consider moving to a client-server configuration, or whether it might be possible to downsize in some other way. Chapter 16, *Tuning in the Client-server Environment*, describes in some detail how you can get the best performance out of a client-server model.

Here are some suggestions for gathering the information you need to make a solid decision about what equipment you need:

1. Ask other organizations that may be running the equipment you're considering about their experiences. Do this for hardware, but also for software, including software packages developed by ORACLE. Be sure to focus your questions on the performance of the products they're running.

2. Do a capacity planning study for your site. In this study, you perform benchmarks on your site's current use of memory, disk, CPU MIPS, and the network, and calculate what additional equipment is needed to produce acceptable performance. You'll usually ask your system administrator to perform this study, as described in Chapter 17, *Capacity Planning*.

3. Shop around for the best equipment and prices. Before you buy anything, ask your vendors to let you run some sample programs on the type of computer you're planning to buy, or to add memory or disk on a trial basis to see how well it meets your performance needs. Most vendors will go along with this plan.

4. Make sure that whatever equipment you buy can be readily upgraded so you'll be able to cope with more users, additional applications, or new functions within existing applications. One of the big advantages of a client-server architecture is that you can add power to the client side without disrupting overall processing.

Remember that, because ORACLE products are so portable, most applications can be developed on a small computer and later ported to your larger production machine.

Management Checkpoints

Figure 3-1 shows the key checkpoints you'll need to be aware of as a manager or system planner. The section in Chapter 1 called "When Do You Tune?" introduces each of these major processes and their effect on performance.

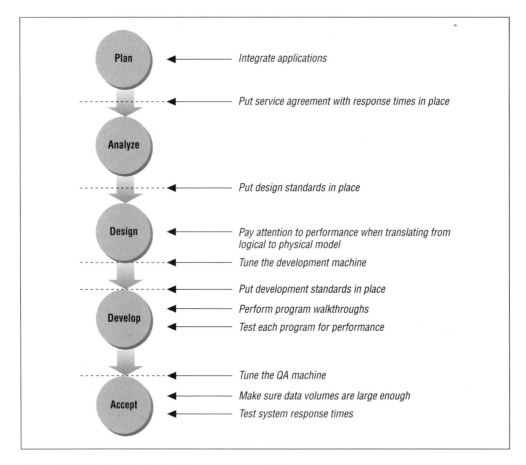

Figure 3-1: Tuning checkpoints for managers and planners

Checkpoint 1: Integrate applications. Your data model, applications, RDBMS, hardware, and other software aren't all stand-alone entities. Each affects the other. If you develop an application without considering its impact on other hardware and software in your system, or vice versa, you're very likely to end up having performance problems. Figure out ahead of time, not afterwards, how your systems will communicate. An important point to consider here is how to transfer data between applications. If you don't carefully plan ahead of time for how applications will exchange data, data transfer might impose a huge burden on your computer resources.

Checkpoint 2: Put tuning service agreement in place. A tuning service agreement is a good idea for just about any site. The section earlier in this chapter called "Considering a Tuning Service Agreement" describes briefly how you establish agreed-upon response times for different types of functions, as well as system up-time and disaster recovery plans.

Checkpoint 3: Put design standards in place. Most analysts and designers are skilled at designing data models and normalizing data. But few of them have much experience designing from a performance point of view. For best results, be sure to include your DBA in the design effort. The DBA can work with the designers to review the data model from a performance point of view, can figure out where performance requirements demand that data be denormalized (described in Checkpoint 4 below), and can help designers meet the requirements you've specified at your site for acceptable response times.

Checkpoint 4: Pay attention to performance when translating from logical to physical model. The physical data model specifies how data is going to be stored in your database and the indexes that will be created to provide fast access to the data. The logical model specifies the abstract relationships between entities. Often, in translating from the logical model to the physical model, your designers will have to compromise the goal of perfectly normalized data in order to achieve good performance. If you don't pay attention to performance at this stage, the costs to repair performance problems later on will be huge, as we show in Chapter 2. Regardless of how talented your programmers, DBAs, and system administrators may be, they will be fighting a losing battle in their efforts to make an inadequate physical data model perform well.

A note about CASE tools. Although CASE tools can be very helpful, they sometimes do not take real-world constraints and requirements into account. If you follow CASE guidelines to the letter, you're likely to end up with beautifully normalized data that may slow your system to a crawl. Many CASE tools don't even offer options for translating logical to physical models in a way that provides for performance.

One of the things CASE methods often don't address is denormalization, which we mention briefly above. Denormalization is the process of storing redundant data to lessen the number of database reads necessary to retrieve that data. Although the goal in any relational database system is normalization to the fullest extent possible, sometimes denormalization is needed to make programs meet the response time goals established for them. In Chapter 5, *Designing Your Data Model for Performance*, we describe some situations in which you'll need to denormalize your data to achieve better performance.

Make sure that your physical data model is reviewed by the DBA to ensure that it provides the best performance possible for your system.

Checkpoint 5: Tune the development machine. Good performance isn't a privilege of production users alone. Don't forget that your programmers may be laboring under tight deadlines. They'll never meet these deadlines if they're waiting half the day for the system to respond.

Checkpoint 6: Put development standards in place. Performance is a programming goal too. Include performance in your programming standards. Optimize each SQL statement so you get the best possible response time out of it. Code all programs carefully and neatly so it's easier to read through program code during tuning.

Checkpoint 7: Perform program walk-throughs. Perform a program walk-through before any programming begins at your site. Make sure all technical specifications are reviewed from a performance, as well as a functional, perspective. For each program, limit the walk-through to a one-hour session, which should be attended by the designer, one or more of your programmers, and the DBA. If the walk-through uncovers any inadequacies in performance, make sure these are remedied before programming begins. This will keep your developer from having to make major changes after the code has been completed, and will result in better overall performance.

Checkpoint 8: Test each program for performance. Make sure your programmers test each of their programs for performance before they release them for testing in the quality assurance environment. Let them know that it isn't professional to send untuned programs to QA and expect the testers to find response time problems. Make sure your programmers are using the ORACLE tools designed to diagnose performance problems and improve performance. See the discussion of EXPLAIN PLAN, TKPROF, and other tools in Chapter 12, *Diagnostic and Tuning Tools.*

Checkpoint 9: Tune the quality assurance machine. Your quality assurance machine must be tuned so it does realistic performance testing of all programs. The quality assurance environment is your last chance to test programs for functionality and performance before moving them into production. If all your QA response times are poor, it will be difficult to gauge how effectively a program will perform in production. Poor response times caused by an inefficiently tuned machine will also increase the time it takes to test programs. Make sure the environment you use for testing is consistent with the production environment (e.g., client-server), and make sure you are testing on a configuration that runs the same or slower than the production machine.

Checkpoint 10: Make sure test data volumes are large enough. If quality assurance data volumes are not large enough, programs will perform well in testing, but may perform abysmally in the production environment. Make sure that your QA data volumes are as similar as they can be to those that will be used in production.

Checkpoint 11: Test response times. You must reject any program that doesn't meet the response time standards specified in your site's tuning service agreement. The DBA should work with the QA staff to investigate the reasons for the poor response time. Once they have a hypothesis, report the information to the programmer who will be fixing the offending program.

Performance Hints for Managers

Here is a summary list of key performance hints that will help you plan and manage your ORACLE system to get the best performance out of it. We've touched on some of the more important of these in this chapter and in earlier chapters.

- If possible, make sure your development staff consists of people who have worked on highly-tuned ORACLE applications in the past. There is no substitute for experience.

- Identify and correct potential problems early in the development life cycle. If poor decisions are made during analysis and design, fixing the problem later on will take a lot longer and cost a lot more money.

- Make sure you have solid standards (for software selection, version control, modular programming, system libraries, and other such topics) in place at all stages of the development life cycle.

- Put in place a tuning service agreement that includes strict response time requirements. If you are buying a canned package, make sure that package also meets your standards for response time.

- Do not allow developers and quality assurers to work on the same machine as production users.

- Remember that, like one bad apple in the barrel, one ORACLE program, or even one SQL statement, that performs very poorly has the potential to degrade the performance of all of the functions in the system. Worse still, if you put an untuned application on a machine that was previously running tuned applications, the untuned application will degrade the performance of all of the applications on the machine.

- Make sure that programs are developed and maintained in a modular fashion. This will decrease development time and memory requirements, and it will make the application easier to maintain.

- Make sure to log inactive users off the system after a specified period of time. Also, monitor those users who repeatedly log on two or three times, making sure there is a genuine need for their behavior.

- Code applications to best suit the particular configuration you are running. For example, make sure that your staff members are aware of the additional coding considerations for tuning client-server.

- Do not allow users to submit untuned ad hoc queries that will compete with online transaction processing users on your system. Set up a procedure to review and tune all such ad hoc queries before they are run.

4

Defining System Standards

As part of planning and managing your ORACLE system, you and the other members of your project team need to establish rigorous system standards for design, programming, and testing. This book does not dictate any particular set of standards, nor does it describe standards in any detail. There are a number of good reference books on design, programming, and testing methodologies. To these general recommendations, you'll have to add and customize areas of particular concern to your own organization.

In this chapter, we remind you that performance, both the performance of your final application and even the performance of your project development team, depends largely on how carefully you have set standards for design, programming, and testing, and of how rigorously you have enforced those standards.

Selecting a Common Design Methodology

There are many methodologies you can choose from to design and develop your system. Your selection ranges from crude in-house products to complex CASE tools, for instance, ORACLE*CASE, as well as many third-party products. The choice is up to you. You will have to take into account such factors as the complexity of your application, your budget, your schedule for development, the experience of your project team, and even the style and communication channels of your organization.

Whatever you select, select it early. We can't stress too emphatically the importance of having a standard methodology in place from the beginning of a project. Organizations that decide, in the middle of a project, to adopt even the most powerful CASE tool, for example, find that it's very hard, and disruptive in terms of both time and budget to switch horses in mid-stream.

Selecting Software

At the very start of the project, you also need to choose the set of development tools you'll be using. There are a large number of ORACLE and third-party tools. Here too, your choice depends on a myriad of considerations, including hardware configuration, in-house staff experience, the availability of supplementary consultants with certain credentials, geography, project deadline, and budget.

There are a number of software decisions you need to make, but chief among them are the choices of an online interface and a report interface. Examples of online interfaces from which you're likely to choose are:

- SQL*Forms
- SQL*Plus
- Third-party GUIs such as Gupta, Forest & Trees, and Quest
- Pro*C, Pro*COBOL, or one of the other Pro* tools
- ORACLE Call Interface (OCI)

Examples of report interfaces from which you're likely to choose are:

- SQL*Reportwriter
- SQL*Plus
- SQL*Report
- SQR
- Pro*C, Pro*COBOL, or one of the other Pro* tools
- ORACLE Call Interface (OCI)

You'll also typically use a spreadsheet package such as Lotus 1-2-3 or Excel that is able to communicate with your database.

Make sure to select readily available, easy-to-learn tools, and make sure all of your developers actually are using them. Although in theory it may seem like a good idea to let individual programmers code in whatever language they're most productive in, this *laissez-faire* attitude can wreak havoc on your project. At one organization we worked in, a high-powered consultant was allowed to code in Assembler, and he worked miracles by generating a huge amount of code in a short amount of time. Unfortunately, the miracle worker couldn't follow through. He left for Cuba, and left a half-finished debugging nightmare behind.

Remember too that the choices you make have financial consequences. At another organization, we saw a superb system developed on time and meeting all user requirements. Unfortunately, this system called for the use of a GUI that necessitated a minimum 66-megahertz 486 processor on every user desk. There went the development budget!

Setting Up Screen and Report Skeletons

A critical way to ensure the continuity of system development is to make sure that skeletons of all screens and reports in the system are stored in default libraries. Make sure that a senior staff member develops these skeletons after consulting with representatives of the user base that will be using the screens and reports.

Here are the key elements in any skeletons you develop:

Program name. Include it in the header at the top of any screen or report, as shown in Figure 4-1. Specifies the name of the program that produces the screen or report. This program name allows programs to be identified easily—for example, when users need to communicate over the telephone, when they identify user screen dumps, etc. Also include the program version where possible.

Program description. Include it in the header at the top of any screen or report. Identifies as precisely as possible the function of the program that produces the screen or report. By setting up this description to be modifiable by users, you can allow individual users to customize their screens.

Usercode. Include it in the header at the top of any screen or report. Specifies the usercode of the user who requested the screen or report. Including the usercode enables problems to be tracked and fixed more easily, and allows reports to be distributed to users.

Date and time. Include them in the header at the top of any screen or report. Including the current date and time on each screen and report page allows problems to be tracked more easily and enforces version control.

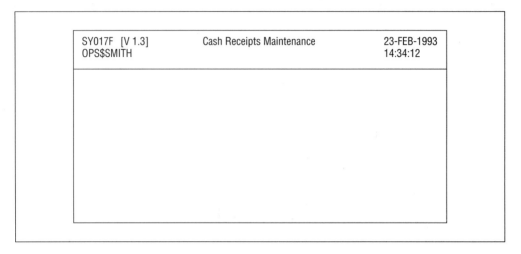

Figure 4-1: Sample screen header

Screen layout. Define common conventions for all screens displayed by the system so each screen has a common look and feel, as shown in Figure 4-2. Choices you will need to make about the screen layout include:

- Should fields be left- or right-justified?

- How should numeric field displays be formatted?

- How should date displays be formatted?

- Should field prompts be left- or right-justified? Should they be followed by a colon?

Field naming. Establish strict guidelines for the naming of fields. Fields must have consistent names from screen to screen. For example, a field that's called ACCOUNT_CODE on one screen should not be called ACC_CODE, ACCT, A/C, etc., on other screens. Select one name and use it everywhere, including on report headers. You'll make life simpler for programmers and users alike.

Pop-up position. Anchor your layered pop-up screens at a common screen location, as shown in Figure 4-3. Windows at specific levels should all look the same from one program to the next. (For an additional discussion of pop-up windows defined via SQL*Forms, see Chapter 9, *Tuning SQL*Forms*.)

Key redefinition. Establish a consistent set of standard keys to be used system-wide. SQL*Forms provides more than 40 standard key functions per screen. Some have well-recognized functions and should be used consistently across programs and screens; some are there only to support compatibility with previous versions; and some are downright risky to use. Decide which essential keys you want to standardize and which

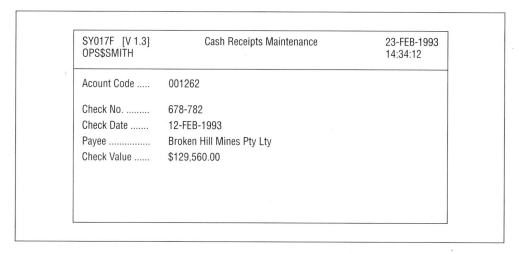

Figure 4-2: Sample screen skeleton

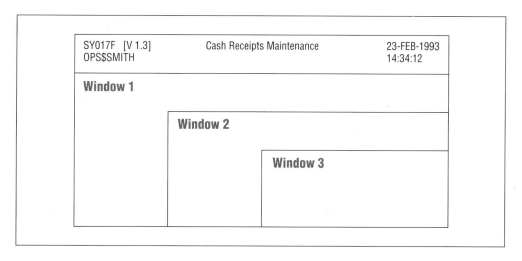

Figure 4-3: Pop-up windows

you might wish to redefine or disable. Make sure that key defaults are consistent for all screens in your application by specifying them in standard skeletons.

For example, on an IBM PC you will probably want to preserve PF1 as the help key in all applications, and PF2 as the select key. PF3 (duplicate field) and PF4 (duplicate record) may also be appropriate, although PF4 sometimes presents problems (see the ORACLE documentation). Be sure to redefine PF5 (call SQL*Forms Menu), which provides no security.

Using Modular Programming Techniques

During this early standardization phase, make sure that all developers know how important it is to use modular programming techniques. Don't let them develop large, complex programs, even if these programs are going to perform miracles. It's in the interest of a working, efficient system to break all tasks down to their lowest manageable units. In addition to making programs easier to develop and test, the modular approach also allows applications to share software modules and build generic system libraries.

SQL*Forms is an apt example of modular programming, shown in Figure 4-4 and Figure 4-5. With SQL*Forms it makes a lot of sense to develop small forms and link them together via the CALL or the CALLQRY macros, rather than to develop enormous, unmaintainable programs. This modular approach is completely invisible to the program user, but enormously simplifies development. It also allows modules to be shared more easily and facilitates recursive functionality.

In addition to increasing the performance of system developers, modularization also increases run time performance. As each function is exited, it releases individual module resources, so overall resource overhead is significantly reduced. In contrast, a program that contains all system functions has only two choices—release all of its resources, or release none of them.

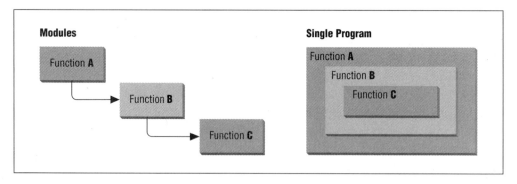

Figure 4-4: Modular versus single program

Breaking functions down during program development also permits the sharing of common routines. This one aspect alone can greatly affect the development cycle of an application. A single program module can be shared by many routines.

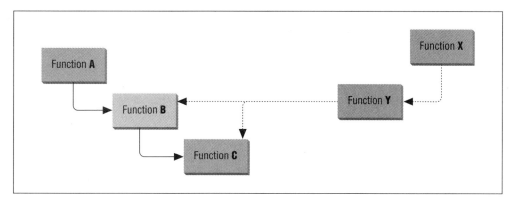

Figure 4-5: Modular programming

Defining System Libraries

During the design phase, and continuing into the start of programming, a senior staff member, typically an analyst/programmer, needs to take responsibility for the defining and coding of as many as possible of the standard system libraries. These libraries are invaluable in speeding up the coding process, controlling system functionality, and performing system-wide maintenance. In addition, your programmers will often be able to put system libraries together to perform many of the functions that would otherwise require custom programming.

Following are a number of standard libraries we have found helpful within our own organizations:

- Validate that user has authority over the report
- Determine the user's destination printer
- Determine the report's stationery code (plan, invoice, etc.)
- Calculate the user's report priority level (online/immediate, deferred, overnight)
- Build the report request definition
- Initiate or schedule the report
- Inform the user of the outcome of the request

Another very useful library to define is one that provides context-sensitive help, that is, a help screen that is aware of what screen you are using. You can define such a library as a default function available from all screens in the system in a consistent way by redefining an unwanted SQL*Forms key. For best results, allow the help text to be able to be entered by users.

We have also found it very useful to define a pop-up screen that allows users to navigate instantly to anywhere in the system (subject to security restrictions). This approach is an application shortcut that saves users from having to navigate back to the menu, traversing the menu to the next function, and selecting it. In this case too, define this library as a default function available from all screens in the system in a consistent way by redefining an unwanted SQL*Forms key.

Be sure to document all common functions and procedures, and make sure your entire programming staff is aware of what functions and procedures are available to them. If they don't know what's already been coded, how can they take advantage of them?

Enforcing Program Version Control

Because ORACLE runs on so many platforms, no one version-control utility can handle all developer and user needs. As a consequence, developers frequently argue about which utility is best to use. For most platforms, there are several viable possibilities for version control. For example, UNIX provides SCCS or RCS, VMS supports CMS, and a number of proprietary utilities are available for MS-DOS. The important thing is that you select one system and stick with it.

Make sure you are using a version-control utility that has won the trust of the people in your organization, and make sure you enforce its use. We can't overemphasize how important it is to use version control, particularly when you are migrating your programs. We've seen many days and weeks of back-breaking development quickly disappear when an incorrect program migration erases all evidence of the correct version!

SQL*Forms presents a particular version control problem. Even a single, unimportant change within an SQL*Forms application—for example, changing the field sequencing within a block—can result in several hundred lines of altered code for the version utility. Although not a single line of code has actually been changed, you'll have to wade through a maddening amount of output.

After some debate, ORACLE has decided to continue support for the *ASCII.INP* format file in SQL*Forms Version 4. We're relieved. Where would existing version control utilities be if this support ceased?

Establishing Documentation Standards

Everybody complains about documentation—writing it and using it. But don't underestimate its importance. The standardization phase is the time to draw up a documentation methodology and establish a uniform style of presentation for all documentation of programs, screens, reports, etc. Now is also the time to decide what products you'll be using for word processing and other documentation tasks. Make sure everybody on the project team knows what is expected of them in terms of documenting whatever design or code they are responsible for, what products they are to use, and where the documentation is to be stored.

These are the documentation areas you'll need to standardize:

- Program specifications: how to present them
- Program functionality: how to present it
- Unit testing: plans and results
- Module testing: plans and results
- System testing: plans and results
- User modifications: what's allowed and how to report them
- Bugs: how to report them
- Migration: what are the plans
- Version control: what type and how to enforce it

III

Tuning for Designers and Analysts

Part III describes what ORACLE system designers and analysts need to know about tuning. How can you best design your data model for performance? How far should data normalization go, and when can you improve performance by denormalizing data? What is the special role of indexes in improving database design?

5

Designing Your Data Model for Performance

The most fundamental part of tuning your ORACLE system is to make sure at the outset that your data model is well structured and normalized. If your tables and columns are not initially structured in a way that enforces simplicity and efficiency, your applications are doomed to failure. The most powerful hardware, the most sophisticated software, and the most highly-tuned data and programs won't succeed in manipulating your database in an acceptable amount of time.

In non-relational databases—those based on hierarchical or network models—structures and programs are designed and implemented as a unit. The relational data model is different. Designing according to a relational model is both simpler and more powerful than designing according to one of the older models. With a relational design, you can design the database as a completely separate step from the design of the procedures that access these structures. The physical design of the database can be completed and verified before any procedural design begins.

There are four important rules to follow in designing your database and making sure your design goals become reality:

1. Develop a sound and thorough database design, as well as a comprehensive overall system design, before you allow any coding to begin.

2. Monitor carefully how well your logical data model (e.g., the abstract definition of the data your system needs and how that data is to be structured into tables) can be translated to a physical data model (e.g., the actual arrangement of data in files).

3. Test, test, test! Throughout detailed design and coding, keep testing to be sure your design is a sound one, and make adjustments for performance as needed.

4.   Make sure you coordinate your efforts with others at your site. Because the DBA is so often aware of database performance issues, he or she can lend expertise to the design effort. And, because programmers have experience coding around bad design decisions, they too can provide input to the overall design.

Although the goal of any relational database system is a fully normalized database, performance is sometimes at odds with the abstractions of normalization. This chapter describes situations in which you'll get much better performance out of your system by denormalizing certain tables in your database.

Indexes are an important part of the design effort. Too often, designers don't take the time to index. Chapter 6, *Defining Indexes*, describes design goals for indexes. The section in Chapter 7, *Tuning SQL*, called "Using Indexes to Improve Performance" supplements this discussion by describing how indexes affect the performance of your SQL statements.

Database Definitions: A Quick Review

We assume, in this book, that you know at least the basics about relational databases and how data is structured and handled in such a system. There are many excellent books on relational design, including, of course, the classic works of E.F. Codd and C.J. Date. We do think it might be helpful to include some brief definitions of the terms that underlie any discussion of database design:

Entity. An entity is any person, place, or thing in your system. For example, an entity might be an employee, a location of a branch office, or an invoice in a financial system. You define these entities in the form of tables.

Table. A table is the basic unit of data storage in the database. A table is a uniquely named, two-dimensional array made up of columns and rows. A table may represent a single entity in your system (e.g., bank accounts), or it may represent a relationship between two entities in your system (e.g., the relationship between a bank account and the prevailing interest rate). In formal relational database language, a table is called a relation.

Column. A column is one attribute of an entity (e.g., name or interest rate or homeroom number). A column has a unique name within a table. Columns within a table are non-decomposable, that is, they can't be broken down further. Columns are arranged in an arbitrary order, that is, their order is not significant. Typically, the number of columns in a table remains constant over time.

Row. A row is a unique entry within a table (e.g., one student, one order, or one bank account). A row contains the actual data describing the student, order, or account. A row is equivalent to a record. Because row data often changes over time, rows, unlike columns, are dynamic. Rows within a table are also arranged in an arbitrary order; their order is not significant.

Primary Key. A primary key is a column (or a group of columns) within a table that can be used to uniquely identify a row in that table. The choice of primary keys is a very important design decision. Meaningful primary keys simplify the relationships between tables and increase the performance of your applications.

Every table must have a primary key. All of the other columns in the table depend on the primary key. If a primary key consists of more than one column, it is known as a composite, or concatenated, key. It is not always easy to identify a primary key in a file. According to Third Normal Form (see the definition below), a key must satisfy these three rules to qualify as a primary key:

- The primary key must uniquely identify each row in the table. For example, a student identification number uniquely identifies each row in the student table because each student has a unique ID.

- If a primary key consists of more than one column, each column of the concatenated primary key is required to uniquely identify each row. For example, a primary key might be a homeroom number. Because a particular school has several buildings, with duplicate room numbers, you must know the building number as well as the room number. The composite primary key is the combination of these two numbers.

- Each row can be uniquely identified by only one primary key. If the student ID is the primary key, only the student ID identifies the student. There must be no other unique ID in the rows of the student table.

Foreign key. A foreign key is a column (or, for a composite key, a group of columns) in one table that corresponds to a primary key in another table. Foreign keys are used to show relationships between tables. For example, each row in a student table contains information about one student. One column in the student table is the student's homeroom (HMRM_NO). A second table, the homeroom table, contains one row for each homeroom in a school. HMRM_NO is the primary key in the homeroom table. In the STUDENT table, the corresponding HMRM_NO column is the foreign key.

Association. An association is a relationship between entities. Several different types of relationships may exist, as shown in Figure 5-1. The three basic types are:

- One-to-one (1:1). For example, an employee can have one, but only one, spouse defined in the employee table.

- One-to-many (1:M). For example, an employee can have many children defined in the children table.

- Many-to-many (M:M). For example, a company can produce many parts. A part can be produced by many companies. Companies and parts are in a many-to-many relationship.

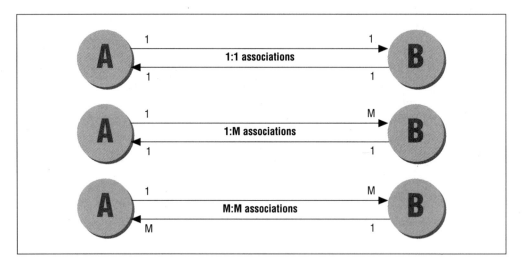

Figure 5-1: Types of associations

Attribute. An attribute is a characteristic or a quality of an entity or an association. For example, an attribute of a employee ID might be that it is in the range 1-100. An attribute of a student might be the student name.

Prime table. A prime table is a core application table around which an application revolves (e.g., EMP in a personnel system, LOAN_MASTER in a credit union system).

Dependent table. A dependent table is a table that cannot exist on its own. It has a composite (multi-column) primary key, at least part of which is the primary key of a prime table. For example, the PURCHASE_ORDER table has a purchase order as its key. The dependent table, PO_LINE_ITEMS, has PO/ITEM_NUM as its key and cannot contain records that do not have a corresponding prime table record.

Associative table. An associative table is a table that links two tables together (e.g., parts and suppliers). The PARTS table is a prime table; the SUPPLIERS table is a prime table, and the PARTS/SUPPLIERS table links which parts are available from a single supplier, or which supplier a part can be purchased from.

History table. A history table usually contains a date column (and possibly a time column) as part of a composite primary key. A history table for a supplier might be SUPPLIER/DATE/PART/QTY. This would simply list all parts sold by a supplier since the company began.

Recursive table. A recursive table is a table that has a foreign key that actually references other rows from the same table. For example, suppose every employee has a manager who is also an employee. The MGR_CODE is a foreign key to the same EMP table.

Normalization. Normalization is a term heard often during the early stages of database design. It is the process of breaking down all items to their lowest level, making sure that each piece of data can be uniquely identified and is not duplicated. There are three basic principles of data normalization:

- A normalized table does not contain any redundant information.

- A normalized table does not contain any repeating columns.

- A normalized database contains only the tables necessary to define the data.

Normalization is the ideal in any relational system, although as we discuss later in this chapter, it is necessary in certain circumstances to violate some of the principles of normalization in order to increase performance.

First Normal Form (1NF). Putting data in first normal form means arranging data in separate tables where the data in each table is similar, and each table has a primary key. Each attribute can be represented by an individual value. 1NF tables cannot have any attribute with multiple values; in other words, repeating groups are not allowed. Figure 5-2 illustrates First Normal Form.

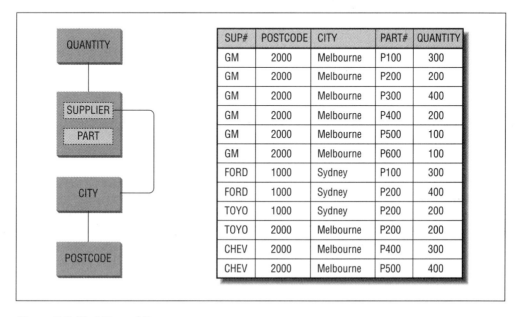

SUP#	POSTCODE	CITY	PART#	QUANTITY
GM	2000	Melbourne	P100	300
GM	2000	Melbourne	P200	200
GM	2000	Melbourne	P300	400
GM	2000	Melbourne	P400	200
GM	2000	Melbourne	P500	100
GM	2000	Melbourne	P600	100
FORD	1000	Sydney	P100	300
FORD	1000	Sydney	P200	400
TOYO	1000	Sydney	P200	200
TOYO	2000	Melbourne	P200	200
CHEV	2000	Melbourne	P400	300
CHEV	2000	Melbourne	P500	400

Figure 5-2: First Normal Form

Second Normal Form (2NF). Putting data in second normal form means removing data that is dependent on only part of the key. Each row of a table must be uniquely identified by key value(s) within the row. In a table, every 2NF non-key attribute must be fully dependent on the primary key. Figure 5-3 illustrates Second Normal Form.

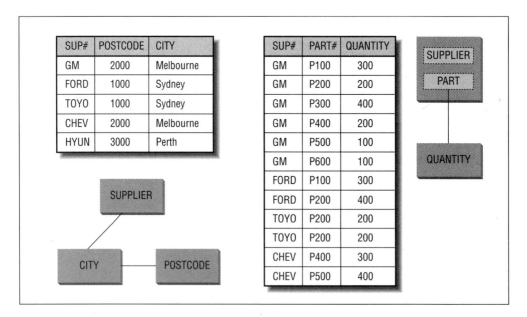

Figure 5-3: Second Normal Form

Third Normal Form (3NF). Putting data in third normal form means eliminating everything in tables that does not depend on a primary key. Each row attribute must be identified only by the key value(s); that is, every non-key column is solely dependent on the primary key. Figure 5-4 illustrates Third Normal Form.

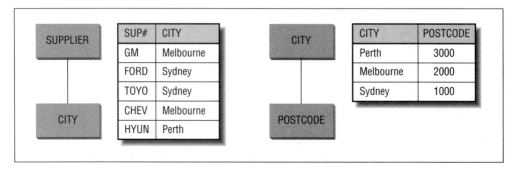

Figure 5-4: Third Normal Form

Fourth Normal Form (4NF). Identical to 3NF, but some non-key attributes have multi-valued dependencies, independent of other attributes. For example, consider the example in Figure 5-5; MVD is a multivalued dependency.

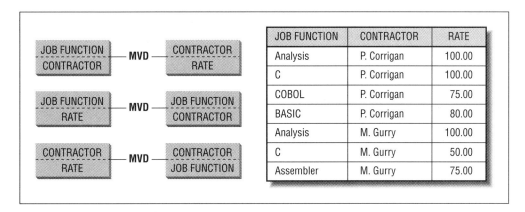

JOB FUNCTION	CONTRACTOR	RATE
Analysis	P. Corrigan	100.00
C	P. Corrigan	100.00
COBOL	P. Corrigan	75.00
BASIC	P. Corrigan	80.00
Analysis	M. Gurry	100.00
C	M. Gurry	50.00
Assembler	M. Gurry	75.00

Figure 5-5: Fourth Normal Form

Normalizing a Database

Normalizing a database is a straightforward, but rather detail-oriented, process. A detailed discussion of normalization is beyond the scope of this book. However, because normalization is basic to designing a high-performance system, we've included some summary information here on the normalization steps, just as a reminder. Refer to more detailed references on relational design for complete information.

1. Identify all of the entities that make up your system, and organize them into tables.

2. Identify all of the relationships between the entities in your system. Add to your tables, as necessary, or create new tables that express these relationships.

3. Identify all of the attributes of the entities in your system. Add to your tables, as necessary, or create new tables that express these attributes.

Within each of these steps, there are several substeps, described in the sections that follow.

NOTE

In addition to these abstract design steps, remember that you must always test every system model with real sample data. By testing your design on current, real data, you'll find that you can often avoid obvious and costly omissions and duplications in your data. This involves obtaining such items as purchase orders and other forms, and making sure that every field on these forms is covered in your data analysis.

Defining Entities

An entity is any person, place, or thing in your system. Entities are related to each other, and have attributes. During this first phase of analysis, determine which entities are within the scope of the system or within a particular module of the system. Remember, you do not necessarily need to include every known piece of information in your database tables. For example, there might be a great deal of information that could be maintained on every student who attends a university. However, not every piece of data might need to be included in your database tables—only data that needs to be available for retrieval or processing. If you aren't sure what falls in the scope of your system, verify your initial database design by running your application against sample data. Follow these steps to define the entities in your system:

Identify all entities in your system. As we've mentioned, an entity is any person, place, or thing that has meaning to the system that is being defined (that is, it falls within the scope of the system). Entities may be tangible (employees, trucks) or intangible (departments, budgets). To be defined as an entity, an entity must exist in or by itself, and must not be dependent upon, or subordinate to, other entities. You must construct a table describing each entity in your system.

Often, minor entities do not become apparent until they are identified as attributes of initial entities. Whenever you become aware of the existence of a new entity during analysis, be sure to record it immediately before proceeding.

Define the primary key for each entity. By definition, an entity—and the table that represents that entity—must have a primary key. The key must uniquely identify each element of the entity. The primary key can never be null and must never change over time. Ask yourself these questions:

- How can the key be uniquely identified?
- Does the primary key always exist?
- Is there only one primary key?
- Is there only one entity per primary key?
- Is the primary key subject to change?

Don't define as a primary key any data whose contents have embedded or implied meaning—sometimes known as an intelligent key. If you want to define such a key, break it down into its component parts, and define the whole as a composite key. For example, instead of defining as a primary key an account number whose individual columns have significance, define individual REGION_ID, CATEGORY, and SEQUEN-CE_NO columns, all making up a composite ACCOUNT_ID.

Verify the scope of the entities. Using simple sample data, test the scope, or domain, of the entity. You need to figure out the values, or range of values, that are valid for each entity. Here we are talking about logical testing, not the thorough testing of the database and code you'll perform later on. At this point, make sure that your sample data thoroughly tests the limits of your domain (for example, the smallest value, the largest value). During this step define the scope by specifying values or ranges for each entity, as in the following:

DATE_OF_BIRTH: Make sure the date is not in the future.

EMP_NO: Make sure employee numbers are in the range 1000 through 9999 available for this organization.

LOC_KEY: If there are currently 250 locations for this organization, make sure this field is three digits.

Document your findings. Document all findings, restrictions, and limitations you discover while you are defining entities. If you're using a formal design methodology such as a CASE tool, most of this documentation will be created automatically. If you're using other, less sophisticated methods, you should keep a project notebook that documents your findings, in accordance with your own organization's standards. (Refer to Chapter 4, *Defining System Standards*.) Remember, if a point is worth noticing, it must be worth remembering, even if all you are doing is noting that a particular topic needs to be revisited and rehashed at a later date. For each entity, you document, at the very least:

- The name of the table
- The primary key
- The set of sample data you used for testing

All of this information will be invaluable during later, more detailed design phases.

Defining Relationships

Once you have defined all entities in your system in tables, determine exactly what relationships exist between these entities. Then, verify all relationships by testing with sample data. Follow these steps:

Identify all relationships. Relationships are direct, logical associations between two or more entities that have already been defined. Not every relationship needs to be stated, only those of concern to your system. One possible relationship is a student table and a homeroom table. Another is a bank account table and an interest rate table.

Determine each relationship type. What is the type of relationship? The following are supported:

> One-to-one (1:1)
>
> One-to-many (1:M)
>
> Many-to-many (M:M)

Verify the scope of the relationships. Verify that all of the relationships you've defined are actually relevant to your system. Verify that the association has been correctly identified (1:1, 1:M, M:M). This can only be proven with real, sample data, provided by your users. For example, suppose you have specified a one-to-one relationship between an employee and her children. If there are two children in the test data, the relationship will fail. You'll need to specify a 1:M relationship instead. Test data may raise other questions as well about this relationship. What happens if an employee has twins? Will the relationship break down (along with the employee!)? Do you need to put an expanded primary key in the CHILDREN table to qualify child sequencing? Is the relationship actually of any importance to the system? These are the kinds of questions that should come up when you are logically testing a relationship.

Document your findings. Document all findings, restrictions, and limitations of each relationship. For each relationship, define the keys (both primary and foreign) and any constraints on the keys (e.g., non-null). Include the set of sample data you used in testing.

Defining Attributes

Finally, you must define attributes (characteristics) for all entities and relationships. Derivable data (that which can be calculated from existing data, such as the sum of other data, a running total, etc.) is not an attribute. Make sure you don't include any derivable data in your original (normalized) database design. As we'll see later in this chapter, you may find that in certain situations you will choose to include derivable data in particular tables to increase performance. However, during this initial stage, we are creating a fully normalized database design. Follow these steps:

Identify all attributes of your entities. An attribute is a characteristic or quality of an entity or relationship of concern to the user. Attributes are simply pieces of information that you need to display, correlate, or maintain within the system. In theory, every column of a table is an attribute. Attributes can be directly related to entities (employee name), or associations (years an employee has been a member of a department).

Verify the scope of the attributes. Attributes must be of value to the user and the project. Again, sample data must be carefully correlated to demonstrate the correctness of the attribute. Attribute ownership is not always straightforward. It is normally during the defining of attributes that new (minor) entities and associations are discovered. These new attributes are attributes of the new entity. You'll need to keep looping through the normalization process until all entities, relationships, and attributes have been completely defined. Now the analysis phase should return to step one: define, record, and test the new entity and its associations, before proceeding.

Document your findings. Document all findings, restrictions, and limitations of each attribute. Include the set of sample data you used in testing.

Denormalizing a Database

Normalization of data is always the goal of database design. In general, good design calls for a database that has no redundant data—that is, a database that is fully normalized. But, a fully normalized database, and one that stays normalized over time, is something of a Platonic ideal. In the real world, a world where performance may be more important than abstract perfection, you may find that you need to compromise your commitment to normalization and be flexible about dealing with real data. In other words, you may need to embrace the necessary evil of denormalization.

You'll need to know how to denormalize in order to optimize certain types of transactions and to help you achieve minimally acceptable physical response times on certain systems. In a number of cases, you can substantially improve response times (by reducing physical disk I/Os) by *not* enforcing system design to the third normal form.

It's important to go about denormalization in the proper way. Make sure that the data model is fully normalized before contemplating denormalization. And, don't assume that you will always need to denormalize. Consider each case on its own merits. Some of the aspects of system operation that you'll have to consider are data volumes, query frequency, update frequency, and minimum required retrieval times.

When should you denormalize? There are a number of situations in which you may improve performance by denormalizing your data. If you find that your application is performing repetitive SQL table joins and sort/merges on large tables, you may be able to avoid or reduce the need for these operations if you denormalize some parts of your database.

Denormalization isn't a panacea. Whenever you denormalize, you must accept the consequences:

- Denormalization makes coding more complex
- Denormalization often sacrifices flexibility
- Denormalization will speed up retrieval but slow updates

Figure 5-6 shows how you need to weigh these two types of activities (retrieval and update).

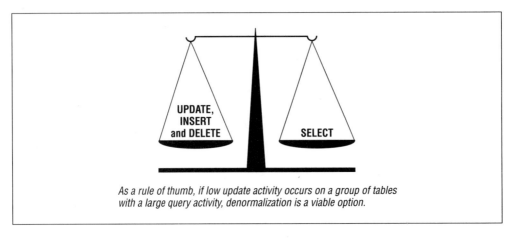

As a rule of thumb, if low update activity occurs on a group of tables
with a large query activity, denormalization is a viable option.

Figure 5-6: Denormalization as an option

In the following sections, we outline a number of cases in which denormalizing your data will substantially improve your system's performance. We're not arguing for the general case. In most situations, a fully normalized database is clearly the way to go. But, in these specific cases, try these denormalization tricks and watch your system fly.

Including Children in the Parent Record

In most cases, when your data has a parent-child relationship, you'll define separate records for the parent and each of the children. For example, consider the case of a bank account table. The basic information about the account (ID, name, etc.) would typically be stored in the parent record. Each of the quarterly balances might appear in a separate child record. Each of the child records will contain a key and a balance field.

But, in a case like this, you will often find that you'll get better performance not by specifying individual child records but by including a set of columns, one for each of the quarterly balances, in the parent record, as shown in Figure 5-7.

It doesn't always make sense to incorporate child columns into the parent record. In general, you should consider doing this when your data meets three criteria:

1. The absolute number of children for a parent is known (in this case, you know there are four quarterly records).

2. This number will not change over time, that is, it is static (the number of quarters in a year is not going to change!).

3. The number is not very large. "Large" is a hazy notion. Somewhat arbitrarily, we'll say that 20 is the limit. To be more precise, though, the fact that the number is fixed and will not increase over time is more important than the absolute number.

Storing child, or subordinate, data in the parent record in this way reduces the overhead required to perform table joins and propagated keys. The total performance improvement is, of course, a function of how many records you are processing and what you are doing with them. You'll realize the biggest performance gains if by including subordinate data in this way you avoid having to join thousands of parent and child records during application processing.

EMP#	NAME	QRT_1	QRT_2	QRT_3	QRT_4
0012745	Smith	1,000	1,500	1,750	2,500
0017346	Jones	12,400	12,700	14,000	15,500

Figure 5-7: Storing child data in the parent record

NOTE

There is a down side to incorporating child records into a parent record. (Isn't there always a down side to everything?) You will note an increase in the complexity of your data manipulation and retrieval statements. You'll have to assess the relative advantages and disadvantages of denormalizing your data before making a decision about what to do.

Storing the Most Recent Child Data in the Parent Record

Now, consider the case where a parent record is associated with a series of child records, each arranged in a kind of sequence. For example, the parent record might contain information about a particular bank account whose interest rate fluctuates over time (perhaps each month or quarter). Each child record might contain an effective date and a particular interest rate. Although, in this case it makes sense to maintain the individual child records, you can improve performance quite a bit by storing the most recent child record (the record containing the interest rate currently in effect) in the parent record, as shown in Figure 5-8. Because it's very likely that data retrievals will request the current rate, you'll be able to satisfy something like nine out of ten queries without ever needing to access a child record.

Storing the most recent child record in the parent is an appropriate choice when there is an unknown number of children and when each child has a sequencing attribute of some kind (in this case, an effective date). Of course, there are cases in which a data retrieval will require access to additional child records (history data). In these cases, a normal table join is performed. But, if few such accesses are expected, you'll find that storing the most recent child record will satisfy most of your access needs.

EMP#	NAME	CURRENT_RATE
0012745	Smith	15.75
0017346	Jones	10.75

EMP#	EFFEC_DATE	RATE
0012745	10-Jan-91	21.00
0012745	30-Jun-91	19.50
0012745	16-May-92	17.25
0012745	01-Jan-93	15.75
0017346	16-Dec-92	12.50
0017346	01-Feb-93	11.75
0017346	01-Jul-93	11.00
0017346	26-Sep-93	10.75

Figure 5-8: Storing the most recent child data in the parent record

What's the down side? Your database will have to contain an additional child record (the record containing the data that is duplicated in the parent record), and you'll have to maintain duplicate update routines for this record.

Hard-coding Static Data

Every good relational analyst shudders at the words "hard-coding," that is, including specific values in your program code, as opposed to references to table entries that may contain those values. And, for good reason. There are few examples where hard-coding makes sense.

But, there are a few. When the codes your programs will test for are very common, and very simple—for example, "Yes" and "No"—you'll find that hard-coding these codes into your programs (rather than creating a separate table for them) improves performance and doesn't create any problems for your clean relational design.

If we were to follow the rules of normalization in slavish fashion, we'd have to create a table to contain the "Yes" and "No" codes. A program would have to search the table each time it needed to test for a response. But third normal form isn't always the preferred choice. You may not think of a simple Yes/No, or Male/Female, test as a denormalization of data, but technically it is. When your programs are going to be testing frequently for such simple choices, you'll find that you can improve performance by hard-coding such choices. Here is an example of such hard-coding.

```
IF :BLK.SEX NOT IN ('M','F','N') THEN
    MESSAGE ('INVALID INPUT - (M)ALE, (F)EMALE OR (N)EITHER!);
    RAISE FORM_TRIGGER_FAILURE;
END IF;
```

Storing Running Totals

Earlier in this chapter, we told you never to store derivable data in a database table. Derivable data is data that can be computed from other data in the table—for example, a total of some values in that table, or some other statistical result. It is an axiom of relational design that we don't store derivable data. Because all necessary information is already contained in the system, it's considered unnecessary overhead—a duplication of effort and storage—to keep a total in a record.

But, there are cases in which you can greatly improve the performance of online inquiries by storing a running total in a record. For example, in the denormalized table on the left in Figure 5-9, we've stored AMT_TO_DATE as a running total. This data was derived from the normalized SALES table on the right. This example is a trivial one, but remember that the SALES table could contain hundreds of thousands of records, so the savings you gain by keeping running totals in the other denormalized table may be substantial.

EMP Table				SALES Table		
EMP#	**NAME**	**AMT_TO_DTE**		**EMP#**	**QRT_NO**	**AMOUNT**
0012745	Smith	6,750		0012745	1	1,000
0017346	Jones	54,600		0012745	2	1,500
				0012745	3	1,750
				0012745	4	2,500
				0017346	1	12,400
				0017346	2	12,700
				0017346	3	14,000
				0017346	4	15,500

Figure 5-9: Storing running totals in a table

What's the down side of storing derivable data? You do incur additional storage and data manipulation overhead. Storing running totals also opens up a potential can of worms. You may sometimes run into data consistency problems (inconsistencies may occur between the total you've stored and the total you've calculated), and tracking down the cause of such inconsistencies can be a real nightmare. You'll have to decide whether your expected performance gains compensate for these risks.

Using System-assigned Keys as Primary Keys

When you create database data, you may decide that you don't want to use any of the entities defined in the table as the primary key. Instead, you can ask ORACLE to assign an internally generated unique key to use as the primary key. The internal primary key is stored as another column of the table. Typically, it is indexed. (See the discussion of indexing in Chapter 6.)

The system-assigned key is known as an internal primary key, or a surrogate key, whereas the traditional primary key is known as the natural key. Table and column names, which may be very long, are compressed to unique numeric identifiers in a one-to-one relationship. Each record is identified by a system-assigned number, typified by ORACLE's own data dictionary tables *col$* and *tab$,* which have system-assigned primary keys (*col#* and *tab#,* respectively), in addition to the natural primary keys (*col$.name* and *tab$name*).

In Figure 5-10, notice that a table is referenced three times (in disk storage areas 1, 2, and 3). Rather than using the original name, APPROPRIATION_BALANCES_ MTD, for each row, the system assigns key 1 instead. The physical table name becomes simply a label for the real primary key.

TNAME Table			STORAGE Table				
TABLE#	TABLE_NAME		TABLE#	EXTENT#	FILE#	SIZE	TYPE
1	Appropriation_Balances_MTD		1	1	1	50	M
2	Appropriation_Balances_YTD		1	2	1	25	M
			1	3	3	25	K

Figure 5-10: Using system-assigned keys

In addition to guaranteeing the uniqueness of the primary key, using a system-assigned key also avoids the problems that can occur if an external primary key is null or if, for some reason, the external primary key needs to be changed.

There is another potential benefit to using internal keys. Because a system-assigned number is so much smaller than a typical table or column name (up to 30 alphanumeric characters), you'll potentially save a lot of storage, particularly if your internal key is propagated as a foreign key throughout large tables in the database.

The down side of using system-assigned primary keys is that these keys require storage, programming, and maintenance and that an extra table column and index has to be carried for the surrogate key. There will also be extra overhead associated with having to query through the natural key, rather than through a more efficient surrogate key.

Combining Reference or Code Tables

Just about every application contains quite a few small, referential validation tables, or code tables; a typical application might have between 10 and 100 such tables. Code tables are used for lookups and usually contain a small handful of records describing such information as country codes, interest category codes, education standards, and other reference information. Typically, each record contains only a single primary key and a description. Figure 5-11 shows two such tables.

LOAN_STATUS Table

LOAN_CODE	DESCRIPTION
10	Application
20	Approved
30	Current
40	Default

STATES Table

STATE_CODE	STATE
VIC	Victoria
NSW	New South Wales
QLD	Queensland

Figure 5-11: Original code tables

Although in theory combining such code tables is considered to be a serious breach of normalization policy, you can often improve system performance by doing so. These tables are accessed quite frequently, usually to look up descriptions (for example, the name of a state or the type of bank loan) so they can be displayed. You will find that if you combine all such code tables implemented for your system into a single global table, you'll improve performance in a number of ways.

In your combined global table, you'll need to create a concatenated primary key, as shown in Figure 5-12 (the CODE_CODE column) because the primary keys of the original tables are no longer likely to be unique.

CODE_TYPE	CODE_CODE	DESCRIPTION
Loan_Status	10	Application
Loan_Status	20	Approved
Loan_Status	30	Current
Loan_Status	40	In Default
States	VIC	Victoria
States	NSW	New South Wales

Figure 5-12: Combining code tables

The performance benefits of combining small code tables in this way can be substantial. Because only one table definition, only one synonym and grant (for the unified code table), and only one index definition need to be loaded into memory; there is a substantial savings in data dictionary cache (DC).

The code table approach we have described almost guarantees that all code tables will be resident (cached) in memory at any time. With the other approach (separate code tables), only the more frequently referenced tables will tend to be in memory. You can also realize additional performance gains by reducing the programming overhead needed to deal with combined code tables. You can create generic lookup and referential integrity routines, store them as standard library procedures, and access them by passing a table identifier plus primary key value(s).

A reduced number of data DB_BLOCK_BUFFERS is needed with this approach. ORACLE must store a minimum of one ORACLE block per table and one per index. Several (and perhaps all) of these minor code tables can fit into a single ORACLE block buffer. This can lead to substantial savings. Suppose you have defined 25 individual code tables. What physical tables, cache buffers, and possible indexes do you need?

- 25 physical tables
- 25 possible indexes
- Up to 50 ORACLE cache buffers

Now, suppose you combine the 25 small code tables into one. What do you need?

- One physical table

- One physical index

- A maximum of two ORACLE cache buffers

You can see that the savings are significant.

Creating Extract Tables

An important benefit of a relational system is the ability to create reports containing up-to-date information that can combine values from various individual tables and create summary data from them. Despite the enormous benefits of accessing fully normalized data in this way, you will find that some reports often are a huge performance drain on the system. Consider the case in which a number of users in your system need to create high-level management reports on a regular basis. The information needed to produce such a report is consolidated; it comes from many tables and involves a good deal of calculation and combination of data. Producing the report requires a large number of table joins, as well as quite a bit of repetitive and expensive table summing.

Although timely information is beneficial, you may find that in your organization it's not imperative that a report reflect the most recent updates to the database. In a case like this, you can improve system performance by completely denormalizing your relational tables and creating a single, consolidated extract table, a type of spreadsheet that actually duplicates the information in the database that is needed by the management report.

Figure 5-13 shows an abbreviated example of the kind of information a consolidated table (extracted from various other tables—EMP, DEPT, MGR, etc.) might contain.

DEPT#	DEPT_NAME	MGR#	MGR_NAME	EMP#	CLASS	CLASS_NAME
0010	Accounts	04562	Smith	134	A	Profitable
0020	Sales	05664	Brown	180	A	Profitable
0030	Purchasing	34529	Jones	56	A	Profitable
0040	Systems	45230	Green	36	D	Huge Money Pit

Figure 5-13: Creating extract tables

The most common method for producing such an extract table is to run an automated process overnight, when system performance needs are not so pressing, to populate the table. The major advantage of such an approach is that you incur the overhead of table joins and data summation only once, instead of each time a user of a management report needs to look at this consolidated data. The more report and query users, the greater your performance gains will be. You'll also find that this approach is especially beneficial, from a performance point of view, if users typically use GUI interfaces for their management reporting. Once the extract table has been created, programs that use it can do very simple and highly efficient table scans of that table only. Ensure that you add indexes to the extract table as required.

In helping sites tune their systems, we've found the "denormalized extract" approach very helpful. At one site, we reduced the amount of time needed for overnight processes by several hours. We also made managers very happy when the response time for their consolidated online queries decreased from 40 minutes to 45 seconds!

So, what's the down side? The obvious drawback to the use of extract tables for consolidated queries is that the data is not current. Remember, if you populate an extract table during an overnight process, the queries and reports performed during the next day will be using data that is many hours old. Other reports—and decisions—based on this data may suffer as a consequence. Only you, in conjunction with your users, can decide whether the performance gains you'll realize by using extract tables are worth the risk of using data that may have aged in this way.

However, even if the extract table(s) are used only for the overnight reporting routine, they will almost certainly provide significant performance gains over individual reports traversing through the database, across the same data, time and time again.

Duplicating a Key Beyond an Immediate Child Record

A principle of relational design is that a table never contains more information than it needs. In particular, when you are working with parent and child records, you must be sure that child, and other subordinate, records do not duplicate information that properly belongs only in the parent record.

But, there's always an exception. In some cases it is desirable to actually carry a primary key down even beyond the child record to the record of the child's child. In general, this approach is advantageous only in cases where multi-table joining may frequently be needed to satisfy queries.

For example, suppose that you have three tables: ORDERS, PARTS, and CLASS. In a normalized relational database, these tables contain only the data they need to contain. When an order needs to be printed, your application typically needs to access both the ORDERS table and the PARTS table so it can print both the part number and the part description. But in quite a few cases, the CLASS code for the part must also be included on the invoice. In these cases, you need to do a three-table join: from the ORDERS table you go to the PARTS table to pick up the part description and, in these cases, the CLASS code. Then, you need to go to the CLASS table to get the CLASS description. If the ORDERS table has many thousands (or even many hundreds) of records, and if orders are frequently reported within class, then you will improve performance by duplicating the CLASS code on the individual child record, as shown in Figure 5-14. Having it available on that record speeds up response time.

PARTS Table

PART#	DESCRIPTION	CLASS
A1284	Front Widget	A+
A345/1	Rear Widget	B-

ORDERS Table

PART#	ORDER#	CLASS
A1284	01237	A+
A1284	00546	A+
A345/1	00002	B-

Figure 5-14: Duplicating a key

Here is the SQL code that does the retrieval.

For the normalized database:

```
SELECT PART_NO, ORDER_NO, CLASS, CLASS_DESC
    FROM CLASS C,
    PART P,
    ORDER O
    WHERE O.PART_NO = P.PART_NO
    AND P.CLASS = C.CLASS;
```

For the denormalized database:

```
SELECT PART_NO, ORDER_NO, CLASS, CLASS_DESC
    FROM CLASS C,
    ORDER O
    WHERE O.CLASS = C.CLASS;
```

Note that you do incur additional overhead for the duplicated data within the PART table, so it makes sense to denormalize in this way only if you do this kind of retrieval frequently.

6

Defining Indexes

Indexes provide a powerful way to speed up the retrieval of data from an ORACLE database. Yet, indexes are often neglected as a performance tool by both designers and programmers. During the system design phase, analysts and designers typically spend many weeks, even months, identifying entities, relationships, and attributes. They extract primary keys, propagate foreign keys, and define one-to-one, one-to-many, and many-to-many relationships. These initial steps are vital, of course, to developing a sound database design. But designers too frequently omit one final step in database design: the defining of indexes. By defining and using indexes properly, you can get much better performance out of your ORACLE system.

In theory, you should define all indexes during the system design phase, well before programming begins. If developers know what indexes exist, they will keep these retrieval paths in mind as they code; this will result in better-tuned programs. In practice, there will be cases in which developers discover that they can tune existing SQL statements by specifying indexes. Make sure developers know that they must check out all decisions with the DBA or project leader to avoid defining duplicate indexes or indexes that actually end up degrading system performance.

What is an Index?

An index is a conceptual part of a database table that may be used to speed up the retrieval of data from that table. (Internally, ORACLE uses a sophisticated, self-balancing B-tree index structure.) If an index is defined for a table, via a CREATE INDEX clause on a column of the table, the index associates each distinct value of a column with the rows in the table that contain the value.

Indexes provide a number of benefits. Indexed retrieval of data from a database is almost always faster than a full-table scan. The ORACLE optimizer uses the indexes defined for a table when it figures out the most efficient retrieval path for a query or update statement. (The optimizer is described in Chapter 7, *Tuning SQL*.) ORACLE also uses indexes in performing more efficient joins of multiple tables. Another benefit of indexes is that they provide a way to guarantee the uniqueness of the primary key in a table. (You must create an index with the UNIQUE option if you want to enforce uniqueness.)

When is an index helpful? If one or two columns in your table are the most likely to be used as criteria for retrieval, those are the columns you'll want to index. For example, consider an employee rating system in which employee performance is rated on a one-to-ten scale.

```
SELECT NAME, DEPT, RATING
    FROM EMP
    WHERE RATING = 10;
```

To speed up the retrieval of employees with the highest ranks, you may want to create an index on the RATING column. Without an index, the application will have to scan through every row of the table until it finds matches.

You can index any column in a table except those defined with data types of LONG or LONG RAW.

All indexes are not equal. Large numbers of indexes specified over stable tables that mainly perform queries are not as resource-hungry as those that are specified over volatile tables. In general, indexes are most useful when they are specified on large tables. If small tables are frequently joined, however, you'll find that performance improves when you index these tables too.

Indexes aren't always the solution to database performance problems. Although indexes usually provide performance gains, there is a cost to using them. Indexes require storage space. They also require maintenance. Remember that every time a record is added to or deleted from a table, and every time an indexed column is modified, the index(es) itself must be updated a well. This can mean four or five extra disk I/Os per INSERT, DELETE, or UPDATE for a record. Because indexes incur the overhead of data storage and processing, you can actually degrade response time if you specify indexes that you don't use.

Although it is wise not to create indexes unless your application can benefit from them, you should be aware that the internal overheads for indexes are not huge. We have done some benchmark testing which showed that a row could be inserted into the EMP table in less than 0.11 seconds. After we added eight indexes to the table—many more than is normally recommended, the row INSERT was increased to only 0.94 seconds.

Although more than eight times the original overhead, this timing is still well within acceptable overall response time limits.

Some sites have firm standards controlling the maximum number of indexes that can be created for a table. This maximum is usually between four and six indexes per table. In reality, a hard-and-fast rule for indexes is unworkable. Our recommendation: do keep the number of indexes over a single table to a minimum, but if an index is useful, and response times can be kept below the agreed-upon limit for your site, then don't hesitate to create the index. We know of a site that has created 16 indexes on a table! This particular table is actually an extract table that is down-loaded from another application each night and can never be modified by the application, just queried. This is a case in which all of the indexes are useful and incur no ongoing overheads, only the initial overheads associated with creating the index and its required disk space.

An Indexing Checklist

These are the questions you'll need to answer before you assign any indexes. The section in Chapter 7 called "Using Indexes to Improve Performance" explains the SQL performance reasons behind these choices.

Should I index the primary key of a table?

Is the primary key unique?	If yes, define an index; indexes can enforce uniqueness.
Is the primary key used in table joins?	If yes, define an index (usually).
What is the table's expected volume?	If the volume is less than 250 items and not used within SQL JOIN statements, do not define an index. If the volume is greater than or equal to 250, or the table is used within SQL JOIN statements, define an index.

Should I index the foreign keys of a table?

Is the foreign key used as an online access path?	If yes, ask the primary key questions. If no, do not define an index.
Is the foreign key used within table joins?	If yes, define an index (usually).

Does the foreign key have an even table spread, or do the foreign key values in question (those needing to be queried) make up less than about 20% of the table?	If yes, define and index. If no, an index may or may not help.
Is the foreign key frequently updated?	If yes, the index will add overhead. If no, the index will add minimal overhead.
Is the foreign key usually part of a WHERE clause?	If yes, define an index. If no, do not define an index.
Is the foreign key used in table joins?	If yes, define an index.
Is the foreign key used for Version 7 referential integrity?	If yes, define an index. If no, an index may or may not help.

Should I index composite columns of a table?

| Will it give me improved data spread? | Two or more columns can often be united to get better selectivity, which might not be available from the poorer data spread of individually indexed columns. |
| Are all queried columns indexed? | If all queried columns are held within the actual index, no data base read is needed; this is particularly useful in SQL*Forms' list of values functions. |

What is the table's expected volume?

If the table has many thousands of entries, extra indexes will help you avoid lengthy full-table scans.

Can index numbers be reduced by combining LIKE indexes?

Consider this example:

```
TABLE_IDX1 LOAN_NUM
TABLE_IDX2 LOAN_NUM TRAN_ID
```

These two indexes can be combined into one if the first index is non-UNIQUE. (Uniqueness will otherwise be lost):

```
TABLE_IDX2
```

How can you enforce the use of indexes?

> Coordinate index definition and use with the DBA, the programmer, and the QA team.

How Many Indexes?

The actual number of indexes that makes sense for a table depends on the application and how the table is used in it. If a table is the hub of an application and is queried from many different directions, you'll have no choice but to define a large number of indexes for it. As we mention in the section above called "What is an Index?," some sites have firm, though often unworkable, standards for the maximum number of indexes that can be created for a table.

Here is an example of indexing a table that is vital to the work of the application. The EMPLOYEE_MASTER table is a core table. Most of the work of the application involves accessing and updating this table. You'll have to specify indexes if your users are going to be able to display online information quickly and in the desired format. The overhead incurred by all these indexes is clearly outweighed by the need to meet user requirements.

```
EMPLOYEE_MASTER
EMP_NO          INDEXED     PK
EMP_NAME
EMP_TYPE        INDEXED     FK
EMP_CLASS
EMP_SEX
DEPT_CODE       INDEXED     FK
SALARY_GRADE    INDEXED     FK
SALARY_AMT
DATE_OF_BIRTH
HIRE_DATE
NEXT_OF_KIN
NO_OF_CHILDREN
SUPER_FUND      INDEXED     FK
BANK_ACCOUNT    INDEXED
MARITAL_STATUS
ADDR_LINE1
ADDR_LINE2
ADDR_LINE3
POST_CODE
APPRAISAL_DUE   INDEXED
HOME_PHONE
BUSINESS_PHONE
TAX_FILE_NO     INDEXED
```

ORACLE actually imposes its own internal controls on the number of indexes allowed. In any one SQL statement, ORACLE evaluates a maximum of five indexes over each table. The system merges rows from each index, and individually validates all other predicate conditions.

One way in which you can reduce the number of indexes specified over a table is to combine similar indexes. For example, suppose you need to specify these two indexes:

```
EMP.EMP_TYPE
EMP.EMP_TYPE, EMP.EMP_CLASS
```

If EMP_TYPE is not a unique column of the EMP table, then you can omit the first index because ORACLE will still use the first part of the second index if the second field is not referenced. If EMP_TYPE is a unique column, omit the second index. It is superfluous.

Using Indexes to Improve Performance

Developers can code their SQL statements to take best advantage of the indexes that have been specified for the tables in the application. The section in Chapter 7 called "Using Indexes to Improve Performance" describes how ORACLE uses indexes to help develop the most efficient execution plan and how you can modify your indexes to further tune SQL performance.

IV

Tuning for Programmers

Part IV describes what ORACLE programmers need to know about tuning. It looks at how statements can be tuned in the SQL, PL/SQL, and SQL*Forms environments, and it takes a look at the special tuning considerations presented by table-level and row-level choices in the ORACLE system.

7

Tuning SQL

SQL (Structured Query Language) is the heart of the ORACLE system. Developed originally by IBM in the mid-1970s, SQL has become a standard for database query, retrieval, and reporting. The American National Standards Institute (ANSI) has adopted SQL as a standard (X3.135-1986, with substantial enhancements in 1989), as has the International Standards Organization (ISO) (9075). SQL-2 is the lowest common ANSI standard that has been implemented as an RDBMS engine. SQL is also a U.S. Federal Information Processing Standard (FIPS 127). ORACLE, along with many other database vendors, has extended the SQL standard by adding features to its implementation of SQL. For example, functions like DECODE and CONNECT BY PRIOR are extensions that are beyond the scope of the original standard.

ORACLE's SQL is a very flexible language. You can use many different SQL statements to accomplish the same purpose. Yet, although dozens of differently constructed query and retrieval statements can produce the same result, in a given situation only one statement will be the most efficient choice.

As a programmer, your responsibility for tuning revolves around SQL (and related tools like PL/SQL and SQL*Forms, described in subsequent chapters). Too many programmers forget that SQL choices are within their power. They somehow believe that as long as a SQL statement returns the expected result, it must be correct. Wrong! An SQL choice is correct only if it produces the right result in the shortest possible amount of time, without impeding the performance of any other system resource. You have the ability, and the responsibility, to tune every SQL statement so it works as efficiently as it can in each application. In each case, you'll have to consider the purpose of your application, where the bottlenecks are, and what your choices of statements and options might be. This section outlines the major performance problems we see in SQL statements that are entered via SQL*Plus or that are embedded in PL/SQL blocks or SQL*Forms specifications. Refer to Chapter 8, *Tuning PL/SQL*, and Chapter 9, *Tuning SQL*Forms*, for specific suggestions on tuning SQL for best performance in those products.

Remember, no matter how well tuned your hardware and other software resources might be, even a single, badly constructed SQL statement can demolish the performance of your system.

How can you tell which SQL statement or option results in the best performance for your system? With Version 7, ORACLE optimizes execution to a large degree. If you are still running Version 6, you will need to do a lot more manual tuning. Analyzing the physical execution of an individual SQL statement can be a complex process. To judge a statement's performance, you need to examine the use of alternative WHERE clauses, the role that might be played by indexes, and the impact of your statement structure on the ORACLE optimizer.

How Does the Optimizer Work?

The ORACLE optimizer is a hidden but extremely important system resource. A part of the ORACLE kernel, the optimizer examines each SQL statement it encounters in your query or program, and chooses the optimal execution plan, or retrieval path, for the statement. The execution plan is the sequence of physical steps the RDBMS must take in order to perform the operation (e.g., retrieval, update) that you've specified.

To figure out the optimal path, the optimizer looks at the following:

- The details of the syntax you've specified for the statement
- Any conditions the data must satisfy (the WHERE clauses)
- The database tables your statement will access
- Any indexes that can be used in retrieving data from the table
- Version 7 hints
- Version 7 statistics via the ANALYZE command

Based on this information, the optimizer figures out the optimal retrieval path for the SQL statement that is being executed.

In most situations, the optimizer's efforts remain hidden from your view. But, it is possible for you to look more closely at how the optimizer works. If you're trying to improve the performance of your system, you'll want to work closely with the optimizer to select the most efficient SQL statements. The EXPLAIN PLAN diagnostic statement gives you an inside look at how the optimizer is planning to process your SQL statements. By running EXPLAIN PLAN and examining its output for several alternative SELECT statements, for example, you'll be able to see which statement is the most efficient. See Chapter 12, *Diagnostic and Tuning Tools,* for a discussion of how you can use EXPLAIN PLAN and other diagnostics to tune your ORACLE system.

ORACLE Version 7 brings you closer to the inner workings of the optimizer by giving you a choice of two optimizing alternatives: the rule-based optimizer (the only optimizer available in Version 6 and earlier) and the more intelligent cost-based optimizer.

How do these optimizers differ? The Version 6 rule-based optimizer uses a predefined set of precedence rules and indexes to figure out which path it will use to access the database. For example, if there is an index on a column, the optimizer will use that index without considering whether the index actually improves performance in this particular case.

The Version 7 cost-based optimizer is a more sophisticated facility. It uses database information (e.g., table size, number of rows, key spread) rather than rigid rules. This information is available once the table has been analyzed via the Version 7 ANALYZE command (described in Chapter 12). If a table has not been analyzed, the cost-based optimizer can use only rule-based logic to figure out the costs of accessing your data and to select the best access path, that is, the path that incurs the least overhead. ANALYZE collects statistics about tables, clusters, and indexes, and stores them in the data dictionary. Because the ANALYZE command incurs substantial overhead of its own, it is not always the best option. An SQL statement will use the cost-based optimizer if any one of the tables involved in the statement has been ANALYZEd. The optimizer makes an educated guess as to the best access path for the other tables based on information in the data dictionary.

If you are running Version 7, you can also explicitly select which optimizer you want to use. For example, if you have carefully tuned your SQL statements under Version 6, you might want to continue using the rule-based optimizer, at least until you've had a chance to test your SQL's behavior under Version 7. There may not be much room for improvement. The cost-based optimizer gives you the most significant performance improvements on SQL statements that have not been tuned under Version 6.

Regardless of which optimizer you use, you need to realize that the optimizer doesn't know as much as you do about how the database is constructed and what you and your system's users want to do with that database. For example, the rule-based optimizer (Version 6) and the unANALYZEd cost-based optimizer (Version 7) are not aware of:

- Physical table volumes

- Actual data distribution within a table

- Actual data distribution within the indexed columns

- Logical data connections between associated tables

- Future index modifications

You'll need to supplement the optimizer's work by manually tuning SQL statements, using the suggestions we provide in this chapter.

Manually Tuning SQL Statements

With Version 7, you can manually tune individual SQL statements, overriding the optimizer's decisions for that statement by including your own optimization hints within the SQL statement. This is a helpful option if you have manually tuned some, but not all, of Version 6 SQL statements that are now being converted to Version 7. By including your own optimization hints as comments within the SQL statement, you force the statement to follow your retrieval path, rather than the one worked out by the optimizer. In the following example, by including /*+ RULE */ inside the SELECT statement, you tell SELECT to use the Version 6 rule-based optimizer, rather than the Version 7 cost-based optimizer:

```
SELECT . . .
    FROM /*+ RULE */
    FROM EMP, DEPT
    WHERE . . .
```

Including optimization hints as comments is a somewhat clumsy way to tune, and later versions of ORACLE may provide a more convenient way to override the optimizer's actions. But this new feature does provide a better way to do manual tuning than anything available in earlier versions. Hints you can include as comments in SQL statements are listed in Table 7-1.

Table 7-1: Optimization Hints

Comment	Description
/*+ ALL_ROWS */	Optimize SQL for best throughput.
/*+ AND_EQUAL */	Use index merging on specified tables.
/*+ CLUSTER */	Use a cluster scan for a specified table.
/*+ COST */	Use cost-based optimizer always.
/*+ FIRST_ROWS */	Optimize SQL for best response times.

Table 7-1: Optimization Hints (Continued)

Comment	Description
/*+ FULL */	Use a full-table scan on a specified table.
/*+ HASH */	Use a hash search on a specified table.
/*+ INDEX */	Force the use of a specified index for a specified table (assuming that the index and the predicates exist for the index).
*+ INDEX_ASC */	Same as INDEX.
*+ INDEX_DESC */	Same as INDEX, but in descending order.
/*+ ORDERED */	Use the FROM clause join sequence.
/*+ ROWID */	Use ROWID (row identifier) access method.
/*+ RULE */	Use rule-based optimizer only.
/*+ USE_MERGE */	Use sort merge join technique on specified tables.
/*+ USE_NL */	Use nested loop join technique on specified tables.

Sharing SQL Statements

Because parsing a SQL statement and figuring out its optimal execution plan are time-consuming operations, ORACLE holds SQL statements in memory after it has parsed them, so the parsing and analysis won't have to be repeated if the same statement is issued again. In Version 6, each process has its own context area in the process's Program Global Area (PGA), in which it holds these statements in case that process issues the same statement again. In Version 7, there is a single, shared context area in the shared buffer pool of the System Global Area (SGA). The big advantage of the Version 7 implementation is that this area is shared by all users. Thus, if you issue a SQL statement, sometimes known as a cursor, that is identical to a statement another user has issued, you can take advantage of the fact that ORACLE has already parsed the statement and figured out the best execution plan for it. This represents major performance improvements and memory savings.

The DBA at your site must set the appropriate INIT.ORA parameters for the context areas. Obviously, the larger the area, the more statements can be retained there, and the more likely statements are to be shared. Part IV of this book describes ways the DBA can monitor the performance of context areas.

Whenever you issue a SQL statement, ORACLE first looks in the context area to see if there is an identical statement there. Unfortunately, ORACLE does an exact string comparison on the new statement and the contents of the context area. To be shared, the SQL statements must truly be the same: carriage returns, spaces, and case (upper versus lower) all affect the comparison. For example:

```
SELECT * FROM EMP;
```

is not the same as any of these:

```
SELECT * from EMP;
Select * From Emp;
SELECT     *     FROM EMP;
SELECT *
   FROM EMP;
```

Statements are also classified as equal only if the underlying objects are the same. If two users both select the same data from the EMP table, both must be referencing the exact same table. Synonyms cannot be used to reference another table, and users cannot have their own local copy of the table.

Note, though, that the values of bind variables do not need to be identical for two statements to be considered identical. If the bind variable references themselves are the same, the parsed form of the statement is considered to be the same. Bind variables are not actually substituted until the statement has been successfully parsed. The actual values of the bind variables are not considered when selecting a statement's execution plan. Only the parsed form of the statement is shared in the context area, and binding is always performed. For example:

```
SELECT * FROM EMP WHERE EMP_NO = :B1;     Bind value: 123
```

is actually the same as:

```
SELECT * FROM EMP WHERE EMP_NO = :B1;     Bind value: 987
```

NOTE

For static application interfaces such as SQL*Forms, Pro*C, etc., statement case, white space, and bind variables will always be the same for the same statements. All users execute the identical SQL statement when using the same program, regardless of bind variable name or value supplied.

Some Preliminary SQL Questions

Before you begin to tune individual SQL statements, there are a few general questions that you need to answer. Be sure to do your homework by answering these questions and studying your database design with care. A little knowledge is a dangerous thing— here, as elsewhere. If you don't really know how your data and programs are constructed, or if those structures are likely to change in the near future, then you may find that by applying the tuning suggestions included in this chapter you'll actually degrade performance, rather than improve it.

A reminder: Make sure that your statements all work before you start trying to tune them. Although producing working code is only the first step to a well-tuned system, it is an important step.

How long is too long? Before you can improve system performance by reducing the amount of time your SQL statements take to retrieve data, you must figure out how long the retrieval *should* take? That's a rather amorphous question. You'll need to take a look at comparable systems, examine your own system's needs, and do some testing of alternative statements. You'll also need to consult with your organization's management to find out what response time policies are in effect for your system. (Chapter 2, *What Causes Performance Problems?*, addresses the overall question of response time.)

If you decide that a retrieval can and should run faster, you'll find the TKPROF and EXPLAIN PLAN diagnostic utilities very helpful. See Chapter 12 for information about these utilities.

Is the statement running over real production volumes? The common, plaintive cry of developers everywhere is, *"But it worked during testing."*

Poor database queries are often due to poor testing environments. To produce well-tuned SQL statements, you must take the time to test your statements thoroughly when you first build them.

Too often, developers do their testing with a test database that's simply too small to be realistic. Many problems are revealed only when you test with a large enough amount of data. If your test database is unrealistically small, you won't really be putting your statements through their paces. For example, full-table scans are usually a major drain on performance. But, if you test using a master table containing only ten records, you'll never see a true full-table scan in action. Performance problems will remain dormant until your application goes live with real data.

Is the optimal retrieval path being used? Figuring out the optimal path for retrieval is a joint effort between you and the optimizer. Let the optimizer figure out a retrieval path. Then, examine your statements yourself using the EXPLAIN PATH utility to determine the best choice of a retrieval path. Only one of the many variants on SELECT statements will retrieve data most efficiently.

Will future events and/or database changes have an effect on optimization? Optimization may not be forever. Remember, a SQL statement is parsed every time it is encountered. For example, if you add or delete an index for an associated table, you may find that the SQL statements that access that table no longer work as efficiently as they did. You'll need to keep testing and checking and tuning for the life of your database and application.

Selecting the Most Efficient Table Name Sequence

One of the most important ways you can tune SQL statements under Version 6 is to make sure your SELECT statements reference tables in the most efficient sequence. Although this discussion is less relevant for Version 7, in which the cost-based optimizer makes its own determination of the most efficient retrieval path, you may encounter situations in which you'll need to do manual tuning using the suggestions we include here.

NOTE

The sequence of conditions in your WHERE clause (described in the section below called "Selecting the Most Efficient WHERE Clause Sequence") is of higher priority to the rule-based optimizer than the FROM sequence. If two index paths over two tables have different rule-based rankings, then the table with the lowest numeric ranking will be the driving table. Only when the two tables have equal query path rankings does the FROM sequence come into play.

If you specify more than one table name in the FROM clause of a SELECT statement— for example:

```
SELECT COUNT ( * ) FROM EMP, DEPT
```

the order in which you specify the tables may have a significant impact on performance.

Regardless of the order in which you specify table names, the optimizer tries to reorder table processing based on what is most efficient. It takes into account such factors as the indexes specified for the tables. However, if you are running the rule-based optimizer, and the optimizer cannot make an intelligent decision, then ORACLE simply executes the statement in the order in which the tables are parsed. Because the parser processes table names from right to left, the table name you specify last (e.g., DEPT in the example above) is actually the first table processed.

Because indexes are so often specified in a well-designed, online system, table name sequence is usually less an issue for online jobs than it is for overnight updating and reporting routines. Often, programs producing reports during lengthy overnight runs tend to scan entire tables, simultaneously joining (i.e., sorting/merging) many tables.

If you suspect that a SQL statement referencing multiple tables is taking longer than is acceptable, you should examine the effects of table sequence on your retrievals.

Chapter 12 describes the TKPROF and EXPLAIN PLAN facilities, which can help localize table sequencing problems.

Obviously, if your SQL statement references only a single table, then table sequencing is not an issue. If you have more than one table referenced (in a single FROM clause), then a driving table must be set.

The Driving Table

The object of all your SQL query and update statements is to minimize the total physical number of database blocks that need to be read. If you specify more than one table in a FROM clause of a SELECT statement, you must choose one as the driving table. By making the correct choice, you can make enormous improvements in performance.

NOTE

Most of the following examples show Version 6 comparisons. Results will be virtually identical if you run a program under Version 7 that does not make use of the ANALYZE command. Chapter 12 describes the tools that produce the output shown in these examples.

Consider the following example of two tables processed by the Version 6 optimizer:

```
Table TAB1  has 16,384   rows
Table TAB2  has 1        row.
```

Suppose you select TAB2 as the driving table (by specifying it second in the FROM clause):

SELECT COUNT (*) FROM TAB1, TAB2   *0.96 seconds elapsed*

	count	phys	cr	cur	rows
Parse	1	0	0	0	
Execute	1	**95**	**100**	**4**	0
Fetch	1	0	0	0	1

Now, suppose that you select TAB1 as the driving table:

SELECT COUNT (*) FROM TAB2, TAB1   *26.09 seconds elapsed*

	count	phys	cr	cur	rows
Parse	1	0	0	0	
Execute	1	**95**	**49247**	**32770**	0
Fetch	1	0	0	0	1

You can see that specifying the correct driving table makes a huge difference in performance (0.96 versus 26.09 seconds). What's going on? When ORACLE processes multiple tables, it uses an internal sort/merge procedure to join your two tables. First, it scans and sorts the first table (the one specified second in the FROM clause). Next, it scans the second table (the one specified first in the FROM clause), and merges all of the rows retrieved from the second table with those retrieved from the first table.

The 95 physical reads shown on the Execute line in the examples above are the minimum number of database "block reads" needed to retrieve all rows from the two tables. The large overhead differences arise from the ensuing number of consistent buffer "cr" and current mode buffer reads "cur."

If TAB1 is processed first, then all 16,384 rows (from TAB1) must be read first. These records are sorted, but cannot fit into the area of memory allocated for each user's sort/merges (specified in the INIT.ORA parameter, SORT_AREA_SIZE). Consequently, these records are sorted in small runs with the data stored in temporary segments on disk. After all runs are completed, ORACLE merges your data to produce the sorted data. The single TAB2 data is read and joined with the TAB1 data.

By comparison, if TAB2 is processed first, only one row needs to be read (from TAB2), and this row can be sorted within the sort area. The TAB1 table is then joined with the TAB2 table.

Now, consider an example in which the number of rows in TAB2 is slightly greater—four instead of one. The performance differential is not quite as extreme in this case.

```
Table TAB1   has 16,384    rows.
Table TAB2   has 4         rows.

SELECT COUNT ( * ) FROM TAB1, TAB2          4.00 seconds elapsed
```

	count	phys	cr	cur	rows
Parse	1	0	0	0	
Execute	1	384	386	10	0
Fetch	1	0	0	0	1

```
SELECT COUNT ( * ) FROM TAB2, TAB1          37.32 seconds elapsed
```

	count	phys	cr	cur	rows
Parse	1	0	0	0	
Execute	1	95	49247	32770	0
Fetch	1	0	0	0	1

If you are using Version 7 and have run the ANALYZE command, the comparisons are much less pronounced:

```
Table TAB1  has 16,384   rows
Table TAB2  has 1        row.
```

SELECT COUNT (*) FROM TAB1, TAB2   *1.20 seconds elapsed*

	count	phys	cr	cur	rows
Parse	1	0	0	0	
Execute	1	0	0	0	0
Fetch	1	**123**	**124**	**5**	1

SELECT COUNT (*) FROM TAB2, TAB1   *1.32 seconds elapsed*

	count	phys	cr	cur	rows
Parse	1	0	0	0	
Execute	1	0	0	0	0
Fetch	1	**123**	**124**	**5**	1

You can see that, while some performance improvements result from changing table order, Version 7's ANALYZE capability is responsible for most of the improvement.

Joining Three Tables

If three tables are being joined, select the intersection table as the driving table. The intersection table is the table that has many tables dependent on it. In the following example, the EMP table represents the intersection between the LOCATION table and the CATEGORY table. This first SELECT:

```
SELECT . . .
    FROM    LOCATION L,
            CATEGORY C,
            EMP E
    WHERE   E.EMP_NO BETWEEN 1000 AND 2000
    AND     E.CAT_NO =  C.CAT_NO
    AND     E.LOCN   =  L.LOCN
```

is more efficient than this next example:

```
SELECT . . .
    FROM    EMP E,
            LOCATION L,
            CATEGORY C
    WHERE   E.CAT_NO =  C.CAT_NO
    AND     E.LOCN   =  L.LOCN
    AND     E.EMP_NO BETWEEN 1000 AND 2000
```

NOTE

Placing the intersection table as the last table in the FROM clause does assume that all tables have equal index rankings (or no indexes at all). Many table joins will also be affected by the WHERE clause access paths, and you must also consider these when you are constructing a multi-table join statement.

Selecting the Most Efficient WHERE Clause Sequence

The way you specify conditions in the WHERE clauses of your SELECT statements has a major impact on the performance of your SQL in Version 6. In the absence of any other information, the ORACLE optimizer uses these conditions to determine the best retrieval path for the database. If you are able to specify the most efficient conditions early in your WHERE clauses, the rule-based optimizer will be more effective in selecting the most efficient path from the available paths with equal optimizer rankings.

Although the suggestions included in this chapter are less relevant for Version 7, they are still worthwhile, particularly if you do manual tuning of certain statements.

Condition Rankings

As we discussed earlier in this chapter, the Version 6 rule-based optimizer calculates the fastest path to the database by evaluating a set of predefined precedence rules. The optimizer has available to it a list of conditions, some of which are more efficient than others; these conditions are shown in the following table. (One is considered the most efficient condition, and 14 the least efficient condition.) ORACLE uses the rankings shown in Table 7-2 to determine which index to apply to a database retrieval. If two indexes are specified over the same table, ORACLE figures out which one to use by looking at the rankings shown below. If two indexes have the same ranking for the same table (e.g., both are non-UNIQUE indexes), or if no index is specified for the table, ORACLE follows the sequence of conditions specified in the WHERE clause.

WARNING

The rankings shown here are not the same as those shown in the most recent ORACLE manuals, but they represent our best information about the actual current state of the optimizer, as detailed in the ORACLE release notes. The optimizer is continually being enhanced by ORACLE. You should be aware that this process of enhancement will continue, so it will be difficult to be absolutely sure of the order of these conditions. The DBA at your site must stay aware of all optimizer changes by reading the README notes that accompany each version upgrade.

Table 7-2: Condition Rankings

Rank	Condition
1	ROWID = constant
2	Entire UNIQUE concatenated index = constant
3	UNIQUE indexed column = constant
4	Entire cluster key = corresponding cluster key of another table in the same cluster
5	Entire cluster key = constant
6	Entire non-UNIQUE concatenated index = constant
7	Non-UNIQUE single-column index merge
8a	More than one column of leading concatenated index = constant
8b	First column of leading concatenated index = constant
9	Indexed column BETWEEN low value and high value or indexed column LIKE "C%" (bounded range)
10	Sort/merge within table joins
11	MAX or MIN of single indexed columns
12	ORDER BY entire index
13	Full-table scans
14	Unindexed column = constant or column is null or column like "%C%"

Using ROWID When Possible

The ROWID for a record is the single fastest method of record retrieval. ROWID is actually an encoded key representing the physical record number within an actual ORACLE database block on the database. Use ROWID whenever possible to get the best performance out of your retrievals.

You can improve performance by selecting a record before updating or deleting it, and including ROWID in the initial SELECT list. This allows ORACLE to perform a much more efficient second record access. Remember, when you first query the record, to select the record FOR UPDATE. This keeps another process from being able to update the selected record and change its ROWID out from under you. For example:

```
SELECT   ROWID, . . .
   INTO   :EMP_ROWID, . . .
   FROM   EMP
   WHERE  EMP.EMP_NO  = 56722
   FOR UPDATE OF EMP.NAME ;
```

```
UPDATE      EMP
    SET     EMP.NAME    = . . .
    WHERE ROWID = :EMP_ROWID ;
```

Reducing the Number of Trips to the Database

Every time a SQL statement is executed, ORACLE needs to perform many internal processing steps; the statement needs to be parsed, indexes evaluated, variables bound, and data blocks read. The more you can reduce the number of database accesses, the more overhead you can save. Reducing the physical number of trips to the database is particularly beneficial in client-server configurations where the database may need to be accessed over a network.

The following examples show three distinct ways of retrieving data about employees who have employee numbers 0342 or 0291. Method 1 is the least efficient, method 2 the next most efficient, and method 3 the most efficient of all.

Method 1 shows two separate database accesses:

```
SELECT  EMP_NAME, SALARY, GRADE
    FROM  EMP
    WHERE EMP_NO = 0342;


SELECT  EMP_NAME, SALARY, GRADE
    FROM  EMP
    WHERE EMP_NO = 0291;
```

Method 2 shows the use of one cursor and two fetches:

```
DECLARE
    CURSOR  C1 (E_NO  NUMBER)   IS
    SELECT  EMP_NAME, SALARY, GRADE
        FROM  EMP
        WHERE EMP_NO = E_NO;
BEGIN
    OPEN   C1 (342);
    FETCH  C1 INTO ..., ..., ...;
    .
    .
    .
    OPEN   C1 (291);
    FETCH  C1 INTO ..., ..., ...;
    CLOSE  C1;
END;
```

Method 3 shows a SQL table join:

```
SELECT      A.EMP_NAME,  A.SALARY,  A.GRADE,
            B.EMP_NAME,  B,SALARY,  B.GRADE
```

```
FROM      EMP   A,
          EMP   B
WHERE     A.EMP_NO  =  0342
AND       B.EMP_NO  =  0291 ;
```

In this last example, the same table is identified by two aliases, A and B, that are joined by a single statement. In this way, ORACLE uses only one cursor and performs only one fetch.

NOTE

One simple way to increase the number of rows of data you can fetch with one database access, and thus reduce the number of physical calls needed., is to reset the ARRAYSIZE parameter in SQL*Plus, SQL*Forms, and Pro*C. We suggest a setting of 200.

Using Null Values

ORACLE's treatment of null conforms to ANSI standards. In general:

- Null is never equal (=) to anything (including zero, space, or null)

- Null is never NOT equal (!= or <>) to anything

- Null is never less than (<) or less than or equal to (<=) anything

- Null is never greater than (>) or greater than or equal to (>=) anything

Never compare null to anything else. In general, if you perform a comparison to a null value, the record will be rejected

None of the following SQL statements will return a row:

```
SELECT    'X'
    FROM   DUAL
    WHERE  'X'   =,  NULL ;

SELECT    'X'
    FROM   DUAL
    WHERE  'X'   <>  NULL ;

SELECT    'X'
    FROM   DUAL
    WHERE  NULL  =   NULL ;

SELECT    'X'
    FROM   DUAL
    WHERE  NULL  <>  NULL ;
```

```
SELECT      'X'
    FROM    DUAL
    WHERE   NULL IN ('A','B',NULL);

SELECT      'X'
    FROM    DUAL
    WHERE   NULL NOT IN ('A', 'B', NULL);
```

Each of the following SQL statements will return one row.

```
SELECT      'X'
    FROM    DUAL
    WHERE   'X'  =   NVL(NULL, 'X');

SELECT      'X'
    FROM    DUAL
    WHERE   'X'  <>  NVL(NULL, 'Y');

SELECT      'X'
    FROM    DUAL
    WHERE   NULL IS NULL;

SELECT      'X'
    FROM    DUAL
    WHERE   'X'  IS NOT NULL ;
```

There are a few exceptions to the rule of nulls. Null is equal to null in the following situations:

```
DECODE (FLAG, 'Y', 'YES', 'N', 'NO', NULL, 'N')

GROUP BY E.EMP_NO, E.NAME        Where a column is null

SELECT DISTINCT (E.NAME)

UNION/MINUS/INTERSECT            Where a column is null
```

Certain indexed columns   *Where the whole key is not null; see the section below called "Avoiding Nulls in Indexes"*

Using DECODE

Programmers often need a way to count and/or sum variable conditions for a group of rows. The DECODE statement provides a very efficient way of doing this. Because DECODE is rather complex, few programmers take the time to learn to use this statement to full advantage. This section describes some common ways you can use DECODE to improve performance.

Using DECODE to Reduce Processing

The DECODE statement provides a way to avoid having to scan the same rows repetitively, or to join the same table repetitively. Consider the following example:

```
SELECT  COUNT(*), SUM(SALARY)
    FROM  EMP
    WHERE DEPT_NO  =  0020
    AND   EMP_NAME LIKE 'SMITH%' ;

SELECT  COUNT(*), SUM(SALARY)
    FROM  EMP
    WHERE DEPT_NO  =  0030
    AND   EMP_NAME LIKE 'SMITH%' ;
```

You can achieve the same result much more efficiently with DECODE:

```
SELECT  COUNT(DECODE     ( DEPT_NO, 0020, 'X', NULL )) D0020_KOUNT,
    COUNT (DECODE        ( DEPT_NO, 0030, 'X', NULL )) D0030_KOUNT,
    SUM   (DECODE        ( DEPT_NO, 0020, SALARY, NULL )) D0020_SAL,
    SUM   (DECODE        ( DEPT_NO, 0030, SALARY, NULL )) D0030_SAL
    FROM EMP
WHERE  EMP_NAME LIKE 'SMITH%';
```

Remember, null values are never included in, nor do they affect the outcome of, the COUNT and SUM functions.

Using DECODE in ORDER BY and GROUP BY Clauses

You may need to specify many ORDER BY clauses to get the result you want. Rather than coding many identical queries, each with a different ORDER BY clause, you can specify a DECODE function such as the following:

```
SELECT  . . .
    FROM  EMP
    WHERE  EMP_NAME  LIKE  'SMITH%'
    ORDER BY  DECODE (:BLK.SEQN_FLD 'E', EMP_NO, 'D', DEPT_NO);
```

This approach can be extended further to include the GROUP BY clause:

```
SELECT  . . .
    FROM  EMP
    WHERE  EMP_NAME  LIKE  'SMITH%'
    GROUP BY  DECODE (:INPUT, 'E', EMP_NO, 'D', DEPT_NO);
```

DECODE verbs within ORDER BY and GROUP BY statements cannot use indexes. Instead, an internal sort/merge is required. Because this is a slow process, use DECODE within ORDER BY only for online statements where the number of rows returned by the WHERE clause is small. For reports, you need not worry about limits.

SQL Performance Hints

This section describes some additional ways you can improve the performance of your SQL statements.

Combining Simple, Unrelated Database Accesses

If you are running a number of simple database queries, you can improve performance by combining them into a single query, even if they are not related. Examples of queries that are particularly suitable to this approach are those that set up default screen headers or report banners by obtaining program initialization information from a number of database tables. The usual approach is to perform one query after another, as shown below:

```
SELECT  NAME
    FROM    EMP
    WHERE   EMP_NO = 1234;

SELECT  NAME
    FROM    DPT
    WHERE   DPT_NO = 10;

SELECT  NAME
    FROM    CAT
    WHERE   CAT_TYPE = 'RD'  ;
```

To combine all these separate queries into one SQL statement, you must perform an outer join on each table with a table which will always be valid (i.e., one that will return at least one row). The easiest way to assure this is to set up a dummy outer join with the system table DUAL as shown in the following example:

```
SELECT  E.NAME, D.NAME, C.NAME
    FROM    CAT C,
            DPT D,
            EMP E,
            DUAL X
    WHERE   NVL('X', X.DUMMY)  = NVL('X', E.ROWID (+))
    AND     NVL('X', X.DUMMY)  = NVL('X', D.ROWID (+))
    AND     NVL('X', X.DUMMY)  = NVL('X', C.ROWID (+))
    AND     E.EMP_NO    (+)    = 1234
    AND     D.DEPT_NO   (+)    = 10
    AND     C.CAT_TYPE  (+)    = 'RD'
```

This type of processing gives you the best performance payoff on machines connected to busy networks. Every time a SQL statement is executed, the RDBMS kernel is visited a number of times: at least once to parse the statement, once to bind the variables, and once to retrieve the selected rows. With this simple example, you reduce network overhead by two-thirds. (See Chapter 16, *Tuning in the Client-server Environment*, for more information about this approach.)

Deleting Duplicate Records

The following example shows a particularly efficient way to delete duplicate records from a table. It takes advantage of the fact that a row's ROWID must be unique.

```
DELETE    FROM EMP    E
    WHERE E.ROWID   >   (   SELECT   MIN(X.ROWID)
                    FROM   EMP   X
                    WHERE X.EMP_NO   =   E.EMP_NO    );
```

Counting Rows from Tables

Contrary to popular belief, COUNT (*) is faster than COUNT (1). If the rows are being returned via an index, counting the indexed column—for example, COUNT (EMP_NO) is faster still. The optimizer realizes from the existence of the index that the column must also exist. We tested the following statements on several different computers and found that COUNT (*) consistently runs between 15% and 20% faster than COUNT (1), and that COUNT (INDEX_COLUMN) is 5% faster again.

The following runs counted 65,536 rows from a table:

```
SELECT COUNT                      unique index column
    FROM TRANSACTIONS;            2.43 seconds

SELECT COUNT (*) FROM TRANSACTION;    2.59 seconds

SELECT COUNT (1) FROM TRANSACTION;    3.47 seconds
```

Using WHERE in Place of HAVING

In general, avoid including a HAVING clause in SELECT statements. The HAVING clause filters selected rows only after all rows have been fetched. This could include sorting, summing, etc. Restricting rows via the WHERE clause, rather than the HAVING clause, helps reduce these overheads. For example:

```
SELECT REGION, AVG(LOC_SIZE)
    FROM       LOCATION
    GROUP BY   REGION
    HAVING     REGION    != 'SYDNEY'
    AND        REGION    != 'PERTH'
```

You'll find the following more efficient:

```
SELECT REGION, AVG(LOC_SIZE)
    FROM       LOCATION
    WHERE      REGION    != 'SYDNEY'
    AND        REGION    != 'PERTH'
    GROUP BY   REGION
```

Tuning Views

Many people think that views are untunable. In fact, views are effectively SELECT statements and can be tuned, just as any other type of SELECT statement can. Remember, though, that views cannot retrieve data any faster than the originating SQL can. Views are not subsets of data, nor are they snapshots of data.

At all costs, avoid specifying views of views or views within SQL sub-query clauses. These statements tend to confuse the optimizer, resulting in full-table scans.

Minimizing Table Lookups in a Query

To improve performance, minimize the number of table lookups in queries, particularly if your statements include sub-query SELECTs or multi-column UPDATEs. For example, instead of specifying:

```
SELECT  TABLE_NAME
    FROM  TABLES
    WHERE TABLE_NAME =      (SELECT  TABLE_NAME
                             FROM    TAB_COLUMNS
                             WHERE   VERSION = 604 )

    AND DB_VERSION =        (SELECT  DB_VERSION
                             FROM    TAB_COLUMNS WHERE VERSION = 604 )
```

specify the following instead:

```
SELECT  TABLE_NAME
    FROM  TABLES
    WHERE ( TABLE_NAME,
            DB_VERSION ) = (SELECT  TABLE_NAME, DB_VERSION
                             FROM    TAB_COLUMNS
                             WHERE   VERSION = 604 )
```

Using Table Aliases

Use table aliases, and prefix all column names by their aliases where there is more than one table involved in a query. This will reduce parse time and prevent syntax errors from occurring when ambiguously named columns are added later on. Consider the following example:

```
SELECT E.EMP_NO, NAME, TAX_NO, C.COMP_CODE, COMP_NAME
    FROM   COMPANY  C,
           EMP  E
    WHERE E.COMP_CODE = C.COMP_CODE;
```

This SQL will work properly until, without your knowledge, the TAX_NO column is added to the COMPANY table:

```
ALTER TABLE COMPANY  ADD  (TAX_NO CHAR (20) );
```

Many programs will now begin to fail. You'll see messages such as the following:

```
ORA-00918 : COLUMN AMBIGUOUSLY DEFINED
```

To avoid problems of this kind, use table aliases as shown below:

```
SELECT  E.EMP_NO,E.NAME,E.TAX_NO,C.COMP_CODE,C.COMP_NAME
    FROM   COMPANY  C,
           EMP  E
    WHERE E.COMP_CODE = C.COMP_CODE;
```

Using NOT EXISTS in Place of NOT IN

In sub-query statements such as the following, the NOT IN clause causes an internal sort/merge.

```
SELECT . . .
    FROM   EMP
    WHERE DEPT_NO  NOT IN  (SELECT  DEPT_NO
                            FROM    DEPT
                            WHERE   DEPT_CAT = 'A');
```

To improve performance, replace this code with:

```
SELECT  . . .
    FROM   EMP  E
    WHERE NOT EXISTS  (SELECT  X'
                       FROM    DEPT
                       WHERE   DEPT_NO  =  E.DEPT_NO
                       AND     DEPT_CAT =  'A');
```

Using Joins in Place of EXISTS

In general, join tables rather than specifying sub-queries for them such as the following:

```
SELECT . . .
    FROM  EMP  E
    WHERE  EXISTS  (SELECT  X'
                    FROM    DEPT
                    WHERE  DEPT_NO  =  E.DEPT_NO
                    AND    DEPT_CAT  =  'A');
```

To improve performance, specify:

```
SELECT . . .
    FROM  DEPT  D, EMP  E
    WHERE E.DEPT_NO = D.DEPT_NO
    AND   DEPT_CAT  = 'A';
```

Using EXISTS in Place of DISTINCT

Avoid joins that require the DISTINCT qualifier on the SELECT list when you submit queries used to determine information at the owner end of a one-to-many relationship (e.g., departments that have employees). An example of such a query is shown below:

```
SELECT  DISTINCT  DEPT_CODE, DEPT_NAME
    FROM  DEPT  D, EMP E
    WHERE D.DEPT_CODE  =  E.DEPT_CODE
```

EXISTS is a faster alternative because the RDBMS kernel realizes that when the sub-query has been satisfied once, the query can be terminated.

```
SELECT  DEPT_CODE, DEPT_NAME
    FROM  DEPT  D
    WHERE EXISTS  (SELECT 'X'
                   FROM  EMP E
                   WHERE E.DEPT_CODE  =  D.DEPT_CODE);
```

Using Indexes to Improve Performance

This section explains how ORACLE uses indexes to help develop the most efficient execution plan. You can code your SQL statements to take best advantage of the indexes that have been specified for your tables. Be sure to read Chapter 6, *Defining Indexes*, about creating indexes on tables.

Which is Faster: Indexed Retrieval or a Full-table Scan?

There is a lively debate in the ORACLE community about the relative advantages of indexed retrievals and full-table scans. At what point does a full-table scan become more efficient than an indexed retrieval? What are the relative costs of the two approaches?

There are pros and cons on both sides. Full-table scans can be efficient because they require little disk head movement. The disk starts reading at one point and continues reading contiguous data blocks. Indexed retrievals are usually more efficient, as you would expect. But, because indexes retrieve records in a logical sequence, not in the order in which they are physically located on disk, indexed retrievals may result in a lot of disk head movement—perhaps retrieving only one record per read.

To a large extent the choice between an indexed retrieval and a full-table scan depends upon the size of the table and the pattern of access to that table. For example, if large portions of a large table are being processed, a serial search can actually be faster. If the rows being accessed sequentially are randomly dispersed throughout the table, processing them in sequence might be quite slow. In addition to the disk head move-ment required to retrieve the records, remember that every read of a row requires an additional read of the index.

If each read of the index and row were performed by a physical disk read, the break-even point for reading the entire table would be 50.1%. (one index and one table read per table record). Because use of the System Global Area (SGA) cache reduces the number of physical reads necessary, the actual break-even point is not quite so obvious. Where do you draw the line between a full-table scan and an indexed retrieval?

ORACLE Corporation recommends that if tables with fewer than eight data blocks are specified in a query, then a full-table scan is more efficient than an indexed retrieval. For larger tables, an indexed retrieval is usually faster. There is a lot of debate about where to draw the line.

In one article we have read, the author called this dilemma the "10, 20, 30 percent rule," because nobody could agree on how much of the table needs to be read before a full-table scan is more efficient. Our own investigations have indicated that each of the "10, 20, 30" figures might be correct in certain situations.

We've done a good deal of testing to try to refine these numbers. Our tests have shown that choosing a full-table scan over an indexed retrieval depends directly on how many rows of the table can fit into a single ORACLE block. ORACLE blocks are read, written, and cached in the SGA as entire blocks. The more rows contained within a block, the fewer physical reads are needed to scan the entire table. The more dispersed the (indexed) consecutive rows are throughout the table, and the fewer the number of rows that can be contained within an ORACLE block, the less the likelihood of the next row's being within the SGA cache.

If the only columns being selected were the indexed columns or pseudo columns (USER, SYSDATE, COUNT(*), etc.), an index read would always be the most efficient. In such a case, only the index would need to be read. The physical rows would never actually be retrieved.

If data is being retrieved from each row, the break-even point is a combination of the number of rows being read and the number of rows that a single ORACLE block can contain.

In the following examples, the left most column shows how much of the table (number of records) met the SQL selection criteria. The first example shows that if more than (approximately) 52% of the table needed to be read, a full-table scan performs better. It simply reads every record and picks out the ones that qualify.

The results below are based on the EMP table, which contains 26,000 rows, with seven rows per ORACLE block:

	Index Only	Index Table Read	Full Table Scan
Percentage Of table read	SELECT COUNT(*) FROM EMP WHERE EMP_NO > 0	SELECT EMP_NAME FROM EMP WHERE EMP_NO > 0	SELECT EMP_NAME FROM EMP WHERE EMP_NO + 0 > 0
8.5 %	0.66 seconds	12.03 seconds	35.70 seconds
15.5 %	1.04 seconds	16.21 seconds	35.70 seconds
25.2 %	1.54 seconds	25.45 seconds	35.70 seconds
50.7 %	**2.80 seconds**	**33.89 seconds**	**35.70 seconds ** **
100 %	5.72 seconds	87.23 seconds	35.70 seconds

** **break-even**

In the next example, the break-even point is only 15.5% of the table. This difference is a result of the physical size of the table and is directly determined by the number of rows that can fit in a single ORACLE block—the number read by a single read. The more rows per block, the less reading is required by a full-table scan to read the entire table.

The results below are based on the EMP_SMALL table, which contains 26,000 rows, with 258 rows per ORACLE block:

	Index Only	Index Table Read	Full Table Scan
Percentage of table read	SELECT COUNT(*) FROM EMP_SMALL WHERE EMP_NO > 0	SELECT EMP_NAME FROM EMP_SMALL WHERE EMP_NO > 0	SELECT EMP_NAME FROM EMP_SMALL WHERE EMP_NO + 0 > 0

8.5 %	0.66 seconds	02.31 seconds	04.52 seconds	
15.5 %	**1.05 seconds**	**04.01 seconds**	**04.52 seconds**	**
25.2 %	1.59 seconds	06.37 seconds	04.52 seconds	
50.7 %	2.91 seconds	12.69 seconds	04.52 seconds	
100 %	6.01 seconds	25.37 seconds	04.52 seconds	

** break-even

Although we've presented some guidelines, remember that you must test each table separately; one rule does not fit all. You must also allow for differing numbers of rows per ORACLE block and for selected columns being contained within the index

Once you've examined your own table situation, you might want to consider dropping indexes before you perform a large data load and then recreate them after the load has been completed. With very large tables, you can potentially increase performance by a factor of ten. In addition to the time savings, you'll find that the physical resources required to generate each index (after the data load) are substantially less than the overheads required to update each index during the data load. Exceptions to this rule occur when less than ten percent of the size of the table is being inserted (for example, via SQL*Loader or SQL*Plus). In this case it is preferable to leave the indexes intact.

Combining Indexes

Database retrieval using indexes is usually much faster than retrievals without indexes. Nevertheless, if you specify too many indexes over a table, performance will suffer as well. To increase performance, ORACLE tries to merge or otherwise combine the indexes for a table whenever it can. ORACLE follows certain rules in determining whether it can combine indexes. (Note that these rules apply only in ORACLE Version 6.0.33 and later.)

Two or more equality indexes. When a SQL statement has two or more equality indexes over different tables (e.g., WHERE = value) available to the execution plan, ORACLE uses both indexes by merging them at run time and fetching only rows that are common to both indexes. If two indexes exist over the same table in a WHERE clause, ORACLE ranks them as described below.

The index having a UNIQUE clause in its CREATE INDEX statement ranks before the index that does not have a UNIQUE clause. If neither has a UNIQUE clause, or if both have one, the effect depends on whether the indexes were specified over the same or different tables. If the two equal indexes are over two different tables, table sequence determines which will be queried first; the table specified last in the FROM clause outranks those specified earlier. If the two equal indexes are over the same table, the index referenced first in the WHERE clause ranks before the index referenced second.

Consider the following example; there is a non-unique index over DEPT_NO, and a non-unique index over EMP_CAT:

```
SELECT    EMP_NAME
    FROM  EMP
    WHERE DEPT_NO  =  0020
    AND   EMP_CAT  =  'A' ;


Explain Plan  Query Plan
-----------------------------------------------------------------
Table Access By Rowid on EMP
    And-Equal
        Index Range Scan on Dept_Idx
        Index Range Scan on Cat_Idx
```

The DEPT_NO index is retrieved first, followed by (merged with) the EMP_CAT rows.

Many programmers share the misconception that unique (and non-unique) comparative WHERE clauses rank very high on the optimizer's ranked list. This is true only when they are compared against constant predicates. If they are compared against other indexed columns from other tables, such clauses are much lower on the optimizer's list. For example, consider the statement:

```
SELECT . . .
    FROM  DEPT D, EMP E
    WHERE E.EMP_CAT = 'A'            Non-unique index;  rank 6
    AND   E.NAME LIKE 'SMITH%'       Indexed range;  rank 9
    AND   E.DEPT_NO = D.DEPT_NO      Sort/merge join;  rank 10
```

People assume that because DEPT has a UNIQUE index over DEPT_NO, it will rank very high. This is true, however, only when comparing against constants (or bind variables).

Equality and range predicates. When indexes combine both equality and range predicates over the same table, ORACLE cannot merge these indexes. In such cases, it uses only the equality predicate. Each row is individually validated against the second predicate. For example, in the following there is a non-unique index over DEPT_NO and a non-unique index over EMP_CAT:

```
SELECT    EMP_NAME
    FROM  EMP
    WHERE DEPT_NO  >  0020
    AND   EMP_CAT  =  'A' ;


Explain Plan Query Plan
--------------------------------------------------------
Table Access By Rowid on EMP
    Index Range Scan on Cat_Idx
```

The EMP_CAT index is utilized, and then each row is validated manually.

No clear ranking winner. When there is no clear index "ranking" winner, ORACLE will use only one of the indexes. In such cases, ORACLE uses the first index referenced by a WHERE clause in the statement (Version 6.0.33 and after). For example, in the following there is a non-unique index over DEPT_NO and a non-unique index over EMP_CAT:

```
SELECT      EMP_NAME
    FROM    EMP
    WHERE   DEPT_NO    >   0020
    AND     EMP_CAT    >   'B' ;


Explain Plan Query Plan
------------------------------------------------------------------
Table Access By Rowid on EMP
    Index Range Scan on Dept_Idx
```

The DEPT_NO index is used, and then each row is validated manually.

Explicitly Disabling an Index

If two or more indexes have equal ranking, according to the method described above, you can improve performance by choosing to use only the index that has the least number of rows satisfying the query. In the following example, concatenating | |" to a character column suppresses the use of the index on that column; concatenating +0 to numeric columns suppresses the use of the index on that column.

```
SELECT      . . .
    FROM    EMP
    WHERE   EMP_NO           =   12893
    AND     DEPT_CODE + 0    =   0010
    AND     EMP_TYPE || ''   = 'A';
```

This is a rather dire approach to improving performance because disabling the WHERE clause means not only disabling current retrieval paths, but also disabling all future paths. You should resort to this strategy only if you need to tune a few particular SQL statements individually.

Here is an example of when this strategy is justified. Suppose you have a non-unique index over the EMP_TYPE column of the EMP table, and that the EMP_CLASS column is not indexed:

```
SELECT      . . .
    FROM    EMP
    WHERE   EMP_TYPE   =   'A'
    AND     EMP_CLASS  =   'X' ;
```

The optimizer notices that EMP_TYPE is indexed and uses that path; it is the only choice at this point. If, at a later time, a second, non-unique index is added over EMP_CLASS, the optimizer will have to choose a selection path. Under normal circumstances, the optimizer would simply use both paths, performing a sort/merge on the resulting data. However, if one particular path is nearly unique (perhaps it returns only four or five rows), and the other path has thousands of duplicates, then the sort/merge operation is an unnecessary overhead. In this case, you will want to remove the EMP_CLASS index from optimizer consideration. You can do this by recoding the SELECT statement as follows:

```
SELECT      . . .
    FROM    EMP
    WHERE   EMP_TYPE         = 'A'
    AND     EMP_CLASS || ''  = 'X' ;
```

Avoiding Calculations on Indexed Columns

The optimizer does not use an index if the indexed column is a part of a function (in the WHERE clause). In general, avoid doing calculations on indexed columns. When the optimizer encounters a calculation on an indexed column, it will not use the index and will perform a full-table scan instead.

In this example, the optimizer does not use the index:

```
SELECT . . .
    FROM DEPARTMENT
    WHERE SALARY * 12  >  25000;
```

Often, you can get around this problem simply by moving the function to the other side of the equation. For example, in the following case, the optimizer uses the index:

```
SELECT
    FROM DEPARTMENT
    WHERE SALARY > 25000  / 12;
```

In some cases, you may want to take advantage of this behavior to keep certain columns from ever being considered by the optimizer. (See the discussion in the previous section.) Note that the SQL functions MIN and MAX are exceptions to this rule and will utilize all available indexes.

Automatically Suppressing Indexes

Under certain circumstances, the RDBMS kernel actually omits particular indexes from the query plan. Assume that a table has two (or more) available indexes, and that one index is unique and the other index is not unique. In such cases, ORACLE uses the unique retrieval path and completely ignores the second option. In the following example, there is a unique index over EMP_NO and a non-unique index over EMP_DEPT.

```
SELECT    EMP_NAME
    FROM   EMP
    WHERE EMP_NO    =  2362
    AND    EMP_DEPT =  0020 ;


    Explain Plan Query Plan
    ----------------------------------------------------
    Table Access By Rowid on EMP
        Index Unique Scan on Emp_No_Idx
```

The EMP_NO index is used to fetch the row. The second predicate (EMP_DEPT = 0020) is then evaluated (no index used).

Inserting Additional Columns in Indexes

In some cases, you'll gain performance benefits by including additional columns (that is, columns that you would not ordinarily specify for indexing) in a concatenated index. Why would you do this? The short answer is that it may allow you to satisfy queries without having to perform a physical read of the actual table at all.

Although most of the overhead for record retrieval is incurred simply by having to locate the address of the record (the row identifier, or ROWID), you can still save a substantial amount of overhead by avoiding a physical read of the record. Because indexes return records in an ordered sequence, not a physical sequence, actually having to retrieve the record also requires extensive head movement on the disk.

Consider the table definition for the DEPARTMENT table. The primary key is DEPT_CODE, and an index is created over this column.

```
TABLE DEPARTMENT
DEPT_CODE     PK    NOT NULL
DEPT_DESCRIPTION    NOT NULL
DEPT_TYPE           NULL
```

Now, suppose that when the DEPARTMENT table is referenced, the DEPT_TYPE column is almost always retrieved as well. By concatenating DEPT_TYPE with DEPT_CODE to create the index, you'll ensure that most retrievals can be satisfied without ever needing to physically read the database:

```
INDEX (DEPT_CODE, DEPT_TYPE)
```

This approach works only for small, frequently referenced fields. Because each index adds storage and updating requirements, you would not realize any performance gains by including long (for example, DEPT_DESCRIPTION, a 30-character field) or infrequently referenced fields in the index.

A drawback of including additional fields in an index is that your index will have to be altered from UNIQUE to NON-UNIQUE.

Avoiding NOT on Indexed Columns

In general, avoid using NOT when testing indexed columns. The NOT function has the same effect on indexed columns that functions do. When ORACLE encounters a NOT, it will choose not to use the index and will perform a full-table scan instead. For example, in the following case, an index will be used:

```
SELECT . . .
    FROM  DEPARTMENT
    WHERE DEPT_CODE  > 0;
```

And in the next case, an index will not be used:

```
SELECT . . .
    FROM  DEPARTMENT
    WHERE DEPT_CODE NOT  = 0;
```

In a few cases, the ORACLE optimizer will automatically transform NOTs (when they are specified with other operators) to the corresponding functions:

```
NOT >      to      <=
NOT >=     to      <
NOT <      to      >=
NOT <=     to      >
```

Using UNION in Place of OR

In general, always consider the UNION verb instead of the OR verb in WHERE clauses. Using OR on an indexed column causes the optimizer to perform a full-table scan rather than an indexed retrieval. Note, however, that choosing UNION over OR will be effective only if both columns are indexed; if either column is not indexed, you may actually increase overheads by not choosing OR.

In the following examples, both LOC_ID and REGION are indexed. Specify the following:

```
SELECT    LOC_ID, LOC_DESC, REGION
    FROM  LOCATION
    WHERE LOC_ID =  10
    UNION
```

```
SELECT    LOC_ID, LOC_DESC, REGION
   FROM   LOCATION
   WHERE  REGION  = 'MELBOURNE'
```

instead of:

```
SELECT    LOC_ID, LOC_DESC, REGION
   FROM   LOCATION
   WHERE  LOC_ID  =   10
   OR     REGION  =   'MELBOURNE'
```

If you do use OR, be sure that you put the most specific index first in the OR's predicate list, and put the index that passes the most records last in the list.

Note that the following:

```
WHERE KEY1 = 10                          Should return least rows
OR KEY2 = 20                             Should return most rows
```

is internally translated to:

```
WHERE KEY1 = 10
AND (KEY1 NOT = 10 AND KEY2 = 20)
```

Avoiding Null in Indexes

As we have discussed earlier in this chapter, null has several special properties. Because null can never be equated or compared, avoid using any column that contains a null as part of an index. ORACLE can never use an index to locate rows via a predicate such as IS NULL or IS NOT NULL. Indexes are often used to guarantee uniqueness. If an indexed column is null, you could potentially have two rows with the same key—a situation that could wreak havoc with your application.

In a single-column index, if the column is null, there is no entry within the index. For concatenated indexes, if every part of the key is null, no index entry exists. If at least one column of a concatenated index is non-null, an index entry does exist.

The treatment of nulls by ORACLE is somewhat quirky. Consider this example. If a UNIQUE index is created over a table for columns A and B, and a key value of (123, null) already exists, the system will reject the next record with that key as a duplicate. This is a case where ORACLE does recognize that a null does equal a null.

However, if all of the index columns are null (e.g., (null, null)), the keys are not considered to be the same, because in this case ORACLE considers the whole key to be null, and null can never equal null. You could potentially end up with 100 rows all with the same key, a value of null!

The following example illustrates a situation in which you could insert two distinct rows into the DEPARTMENT table, both with the primary key null. Don't try this at home!

```
TABLE DEPARTMENT

    DEPT_CODE          PK     NULL
    DEPT_DESCRIPTION          NULL
    DEPT_TYPE                 NULL

UNIQUE INDEX ( DEPT_CODE )

INSERT INTO DEPARTMENT VALUES   ( NULL, 'ACCOUNTS PAYABLE', 'A' );
INSERT INTO DEPARTMENT VALUES   ( NULL, 'ACCOUNTS RECEIVABLE', 'C' );
```

Using null improperly can hurt performance. Because null values are not a part of an index domain, specifying null on an indexed column will cause that index to be omitted from the execution plan. For example, the index will be used if you specify the following:

```
SELECT . . .
    FROM DEPARTMENT
    WHERE DEPT_CODE >= 0;
```

But, it will not be used if you specify the following:

```
SELECT . . .
    FROM DEPARTMENT
    WHERE DEPT_CODE  IS NOT NULL;
```

Using Null to Flag Record Subsets

Although null values frequently cause problems in retrievals, sometimes they can be used to increase performance.

Consider the case of a very large table (20,000,000 rows) to which new records are added daily (usually about 500 of them). Every night you need to report these additions on an audit trail. Rather than scan the whole table looking for changes, of course you will want to use an index. But the index would need to be huge. This is a case where your index is over the entire table, although you are actually interested only in the 500 or so records added today. The actual index is physically many times larger than it needs to be, and it uses many more disk I/Os to traverse the binary tree to the leaf data.

Now, suppose you add a special nonprinting column to the table that distinguishes between the records that need to be printed, and the records that need not be printed; this column will contain "U" for unprinted, and "P" for printed. This gives you a good way to find the records you are looking for, but it still requires that your index contain 20,000,000 entries, just to find the 500 you need to print.

By taking advantage of the special qualities of null, you can avoid having to create all of these index entries. When the print job actually prints the new records later on, it prints each record containing a "U" flag. Once the record has printed successfully, the print routine resets this column to null, thus removing all references to those unprinted (and not new) records from the index. Thus, the index will never grow any larger than the approximately 500 records you have added today. By doing this, you reduce the expected size of the index from approximately 20 megabytes to approximately 20K. The reduction in size easily justifies the additional overhead (a new sub-index and extra column update).

Using WHERE Instead of ORDER BY

One of the major errors made by SQL*Forms users is to specify an ORDER BY clause, rather than a WHERE clause, on the SELECT statement for an indexed column that may have null values (i.e., created without the NOT NULL clause). For the reasons described here, SELECT statements specified with such clauses cause the indexes to be discarded. As a result, the application performs a full-table scan, usually a major performance drain.

ORDER BY clauses use an index only if they meet two rigid requirements:

1. All of the columns that make up the ORDER BY clause must be contained within a single index in the same sequence.

2. All of the columns that make up the ORDER BY clause must be defined as NOT NULL within the table definition. Remember, null values are not contained within an index.

These two requirements tend to rule out most indexes.

Another problem sometimes arises when a WHERE clause is inadvertantly added to the statement (e.g., SQL* Forms "user-entered" queries). WHERE clause indexes override ORDER BY indexes. If the ORDER BY clause did manage to use an index, the WHERE clause will force a new index path to be used instead (satisfying the WHERE), and the ORDER BY will then be forced to perform a sort.

Fortunately, there is a way around this maze of conditions and problems. If you add a dummy WHERE clause (e.g., WHERE DEPTNO > 0) instead of an ORDER BY, you can trick the optimizer into using the correct index (by accident!). The statement will return data in the required order without doing a sort and without including an ORDER BY clause. If you add a new WHERE clause, the new index(es) and the existing (dummy ORDER BY) index will be used in parallel.

NOTE

WHERE clause indexes and ORDER BY indexes cannot be used in parallel.

Here is a more detailed example of what goes on behind the scenes when you specify WHERE and ORDER BY clauses. Note that DEPT_TYPE is defined as allowing NULL, and that column has the index over it:

```
TABLE DEPARTMENT

DEPT_CODE       PK      NOT NULL
DEPT_DESCRIPTION        NOT NULL
DEPT_TYPE               NULL

NON UNIQUE INDEX  (DEPT_TYPE)
```

In the following statement, the index will be used:

```
SELECT     . . .
    FROM  DEPARTMENT
    WHERE DEPT_TYPE  >  0

    Explain Plan Query Plan
    ---------------------------------------------------------------
    Table Access By Rowid on EMP
        Index Range Scan  on Dept_Idx
```

In the following statement, the index will not be used:

```
SELECT . . .
    FROM DEPARTMENT
    ORDER BY  DEPT_TYPE

    Explain Plan Query Plan
    ---------------------------------------------------------------
    Sort Order By
        Table Access FULL
```

Problems When Converting Index Column Types

In both Version 6 and Version 7, ORACLE automatically performs simple column type conversion, or casting, when it compares two columns of different types. If a numeric column is compared to an alphabetic column, the character column automatically has its type converted to numeric.

Assume that EMP_NO is an indexed numeric column.

```
SELECT . . .
    FROM EMP
    WHERE EMP_NO = '123'
```

In fact, because of conversion this statement will actually be processed as:

```
SELECT . . .
   FROM EMP
   WHERE EMP_NO = TO_NUMBER('123')
```

Even though a type conversion has taken place, in this example index usage is not affected. Unfortunately, this is not the case in the next example. Here, assume that EMP_TYPE is an indexed CHAR column:

```
SELECT  . . .
   FROM EMP
   WHERE EMP_TYPE = 123
```

This statement will actually be processed as:

```
SELECT  . . .
   FROM EMP
   WHERE TO_NUMBER(EMP_TYPE) = 123
```

Indexes cannot be used if they are included in a function. Therefore, this internal conversion will keep the index from being used. This automatic type conversion can cause strange performance anomalies when the columns are indexed. Note that TKPROF (described in Chapter 12), cannot detect or identify these problems; it simply assumes that all bind variables are of the correct type.

Beware of the WHEREs

Some SELECT statement WHERE clauses do not use indexes at all. If you have specified an index over a table that is referenced by a clause of the type shown in this section, ORACLE will simply ignore the index. For each clause that cannot use an index, we have suggested an alternative approach which will allow you to get better performance out of your SELECT statements.

In the following example, the SUBSTR function disables the index when it is used over an indexed column:

Do Not Use:

```
SELECT  ACCOUNT_NAME, TRANS_DATE, AMOUNT
   FROM  TRANSACTION
   WHERE SUBSTR(ACCOUNT_NAME,1,7) = 'CAPITAL';
```

Use:

```
SELECT  ACCOUNT_NAME, TRANS_DATE, AMOUNT
   FROM  TRANSACTION
   WHERE ACCOUNT_NAME LIKE 'CAPITAL%';
```

In the following example, the != (not equal) function cannot use an index. Remember, indexes can tell you what is in a table, but not what is not in a table. All references to NOT, !=, and <> disable index usage:

Do Not Use:

```
SELECT  ACCOUNT_NAME,TRANS_DATE,AMOUNT
    FROM  TRANSACTION
    WHERE AMOUNT != 0;
```

Use:

```
SELECT  ACCOUNT_NAME,TRANS_DATE,AMOUNT
    FROM  TRANSACTION
    WHERE AMOUNT > 0 ;
```

In the following example, the TRUNC function disables the index:

Do Not Use:

```
SELECT  ACCOUNT_NAME, TRANS_DATE, AMOUNT
    FROM   TRANSACTION
    WHERE TRUNC(TRANS_DATE) = TRUNC(SYSDATE);
```

Use:

```
SELECT  ACCOUNT_NAME, TRANS_DATE, AMOUNT
    FROM  TRANSACTION
    WHERE TRANS_DATE BETWEEN TRUNC(SYSDATE)
          AND TRUNC(SYSDATE) + .99999;
```

When using dates, note that, if more than five decimal places are added to a date, the date is actually rounded up to the next day! For example:

```
SELECT  TO_DATE('01-JAN-93') + .99999
    FROM DUAL;
```

returns:

```
'01-JAN-93 23:59:59'
```

and:

```
SELECT TO_DATE('01-JAN-93') + .999999
    FROM DUAL;
```

returns:

```
'02-JAN-93 00:00:00'
```

In the following example, || is the concatenate function; it strings two character columns together. It, like other functions, disables indexes.

Do Not Use:

```
SELECT  ACCOUNT_NAME, TRANS_DATE, AMOUNT
    FROM  TRANSACTION
    WHERE ACCOUNT_NAME || ACCOUNT_TYPE = 'AMEXA';
```

Use:

```
SELECT  ACCOUNT_NAME, TRANS_DATE, AMOUNT
    FROM   TRANSACTION
    WHERE ACCOUNT_NAME  =  'AMEX'
    AND    ACCOUNT_TYPE  =  'A' ;
```

In the following example, addition (+) is a function and disables the index. The other arithmetic operators (-, *, and /) have the same effect.

Do Not Use:

```
SELECT  ACCOUNT_NAME, TRANS_DATE, AMOUNT
    FROM   TRANSACTION
    WHERE AMOUNT+3000 < 5000;
```

Use:

```
SELECT  ACCOUNT_NAME, TRANS_DATE, AMOUNT
    FROM   TRANSACTION
    WHERE AMOUNT <  2000;
```

In the following example, indexes cannot be used to compare indexed columns against the same index column. This causes a full-table scan.

Do Not Use:

```
SELECT ACCOUNT_NAME, TRANS_DATE, AMOUNT
    FROM   TRANSACTION
    WHERE ACCOUNT_NAME=NVL(:ACC_NAME, ACCOUNT_NAME);
```

Use:

```
SELECT ACCOUNT_NAME, TRANS_DATE, AMOUNT
    FROM   TRANSACTION
    WHERE ACCOUNT_NAME LIKE NVL(:ACC_NAME, '%');
```

Auditing

The dynamic SQL column reference (*) gives you a way to refer to all of the columns of a table; for example, if you specify:

```
SELECT * FROM EMP
```

ORACLE references each column in the EMP table in turn. This is a helpful feature because it keeps you from having to identify every individual field. The SQL parser handles all the field references by obtaining the names of valid columns from the data dictionary and substitutes them on the command line.

Usually, we recommend that you do not use the * feature because it is a very inefficient one (the * has to be converted to each column in turn). However, you can use this feature very effectively in auditing. Prefix the * operator with a table alias and use it with other columns from other tables. For example, you can specify:

```
SELECT 'A', 'B', E.* FROM EMP E
```

You cannot specify:

```
SELECT 'A', 'B', * FROM EMP
```

You can easily develop a mirror image audit trail of a table, for example:

```
INSERT INTO  EMP_AUDIT
SELECT USER, SYSDATE, A.*
    FROM  EMP A
    WHERE EMP_NO = :EMP_NO;
```

If two tables are identical (e.g., a source table and a mirrored audit table), you can copy data easily from one to the other this way. Mirrored audit tables have a completed, post-updated copy of the record written to the audit table after the update takes place. This means that the audit table has a complete modification history of the table.

There is a big advantage to using the * operator. If you keep the audit table up to date (i.e., identical in field number, type, and sequence to the source table), you never need to maintain the audit routines. If you add a column to the EMP table and the EMP_AUDIT table, the routines that access these tables will continue to work; you won't have to modify all of the routines in the EMP audit procedure that deal with updates. For example, you might specify:

```
INSERT INTO EMP_AUDIT
SELECT 'WHO', 'WHEN', 'WHERE', E.*
    FROM  EMP  E
    WHERE  E.EMP_NO  = 123;
```

This simple idea can be extended to simplify many programming situations. Another example is shown below:

```
SELECT  E.EMP_NO, E.EMP_NAME, D.*, C.*
    FROM CAT  C,
         DPT  D,
         EMP  E
    WHERE E.DEPT_NO  =  D.DEPT_NO  (+)
    AND E.CAT_TYPE  =  C.CAT_TYPE  (+);
```

Adjusting SQL Statements Over Time

You are not finished after you have tuned your SQL statements for best performance. You'll have to keep monitoring system performance and adjusting your SQL to take advantage of changing times and situations. Here are some reasons why you may find that today's most efficient SQL statements are not tomorrow's:

Physical table volumes. Driving tables may grow, or shrink, over time. For example, the CREDITORS table might have had only 25 records when the system was launched, but now, after five years of recession, the table may contain 25,000 records.

Indexes. The number of indexes available at execution time may change over time. Indexes come and go. Even adding a single index on a minor application table can affect the entire execution plan of certain crucial statements in your application.

Key field data spread. As data is added to the database over time, it may turn out that an indexed column actually has the same value for most rows. In this case, defining an index over a table in fact adds overhead to that table. ORACLE provides a SQL script, *ONEIDXS.sql* (found in the *..\dbs* directory; the actual directory name is operating system-dependent), which actually plots an index spread over the key fields.

The ORACLE version. As new versions of the ORACLE RDBMS and associated tools are released, new features may affect your SQL. For example, the rule-based optimizer has frequently been altered and refined over time. And with Version 7, a new cost-based optimizer has been introduced.

Physical location. The physical distance between client-server machines makes a big difference in SQL performance. For example, certain statements take only two seconds to process on a unitary machine, but take 22 seconds to process over the network connecting Sydney and Melbourne.

SQL Security

This section describes a few particular security issues that have an impact on the security of your SQL statements. For additional information about security changes for Version 7 that affect the DBA, see Appendix A, *Planning for Version 7.*

SQL*Plus Login Automation

SQL*Plus allows you to automatically execute two different SQL scripts when you first begin SQL*Plus operation. This feature allows you or the DBA to create crude security scripts that record when a user logs on, and may also protect automatically against invalid logon access. You can also use this feature simply to initialize a number of default parameters you will use in your SQL*Plus session.

GLOGIN.sql is the first script initiated. It resides in the default ORACLE directory, *$ORACLE_HOME\dbs*. You can include in this script a variety of parameters you might want to initialize at this time. For example, the following assignment sets the default UNIX editor for the SQL*Plus session:

```
DEFINE _EDITOR = "/usr/ucb/vi"
START /usr/dba/SECURITY.sql
```

When a user logs on, this script runs automatically.

LOGIN.sql is the second script initiated. This script can reside only in the user's home directory and is used to customize the user's SQL*Plus connection. For example, the following sets a variety of initial parameter, including setting up the trace file for debugging:

```
SET PAGESIZE  66
SET LINESIZE  80
SET TIMING    ON
ALTER SESSION SET  SQL_TRACE TRUE;
```

Using the PRODUCT_USER_PROFILE Table

The PRODUCT_USER_PROFILE table available only through SQL*Plus allows you to implement a degree of security beyond standard application security. You can use this table to limit a user's or a group of users' ability to use particular operations of an ORACLE tool.

Applications that support OPS$ logins can restrict user access. You can even use this feature to prevent SQL*Plus access altogether, while still permitting normal secured access, via RUNFORM. Note that all SQL*Plus commands are valid attributes here (e.g., ALTER, AUDIT, CONNECT, CREATE, DELETE, DROP, EDIT, HOST, etc.)

Following are the columns contained in the PRODUCT_USER_PROFILE table:

PRODUCT	SQL*Plus only; case-sensitive
USERID	Can be username or wild-card (e.g., SCOTT, OPS$SMITH, OPS$%
ATTRIBUTE	SQL command to disable
SCOPE	Not used
NUMERIC_VALUE	Not used
CHAR_VALUE	String "DISABLED"
DATE_VALUE	Not used

For example:

```
INSERT INTO SYSTEM.PRODUCT_USER_PROFILE
    ( PRODUCT, USERID, ATTRIBUTE, CHAR_VALUE )
    VALUES ( 'SQL*Plus', 'SCOTT', 'CONNECT', 'DISABLED' );
```

Applications that access many physical databases, connected via database links and SQL*Net, can use the PRODUCT_USER_PROFILE feature to keep each user from being unnecessarily enrolled on every database instance. By creating the database link with hard-coded user code, and suppressing any connection to the remote nodes via SQL*Plus, you can effectively define only one user and one set of accesses. For example:

```
CREATE PUBLIC DATABASE LINK PRD
    CONNECT TO SCOTT IDENTIFIED BY TIGER USING 'X:ORASRV';
    INSERT INTO SYSTEM.PRODUCT_USER_PROFILE
            ( PRODUCT,  USERID,  ATTRIBUTE,  CHAR_VALUE  )
    VALUES  ( 'SQL*Plus',  'OPS$%',  'CONNECT', 'DISABLED' );
```

NOTE

The ORACLE PRODUCT_USER_PROFILE functionality is available only within SQL*Plus and is not applicable to the ORACLE users SYSTEM or SYS.

8

Tuning PL/SQL

PL/SQL (Procedure Language/SQL) is a set of procedural capabilities that extends the power of traditional SQL. PL/SQL statements can be combined with traditional SQL in a variety of ORACLE products to increase the ease of application programming, allow SQL to perform control and procedural functions previously beyond its powers, and considerably improve overall system performance.

PL/SQL is essentially a procedural extension of SQL. It allows all of the procedural constructs available in traditional third-generation languages to be specified directly within the ORACLE SQL environment—for example, conditional control (IF, THEN, ELSE), local variable and constant declarations, etc., rather than through complex user exits.

PL/SQL is incorporated into the more recent versions of all the current ORACLE tools, as shown below:

SQL*Forms	Version 3.0 and above
SQL*Reportwriter	Version 2.0 and above
SQL*Plus	Version 3.0 and above
SQL*Menu	Version 5.0 and above
SQL*DBA	All versions

In most cases, you can choose whether or not to use the PL/SQL facilities. With SQL*Forms, for example, PL/SQL is included by default, but you can remove it for performance reasons, as discussed in Chapter 9, *Tuning SQL*Forms*.

Regardless of which ORACLE tool you are using, the tool passes PL/SQL blocks to the PL/SQL engine, which executes the code and then passes SQL statements, as appropriate, to the database.

PL/SQL and SQL

From our point of view, the most important feature of PL/SQL is its dramatic effect on performance. Database accesses and network communications are usually the slowest aspects of ORACLE processing. PL/SQL improves performance by dramatically reducing the number of calls the application must make to the database. Because PL/SQL allows multiple SQL statements to be included in a single block, PL/SQL cuts down on database accesses by passing the whole block at once. With one database access, PL/SQL can process many statements that, with traditional SQL, would have to be passed to the database one at a time. In fact, if a PL/SQL block contains no traditional SQL statements at all, the application doesn't even need to call the database.

The reduction in database calls is demonstrated in Figure 8-1.

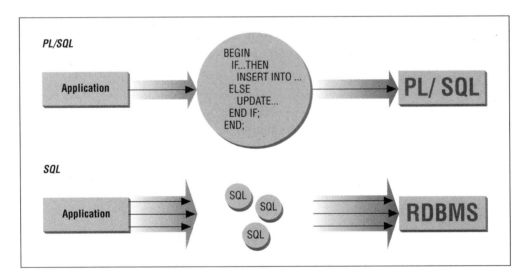

Figure 8-1: Contrast between SQL and PL/SQL

The inclusion of PL/SQL capabilities in a variety of ORACLE tools (e.g., SQL*Forms, SQL*Plus) significantly increases the performance of all of these tools. The greatest performance gains of all are realized when client-server applications are being run.

What Does PL/SQL Offer?

With traditional SQL, each statement is a single entity, with no particular relationship to the other SQL statements you issue. ORACLE executes each SQL statement separately. It accesses the database for each distinct SQL statement.

With PL/SQL, on the other hand, you can group many SQL statements into a single block. ORACLE processes this group as a unit, accessing the database only once for each block. In PL/SQL, you typically specify statements in a block structure, as shown in Figure 8-2.

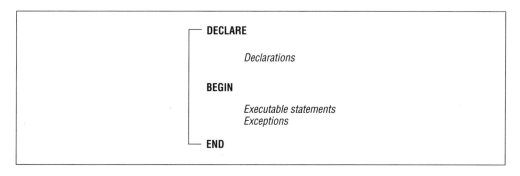

Figure 8-2: PL/SQL block structure

Types of PL/SQL Statements

In a PL/SQL block, you can include traditional SQL statements as well as special PL/SQL statements. You can include the following statements, as shown in Table 8-1.

Table 8-1: Statements Allowed in PL/SQL Blocks

SQL Statements	Type
Query and data manipulation language statements	SELECT, INSERT, UPDATE, DELETE
Cursor control statements	DECLARE, OPEN, FETCH, CLOSE
Transaction processing statements	COMMIT, ROLLBACK, SAVEPOINT

Table 8-1: Statements Allowed in PL/SQL Blocks (Continued)

PL/SQL Statements	Type
Control statements	IF...THEN...ELSE, EXIT, GOTO
Looping statement	FOR...LOOP, WHILE...LOOP
Assignment statements	X := Y + Z and similar statements
Block control statements (you can nest PL/SQL blocks within other blocks)	DECLARE, BEGIN, END
Error exception statements (beyond those supported by SQL)	RAISE statements that handle errors supported by SQL for such conditions as STORAGE_ERROR, NO_DATA_FOUND, and ZERO_DIVIDE.

Portability

Like SQL, PL/SQL is completely portable across all ORACLE platforms and versions (RDBMS Version 6 and above). You can develop applications that incorporate PL/SQL code in SQL*Forms, SQL*Menu, or SQL*Plus applications (as well as others), without regard for whether the final production platform will be a PC running DOS, a Sun workstation running UNIX, or an IBM mainframe running MVS.

Use of Variables and Constants

The PL/SQL parser and interpreter are incorporated directly into the RDBMS kernel. This allows variables and constants to be identified by the RDBMS data dictionary. This means any variables referenced within a PL/SQL block can be part of the actual procedure. Processing of the routine (at the RDBMS) does not have to be continually paused while a variable value is retrieved from the source application.

The following SQL*Forms routine demonstrates how to reduce the number of application variable calls while executing the PL/SQL block. This example performs only one GET of :BLK.EMP_SAL, storing it in a local PL/SQL block variable (SAL_VAL), and it performs only one PUT of the calculated result into the :BLK.EMP_INT field.

NOTE

In the PL/SQL examples in this chapter and in Chapter 9, we occasionally include blank lines to set off individual blocks. This is done only for clarity and is not a necessary part of PL/SQL.

```
DECLARE
     SAL_VAL  NUMBER;
     TAX_VAL  NUMBER;
BEGIN
```

```
SAL_VAL   :=   :BLK.EMP_SAL;

   IF  SAL_VAL <= 2000  THEN
       TAX_VAL := 0;
   END IF;

   IF  SAL_VAL >= 2001  AND
       SAL_VAL <= 8000  THEN
       TAX_VAL := (SAL_VAL * 15 ) / 100;
   END IF;

   IF  SAL_VAL >= 8001  THEN
       TAX_VAL := (SAL_VAL * 25 ) / 100;
   END IF;

   :BLK.EMP_INT := TAX_VAL;
END;
```

Using PL/SQL in Procedures and Functions (Version 7 Only)

Both stored library procedures and system library functions support PL/SQL. Procedures and functions are globally stored within the database and are available to all application products. Using PL/SQL, you can code powerful generic routines and thus reduce the number of application-specific libraries needed.

PL/SQL Limitations

Although PL/SQL offers many benefits, it does have some limitations you'll need to be aware of to get the best performance from the product. In this section, we describe strategies you may need to follow to use PL/SQL to best advantage.

Block Size

PL/SQL blocks do have a physical size limit. This limitation depends on the number and type of commands included in the block. This restriction is approximately 32K per block (after compressing all unrequired "white space," etc.). ORACLE raises the following error when your block is too large:

```
ORA-4031 : out of shared memory - RAM Buffer exceeded
```

The original versions of PL/SQL were limited to approximately 200 lines per block.

You can get around the problem of block limitation very easily. Simply break your blocks into sub-blocks, as shown in Figure 8-3.

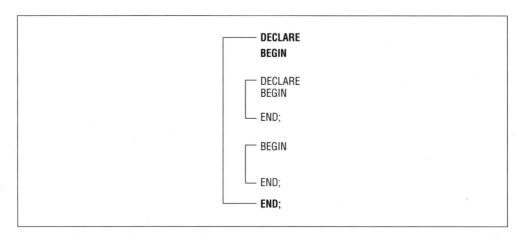

Figure 8-3: Use of sub-blocks

No Support Of DDL or DCL

PL/SQL is a procedural engine only. It does not support SQL statements that manipulate the data dictionary. PL/SQL does not support such data dictionary manipulation (DDL) statements as the following: CREATE TABLE, CREATE INDEX, DROP TABLE, ALTER TABLE, and CREATE SEQUENCE.

PL/SQL does not support such data control language (DCL) statements as the following: CONNECT, GRANT, and REVOKE.

No Screen or Printer I/O

PL/SQL does not support screen or printer I/O. In fact, PL/SQL has no ability to communicate outside its block except via table updates, updates of application variables, and error exceptions. Although this may seem to be a major limitation, in practice it is rarely an issue. Just remember that the fundamental function of PL/SQL is to group many SQL statements into a single processing unit. Any other function (e.g., I/O) can be handled via the more global tool you're using (e.g., SQL*Forms and user exits, Pro*C, etc.)

Limited LONG Support

PL/SQL does not directly support LONG data types (up to two gigabytes for RDBMS Version 7). If you select a column into a variable defined as LONG, you will not get an error message, but your value will be truncated.

You can get around the LONG limitation by creating, through PL/SQL, a local character field. This field can hold as many as 32,767 characters.

Problems with Duplicate Names

As we've mentioned earlier, PL/SQL allows you to declare local variables. If you inadvertently give a local variable the same name as a column from a table that you are referencing, the PL/SQL routine compiles successfully and no error is reported. If in your code the local variable is compared or referenced within an SQL statement, undesirable results may occur. The following example of such a situation may seem an obvious and simplistic one, but it's one that actually occurred and disrupted an organization's processing for many weeks. Be careful that you don't make the same mistake.

```
PROCEDURE SYSTEM_ERROR (MSG_NO IN NUMBER) IS
BEGIN
    DECLARE
        CURSOR C1 IS
        SELECT MSG_TEXT
            FROM SYSTEM_MESSAGES
            WHERE MSG_NO = MSG_NO;
                    ↑          ↑
            table column    procedure variable


    BEGIN
        .
        .
        .
    END;
END;
```

Problems with GOTO

Many programmers have complained to us about the behavior of the PL/SQL GOTO macro. This macro provides a valuable way of breaking loops, and you'll often find that you want to use it to simplify processing of complex routines.

But, be prepared for an odd and annoying characteristic of GOTO. You can't GOTO the end of a PL/SQL block directly. You must include a NULL statement in your PL/SQL block immediately following the exit label and preceding the END statement. We haven't been able to fathom why this is necessary, but if you insert the NULL, as shown, following <<EXIT_LABEL>> in the following example, you won't run into trouble.

```
DECLARE
    LOOP_NO NUMBER := 0;
BEGIN
    .
    .
    .
    WHILE LOOP_NO <= 10 LOOP
        .
        .
        .
        IF   ABC > XYZ    THEN
            GOTO EXIT_LABEL;
        END IF;
        .
        .
        .
    END LOOP;
    .
    .
    .
    <<EXIT_LABEL>>
    NULL;
END;
```

Using Explicit and Implicit Cursors in PL/SQL

Two types of cursors are available to PL/SQL programmers: explicit and implicit. When it processes an SQL statement, PL/SQL opens a work area called the context area. A cursor gives you a way to name a portion of this context area. You'll commonly use a cursor to access the current row obtained from queries.

You define an explicit cursor by specifying it in a DECLARE statement. You include this DECLARE in your PL/SQL code (before you specify any BEGIN blocks). Then, within your block you may include OPEN, FETCH, and CLOSE statements. OPEN opens and parses the cursor and is required. FETCH fetches the cursor's current row and is also required. CLOSE closes the cursor after all fetches have been completed and is optional. For example:

```
DECLARE
CURSOR C IS
SELECT     EMP_NAME
    FROM   EMP
    WHERE  EMP_NO = 1234;
```

```
BEGIN
    OPEN  C;
    FETCH C INTO . . . ;
    CLOSE C;
END;
```

If you do not specify an explicit cursor for a SELECT statement, PL/SQL will implicitly open a cursor to use when it processes each SQL statement, as shown below.

```
SELECT      EMP_NAME
    INTO   :BLK.EMP_NAME
    FROM    EMP
    WHERE   EMP_NO = 1234;
```

You will get better performance if you declare explicit cursors. PL/SQL handles the two types of cursors differently. When PL/SQL is handling implicit cursors, it performs a second fetch for each row to be sure that nothing else meets the SQL selection criteria— for example, in the example above, a second employee with an EMP_NO of 1234. If a second row is found, PL/SQL displays the message, "MORE THAN ONE ROW RETURNED," as required by ANSI standards.

The savings associated with using explicit, rather than implicit, cursors are significant. Suppose that an application needs to perform 100 SELECTs using an implicit cursor within a session. The application would perform 100 unnecessary extra FETCHes. (Remember, though, that although each FETCH is performed twice, the parse is performed only once.) Use of explicit cursors is especially important in the client-server environment. (See Chapter 16, *Tuning in the Client-server Environment.*)

Using PL/SQL to Expand the Functionality of Other Tools

By incorporating PL/SQL into ORACLE tools, such as SQL*Forms and SQL*Plus, you expand the capabilities of these tools by allowing them to perform functions not normally available to them. For example, SQL*Forms ordinarily does not allow DML statements (UPDATE, INSERT, DELETE, COMMIT, ROLLBACK) to be specified outside the scope of a commit phase (the normal scope is between pre-COMMIT and post-COMMIT). You can get around these limitations by including such statements in PL/SQL blocks.

In the following example, SQL*Forms updates information when a user enters the form. Within the KEY_STARTUP trigger, you cannot specify a COMMIT statement directly.

However, by including COMMIT inside a PL/SQL block (delimited by BEGIN and END), you can get around this limitation.

```
KEY-STARTUP :   BEGIN
                    UPDATE USER_FORM
                    SET    CURR_FORM = "XXXXXX:,
                           FORM_TIME = SYSDATE
                    WHERE  USER_CODE = USER;

                    :SYSTEM.MESSAGE_LEVEL  := 25;
                    COMMIT;
                    :SYSTEM.MESSAGE_LEVEL  := 0;
                END;
```

:SYSTEM.MESSAGE_LEVEL needs to be set to level 25 to suppress the message "NO OUTSTANDING COMMITS". This message is a side effect of no outstanding base-table commits. The PL/SQL update proceeds regardless.

Using PL/SQL to Speed Up Updates

The use of PL/SQL provides especially noticeable performance gains when you are running a large batch update job in which parent/child updating plays a part.

Consider a system in which the ACCOUNT_TOTALS table is updated every night from various systems to post each account's current expenditures against its budget. There are approximately 10,000 rows in the ACCOUNT_TOTALS table and about 200 rows in the TRANSACTION table (containing the day's transactions). The system is not an integrated one in which data loaded into the TRANSACTION (child) table automatically updates the ACCOUNT_TOTALS (parent) table. You need to run a program that posts the updates to ACCOUNT_TOTALS as a separate step.

Using SQL only, you would update as follows. This type of update would take several minutes to run.

```
UPDATE ACCOUNT_TOTALS A
SET CURRENT_EXP = CURRENT_EXP + ( SELECT DAILY_EXP
                                  FROM TRANSACTION T
                                  WHERE T.ACC_NO = A.ACC_NO )
WHERE EXISTS ( SELECT  'X'
                 FROM TRANSACTION T
                 WHERE T.ACC_NO = A.ACC_NO  );
```

Now, suppose you used PL/SQL to achieve the same result. You'd accomplish the update in seconds!

```
DECLARE
    CURSOR READ_TRAN  IS
    SELECT ACC_NO, DAILY_EXP
        FROM TRANSACTION;

    ACC_NO_STORE       NUMBER (6);
    DAILY_EXP_STORE    NUMBER (9,2);
BEGIN
    OPEN READ_TRAN;
    LOOP
        FETCH READ_TRAN INTO ACC_NO_STORE, DAILY_EXP_STORE;
        EXIT WHEN READ_TRAN%NOTFOUND;

        UPDATE ACCOUNT_TOTALS A
        SET CURRENT_EXP = CURRENT_EXP + DAILY_EXP_STORE
        WHERE ACC_NO = ACC_NO_STORE ;
    END LOOP;
END;
```

Although using PL/SQL instead of traditional SQL results in a substantial performance gain, PL/SQL does not always produce such results. What if the TRANSACTION table contains 1000 or more rows, rather than 200. If a daily child transaction table updates more than about 10 to 15% of the parent table (ACCOUNTS_TABLE, in the example), PL/SQL will actually make the update run more slowly. PL/SQL uses the table's indexes and performs more physical reads against the database than the SQL method, which performs a full-table scan in this case.

Inconsistencies in PL/SQL Statements

PL/SQL surprises some ORACLE users by operating somewhat differently from one ORACLE tool to another. Even when you use the same product on a multi-platform network, you may even find that the PL/SQL on one platform (e.g., a PC running DOS) operates differently from the PL/SQL on another platform (e.g., a Sun workstation running UNIX). Finally, you may find that there are subtle differences between versions of PL/SQL.

PL/SQL is incorporated into different tools in different ways. PL/SQL is bound directly into the ORACLE RDBMS kernel and into the SQL*Forms executable. To achieve the best performance, some SQL functions use the RDBMS SQL engine, while others that do not need to access the RDBMS engine have been coded directly into the PL/SQL kernel (for example, the TO_DATE macros are coded in this way). So, you need to be aware that behavior in PL/SQL statements may differ, and test all of your implementations thoroughly.

For example, all of the following statements are invalid in SQL*Forms, but all are valid in SQL (via SQL*Plus) and return 01-JUN-92.

```
SELECT TO_DATE ('01JUN92', 'DD-MON-YY') FROM DUAL;
SELECT TO_DATE ('01JUN92', 'DD/MON/YY') FROM DUAL;
SELECT TO_DATE ('1JUN92',  'DD-MON-YY') FROM DUAL;
```

A second, even worse anomaly is when two ORACLE tools return different results altogether. The SQL statement:

```
SELECT TO_DATE ('10011993', 'DD/MM/YYYY') FROM DUAL;
```

returns the date 10-OCT-1993 in SQL*Plus and 10-JAN-0093 in SQL*Forms!

9

*Tuning SQL*Forms*

You use SQL*Forms to develop and run interactive applications based on forms. SQL*Forms provides a complete default structure for your applications so you don't need to be concerned with all of the details of data type validation, navigation from field to field on a form, and database access. SQL*Forms gives you a very productive environment in which to develop interactive applications that provide a fill-in-the-form user interface. Because SQL*Forms has so many built-in capabilities and defaults, much of the product tuning is beyond your reach. However, there are a number of ways in which you can subtly manipulate SQL*Forms to get better performance. Because SQL*Forms is built on SQL and PL/SQL, most of the performance problems you encounter in SQL*Forms are actually the result of poorly tuned SQL or PL/SQL statements whose inefficiencies are compounded in the SQL*Forms environment. Be sure to read Chapter 7, *Tuning SQL*, and Chapter 8, *Tuning PL/SQL*, before you read this chapter.

This chapter describes how to tune SQL*Forms Version 3. This release is supported across all versions of the ORACLE RDBMS from Version 5 to Version 7. Although Version 3 provides additional power, it also can cause performance problems. The Version 3 executables are almost twice as large as those for Versions 2 and 2.3 and require twice as much memory. Adding PL/SQL processing overheads can increase resource use still more. The extra memory requirement can spell the difference between a machine's being able to function adequately, with sufficient spare memory, and the machine's laboring to perform despite paging and swapping overhead. With Version 3, it is all the more important that you tune SQL*Forms as best you can.

When you run SQL*Forms, your input is usually an *.INP* ASCII source statement file. SQL*Forms generates this input into interpretive code and places it in a *.FRM* object file, which is then executed by RUNFORM (the SQL*Forms executable). There has been some discussion about dropping support of the *.INP* file in future releases of SQL*Forms. However, we understand that ORACLE Corporation has agreed to continue support for this file in Version 4 and probably beyond.

NOTE

When you specify triggers in SQL*Forms, always use Version 3, rather than Version 2, triggers. Because Version 3 triggers support the PL/SQL database interface, they provide better performance and more flexibility. Always begin coding a new form from a standard SQL*Forms skeleton. It will simplify your work, enforce system-wide standards, and improve application performance.

SQL and SQL*Forms

Whenever you encounter a SQL*Forms performance problem, look first at the SQL statements you have specified. Nine times out of ten an offending SQL statement, rather than a poorly written form, is the cause of a performance problem. (Remember, SQL syntax does not vary from tool to tool; the discussion in Chapter 7 applies to SQL*Forms too.)

You need to be aware of the way that the settings of certain INIT.ORA parameters affect SQL*Forms processing. If you are developing forms, you may need to change the settings of some of these parameters.

The number of cursors you can have open simultaneously in SQL*Forms is limited by the setting of the OPEN_CURSORS parameter. This parameter has a default of 50, but we recommend that you increase it to 100 for complex SQL*Forms applications. Your SQL*Forms applications tend to use more cursors than you may expect. For example, RUNFORM uses four cursors during initialization. The simplest SQL*Forms base table block uses five cursors (one each for LOCK, QUERY, INSERT, UPDATE, and DELETE). SQL*Forms does not release these cursors or their associated resources until the form that owns the cursors is exited. Therefore, if a form has five base tables (and all are visited), the form will hold a minimum of 29 cursors.

You can find out how many cursors a form actually uses by executing the form with the -S (statistic) option set:

```
RUNFORM form usercode/password -S
```

When you exit the RUNFORM session, SQL*Forms displays all cursors used in the session, as shown below:

```
Total cursors used    9
```

PL/SQL and SQL*Forms

The ability to include PL/SQL statements in SQL*Forms specifications gives SQL*Forms procedural capabilities previously beyond it, including the ability to open and close cursors. PL/SQL is available only in SQL*Forms Version 3, and will be supported by future releases. Because some of the performance problems you might encounter in SQL*Forms may be the result of PL/SQL problems, check out the recommendations in Chapter 8 before you assume that there is a problem with your forms.

PL/SQL allows you to open and close cursors, as described in the section in Chapter 8 called, "Using Explicit and Implicit Cursors in PL/SQL." When a cursor is closed, the ORACLE kernel does not immediately discard the cursor information. Instead, it retains the cursor for possible shared use, as described in the next section. You can close a cursor manually (CLOSE), or allow it to be closed automatically when the block that owns the cursor ends. (Remember from Chapter 8 that PL/SQL statements can be structured in blocks delimited by BEGIN and END statements.)

PL/SQL is directly linked into the SQL*Forms executable. This allows SQL*Forms to execute Version 3-type triggers without having to call the RDBMS kernel, provided that the triggers do not contain SQL statements. This feature improves performance a great deal, particularly if SQL*Forms is running in a client-server configuration, reducing database overheads and network traffic. It also reduces memory and processor requirements at the database server end.

There is a potential problem with having PL/SQL linked directly into SQL*Forms. It can lead to strange anomalies when the PL/SQL version for the RDBMS differs from the PL/SQL version for SQL*Forms. When your environment includes multiple remote databases on multiple hardware platforms, all linked by SQL*Net and possibly running different ORACLE releases, this problem is magnified. Check to make sure your versions are consistent.

If you are not using PL/SQL capabilities, you can save memory by not including PL/SQL in your RUNFORM executable. For example, if you use only SQL*Forms Version 2 triggers, not Version 3 triggers, you do not need PL/SQL support. The tools bound into SQL*Forms differ for different platforms. For example, under MS-DOS, both PL/SQL and

SQL*Menu are bound into the RUNFORM executable by default. You can reduce the size of RUNFORM by about 10% by relinking it without SQL*Menu. You can reduce the size by more than 15% by relinking it without either PL/SQL or SQL*Menu.

Reducing SQL*Forms Cursor Overhead

A lot of SQL*Forms overhead comes from dealing with cursors. When you define a cursor via a SQL SELECT statement, that cursor is put into an area of memory so that it can potentially be used again, either by the user who issued it or by another user. When another SQL statement is issued, ORACLE looks first in this shared area for an identical statement before parsing the statement and calculating an execution path for the statement. In Version 6, cursors are stored in each process's own context area in its PGA. Here, they are available only for use by that process. In Version 7, cursors are stored in the shared buffer pool in the SGA in which dictionary information also resides. Here, cursors are available for use by all processes. As the cursor area fills up, older cursors (those that have not been referenced recently) are removed to make room for newer ones. (For more information about the shared areas and cursor sharing, see the section in Chapter 7 called "Sharing SQL Statements.")

As we discussed in Chapter 8, there are two types of cursors used in defining SELECT statements: explicit and implicit. Explicit cursors are those you define in a DECLARE statement at the start of a PL/SQL block. Within the block, you can OPEN, FETCH, and CLOSE the cursor. If you do not define an explicit cursor, PL/SQL creates an implicit one when you specify an INTO clause of a SELECT statement; for example:

```
SELECT EMP_NAME
    INTO :BLK.EMP_NAME . . .
```

Although explicit cursors require more programming, they use fewer system resources and thus produce better performance. Use explicit cursors, whenever possible, to improve SQL*Forms performance.

Avoiding Unnecessary Use of Cursors

Try to limit the total number of cursors you use in an application. Every cursor requires memory and CPU, resources that might better be deployed elsewhere. One good way to reduce the number of cursors is to combine a number of simple SQL statements into one. Issuing fewer SQL statements increases the probability that statements will be able to be kept in the context area of memory and shared by other users, and reduces the likelihood that frequently used cursors will have to be reparsed over and over again.

As we described in Chapter 7, for a cursor to be reused the SQL statement that is issued must be identical to the one that created the cursor. Remember, even the case must be the same: "EMP" is not the same as "Emp". Many consistency problems can be avoided by establishing programming standards at the outset of a project and enforcing them throughout.

In SQL*Forms, the use of procedure and function libraries helps to reduce the number of cursors used by an application by creating application-wide libraries for common business activities. Because common operations are defined in a central place, individual users are much less likely to issue SQL statements that can't be shared because of small differences.

Combining Similar Cursors with Table Joins

There are a number of ways in which you can combine SQL statements. By planning ahead, you can improve performance by reducing the overall number of cursors and the number of retrievals in a single statement. Consider the following SQL statements:

```
SELECT EMP_NAME, EMP_MGR
    INTO  :BLK.EMP_NAME, :BLK.EMP_MGR
    FROM  EMP
    WHERE EMP_NO = :BLK.EMP_NO;

SELECT EMP_NAME
    INTO  :BLK.MGR_NAME
    FROM  EMP
    WHERE EMP_NO = :BLK.EMP_MGR;
```

Using SQL*Forms you can create common triggers to pass and retrieve parameter information. These triggers can use non-base-table page zero fields, as shown below. The one cursor is used to satisfy both selection criteria (via a table join). If one selection criteria may not always exist, remember to use the outer join function (+).

```
DEFINE TRIGGER LOOKUP_EMP_MGR
    DECLARE
        CURSOR C IS
        SELECT E.EMP_NAME, E.EMP_MGR, M.EMP_NAME
            FROM EMP M, EMP E
            WHERE E.EMP_NO = :BLK.E_NO
            AND E.EMP_MGR = M.EMP_NO (+);

    BEGIN
        OPEN C;
        FETCH C INTO :BLK.EMP_NAME,:BLK.EMP_MGR, :BLK.MGR_NAME;

        IF C%NOTFOUND THEN
            CLOSE C;
            MESSAGE ('INVALID EMPLOYEE NUMBER ENTERED ....');
            RAISE FORM_TRIGGER_FAILURE;
```

```
    ELSE
        CLOSE C;
    END IF;
END;
```

Performing Multiple Fetches from the Same Cursor

Another way to reduce cursor overhead is to manipulate the way you fetch when you perform many lookups on the same table. Controlling the physical order in which the rows are retrieved means that we only have to perform a second fetch, rather than another whole cursor. Consider the way the ORDER BY clause is specified in the following statement:

```
DEFINE TRIGGER LOOKUP_EMP_MGR

    DECLARE
        CURSOR C IS
        SELECT E.EMP_NAME
            FROM EMP E
            WHERE E.EMP_NO IN (:BLK.E_NO, :BLK.M_NO)
            ORDER BY DECODE (E.EMP_NO, :BLK.E_NO, 'A', 'Z');

    BEGIN
        OPEN   C;
        FETCH C INTO :BLK.EMP_NAME,

        IF C%NOTFOUND THEN
            CLOSE C;
            MESSAGE ('INVALID EMPLOYEE NUMBER ENTERED ....');
            RAISE FORM_TRIGGER_FAILURE;
        ELSE
            IF :BLK.EMP_MGR IS NOT NULL THEN
                FETCH C INTO :BLK.MGR_NAME;

                IF C%NOTFOUND THEN
                    MESSAGE ('WARNING - EMPLOYEE HAS INVALID MANAGER');
                END IF;
            END IF;

            CLOSE C;
        END IF;
    END;
```

Passing Parameters via Procedures

SQL*Forms procedures provide a good way to reduce the number of cursors in an application. Unlike triggers, procedures support the substitution of variables at run time, so cursors can be used throughout forms processing. Consider the following example:

```
PROCEDURE procedure_name [argument_list]   IS
       local_variable_declaration
   BEGIN
       .
       .

       .
       PL/SQL block(s)
       .
       .

       .
   END;
```

Procedures allow you to pass run time parameters, as shown by the IN, OUT, and IN OUT parameters in the example below. These parameters help reduce the number of procedures needed for an application. The two SQL statements shown in earlier examples can be programmed as a single procedure as follows:

```
DEFINE PROCEDURE LOOKUP_EMP (ENO   NUM    IN,
                             MGR   NUM    IN OUT,
                             NAME  CHAR   IN OUT )   IS
   BEGIN
      DECLARE
         CURSOR C1 IS
         SELECT EMP_MGR, EMP_NAME
         FROM EMP
         WHERE EMP_NO = ENO;
      BEGIN
         OPEN  C1;
         FETCH C1 INTO :BLK.EMP_MGR, :BLK.EMP_NAME;
         CLOSE C1;
      END;
   END;

TRIGGER XYZ;

   BEGIN

      LOOKUP_EMP (:BLK.EMP_NO, :BLK.EMP_MGR, :BLK.EMP_NAME);

      LOOKUP_EMP (:BLK.EMP_MGR, :BLK.DUMMY, :BLK.MGR_NAME);

   END;
```

Note that SQL*Forms triggers do not allow you to pass parameters. If you use triggers, you will have to rely on background fields and/or global variables to pass and return data.

Speeding Up Field References

A substantial amount of overhead is required to reference an individual field in a SQL*Forms application. This section describes several ways you can reduce that overhead.

Pseudo-field Reference Overheads

You can use PL/SQL features to reference pseudo-information implicitly in a SQL*Forms application. When you reference pseudo fields, such as USER, SYSDATE, and USERENV, SQL*Forms translates each reference to a database SELECT statement over the dummy table DUAL. For example:

```
:BLK.USER_CODE = USER;
    .
    .
    .
IF :BLK.DATE_EFF <= TRUNC (SYSDATE) THEN
    .
    .
    .
END IF;
```

If you reference these fields regularly, you can improve performance by initializing them into background fields or global variables, and referencing them as shown below:

```
PRE-FORM TRIGGER

BEGIN
    SELECT TRUNC(SYSDATE), USER
    INTO :GLOBAL.SYS_DATE,
         :GLOBAL.USER_CODE
    FROM DUAL;
END

TRIGGER ABC
    .
    .
```

```
      .
   IF :BLK.HIRE_DATE > TO_DATE(:GLOBAL.SYS_DATE) THEN
        MESSAGE ('INVALID HIRE DATE . . .);
   END IF;
      .
      .
      .
```

Using a Block Prefix in Field References

It's a good idea to prefix all field references within SQL*Forms with block names. Although this approach is not required, it does have the effect of improving performance. If you do not use block prefixes, SQL*Forms has to scan an internal block/field stack to identify which block owns a field and to determine if a field has been defined more than once. If you do use block prefixes, SQL*Forms needs only to validate the field's existence. For example, specify:

```
   :EMPLOYEE.EMP_NO := 123456;
```

Although the overhead you save each time by doing this is almost undetectable, using block prefixes adds up if you have large forms with many blocks and many fields. Using block prefixes offers other benefits too. Your program code will be clearer and less ambiguous. And, if you add another field by the same name in another block, SQL*Forms will not display the error message, "UNRESOLVED DUPLICATE REFERENCED FIELD" at compile (generate) time, only at run time.

Storing Fields in PL/SQL Local Variables

As we described in Chapter 8, PL/SQL processes a block of SQL statements as a single unit, reducing the number of database accesses by executing these statements as a group. Unfortunately, field variables are not bound into PL/SQL blocks at parse time. Every time a PL/SQL block encounters a SQL*Forms field (*:block.field*), it must suspend processing of the PL/SQL block, retrieve the field value, and then resume processing. You can improve performance by setting up frequently referenced fields in local PL/SQL variables and thus incurring the variable GET and PUT overhead only once. For example:

```
   DECLARE
       SAL_VAL    NUMBER;
       INT_VAL    NUMBER;
   BEGIN
       SAL_VAL := :BLK.EMP_SAL;
```

```
IF SAL_VAL <= 2000    THEN
     INT_VAL := 0;
END IF;

IF  SAL_VAL >=  2001  AND
     SAL_VAL <=  8000  THEN
     INT_VAL :=  (SAL_VAL * 15 ) / 100;
END IF;

IF  SAL_VAL >= 8001    THEN
     INT_VAL := (SAL_VAL * 25 ) / 100;
END IF;

:BLK.EMP_INT := INT_VAL;
END;
```

Differences Between Fields and Global Variables

The following lists a number of other things you should know about referencing fields and global variables in SQL*Forms:

- Fields require a longer setup time during the startup phase. At this time, the *.FRM* file needs to be interpreted, fields identified, and memory allocated each time a form is called.

- Unlike global variables, fields can be referenced within a DEFAULT attribute, a WHERE clause, and an ORDER BY clause.

- The overhead you incur by using fields prefixed by block names is comparable to the overhead incurred by using global variables.

- Global variables are characters only. When you store numbers or dates within a global variable, make sure you perform data type conversion on TO_DATE and TO_NUMBER functions. For example:

```
:BLK.DATE_FROM := TO_DATE (:GLOBAL.DATE_FM);
```

Remember that these functions incur their own overheads.

- The following functions clear out corresponding fields by initializing them to null:

```
CLEAR_RECORD
CLEAR_BLOCK
CLEAR_FORM
```

They do not initialize global variables in the same way. Note that if you use global variables to hold special block data, you need to initialize them individually when the respective block is cleared.

- When you assign a value, you effectively create an uninitialized, unreferenced global variable. If you misspell the name of a global variable, you may have trouble debugging because no error is reported. SQL*Forms requires that all fields be correctly defined before any reference can be made to them. For example, the following global variable is created automatically.

  ```
  :GLOBAL.DATE_FM:='01-JUL-92';
  ```

- Referencing an uninitialized global variable results in an annoying run time error. Referencing an undefined field variable gives an immediate compile (generate) error.

- Memory is allocated to global variables only on an as-needed basis. The ERASE function relinquishes this memory. Field variables that are set up on entry to a form retain their associated resources for the duration of the form. These new field overheads are not released when the CALL or NEW_FORM statement navigates to another form, only when the owning form is exited. For example:

  ```
  ERASE ('GLOBAL.DATE_FM');
  ```

- Global variables are retained across forms, but field variables are local only to a form. The only way to pass information from one form to the next, other than physically writing the information to the database and then selecting the information from within the called form, is via global variables. Global variable overheads are relinquished only by an ERASE macro or when the user exits the current RUNFORM session.

Overhead for Types of Fields

There are a number of different ways to hold temporary fields within a SQL*Forms application. Each has advantages, and each has its own degree of overhead, as shown below; all byte counts are approximate. This information may be helpful if you are trying to reduce memory requirements for large forms.

```
Database (base table) field:    (field size * 2)   + 100 bytes
Non-database field:             (field size * 1)   + 100 bytes
Global variable:                255 bytes (data)   +  20 bytes
```

You can see that non-database fields are more memory-efficient than global variables if the field length is less than (approximately) 175 bytes long. If a field is only one character in length, use these byte counts:

```
Database field       = 102 bytes
Non-database field   = 101 bytes
Global variable      = 275 bytes
```

Other Ways to Conserve Memory

This section describes a number of other ways to improve the use of memory when you are using SQL*Forms.

Using NEW_FORM Versus CALL and CALLQRY Macros

Use the SQL*Forms NEW_FORM function, and not CALL, whenever possible. If you use CALL or CALLQRY, SQL*Forms keeps the calling form in memory and releases it, along with DDL table locks, cursor overheads, and memory, only when you exit a form, not when you navigate to a lower level. NEW_FORM, on the other hand, saves memory by releasing the current form, and all of its resources, before navigating to the specified form.

NEW_FORM does not release all form stacking when it is executed. It discards only the initiating form's information and resources. It retains all form stacking above that level. When the next form is exited, the user navigates back through these levels.

Consider the example shown in Figure 9-1. When Form 3 exits from the first example, control returns to Form 2. All overhead associated with Form 2 is retained. When Form 3 exits from the second example, control returns to Form 1. All overhead associated with Form 2 is released when Form 3 is entered.

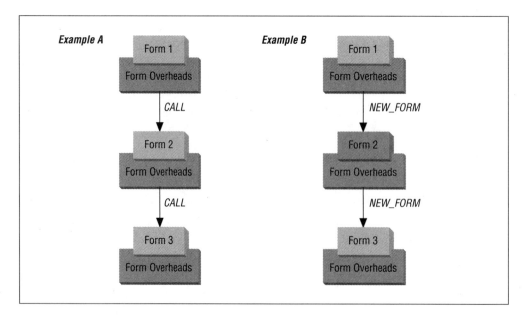

Figure 9-1: NEW_FORM macro

Using the RECORDS BUFFERED Option

The RECORDS BUFFERED parameter within SQL*Forms specifies the number of records stored in memory for a base table query. Setting RECORDS BUFFERED does have memory consequences. Every extra record buffer you specify needs working memory to accommodate it. If you are short of memory, you can set RECORDS BUFFERED to be equal to the number of rows on the screen for the relevant block. If you have extra memory, however, set RECORDS BUFFERED to a value that is a multiple of the number of rows on the screen. Any records retrieved beyond this buffer size will be temporarily written to disk. This allows the application to buffer many unqueried rows, making them available for the user to review. We recommend that you make RECORDS BUFFERED this large only in exceptional cases. You will get excellent performance in this case. Before you increase RECORDS BUFFERED, think carefully about how the user will typically use the form. Only if the user typically queries many pages of records, time after time, should you increase this parameter dramatically over its default. The maximum number of rows you can buffer is 999.

For best results, set the SQL*Forms ARRAYSIZE parameter, described below, as well, so it is equal to the RECORDS BUFFERED value. Otherwise, there will be a delay when you do the initial fetch from the database.

Setting the ARRAYSIZE Parameter

The SQL*Forms parameter, ARRAYSIZE, specifies the maximum number of records that can be fetched from the database in a single access. By increasing this value, you cut down on the number of database accesses that are required, and you improve performance. (Actually, increasing ARRAYSIZE will increase the time needed to perform each fetch from the database, but it will improve overall fetch performance.)

As with RECORDS BUFFERED, make sure before you increase ARRAYSIZE that your situation is suitable. Otherwise, preserve the default value. ARRAYSIZE has a minimum value of 1 and a maximum value equal to the number of records buffered.

ARRAYSIZE has always been available within the ORACLE precompilers, but only recently has it been available within SQL*Forms. Note that there has been a bug in certain releases of SQL*Forms (V3.0.16.7, reported in ORACLE bugs 97173 and 79733). If you are having a problem with ARRAYSIZE, check to see if this bug has been corrected in your system.

Tuning Base Tables

A great many SQL*Forms applications involve SQL SELECT statements for one or more base tables. In Chapter 7 we describe how to tune SQL statements, and how the choice of a driving table for SELECT statements can improve performance. This section describes special considerations for SQL*Forms.

Using Unqualified ORDER BY Clauses

The single, most common problem SQL*Forms programmers encounter is actually not a SQL*Forms problem at all. It is a SQL and indexing problem. As we mention in the section in Chapter 7 called "Using WHERE Instead of ORDER BY," including the ORDER BY clause in a SELECT statement can cause a major performance problem. Unless ORDER BY clauses and associated indexes are correctly structured, they will not be able to use any available indexes, and will fall back to a full-table scan. They usually cause ORACLE to do a complete internal data sort of all records that satisfy the conditions specified in the clause.

ORDER BY clauses use an index only if they meet two rigid requirements:

1. All of the columns that make up the ORDER BY clause must be contained within a single index in the same sequence.

2. All of the columns that make up the ORDER BY clause must be defined as NOT NULL within the table definition. Remember, null values are not contained within an index.

For example, consider the base table EMP, which has several thousand rows and a concatenated index over the columns, EMP_NO and DPT_NO. A common base table query over the table might contain the clause:

```
ORDER BY EMP_NO
```

This statement will not use the index. In fact, it will perform a sort of the entire table to return the records in the required sequence. However, if you code this clause in one of the following ways instead, it will use the index:

```
WHERE EMP_NO > 0

ORDER BY  EMP_NO,
          DPT_NO
```

Preventing Open Base Queries

Most large tables have many indexes over the common primary and foreign key paths for the table. But you can't define an index over every column of every table. What happens when a user submits an open query via the ENTER_QUERY function, a query for which none of the table's indexes applies? How can you keep obscure query combinations from slowing down performance by undertaking full-table scans of tables that may contain thousands of records? There are several ways to plan for such searches.

First, you could disable the QUERYABLE attribute for non-indexed database fields. Although this approach is effective, it is often not desirable. SQL*Forms goes to great pains to provide a powerful and complete query interface. Disabling fields in this way is admitting defeat!

Note that even indexed columns will not use the database index path if the user enters query conditions that are prefixed by operands. For example:

```
%SMITH%
<> 100
```

Another approach is to define a block-level PRE-QUERY trigger to prevent unwanted query combinations from being entered for each queryable SQL*Forms block. This method is more palatable than disabling queries completely, because all fields are still potentially queryable. The PRE_QUERY trigger must ensure that at least one indexed column is included within each query selection, thus preventing wild, unchecked base table searches. For example:

```
PRE-QUERY TRIGGER

    BEGIN
        IF    :BLK.FLD1 IS NULL
        AND   :BLK.FLD2 IS NULL
        AND   :BLK.FLD3 IS NULL    THEN
            MESSAGE ('INVALID QUERY - ...');
            RAISE FORM_TRIGGER_FAILURE;
        END IF;
    END;
```

You may need to define a PRE-QUERY trigger, not only to ensure that at least one indexed column has been included, but also to check that the query condition will actually use the index. Leading, wildcard query conditions behave like functions, which rules indexes out of contention. For example, an indexed character key will not use an index if the first character is % or _. To prevent these characters, do this:

```
PRE-QUERY TRIGGER
    BEGIN
        IF :BLK.FLD1 IS NULL
```

```
OR SUBSTR(:BLK.FLD1,1,1) IN ('%' , '_') THEN
    MESSAGE ('INVALID QUERY - . . .');
    RAISE FORM_TRIGGER_FAILURE;
END IF;
END;
```

SQL*Forms does not check field attributes during the PRE-QUERY phase of execution. It allows wildcard query criteria to be for *all* field data types, criteria that would otherwise be illegal. Here are some examples of date field values that would be illegal during input mode, but are legal during query mode.

```
%JUN-92
>02-JUN-92
```

Here are some examples of numeric field values that would be illegal during input mode, but are legal during query mode.

```
<100
120%
<>100
```

If you reference (validate) a field during a PRE-QUERY trigger, SQL*Forms automatically performs field attribute editing. This could result in raising the run time error, "FRM-40735 PRE-QUERY TRIGGER RAISED UNHANDLED EXCEPTION VALUE-ERROR." To avoid this problem, reference each field's contents indirectly, rather than directly. Code the trigger like this:

```
PRE-QUERY TRIGGER

    DECLARE
        TMP CHAR(240);
    BEGIN
        TMP := NAME_IN ('BLK.FLD');          Indirect reference

        IF TMP IS NULL THEN
            MESSAGE  ('INVALID QUERY - ...);
            RAISE FORM_TRIGGER_FAILURE;
        END IF;
    END;
```

Using UNION Clauses on Base Tables

Too often, programmers try to satisfy all kinds of contorted and unlikely situations with a single SELECT statement. This is an especially serious problem with SQL*Forms and base tables. Often, we find that when poor performance occurs the underlying problem is the multiple combinations of AND and OR operations. More often than not, these complicated SELECT statements do achieve the desired result when you test them with small amounts of data. However, when they are run on larger data volumes, they drag down performance. Consider the following example.

Assume that the EMP table has an index over the foreign key EMP_DEPT. A query screen needs to display the following categories of employees:

- All employees from department 0010, or
- Employees from department 0020 with salaries greater than $25,000, or
- Employees from department 0030 with salaries greater than $50,000.

The following single SQL statement against a base table works, but cannot use the index efficiently. Each occurrence of an OR clause causes the optimizer to perform a CONCATENATING sort/merge of all the rows returned by each OR clause. Worse still, to satisfy the ORDER BY clause, it has to perform a sort/merge operation on all of the returned records.

```
WHERE
    ( EMP_DEPT = 0010 )
OR
    ( EMP_DEPT = 0020
    AND EMP_SALARY > 25000 )
OR
    ( EMP_DEPT = 0030
    AND EMP_SALARY > 50000 )
ORDER BY EMP_NO
```

By modifying the WHERE clause to something a bit more complicated, we can achieve astounding results. By slightly contorting the original intentions of SQL*Forms base tables and writing several complementary SELECT statements, we are able to use all of the indexes under all conditions.

```
WHERE EMP_DEPT   = 0010
UNION
    SELECT..., ..., ..., ROWID
        FROM EMP
        WHERE EMP_DEPT = 0020
        AND EMP_SALARY > 25000
UNION
    SELECT..., ..., ..., ROWID
        FROM EMP
        WHERE EMP_DEPT = 0030
        AND EMP_SALARY > 50000
ORDER BY 1
```

There are a number of advantages to using the UNION clause on base tables.

- Each (sub) statement uses its own index, instantly selecting and omitting all rows.

- SQL*Forms appends the pseudo-column, ROWID, as the last field of the SELECT list, and you must allow for this column when you do joins with other statements.

  You can manufacture this ROWID column as:

  ```
  CHARTOROWID('0').
  ```

  Note that earlier versions of SQL*Forms (Version 2 and earlier) actually prefix, rather than suffix, the SELECT list with the column ROWID.

- UNION statements implicitly exclude duplicates, so you don't run the risk that the same record will be selected by more than one statement.

- You can often omit the ORDER BY clause, thus saving on sort/merge overhead, by carefully sequencing the columns selected. Because the UNION clause causes the database to perform an internal sort of the rows returned (to eliminate all duplicates), you can take advantage of this internal sort and return the rows in the required sequence, rather than sorting them all over again.

- UNION saves the DBA from having to generate a database view just to satisfy a single SQL*Forms query condition. A view will incur slightly more overhead than a base table UNION, and runs the risk of confusing the optimizer when it is calculating the execution path.

- Subordinate tables do not have to be the same as the originating base table. This means that several differing tables with a common underlying connection can be linked with one base table query. You can take advantage of this behavior to generate very sophisticated query screens, satisfying a number of different conditions with one action. Consider the following example of querying the complete purchasing history for an employee with one base table query:

In this example, a single query displays all of the requisitions, purchase orders, and invoices connected to an employee in a simple, logical, inter-connected sequence. This is much more attractive than three separate screens, or a single screen containing three separate blocks. For example:

```
BASE TABLE : REQUISITIONS.

DATABASE FIELDS : REQ_NUM,
                  REQ_DATE,
                  REQ_AMT,
                  EMP_NO.
WHERE EMP_NO = :BLK.EMP_NO
UNION
    SELECT PO_NUM, PO_DATE, PO_AMT, EMP_NO, ROWID
        FROM   PURCHASE_ORDERS
```

```
            WHERE EMP_NO = :BLK.EMP_NO
    UNION
        SELECT INV_NUM, INV_DATE, INV_AMT, EMP_NO, ROWID
            FROM INVOICES
            WHERE EMP_NO = :BLK.EMP_NO
    ORDER BY 4, 2
```

There are also some disadvantages to using the UNION clause on base tables.

- User-entered ENTER_QUERY mode selections are of little use with the UNION clause. SQL*Forms appends the query condition to the end of the WHERE clause, and thus only to the last UNION statement.

- Updates cannot be performed directly via UNION base tables. (This is similar to the UPDATE restrictions on views.) If updating is necessary, you must handle it via special ON-LOCK, ON-INSERT, ON-UPDATE, and ON-DELETE triggers, described later in this chapter.

- If correct indexes do not exist (or are removed at a later date), a UNION clause will actually multiply the original overheads. Rather than resulting in a single full-table scan, you might end up with three or four of them!

- Each sub-query should return only a handful of records. UNION clauses actually perform a sort/merge operation between each sub-query. If one side of the equation returns many thousands of rows, the sort/merge might actually take longer than a full-table scan.

Simplifying Complex Base Table Statements

You can often simplify and improve complex base table SQL queries by stripping the sub-query portion of the statement. If you know that the sub-query returns only a few rows (fewer than ten), try executing the sub-query as a PRE-QUERY trigger. All returned values are fed back into the base table query as constants.

```
SELECT ..., ..., ...
    FROM EMP
    WHERE EMP_DEPT IN (SELECT MAX (DEPT_CODE),
                              MIN (DEPT_CODE)
                       FROM DEPARTMENTS);
```

Replace the previous sub-query with:

```
PRE-QUERY TRIGGER

    SELECT MAX (DEPT_CODE),
           MIN (DEPT_CODE)
    INTO :BLK.MAX_DPT,
         :BLK.MIN_DPT
    FROM DEPARTMENTS
```

```
AND "BASE TABLE QUERY"

SELECT..., ..., ...
     FROM EMP
     WHERE EMP_DEPT IN (:BLK.MAX_DPT, :BLK.MIN_DPT);
```

Using EXISTS in Place of IN for Base Tables

Many base table queries have to actually join with another table to satisfy a selection criteria. As we show in Chapter 7, a simple two-table join is the most efficient type of join. Because SQL*Forms base tables can reference only a single table and cannot be assigned a table alias, the only way to perform a table join is with a sub-query. Most programmers use IN (or NOT IN) clauses to do sub-queries. However, the EXISTS (or NOT EXISTS) clause is often a better choice for performance.

Suppose that all employees whose records are being queried work in departments at the Melbourne office. You might specify:

```
BASE TABLE : EMP

WHERE EMP_NO > 0
AND
     DEPT_NO IN (SELECT DEPT_NO
                        FROM DEPARTMENTS
                        WHERE DEPT_LOCN   = 'MELB' )
```

However, the following query is more efficient:

```
BASE TABLE : EMP

WHERE EMP_NO > 0
AND
     EXISTS (SELECT 'X'
                 FROM DEPARTMENTS
                 WHERE DEPT_NO = EMP.DEPT_NO
                 AND DEPT_LOCN = 'MELB')
```

Performing Pseudo-dynamic Base Table Queries

Unfortunately, SQL*Forms does not support genuine dynamic SQL statements, which often leads to confusing and inefficient base table WHERE clauses. However, you can issue what we call pseudo-dynamic SQL statements.

SQL*Forms supports extended queries. By including the & character or a text string in a queryable field from ENTER_QUERY mode, you can perform a limited form of dynamic

SQL, triggered by ENTER_QUERY and EXECUTE_QUERY actions. Consider the following example. When & or a text string (*text*) is entered into the field, FLD, during ENTER_ QUERY mode, the base table query is altered as shown below.

&	**text**
SELECT . . .	SELECT . . .
FROM BASE_TABLE	FROM BASE_TABLE
WHERE . . .	WHERE . . .
AND (*string*)	**AND (FLD [LIKE] *text*)**

You can see that the only difference between the two extended query functions is the automatic inclusion of the receiving field name within the *text* SQL clause. Within application code, you can use only the *text* alternative. Both are equally efficient.

There are a number of limitations to creating pseudo-dynamic SQL in this way:

- The database field can be only of data type CHAR.

- The database field cannot be null if you use the *text* alternative. (Remember, null can never equal anything.)

- The query length of the field must be long enough to contain the extra SQL. This often means defining the field length and query length as CHAR (255).

- The extra *text* clause is limited to a maximum of 255 characters in length, or the extra *text* must be broken up over many fields. This is not always syntactically possible.

The pseudo-column, USER, is a good candidate for the receiving field for "query-only" base tables. This column is valid for all tables. It simply needs to be defined as a base table field. It has a data type of CHAR, is always non-null, and can be extended to 255 characters in length. The USER column cannot be used if the base-table block will be performing updates; because the USER column is not real it cannot be updated.

The major advantage of dynamic SQL is the ability to manipulate index usage. Often, the only way to achieve variable SELECT conditions without dynamic SQL is to issue a complicated series of AND and OR clauses. These clauses often confuse the optimizer and limit or destroy indexes.

Here are several examples of how you can replace non-dynamic SQL base table queries with their dynamic equivalents. The first example shows a wild-card search of a name field (disregarding case):

```
SELECT . . .
    FROM  EMP
    WHERE . . .
    AND ( UPPER(NAME) LIKE UPPER(:BASE.NAME )
    OR :BASE.NAME IS NULL )
```

You can replace the previous with the following type of query:

```
SELECT . . .
    FROM  EMP
    WHERE . . .
```

and a PRE-QUERY trigger:

```
BEGIN
    IF :BASE.FLD IS NOT NULL THEN
        :BASE.NAME  :=  '=NAME AND UPPER(NAME) LIKE '
            || '''' || UPPER (:BASE.NAME) || '''';
    END IF;
END;
```

With the second example, you can omit the OR clause, which means that the unavoidable full-table scan is performed only when necessary and when it does not disrupt any other selection criteria. For example, when a value is entered into :BLK.NAME, the SQL is transposed as:

```
SELECT . . .
    FROM EMP
    WHERE . . .
    AND ( UPPER(NAME) LIKE UPPER(:BASE.NAME) ) ;
```

When no value is entered into :BLK.NAME, the SQL is transposed as:

```
SELECT . . .
    FROM EMP
    WHERE . . .
```

Now, consider the use of an ORDER BY clause in a dynamic base table:

```
SELECT . . .
    FROM EMP
    WHERE . . .
    ORDER BY DECODE (:BLK.SORT_SEQ,  'E',    EMP_NO,
                                     'M',    EMP_MGR,
                                             EMP_DEPT)
```

You can replace the previous with the following query:

```
SELECT . . .
    FROM EMP
    WHERE . . .
```

and the PRE-QUERY trigger:

```
BEGIN
    IF :BLK.SEQN = 'E' THEN
        :BASE.FLD := '=FLD) ORDER BY (EMP_NO ';
```

```
        ELSIF
            :BLK.SEQN = 'M' THEN
            :BASE.FLD := '=FLD) ORDER BY (EMP_MGR ';
        ELSE
            :BASE.FLD := '=FLD) ORDER BY (EMP_DEPT ';
        END IF;
   END;
```

In this particular example, the syntax of the *text* clause has been contorted slightly to allow for the ORDER BY clause. Actually, the *text* clause must be enclosed within parentheses. We must insert extra parentheses like this:

```
WHERE . . .
AND (FLD = FLD) ORDER BY (EMP_NO)
```

If you need to add a dynamic ORDER BY DESC clause, this will take a bit more imagination. You must add a dummy column to the end of the ORDER BY list to fool the syntax checker. For example:

```
WHERE . . .
AND (FLD = FLD) ORDER BY EMP_NO DESC, ( 'A' )
```

Remember, if you are using this method, you cannot hard-code an ORDER BY clause as part of the default base table query.

Sometimes, the dynamic *text* may actually appear in the form:

```
BEGIN
    :BASE.FLD := '# = FLD AND UPPER(NAME) LIKE
            ' || '''' || UPPER (:BASE.FLD) || '''';
END;
```

The # statement simply removes the requirement that the first character of the string be an operator (e.g., LIKE, =, >). Instead, the *text* string can be anything that forms correct syntax when it is suffixed to the receiving field. It is a good idea to prefix all such statements with the #. Note that using # also means that the field doesn't need to be defined as being NOT NULL. Consider the following example:

```
:BASE.FLD := '# || ''X'' IS NOT NULL AND UPPER(NAME) LIKE
                '' || '''' || UPPER(:BASE.NAME) || '''';
```

This SQL is transposed as:

```
SELECT . . .
    FROM EMP
    WHERE  . . .
    AND (NAME || 'X' IS NOT NULL AND
        UPPER(NAME) LIKE UPPER(:BASE.NAME) ) );
```

Using the OR Clause with Dynamic Base Table Queries

Default operator rankings are another source of problems with dynamic SQL*Forms base tables. By definition, AND clauses bind tighter than OR clauses. If a base table is defined with an OR clause, and a user enters an ENTER_QUERY mode condition (automatically suffixed to the end), abnormal behavior results. Consider the following example of the base table EMP:

```
EMP                                  Base table
   WHERE  DEPT_NO = 10               Base table clause
      OR  DEPT_NO = 20


   FIELD_NAME : [ SMITH% ]           User-entered query condition

SELECT ..., ..., ROWID               Actual SQL statement
   FROM EMP
   WHERE  DEPT_NO = 10
      OR  DEPT_NO = 20
         AND ( NAME LIKE SMITH%' )
```

Before the user condition was entered, only employees for departments 10 and 20 were fetched. When a user query condition is added, the AND clause binds with the second OR clause, giving a completely different meaning.

The translated SQL statement is now:

```
SELECT ..., ..., ROWID
   FROM EMP
   WHERE DEPT_NO    = 10
      OR ( DEPT_NO = 20
      AND  ( NAME LIKE SMITH%' ) )
```

The base table statement now fetches all employees in department 10, or employees in department 20 with a name like SMITH. This is not what was intended. To avoid confusion of this kind, always enclose base table statements in parentheses. This is the only way to guarantee consistent results. For example:

```
EMP                                  Base table
   WHERE   ( DEPT_NO = 10            Base table clause
      OR  DEPT_NO  = 20 )


   FIELD_NAME : [ SMITH% ]           User-entered query condition

SELECT ..., ...,  ROWID              Actual SQL statement
   FROM EMP
   WHERE   ( DEPT_NO = 10
      OR  DEPT_NO  = 20 )
         AND ( NAME LIKE 'SMITH%' )
```

Viewing Dynamic Base Table Queries

Because of the contorted way we have to construct some base table statements to take advantage of SQL*Forms' dynamic behavior, many of these statements don't always come out as expected. Programming dynamic base table SQL is often difficult because you cannot actually see what the final outcome is, and SQL*Forms insists on enclosing each dynamic portion of the statement within parentheses. Operator-entered ENTER_ QUERY mode operations magnify the debugging problems associated with dynamic base table statements. These query conditions are simply suffixed onto the end of the existing statement.

So, when a statement is not performing as expected, or when a particular user-entered query condition mysteriously ruins the application performance, how can you view the offending statement? If you can't see it, you can't fix it!

There is a way. To view the SQL statement after the base table query has been performed, display the system variable, "SYSTEM.LAST_QUERY":

```
MESSAGE ( :SYSTEM.LAST_QUERY );
```

To view an offending base table statement as it occurs (i.e., at the user's terminal), simply force an ORACLE SQL error. When SQL*Forms base table queries encounter an ORACLE error, the default SQL*Forms function, DISPLAY_ERROR, shows the complete offending SQL statement and an extended error message. To force a base table SQL statement error, enter an illegal SQL operand during ENTER_QUERY mode. For example:

```
Numeric Field     [>A ]      SQL Error 0904     Invalid column name
Character Field   [>A ]      SQL Error 0904     Invalid column name
```

This should have been entered as:

```
Numeric Field     [>0  ]
Character Field   [>'A']
```

Updating Base Table Views

You can update base table views via normal, default SQL*Forms functionality if they are over only one table and they satisfy all non-null field requirements. However, you cannot perform default updates if you are using complex views (made up of UNION and/or multi-table joins) as SQL*Forms base table statements. If you need a full base table updating capability, you must define the following triggers within the block:

```
ON-LOCK   :    SELECT   . . .
               FROM TABLE_NAME
               FOR UPDATE OF . . .
```

```
ON-INSERT   :    INSERT
ON-UPDATE   :    UPDATE
ON-DELETE   :    DELETE
```

NOTE

The ON-LOCK trigger will need special error logic to deal with the rows already being locked via another process. You can reduce overheads for each of the "update" triggers by actually selecting each row's ROWID when you are doing the initial record lock. Subsequent updates can then be done via the record's ROWID, rather than its primary key. Remember, ROWID is the single fastest path into an ORACLE database; always use it ahead of other alternatives.

Tuning the List of Values Function

The SQL*Forms list of values (LOV) function allows you to define a mini-pop-up window that shows the values for a field that is currently displayed on the screen. Version 3 extends the list of values beyond the capabilities available in Version 2.3. You can now define the pop-up window and display field descriptions and associated columns. You can return more than one column to the calling form. You can even base the list of values query over a multi-table join expression.

The SQL*Forms LIST_VALUES macro is powerful, but demands extensive system resources when it is used over tables with large numbers of records. The enormous overhead required by this macro is the result of the fact that the macro fetches all records into a temporary user buffer before the first one is displayed. For larger tables, this buffer fills up and SQL*Forms needs to use a temporary disk file for the excess. We find that if you run the LIST_VALUES macro over an entire table, you will encounter performance problems if your table has more than about 500 rows.

Running LIST_VALUES Over a Large Table

Because the LIST_VALUES macro retrieves all eligible rows before performing an operator-entered LIKE function on selected fields, this macro will need to read and buffer to disk thousands of rows before it can display the first one. Although the macro provides a RESTRICT function, this function begins restricting records only after all of the records have been fetched.

The easiest way to improve performance for LIST_VALUES is to code a special SQL*Forms pop-up window in place of the default pop-up window. By defining a field-level KEY-LISTVAL trigger for primary key fields of the larger tables (more than 500 lines), you can override the default LIST_VALUES functionality. In this way, you can define a new record buffer and avoid retrieving all records for each fetch. With the new

Version 3 features, you can display pop-up windows that are dynamically sized and positioned. This provides a layered effect which cannot be achieved via SQL*Forms Version 2.3.

Here is an example of a KEY-LISTVAL trigger:

```
TRIGGER KEY-LISTVAL

    BEGIN
        IF :SYSTEM.CURSOR_FIELD = 'EMP_NO' THEN

            :GLOBAL.LVAL := '';
            CALL_QUERY ('NEW_LISTVAL', NO_HIDE);

            IF  :GLOBAL.LVAL IS NOT NULL THEN
                :SYSTEM.CURSOR_FIELD := :GLOBAL.LVAL;
            END IF;

            ERASE ('GLOBAL.LVAL');
        ELSE
            LIST_VALUES;
        END IF;
    END;
```

This solution works well in all cases except ENTER_QUERY mode. In this mode, only a handful of keys are operative, and all user-defined keys are overridden by their SQL*Forms default definitions. To overcome this problem, you need two additional triggers. The new LOV text causes a run time error to be raised (dividing by zero) whenever the default list of values function is executed. This approach works in ENTER_QUERY mode as well. The statement also prompts SQL*Forms to display the LOV hint at the bottom of the screen, showing that the current field has the extended list of values functionality. Specify this dummy list of values SQL statement:

```
LOV TEXT : SELECT 1 FROM DUAL
                WHERE 1 = 1 / NVL(0, 0)
```

Next, you must define a field-level ON-ERROR trigger to trap the error and perform the necessary processing:

```
TRIGGER ON-ERROR
    BEGIN
        IF ERROR_CODE = 40502 THEN
        :GLOBAL.LVAL := '';
        CALL_QUERY ('NEW_LISTVAL', NO_HIDE);

        IF :GLOBAL.LVAL IS NOT NULL THEN
            :SYSTEM.CURSOR_FIELD := :GLOBAL.LVAL;
        END IF;
```

```
            ERASE ('GLOBAL.LVAL');
    ELSE
            MESSAGE (ERROR_TYPE ||'-'|| TO_CHAR(ERROR_CODE)
                        ||''||ERROR_TEXT);
            RAISE FORM_TRIGGER_FAILURE;
    END IF;
END;
```

You can further improve this approach by defining the ON-ERROR trigger as follows. This method takes advantage of the fact that you need to define the specialized LIST-VALUES trigger only once, and don't need to duplicate the KEY-LISTVAL trigger code within the ON-ERROR trigger.

```
TRIGGER ON-ERROR

BEGIN
    IF  ERROR_CODE = 40502 THEN
        EXECUTE_TRIGGER ('KEY-LISTVAL');
    ELSE
        MESSAGE (ERROR_TYPE ||''|| TO_CHAR(ERROR_CODE) ||''||
                    ERROR_TEXT);
        RAISE FORM_TRIGGER_FAILURE;
    END IF;
END;
```

Within this modified ON-ERROR trigger, the EXECUTE_TRIGGER function is used instead of the normal DO_KEY macro. In many cases (including in the ON-ERROR trigger), the DO_KEY macro is not allowed, and the system displays the error message "THIS MACRO IS NOT PERMITTED WITHIN THIS OPERATION." On the other hand, the EXECUTE_TRIGGER macro achieves the same result and can be included anywhere. These two statements are equivalent:

```
DO_KEY ('LIST_VALUES')
EXECUTE_TRIGGER ('KEY-LISTVAL')
```

Standardizing the Use of LIST_VALUES

You and the users of your forms will get the best results out of the LIST_VALUES macro if you standardize its use throughout an application. Follow these guidelines:

- Try to anchor list of values windows at a consistent position on the screen.

- Make list of values windows small and concise, rather than large and cumbersome. To reduce the width of the default list of values window, limit the size of the display fields. Obviously, you cannot truncate the primary key data being returned to the application, but you can truncate other fields, for example, EMP_NAME:

```
SELECT    EMP_NO,
     SUBSTR (EMP_NAME, 1, 20 ),
     CURRENT_EMP
     FROM EMP
```

- Sequence list of values data in the most practical way possible. For example, this query:

```
SELECT EMP_NO,
     SUBSTR ( EMP_NAME, 1, 20 ),
     CURRENT_EMP
FROM EMP
WHERE EMP_NO > 0          /* FORCE EMP_NO INDEX */
```

returns the following output:

```
  1  Smith, John     Y
102  Smith, Mark     Y
563  Smith, Peter    N
```

- Format your display data (data not returned to the application) into a more helpful format than the one normally displayed by LIST_VALUES. (List of values windows do not display column headings unless they are specified as the window title, so it's often not clear what is being displayed.) For example:

```
SELECT EMP_NO,
     SUBSTR (EMP_NAME,1,20),
     DECODE ( CURRENT_EMP, 'Y', CURRENT', 'NON CURRENT' )
     FROM EMP
     WHERE EMP_NO > 0
```

displays the following output:

```
  1  Smith, John     CURRENT
102  Smith, Mark     CURRENT
563  Smith, Peter    NON-CURRENT
```

- Display fields in the list of values window in the same format in which they are displayed in the application. If numeric fields have format masks within the application, make sure they have the same masks in the window. For example:

```
SELECT TO_CHAR (EMP_NO, '000009' ),
     SUBSTR ( EMP_NAME,1,20),
     DECODE ( CURRENT_EMP, 'Y', 'CURRENT', 'NON CURRENT' )

     FROM EMP
     WHERE EMP_NO > 0
```

displays the following output:

```
00001  Smith, John       CURRENT
00102  Smith, Mark       CURRENT
00563  Smith, Peter      NON-CURRENT
```

Including Constants in LIST_VALUES

Sometimes, you'll want a LIST_VALUES macro to display a list of constants rather than the contents of a table. For example, if the list of values to display consists of "Y" and "N," there is unlikely to be a physical table for these values. Define the LOV clause as follows:

```
SELECT N', 'NO'
    INTO  . . .
    FROM DUAL
    UNION
SELECT 'Y', 'YES'
    FROM DUAL
```

Protecting Against Risky Macros

Some of the new SQL*Forms macros are downright dangerous in the wrong hands! Each macro serves a valuable purpose, but can also represent a major performance drain when it is used in the wrong way. Abide by the recommendations included here and you'll avoid dangerous pitfalls.

Using the LAST_RECORD Macro

The LAST_RECORD macro positions the cursor at the last record of a SQL base table query. You'll find this macro very helpful if you are running a query that can fetch only a limited number of records.

The problem with LAST_RECORD occurs when the macro is applied to base table queries that have many records (that is, more than one screen full). To navigate to the last record, SQL*Forms must pass through each record, one at a time, executing all of the relevant triggers (e.g., POST-CHANGE, ON-VALIDATE-FIELD, ON-VALIDATE-RECORD, POST-QUERY, PRE-RECORD, POST-RECORD, etc.)

For best results, use this macro only for queries that return a small number of records.

Using the EXECUTE_QUERY Macro

The EXECUTE_QUERY macro is similar to the LAST_RECORD macro when you execute it with the ALL_RECORDS attribute. This macro causes SQL*Forms to retrieve all selected records into its working space before you display the first one. EXECUTE_ QUERY is very helpful if you want to accumulate running totals, for example, when all POST-QUERY and POST-CHANGE triggers need to be triggered for all fetched records. Each of these triggers will fire for each database record fetched.

As with the LAST_RECORD macro, EXECUTE_QUERY causes problems when you run it on base tables with a large number of records selected. For best results, use this macro only for queries that return a small number of records.

Executing Multiple Triggers

When you execute a SQL*Forms trigger you incur a good deal of system overhead, over and above whatever action the trigger itself has to take. SQL*Forms has to navigate to the trigger (allowing for cursor scope), parse it, execute it, and then navigate to the next trigger. Each navigation depends on the outcome of the last action. In a query that retrieves a single record from a base table, this overhead is minor. But overheads mount rapidly when you retrieve multiple records from base tables. The overhead of retrieving a single record might be multiplied as many as 20 times.

To demonstrate this problem, we look in this section at two methods of highlighting (displaying in bold face) fields for the current record of a multiple-record block. Remember, when a full screen of records is retrieved, each row is processed individually before the next is returned.

The first solution (solution A) uses the fact that the current record will always be the last record to fire the SQL*Forms PRE-RECORD trigger. It also assumes that any records previously navigated to will have fired the POST-RECORD trigger when leaving. These two simple triggers work well together, guaranteeing that the current record is always highlighted in bold face:

```
PRE-RECORD  :  DISPLAY_FIELD ('BLK.FLD', 'BOLD');

POST-RECORD :  DISPLAY_FIELD ('BLK.FLD', 'NORMAL');
```

The second solution (solution B) resets the current record first, executes the macro, and then sets to bold the final record that the cursor is in.

```
KEY-STARTUP :  DISPLAY_FIELD ('BLK.FLD', 'BOLD');

KEY-ENTQRY  :  DISPLAY_FIELD ('BLK.FLD', 'NORMAL');
               ENTER_QUERY;
               DISPLAY_FIELD ('BLK.FLD', 'BOLD');
```

```
KEY-EXEQRY  :  DISPLAY_FIELD ('BLK.FLD', 'NORMAL');   .
               EXECUTE_QUERY;
               DISPLAY_FIELD ('BLK.FLD', 'BOLD');
```

Other active triggers (those not disabled) that need to be coded in a similar way are:

KEY-DOWN	KEY-UP	KEY-NXTSET	KEY-NXTKEY
KEY-NETREC	KEY-PRVREC	KEY-SCRDOWN	KEY-SCRUP
KEY-DELREC	KEY-CREREC	KEY-CLRREC	

At first glance, solution A is more appealing, from a programming point of view, than solution B. Naturally, the more appealing solution is not always the more efficient. In fact, solution A executes more than 42 PRE-RECORD and POST-RECORD triggers for every EXECUTE_QUERY action. Solution B, on the other hand, needs to execute only the originating (extended) EXECUTE_QUERY trigger. Although you may not want to go through the trouble of coding and maintaining solution B for every application, it is definitely worth considering for vital, frequently used application forms.

We developed an application recently that had its own SQL*Forms menu and security module. Every user accessed the application via this dynamic menu. The menu system could display as many as 20 menu options (records) per screen. Using solution A, the overall elapsed time for a fully populated menu query was 2.5 seconds. Although this response was acceptable, the fact that this screen was used so frequently led us to try to tune it further. By switching from solution A to solution B, we reduced the overall elapsed time for a fully populated menu query from 2.5 seconds to 1.1 seconds.

Remember, not all triggers are enabled in all forms. We have identified 14 triggers as potentially needing redefinition, but find that only four or five are needed for any particular form.

*Using SQL*Forms Libraries*

For the first time, SQL*Forms Version 3 allows applications to use centrally defined libraries. Libraries can be shared by many forms or can be limited to individual forms. We recommend that you use common procedure, trigger, and function libraries as much as possible. Doing so helps application performance by reducing memory requirements and increasing the likelihood that system cursors will be able to be shared. The use of libraries also eases the transition to ORACLE Version 7 and its support of stored procedures, triggers, and functions.

For best results, incorporate system libraries into each form by reference, rather than by copy. You can modify and automatically refresh referenced modules throughout the application, as you generate relevant forms. You cannot do this with copied modules.

You can also include common database field definitions such as primary keys in system library forms. You should include in these field definitions all field edits, list of values definitions, and associated POST-CHANGE, ON-VALIDATE-FIELD, and ON-ERROR triggers. These triggers are copied automatically into the new form when the field that owns them is copied. Doing this has a number of advantages: it reduces the overhead involved with having many complex key fields, ensures that standard business rules are applied against critical fields, and implements the extended list of values definition described earlier.

We also recommend that during the initial design stage of all new applications, you design a number of dummy triggers and procedures in a form skeleton. These dummy procedures and triggers contain no code and perform no functions. They do allow you, or your site's DBA or analyst, to retrospectively fit a system-wide change at a later date. Such dummy procedures and triggers will even let you add whole new functions, such as context-sensitive help text or application navigation shortcuts to the entire application.

Library triggers work just the way traditional Version 2 and 2.3 triggers do, except that they are referenced from a central repository. Procedures and functions are new to Version 3 and provide the greatest potential for both performance improvement and possible confusion. We concentrate on these features in the sections below.

SQL*Forms Procedures

SQL*Forms allows you to create user-defined, form-level procedures. These let you develop common library routines that can be shared. The availability of such routines simplifies development, eases future maintenance, and lets later changes in an application be folded easily into existing code.

The typical approach is that the DBA creates a common public library repository. Public SQL*Forms code is defined, for example, in *SYSLIB/SYSLIB*, and its usercode and password are shared with developers. A single form containing all libraries is placed in this library. The generic library form does not have to generate (compile) cleanly. It is available for programmers to include (remember to do this by reference rather than by copy) into their own forms. Whenever a programmer generates a form, all referenced libraries are refreshed automatically.

(In RDBMS Version 7, globally stored procedures and functions provide even greater efficiency, but these are not available in RDBMS Version 6. See Appendix A, *Planning for ORACLE7*, for details.)

Error (exception) handling works differently for procedures and triggers. Triggers are self-contained modules and do not pass exception conditions back to the calling trigger. You must interrogate the FORM_SUCCESS Boolean to determine the outcome of a called trigger. Procedures, on the other hand, work just like copy libraries. They are transposed directly into the calling trigger and act upon that trigger's own exception handling logic. If a trigger calls a procedure, which in turn calls another procedure, error processing still passes back to the originating trigger, even from the second nested procedure.

If a trigger does not contain an exception clause, and the trigger or a dependent procedure raises an error exception, control still passes back to the end of that trigger. SQL*Forms assumes that all triggers at least have a default (dummy) exception clause. Figure 9-2 compares error processing for procedures and triggers.

SQL*Forms Functions

SQL*Forms user-defined functions are effectively procedures that can be defined within the SQL*Forms procedure window. Functions are available in Version 3, although many developers don't know about them because they are not well-documented. Fundamentally, the difference between functions and procedures is that functions are actually user-defined verbs, not routines.

In the following simplified example, a function returns an employee's estimated income tax withholding, based on the employee's salary:

```
Function EMP_TAX ( SAL IN NUMBER ) RETURN NUMBER IS
    TAX NUMBER;
BEGIN
    IF   SAL  <=  20000 THEN
        TAX  :=  SAL * 20 / 100 ;
    ELSIF
        SAL  <=  30000 THEN
        TAX  :=  SAL * 25 / 100 ;
    ELSE
        TAX  :=  SAL * 30 / 100;
    END IF;

    RETURN ( TAX );
END;
```

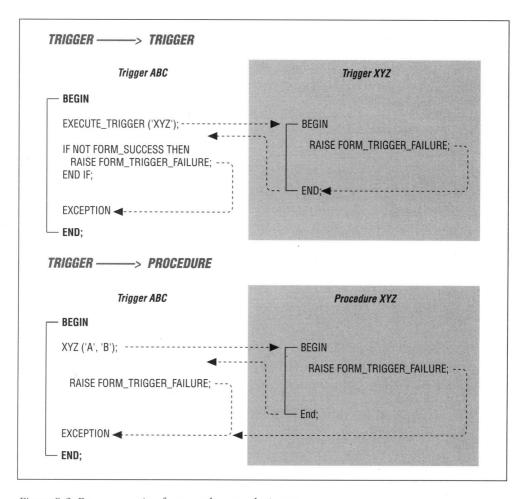

Figure 9-2: Error processing for procedures and triggers

Now you can access this function from within a SQL*Forms trigger or procedure as shown below:

```
BEGIN
    .
    .
    .
    IF EMP_TAX ( EMP_SALARY ) > BANK_BALN THEN
        MESSAGE ( 'EMPLOYEE CANNOT PAY INCOME TAX - REAL TROUBLE !!);
    END IF;
    .
    .
    .
END;
```

The most obvious difference between functions and procedures is that you must include a RETURN clause in the function block.

You can use a function effectively as if it is another PL/SQL verb. In the following, we implement our version of the SQL DECODE statement, a verb that, for some reason, is not allowed in standard PL/SQL blocks. (Because DECODE itself is a reserved word, we've called this one XDECODE.)

```
FUNCTION XDECODE (  TOK   IN  CHAR,
                    FM1  IN  CHAR,  TO1  IN  CHAR,
                    FM2  IN  CHAR,  TO2  IN  CHAR,
                    FM3  IN  CHAR,  TO3  IN  CHAR ) RETURN CHAR IS
BEGIN
    IF  TOK  =  FM1    THEN
        RETURN  ( TO1 );
    ELSIF
        TOK  =  FM2    THEN
        RETURN  ( TO2 );
    ELSIF
        TOK  =  FM3    THEN
        RETURN  ( TO3 );
    ELSE
        RETURN  ( NULL );
    END IF;
END;
```

Now, you can access this function within a SQL*Forms trigger or procedure as follows:

```
BEGIN
    .
    .
    .
    :BLK.SEX_DESC := XDECODE (:BLK.SEX,  'M','MALE',
    .                                    'F','FEMALE',
    .                                    'O','OTHER');
END;
```

Optional Procedure and Function Parameters

As we have shown, SQL*Forms allows procedures and functions to pass and receive parameters. Sometimes you'll find that certain forms don't need all parameters. Rather than passing dummy field references, you can give the procedures and functions default settings. For example, in the following, the previously defined XDECODE function passes parameters that have default settings.

```
FUNCTION XDECODE ( TOK  IN  CHAR,
            FM1  IN  CHAR := NULL,  TO1  IN  CHAR := NULL,
            FM2  IN  CHAR := NULL,  TO2  IN  CHAR := NULL,
```

```
                    FM3  IN  CHAR := NULL,  TO3  IN  CHAR := NULL )
                    RETURN CHAR IS
   BEGIN
           .
           .                   As defined previously
           .
   END;
```

You can now access this function from within a SQL*Forms trigger or procedure as follows:

```
   BEGIN
           .
           .
           .
   :BLK.SEX_DESC := XDECODE(:BLK.SEX, 'M', 'MALE');
           .
           .
           .
   :BLK.SEX_DESC := XDECODE(:BLK.SEX, 'M', 'MALE','F','FEMALE');
           .
           .
           .
   :BLK.SEX_DESC:=XDECODE(:BLK.SEX,'M','MALE',
                         'F','FEMALE','O','OTHER');
           .
           .
           .
   END;
```

You can also initialize parameters to constants, as shown below:

```
   PROCEDURE EMP_TAX ( FLD1 IN NUMBER  := 0,
                       FLD2 IN CHAR    := 'ABC',
                       FLD3 IN BOOLEAN := TRUE )    IS
       BEGIN
           .
           .
           .
       END;
```

Common SQL*Forms Triggers and Procedures

This section contains some examples of SQL*Forms procedures and functions we have used to solve common problems. You may wish to include them in your common system library routines or to implement them as Version 7 stored procedures and functions.

Checking for outstanding commits

This routine checks to make sure there are no outstanding commits in a block. Such a routine is helpful when you are moving between logically linked blocks. When one block depends on another, you must commit all outstanding changes before moving control to that dependent block. You might also use it in forms that include special key triggers (e.g., print the current row's employee history details) that need all changes committed to the database before they can proceed.

```
BEGIN
    IF :SYSTEM.CURSOR_VALUE IS NOT NULL THEN
        ENTER;
        IF NOT FORM_SUCCESS THEN
            RAISE FORM_TRIGGER_FAILURE;
        END IF;
    END IF;

    IF :SYSTEM.FORM_STATUS != 'CHANGED' THEN
        .
        .
        .
        GO_BLOCK ( 'XXXX' );
        .
        .
        .
    ELSE
        MESSAGE ('INVALID ACTION - COMMITS ARE OUTSTANDING');
        RAISE FORM_TRIGGER_FAILURE;
    END IF;
END;
```

Within SQL*Forms, this routine may work best as a system Boolean library function, which allows the routine to be referenced in-line:

```
IF OUTSTANDING_COMMITS THEN
    MESSAGE ( 'INVALID ACTION - COMMITS ARE OUTSTANDING' );
ELSE
    .
    .
    .
END IF;
```

Checking whether a field can be updated

This procedure checks to find out whether a field can be updated by a SQL*Forms user. It may be useful when you are coding a non-standard function into a user's trigger. If a user chooses a trigger that would ordinarily result in the error "FIELD IS PROTECTED AGAINST UPDATE," but if the programmer has changed the trigger's functionality, the field update is actually allowed. Programmer-defined triggers are always allowed to modify the contents of a field.

```
IF  FIELD_CHARACTERISTIC  (:SYSTEM.CURSOR_FIELD, UPDATEABLE)  = 'TRUE'
OR  (FIELD_CHARACTERISTIC (:SYSTEM.CURSOR_FIELD, UPDATE_NULL) = 'TRUE'
        AND :SYSTEM.CURSOR_VALUE IS NULL )
OR  :SYSTEM.RECORD_STATUS IN ('INSERT', 'NEW') THEN
    .
    .
    .
ELSE MESSAGE ('INVALID ACTION - FIELD CANNOT BE UPDATED');
END IF;
```

Enforcing commits on exits

When a form needs to perform some special action in addition to the commit logic, it is possible that the trigger flow can be altered, and disastrous results will occur. For example, suppose a user chooses to exit or abort and answers "YES" to the fail-safe pop-up window. This results in an abnormal commit cycle. If the programmer has implemented an enhanced KEY-COMMIT trigger, that altered commit trigger and (if defined) the POST_RECORD, POST_BLOCK, and POST_FORM triggers are ignored.

By restricting (enforcing) the commit phase to only the KEY-COMMIT trigger key, we can avoid this potential problem. In fact, many users prefer the commit restriction because they find it less confusing. Data changes can be actioned (commited) only via a single key. You must use the following triggers together to restrict the commit routine:

TRIGGER KEY-COMMIT

```
:GLOBAL.COMMIT_FLAG := 'Y';
COMMIT;
:GLOBAL.COMMIT_FLAG := NULL;
```

TRIGGER PRE-COMMIT

```
IF  NVL(:GLOBAL.COMMIT_FLAG, 'N') <> 'Y' THEN
    MESSAGE ('INVALID ACTION - MAY ONLY COMMIT VIA COMMIT KEY ');
END IF;
```

Performing full-block scrolling

Many SQL*Forms developers complain about the default operation of the SQL*Forms macros SCROLL_DOWN and SCROLL_UP. These macros scroll only about 80% of the current screen block. This often confuses users because they have no way of telling which rows are new and which have simply been moved up or down on the screen.

The following triggers use the number of displayed rows for the current SQL*Forms block, and automatically scroll the screen that number of records.

TRIGGER KEY-SCRDOWN

```
DECLARE
    XNUM  NUMBER;
    XBLK  NUMBER;
    XREC  NUMBER  := 0;
BEGIN
    IF BLOCK_CHARACTERISTIC (:SYSTEM.CURSOR_BLOCK, BASE_TABLE)
        IS NOT NULL
    THEN
        XBLK  := :SYSTEM.CURSOR_BLOCK;
        XNUM  := BLOCK_CHARACTERISTIC ( XBLK, RECORDS_DISPLAYED );

        GO_RECORD(TO_NUMBER(BLOCK_CHARACTERISTIC(XBLK, TOP_RECORD))
            + XNUM;

        WHILE XREC < XNUM  AND :SYSTEM.LAST_RECORD = 'FALSE' LOOP
            NEXT_RECORD;
            XREC := XREC + 1;
        END LOOP;

        GO_RECORD (TO_NUMBER(BLOCK_CHARACTERISTIC
            (XBLK,TOP_RECORD) );
    ELSE
        MESSAGE ('THIS FUNCTION NOT ALLOWED FOR THIS BLOCK');
    END IF;
END;
```

TRIGGER KEY-SCRUP

```
DECLARE
    XBLK  NUMBER;
    XREC  NUMBER;
BEGIN
    IF BLOCK_CHARACTERISTIC (:SYSTEM.CURSOR_BLOCK, BASE_TABLE)
        IS NOT NULL
    THEN
        XBLK  := :SYSTEM.CURSOR_BLOCK;
        XREC  := BLOCK_CHARACTERISTIC ( XBLK, RECORDS_DISPLAYED );

        WHILE  XREC > 0 AND :SYSTEM.CURSOR_RECORD != 1 LOOP
            PREVIOUS_RECORD;
            XREC := XREC - 1;
        END LOOP;

        GO_RECORD(TO_NUMBER(BLOCK_CHARACTERISTIC(XBLK,TOP_RECORD);
```

```
        ELSE
            MESSAGE ('THIS FUNCTION NOT ALLOWED FOR THIS BLOCK');
        END IF;
    END;
```

Positioning a query at a particular record

Occasionally, you will need to position a particular base table query at a particular record (returned via the FETCH macro). You will find this routine helpful if the SQL*Forms developer wants to display returned records for the current month, but also wants to be able to go back to historic records (via KEY-PRVREC, KEY-UP). It keeps you from having to execute different base table queries to satisfy these two alternative scenarios (pre-current month, and post-current month). With this procedure, you can position the query function at the desired record after each EXECUTE_QUERY operation. This allows the user to scroll back and forth through the data. In the following, 'BLK' stands for the current SQL*Forms block.

```
    PROCEDURE POSITION_AT_FIRST_RECORD

    DECLARE
        XREC    NUMBER;
        XMTH    DATE;
    BEGIN
        XMTH := TO_DATE ('01' || (TO_CHAR (SYSDATE, 'MMYYYY'),
            'DDMMYYYY');

        WHILE :BLK.ROWID IS NOT NULL AND :BLK.DATE_EFF < XMTH LOOP
            NEXT_RECORD;
        END LOOP;

        XREC := TO_NUMBER(:SYSTEM.CURSOR_BLOCK);

        WHILE TO_NUMBER(BLOCK_CHARACTERISTIC('BLK',TOP_RECORD))<>XREC
            AND :SYSTEM.LAST_RECORD = 'FALSE' LOOP
            NEXT_RECORD;
        END LOOP;

        GO_RECORD (TO_NUMBER(BLOCK_CHARACTERISTIC('BLK',TOP_RECORD)));
    END;
```

SQL*Forms Pop-up Windows

Pop-up windows, available only in SQL*Forms Version 3 applications, give your applications a more elegant look and feel. The ability to layer information makes it possible to show which information is subordinate. We recommend that you use these pop-up windows as much as possible to improve the look of your applications as well as overall performance. Here we present some personal recommendations for using this feature to best advantage:

- Redefine the key KEY-PRVBLK to allow pop-up forms to perform the EXIT macro. In this way, the user doesn't have to distinguish between pop-up blocks and pop-up forms.

- Anchor your pop-up pages in the bottom, right-hand corner of the screen, as shown in Figure 9-3. Layer each subordinate page over its parent page, always leaving the parent keys exposed.

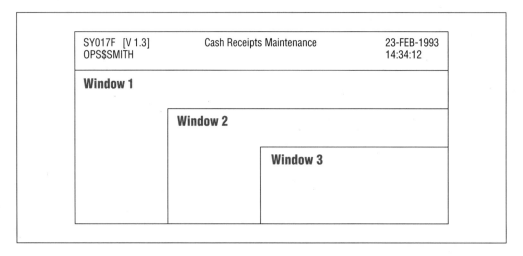

Figure 9-3: Anchoring pop-up pages

- Box all pop-up blocks and forms, and highlight the boxing of the current page, as shown in Figure 9-4.

```
ANCHOR_VIEW     (2, 10, 14);
DISPLAY_PAGE    (2, 'BOLD');
```

- Set the primary key(s) of the parent block to bold face, as shown in Figure 9-5. In multi-record parent blocks, you must be able to identify which record is actually the parent.

```
ANCHOR_VIEW     (2, 10, 14);
DISPLAY_FIELD   ('BLK.FLD', 'BOLD');
DISPLAY_PAGE    (2, 'BOLD);.
```

- Commit all outstanding commits before returning from a pop-up block. The user can propagate outstanding commits down into subordinate blocks, but not back up out of the block.

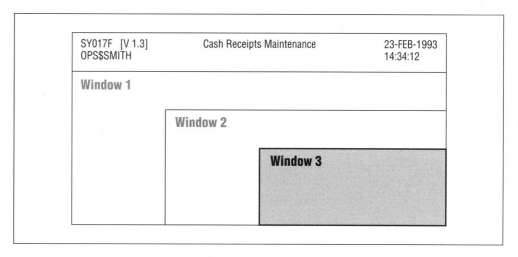

Figure 9-4: Highlighting pop-up pages

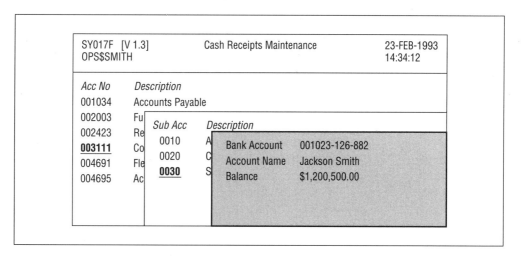

Figure 9-5: Highlighting primary keys

- Set the attribute HIDE ON EXIT for all pop-up blocks. This means that the block is automatically removed when the operator navigates up, back to the parent block. Doing this saves an enormous amount of programming effort in trying to coordinate parent/child blocks. If you do not set HIDE ON EXIT, then the child block remains exposed and needs to be refreshed every time the current record of the parent block is changed. Simply scrolling through the parent block can consume a large amount of resources by continually redisplaying the child block information.

SQL*Forms V3 supports (automatically creates) a default set of triggers and procedures to automatically coordintate parent-child block relationships. This approach
should never be adopted unless absolutely necessary. By only displaying the child
block when the operator navigates to it, and hiding it when the operator leaves the
block, data within it does not need to be coordinated when the operator steps
through the parent block.

SQL*Forms User Exits

User exits are 3GL subroutines that are linked directly into the SQL*Forms executable
(RUNFORM). User exits allow you to use facilities that are outside the normal
SQL*Forms or even ORACLE arena. User exits support a number of different 3GL
languages, including Ada, C, COBOL, FORTRAN, Pascal, and PL/I. Each 3GL language
has its own specialty; for example, FORTRAN is a scientific language; C excels in string
manipulation.

You must include all user exit references in the GENXTB source, and compile it. Then,
you must link both the user exit and the GENXTB object with the other ORACLE object
files. There are many good reasons to use user exits, as described below.

Outside access. Allow access to devices and to non-ORACLE products and databases
that can't be accessed through normal ORACLE tools. For example, through user exits
you can control peripheral devices such as printers, plotters, bar-code readers, modems,
and even sophisticated equipment like robotic devices. User exits allow any third-party
product to communicate with an ORACLE database.

Additional facilities. Extend the power of certain ORACLE tools beyond the facilities
available in them. For example, you can't normally do array processing for inserts,
updates, or deletes through SQL*Forms. If your application must do processing of this
kind, you can write a user exit to do it. Precompiler and OCI exits support dynamic
SQL. For earlier versions of SQL*Forms, they support an interface to pop-up window
libraries.

Different data types. Allow you to process different types of data. For example, within
SQL*Forms, you can manipulate a field defined as LONG (via PL/SQL variables), but
you cannot reference a single field that is longer than 32K.

Security. A common user exit is a secure, application-dependent password algorithm.
The physical code for this routine will be restricted to one senior person at your site, but
the object code (in the form of a user exit) will be available to all developers.

Performance. Because user exits are compiled, not interpreted, they are more efficient
to execute. If you are doing a lot of complex data manipulation, you might want to
consider user exits as a performance aid.

Many developers shy away from user exits because they think they are too difficult to use. While they are more complex than inserting a trigger, they are not overly difficult. In fact, sometimes trying to make a trigger handle some very difficult logic is actually a lot harder than coding a concise user exit. Consult your standard ORACLE documentation for how to code and call user exits.

ORACLE Precompiler Exits

Precompiler user exits use ORACLE's precompiler interface. By embedding SQL statements in these user exits, you can access the ORACLE database, SQL*Forms variables, global variables, and fields. Precompiler user exits support dynamic SQL. All fields you use to communicate with the database must be included between the BEGIN DECLARE and END DECLARE statements of the program.

You must execute the precompiler for each user exit before you can do the normal 3GL compile. During this phase the precompiler converts all precompiler statements (via EXEC SQL) within the program, automatically replacing them with low-level ORACLE routines.

ORACLE Call Interface (OCI) User Exits

ORACLE Call Interface (OCI) user exits are more complicated than precompiler user exits. OCI supports lower-level ORACLE interfaces (libraries), which allow you to manipulate cursors in any way you wish. You can share them, change them, or discard them, as required by the application. OCI user exits support dynamic SQL.

Note that a user call that incorporates only OCI cannot access SQL*Forms variables or fields. Usually, OCI libraries are the most efficient way to manipulate application data and machine resources.

Non-ORACLE User Exits

Non-ORACLE user exits often are written to communicate with raw devices in order to reset printers or to check for disk free space. A user exit of this kind does not use the precompiler interface or the OCI. Non-ORACLE user exits cannot access ORACLE databases or SQL*Forms variables and fields.

10

Selecting a Locking Strategy

How well your application performs often depends directly on the data locking strategies you adopt. Yet, unlike many performance decisions, locking decisions are often overlooked by designers and unappreciated by application users. If you plan carefully what row and table locking strategies your application will use, your smart thinking will tend to go unnoticed. Your application will simply chug along, performing efficiently and keeping users happy. If you make the wrong choices, however, your application may be completely crippled.

Time and time again, we've found that poor performance is linked directly to poor selection of locking strategies. We've also found that application designers and developers tend to overlook locking as a critical issue. More than anything, this is a testing problem. When application modules are being developed—and even into the acceptance phases of a project—testing is too often limited to looking at modules and programs as single, independent units, not as small pieces of the larger application jigsaw. Unfortunately, locking problems often remain hidden until full and rigorous system testing puts all the pieces together by simultaneously executing all of the programs that make up an application. Until they are revealed by full testing, locking problems will linger in your application as potential time bombs that threaten to blow up your application's performance when that performance is most critical.

What is Locking?

ORACLE is a large, multiuser system. Many users are issuing many transactions—perhaps concurrently. What if two or more users are trying to update the same table or row simultaneously? ORACLE's locking facilities keep concurrent users and transactions from clashing. If updating isn't controlled in some way, you might find your data changed out from under you; even as you are updating a value in the database, another user might be changing that value too. The integrity of the data is at risk.

The basic idea of locking is a simple one: when one transaction is issued, it acquires a lock on the data it needs to access. Until the lock is released, no other transaction can access that data. But, the reality of locking can be more complex. Because performance will obviously suffer if locks are maintained for too long, it's in the interest of overall system performance to lock the smallest amount of data for the shortest amount of time.

Although locks are vital to enforcing database consistency and performance, they can create performance problems as well. Every time one process issues a lock, another user may be shut out from processing the locked row or table. ORACLE allows you to lock whatever resources you need—a single row, many rows, an entire table, even many tables. But, the larger the scope of the lock, the more processes you potentially shut out.

ORACLE provides two different levels of locking:

- **Row-level locking.** When one transaction updates a table, only the table row that is actually being updated is locked to other transactions. Other transactions can continue to update other rows in the table, but can't access the particular row locked by the first transaction until the row lock is released. To use row-level locking, your system must have installed the Transaction Processing Option (TPO).

- **Table-level locking.** When one transaction updates a table, the entire table is locked to other transactions. Other transactions can't update any of the table's rows until the table lock is released.

With either level of locking, although one transaction may have an update lock on a particular table or row, other transactions can still read that table or row. They just can't update it.

As you'd expect, your application realizes substantial performance gains with row-level, as opposed to table-level, locking because a row lock ties up only one row of a table. Row-level locking is especially effective for large, online transaction processing (OLTP) applications because it allows many users to simultaneously update, insert, and delete different rows in the same table. By contrast, with table-level locking, the entire table is locked (although briefly) during the time that an actual update takes place.

Versions of ORACLE prior to Version 6 support only table-level locking, but Versions 6 and 7 allow the selection of either strategy (TPO or non-TPO). Although row-level locking tends to provide far better performance, there are certain situations in which you'll want to select table-level locking, or will want to issue explicit table locks for certain transactions. These special situations are described in this chapter.

Row-level Locking

With a row-level locking strategy, each row within a table can be locked individually. Locked rows can be updated only by the locking process. All other rows in the table are still available for updating by other processes. Of course, other processes continue to be able to read any row in the table, including the one that is actually being updated. When other processes do read updated rows, they see only the old version of the row prior to update (via a rollback segment) until the changes are actually committed. This is known as a "consistent read."

When a process places a row level lock on a record, what really happens? First, a data manipulation language (DML) lock is placed over the row. This lock prevents other processes from updating (or locking) the row. This lock is released only when the locking process successfully commits the transaction to the database (i.e., makes the updates to that transaction permanent) or when the process is rolled back. Next, a data dictionary language (DDL) lock is placed over the table to prevent structural alterations to the table. For example, this type of lock keeps the DBA from being able to remove a table by issuing a DROP statement against the table. This lock is released only when the locking process successfully commits the transaction to the database, or when the process is rolled back.

With ORACLE Versions 6 and 7, you don't need to choose row-level locking explicitly. Row-level locking is the default. Later sections describe how you can explicitly override row-level locking.

Table-level Locking

With table-level locking, the entire table is locked as an entity. Once a process has locked a table, only that process can update (or lock) any row in the table. None of the rows in the table are available for updating by any other process. Of course, other processes continue to be able to read any row in the table, including the one that is actually being updated.

If you have not installed the TPO in your system, table-level locking is the default. If TPO is installed (and row-level locking is the default), you can globally select table-level locking by default by setting the INIT.ORA parameter, ROW_LOCKING, to INTENT. This setting overrides the default of ROW_LOCKING = ALWAYS.

How does table-level locking work? The first DML operation that needs to update a row in a table obtains what's called a Row Share Exclusive lock over the entire table. All other query-only processes needing access to the table are informed that they must use the rollback information for the locking process. The lock is released only when the locking process successfully commits the transaction to the database, or when the process is rolled back.

Releasing Locks

Many users believe that they are the only users on the system—at least the only ones who count. Unfortunately, this type of attitude is what causes locking problems. We've often observed applications that were completely stalled because one user decided to go to lunch without having committed his or her changes. Remember, all locking (row or table) will prevent other users from updating information. Every application has a handful of central, core tables. Inadvertently locking such tables can affect many other people in a system.

Many users, and some programmers, don't understand that terminating a process does not release locks. Switching off your workstation before going home also does not release locks. Locks are released only when changes are committed or rolled back. A user's action is the only thing that distinguishes between committing, aborting, and rolling back changes. Make it a priority to train your users to commit or roll back all outstanding changes before leaving their current screens.

Avoiding the Dreaded Deadlock

Locking—in particular, row-level locking—is an excellent way to preserve database consistency while improving performance. But, locking itself can occasionally cause performance problems by creating deadlocks.

What is a deadlock? In rare cases, two (or more) processes each hold resources that the other requires. For example, suppose process A needs to update the EMP table and then the DEPT table. It acquires a lock on the EMP table and maintains that lock until the next resource it needs to lock, the DEPT table, is free. Concurrently, process B needs to update the DEPT table and then the EMP table. It acquires a lock on the DEPT table and maintains that lock until the EMP table is free. Because neither process can lock the other resource it needs, neither will release the lock it holds. The processes could potentially wait forever for the necessary resources to become available. This situation, illustrated in Figure 10-1, is known as a deadlock.

ORACLE doesn't let deadlocks stop your applications dead in their tracks. It has its own strategy for dealing with the deadlocks it encounters. It picks one of the contending processes, and rolls back the updating that it has already performed for that process's locked resources. How does ORACLE decide which process to roll back? It automatically aborts the process requiring the least amount of rollback activity and informs that process about the failure. The aborted process can simply retry the action again.

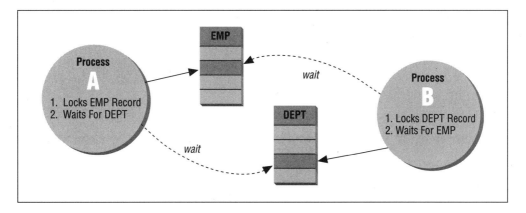

Figure 10-1: Deadlock situation

A Warning About Certain Tools and Products

How can you prevent deadlocks from occurring? Most of the ORACLE tools handle dead-lock detection and rollback very well. SQL*Forms, for example, handles deadlocks and other forms of database errors by default. Although most of the ORACLE tools handle deadlocks properly, some can cause undesirable results.. SQL*Plus, for example, cannot programmatically enforce database validity and consistency. SQL*Plus users have been known to add invalid data to a database, delete vital data, exclusively lock core application tables, and so on.

Third-party products can also cause problems. Even if your own application has been thoroughly tested for deadlocks and other database problems, you sometimes cannot anticipate the impact of another product on your database. Casual users of third-party products like Lotus 1-2-3, Excel, and Forest & Trees have been known to access and inadvertently lock your database via special interface drivers.

How can you protect your database from these errors? There is no single answer. You'll need to set up rules and procedures that make sense for your own organization to protect against the inadvertent locking and destruction of your database by users who may not be aware of the consequences of their actions.

Handling Deadlocks Explicitly

The accidental damage that third-party products could cause is very rare. However, when you use certain third-generation language interfaces (Pro*C, Pro*COBOL, etc.), you need to be aware that these products do not automatically handle deadlock detection. These leave the handling of deadlocks and other types of database errors up to the programmer. If you use these tools, your programs will have to include logic that explicitly detects errors of various kinds.

With some very serious errors, you'll have to abort program execution. Deadlocks, although a nuisance, are not intrinsically serious problems. When your program detects such an error, it should respond by explicitly rolling back changes to the database and beginning the update routine again.

Establishing a Locking Sequence

Even when you use standard ORACLE tools, which provide automatic deadlock detection, you should do all you can to minimize the chances of deadlocks occurring. The best way to prevent deadlocks is to establish a strict locking sequence for tables. It is the job of the DBA to specify, during the initial system design, the physical locking sequence and to document and distribute information about this sequence. It is the job of the application developer to make sure that the program code carries out the locking policy. Both DBA and developer must share in policing these policies within the organization to make sure they adhere to table locking rules.

To specify a locking sequence, you assign a table ranking to each table. Program statements must lock tables strictly in this order. When a process locks a resource, it can do so only by ascending or descending table ranking order.

Although alphabetic ordering is simple and usually effective (e.g., DEPT before EMP), alphabetic locking is not always suitable for more complex applications where many tables are updated in a single transaction state. In general, when you devise table locking rankings, make sure that each table has a higher ranking than any table referenced via a foreign key connection. The following example illustrates only one of many ranking possibilities. The most important thing you can do here is to enforce carefully whatever schema has been adopted for your own application. For example:

```
TABLE EMPLOYEE                 Ranking 1
        .
        .
        .
        DEPARTMENT             Ranking 4
        .
        .
        .
        CATEGORY               Ranking 12
        CLASS                  Ranking 13
        DEPT_TYPE              Ranking 14
```

Remember, rows in tables are not locked in the order in which tables are referenced in the LOCK TABLE statement, but rather in the order in which rows are actually updated.

Consider the following example:

```
LOCK TABLE EMP, DPT, CAT IN ROW SHARE MODE;
UPDATE CAT SET . . . WHERE . . .;
UPDATE EMP SET . . . WHERE . . .;
UPDATE DPT SET . . . WHERE . . .;
```

In this example, the rows will be locked in the sequence CAT, followed by EMP, followed by DPT (instead of EMP, followed by DPT, followed by CAT, as they are specified in the LOCK TABLE statement).

Special Considerations for Version 7

Several of the new Version 7 features introduce the potential for creating locking problems. These problems are unlikely, but are worth knowing about, because, in the worst case, they could cause deadlocks. For a summary of these Version 7 features, see Appendix A, *Planning for ORACLE7.* For complete information about the features, consult your standard ORACLE documentation.

The full import of Version 7 changes on locking is still being explored. If you encounter any of the problems mentioned below, be sure to document exactly what happens, and distribute information about it to other programmers at your site.

Stored triggers

Stored triggers are fired either on a table level (for an INSERT, UPDATE, or DELETE), or on a row level (for a per-row UPDATE). If a table has 100 rows updated by a user, 100 more row-level triggers may be executed, and neither the user nor the programmer will be aware of it. Each of these hidden actions could update other tables and fire other stored triggers.

DELETE CASCADE

If a row is deleted from a parent table, all of the associated children will be automatically purged. A deleted child table might, in turn, have its own child tables. Even worse, the child tables could have table-level triggers that begin to fire. What starts out as a simple, single-record delete from a harmless table could turn into an uncontrollable torrent of cascading deletes and stored table triggers.

Distributed databases

Version 6 supports distributed database queries, but Version 7 supports full distributed updating. When you update a record in another database on the other side of the world, the results might surprise you. Because you have had no input into the database design, you may have no way of appreciating resulting actions upon it. The remote database could trigger a stored trigger at the remote database, for example, which could then perform a remote update back at the originating database.

Overriding the Default Locking Strategy

By default, ORACLE locks a table or row only when it needs to. ORACLE executes the lock only when a DML statement of some kind (UPDATE, INSERT, DELETE) actually executes an update, not when a query is issued against that table or row. .

Because ORACLE does not lock the table or row any sooner than it actually needs to, this default locking strategy usually provides the best performance. For example, suppose that a user selects 100 rows from the database, but updates only one. It would be inefficient to lock the entire set of rows.

Sometimes, though, relying on ORACLE's default locking strategy does not result in the best performance. ORACLE provides statements that allow you to override the default strategy and lock a table or row explicitly. You'll want to use these statements if it is important to your application to lock a table or row before you update the database.

When default locking is in effect, the lock occurs when the database update or deletion is actually performed, not when the query is issued. You'll have to consider your own system needs carefully before selecting an appropriate strategy—row locking, table locking, or the hybrid form we discuss at the end of this chapter.

SELECT...FOR UPDATE OF: Locking a Row Explicitly

The SELECT statement, through the FOR UPDATE OF clause, allows you to explicitly lock a row, or more likely a set of rows, before you perform an update to these rows. This statement is useful if you need to process a number of rows as a single unit. Consider the case in which ORACLE has, by default, locked only one of the rows in your unit, and you've successfully updated it, but another process has acquired a lock on the next row in your unit, changing the data in it before you've been able to lock and update it. Having another process change data out from under you in this way may result in an inconsistency in the data, or even a corrupted database.

Using the FOR UPDATE OF clause in the SELECT statement that selects your desired group of rows issues a preemptive lock. It prevents other processes from locking a row that you will need access to in order to complete your work.

Here's an example of explicitly locking a row in the EMP table:

```
SELECT . . .
    FROM EMP
    FOR UPDATE OF EMP_NO;
```

Remember, even if you have locked several rows of a table, other processes will still be able to lock and update the rows that you have not locked.

Here is an example of using SQL*Forms to lock specific "detail" rows of a table, when the "master" row is locked:

```
TRIGGER ON-LOCK

SELECT  'X'
    FROM  EMP
    WHERE EMP_NO = 1234
    FOR UPDATE OF EMP_NO;
SELECT  X'
    FROM  EMP_HISTORY
    WHERE EMP_NO = 1234
    FOR UPDATE OF EMP_NO;
```

SQL*Forms allows you to override default locking. If you choose to do this, you disable all normal locking routines, and your code is completely responsible for all locking. You must be aware of all of the operations that would otherwise be handled by default. For example, if you are simply locking a second associated table in your code, you must also manually perform the original table lock that would otherwise have been handled by default.

LOCK TABLE: Locking a Table Explicitly

Row locking is not always the most efficient approach to updating a table. If you are updating a large number of rows in a table, you might end up locking, in sequence, each of many thousands of rows. In a case like this, you'll find that an exclusive table lock is more efficient than successive row locks.

The LOCK TABLE statement allows you to lock a table before performing an update on it. This statement prevents other processes from exclusively locking the entire table. You might need to use the LOCK TABLE statement if many rows in a table need to be updated together as a single unit, or if several tables must be treated as a unit. If you have tables with referential connections, such as master/detail relationships, you may want to lock the associated rows of the detail table explicitly when their master record is reserved for deletion.

There are two types of table locks: exclusive and shared. Here is an example of explicitly locking a table with an exclusive lock:

```
LOCK TABLE EMP IN EXCLUSIVE MODE NOWAIT;
```

What does this statement do?

1. It exclusively locks the table. This means that other processes cannot update any part of the table, even rows that your program will not be updating.

2. It takes out a DDL lock, preventing the DBA from dropping or modifying the table-structure.

3. NOWAIT means that, if exclusive mode cannot be acquired (usually because some other process is currently accessing the table), the program reports an error. It does not wait for the offending locks or processes to complete. If a lengthy table is undergoing updating, the wait could take hours!

Here is an example of explicitly locking a table with a shared lock:

```
LOCK TABLE EMP, EMP_HISTORY IN ROW SHARE MODE NOWAIT;
```

What does this statement do?

1. It locks the table in shared mode. This allows other processes to update the rows of the table not affected by this process, and it prevents other processes from locking the table exclusively.

2. It takes out a DDL lock, preventing the DBA from dropping or modifying the table structure.

3. When the process actually updates a row in the locked table, that row has a DML lock placed over it.

4. NOWAIT has the same effect as in the previous example.

Here is an example of locking a table when you're using PL/SQL:

```
      .
      .
      .
LOCK TABLE EMP, EMP_HISTORY IN SHARE MODE NOWAIT;
      .
      .
      .
DELETE FROM EMP
    WHERE EMP_NO = 1234;
      .
      .
      .
DELETE FROM EMP_HISTORY
    WHERE EMP_NO = 1234;
      .
      .
      .
COMMIT;
```

Using Pseudo-code to Lock a Large Table

There are some situations in which neither locking an entire table, nor locking all of the affected rows in that table, seems to be a good choice. Suppose that a large table (e.g., one with more than 1000 rows) is being updated during online access. The obvious way to handle such an update would be to put an exclusive lock on the entire table. Even if row-locking is the default for your system, you can lock the table explicitly using the LOCK TABLE statement described in the previous section. The problem with this approach is that it stops other processes from accessing the table, potentially for a very long time. For large tables, this is a major problem. Updating a table containing 50,000 rows might take many hours.

Now, suppose you lock individual rows of the table instead. Although we generally advise you to lock rows, not whole tables, row locking for a large table may also be problematic. When you use a SELECT statement, you'll need to explicitly mark 50,000 distinct rows for locking (50,000 row latches) before starting the update.

What you need is a way to allow several thousand row updates while allowing other users to continue to have online access to the table. One solution we've used successfully is to write pseudo-code that batches database locking and updating.

In the program example shown below, the SELECT statement for cursor C1 (the driving statement) selects all records for department 20. This cursor assembles all of the rows that meet the first selection criterion (EMP_DEPT = 0020) before the first row is fetched. It does this to enforce consistency in the read. No matter how many rows are selected, the data in the rows represent a consistent snapshot of the table as it was when the first row was selected.

Note, however, that although we have selected all of the rows, we have not locked them. (To do so with a very large table, where we might be selecting 100,000 records, for example, would cause serious performance problems for the whole system.) Therefore, it is possible that the actual data in one of the selected rows might have been modified by another process after cursor C1 selected it, but before cursor C2 locked it.

To get around this problem, we simply re-apply the original condition:

```
SELECT . . .
    WHERE EMP_DEPT = 0020;
```

as well as specifying the unique WHERE clause:

```
SELECT . . .
    WHERE EMP_NO = :XEMP_NO;
```

when we lock and fetch the row.

Here is the full example:

```
DECLARE
    CURSOR C1    IS
        SELECT   EMP_NO
            FROM   EMP
            WHERE   EMP_DEPT = 0020;
CURSOR C2 IS
    SELECT ROWID
        FROM    EMP
        WHERE  EMP_NO    = :XEMP_NO
        AND     EMP_DEPT  = 0020
        FOR     UPDATE OF . . .;

BEGIN
    KOUNTER = 0;
    OPEN C1;

    BEGIN_LOOP;
        FETCH C1 INTO :XEMP_NO;

        OPEN C2;
        FETCH C2 INTO :XROWID;

        IF C2%FOUND THEN
            UPDATE EMP
            SET  . . .  =  . . .
            WHERE   ROWID = :XROWID
            KOUNTER = KOUNTER + 1;
            IF    KOUNTER = 20    THEN
                COMMIT;
                KOUNTER = 0;
            END IF;
        END IF;
    END_LOOP;

    CLOSE C1;
    CLOSE C2;
END;
```

A major advantage of this approach is that it dramatically reduces the overhead that would be incurred by single-row processing. By incrementing KOUNTER and committing the update to the database only every 20 records, rather than every one, performance increases a good deal. This practice does run the risk of having large "update processes" fail when they have only partially completed. Make sure that such update processes are restartable and be sure to commit only "complete" units, never violating the referential integrity of the application.

V

Tuning for Database Administrators

Part V describes what ORACLE database administrators (DBAs) need to know about tuning. How can you tune a new database to best advantage? What can you do to improve the performance of an existing database? What are the special tuning requirements for the ORACLE data dictionary? What diagnostic and tuning tools are available to you?

11

Tuning a New Database

The way you create your database has a significant impact on your site's performance. Not only do programs run faster against a well-tuned database, the database structure also makes it easier for you to monitor performance. The importance of database performance ranks right behind your first database goal: making sure you'll be able to recover data in case of a system crash or data integrity problem. Keep these two goals in mind as you tune your new database.

What does your database contain? There are two main types of files: database files and redo log files. Database files contain tables, indexes, clusters, sequences, the ORACLE data dictionary, temporary segments, and rollback segments. Redo logs contain after-image information—the new values the database will contain after updates have completed.

Because many sites are still running ORACLE Version 6, this chapter describes performance for both Version 6 and Version 7 databases.

Remember, you are responsible for creating and tuning all of the databases at your site—not only the production database, but also the developers' database, the quality assurance database, and the training database. Tuning is important for all of these databases. Your programmers will be better able to meet deadlines and provide good response times if they are doing their work on a well-tuned database. Your QA staff will be able to do accurate response time testing only if the database is properly tuned. And, your users will be better able to learn how to use the production system if they are working on a database that behaves the way it will in production. Remember, too, many organizations have tuning service agreements for specific response times that enforce a certain level of performance.

Your specific hardware configuration determines how much flexibility you will have in tuning your database—in particular, the amount of memory and the size and number of disks. If you don't have enough memory to satisfy demands, memory bottlenecks will occur. The CPU will be consumed by moving whole processes or parts of processes in and out of memory. If one or more of your disk controllers is operating above its recommended maximum, you'll encounter disk bottlenecks too. Make sure you know how to use the memory and disk monitoring commands available for your own particular operating system so you can keep close tabs on memory and disk availability.

WARNING

Never put any part of your database on the operating system disk. And, if you are operating in a client-server environment, make sure you put the database on a dedicated server.

Although as the database administrator you have primary responsibility for database tuning, the entire tuning process is a team effort. Make sure you work closely with the system administrator and the analysts and designers at your site.

What do you need from your system administrator? He or she is responsible not only for ORACLE but also for other non-ORACLE applications such as electronic mail. This person maintains the system hardware and software and makes sure you have enough contiguous disk space for your database files. The system administrator typically creates user accounts in your system, and assigns memory to these users (in operating systems like VMS that support per-user memory assignments). Be aware that if the amount of memory assigned is too low, CPU will be consumed when the system needs to obtain additional memory increments. If the amount of memory assigned is too large, memory is wasted that might be sorely needed by other products. Make sure the system administrator knows what your database needs are.

What do you need from your analysts and designers? They will provide valuable information on the expected size and usage patterns of the various tables, which help determine the types of indexes you need and how much storage to allocate to tables and indexes. This information will also help you spread the disk load across disks to avoid disk I/O bottlenecks. Analysts and designers should also be able to help you determine the number of expected users and what they will be doing in the system.

Here are the basic steps you follow when you set up your database:

1. Obtain from analysts, designers, and/or user representatives background information on numbers of users, their usage patterns, and the expected increase in the number of users.

2. Check with the system administrator to make sure there is adequate memory and disk space. Also, make sure that the disk space is contiguous. This helps performance when you are reading to and writing from database files.

3. With the help of the system administrator, develop comprehensive backup and recovery procedures.

4. Create the INIT.ORA parameter file and set the most efficient values for the parameters.

5. Create the database and tablespaces, with their default storage allocations,

6. Create the users who will own the tables, indexes, sequences, views, and clusters.

7. Create tables, indexes, sequences, views, and clusters.

8. Import the data into the tables (if you are transferring data from an existing ORACLE application).

9. Create all other users with their appropriate synonyms.

Tuning Memory

This section describes the layout of memory and briefly discusses how you can tune memory areas. Because most of the memory tuning you will perform occurs once your system is running (and perhaps experiencing bottlenecks), Chapter 13, *Monitoring and Tuning an Existing Database*, describes memory tuning in greater detail.

Memory Components

The general layout of memory in the ORACLE system is shown in Figure 11-1. Although the physical layout varies slightly for Version 6 and Version 7, the systems are quite similar in how they divide memory. The main difference is that Version 7 stores less of the database in individual processes and more in the System Global Area (SGA).

Figure 11-2 and Figure 11-3 show simplified diagrams of how the SGA differs in Version 6 and Version 7.

By tuning these memory areas (primarily by setting the appropriate INIT.ORA parameters), you can improve performance in your ORACLE system. All of the parameters that affect performance are included in the list in the section at the end of this chapter called "INIT.ORA Parameter Summary."

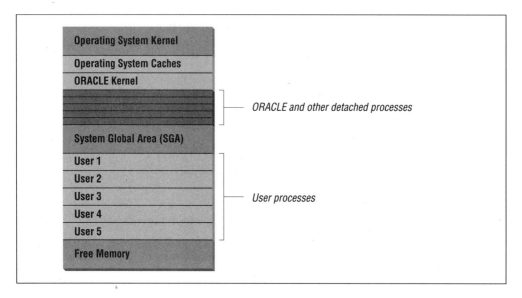

Figure 11-1: ORACLE's use of memory

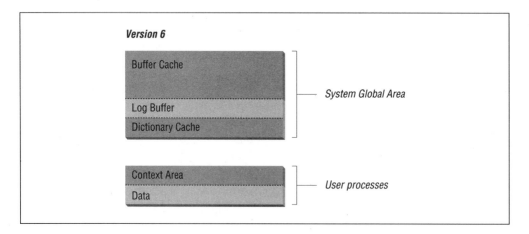

Figure 11-2: SGA and user processes (Version 6)

In Version 6, a number of different parameters, all of which begin with the prefix DC_, control the allocation in the dictionary cache. The CONTEXT_AREA and CONTEXT_ INCR parameters control the storage of SQL and PL/SQL statements in the user processes. In Version 7, on the other hand, a single parameter, SHARED_POOL_SIZE, controls the entire shared area.

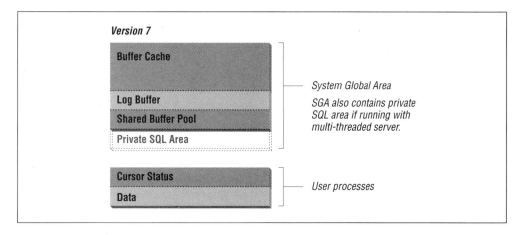

Figure 11-3: SGA and user processes (Version 7)

For Version 6, you can tune the following areas:

Dictionary cache. Holds information on tables, indexes, rollbacks, and other dictionary objects.

Context areas. Holds the SQL statements that are currently being parsed; there are several for each user process.

Buffer cache. Holds copies of database blocks for tables, indexes, rollback segments, and clusters. Each buffer holds one ORACLE data block.

Log buffer. Holds copies of redo log buffers.

For Version 7, you can tune:

Private SQL and PL/SQL areas. Hold the SQL and PL/SQL statements that are not shared.

Shared pool. Holds the library cache (for shared SQL statements being executed), the dictionary cache, and some session information.

Buffer cache. Holds copies of database blocks.

Log buffer. Holds copies of redo log buffers.

Buffer cache

The buffer cache is identical for Version 6 and Version 7. It holds copies of database blocks for tables, indexes, rollback segments, and clusters. Each buffer holds one ORACLE data block. The more blocks you can hold in memory, the better your performance will be. You control the size of the buffer cache with the DB_BLOCK_BUFFERS parameter. The description of this parameter in "INIT.ORA Parameter Summary" contains an initial size recommendation for a new database. Chapter 13, *Monitoring and Tuning an Existing Database*, describes how you can monitor the buffer cache over time and adjust this size to suit your own site's needs.

Log buffer

In both Version 6 and Version 7, the log buffer contains information showing the changes that have been made to database buffer blocks. When this buffer file fills up, the log writer (LGWR) process writes the contents of the buffer out to the redo log files associated with the database. (Chapter 13 describes these files and how to tune them.) The LOG_BUFFER parameter controls the size of this buffer. If the buffer is too small, LGWR will have to write to disk often, slowing performance. The "INIT.ORA Parameter Summary" contains an initial size recommendation for a new database.

Shared buffer pool

In Version 7, a shared buffer pool contains the library cache, the dictionary cache, and, if you are running ORACLE's multi-threaded server, some session data. You control the size of the shared buffer pool with the SHARED_POOL_SIZE parameter. The description of this parameter in the "INIT.ORA Parameter Summary" contains an initial size recommendation for a new database. Chapter 13 describes how you can monitor the shared buffer pool over time and adjust this size to suit your own site's needs. Figure 11-4 shows the contents of the shared buffer pool.

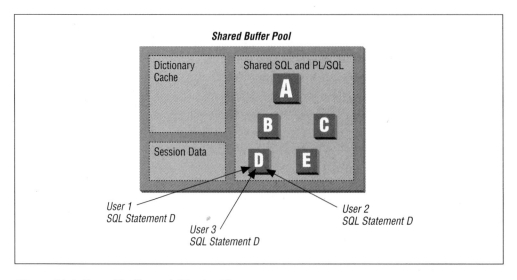

Figure 11-4: Shared buffer pool (Version 7)

Context areas

In Version 6, the PGA has a context area for each user process. In this area, the process holds the information it needs to process an SQL statement:

- The text of the SQL statement

- A translated SQL statement

- One row of the result and some intermediate values

- Cursor status information

- Control information used for sorting

The time required to parse an SQL statement is sometimes significant. If you tune your context areas carefully, you can reduce this time quite a bit by making sure statements are retained in memory after they are parsed the first time; this avoids the need to have to parse them again—a major time drain. You tune the context areas by setting the OPEN_CURSORS, CONTEXT_AREA, and CONTEXT_INCR parameters.

In Version 7, instead of having each process maintain its own context area, there is a single library cache (sometimes called the shared SQL area) in the shared buffer pool of the SGA. (Remember, this pool also contains dictionary information and some session information.) Figure 11-5 illustrates these context areas.

Dictionary cache

In Version 6, there is a separate dictionary cache in the SGA. This cache contains dictionary information on users, tables, indexes, storage information, and database security. To tune this area, you must set a number of dictionary parameters (the INIT.ORA parameters beginning with the DC_ prefix); for example, DC_FILES determines how many file descriptions can fit in the cache.

In Version 7, the dictionary cache is a part of the shared buffer pool. To tune the dictionary, you simply set the SHARED_POOL_SIZE large enough to accommodate dictionary information, as well as shared SQL statements and session information.

Dictionary tuning has a major effect on overall system performance. We have found in testing that poorly tuned dictionaries can result in as much as a 50% performance degradation in an ORACLE system. Chapter 14, *Tuning the Data Dictionary*, describes tuning for both Version 6 and Version 7.

Private SQL and PL/SQL areas

As we mentioned above, the library cache in Version 7 contains shared SQL statements. Included in this area are the parse tree and the execution plan for these statements.

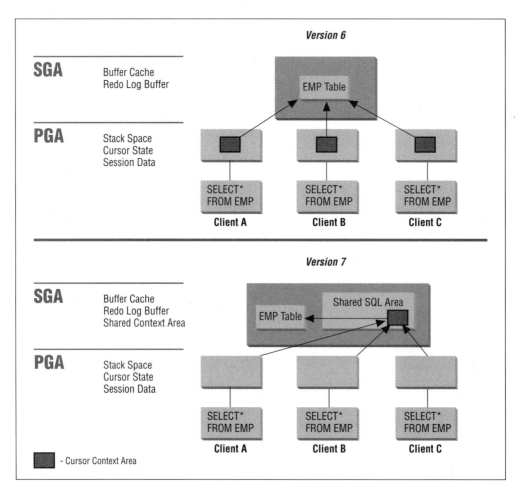

Figure 11-5: SQL context areas

Another separate area contains the bind variables and run time buffers associated with these statements for each user. In the following statement, :1 is a bind variable:

```
SELECT NAME FROM EMP
    WHERE ID = :1
```

The location of the private SQL area depends on whether you are running with the multi-threaded server available in Version 7. If you are, the private SQL area is in the shared buffer pool, along with the dictionary cache. If you are running with a dedicated server, this private area is in the user's own PGA. The number of private SQL areas that an individual user can process is determined by the OPEN_CURSORS parameter, which has a default of 50.

Memory Checklist

Here are some guidelines to help you optimize your memory performance. We'll expand on each of these points in the rest of this chapter:

- Memory access is tens of thousands or even hundreds of thousands times faster than disk access. ORACLE lets you bring items from disk into memory and cache them there for subsequent use. Memory caching saves a lot of disk access time. Make sure you take advantage of this facility to avoid unnecessary disk I/Os and slowdowns in performance.

- Memory is also used to buffer information that is being written to the database and redo logs. By enlarging such buffer areas as the redo log buffer, you will reduce the number of times data needs to be written. This will also significantly reduce the number of disk I/Os.

- Make sure you keep some free memory available (but not too much). Performance suffers drastically if you run out of memory. When additional processes request memory, your CPU will be forced to spend almost all of its cycles managing paging and swapping activities.

- Make sure you know how to use the memory monitoring commands provided by your operating system and use them regularly to ensure that you have free memory.

- If your operating system allows you to install the ORACLE executables as shared, take advantage of this facility. In this way, executables such as *iap30* (SQL*Forms), *dmu50* (SQL*Menu), and SQL*Plus will be stored once in memory and shared between many users, rather than requiring each user process to store its own copy. Unfortunately, many operating systems don't allow shared executables. Check your own system's *ORACLE Installation and Users Guide* to see if it offers the shared executable facility.

- If you are running in a client-server environment, be aware of your memory usage levels at both the client and the server ends. There are ways you can use your memory to reduce the number of packets being transferred across the network. See Chapter 16, *Tuning in the Client-server Environment.*

- Be aware of any memory usage by other ORACLE or non-ORACLE applications which may affect the level of free memory on your machine.

- If your users log on second and subsequent times running products like SQL*Forms Version 3, they are likely to use between one and three megabytes per logon. Make sure that you have planned for this when calculating free memory. If you are running ORACLE Version 7, you can control your users' use of memory by setting the INIT.ORA parameter, RESOURCE_LIMIT.

Setting INIT.ORA Memory Parameters

As we mentioned above, you control memory in your ORACLE database by assigning values to the memory parameters in the INIT.ORA file for your system. The location of this file varies, depending on the operating system you're using. Consult your *ORACLE Installation and Users Guide* for information. Make sure to read all README files as well, to check for any new INIT.ORA parameters or any changes to existing ones.

In some systems, there will be multiple INIT.ORA files; this allows different databases to have their own parameter settings. For example, *INITDEV.ORA* may control the developer database, *INITQA.ORA* the quality assurance database, and *INITPROD.ORA* the production database.

The section at the end of this chapter called "INIT.ORA Parameter Summary" lists all of the INIT.ORA parameters that affect memory tuning, along with default values and recommended values. In addition, there are a few operating system-specific parameters; for example, the SPIN_COUNT parameter applies only to UNIX systems. For information on these parameters, see Chapter 18, *Tuning for Specific Systems.* Don't set the INIT.ORA parameters lower than the defaults, or your database creation may fail. In the next chapter, we'll describe a few situations where you may be able to decrease the values of these parameters later on.

Tuning Disk I/O

You can improve performance a great deal by setting up your disks and your disk parameters carefully. Remember, though, your primary obligation is to set up your disk files in a way that guarantees database recovery. Performance comes second. There are two basic disk performance rules: keep disk I/Os to a minimum, and spread your disk load across disk devices and controllers (this will avoid contention, which is caused when disks operate above their maximum I/O rates per second).

Figure 11-6 shows the basic disk components in an ORACLE system. These are the same for both Version 6 and Version 7.

Disk I/O Checklist

Here are some guidelines to help you optimize your disk performance. We'll expand on these points in the rest of this chapter:

*   Don't allow developers to develop programs on the machine where the production database is running or to make large ad hoc queries against your production database. Programmers typically use many resource-intensive tools (e.g., SQL*Forms generation, linking user exits into RUNMENU and RUNFORM). They also have an

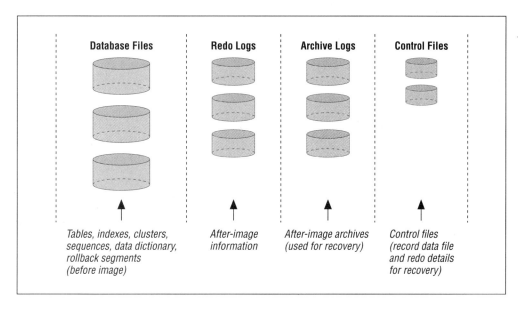

Figure 11-6: Disk components

unfortunate tendency to head straight to the production database and perform the dreaded full-table scans on tens of thousands, hundreds of thousands, or even millions of rows of data! Make sure the programmers at your site know that they must ask you to approve any access to the production database. Otherwise, chaos will reign.

- Don't allow quality assurance staff to test their programs on the machine that is running the production database. Untested programs may also be poorly tuned and may slow your production machine down by causing excessive disk I/Os.

- Know your applications, the tables and indexes defined for them, their usage patterns, and the amount of storage they will require. You'll need to get information from your analyst, designer, and/or user representatives. If the sizes of tables and index extents have not been computed correctly, performance will be seriously affected. A personal note here: we have never seen an ORACLE database in which the default sizes were adequate.

- Separate redo logs and the database files onto different drives. You should have three redo logs, each about five to ten megabytes in size. The availability of three redo logs allows your site to turn archiving on and ensure that the redo being written to the archive log will have time to be written before ORACLE needs to write more redo information to it. In general, five to ten megabytes is adequate to allow sites to operate efficiently, but you'll have to assess this estimate for your own site.

- Do not store any database files on the operating system disk. The operating system disk is normally heavily used for operating system functions such as hard page faulting and swapping.

- Make sure you have more than one control file, and that each one resides on a different disk device and disk controller.

- If you are running ORACLE Version 7, take advantage of multiplexed redo logs and store each redo log group on a different disk device.

- Make sure the archive logs reside either offline on tape or on a different disk from that used for any database file or redo log.

- If you are backing up database files from disk to disk, don't place your backup on the same disk as the one used to store the database file. Obvious, you say? We've seen a number of sites do this.

- If one of your tables has high insert, update, or delete activity, with many indexes continually being modified, consider splitting the indexes for the table onto different disks.

- Split tables and indexes into separate tablespaces. Because indexes and tables are often inserted into and read from simultaneously, splitting them minimizes disk head movement and allows concurrent access.

- Split commonly used tables into separate tablespaces (logical parts of the database). For example, if the users typically access the EMP and DEPT tables together, it may pay to separate EMP and DEPT into separate tablespaces. Also, mix frequently used indexes in the same tablespace as infrequently used ones to avoid constant demand on a particular tablespace.

- If your system has mixed transaction sizes, create one rollback segment for every four concurrent users (if you have up to 40 users) or every eight concurrent users (if you have up to 100 users). If all transactions are small, consider assigning one 10K rollback segment per user process to allow rollback segments to be stored in buffer cache. Most sites create a number of rollback tablespaces and use these exclusively for rollback segments.

- Create one or more separate tablespaces for temporary segments. All users must have this tablespace defined as their temporary tablespace. This tablespace must be at least the size of your largest table. It can be used to monitor temporary table activity (for example, to see if the size of the SORT_AREA_SIZE parameter is adequate) when your database is running.

- Make sure you have enough free space in your database to rebuild your largest table. You must also have enough free storage in your temporary tablespace to create your largest index.

- Spread your disk I/O load across as many disks and as many disk controllers as possible. Many medium-sized disks are preferable to a few very large files. A disk spread keeps one disk from getting overworked.

- Maintain the system tablespace as a separate tablespace of at least 20 megabytes. (Version 7 requires more system tablespace storage because it stores far more information.)

- Ensure that the space available on the disk where database files are to be placed is physically contiguous. You may have to ask your system administrator to do a disk reorganization before creating the database.

- Don't be rigid about where to put database files. Some sites have such inflexible standards that they can't get decent performance. We worked at one site that was experiencing disk I/O problems on all disks except one. That disk contained the system tablespace. Because a site standard stated that the system tablespace must reside on its own disk, everybody was suffering the consequences. Although standards are a good idea, sometimes they can unnecessarily restrict performance.

- If you are performing disk-to-disk-image backups of database files, do not allow the backup devices to contain only backed-up database files. You can use these devices more fruitfully.

Setting Disk Storage Parameters

When you create a table, index, tablespace, cluster, or rollback segment, you tell ORACLE how much disk space to allocate for it. With some database objects, such as tablespaces and clusters, you specify a STORAGE clause in the CREATE statement used to create the object—for example, in CREATE CLUSTER and CREATE TABLESPACE. You can change these via the various versions of the ALTER statement. With other objects, such as tables and indexes, you specify a number of distinct parameters in separate clauses of the CREATE statement; some of these parameters are identical to those available through the STORAGE clause.

Version 6 and Version 7 support somewhat different sets of parameters, as explained below. For either version, you might specify a STORAGE clause in the form:

```
CREATE TABLE . . .
   STORAGE (INITIAL 5M NEXT 1M MAXEXTENTS 110 MINEXTENTS 1 PCTINCREASE 0)
```

For Version 7, you can also specify values for OPTIMAL (rollback segments only) and FREELISTS (which replaces the Version 6 INIT.ORA parameter FREE_LIST_PROC) in this clause. The following list summarizes the STORAGE parameters; the sections that follow describe the specifics of using these parameters with particular data objects.

INITIAL

> Default: 10K
>
> Values: OS-dependent

> Size of the first extent (a contiguous piece of database storage) allocated to the object. Ideally the entire amount of data in the table or other object should fit in this extent. The default is 10K. The minimum size varies by object. For tables it is one ORACLE block; for indexes it is two ORACLE blocks.

NEXT

> Default: 10K
>
> Values: OS-dependent

> Size of the next extent to be allocated after the extent specified in INITIAL has been filled. Set the NEXT parameter to minimize the number of extents in the object while ensuring that there is enough space to create the extent.

PCTINCREASE

> Default: 50
>
> Values: 0 - 100

> Percentage by which the NEXT storage parameter is increased for the next extent. If you set this value to 0, every additional extent is the same as the value of NEXT. (Leaving it at the default causes each of the additional extents to be 50% larger than the previous one.) If your table is sized correctly, set the parameter to 0. Set it to 100 for fast-growing sorts because in this case disk extents may increase quickly.

> Be careful not to set this parameter indiscriminately. Think of how quickly the extent sizes can grow and how little of the last extent may actually be used.

> One particular site we visited complained that their database was now using one gigabyte more storage space than they had estimated. (They had planned that the 2.5 gigabytes they initially allocated would allow for 12 months' growth.) But now the conversion run was using all 2.5 gigabytes and was screaming for more as it crashed. It turned out that they had set PCTINCREASE to 50. When they carefully sized the tables and set PCTINCREASE to 0, they reduced the amount of storage needed to 1.5 gigabytes.

> You cannot set PCTINCREASE for rollback segments in Version 7.

MAXEXTENTS

> Default: OS-dependent
>
> Values: 1 - OS-dependent maximum

Maximum number of extents allowed for this object. Set this parameter to a few extents lower than the maximum allowable number of extents in your database. The particular value you can specify depends on your operating system and the size of its blocks. Each table extent must be recorded in the table header block. A 1K header block allows about 57 extents, 2K about 121 extents, 4K about 249 extents, and 8K about 505 extents.

The reason why we recommend that you specify a few less than the maximum extents is that it allows us the opportunity to allocate a NEXT extent of an optimal size to the table or index. If the table or index exceeds MAXEXTENTS, and MAXEX-TENTS equals the maximum allowable machine limit, you have no choice but to rebuild the table and all its indexes with a new storage allocation. This may take a long time if the table is extremely large and has many indexes. If the MAXEXTENTS parameter is several less than the maximum possible extents on your machine, you can find the largest free extent size available to you and resize your table dynami-cally using a statement like the following one:

```
ALTER TABLE ACCOUNT STORAGE (NEXT 5M);
```

Do not set MAXEXTENTS too low. Too often a long-running job fails because a DBA tried to cut the number of extents too close, and a minor miscalculation resulted in disaster.

NOTE

Version 7 will fail with an error if you specify a value higher than the maximum value for your machine.

MINEXTENTS
Default: 1 (for rollback segments, default is 2)
Values: 1 - OS-dependent maximum

Minimum extents allocated to the table. Leave this parameter at its default value unless the storage allocation is for a striped table, in which case MINEXTENTS must be equal to the number of files across which the table has been striped.

OPTIMAL
Default: Value of INITIAL + MINEXTENTS * NEXT
Values: Default value - OS-dependent maximum
Version: Version 7 only

Optimal size for a rollback segment. ORACLE will automatically shrink the segment back to this setting to maintain the optimal size after the segment has expanded beyond its specified optimal size. This parameter is usually left at its default.

FREELISTS

> Default: 1
>
> Values: 1 - block-dependent maximum
>
> Version: Version 7 only

> Number of free lists for each free list group. Free lists are lists of data blocks allocated for table or index extents. Increase this parameter if your programs are performing a lot of inserts. You should set FREELISTS to the number of concurrent inserts you would expect against your table.

FREELIST GROUPS

> Default: 1
>
> Values: 1 - block-dependent maximum
>
> Version: Version 7 only

> Number of groups of free lists. You set this parameter only if you are using the parallel server option (in parallel mode) for tables or clusters. FREELIST GROUPS allows each database instance to have its own specified number of free lists so multiple inserts can be performed. You cannot specify this parameter for indexes.

Creating the Database

You create a database with the CREATE DATABASE statement. In this statement you specify the files to be used for the database, the files to be used as redo log files, and a number of other options. Try to structure your database so it minimizes disk I/O by spreading I/O evenly across disk drives. The ideal database also can easily be monitored for I/O bottlenecks and easily changed if an I/O bottleneck does occur.

At many sites, the hardware configuration is dictated ahead of time; for example, you may be assigned three disks: one for the operating system and two for your own use. Other sites in which you have more control of the configuration may support many disks. At such sites, you can split the database across disks to get the best possible performance. In general, it is better to have many medium-sized disks rather than a few very large disks, because this type of configuration allows the database load to be shared across disks.

An ORACLE database may have one or more tablespaces, as described in the section below called "Creating Tablespaces."

How Many Data Files Should You Create?

Under normal circumstances, create one contiguous database file per tablespace. The tablespaces you choose must allow you to spread I/O across disks and to cope with all forms of transactions that may be run against the database. If a disk is overworked with excessive I/O, you will find it helpful to move the data files from disk to disk to share the load. (What is considered "excessive" depends on your hardware, but on most computers anything approaching 40 I/Os per second on a consistent basis is regarded as excessive.)

You can include the MAXDATAFILES parameter in the CREATE DATABASE statement to specify the maximum number of data files that your database can contain. Be aware, though, that there is a system-dependent limit (for example, Sequent DYNIX has a limit of 61) which overrides MAXDATAFILES and can cause serious problems, particularly on very large databases. Note the limit shown in your own system's *ORACLE Installation and User's Guide*, and configure your database accordingly.

What Should You Name Your Data File?

What has naming got to do with tuning, you ask? Obviously names are a site standard, but to be able to monitor file activity easily you must have names that indicate the type of file, the application, and the database the file belongs to. For example, *INDEX_ ACCT1_PROD.DBF* is an index (*INDEX*) accounting (*ACCT1*) file that is part of the production (*PROD*) database (*DBF*).

At one site we tuned, the DBA investigated an I/O problem, using the SQL*DBA MON FILE option to obtain information on the types of segments and the application encountering the problem. He found, to his dismay, that all of the files were named *FILE1.DBS*, *FILE2.DBS*, *FILE3.DBS*, etc. Very informative!

What Size Should You Make the Data File?

When you are figuring out the optimal size for your total database, be aware that there is more to an ORACLE database than just the data stored in tables. There is also the ORACLE data dictionary, the tables required to store ORACLE products like SQL*Forms, temporary tables used for sorting, and the indexes placed on tables.

Also keep in mind that even though you may have the physical disk capacity to hold your entire database, it may be on too few disks to provide satisfactory performance. An ORACLE database must be sized to allow the flexibility for future changes in case of poor performance. For example, you may need to add a new index, recreate a table to avoid a chaining problem, or move a tablespace to a different disk device.

You must also plan for growth. Some sites shortsightedly create databases that allow for only a few months of growth. When they suddenly run out of space, their tables and indexes have to expand onto small extents on non-contiguous parts of disk. Undersizing extent allocations often causes dynamic extension problems that can seriously affect performance.

How Many Redo Logs and What Size?

Redo log files are separate from the database itself, but are necessary to its operation. You must protect these files just as you protect the control files. If you lose or damage the redo log files, your only recourse will be to recover the database to its last full backup.

You specify the number of redo log files by setting the LOG_FILES parameter in the INIT.ORA file. The maximum value you can specify is the value of the MAXLOGFILES parameter in the CREATE DATABASE statement. As we've mentioned, you'll get the best performance if you create three redo logs, each between five and ten megabytes.

You must have a minimum of two redo log files to allow a database to operate. In this mode, the two files alternate as the current log file. As soon as the system finishes writing one file, it immediately starts writing to the next file. There is usually no advantage in having the two or three redo log files defined for your database each on separate disks. The system writes only to one file at a time, and only the current log file is needed for recovery. However, when you are running in archivelog mode and experiencing I/O bottlenecks on the redo log disk, you may benefit from placing alternate log files onto different disks so that when one file is being written and another is being archived, the two will be on different disks. You can check the LGWR trace file to see the log sequence.

The physical size of each log file is fixed at the time you create the file. The minimum size is 50K. You don't gain anything by setting redo log files to varying sizes because all log files are used in a cyclical fashion under system control; a transaction cannot select a particular log file.

There is an advantage to placing redo log files on the fastest disk drive available. Never locate a redo log file on the same disk as a database file. The current log file is always required for instance recovery. If a disk crash occurs, you must be able to access either the database or the redo file to be able to recover it. If your system does not have a spare physical disk to hold log files, they can be placed on the same disk as the index data files, but not the same as the actual data file. In this case, if you have ARCHIVE LOG enabled, we recommend that you archive to tape.

Often, the redo file disk will have more I/O activity than the data and index disks. Be sure to monitor the I/O rates on a per-file basis when the database is active. To get the information you need to figure out how to share the I/O load, double-check which files are performing what amount of activity.

In ORACLE Version 7, the multiplexed redo log facility allows the log writer process (LGWR) to enhance recovery by writing to multiple redo logs in different groups simultaneously, as shown in Figure 11-7. This feature is a great benefit, but it does pose some performance problems. The system writes heavily to the redo log files, and we recommend that each redo log file group be on a distinct disk. If you don't have enough disk devices, the next best thing is to put one redo log group on its own disk device and the other on the device that has the least amount of activity. In Figure 11-7, Redo1 file in Group A is written to at the same time as Redo1 in Group B.; Redo2 in Group A is written to at the same time as Redo2 in Group B, and so on.

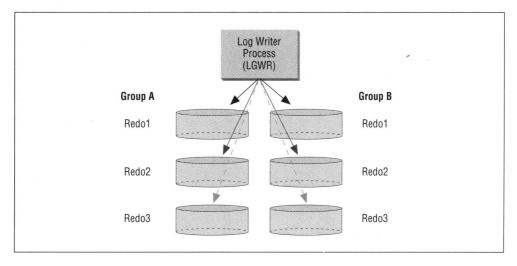

Figure 11-7: Multiplexed redo logs (Version 7)

Creating the Tablespaces

Tablespaces are logical divisions of the database. You create a tablespace with the CREATE TABLESPACE command. A tablespace may contain one or more database files, specified in the DATAFILE clause of the command. These files may reside on any disk drive. You can also specify default storage for the tablespace in the DEFAULT STORAGE clause. Your tables, indexes, the ORACLE data dictionary, and temporary segments will use this default if they don't have specific storage parameters assigned to them.

When you create a table, index, cluster, or rollback segment, it will be created in a tablespace. If you don't specify which tablespace should be used for an object, the system uses the default for the user who owns the object.

To structure tablespaces for best performance:

* Spread the I/O load across disk devices and controllers.

* Allow the monitoring of the use of various parts of the database.

- Apply default storage allocations to speed up certain database options.

- Take a particular application offline without affecting other applications.

- Reduce contention for database objects; for example, new rows can be inserted into the table while the indexes for the table use different tablespaces located on different disk devices.

- Provide logical data separation; for example, accounting data is separate from personnel data.

Do not let tablespaces exceed 500 megabytes unless absolutely necessary. We have seen performance drop on a number of minicomputer systems when files exceeded 500 megabytes. Larger files may also stop you from being able to move database files from one disk to another.

We recommend that, regardless of how many disks you now have available, you create your tablespaces as if your applications are running in an ideal, multi-disk environment. This allows you to monitor the load and spread it between tablespaces with the eventual aim of obtaining more disks and the knowledge of how to spread the database to optimize I/O.

Make sure that before you go into production, when your developers and testers are testing your applications, they give you all of the information they uncover about problems with the use of rollback segments, temporary segments, tables, indexes, and usage patterns of tables and indexes by the major programs in the applications. You can also get valuable information by monitoring disk usage while they test. This will help you figure out how best to place database objects in the various tablespaces.

Figure 11-8 shows a tablespace breakdown that will allow you to spread your I/O load and do performance monitoring.

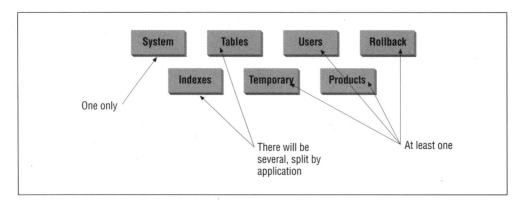

Figure 11-8: Recommended tablespaces

System Tablespace

When you create an ORACLE database, that database is initialized with a system tablespace. The system tablespace contains the ORACLE data dictionary, which holds information on tables, indexes, clusters, views, grants, synonyms, rollback segments, database files, tablespaces and their default storage parameters, valid users, and other information. The system tablespace is also the default home for all tables, indexes, rollback segments, and temporary tables that have not been explicitly directed to another tablespace. The only other information that you may store in the system tablespace is the small rollback segment that must exist before additional tablespaces can be added. Make sure you do not allow any of your database objects to be stored in the system tablespace. If you do, this will limit your option to move different components of your database from one disk to another in order to spread disk I/O evenly and to set variable default storage parameters from one tablespace to the next.

A system tablespace usually requires only a small percentage of the overall database storage requirements. You must ensure, however, that there is enough free space left for growth in the data dictionary and the deferred rollback segments. When you create the system tablespace, make sure it has about 75% free space. Give it a storage allocation of at least 20 megabytes for a medium- to large-size site running Version 6. Give it more if you are running Version 7, because Version 7 also stores procedures, functions, and stored triggers in the dictionary cache. For this reason, a Version 7 data dictionary needs a lot more space than a Version 6 dictionary. Typically, a medium- to large-size Version 6 site will need a data dictionary of 20 to 40 megabytes, and a similar Version 7 site will need a data dictionary of 40 to 60 megabytes. If ORACLE products such as SQL*Forms are going to be stored in the system tablespace (which is not recommended), make the system tablespace even larger.

A good policy is to not allow any database objects to be created in the system tablespace after its initial creation. You must remember to set all new users' default and temporary tablespaces to alternate tablespaces. If you don't, they will default to the system tablespace.

Table Tablespaces

Table tablespaces store tables and clusters. If you have a large database, you will probably have more than one such tablespace. Tables that are commonly used together should ideally be split across multiple tablespaces. For even better performance, place the tablespaces on separate disk devices. It is also a good idea to balance the load by storing some commonly accessed tables in the same tablespace as some of those less commonly accessed.

You can improve performance a lot by splitting application tables into separate table tablespaces. This allows the application to be taken offline by taking the tablespace offline. Tables that are shared between applications can be stored in a separate tablespace.

Index Tablespaces

An index tablespace contains the indexes defined for a table. Try to put the tablespace for a particular index on a different disk device from the one that holds that index's table.

Some sites create one index tablespace per application. As with table tablespaces, it is a good idea to put frequently used indexes in the same tablespace as some that are less frequently used. If one of your tables has a high rate of insertions, you might consider placing some of that table's indexes on one disk and the other indexes on a different tablespace on another disk device.

Temporary Tablespace

It is often handy to put temporary segments in their own separate tablespace. There are two main reasons for this: First, it lets you modify more easily the default table storage allocation so you can make sure that large, long-running jobs (for example, those that create indexes on very large tables) do not fail because they cannot acquire enough temporary segments. Second, it gives you a handy way to monitor the effectiveness of the SORT_AREA_SIZE parameter, which assigns memory to each user for sorting data. As we describe in the section in Chapter 13 called "Reducing Disk I/O by Increasing the Sort Area," ORACLE tries to sort in memory; however, if SORT_AREA_SIZE is not large enough, some sort activity has be moved to the temporary tablespace. By looking at the disk activity on the temporary tablespace, you will be able to figure out how much larger SORT_AREA_SIZE must be.

With tables, indexes, and rollback segments, you create tablespaces via the appropriate version of the CREATE command. You can't use this command for temporary tablespaces. The size of temporary segments depends entirely on the default storage setting you assign to the temporary tablespace using the command:

```
ALTER TABLESPACE temp-tspace DEFAULT [storage parameters]
```

Compute the most effective default storage size as follows:

1. Allocate one block for the segment header.

2. Add to that a size which is a multiple of the SORT_AREA_SIZE.

For example, if you have a DB_BLOCK_SIZE of 4K and a SORT_AREA_SIZE of 64K, you may set the INITIAL and NEXT extents of 64K + 4K = 68K, or 128K + 4K =132K, or any other multiple.

Some sites have two temporary tablespaces, one with small INITIAL and NEXT extent sizes for high volume online transaction processing users, and a second temporary tablespace for longer-running jobs requiring larger sort areas and thus larger INITIAL and NEXT extents. In Chapter 15, *Tuning Long-running Jobs*, the section called "Resizing Temporary Tables for Long-running Jobs," describes a procedure you can follow to define daytime and nighttime temporary tablespaces.

User Tablespaces

In some systems, your users can create their own tables. However, you may want to be able to monitor these tables to make sure performance won't suffer because users are creating an excessive number of tables. If you find that users are indiscriminately creating tables, and performance is suffering, separating this activity into a user tablespace gives you the option to move this activity to a separate database using an extract from the production database or to encourage users to do their work during non-peak hours.

GUI users often make ad hoc requests for application data. To accommodate such users you can create extract tables (which resemble spreadsheets) in overnight batch procedures and place them in the users' tablespaces. These extract tables eliminate the need for the GUI users to have a detailed understanding of complex data modes and avoids having to requery the same foundation tables over and over again. Placing extract tables in the user tablespaces also allows you to monitor all ad hoc GUI queries against your database.

Rollback Segment Tablespace

Because rollback segments usually have such a high level of activity, we recommend that you spread them across a number of disks and put them in separate tablespaces or stripe the rollback segment across the disk using a striped tablespace.

You can monitor rollback segment activity by means of the DBA monitoring screen you invoke via the SQL*DBA function:

```
SQLDBA> MON R
```

(See the discussion of MONITOR in the section in Chapter 12, *Diagnostic and Tuning Tools*, called "MONITOR: Monitoring System Activity Tables.")

If you make sure that rollbacks are put in their own tablespaces, you keep the rollback activity from interfering with the activity of the other tablespaces (for example, a tablespace containing tables that are being monitored).

A new Version 7 option, described in the section below called "Setting Rollback Segment Size," allows a rollback segment to expand as necessary and then to shrink back to an optimal size to save space. ORACLE Version 6 rollback segments cannot shrink back in size without dropping the rollback segment and recreating it. The dropping and recreating of rollback segments causes irregular free extent sizes which can cause problems as other segments need to expand. The irregular free extent sizes may force you to assign inappropriate storage allocations to tables and indexes if they share the same tablespace as rollbacks.

Products Tablespace

If you don't tell ORACLE where to place products such as SQL*Forms and SQL*Menu, the system will put them in the system tablespace. If you have not allocated enough space for these products, serious performance problems can occur. These problems will have an impact both on the programmers who are trying to generate programs using product tables and on QA staff and production users who are using products such as SQL*Menu. Sites that put their products in the system tablespace find themselves struggling for contiguous extents because product tables expand quickly.

For performance reasons, define a separate products tablespace, at least in the development database. Loading large SQL*Forms library forms, SQL*Reportwriter programs, and SQL*Menu menus can cause product tables and indexes to grow in size very quickly. It is quite common to see a table or index exceed the maximum number of extents. For best results, assign a storage allocation of INITAL 200K and NEXT 200K to the products tablespace.

If you want to move your products tables from the system tablespace, export them and rebuild them with new sizes that allow for growth. Then, re-import the product data on a regular basis to maintain acceptable performance.

Number of Database Files per Tablespace

Ideally, you should place each tablespace into a single data file, and make sure the data file is contiguous on the disk. The exception to this rule occurs when you are using table striping. With striping, you create a tablespace with a number of database files where each file is the same size and is placed onto a separate disk. You then create the table to be striped with its minimum number of extents set to the same number as the number of and size of database files. The table is assigned the tablespace containing the multiple files.

If you are forced to add a data file to a tablespace, try to add it to the same disk device as the disk that contains the original data file of the tablespace. The reason for this is that usually the major purpose of creating the tablespace is to spread I/O across disk devices. If the second data file is placed onto a different disk device, this will make it difficult to predict how much of the tablespace load will go onto each disk device. Placing your second data file onto a second disk device may be unavoidable because of the free space available. If several tablespaces contain data files that are spread across multiple disks, consider restructuring your database.

Setting Default Storage for Tablespaces

Before you assign storage allocations for your tablespaces via the DEFAULT STORAGE clause, make sure you understand extents: contiguous pieces of database storage that may contain data or may be free to be used by a table, index, or another object that needs more storage. When a tablespace is first created, it will have one extent which will be equal in size to the tablespace. Figure 11-9 illustrates how extents are used.

When a segment (e.g., a table) is dropped from the database, all its extents become available for other segments. Because this space is a multiple of all other segment storage sizes, when a smaller segment uses the space a usable fragment still remains.

If the minimum application storage size is set to 50K, all subsequent (larger) storage clauses should only be multiples of this base (e.g., 100K, 500K, 750K, 10M, 20M). This prevents the creation of smaller, useless fragments of database storage that cannot be utilized until the database is rebuilt.

Setting default storage parameters

There is no need to assign storage parameters individually on very small tables. Simply leave them with the default storage settings if they have been created appropriately at the tablespace level. All table, system, user, and index tablespaces should have the following default:

```
STORAGE    (INITIAL    10K
            NEXT       10K
            MINEXTENTS  1
            MAXEXTENTS  121
            PCTINCREASE  0 )
```

Version 6 DBAs often assign a MAXEXTENTS size of 999 to avoid having to size more exactly. Unfortunately, Version 7 does not allow you to exceed the maximum possible extents on your machine. If you have a DB_BLOCK_SIZE of 2K, you will have 121

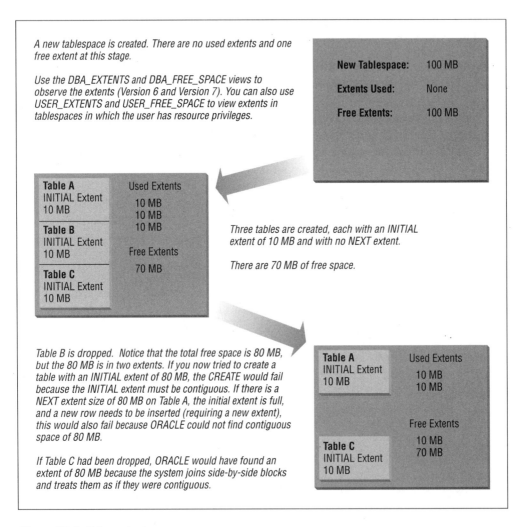

A new tablespace is created. There are no used extents and one free extent at this stage.

Use the DBA_EXTENTS and DBA_FREE_SPACE views to observe the extents (Version 6 and Version 7). You can also use USER_EXTENTS and USER_FREE_SPACE to view extents in tablespaces in which the user has resource privileges.

New Tablespace:	100 MB
Extents Used:	None
Free Extents:	100 MB

Table A INITIAL Extent 10 MB	Used Extents
	10 MB
	10 MB
Table B INITIAL Extent 10 MB	10 MB
	Free Extents
	70 MB
Table C INITIAL Extent 10 MB	

Three tables are created, each with an INITIAL extent of 10 MB and with no NEXT extent.

There are 70 MB of free space.

Table B is dropped. Notice that the total free space is 80 MB, but the 80 MB is in two extents. If you now tried to create a table with an INITIAL extent of 80 MB, the CREATE would fail because the INITIAL extent must be contiguous. If there is a NEXT extent size of 80 MB on Table A, the initial extent is full, and a new row needs to be inserted (requiring a new extent), this would also fail because ORACLE could not find contiguous space of 80 MB.

If Table C had been dropped, ORACLE would have found an extent of 80 MB because the system joins side-by-side blocks and treats them as if they were contiguous.

Table A INITIAL Extent 10 MB	Used Extents
	10 MB
	10 MB
	Free Extents
Table C INITIAL Extent 10 MB	10 MB
	70 MB

Figure 11-9: Using extents

maximum extents, whereas if your machine has a 4K block size, you will have 249 maximum extents.

Set your temporary tablespace default storage parameters as a multiple of the SORT_ AREA_SIZE parameter plus one block for the online transaction processing. If your block size is 4K and your sort area size is 64K, you may specify:

```
4K + (64K * 4) = 260K
```

as both your INITIAL and NEXT extents. With this size, the block is used for the segment header and the multiple of the SORT_AREA_SIZE because this allows a resource-efficient transfer of the sort area memory buffer to the temporary segment. Some sites set the PCTINCREASE to 100, which doubles the size of each NEXT extent.

To help prevent database fragmentation, make sure all segment storage classes have a common denominator. INITIAL extent and NEXT extent values must all be divisible by this denominator.

Setting PCTINCREASE

By setting the PCTINCREASE STORAGE parameter to 0% or 100%, you can prevent accidentally generating storage extents that are not a multiple of the application base. In Figure 11-10 the INITIAL extent is one megabyte, as is the first NEXT extent. Because PCTINCREASE has been set to 50%, each additional NEXT extent will be 50% larger than the previous one.

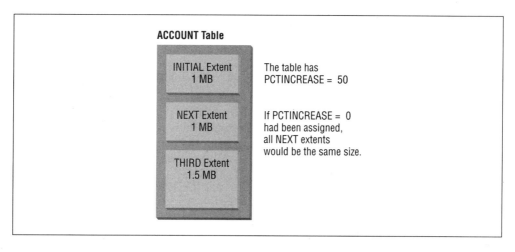

Figure 11-10: Adjusting the PCTINCREASE variable

To appreciate why a PCTINCREASE of 50 is so dangerous, look at the following figures in the following table. Assume that we have a table that has an INITIAL extent of five megabytes and a NEXT extent of one megabyte. Note that Version 7 rounds each NEXT extent up to the nearest five blocks.

Extent	Megabytes
Extent 1	5
Extent 2	1
Extent 3	1.5
Extent 4	2.25
Extent 5	3.37

Extent	Megabytes
Extent 6	5
Extent 7	7.5
Extent 8	11.2
Extent 9	16.8
Extent 10	25.2
Extent 11	37.7
Extent 12	55.7
Extent 13	83.5
Extent 14	125.2

Leaving PCTINCREASE at its default of 50 can be very dangerous. If you add one row of data after the 13th extent, you will require more than 125 megabytes of contiguous extent space. There is a very strong possibility that a contiguous extent of 125 megabytes will not be available. This will produce an ORACLE error message and will disallow the extension. It's also a huge waste of database space.

Segment extents are issued from the free extent list according to a first-fit algorithm. The first free space block large enough to accommodate the extent requirement is used, and any unused portion of the block is returned to the free space list. If a free block cannot be located, a second pass of the free list is made, attempting to join side-by-side blocks into a single extent. Having all database extents as a multiple of the common denominator means joining free blocks to prevent generating useless fragments.

Creating Rollback Segments

Rollback segments enforce read consistency within your database. They store data as it existed before an update. This data can be used to restore the database to a consistent state, as it was at an earlier point in time. If you are changing data and decide, in midstream, that you don't want to commit the changes after all, rollbacks give you a way to "roll back" the changes and return the data to its original form. If other users want to read the data you are in the midst of changing, rollbacks give them a way of reading the data as it was prior to the changes.

You create a rollback segment with the CREATE ROLLBACK SEGMENT statement. You specify the size allocation for a rollback segment in the STORAGE clause of the statement. You can subsequently modify a rollback statement with the ALTER ROLLBACK SEGMENT and DROP ROLLBACK SEGMENT statements. ORACLE also provides public rollback segments which are designed to be used for shared disk systems—those in which multiple instances access one database. Public rollback segments are created, altered, and dropped by adding the word PUBLIC after the CREATE, ALTER, and DROP keywords; for example:

```
CREATE PUBLIC ROLLBACK SEGMENT
```

Rollback segments exist inside database files assigned to a tablespace. If you incorrectly structure your rollbacks, you can seriously degrade the performance of your system by causing excessive disk I/Os or by allowing user transactions to suffer contention for roll-back segment headers. Rollbacks are very I/O-intensive in databases where a lot of data changes occur. If this I/O is not distributed evenly across disk devices, there is potential for I/O bottlenecks. Contention for rollbacks occurs because every time writes are made to a rollback segment, the rollback header segment is locked. The header is freed after the write is completed. This contention is avoided by having sufficient rollback segments.

Rollback segments are the most difficult storage components to understand and tune. Figure 11-11 shows a single rollback segment that may have one or many transactions writing to it. When a transaction makes a change to data, all of the before-image data must be written into the rollback extents. In the figure, if there is insufficient space in the four existing extents, another extent is allocated to the rollback. This now becomes part of the rollback ring that ORACLE will loop around and use for future changes. In Version 6, once additional extents are assigned, they can't be removed without drop-ping and recreating the rollback. In Version 7, it is possible to set the optimal size for the rollback to shrink back to. To force the rollback to shrink back to its original four extents, specify an OPTIMAL 40K clause in the CREATE ROLLBACK statement.

There are some important improvements to rollback segment handling in ORACLE Version 7. In Version 6, if you want to restore a rollback segment back to its original size, you have to perform a frustrating series of steps:

1. Shut down the database

2. Edit the ORA.INIT file to exclude one of the rollbacks

3. Restart the database

4. Drop the offending rollback

5. Recreate the rollback

6. Shut down the database again

7. Adjust the INIT.ORA file to re-include the rollback segment

8. Restart the database

Version 7, by contrast, offers an automated way to change the storage of a rollback segment dynamically, or take the rollback offline, and then shrink the rollback back to its optimal size after expanding it temporarily.

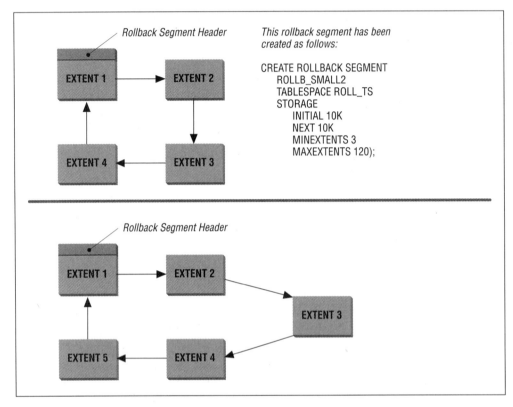

Figure 11-11: Using rollback segments

To structure your rollback segments correctly, you must perform some background research on the number and types of transactions performed at your site. You must know the number of concurrent ORACLE transactions and the type of transaction (online transaction with short, sharp updates or larger, long-running updates or queries).

You must be flexible in your choice of rollback segments. If your site has one type of transaction during prime daily working hours, and another type of transaction for overnight jobs, you may use smaller rollback segments for daily processing and enlarged rollback segments for overnight processing.

We recommend that you place the rollback segments into one or more tablespaces set up specifically for rollback segments.

Be aware that:

- One rollback is created automatically in the system tablespace when the database is first created.

- You must have at least one non-system segment, as well as the system rollback segment which is created at the time of database creation to add additional tablespaces.

- In Version 6 the rollback cannot shrink back as it can in Version 7. In Version 6, if the rollback grows to a huge size, it will stay huge until it is dropped and recreated to its original size.

- Every rollback segment created must have at least two extents.

- Transactions cannot write to multiple rollback segments at once.

- A transaction can write to only one extent at any given time.

- The maximum number of transactions that may simultaneously access a rollback segment is set by the INIT.ORA parameter, TRANSACTIONS_PER_ROLLBACK, which we recommend you leave at the default value.

- In Version 6.0.33 and later, you can specify the rollback segment you wish to use in a transaction by issuing the SET TRANSACTION USE ROLLBACK statement. Take advantage of this but be aware of its limitations. The SET TRANSACTION USE ROLL-BACK statement must be the first statement issued after connecting to ORACLE or immediately following a ROLLBACK or COMMIT statement. If you connect as another user, perform a rollback, or perform a commit, you will have to re-issue the command.

- ORACLE will share rollback segments among the various transactions if you don't specifically assign the transaction to a rollback segment.

How Many Rollback Segments?

As the amount of data being modified in a table increases, the amount of rollback space required increases proportionately. There must be enough space in your tablespace to store your rollback segment data.

The number of rollback segments must be large enough to eliminate contention for rollback segment usage. When you are figuring out how many rollback segments you need, take into account the number of active transactions, the type of transactions, and the transactions per rollback segment.

The maximum transactions that may share a rollback segment is set by the parameter TRANSACTIONS_PER_ROLLBACK. If you have 20 rollback segments and 20 transactions, ORACLE will usually use all 20 rollbacks, assigning one transaction to each rollback. A reasonable rule of thumb is one rollback segment per four transactions for online transaction processing. Although this recommendation provides acceptable performance, for some sites you may want to allocate more. Our tests have shown minor improvements in response times of 5% to 10% when we allocated one rollback segment of 10K to all transactions. Where the transactions are all online transaction processing performing small numbers of database updates, smaller rollback segments increase the chance that a particular rollback is available in the buffer cache in the SGA.

Creating a large number of rollback segments carries an administrative overhead. If you have a large number of small rollback segments (e.g., 10K), ORACLE warns that long-running queries, such as online reports that may run for several minutes, may experience problems if transactions frequently update records required by the query. The message, "SNAPSHOT IS TOO OLD," is displayed because all queries must obtain the data as it was when the query started.

Consider the following example: suppose that a change has been made to a large table which is currently being queried on, and the change has been committed. Committed changes are no longer required and can be overwritten in the rollback segment. Many other updates have also occurred using the same rollback segment. Eventually, the extent that contained the data as it was before the committed change is overwritten by another transaction requiring rollback space in the rollback ring. The query can't obtain the data for the long-running query, as it existed when the query started, and the query fails and must be rerun.

We have discovered that sites that perform large numbers of updates get considerably better performance (often improvements of more than 20%) when they assign larger rollback segments. We recommend that you use fewer, larger rollback segments for overnight processing because such overnight jobs are more likely to contain long-running updates which will speed up considerably by avoiding dynamic extension.

If you are using Version 6.0.33 or later, and your mix of jobs includes a few long-running jobs and many smaller transactions, you will get better performance if you have one or more larger rollbacks, as shown in Figure 11-12. Figure out how large the rollback segment needs to be by looking at the results of QA testing. You can specify the SET TRANSACTION USE ROLLBACK SEGMENT command to set at least one rollback segment to the largest size taken from the production simulation. If you use this statement consistently for all long-running jobs, you will avoid the chance that larger transactions will use rollbacks that are too small and thus need many extents, which would result in bad performance. By using this version of the SET TRANSACTION statement, you will effectively assign the larger transactions to the larger rollbacks. The smaller transactions will then have a high probability of running against the smaller rollbacks. For smaller rollback segments, assign 10K or something similar to increase the possibility that these segments will be able to be held in cache.

Rollback segment usage can be extremely high at some sites. At such sites, some DBAs prefer to place the rollbacks into one or two separate tablespaces. Others prefer to place the rollbacks into other tablespaces, such as those set up to store tables.

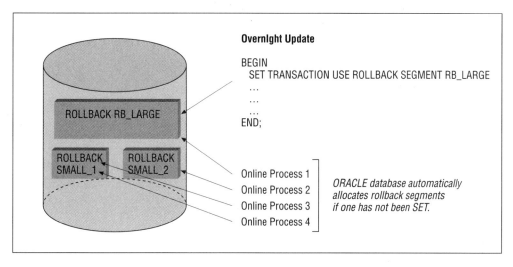

Figure 11-12: Rollback segment for overnight jobs

Remember, from a performance point of view your main goals are to spread I/O evenly across disk drives, avoid dynamic extension, and eliminate contention for rollback segments. You can check to see how effective your rollbacks are by examining the disk I/Os on the tablespaces and disk devices that contain rollback segments. Looking for excessive I/O and the "buffer busy waits" statistic lets you detect rollback contention.

Setting Rollback Segment Size

Picking the right size for your rollback segments can have an important effect on performance. You'll reduce dynamic extension and increase the chances that rollbacks will be stored in the buffer cache when needed.

To specify the size of your rollback segments, use the same STORAGE parameters you use for any other data object. For Version 6, specify a statement such as the following:

```
CREATE ROLLBACK SEGMENT ROLB_ONIGHT
    TABLESPACE ROLB_TSPACE
    STORAGE (INITIAL      5M
             NEXT         5M
             MINEXTENTS   4
             MAXEXTENTS   121
             PCTINCREASE  0)
```

Be sure to keep PCTINCREASE at 0 to allow for increases in rollback segment sizes. In the example above, MINEXTENTS 4 indicates that the rollback is to be created with 4 * 5 megabytes per extent, or a total of 20 megabytes. This is a typical setting for four transactions.

If you are running Version 7, note the following differences from Version 6:

- The PCTINCREASE parameter is not allowed for rollback segments. ORACLE effectively forces a PCTINCREASE value of 0.

- The MAXEXTENTS parameter may not exceed the total possible on your machine. For example, if your DB_BLOCK_SIZE is 2K, you will have a MAXENTENTS of 121. Version 7 will not allow you to exceed this number.

- There is a new parameter called OPTIMAL. This specifies the size that the rollback will shrink back to after it has expanded beyond its specified optimal size. In the example above, the ideal optimal size is 20 megabytes, which is the value you'd get by multiplying MINEXTENTS * extents.

For example, you might specify:

```
CREATE ROLLBACK SEGMENT ROLB_ONIGHT
    TABLESPACE ROLB_TSPACE
    STORAGE (INITIAL      5M
             NEXT         5M
             MINEXTENTS   4
             MAXEXTENTS   121
             OPTIMAL      40M)
```

If the database you are creating is a production database, and you're loading an application that has been tested in a QA environment containing a reasonable amount of data, try running a transaction mix that is similar to the one the application will use in production, and note the rollback segment sizes. If you are running a version of ORACLE prior to Version 6.0.33, use the largest size from the run in the QA environment to size all of your rollback segments. This ensures that the rollback segments will be able to provide satisfactory performance regardless of the rollback selected. It also means, however, that you may be wasting database space on rollbacks.

If your application is an online transaction processing system with only small transactions, keep your rollback segments 10K in size, to increase the chances that they will be able to be stored in cache. If the rollbacks are small, it is common to have one rollback segment per transaction. If you have long-running queries that are querying large amounts of data that are being changed, you may get the error "SNAPSHOT TOO OLD."

Like other segments, rollback segments must be able to acquire enough space to hold their data. From an application perspective, if many extents are required to place the data, serious performance problems will result. Be sure that you set INITIAL and NEXT parameters high enough to reduce the number of extents. Set MAXEXTENTS high enough to ensure that that rollback segments do not exceed the maximum extents.

Rollback Checklist

The following list summarizes the main guidelines to follow when creating rollback segments:

- Use large rollbacks for long-running updates.

- Use small rollbacks for online transaction processing systems.

- Do not have too many transactions per rollback segment because this significantly increases the chance of rollback segment header contention.

- As a rule of thumb, assume four concurrent transactions per rollback for acceptable performance.

- If you are using a version of ORACLE prior to 6.0.33, set all of your rollback transactions to be the size you expect as your largest transaction. It is better to have all rollback segments set to the same size.

- If you are using Version 6.0.33 of ORACLE or later, use the SET TRANSACTION USE ROLLBACK SEGMENT statement to assign users to large rollback segments for all long-running updates. Keep all other rollback segments small to increase their chances of being held in buffer cache.

- If you are using ORACLE Version 7, take advantage of the OPTIMAL option in the STORAGE clause that allows rollbacks to shrink back in size.

- Be aware that PCTINCREASE is no longer a valid parameter in Version 7. Make sure the value is always 0 if you are using Version 6.

- Never set MAXEXTENTS higher than your maximum allowable. Version 7 will report an error if the amount is exceeded.

Creating Tables

Setting appropriate sizes for your tables boosts performance in your system. If you don't allocate enough space for a table, ORACLE will be forced to perform dynamic extension on your tables (i.e., allocate more space for them during processing). Dynamic extension, described in the section below called "Reducing Dynamic Extension," has an extremely bad effect on performance.

You create a table with the CREATE TABLE statement. In this statement, you specify a size allocation in a series of parameter clauses, described below. You can associate a table with a tablespace via the TABLESPACE clause. You can later modify a table via the ALTER TABLE statement or by dropping the table via DROP and then recreating it. Note that the INITIAL extent size and the tablespace assigned to the table cannot be changed via the ALTER command. To change these, you must drop and recreate the table.

Specifying the Tablespace

When you create a table, you can specify its tablespace in the TABLESPACE clause of the CREATE TABLE statement. If tables are frequently joined during processing (e.g., EMP and DEPT), separating these tables into separate tablespaces on different disks will usually improve performance, especially if the tablespaces can be placed onto separate devices. Place all of your tables into a dedicated table tablespace (that is, a tablespace that is used only for table storage).

Calculating the Size of the Table

If at all possible, size your tables so each table fits into one contiguous extent, with no chaining. (Figure 2-7 in Chapter 2, *What Causes Performance Problems?*, shows an example of chaining.) Be sure to set up the table so it can grow over time and still fit in the single extent. A rule of thumb is to allow for 12 months' growth, but be prepared to rebuild the table every nine months or so.

To be able to allocate the proper size for a table, you must know the following: how many rows the table will contain when the database is first created, how much the rows will expand after the row has been created, and the expected growth in number of rows over the next year. Try to estimate as well how many rows are likely to be deleted from the table. By looking at the results of QA testing at your site, you should be able to get a more precise estimate of how quickly a row is likely to grow. Find out the length of the rows when first created and after processsing. For example, if a row grows in length by 40%, on average, make sure you set the PCTFREE parameter on the table to 50% to avoid chaining.

Here is a simple example of a row analysis. Assume that the APPLICATION table has four columns:

```
APPLIC_ID        NUMBER(6)
CATEGORY         CHAR(10)
CHANGED_DATE     DATE
DESCR_LINE       CHAR(80)
```

When the row was first inserted, it had all this information except for DESCR_LINE. This line is always filled in, but only after the initial insertion of the row. To obtain the length of the rows before and after the DESCR_LINE update, perform this query to calculate the average row length:

```
SELECT AVG ((NVL(VSIZE(APPLIC_ID),0)+1)
    +   (NVL(VSIZE(CATEGORY),0)+1
    +   (NVL(VSIZE(CHANGED_DATE),0)+1)
    +   (NVL(VSIZE(DESCR_LINE),0)+1)) +5
    FROM APPLICATION;
```

Ideally the table will contain only the rows that have been updated with the query being run once before the update to the DESCR_LINE column and then after the update.

In the CREATE TABLE statement, you can specify the following storage parameters. You can also specify a STORAGE clause to set the same values available to other data objects (e.g., INITIAL, NEXT, MINEXTENTS, MAXEXTENTS).

INITRANS

> Default: 1 for tables, 2 for indexes
>
> Values: 1 - 255
>
> Initial number of transactions that can simultaneously update a block of data. Increase the default value if many transactions are likely to be accessing a single block in the table. Each transaction has 23 bytes reserved for it.

MAXTRANS

> Default: OS-dependent
>
> Values: 1 - OS-dependent maximum
>
> Maximum number of transactions that can simultaneously update a block of data. There is no performance advantage to changing this default.

PCTFREE

> Default: 10
>
> Values: 0 - 99
>
> Percentage of space ORACLE will leave in the current block when inserting a row into a table. PCTFREE + PCTUSED must not exceed 100.

PCTUSED

> Default: 40
>
> Values: 0 - 99
>
> Percentage minimum of available space in a block that has to be reached before ORACLE can start inserting rows into it again. PCTFREE + PCTUSED must not exceed 100.

Determining INITIAL

In a perfectly-tuned system, the initial extents allocated for a table (specified in the INITAL parameter in the STORAGE clause) will contain all of a table's data (unless striping is being performed). To work out the size of the INITIAL extent, you will need to determine the number of rows the table will contain and its likely growth rate over the next 12 months.

Use the following formula to determine the INITIAL value:

$$\text{Size(bytes)} = \text{blocksize} \times \frac{(\text{rows in 12 months} \times \text{average row length})}{(\text{blocksize} - 90) \times (1 - \text{PCTFREE}/100)}$$

In this calculation, "average row length" is the average row length from the previous calculation. Notice that each block has an overhead of 90 bytes.

Determining PCTFREE

PCTFREE is the percentage of the block that must be left free when rows are being inserted into a table. This free space is set aside for future row expansion. DBAs too often neglect to set an appropriate value for PCTFREE.

If you set a high value for PCTFREE, more physical reads will be required if full-table scans are made on the table. A low PCTFREE may cause chaining; that is, a single row may span several physical blocks. In general it is best to avoid chaining at all costs. Some sites modify PCTFREE to a low value when they do a reorganization of the table and change PCTFREE back to a larger value after the table has been rebuilt. This method can be used to minimize storage and avoid chaining at the same time. There are fewer physical blocks in the table for ORACLE to read because every block that has a PCTFREE specified above 0 has to reserve that amount of free space for row expansion.

Chapter 15 describes a chaining situation. In one example an update involving 8000 rows with a chained table took 58.82 seconds to complete processing. On the other hand, a table with an appropriately sized PCTFREE, and therefore no chaining, took 27.24 seconds. Queries of chained rows take approximately twice the time it takes to query unchained rows.

When a table grows, each column it grows by requires one byte of overhead; each row requires five bytes of overhead. By looking at the average length before and after the update, you'll determine the percentage by which the rows are going to increase. This supplies a value for PCTFREE. For example, growing from an average of 30 characters to an average of 100 characters indicates a growth rate of 70% . Set PCTFREE as follows:

$$\text{growth rate} = \frac{\text{end row length} - \text{start length}}{\text{end row length}} \times 100$$

where:

end row length	is 100 in the above example or the length of the row after the update.
start length	is the length of the row when it is first inserted.

Determining PCTUSED

The previous section showed how to select a value for PCTFREE that reduces the possibility of chaining. Most applications will perform optimally with a PCTFREE set high enough to avoid all chaining, but there are some exceptions. One exception occurs when there are many full-table scans against the table and very few updates or indexed lookups of individual rows. There are fewer physical blocks in the table for ORACLE to read because every block that has a PCTFREE specified above 0 has to reserve that amount of free space for row expansion.

The PCTUSED value you specify can also have an impact on performance. PCTFREE is reserved for row expansion, whereas PCTUSED attempts to keep the PCTUSED percentage of the block filled with data. If the percentage used in the block falls below the PCTUSED value, ORACLE is informed that there is free space and new rows may be added. A high PCTUSED indicates that the data will be stored very efficiently in terms of space usage, but the likelihood of chaining is increased.

Note that the sum of PCTFREE + PCTUSED cannot exceed 100.

Determining INITRANS and MAXTRANS

The INITRANS and MAXTRANS parameters specified at the time of table creation control the number of transactions able to access a block. INITRANS specifies the minimum number of concurrent transactions per block for which space is reserved. MAXTRANS is the maximum number of transactions that a block will support. Each entry for a transaction that is currently accessing a block uses about 23 bytes of free space. The INITRANS parameter is set at 1 and should be increased to the number of transactions that will be accessing a single block in the table simultaneously.

Determining FREE_LIST_PROC or FREELISTS

If a table is likely to have a large number of insertions from many simultaneous processes, check the value of FREE_LIST_PROC (an INIT.ORA parameter in Version 6) or FREELISTS (an option in the STORAGE clause in Version 6.0.36 and later in Version 7) . A free list is a list of data blocks in a table that contain free space. This list is checked before inserting new rows. We recommend that you set the free lists to the number of transactions that will be simultaneously inserting into your table. Ideally, set free lists for each table that has a high number of inserts.

A value of 6 for FREE_LIST_PROC is adequate for most applications, but you may consider a value as high as 32 (the maximum allowable) if a table has a massive number of simultaneous inserts. The FREE_LIST_PROC parameter can be applied at the time of table creation and cannot be modified without rebuilding the table. If you shut down ORACLE, specify a new value for FREE_LIST_PROC, and then restart ORACLE, the new value will take effect for all tables subsequently created.

In Version 7, you specify the FREELISTS parameter in the STORAGE clause in place of FREE_LIST_PROC. If you experience free list contention, you will have to rebuild your table using an increased FREELISTS parameter. This can be very time consuming on a large table with several indexes. We recommend that you make every effort to put the appropriate FREELISTS parameter in place at the time you create the table.

Reducing Dynamic Extension

Dynamic extension is the process of acquiring more disk space for tables and indexes that have not been allocated enough to begin with. When you first create a database object such as a table or an index, ORACLE determines the size to be allocated by looking for a STORAGE clause in the CREATE command or by assigning a default allocation from the tablespace in which the object is created. When the INITIAL extent size is exceeded for that object, ORACLE must dynamically create an extent based on the NEXT parameter in the STORAGE clause. This creation of additional extents is referred to as dynamic extension.

In almost all cases, you'll get far better performance if the disk allocation for a table or any other object is in one contiguous extent. With one large extent available, ORACLE is able to read a large amount of data from disk in a single multi-block read with less disk movement.

If a table consists of many discontiguous areas of data scattered across the disk, ORACLE is forced to scan all of these areas, as well as having to access the table segment header before obtaining each extent. The database functions that suffer the most from discontiguous extents are full-table scans, table drops, deletes of many rows from tables, and inserts of many rows into tables.

Be sure to think carefully when you first create your database about how big your tables and indexes are likely to be, and assign storage parameters that allow for enough contiguous space, and as few extents, as possible. Figure 11-13 shows the way a table can be distributed around the disk when dynamic extension occurs.

Dynamic extension is a particularly serious problem with long-running jobs, as described in Chapter 15. Consider the following example of how much more quickly an operation can be performed on a contiguous, rather than a fragmented, table:

Operation	Contiguous	Fragmented
Inserting 4000 rows	.76 seconds	3.62 seconds
Dropping the table	5.29 seconds	1 minute, 31 seconds

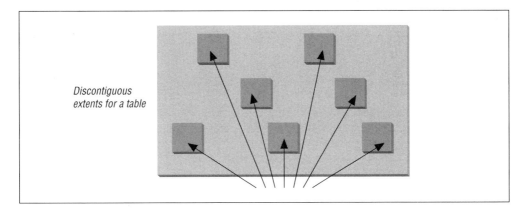

Figure 11-13: Dynamic extension

The section in Chapter 13 called "Reducing Dynamic Extension" describes how you can monitor activity in an existing database to detect dynamic extension, and how you can tune your database to avoid dynamic extension as much as possible.

Creating Indexes

As we've discussed in earlier chapters, specifying the appropriate indexes over columns in your tables can greatly increase performance in your system. You create an index and allocate its size with the CREATE INDEX statement.

Specifying the Index Tablespace

Place all indexes in tablespaces that are dedicated to use by indexes. If possible, place index tablespaces on their own disk drive or, at the very least, on a different drive from the one used by the corresponding table tablespace.

Calculating the Size of an Index

Sizing indexes, like sizing tables, requires knowledge of the number of rows in the table (with growth for the next 12 months allowed) and the average length of the columns. The following calculation determines the size of the index, assuming that the APPLICA-TION table is being indexed on the APPLIC_ID and CATEGORY columns:

```
SELECT AVG((NVL(VSIZE(APPLIC_ID),0)+1)
    + (NVL(VSIZE(CATEGORY),0)+1))
    FROM APPLICATION;
```

This calculation gives the average length in bytes of the indexed columns:

$$\text{leaf size} = \text{Bsize} \times \frac{(\text{rows in 12 months}) \times (11 + \text{average row length})}{(\text{Bsize} - 90) \times (1 - \text{PCTFREE}/100)}$$

where:

Bsize   is the block size set in the INIT.ORA file.

index size   approximately equals leaf size * 1.1.

1.1   is the overhead for storing the branch blocks.

This is the value that should be assigned to the INITIAL extent of the index. As with tables, make every attempt to store the index in one physical extent.

You can also use the VALIDATE INDEX command to determine the size of the index, particularly when you are sizing a production database and have a test database at your disposal that contains sound information that could be used for sizing. This command places index information into a table called INDEX_STATS. For Version 6 or Version 7, specify:

```
VALIDATE INDEX index_name;
```

For Version 7, you can use the ANALYZE command described in Chapter 12. Specify:

```
ANALYZE INDEX index_name
    VALIDATE STRUCTURE;
```

To obtain information on the index, select from the view INDEX_STATS containing the following definitions:

INDEX_STATS Statistic	Description
HEIGHT	Height of B-tree
BLOCKS	Blocks allocated to the index
NAME	The name of the index
LF_ROWS	Number of leaf rows
LF_BLKS	Number of leaf blocks in the B-tree
LF_ROWS_LEN	Sum of the lengths of all leaf rows
LF_BLK_LEN	Usable space in leaf block
BR_ROWS	Number of branch rows
BR_BLKS	Number of branch blocks in the B-tree
BR_ROWS_LEN	Sum of lengths of all branch rows
BR_BLK_LEN	Sum of lengths of all branch blocks
DEL_LF_ROWS	Number of deleted leaf rows in the index

INDEX_STATS Statistic	Description
DEL_LF_ROWS_LEN	Total length of all deleted rows in the index
DISTINCT_KEYS	Number of distinct keys in the index
MOST_REPEATED_KEY	How many times most repeated key is repeated
BTREE_SPACE	Total space allocated to B-tree
USED_SPACE	Total space currently used
PCT_USED	Percent of space allocated being used
ROWS_PER_KEY	Average rows per distinct key
BLKS_GETS_PER_ACCESS	When a row is searched for, using the index, the number of blocks read to satisfy that search

Two columns of particular interest in this view are the HEIGHT and DEL_LF_ROWS columns. If either of these figures become too large, (that is, if HEIGHT is greater than 4 or if DEL_LF_ROWS is greater than 25%), the index is a candidate for dropping and recreating.

To obtain the storage allocated, storage used, and percentage used, perform the following calculation. Remember to attempt to store the index in one contiguous extent and to allow for 12 months' growth.

```
SELECT NAME  "INDEX NAME",
    BLOCKS * 4096 "BYTES ALLOCATED",
    BTREE_SPACE "BYTES UTILIZED",
    (BTREE_SPACE / (BLOCKS * 4096)) * 100 "PERCENT USED"
    FROM INDEX_STATS;
```

NOTE

The 4096 in this calculation refers to the DB_BLOCK_SIZE setting on the database from which you are selecting. You can obtain the same output by observing the PCT_USED statistic in the INDEX_STATS view.

You must closely monitor all space usage within dynamic indexes. Make sure that INITIAL extent sizing is always large enough to hold all indexed rows. Once this has been established, index growth needs to be monitored. Indexes do not release space when a row is deleted from the table. Index leaf blocks will be released only when all indexed rows within a leaf block have been deleted. Space is reused if a new row is added to the table with a record key that causes the index entry to be placed within the same index leaf block.

Dynamic tables can become a space management problem when rows are spasmodically deleted from tables. Under certain conditions, the physical size of the index can even exceed the physical size of the table that owns that index.

Creating Views

Too often, DBAs don't create and tune views with the same enthusiasm with which they tune tables and indexes. This is unfortunate, because untuned views can badly damage performance in your system. You create a view with the CREATE VIEW statement.

Check that the statements that create the view have been written efficiently. A fast way of checking the effectiveness of views is to specify:

```
SELECT  *
    FROM VIEW_NAME
    WHERE ROWNUM < 5;
```

If the view contains a GROUP BY, such as the one in the following statement:

```
CREATE VIEW RUNNING_TOTALS
SELECT     D.NAME, SUM(T.FIGURE)
    FROM  DOMAIN D, TRANSACTION T
    WHERE D.ACC_NO = T.ACC_NO
    GROUP BY D.NAME;
```

the entire transaction table will be scanned because there are no qualifying conditions. In reality, the view will always have an ACC_NO provided. To test a view that contains a GROUP BY simply dissect the statement as follows:

```
SELECT     D.NAME
    FROM  DOMAIN D, TRANSACTION T
    WHERE D.ACC_NO - T.ACC_NO
    AND    ROWNUM < 5;
```

If the view or the statement above does not return the rows instantly, the chance of the view being badly tuned is high. Remember, views are simply SQL statements and should be tuned as such. The most common performance problems with views are caused by the use of an incorrect driving table or a missing index. A more sophisticated method of checking a view is to extract the SQL used in the view and run it through the EXPLAIN PLAN or TKPROF facilities to ensure all the necessary indexes are being used. (See Chapter 12 for a discussion of these facilities.)

Creating Users

When you create a user via the CREATE USER statement, you create a user account that has certain specific privileges and storage allocations. When you create your users, you can assign them resource privileges that allow them to create tables. You can also assign them a default tablespace for any tables and indexes they create, and a temporary tablespace where their sort processing will be performed if it can't be done in memory.

It is good practice to assign all of your users to a separate default tablespace so you can monitor the processing they do. By assigning a space quota to this tablespace, you can prevent the indiscriminate creation of large, ad-hoc tables.

In Version 6, issue commands like the following:

```
ALTER USER GURRY DEFAULT TABLESPACE USER_TSPACE
    TEMPORARY TABLESPACE OLTP_TEMP_TSPACE;
GRANT RESOURCE (5M) ON USER_TSPACE TO GURRY;
```

In Version 7, issue:

```
ALTER USER GURRY DEFAULT TABLESPACE USER_TSPACE
    TEMPORARY TABLESPACE OLTP_TEMP_TSPACE;
ALTER USER GURRY QUOTA 5M ON USER_TSPACE;
```

If you are using ORACLE Version 7, you can also take advantage of resource profile limits, which let you control the resources you assign a user. You can set the folllowing resource limits for a user profile:

Resource Limit	Description
SESSIONS_PER_USER	Total concurrent sessions per username
CPU_PER_SESSION	Maximum CPU per session
CPU_PER_CALL	Maximum CPU per call
CONNECT_TIME	Maximum continuous connect time per session
IDLE_TIME	Maximum allowable idle time before user is disconnected
LOGICAL_READS_PER_SESSION	Maximum database blocks read per session
LOGICAL_READS_PER_CALL	Maximum database blocks read per database call
PRIVATE_SGA	Maximum number of bytes of private space within SGA
COMPOSITE_LIMIT	Maximum weighted sum of:
	CPU_PER_SESSION, CONNECT_TIME, LOGICAL_READS_PER_SESSION, and PRIVATE_SGA.

Note that it is possible to impose explicit resource limits on some parameters, combined with the composite limit on other parameters. To impose the resource limits, issue the CREATE PROFILE or ALTER PROFILE statements or the SQL*DBA ALTER PROFILE facility. To assign a user to a profile with a resource limit, use the CREATE USER or ALTER USER commands or the SQL*DBA dialogue to create and alter users. The following example creates the AD_HOC profile and then assigns user GURRY to it.

```
CREATE PROFILE AD_HOC
LIMIT
```

```
SESSIONS_PER_USER            2
CPU_PER_SESSION              20000
CPU_PER_CALL                 20000
CONNECT_TIME                 120
IDLE_TIME                    30
LOGICAL_READS_PER_SESSION    UNLIMITED
LOGICAL_READS_PER_CALL       UNLIMITED;

ALTER USER GURRY PROFILE AD_HOC;
```

INIT.ORA Parameter Summary

This section summarizes the INIT.ORA parameters that allow you to tune memory and disk performance. For a complete discussion of these and the other INIT.ORA parameters, see ORACLE's standard DBA documentation.

NOTE

Some parameters apply only to Version 6 or only to Version 7. We note these cases. If no version is specified, the parameter is in effect in both versions.

A special note about the dictionary cache parameters. These parameters, which all begin with the DC_ prefix, can be set only in Version 6. For a discussion of these parameters, refer to Chapter 14.

CHECKPOINT_PROCESS
    Default: FALSE
    Values: TRUE or FALSE
    Version: Version 7 only

Turns the new background process, CKPT, on (TRUE) or off (FALSE). Checkpoints can have a negative impact on performance, as the DBWR process writes data to the database and the LGWR updates the database and control files to record the current log sequence number (required for archive recovery) and writes entries from the redo log buffer to the redo log file. CKPT updates the database and control files; this takes a load off the LGWR process and allows it to concentrate on the task of clearing the log buffer to the redo log. CHECKPOINT_PROCESS has a greater influence if the frequency of checkpoints is high and there are numerous database files.

CONTEXT_AREA
    Default: 4096 (4K)
    Values: 1K - 130K
    Version: Version 6 only

Specifies an initial size for the shared SQL context area. This parameter allocates bytes in memory for each user to store the data structures required for an SQL statement. Increasing the value improves CPU activity (because of the reduced amount of dynamic extension) but uses more memory. Keep the default value unless you're running an application where many of the SQL statements are exceptionally large.

CONTEXT_INCR

Default: 4096 (4K)

Values: 1K - 130K

Version: Version 6 only

Amount of memory (in bytes) by which the shared context area grows each time it is extended. Most sites keep the default. Changing it to equal your own machine's paging size (if that is larger than the default) may improve performance.

CURSOR_SPACE_FOR_TIME

Default: FALSE

Values: TRUE or FALSE

Version: Version 7 only

Turns waiting for application cursors on (TRUE) or off (FALSE). Setting this parameter to TRUE gives you a minor performance improvement by pinning SQL areas in the shared context area and stopping private SQL areas from being deallocated until the application cursors are closed. If the parameter is set to FALSE, a check has to be made to see if the SQL statement is contained in a shared SQL area in the library cache. You must allocate a shared pool that is large enough (see the SHARED_POOL_SIZE parameter). If it is not large enough and this parameter is set to TRUE, ORACLE will display a message telling you that it can't parse the statement. If it can't maintain the private SQL area because of insufficient memory, ORACLE displays a message telling you it has run out of memory.

DB_BLOCK_BUFFERS

Default: 32

Values: 4 - unlimited

Sets the size of the database buffer cache in memory. You must set this parameter, and the dictionary cache parameters described later, to get optimal performance by caching data from the database in memory. The buffer cache stores tables, indexes, clusters, and rollback segments. Our testing shows that the higher the number of block buffers, the less I/O and the better your system will perform. If excessive paging and swapping activity occurs for user processes or if any paging or swapping of the SGA occurs, you will have to reduce DB_BLOCK_BUFFERS to free memory. You should enlarge this parameter only after you are certain that the DC parameters (dictionary cache) in Version 6 or the SHARED_POOL_SIZE parameter (dictionary and library caches) in Version 7 have been adequately tuned.

For a typical medium-sized system, set this parameter to 500 or more; for a larger system, set it to 4000 or more.

DB_BLOCK_CHECKPOINT_BATCH

Default: DB_BLOCK_WRITE_BATCH / 4

Values: 0 - value of DB_BLOCK_WRITE_BATCH

Version: Version 7 only

Number of blocks the DBWR background process uses at any one time. You can increase this parameter to allow checkpoints to complete a fraction faster. If you make the parameter lower, you'll give a higher share of database writes to other modified blocks. We recommend that you make this parameter the same size as DB_BLOCK_WRITE_BATCH to speed up the checkpoint write process.

DB_BLOCK_MAX_SCAN_CNT

Default: 30

Values: 0 - value of DB_BLOCK_BUFFERS

The equivalent Version 7 parameter is _DB_BLOCK_MAX_SCAN_CNT.

Maximum number of buffers that the user will scan before DBWR is invoked. This parameter can use an excessive amount of CPU if it is set too high, particularly for a database that has a very high percentage of queries and very few updates. DBWR scanning will continue until either the number of modified blocks specified in DB_BLOCK_WRITE_BATCH has been found or the DB_BLOCK_MAX_SCAN_CNT number of blocks has been scanned. The default value is adequate for most sites. If you have a DB_BLOCK_BUFFER size greater than 10 megabytes, though, consider increasing this parameter, especially if you are experiencing CPU problems.

DB_BLOCK_WRITE_BATCH

Default: 8

Values: 1 - 128

Number of blocks DBWR passes at one time to the operating system for writing. Setting this parameter higher allows the operating system to write to different disks in parallel and to write adjacent blocks in a single I/O (if your operating system allows these features). If your buffer cache is small, having a high value will increase the wait time to modify a block that is in the batch being written.

DB_BLOCK_SIZE

Default: OS-dependent (often 2048)

Values: OS-dependent (normally 1K - 4K)

Size of each database buffer. ORACLE recommends that, unless your rows are very long or short, you should preserve the default value. We agree. We performed a simple test, creating a small database on an ULTRIX system with a DB_BLOCK_SIZE twice the default size. (The default was 2048 and the range 1024 to 8192.) There was no improvement in response times. It is easy to experiment with this parameter by creating a small database using a different DB_BLOCK_SIZE and noting the effect.

This parameter takes effect only at the time the database is created. Remember that if you adjust the parameter, the sizes of other parameters are also changed (e.g., DB_BLOCK_BUFFERS).

DB_FILES

Default: 32

Values: 2 - value of MAXDATAFILES

The number of database files that can be open when the database is running. Set this value lower than the default if you are not using 32 data files (to reduce the space used in the SGA). You can increase this value by shutting down your database, changing the parameter value, and restarting the database.

DB_FILE_MULTIBLOCK_READ_COUNT

Default: OS-dependent (often 1)

Values: OS-dependent (normally 1 - 32)

Number of blocks read at once when performing a sequential scan. This parameter is often set higher for full table scans performed by overnight runs, and is then adjusted back for high-volume daily processing. At the time the database is created, there will often be sequential scans of tables to create indexes.

For best performance, set this parameter higher than the default. For example, on ULTRIX set it to 20. For a typical medium-sized system, set this parameter to a value from 8 to 20; for a larger system, set it to the same range.

DDL_LOCKS

Default: 5 * value of SESSIONS

Values: OS-dependent

Version: Version 6 only

Maximum number of parse locks held simultaneously. If five users are modifying data in five tables, five locks are required. Although this parameter has no bearing on performance, it must be set large enough for your applications to operate. A typical setting is 20 * SESSIONS (the INIT.ORA parameter representing the number of sessions).

Note that SESSIONS has a default of:

```
1.1 * PROCESSES
```

and PROCESSES has a default of 25.

DISCRETE_TRANSACTIONS_ENABLED
    Default: FALSE
    Values: TRUE or FALSE
    Version: Version 7 only

Enables (TRUE) or disables (FALSE) discrete transactions. Such transactions are available for non-distributed systems and can be used only for the following types of transactions:

- Transactions that update only a small number of blocks (ideally, one).

- Transactions that will not change an individual database block more than once and will not insert more than one row into the same table.

- Transactions that will not modify data and commit the changes against the same data that long-running queries are running against (this will cause an abort on the query with the message, "SNAPSHOT TOO OLD").

- Transactions that do not have to refer to the data they have changed.

- Transactions that do not modify a table containing a long column.

Discrete transactions can be run with non-discrete (normal) transactions. The reason why discrete transactions run faster is that there is no undo (rollback) information stored. Instead, the redo information is stored in a separate location in memory, and all changes made to the data are committed when data is transferred to the redo log buffer and updates to the database are performed as usual.

Use discrete transactions only when you are absolutely certain that the transaction falls into the category specified here, and only when your database is experiencing excessive rollback activity.

DML_LOCKS
    Default: 4* value of PROCESSES
    Values: 20 - unlimited

Maximum number of data manipulation language (DML) locks. If three users are modifying data on two tables, you will need six DML locks. This parameter has no effect on performance, but if it is set too low transactions will fail with a "DML LOCK" error. It is therefore essential to set this parameter high enough. Usually, a site requires a value of 8 * number of transactions.

LOG_ARCHIVE_DEST
    Default: OS-dependent
    Values: OS-dependent

Specifies the location of the archive log. For recovery purposes, be sure to keep this log separate from all database files. The writing of the archive logs can have some impact on the performance of lower-end machines (for example, when the archive logs are being written to a disk using the same disk as database files or redo logs). Try to keep the destination on a separate disk (and controller) from the database files.

LOG_ARCHIVE_BUFFERS
> Default: OS-dependent
> Values: OS-dependent
> Version: Version 7 only

> Number of buffers to allocate for archiving. This parameter can be adjusted, along with LOG_ARCHIVE_BUFFER_SIZE, to tune the archiving process so it has as little impact as possible on your site's performance. The more buffers you allocate, the faster the archiver will run. But, this parameter will also take a larger slice of your site's CPU resources, which could otherwise be used for other functions such as writing to or querying your database.

> As a rule of thumb, the faster the device being written to, the larger the number of buffers you can have. Typically a value of 3 is appropriate if you are archiving to disk or a high-speed tape device. Reduce the number of buffers if archiving is having an impact on performance.

LOG_ARCHIVE_BUFFER_SIZE
> Default: OS-dependent
> Values: OS-dependent
> Version: Version 7 only

> Buffer size for archive log. This parameter is used with the LOG_ARCHIVE_BUFFER parameter to tune the archiving process. If you specify a larger number, more archive data is stored in the archive buffer before writes are performed. If you specify a smaller number, you increase archive write activity.

> We recommend that you increase the buffer size to the maximum possible (operating system dependent), and decrease the parameter only if you are experiencing overall performance problems.

LOG_ALLOCATION
> Default: 200
> Values: 1 - size of redo log file +1

> Number of blocks in a redo log file allocated to each instance time that the file needs more space in the redo log currently being used. For single-instance databases, set this parameter equal to the size of your redo logs. (All redo logs should be the same size.) If this parameter is smaller than your redo logs, database creation performance will suffer because more redo chunk allocations will be required.

If your system is a shared disk system, that is, many instances share the same database, do not let the total log allocation of all instances exceed the redo log file size. Otherwise, a log switch and checkpoint will occur every time the subsequent instance requests a write to the redo log. We agree with the recommendations in the *ORACLE Database Administrators Guide:*

- Make LOG_ALLOCATION at least 1000 blocks.

- Make each log file at least 2000 blocks times the number of instances.

- Allow 4-5 allocations per redo log per instance.

LOG_ARCHIVE_START
Default: FALSE
Values: TRUE or FALSE

Enables (TRUE) or disables (FALSE) archiving.

LOG_BUFFER
Default: 4 * block size
Values: OS-dependent

Number of bytes allocated to the redo log buffer in the SGA. The log buffer can affect the performance of the RDBMS by buffering information before writing to the redo logs. If you are experiencing I/O bottlenecks on the disks that contain the redo logs, increase this parameter. For high-volume, intensive-update applications, we have noticed response improvements of 7% to 10% by increasing the buffer size from 64K to one megabyte. There were no advantages increasing beyond one megabyte.

The tradeoff is that if you specify a larger value, more memory is used in the SGA. If your system is tight on memory and is likely to experience paging and swapping activity, keep this buffer at its default. If there is abundant memory, set the buffer size at about one megabyte and monitor its performance.

For a typical medium-sized system, set this parameter to 64K; for a larger system, set it to somewhere between 640K and one megabyte. You specify this value in blocks. Under VMS, your block size is 2048 (so the LOG_BUFFER default would be 8192). On a Sun workstation, the block size is 8192; on an Amdahl it is 16384.

LOG_CHECKPOINT_INTERVAL
Default: OS-dependent
Values: 2 - unlimited

Number of new redo log file blocks needed to trigger a checkpoint. Note that these blocks are operating system blocks, not ORACLE blocks. If you set this parameter smaller than the sizes of the redo log files, it will cause a checkpoint to occur. A checkpoint causes all modified database buffers to be written to disk, and stores the location from the redo log where checkpointing has occurred in the control file and database files. Keep in mind that ORACLE writes modified buffers regardless of checkpointing, so many of the buffers in the redo log since the last checkpoint have probably already been written to the database.

If fast recovery time is required, keep the LOG_CHECKPOINT_INTERVAL at a value lower than the size of the redo logs and at a size that is a whole fraction of the redo log size. If performance is the more important consideration, make your LOG_CHECKPOINT_INTERVAL equal to or greater than the size of the redo logs; this will force less frequent checkpoints and will minimize the amount of I/O in your system caused by the checking and writing required to perform the checkpoint. To check the frequencies of checkpoints, run SQL*DBA and observe the DBWR CHEKPO value in the MON STATS output.

Typically this parameter is set to a high value (e.g., 10,000).

LOG_CHECKPOINT_TIMEOUT

Default: 0
Values: 0 - unlimited
Version: Version 7 only

Forces more frequent checkpoints. If you set this parameter to a non-zero value, checkpoints will occur more often than when a redo log fills and the associated redo log switch takes place. You can achieve the same effect by setting the LOG_CHECKPOINT_INTERVAL to a size less than the redo log file size. The difference is that the timeout parameter works in seconds since the last checkpoint; the LOG_CHECKPOINT_INTERVAL parameter, on the other hand, uses the number of buffers filled as its indicator of when to throw a checkpoint.

You'll get the best performance by leaving the LOG_CHECKPOINT_TIMEOUT parameter at its default value of 0, which causes a checkpoint only on a change of redo log. Make sure that you set LOG_CHECKPOINT_INTERVAL to a size larger than that of the redo log.

LOG_ENTRY_PREBUILD_THRESHOLD

Default: 0
Values: 0 - OS-dependent maximum

Maximum number of bytes to collect from the redo logs before copying them to the log buffer. This parameter is used only for multiple-CPU systems. If you are running a single-CPU system, do not change the default. By increasing the default to a value of either 2048 or 4096, you can improve performance, especially by helping to eliminate latch contention. (See the discussion of latches in Chapter 18.)

LOG_FILES

> Default: 16
>
> Values: 2 - 255

Maximum number of redo logs that can be opened when the database is running. The value of LOG_FILES must not exceed the value of MAXLOGFILES, which is set when the database is created. Set this parameter to 3 to reduce the space used in the SGA. You can increase this value by shutting your database down, changing the parameter, and restarting the database.

LOG_SIMULTANEOUS_COPIES

> Default: CPU_COUNT
>
> Values: 0 - unlimited

Maximum number of redo buffer copy latches that can write log buffers simultaneously. Specify this parameter only for multiple-CPU systems. We recommend that you set this parameter to twice the number of CPUs in systems that have high transaction rates (although we don't typically see much performance improvement beyond 2). This reduces contention for redo copy latches. Note that if you set this parameter to zero, redo copy latches are turned off.

LOG_SMALL_ENTRY_MAX_SIZE

> Default: OS-dependent
>
> Values: OS-dependent

Size in bytes of the largest copy to log buffers that may occur without obtaining a redo copy latch. This parameter applies only when the LOG_SIMULTANEOUS_COPIES is greater than zero. If the entry to be written to the buffer is larger than 0, user processes will release the latch after allocating space in the log buffer and getting a redo copy latch. If the entry to be written is smaller than this size, the user process releases the redo allocation latch after the copy.

Leave this parameter at its default value for your operating system. It may need to be decreased later if you are experiencing redo allocation latch contention. (See the discussion of this point in Chapter 13.)

MTS_DISPATCHERS

> Default: null
>
> Values: Not applicable
>
> Version: Version 7

Number and type of dispatcher processes to be created when a database or database instance starts up. You must specify a string that shows your network protocol; for example:

```
MTS_DISPATCHERS = TCP,4
MTS_DISPATCHERS = DECNET,4
```

MTS_MAX_DISPATCHERS

Default: 5

Values: OS-dependent

Version: Version 7 only

Maximum number of dispatchers that can run simultaneously.

MTS_MAX_SERVERS

Default: 0

Values: OS-dependent

Maximum number of server processors that can run simultaneously.

OPEN_CURSORS

Default: 50

Values: 0 - 255

Maximum number of context areas a user process can have open at any one time. To avoid your users getting the error "MAX OPEN CURSORS EXCEEDED" and thinking it is a response time problem, set the parameter to 255.

OPTIMIZER_MODE

Default: CHOOSE

Values: CHOOSE and RULE

Version: Version 7 only

Selects the Version 7 cost-based optimizer (CHOOSE) or the Version 6 rule-based optimizer (RULE) (introduced in Version 6.0.33) used to select the most efficient retrieval path for your SQL statements. In most cases, we recommend that you take advantage of the performance improvements you'll get from the Version 7 optimizer. However, if you are transferring a fully-tuned application from Version 6 to Version 7, you will probably want to start out by setting OPTIMIZER_MODE to RULE and then taking your time testing the performance of your application with the new optimizer.

_OPTIMIZER_UNDO_CHANGES

Default: FALSE

Values: TRUE and FALSE

Version: Version 6.0.32 and after

Ignores (TRUE) or does not ignore (FALSE) changes that the optimizer makes in the hope of improving system performance. Sometimes, these changes rebound and actually degrade performance. Set this parameter to TRUE until you have been able to test carefully the effect of optimizer changes on your system by checking the README file that comes with your system and testing all of your programs in the Version 7 QA environment. (See the note at the end of this section.)

RESOURCE_LIMIT
>   Default: FALSE
>   Values; TRUE and FALSE
>   Version: Version 7 only

Limits (TRUE) or does not limit (FALSE) a user's database resources to those defined in his or her profile. Your setting takes effect after the database has been shut down and restarted. You can enable resource limits by issuing the command:

```
ALTER SYSTEM SET RESOURCE_LIMIT TRUE
```

After you issue this command, the resource limits are returned to the INIT.ORA value after the database has been shut down and restarted. (See the section above called "Creating Users," for information.)

We strongly recommend that you set RESOURCE_LIMIT to TRUE (and manage the way users are using your site's resources). Our testing indicates that setting this parameter to TRUE does not slow performance.

SEQUENCE_CACHE_ENTRIES
>   Default: 10
>   Values: 10 - 32000

Number of sequences that will be cached in memory (in the SGA). Set this parameter to the number of sequences that will be used by your instance at one time. Setting this parameter too low affects response times because a disk read is required to obtain each sequence number.

If you have the NOCACHE option set when you create the sequence in the CREATE SEQUENCE command, the sequence will not reside in this cache; it will have to be brought in from disk. Many sites use the NOCACHE option, however, because they cannot skip sequence numbers which can occur when the sequence cache facility is used.

For a typical medium-sized system, set this parameter to 50 or higher; for a larger system, set it to 100 or higher.

SHARED_POOL_SIZE
>   Default: 3.5 megabytes
>   Values: 300K - OS-dependent maximum
>   Version: Version 7 only

Size of the shared buffer pool in the Version 7 SGA. This pool stores shared SQL and PL/SQL blocks, the data dictionary cache, and (if your site is using a multi-threaded server architecture) some session information.

Make the shared pool large enough, but not too large. If your shared pool is too large, you are wasting memory that could otherwise be used to enlarge the buffer cache. If you set it too low, you'll need to do too many disk accesses and performance will suffer—sometimes as much as 50%. Make sure you have some free memory after increasing this parameter, or the resulting paging and swapping will seriously degrade performance. Tune this parameter before you tune the buffer cache (see the DB_BLOCK_BUFFER parameter) because having an undersized shared pool will degrade performance even more than an undersized buffer cache will.

The maximum size allowed for the shared pool in your own system is shown in your *ORACLE Installation and User's Guide.*

For a small system, we recommend that you reduce the default value to about one megabyte; for a small- to medium-sized system, keep the default; and, for a medium- to large-sized system, increase it to 10 megabytes. You must monitor the performance of the shared pool cache regularly and adjust the shared pool size to optimize your site's performance.

SMALL_TABLE_THRESHOLD

> Default: 4
> Values: 0 - OS maximum
> Version: Version 7 only

Number of blocks that will be stored in the most-recently-used end of the buffer cache before the rest of the blocks from the same table will be stored in the least-recently-used end of the list.

This parameter keeps in the buffer cache for a longer time the data read using full-table scans. If you perform a query that uses a full-table scan and then repeat the query, the same or a similar number of physical reads from the database will occur in both situations. The reason is that, for a full-table scan, ORACLE assumes that the data will be needed only briefly. It places the first four blocks into the most-recently-used end of the list, and all data after the first four blocks read into the least-recently-used end of the list. As new data is read from the table, the new data replaces the least-recently-used blocks in the buffer.

ORACLE recommends that you keep the default for this parameter. We have tested the impact of increasing the value and have found that increasing the value neither improves nor degrades performance. This is partly due to the fact that most of the tables we would like to have in cache consist of more than four blocks, as well as to the fact that indexed retrieval overrides the need for more room in the cache.

We would prefer to see a way of holding specified indexes or entire tables in cache, by specifying the index or table name we would like cached, but we'll have to talk to ORACLE about that!

SORT_AREA_SIZE

> Default: OS-dependent
>
> Values: OS-dependent

Size in bytes that a user process has available for sorting. If the machine that the database is being created on has an abundance of memory, you can increase this parameter beyond the default (for example, 2097152).

The performance improvements can be substantial, especially when your site is running long-running overnight jobs such as sorted reports. Some sites adjust this parameter upwards for overnight processing (when there are fewer users logged onto the system and more free memory). They then set it back to its smaller number for daytime processing after the nightly runs complete. Because SORT_AREA_SIZE is allocated on a per-user process basis, free memory will disappear very quickly if the parameter is left high during peak system usage times.

SORT_AREA_RETAINED_SIZE

> Default: value of SORT_AREA_SIZE
>
> Values: 0 - value of SORT_AREA_SIZE
>
> Version: Version 7 only

Size in bytes to which ORACLE will reduce your sort area if sort data is not being referenced. Memory is reduced only after all of the rows have been fetched from the sort space. Sometimes, a number of concurrent sorts may be required, and each is given its own memory allocation of a size determined by this parameter.

SQL_TRACE

> Default: FALSE
>
> Values: TRUE or FALSE

Enables (TRUE) or disables (FALSE) the SQL trace facility. Make this parameter FALSE when creating your new database; setting it to TRUE slows down database creation. We recommend that you leave SQL_TRACE set to FALSE. We tend to leave SQL_TRACE on in QA databases, and then run TKPROF against all trace files and interrogate the output nightly to identify any poorly-tuned statements. We turn this parameter on against a production database only when a site has serious response time problems and the site has already tuned its database and system administration component. In tests we have run, turning SQL_TRACE on has degraded our performance by as much as 27%.

TIMED_STATISTICS

Default: FALSE

Values: TRUE and FALSE

Enables (TRUE) or disables (FALSE) timed statistics from certain SQL*DBA MONITOR screens. Set this parameter to TRUE; it provides needed timing information and we have found that its setting does not affect response time.

USER_DUMP_DEST

Default: OS-dependent

Values: OS-dependent

Specifies the directory to which to write user process trace files. Usually, output is placed into a subdirectory of the ORACLE RDBMS's home directory. This default is acceptable for use during database creation.

NOTE

In addition to the parameters shown above (and those that do not affect performance, described in standard ORACLE documentation), there are several "hidden parameters." These parameters are not displayed by the SQL*DBA SHOW PARAMETERS command, nor are they shown in the V$PARAMETERS view. These parameters are all prefixed by an underscore (_) in Version 6.0.36 and later and are used primarily for internal testing and support. The one hidden parameter you are likely to care about is _OPTIMIZER_UNDO_ CHANGES. If you set this parameter to TRUE, it tells an application to ignore the execution plan worked out by the optimizer and to use its own execution plan. If you are curious about these parameters, you can connect as SYS and run the following query to display them:

```
SELECT KSPPINM FROM X$KSPPI
    WHERE  SUBSTR (KSPPINM, 1,1) = '_';
```

Do not attempt to change any hidden parameter (except for _OPTIMIZER_UNDO_ CHANGES) unless ORACLE support advises you to.

12

Diagnostic and Tuning Tools

This chapter describes a number of ORACLE database monitoring and diagnostic tools that help you to examine system and database statistics so you can tune more effectively. Chapter 11, *Tuning a New Database*, introduced the memory and disk areas that you can examine and tune with these tools. Chapter 13, *Monitoring and Tuning an Existing Database*, shows how you can use these tools in specific tuning situations. For complete information about tuning tools and their options, consult standard ORACLE documentation.

This chapter describes:

MONITOR	A SQL*DBA facility that lets you look at various system activity and performance tables.
SQL_TRACE	A utility that writes a trace file containing performance statistics.
TKPROF	A utility that translates the SQL_TRACE file into readable output, and can also show the execution plan for a SQL statement.
EXPLAIN PLAN	A statement that analyzes and displays the execution plan for a SQL statement.
ANALYZE	A statement that compiles statistics the Version 7 cost-based optimizer can use to construct its execution plan.

BSTAT (begin) and ESTAT (end)

> Version 6 scripts that produce a snapshot of how the database is performing. The Version 7 equivalents are *UTLBSTAT.sql* and *UTLESTAT.sql.*

ORACLE scripts   A number of additional diagnostic and tuning scripts provided by ORACLE.

Custom scripts   A number of diagnostic and tuning scripts we have developed ourselves.

V$SYSSTAT   A table that contains a variety of processing and performance statistics which can be queried in a variety of ways.

There are also diagnostic and tuning tools available for the various operating systems that support ORACLE. For example, in a UNIX environment, you might use *iostat* to look at disk activity in your system. In VMS, you might use MON PAGE to examine memory. For information about these system-specific tools, consult your operating system documentation.

In addition to the standard ORACLE and operating system facilities, every database administrator develops his or her own set of handy scripts and modified utilities. As mentioned above, we've included a few of our own favorites in this chapter. We encourage you to save any diagnostic and tuning scripts you develop in your own system toolbox so they will be available next time you need them. If you think ORACLE DBAs or other users could benefit from what you've learned about improving system performance, we encourage you to send us a copy and we'll include the best scripts and other tools in the next edition of this book.

The tools described in this chapter help you identify potential and real database problems. By using them on a regular basis to monitor system activity and performance, you can detect when a potential problem is becoming a real one, and when a real problem is turning into a true disaster. You'll notice that some of the tools overlap in function. Choose the tools and options that best suit your style and your system, and use them on a regular basis to monitor system, memory, and disk usage. Things can change rapidly in a dynamic system like ORACLE.

MONITOR: Monitoring System Activity Tables

The SQL*DBA MONITOR facility allows you to monitor activity and performance in your system by looking at the views of a variety of read-only system performance tables that are held in memory. The way you use this facility depends on your particular platform, but its function is consistent across platforms. If you are using a command line interface (e.g., VMS), you'll type a command line in response to the SQLDBA prompt, such as:

SQLDBA> MON FILES

to display information about file activity. If you're running a GUI (e.g., Macintosh), you'll select a MONITOR function, such as Files, from a pull-down menu. Table 12-1 shows the available MONITOR displays. For reference purposes, Appendix D shows what views of the dynamic performance tables each MONITOR function accesses for information.

This chapter and Chapter 13 show how you can use the MONITOR facility to look at memory and disk performance. For complete information about that facility and how you invoke it in your own system, refer to the *ORACLE Database Administrator's Guide.*

NOTE

All MONITOR displays have a default of five seconds, which means that the information in the tables is refreshed every five seconds. To change the default, issue the following:

SQLDBA > MON CYCLE *number*

where *number* is the number of seconds, in the range 1 to 3600.

Table 12-1: MONITOR Displays

Version 6	Version 7	Description
FILES	FILE IO	Read/write activity for database files in the system. In Version 7, you can select an individual file or set of files. Pay particular attention to the "Request Rate" columns.
IO	SYSTEM IO	Logical and physical reads in writes, cumulative figures, and interval.
LATCH	LATCH	Internal latches in the system. in Version 6, pay particular attention to "Timeouts." In Version 7, pay particular attention to "No Wait Request Misses," which must be kept as low as possible.
LOCK	LOCK	Locks in the system. We recommend that you use the locking scripts instead because, for a reasonably-sized system, it is impossible to see all of the locks on the screen at once.

Table 12-1: MONITOR Displays (Continued)

Version 6	Version 7	Description
PROCESSES	PROCESSES	Process IDs for ORACLE and operating system, username, terminal, and executing program.
ROLLBACK SEGMENTS	ROLLBACK SEGMENTS	Extents, transactions, size, writes, and waits for rollbacks. Pay attention to extents (should be as low as possible) and waits (should not be any).
STATISTICS	STATISTICS	Run time statistics on system or session use and performance (includes user, enqueue, cache, and redo).
TABLE	TABLE	Table statistics. In Version 7, you can display an individual table and its owner.
USER	SESSION	Session ID for user ID, process ID, session status, username, and most recent SQL statement executed.
	CIRCUIT	(Multi-threaded server only.) Status, currently active queue, number of messages, and total bytes transferred for each path.
	DISPATCHER	(Multi-threaded server only.) Total messages, bytes, idle time, busy time, and load.
	LIBRARYCACHE	Parts of the cache and the hit ratio. Pay particular attention to the "Gets" ratio, which must be kept as close to 1 as possible.
	QUEUE	(Multi-threaded server only.) Current number of messages in dispatcher queue, total messages, and average wait time.
	SHARED SERVER	(Multi-threaded server only.) Requests from server, idle time, and load (which should be kept balanced).
	SQLAREA	SQL statements being executed and contained in cache. Pay attention to whether almost identical statements are in the cache.

SQL_TRACE: Writing a Trace File

The SQL trace facility writes a trace file containing performance statistics for the SQL statements being executed. These include:

- The number of parses, executes, and fetches performed

- Various types of CPU and elapsed times

- The number of physical and logical reads performed

- The number of rows processed

This trace file provides valuable information that you can use to tune your system. You should be sparing about running it, however. When you have globally enabled SQL_TRACE by setting the appropriate parameters in the INIT.ORA file, your overall response times are likely to degrade as much as 20% to 30%.

The exact form of the trace file name written by SQL_TRACE is system-dependent, but usually it is in the form *filename.TRC.* You cannot read this file directly, but you can run the TKPROF utility against it to produce a readable version. (TKPROF is discussed in the section later in this chapter, "TKPROF: Interpreting the Trace File." That section shows the particular statistics collected by SQL_TRACE.)

To globally enable SQL_TRACE, you must set a number of INIT.ORA parameters:

Parameter	Setting	Description
SQL_TRACE	TRUE	Enables the trace for all application users. A setting of FALSE disables the trace. FALSE is the default.
USER_DUMP_DEST	*directory*	The directory where SQL_TRACE writes the trace file. The default is system-dependent, but generally is the directory that holds your system dumps (e.g., *$ORACLE_HOME/rdbms/log*).
TIMED_STATISTICS	TRUE	Causes the RDBMS to collect additional timing statistics. These timing statistics are useful to SQL_TRACE and also to the SQL*DBA MONITOR command. The default is FALSE.
MAX_DUMP_SIZE	*number*	Limits the physical size of the trace file to the specified number of bytes. If you enable the SQL_TRACE parameter for the entire database, this option helps control the amount of disk space used. To find out what size to specify, find out the number of operating system blocks available in your system. If SQL_TRACE runs out of space, it will truncate your output; you'll have to allocate more space and start again.

The way you invoke SQL_TRACE for individual ORACLE tools and user sessions depends on the ORACLE program you are running:

For:	Do This:
SQL*Forms	`RUNFORM formname usercode/password` -S (Version 3 and later)
SQL*Plus	ALTER SESSION SET SQL_TRACE TRUE
SQL*Reportwriter	Create a field called SQL_TRACE and a group report with an attribute of CHAR(40). Specify the following statement against the column: `&SQL ALTER SESSION SET SQL_TRACE TRUE`
Pro* tools	EXEC SQL ALTER SESSION SET SQL_TRACE TRUE

TKPROF: *Interpreting the Trace File*

The TKPROF utility translates the trace file generated by the SQL trace facility (described in the previous section) to a readable format. You can run TKPROF against a trace file that you have previously created, or you can run it while the program that is creating the trace file is still running. You can optionally tell TKPROF to invoke the EXPLAIN PLAN statement (described in the next section) for the statements being analyzed.

You invoke TKPROF by issuing the command:

```
TKPROF tracefile listfile [SORT = parameters] [PRINT = number]
    [EXPLAIN = username/password]
```

where:

tracefile   Is the name of the trace file containing the statistics gathered by the SQL trace facility.

listfile   Is the name of the file where TKPROF writes its output.

SORT=*parameters*   Is the order in which to display output. You can specify, as parameters, any of the statistics collected by SQL_TRACE. (These are listed in Table 12-3.) TKPROF outputs statistics in the descending order of the values of these parameters. For example, if you specify:

```
SORT = EXECPU
```

TKPROF first displays statistics for the statements that had the worst EXECPU values (that is, required the most CPU time).

If you specify more than one parameter, for example:

```
SORT = (FCHPHR, PRSCPU)
```

TKPROF adds the statistics you specify. The output that appears first is for statements where the sum of these two statistics was the worst.

PRINT = *number*
The number of statements included in the output. You might want to limit the amount of output to the worst-performing statements.

EXPLAIN = *username/password*
Run the EXPLAIN PLAN statement on all of the statements in the trace file, logging in under the account specified.

For example, you might specify:

```
TKPROF 12_12626.TRC TRACE.LIS SORT=(EXECPU)
    [EXPLAIN = username/password]
```

When you run TKPROF, it interprets the trace file and puts the readable output in the file you specify. TKPROF produces a formatted listing. The rows and columns in the TKPROF output have the meanings shown in Table 12-2.

Table 12-2: TKPROF Output Rows and Columns

Row/Column	Description
Parse	Statistics for the parse steps performed by SQL statements.
Execute	Statistics for the execute steps performed by SQL statements. UPDATE, DELETE, and INSERT statements show the number of rows processed here.
Fetch	Statistics for the fetch steps performed by SQL statements. SELECT statements show the number of rows processed here.
count	Number of times a SQL statement is parsed or executed, plus the number of times a fetch is performed in order to carry out the operation.
cpu	CPU time for all parses, executes, and fetches, in one-hundredths of seconds.
elap	Elapsed time for these operations, in one-hundredths of seconds.
phys	Number of data blocks read from disk.
cr	Number of times an older version of a buffer is needed (consistent reads).
cur	Number of times the current version of a buffer is needed (current reads).
rows	Number of rows processed by a SQL statement (only queries, not subqueries).

Following is an example of TKPROF output showing the rows and columns shown in Table 12-2.

```
Overall Totals For All Statements
            count    cpu    elap    phys    cr     cur    rows
Parse:      38       360    1520    66      155    0
Execute:    38       197    700     69      70     184    10
Fetch:      101      100    230     46      57     0      90

Total Number of SQL statements: 36
```

You can select any of the statistics shown in Table 12-3, computed by SQL_TRACE and interpreted by TKPROF, in the SORT clause. Of these, EXECPU is probably the most useful; it shows the total CPU time spent executing the statement. If you have not collected timed statistics (that is, you have set the INIT.ORA parameter TIMED_STATISTICS = FALSE), you'll find EXECR the most useful; it shows the number of consistent reads during execution.

Table 12-3: TKPROF SORT Parameters

Parameter	Description
PRSCNT	Number of times parsed
PRSCPU	CPU time spent parsing
PRSELA	Elapsed time spent parsing
PRSPHR	Number of physical reads during parse
PRSCR	Number of consistent mode reads during parse
PRSCU	Number of current mode block reads during parse
EXECNT	Number of executes
EXECPU	CPU time spent executing
EXEELA	Elapsed time spent executing
EXEPHR	Number of physical reads during execute
EXECR	Number of consistent mode block reads during execute
EXECU	Number of current mode block reads during execute
EXEROW	Number of rows processed during execute
FCHCNT	Number of fetches
FCHCPU	CPU time spent fetching
FCHELA	Elapsed time spent fetching
FCHPH	Number of physical reads during fetch
FCHCR	Number of consistent mode blocks read during fetch
FCHCU	Number of current mode blocks read during fetch
FCHROW	Number of rows fetched

TKPROF formulates its output for each individual SQL statement and then at the user session level. It often pays to look at the "Overall Totals For All Statements" before you examine individual statement performance. The overall totals will tell you what general problems exist.

Here are some rules for interpreting these statistics; these rules apply to all types of systems and jobs:

- If the "cpu", "elap", and "phys" figures in the Parse row are high relative to the Execute and Fetch rows, you probably need to do some dictionary cache tuning so you'll be able to store more of the dictionary in memory. This will reduce the required amount of disk I/O.

- If the Parse "count" figure is relatively high, you may need to do open cursor tuning on the application.

- If the sum of Execute "phys" + Fetch "phys" is more than 10% of the sum of Execute "cr" + Execute "cur" + Fetch "cr" + Fetch "cur", the hit ratio of finding data in the cache is too low. See if you can increase the buffer cache.

- If the Fetch "count" is about twice Fetch "rows", and if PL/SQL is being used, it's likely that implicit cursors are in use. (Implicit cursors are SQL statements that are not declared; they are less efficient than explicit cursors.) Ask your analysts/programmers to investigate.

- If the total of the "elap" column is greater than 250 (i.e., greater than 2.5 seconds), and if the query is an interactive, online one, investigate the SQL statements. The response times indicated by these statistics exceed the standards for most sites.

- If Execute "cr" is high, and Execute "rows" and Execute "cur" are markedly lower, investigate your indexes. Your tables probably do not have enough indexes or have inadequate indexes defined for them.

The following additional rules apply only to online transaction processing systems that require excellent response time (e.g., 2.5 seconds elapsed for all online queries):

- Make sure all Execute "cpu" times are less than one second.

- Make sure Parse "cpu" times are less than one second.

- Allow full-table scans only on small tables. Don't allow them on tables with more than 200 rows, or on tables that are frequently used in multiple-table joins. (See the discussion later in this chapter on confusing full-table scan reports in Version 6.)

- Remove all unnecessary calls to the system table, DUAL.

- Declare all PL/SQL SELECTs unless absolutely necessary.

- Make sure ORACLE chooses the appropriate driving table (described in Chapter 7, *Tuning SQL*, in the section called "The Driving Table.")

There is a problem with output from TKPROF under Version 6. If we write the following simple PL/SQL script, with SQL_TRACE set to TRUE, and then run TKPROF against the trace file, the following output appears:

```
/* SAMPLE PL/SQL SCRIPT TO DEMONSTRATE HOW A FULL TABLE SCAN IS SHOWN
IN THE TKPROF OUTPUT, EVEN THOUGH ONE IS NOT ACTUALLY PERFORMED */

DECLARE CURSOR GET_ACCT IS
     SELECT ACC_NAME FROM ACCOUNTS
         WHERE ACC_ID = 1;
         ACC_NAME_STORE CHAR(30);
BEGIN
       OPEN GET_ACCT;
       FETCH GET_ACCT INTO ACC_NAME_STORE;
       CLOSE GET_ACCT;
END;
```

You must ignore the following statement that appears in the TKPROF output. Every table which is declared shows the table being accessed in this fashion. This is the result of the PL/SQL block "parse and syntax check," as shown below.

```
SELECT * FROM ACCOUNTS
```

	count	cpu	elap	phys	cr	cur	rows
Parse:	1	0	0	0	0	0	
Execute:	0	0	0	0	0	0	0
Fetch:	0	0	0	0	0	0	0

Execution plan:

	count	cpu	elap	phys	cr	cur	rows
Parse:	1	4	4	0	0	0	
Execute:	1	3	10	0	4	0	1
Fetch:	0	0	0	0	0	0	0

Execution plan:

```
SELECT ACC_NAME FROM ACCOUNTS WHERE ACC_ID = 1
```

	count	cpu	elap	phys	cr	cur	rows
Parse:	1	0	0	0	0	0	
Execute:	1	0	0	0	0	0	0
Fetch:	1	0	2	0	4	0	1

The actual execution plan is shown below. Notice that a full-table scan is not performed.

```
Execution plan:
    TABLE ACCESS (BY ROWID) OF 'ACCOUNTS'
    INDEX (RANGE SCAN) OF 'ACC_NDX1' (NON-UNIQUE)
```

EXPLAIN PLAN: Explaining the Optimizer's Plan

EXPLAIN PLAN is a statement you can include in your SQL to explain the execution plan, or retrieval path, that the optimizer will use to do its database retrievals. The execution plan is the sequence of physical operations that ORACLE must perform to return the data requested (See the discussion of the optimizer in the section in Chapter 7 called "How Does the Optimizer Work?") By looking at the execution plans for SQL statements, you can see which ones are inefficient, and you can compare alternatives to find out which will give you better performance.

If you are going to issue the EXPLAIN PLAN statement, you need to create a table called PLAN_TABLE which will hold the data to be displayed. You do this by running a script. The name of this script is system-dependent, but is likely to be *XPLAINPL.sql*. (You can use your own table instead, if you define it properly and reference it in the INTO clause described below.)

You issue the EXPLAIN PLAN statement as follows:

```
EXPLAIN PLAN [SET STATEMENT_ID = 'identifier']
    [INTO tablename]
    FOR statement
```

where:

STATEMENT_ID = 'identifier'
             Is an optional description of 1-30 characters for this statement.

INTO tablename   Is the name of the table in which to store output; specify only if you don't use PLAN_TABLE.

FOR statement   Is a SQL statement (SELECT, INSERT, DELETE, UPDATE) being explained.

For example, you might specify:

```
EXPLAIN PLAN   SET STATEMENT_ID = 'EMP FILE SELECT'
    FOR SELECT . . .
```

To display the table built by EXPLAIN PLAN, issue a statement like the following one:

```
SELECT   LPAD(' ', 2*LEVEL) || OPERATION || '' || OPTIONS || ' ' ||
        OBJECT_NAME EXPLAIN_PLAN
    FROM  PLAN_TABLE
    CONNECT BY  PRIOR ID = PARENT_ID AND
                STATEMENT_ID ='EMP FILE SELECT'
    START WITH ID = 1
    WHERE STATEMENT_ID  = 'EMP FILE SELECT'
```

Table 12-4 shows the format of PLAN_TABLE into which EXPLAIN PLAN puts its output.

Table 12-4: EXPLAIN PLAN PLAN_TABLE Format

Field	Description
STATEMENT_ID	From your EXPLAIN PLAN statement
TIMESTAMP	Date and time analyzed
REMARKS	Your comment (up to 80 characters)
OPERATION	See Table 12-5
OPTIONS	See Table 12-5
OBJECT_NODE	Database link
OBJECT_OWNER	Owner of the object
OBJECT_NAME	Name of table or index
OBJECT_INSTANCE	Column in output from left to right in which this operation appears
OBJECT_TYPE	Type of object (e.g. non-unique index)
SEARCH_COLUMNS	Not used
ID	Number assigned to each step in execution plan
PARENT_ID	ID of the parent of this step
POSITION	Order of processing of steps that all have the same parent ID
OTHER	Long field that stores other useful text

Sample output is shown below:

```
Query plan

----------------------------------------------------
filter
    merge join
        sort join
            table access full dept
        sort join
            table access full emp
    table access full salgrade
```

Table 12-5 lists the operations (and their options, where relevant) that will be displayed in the EXPLAIN PLAN output.

Table 12-5: Operations Displayed in EXPLAIN_PLAN Output

Operation	Option	Description
AGGREGATE	GROUP BY	A single row that is the result of a GROUP BY (Version 7 only)
AND-EQUAL		Accepts multiple ROWIDs and returns the intersection of the sets with no duplicates

Table 12-5: Operations Displayed in EXPLAIN_PLAN Output (Continued)

Operation	Option	Description
CONNECT BY		Tree-walks rows using a CONNECT BY query
CONCATENATION		Returns UNION all rows
COUNTING		Counts number of rows from a table
FILTER		Accepts some rows and eliminates others using WHERE conditions in statement
FIRST ROW		Returns only first row of query
FOR UPDATE		Places row locks on selected rows
INDEX	UNIQUE	Uses UNIQUE index (one row)
	RANGE SCAN	Uses non-UNIQUE index (more than one row)
	RANGE SCAN DESCENDING	Same as RANGE SCAN, but returns all rows in descending order
INTERSECTION		Returns intersection rows (no duplicates)
MERGE JOIN		Gets two sets of rows, both sorted, and combines each row from one with the other
	OUTER	Same as above but with an outer join
MINUS		Uses MINUS function
NESTED LOOPS		Compares two sets of rows and checks each row or a condition before returning data
	OUTER	Same as above but includes outer join
PROJECTION		Returns a subset of columns from a table
REMOTE		Uses database link to access another database
SEQUENCE		Accesses a sequence
SORT	UNIQUE	Sorts rows to eliminate duplicates
	GROUP BY	Sorts as result of a GROUP BY clause
	JOIN	Sorts rows prior to a merge join
	ORDER BY	Sorts as result of an ORDER BY clause
TABLE ACCESS	FULL	Performs a full-table scan
	CLUSTER	Accesses a cluster
	HASH	Uses hashing algorithm based on the key (Version 7 only)
	ROWID	Accesses a table by its ROWID
UNION		Uses UNION statement
VIEW		Does a retrieval from a virtual table

ANALYZE: *Validating and Computing Statistics*

The ANALYZE statement is a SQL*Plus statement that allows you to validate and compute statistics for an index, table, or cluster. These statistics are used by the Version 7 optimizer when it calculates the most efficient plan for retrieval. In addition to its role in statement optimization, ANALYZE also helps in validating object structures and in managing space in your system. You issue this command as follows:

```
ANALYZE  object-clause  operation  STATISTICS
    [VALIDATE STRUCTURE [CASCADE]]
    [LIST CHAINED ROWS [INTO table]]
```

where:

object-clause	TABLE, INDEX, or CLUSTER, followed by a name. You can run ANALYZE on any one of these.
operation	You can choose one of these operations:

	COMPUTE	Calculates each value. This option provides the most accurate statistics, but is the slowest to run.
	ESTIMATE	Estimates statistics by examining data dictionary values and performing data sampling. this option provides less accurate statistics, but is much faster.
	DELETE	Removes all table statistics (freeing space).

ANALYZE produces the following statistics; depending on whether you have specified COMPUTE or ESTIMATE, these statistics will be exact or estimated.

For tables:

> Number of rows
> Number of blocks
> Number of blocks unused
> Average available free space
> Number of chained rows
> Average row length

For indexes:

> Index level
> Number of leaf blocks
> Number of distinct keys
> Average number of leaf blocks/key
> Average number of data blocks/key
> Clustering factor

Minimum key value (exact only)

Maximum key value (exact only)

For columns:

Number of distinct values

For clusters:

Average cluster key chain length

ANALYZE stores these statistics in the views, USER_TABLES and USER_TAB_COLUMNS.

ANALYZE has many uses. In addition to its use in optimization, ANALYZE can be used to look for chained rows (a performance drain on the system). See Chapter 13 and consult your Version 7 documentation for complete information.

BSTAT.sql, ESTAT.sql, UTLBSTAT.sql, and UTLESTAT.sql

BSTAT.sql and *ESTAT.sql* are Version 6 scripts provided by ORACLE that allow you to take a snapshot of how the database is performing. They provide information that may help you identify problems and give you guidance about what needs tuning. BSTAT tells ORACLE to start writing system statistics into a table. ESTAT stops this writing and displays the report. Keep in mind that the statistics provided by these scripts are system-wide, but only for the interval between BSTAT and ESTAT. BSTAT and ESTAT cannot be executed for an individual user connection.

In Version 7, use the SQL scripts, *UTLBSTAT.sql* and *UTLESTAT.sql*, in place of BSTAT and ESTAT. They perform the same function. For an example of output and using these scripts to diagnose dictionary problems see in Chapter 14, *Tuning the Data Dictionary*, the section called "Running the UTLBSTAT.sql and UTLESTAT.sql Scripts (Version 7)."

Be sure to run these scripts when your system is doing ordinary processing. If you run them when there are no users on the system, they will give unrealistic and misleading results. You may also get distorted results if you run them all day (24 hours) on a system in which users are normally logged on for only the workday (eight hours). Most sites run BSTAT and ESTAT from 10:00 a.m. to 12:00 p.m. and again from 2:00 p.m. to 4:30 p.m. These periods normally reflect peak production load and consistent application transaction activity.

In testing, we have found that BSTAT and ESTAT incur very little system overhead.

To start the snapshot, type:

> **SQLDBA>** @BSTAT

Let BSTAT run for as long as you want to gather information. Then, end the snapshot by typing:

> **SQLDBA>** @ESTAT

To start the snapshot for a Version 7 database, type:

> **SQLDBA>** @UTLBSTAT

Note that you must set the INIT.ORA parameter, TIMED_STATISTICS, to TRUE (the default is FALSE) to produce the timing statistics (e.g., "current lock get time") shown in the output.

```
SQLDBA> set charwidth 30;
SQLDBA> set numwidth 11;
SQLDBA> rem    Total is the total value of the statistic between the time
SQLDBA> rem    bstat was run and the time estat was run.
SQLDBA> select n1.name Statistic",
    2> n1.change "Total",
    3> trunc (n1.change/n2.change,2)  "Per Trans"
    4> from stats$stats n1, stats$stats n2
    5> where n2.name='user commits'
    6> order by n1.name;
```

The following output example was produced from a Version 6 database. However, Version 7 output is very similar.

NOTE

> If you find any negative values (except those beginning with "current") in the output, ignore the output. The database must have been shut down and then restarted across the boundary of the BSTAT/ESTAT snapshot.

We have annotated the following output by highlighting certain statistics and including comments suggesting simple things you can do to improve performance when you notice suspicious statistics. For a discussion of Note (1), see the first section of the following list; for Note (2), see the second section; and so on. These sections show specifically how to interpret BSTAT/ESTAT output. Chapter 13 expands on this discussion and suggests other ways to tune the areas of memory and disk mentioned below.

Statistic	Total	Per Trans
DBWR exchange waits	0	0
background timeouts	15505	1292.08

Statistic	Total	Per Trans
buffer busy waits (2)	1	.08
busy wait time	11	.91
calls to kcmgcs	3316	276.33
calls to kcmgns	29	2.41
calls to kcmgrs	116	9.66
change write time	35	2.91
cluster key scan block gets	50	4.16
cluster key scans	16	1.33
consistent changes	17	1.41
consistent forceouts	0	0
consistent gets(1) (2)	35869	2989.08
consistent lock get time	0	0
consistent lock gets	0	0
cumulative opened cursors	1679	139.91
current lock get fails	0	0
current lock get time	0	0
current lock gets	0	0
current logons	2	.16
current open cursors	28	2.33
db block changes	1781	148.41
db block gets(1) (2)	3545	295.41
dbwr buffers scanned	4559	379.91
dbwr checkpoints	0	0
dbwr free low (3)	0	0
dbwr free needed (3)	0	0
dbwr interrupts	0	0
dbwr interrupts deferred	0	0
dbwr timeouts	7748	645.66
enqueue conversions	10	.83
enqueue deadlocks	0	0
enqueue releases	9976	831.33
enqueue requests	9958	829.83
enqueue timeouts	0	0
enqueue waits[a]	0	0
exchange deadlocks	0	0
free buffer inspected	0	0

Statistic	Total	Per Trans
free buffer requested	4561	380.08
free buffer scans	4561	380.08
free buffer waits	0	0
free wait time	0	0
instance lock convert time	0	0
instance lock converts (async)	0	0
instance lock converts (non async)	0	0
instance lock get time	0	0
instance lock gets (async)	0	0
instance lock gets (non async)	0	0
instance lock release time	0	0
instance lock releases (async)	0	0
instance lock releases (non async)	0	0
logons	69	5.75
messages received	43	3.58
messages sent	43	3.58
parse count	2032	169.33
parse time cpu	678	56.5
parse time elapsed	3559	296.58
physical reads (1)	4530	377.5
physical writes	208	17.33
recursive calls[b]	5225	435.41
redo blocks written	71	5.91
redo buffer allocation retries	0	0
redo chunk allocations	0	0
redo delayed write sync	0	0
redo entries	734	61.16
redo entries linearized	734	61.16
redo log space requests	0	0
redo log space wait time	0	0
redo log switch interrupts	0	0
redo log switch wait failure	0	0
redo size	174626	14552.16
redo small copies	727	60.58
redo synch time	198	16.5
redo synch writes	25	2.08

Statistic	Total	Per Trans
redo wastage	114912	9576
redo write time	432	36
redo writer latching time	2	.16
redo writes	50	4.16
sorts (disk)[c]	0	0
sorts (memory)[c]	499	41.58
sorts (rows)[c]	1962	163.5
table fetch by rowid (4)	12172	1014.33
table fetch continued row(4)	0	0
table scan blocks gotten	6635	552.91
table scan rows gotten	130247	10853.91
table scans (long tables) (4)	263	21.91
table scans (short tables) (4)	258	21.5
user calls[d]	15230	1269.16
user commits	12	1
user rollbacks	4	.33
write complete waits (3)	0	0
write wait time	0	0

92 rows selected.

[a]If enqueue waits is > 0, you must increase the ENQUEUE_RESOURCE parameter in the INIT.ORA file.

[b]If recursive calls /user calls > .1, tune the dictionary cache and/or try to eliminate dynamic extension.

[c]The three sort statistics above are useful in determining the need to increase SORT_ AREA_SIZE.

[d]If recursive calls /user calls > .1, tune the dictionary cache and/or try to eliminate dynamic extension.

Note that ORACLE provides a number of other ways you can derive this same information on system activity, as described later in this chapter and in Chapter 13.

Tuning the Buffer Cache Hit Ratio

The goal of this performance test is to find as much application data in memory as possible. If you tune the buffer cache correctly, you can significantly improve database performance. The hit ratio computed below is the rate at which ORACLE finds the data blocks it needs already in memory. The closer the hit ratio approaches 100%, the better your system will perform. Use the statistics from BTAT/ESTAT above to do the following calculation:

```
Hit ratio = (logical reads - physical reads) / (logical reads)
Logical reads = consistent gets + db block gets = 35869 + 3545 = 39414
Hit ratio = (39414 - 4530) / (39414) = (34884) / (39414) = 89%
```

The general rule of thumb is that if the hit ratio is below 0.90, and the dictionary cache has been tuned, increase the buffer cache value to the point where at least 5% free memory remains available during peak usage. The system being monitored in this example has a hit ratio of .89 (89%), which is fairly efficient. We usually consider anything below .60 poor, and recommend that anything below .95 could probably be improved given sufficient free memory. The particular threshold for your system depends on your application transaction mix and the amount of free memory you have available.

What can you do to solve this problem? Enlarge the amount of buffer cache in your system by increasing the INIT.ORA parameter, DB_BLOCK_BUFFERS, but make sure you keep 5% of your memory free.

For another example of computing the hit ratio via the MONITOR statistics, refer to Chapter 13, *Monitoring and Tuning an Existing Database.*

Tuning Buffer Busy Wait Ratio

The goal of this performance test is to reduce contention for database data and rollback blocks. Use the BSTAT/ESTAT statistics to perform this calculation:

```
Buffer busy waits ratio=(buffer busy waits) / (logical reads)=(1) / (39414)
= 0.00002
```

If the ratio is greater than 5%, there is a problem. In the sample above, the figure is close to 0%, which is an ideal situation. If there were a problem, you could try adding free lists to table headers (via the INIT.ORA parameter, FREE_LIST_PROC for Version 6, or the FREELISTS parameter on the CREATE command for Version 7). Alternatively, add rollback segments to the rollback tablespace.

Tuning the DBWR

The database writer (DBWR) process handles all writes to the database. The aim of this performance test is to ensure that free buffers are available in the buffer cache as needed. Read-only buffers can always be swapped out, but dirty buffers need to be retained until they have been successfully written to the database. User processes that require DBWR must be functioning efficiently.

If the "DBWR free needed" statistic displayed by BSTAT/ESTAT is greater than zero, there is a problem. With contention that must be remedied immediately. There is no problem in the output above. ("DBWR free needed" is 0). If there were a problem, you could increase the number of free buffers by increasing the INIT.ORA parameter DB_WRITERS and DB_BLOCK_WRITE_BATCH. For an example of using the MONITOR function to look at DBWR performance and a more detailed discussion of this process, see the section called "Tuning the Database Writer" in Chapter 13.

Tuning Table Access Method

The goal of this performance test is to increase the effectiveness with which data is accessed by indexes.

If the result of the following calculation is greater than 10%:

```
Table scans (long tables) / (table scans (short tables) + table scans (long
tables))
```

you must evaluate your use of indexes. This rule may vary depending on the nature of your site's transaction mix. For databases used primarily for reporting, full table scans are sometimes preferable to indexed table lookups. You'll have to select the right approach for your own particular site.

In our example, the calculation is:

```
263 / (258 + 263) = .50
```

This indicates that a large percentage of the tables accessed were not indexed lookups. You need to investigate this situation. If the overhead of running SQL_TRACE is not too great for your site, set the INIT.ORA parameter SQL_TRACE to TRUE. Then, run TKPROF against all trace files with an automatic output scan to find "Full" references (representing full-table scans) in the output files. Remember to reset SQL_TRACE to FALSE for the next day's processing.

What can you do about this problem? Use indexes that give you much faster results. For online transaction processing systems, investigate all full-table scans to see if you can use an index to avoid the need to scan this way. Note, however, that if a particular report or update requires that every row of a table be read, it is more efficient to do a full-table scan. This is because the system needs to read the index (to find out the index on disk) for each row, and then to do a physical read of the database block. With a full-table scan, one table block may contain more than 100 rows, which can all be read with one physical read. (Chapter 6, *Defining Indexes*, and Chapter 7, *Tuning SQL*, describe a number of other indexing and data access considerations.)

Tuning I/O Spread

Check the output of the following query from the BSTAT/ESTAT temporary tables to observe how well the I/O load is distributed across the disk devices in your system.

```
SQLDBA> set charwidth 48;
SQLDBA> set numwidth 12;
SQLDBA> rem  I/O should be spread evenly across drives. A big difference
SQLDBA> rem  between PHYS_READS and PHYS_BLKS_RD implies table
SQLDBA> rem  scans are going on
SQLDBA> select * from stats$files;
```

TABLE_SPACE	FILE_NAME	PHYS_ READS	PHYS_ BLKS_RD	PHYS_ RD_TIME	PHYS_ WRITES	PHYS_ BLKS_WR	PHYS_ WRI_TIM
ROLLBACK	/db/datafile1.ora	0	0	0	78	78	2034
TEMP	/db/datafile2.ora	0	0	0	0	0	0
DATA1	/db/datafile3.ora	202	766	1330	54	54	1058
DATA2	/db/datafile4.ora	62	391	720	29	29	1112
INDEX1	/db/datafile5.ora	37	37	117	3	3	39
SYSTEM	/db/datafile0.ora	740	3353	6779	44	44	1619

6 rows selected.

In the example shown, the system tablespace was the most active, which is not a healthy scenario. The previous tuning steps have uncovered the fact that quite a few unindexed searches have been taking place. The tablespace table shown here indicates that there might be sort activity going on in the system tablespace.

What can you do about this problem? Create a separate tablespace for temporary table activity. With the ALTER USER *username* TEMPORARY TABLESPACE *tablespace* command you can assign each user to this new temporary tablespace. If users do not have a temporary tablespace explicitly assigned, they default to the SYSTEM tablespace, which should not be allowed. If you cannot add a new temporary tablespace because there isn't enough free disk space on your system, assign your users elsewhere—perhaps to the DATA1 tablespace.

Reducing Contention for Internal Latches

If a user process is going to perform an operation such as accessing data in the SGA, it must first obtain a latch from the table and then own the latch. If the process is forced to wait for a latch, because there aren't enough available, a slowdown occurs. Additional CPU is also needed to keep interrogating the latch queue.

This query asks if there is internal latch contention going on:

```
SQLDBA> set charwidth 26;
SQLDBA> set numwidth 9;
```

```
SQLDBA>  rem Timeouts should be low. Successes should be very close to
         nowaits.
SQLDBA>  select name, waits, immediates, timeouts, nowaits, successes
      2> from stats$latches order by name;
```

NAME	WAITS	IMME-DIATE	TIME OUTS	NO WAITS	SUCC-ESSES
archive control	0	0	0	0	0
cache buffer handles	2670	2670	0	0	0
cache buffers chains	92861	92861	0	247997	247997
cache buffers lru chain	20141	20139	2	38481	38481
dml/ddl allocation	3994	3994	0	0	0
enqueues	36941	36939	2	0	0
messages	31468	31465	3	0	0
multiblock read objects	1740	1740	0	0	0
process allocation	432	432	0	0	0
redo allocation	9340	9340	0	0	0
redo copy	0	0	0	198	198
row cache objects	69528	69528	0	0	0
sequence cache	408	408	0	0	0
session allocation	15250	15250	0	0	0
system commit number	4143	4143	0	0	0
transaction allocation	198	198	0	0	0
undo global data	146	146	0	0	0

```
17 rows selected.
```

If the latch ratio of any of the key latches ("cache buffers lru chain", "enqueues", "redo allocation", "redo copy") is greater than 3%, there is latch contention. For example, "cache buffer lru chain" has a ratio of:

```
timeouts / immediates > 35% (2 / 20139 = 0.01% )
```

The section in Chapter 13 called "Monitoring for Redo Log Latch Contention" shows how to deal with this problem. Chapter 18, *Tuning for Specific Systems*, also contains a discussion of how to handle this problem in a UNIX system.

Reducing Rollback-related Transactions

This query asks if transactions are waiting for rollback segments to be released by other transactions:

```
SQLDBA>  set numwidth 19;
SQLDBA>  rem  If TRANS_TBL_WAITS is high, you should add rollback segments.
SQLDBA>  select * from stats$roll;
```

TRANS_ TBL_GE	TRANS_ TBL_WAITS	UNDO_BYTES_ WRITTEN	SEGMENT_ SIZE_BYTEs

| ------ | --------- | ----------- | ---------- |
76	0	0	182790
270	0	13820	29157036
345	0	21048	29157036
293	0	16851	29157036
427	0	27942	8603316

5 rows selected.

Perform the following calculation:

```
Transaction table wait ratio = TRANS_TBL_WAITS / TRANS_TBL_GETS
```

If this ratio is greater than .05, add rollback segments. In our example, there have been no waits at all. If there were, however, you would need to add more to ensure that each transaction can get a rollback segment without having to wait for another transaction to release it.

Other ORACLE Scripts

ORACLE provides a variety of SQL scripts in each system release. In addition to BSTAT and ESTAT (and their Version 7 equivalents, *UTLBSTAT.sql* and *UTLESTAT.sql*), several others allow you to diagnose system problems and tune for better performance. In this section we describe the most commonly used ORACLE tuning scripts.

ONEIDXS.sql: Testing an Individual Index

The *ONEIDXS.sql* script allows you to test a particular index to find out how effective it is. Use this script to identify columns on which you might index in the future, evaluate how selective a current index is, and evaluate whether an existing index is still useful.

This output, from an application master table, shows the column spread for a particular index:

Table_Name	Column_Name	Stat_Name	Stat_Value
LOAN_MASTER	MGR_CODE	Rows - Total	26062
LOAN_MASTER	MGR_CODE	Rows - Null	23991
LOAN_MASTER	MGR_CODE	Total Distinct Keys	34
LOAN_MASTER	MGR_CODE	Rows per key - avg	60.91176
LOAN_MASTER	MGR_CODE	Rows per key - min	1
LOAN_MASTER	MGR_CODE	Rows per key - max	751
LOAN_MASTER	MGR_CODE	Rows per key - dev	125.7822
LOAN_MASTER	MGR_CODE	db_gets_per_key_miss	313.0116
LOAN_MASTER	MGR_CODE	db_gets_per_key_hit	156.916

You can see from this output that the indexed column (MGR_CODE) may not have been the best choice of a column. Nearly all the rows of the table (more than 92%) have a null value as the key. Of the 2071 non-null keys, only 34 distinct key values exist. This means that there are on average, 60.9 rows per key value. To make matters even worse, one key value has 751 rows, more than 36% of the non-null records.

All this tells us, though, is that we need to investigate this index further. In fact, when we looked more carefully, we found out that the indexed column, MGR_CODE, was only the first column of a concatenated index; that accounted for the reporting of poor key spread. But, the large number of null rows did in fact turn out to be a problem that had to be followed up. (In general, Version 7 will not use an inefficient index if the table has been ANALYZEd.)

BLOCKING.sql and LOCKTREE.sql: Version 6 Locking

For Version 6, *BLOCKING.sql* lets you monitor locking problems by creating two views of database locks currently being held: ALL_LOCKS_VIEW and BLOCKING_LOCKS.

ALL_LOCKS_VIEW displays a row for every lock or latch that is being held, and one row for each outstanding request for a lock or latch.

```
TYPE    LMODE   PID       ID1      ID2     REQUEST
----    -----   ---     --------  ------  ----------
LATCH   6       1       01F03757          0
TD      4       2       551       0       0
TM      5       2       108       0       0
TX      6       2       65561     401     0
```

The BLOCKING_LOCKS view displays processes requesting locks that are actually held by another process. The second process is not waiting for other resources (i.e., this view is not detecting deadlock).

Here is the internal description of how these scripts work:

```
DOC> * This script prints the processes in the system that are waiting for
DOC> * locks, and the locks that they are waiting for. The printout is tree
DOC> * structured. If a processid is printed immediately below and to the
DOC> * right of another process, then it is waiting for that process. The
DOC> * process ids printed at the left hand side of the page are the ones
DOC> * that everyone is waiting for.
DOC> *
DOC> * For example, in the following printout process 9 is waiting for
DOC> * process 8, 7 is waiting for 9, and 10 is waiting for 9.
DOC> *
DOC> * PROCESS   TYPE    MODE          MODE HELD       LOCK ID1  LOCK ID2
DOC> * WAITING           REQUESTED
DOC> * -------   ----    -----------   -------------   --------- --------
DOC> * 8         NONE    None          None            0         0
DOC> * 9         TX      Share (S)     Exclusive (X)   65547     16
DOC> * 7         RW      Exclusive (X) S/Row-X (SSX)   33554440  2
```

```
DOC> * 10       RW    Exclusive (X)  S/Row-X (SSX)  33554440    2
DOC> *
DOC> * The lock information to the right of the process id describes the
DOC> * lock that the process is waiting for (not the lock it is holding).
DOC> *
DOC> * You must have the blocking.sql script loaded for this script to work.
DOC> *
DOC> * Note that this is a script and not a set of view definitions because
DOC> * connect-by is used in the implementation and therefore a temporary
DOC> * table is created and dropped since you cannot do a join in a
DOC> * connect-by.
DOC> * This script has two small disadvantages. One, a table is created when
DOC> * this script is run. To create a table a number of locks must be
DOC> * acquired. This  might cause the process running  the script to get
DOC> * caught in the lock problem it is trying to diagnose. Two, if a
DOC> * process waits on a lock held by more than one process (share lock)
DOC> * then the wait-for graph is no longer a tree and the conenct-by will
DOC> * show the process (and any processes waiting on it) several times.
DOC> */
DOC> * pid of the process that holds the lock.
DOC> *   UNION
DOC> * The pids of all processes holding locks that someone is waiting on
DOC> * that are not themselves waiting for locks. These are included so
DOC> * that the roots of the wait for graph (the processes holding things
DOC> * up) will be displayed.
DOC> *
DOC> * pid       - pid of requesting process
DOC> * type      - type of lock being requested
DOC> * id1       - id1 of lock being requested (value is lock type specific)
DOC> * id2       - id2 of lock being requested (value is lock type specific)
DOC> * req       - mode lock is being requested in
DOC> * hpid      - pid of process holding the lock
DOC> * hmod      - mode the lock is held in
```

CATBLOCK.sql and UTILOCK.sql: Version 7 Locking

In Version 7, the *CATBLOCK*.sql scripts create a number of views showing information about locks held in the database.

DBA_LOCKS   This view has a row for each lock and latch that is being held, and one row for each outstanding request for a lock or latch; it is just like the Version 6 ALL_LOCKS_VIEW.

ID	LOCK_TYPE	HELD	RQST	LOCK_ID1	LOCK_ID2
2	Media Recovery	Share	None	6	0
2	Media Recovery	Share	None	2	0
2	Media Recovery	Share	None	1	0

```
2  Media Recovery       Share        None  2                                    0
3  Redo Thread          Exclusive    None  1                                    0
6  Transaction          Exclusive    None  196640                               129
8  DML                  Row-X (SX)   None  1456                                 0
8  Transaction          Exclusive    None  327726                               152
8  DML                  Row-X (SX)   None  1460                                 0
8  DML                  Row-X (SX)   None  1462                                 0
6  Cursor Definition Lock Null       None  SELECT SYSDATE FROM SYS.DUAL    0070E210
6  Cursor Definition Lock Null       None  SELECT USER FROM SYS.DUAL       0072F8A0
6  Cursor Definition Lock Null       None  SAVEPOINT IAP_1                 00825214
6  Cursor Definition Lock Null       None  SAVEPOINT IAP_1                 008254B0
6  Cursor Definition Lock Null       None  SELECT 'C' FROM GROUP_USERS G,  00877F7C
                                           MENU_GROUPS M  WHERE M.MENU_
                                           CODE = :b1  AND M.GROUP_CODE = G.
                                           GROUP_C  AND G.USER_CODE = :b2
                                           AND M.UPD_LEVEL <= G.ACCESS_LVL
6 Cursor Definition Pin Share        None  SELECT 'C' FROM GROUP_USERS G,  00877F7C
                                           MENU_GROUPS M  WHERE  M.MENU_
                                           CODE = :b1  AND M.GROUP_CODE = G.GR
                                           OUP_CODE  AND G.USER_CODE = :b2
                                           AND U.UPD_LEVEL <= G.ACCESS_LVL
```

DBA_DML_LOCKS	This view has one row for each data manipulation language (DML) lock held, and one for each outstanding request for a DML lock.
DBA_DDL_LOCKS	This view has one row for each DDL lock held, and one for each outstanding request for a DDL lock.
DBA_WAITERS	This view shows all sessions waiting for locks and the session that holds that lock.
DBA_BLOCKERS	This view shows all sessions that are holding a lock required by another process.

DBMSLOCK.sql: Requesting, Converting, and Releasing Locks

The *DBMSLOCK.sql* script is a Version 7 script that makes use of the packages and functions available in Version 7. With this script you can request, convert, and release locks managed by the RDBMS lock management service. Such locks have the "UL" identifier, when they appear on the SQL*DBA MONITOR LOCK function and in various views, to avoid confusion with real ORACLE data locks.

NOTE

These are manual locks, not real ORACLE data locks. Be careful with this script, though, because if you are not, you might release or modify ORACLE locks, resulting in unpredictable and possibly disastrous outcomes.

Deadlock detection is performed on these manual user locks, and all locks are released automatically when the owning session terminates.

Services provided by this package include:

Allocate_Unique	Allocates a unique lock identified for a lock name.
Request	Requests a lock for a given mode.
Convert	Converts a lock from one mode to another.
Release	Releases a database lock (ORACLE or user).
Sleep	Sleeps for a specified time.

We generally avoid using this script. We did use it once to release the resource locks of a terminated session that had inadvertently failed and continued to hold vital resources. These locks were only over the table schema, not individual table rows. Nevertheless, they prevented us from performing a table ALTER required by another area of this application.

SYNC.sql: Synchronizing Processes (Version 7 Only)

The *SYNC.sql* script helps you tune SQL statements. Often, these statements do not reveal their tuning flaws until they are run in conjunction with other processes. The *SYNC.sql* script allows you to activate many other processes and synchronize them so they work concurrently. These processes can be different SQL statements or (for testing purposes) the same one multiple times. This script also generates a number of functions (libraries) that you can call via SQL*Plus to coordinate the resulting information.

In the following example, we are synchronizing three user processes in order to process three separate SQL statements at exactly the same time.

Process 1	Process 2	Process 3
EXECUTE SYNC.INIT (3)	EXECUTE SYNC.INIT (3)	EXECUTE SYNC.INIT (3)
EXECUTE SYNC.WAIT	EXECUTE SYNC.WAIT	EXECUTE SYNC.WAIT
. . . SQL statement . . .	. . . SQL statement . . .	. . . SQL statement . . .

Some Scripts of Our Own

Through the years, we've been writing scripts to do all kinds of things. The ones included in this section are our favorite database tuning scripts, developed, begged, and borrowed over the last few years. These scripts aren't definitive in any way; they could have been, and probably have been, written in a dozen alternative ways. But they do get the work done. Unless we say otherwise, each of these scripts can be executed against either a Version 6 or a Version 7 database.

Identifying Database Extents

One of the most common activities you'll find yourself doing as a DBA is scanning the physical database looking for new table and index extents. You ought to do this on a regular basis, ideally as part of an automated daily or weekly overnight procedure. Your goal is to minimize the number of extents on disk. Access to contiguous areas of disk is much faster than access to noncontiguous areas. In one test we did on a 4000-row table, we found that when the entire table fit on one extent, it took .76 seconds to scan it; when the table was spread over 10 extents, it took 3.62 seconds.

We have found that the existence of a small number of such extents (less than five) doesn't seem to affect performance very much, but it is still good practice to remove them all. (In the next section, we describe how to size the table for the reorganization while not wasting valuable disk space.)

Note that this script assumes that the operating system ORACLE block size is 4K and that all ROLLBACK segments were created with 10 initial extents (MINEXTENTS parameter).

```
SELECT SUBSTR(S.SEGMENT_NAME,1,20) OBJECT_NAME,
    SUBSTR(S.SEGMENT_TYPE,1,5) TYPE,
    SUBSTR(S.TABLESPACE_NAME,1,10) T_SPACE,
    NVL(NVL(T.INITIAL_EXTENT, I.INITIAL_EXTENT),R.INITIAL_EXTENT)/ 4096
        FST_EXT,
    NVL(NVL(T.NEXT_EXTENT,I.NEXT_EXTENT),R.NEXT_EXTENT) / 4096 NXT_EXT,
        S.EXTENTS - 1  TOT_EXT,
        S.BLOCKS   TOT_BLKS
    FROM
        SYS.DBA_ROLLBACK_SEGS R,
        SYS.DBA_INDEXES I,
        SYS.DBA_TABLES T,
        SYS.DBA_SEGMENTS S
    WHERE
    S.SEGMENT_NAME     LIKE  UPPER('&S_NAME')  ||  '%'
AND S.TABLESPACE_NAME  LIKE  UPPER('&T_SPACE') ||  '%'
AND S.EXTENTS              >   1
AND S.OWNER            =     T.OWNER (+)
AND S.SEGMENT_NAME     =     T.TABLE_NAME (+)
AND S.TABLESPACE_NAME  =     T.TABLESPACE_NAME (+)
AND S.OWNER            =     I.OWNER (+)
AND S.SEGMENT_NAME     =     I.INDEX_NAME (+)
AND S.TABLESPACE_NAME  =     I.TABLESPACE_NAME (+)
AND S.OWNER            =     R.OWNER (+)
AND S.SEGMENT_NAME     =     R.SEGMENT_NAME (+)
```

```
AND S.TABLESPACE_NAME   =     R.TABLESPACE_NAME (+)
ORDER BY
    S.SEGMENT_NAME,   S.SEGMENT_TYPE
```

OBJECT_NAME	TYPE	T_SPACE	FST EXT	NXT EXT	TOT EXT	TOT BLKS
ALL_TRAN_AUDX_INDX	INDEX	DEV_IDX	125	63	2	251
OBJ$	TABLE	SYSTEM	13	13	1	26
PRODUCT_PROFILE	TABLE	SYSTEM	13	13	1	26
RBACK1	ROLLB	RBK	25	25	9	300
RBACK2	ROLLB	RBK	25	25	9	525
RBACK_BIG	ROLLB	RBK	256	256	9	2560
XREF$	TABLE	SYSTEM	13	13	1	26

Performing Database Table Sizing

This section contains several scripts we use to size a database.

Looking for tablespace space shortages

When tables, indexes, and rollback segments are created, they are preassigned a storage allocation (extent), which is reserved and cannot be used by any other object. Although the objects may not use all of the space allocated at the start, as more information is placed into the area the amount of available free space diminishes. This query helps you instantly find application problems resulting from space shortages. Run it at regular intervals for the best information. Note that this script assumes that you have ORACLE data blocks of 4K (4096 bytes). This size is operating system-dependent, and you will have to modify the query if your block sizes differ.

```
SELECT   SUBSTR(D.TABLESPACE_NAME,1,15)                    TSPACE,
         D.FILE_ID                                         FILE_ID
         D.BYTES / 1024 / 1024                             TOT_MB,
         D.BYTES / 4096                                    ORA_BLKS,
         SUM(E.BLOCKS)                                     TOT_USED,
         ROUND(SUM(E.BLOCKS) / (D.BYTES / 4096), 4) * 100  PCT_USED,
   FROM  SYS.DBA_EXTENTS    E,
         SYS.DBA_DATA_FILES D
  WHERE  D.FILE_ID = E.FILE_ID (+)
  GROUP  BY D.TABLESPACE_NAME, D.BYTES
```

TSPACE	FILE_ID	TOT_MB	ORA_BLKS	TOT_USED	PCT_USED
DEV	4	250	64000	36633	57.2
DEV_AUD	6	100	25600	3691	14.4
DEV_IDX	5	300	76800	61317	79.8
HST	7	200	51200	38400	75.0

INV	8	80	20480	13739	67.1
INV_IDX	9	50	12800	7673	59.9
RBK	3	25	6400	4110	64.2
SYSTEM	1	20	5120	2366	46.2
TMP	2	50	12800		

Looking for tablespace fragmentation

This query of the database gives a detailed breakdown of the fragmentation of each tablespace file within the database.

```
SELECT      SUBSTR(TS.NAME,1,10)                              TSPACE,
            TF.BLOCKS                                         BLOCKS,
            SUM(F.LENGTH)                                     FREE,
            COUNT(*)                                          PIECES,
            MAX(F.LENGTH)                                     BIGGEST,
            MIN(F.LENGTH)                                     SMALLEST,
            ROUND(AVG(F.LENGTH))                              AVERAGE,
            SUM(DECODE(SIGN(F.LENGTH-5), -1, F.LENGTH, 0))    DEAD
FROM        SYS.FET$            F,
            SYS.FILE$           TF,
            SYS.TS$             TS
WHERE       TS.TS#  =  F.TS#
AND         TS.TS#  =  TF.TS#
GROUP BY    TS.NAME, TF.BLOCKS;
```

Tspace	Blocks	Free	Pieces	Biggest	Smallest	Average	Dead
DEV	64000	27366	9	25614	105	3041	0
DEV_AUD	25600	21908	1	21908	21908	21908	0
DEV_IDX	76800	15482	16	175	4	968	2
HST	51200	12799	1	12799	12799	12799	0
INV	20480	6740	12	6740	6740	6740	0
INV_IDX	12800	5126	4	2565	63	1282	0
RBK	6400	2289	1	2289	2289	2289	0
SYSTEM	5120	2753	74	487	3	16	12
TMP	12800	12799	41	1536	11	312	0

The last column, "Dead", is based on the assumption that any contiguous block smaller than five ORACLE blocks (20K for the operating system we used for testing) cannot be used. That is, no table or index has an INITIAL or NEXT extent size less than 20 kilobytes.

Looking at space use by individual tables

This query reports how full a particular table actually is. It compares the number of ORACLE blocks that have at least one record against the total number of blocks allocated to the table extent(s). You can use this query to interrogate table after table; the table name replaces the name, &TAB_NAME, in each statement execution.

```
SELECT    BLOCKS                                          ALLOCATED_BLKS,
          COUNT(DISTINCT SUBSTR(T.ROWID,1,8)
                       || SUBSTR(T.ROWID,15,4))           USED,
          (COUNT(DISTINCT SUBSTR(T.ROWID,1,8)
                       || SUBSTR(T.ROWID,15,4))
          / BLOCKS) * 100                                 PCT_USED
FROM      SYS.DBA_SEGMENTS E,
          &TAB_NAME T
WHERE     E.SEGMENT_NAME = UPPER ('&TAB_NAME')
AND       E.SEGMENT_TYPE = 'TABLE'
GROUP BY E.BLOCKS;


ALLOCATED_BLKS          USED          PCT_USED
--------------          ----          --------
2560                    1728          67.50
```

Looking at the average number of records per block

This query reports the number of rows physically residing in ORACLE blocks of a table. This query can be used to calculate how much space a table will ultimately require.

```
SELECT    SUBSTR(T.ROWID,1,8)  || '-' ||SUBSTR(T.ROWID,15,4)   BLOCK,
          COUNT(*)                                             ROW_CNT,
FROM      &TAB_NAME T
WHERE     ROWNUM  <  2000
GROUP BY SUBSTR(T.ROWID,1,8) || '-' || SUBSTR(T.ROWID,15,4);
```

Output from this query is shown below.

```
BLOCK                   ROW_CNT
-------------           -------
00001F52-0002           93
00001F53-0002           85
00001F54-0002           82
00001F55-0002           100
00001F56-0002           83
00001F57-0002           71
00001F58-0002           82
00001F59-0002           91
00001F5A-0002           93
00001F5B-0002           91
00001F5C-0002           63
00001F5D-0002           69
00001F5E-0002           75
00001F5F-0002           1
00001F60-0002           4
00001F61-0002           5
```

Putting it together

By looking at the results of the set of scripts included in this section, you can do a good job of calculating future table requirements:

Script 1   Tells us that the DEV tablespace is only 43% used. Of the initial 250-megabyte allocation, more than 107 megabytes are still free. This tablespace should not be a problem for some time.

Script 2   Tells us that the 107 megabytes of free space within the DEV tablespace comprises only nine contiguous segments and no dead blocks. This tells us that the free space is indeed free and usable.

Script 3   Tells us that the table being analyzed currently has consumed only 67% of its current extent allocations.

Script 4   Tells us that the table being analyzed can store an average of 80 to 90 records per ORACLE block (4K per block). Therefore, the current volume represents one year of growth and is already 40,000 records in size. What storage will be needed for 10 years' growth?

We advise you to be relatively conservative in making estimates so you don't consume needless amounts of disk space, while being sensible enough not to run out of space too soon. Not always an easy task! Our calculation:

```
Total records      = 40,000 x 10
                   = 400,000 records  (adjust to 500,000)

Records Per Block = 80 . . . 90      (adjust to 75)

Space Requirements = (Total Records / Records Per Block) x Block Size
                   = ( 500,000 / 75 ) * ( 1024 * 4 )
                   = 27,306,667 bytes
                   = 26.4 megabytes
```

Computing the Hit Ratio

Throughout this book we have emphasized how proper sizing of the ORACLE cache buffers can help reduce disk I/O. Computing the hit ratio is a very helpful way to do this sizing. The hit ratio tells us how many times ORACLE has needed to retrieve a database block and has found it in memory (rather than having to access it on disk). Because memory access is so much faster than disk access, the higher the hit ratio, the better your performance.

You can ordinarily obtain the hit ratio for your application only by looking at either the BSTAT/ESTAT statistics or the DBA MONITOR screens, as described earlier in this chapter. The script included below shows how to get the hit ratio from SQL*Plus. If you do this, you can automatically schedule hit ratio queries and can direct the output to a report or another database table. That table can then be used to produce application statistics or management reporting.

NOTE

Actual "STATISTIC#" values depend upon your platform and your ORACLE release.

```
SELECT   A.VALUE + B.VALUE                          LOG_READS,
         C.VALUE                                    PHY_READS,
         ROUND(100 * (A.VALUE + B.VALUE - C.VALUE)
            /(A.VALUE + B.VALUE))                   RATIO,
         D.VALUE                                    PHY_WRITES
FROM     SYS.V_$SYSSTAT A,
         SYS.V_$SYSSTAT B,
         SYS.V_$SYSSTAT C,
         SYS.V_$SYSSTAT D
WHERE    A.STATISTIC#  = 28        /* db block gets   */
         B.STATISTIC#  = 29        /* consistent gets */
         C.STATISTIC#  = 30        /* physical gets   */
         D.STATISTIC#  = 31        /* physical writes */


LOG_READS         PHY_READS        RATIO         PHY_WRITES
----------        ---------        -----         ----------
39,746,936        3,456,039        91.3          149,348
```

Looking at the Dictionary Cache

This script lets you interrogate the ORACLE data dictionary performance tables via SQL*Plus. These tables give you information about all the objects stored in your dictionary (e.g., tablespaces, files, users, rollback segments, constraints, synonyms, etc.). This information is available in other ways, but getting at it through SQL*Plus lets you automate your queries, as we've described for the hit ratio in the previous section.

NOTE

This script applies only to Version 6. In Version 6, there are a number of distinct dictionary cache tables, and INIT.ORA parameters that allocate space in them. In Version 7, there is a single shared pool buffer, and a single parameter, called SHARED_POOL_SIZE. (See Chapter 14 for details.) Nevertheless, you can query the Version 7 variant of V$ROWCACHE as well for information, as described in Chapter 13.

```
SELECT    SUBSTR(PARAMETER,1,20)                              PARAMETER,
          GETS                                                GETS,
          GETMISSES                                           MISSES,
          DECODE(GETS,   0, 100, ROUND( 100 * GETMISSES / GETS)) RATIO,
          COUNT                                               COUNT,
          USAGE                                               USAGE,
          DECODE(COUNT, 0, 100, ROUND(100 * USAGE / COUNT))   CAPACITY,
FROM      SYS.V_$ROWCACHE;
```

PARAMETER	GETS	MISSES	RATIO	COUNT	USAGE	CAPACITY
dc_free_extents	1048	135	13	200	119	60
dc_used_extents	919	121	13	200	121	61
dc_segments	1300	81	6	250	79	32
dc_tablespaces	1825	10	1	10	10	100
dc_tablespaces	493	7	1	10	7	70
dc_tablespace_quo	326	10	3	10	10	100
dc_files	23	9	39	10	9	90
dc_users	654635	92	0	250	92	37
dc_rollback_seg	268257	6	0	25	7	28
dc_objects	1573520	4076	0	5000	4049	81
dc_constraints	85	51	60	500	51	10
dc_object_ids	11050	71	1	50	5	10
dc_tables	916276	350	0	400	362	91
dc_synonyms	465936	223	0	250	223	89
dc_sequences	13632	5	0	10	5	50
dc_usernames	577018	103	0	250	103	41
dc_columns	5339522	3509	0	5000	4080	82
dc_table_grants	258682	62	0	300	159	53
dc_column_grants	0	0	100	10	0	0
dc_indexes	963644	08	0	300	157	52
dc_constraint_defs	0	0	100	10	10	100
dc_sequence_grant	1333	3	0	10	3	30

Looking at the V$SYSSTAT Table

Most of the ORACLE database statistics we have displayed via the various utilities, statements, and scripts described in this chapter and in Chapter 13 actually are stored in one pseudo-table, constructed in memory at the time of database initialization. This table, called V$SYSSTAT, is virtually identical for Version 6 and Version 7. You can look at this table directly, if you prefer. It may reveal performance information you might not have noticed through other means. (Note that there are several other tables you might want to examine; see Chapter 13 for examples.)

S#	NAME	CLASS	VALUE
0	cumulative logons	1	307
1	current logons	1	9
2	cumulative opened cursors	1	19198
3	current open cursors	1	17
4	user commits	1	11048
5	user rollbacks	1	276
6	user calls	1	319471
7	recursive calls	1	300381
8	recursive cpu usage	1	0
9	session logical reads	1	1392435
10	session stored procedure space	1	0
11	CPU used when call started	128	0
12	CPU used by this session	1	0
13	session connect time	1	0
14	process last non-idle time	128	0
15	session memory	1	1201973
16	max session memory	1	9546989
17	messages sent	128	26684
18	messages received	128	26684
19	background timeouts	128	510287
20	session pga memory	1	21449404
21	session max pga memory	1	21478436
22	enqueue timeouts	4	13
23	enqueue waits	4	24
24	enqueue deadlocks	4	0
25	enqueue requests	4	68501
26	enqueue conversions	4	2486
27	enqueue releases	4	68472
28	db block gets	8	146695
29	consistent gets	8	1252109
30	physical reads	8	195243
31	physical writes	8	24202
32	write requests	8	5853
33	summed dirty queue length	8	2079
34	db block changes	8	95001
35	change write time	8	0
36	consistent changes	8	2120
37	write complete waits	8	635
38	write wait time	8	0
39	buffer busy waits	8	89
40	busy wait time	8	0
41	redo synch writes	8	11524
42	redo synch time	8	0
43	DBWR exchange waits	8	0
44	exchange deadlocks	8	0
45	free buffer requested	8	203575

46	dirty buffers inspected	8	1568
47	free buffer inspected	8	3081
48	free buffer waits	8	16
49	free wait time	8	0
50	DBWR timeouts	8	254416
51	DBWR make free requests	8	13071
52	DBWR free buffers found	8	82626
53	DBWR lru scans	8	13182
54	DBWR summed scan depth	8	91466
55	DBWR buffers scanned	8	88365
56	DBWR checkpoints	8	296
57	calls to kcmgcs	128	117246
58	calls to kcmgrs	128	0
59	calls to kcmgas	128	12234
60	redo entries	2	54912
61	redo size	2	17995651
62	redo entries linearized	2	0
63	redo buffer allocation retries	2	26
64	redo small copies	2	54887
65	redo wastage	2	4803610
66	redo writer latching time	2	0
67	redo writes	2	13864
68	redo blocks written	2	46075
69	redo write time	2	0
70	redo log space requests	2	59
71	redo log space wait time	2	0
72	redo log switch interrupts	2	0
73	redo ordering marks	2	0
74	background checkpoints started	8	22
75	background checkpoints completed	8	21
76	table scans (short tables)	64	6817
77	table scans (long tables)	64	5626
78	table scan rows gotten	64	4577154
79	table scan blocks gotten	64	398405
80	table fetch by rowid	64	307729
81	table fetch continued row	64	88
82	cluster key scans	64	11180
83	cluster key scan block gets	64	21331
84	parse time cpu	64	0
85	parse time elapsed	64	0
86	parse count	64	36774
87	sorts (memory)	64	287
88	sorts (disk)	64	0
89	sorts (rows)	64	448
90	cursor authentications	128	64175

13

Monitoring and Tuning an Existing Database

As we described in Chapter 11, *Tuning a New Database*, database tuning has an enormous effect on overall system performance. Tuning a newly created database is only the start. As time goes on, you'll need to monitor your database to make sure it continues to work efficiently. As database administrator, there is a great deal you can do to keep the database tuned as the amount of data, the number of users, and the complexity of queries increase over time. This chapter builds on the concepts introduced in the previous two chapters, describing how you can monitor and tune in three areas: memory, disk I/O, and contention (a situation in which several of your users vie for system resources).

ORACLE provides a number of tools that allow you to observe database performance, diagnose performance problems in the making, and remedy problems when they occur. These tools have been introduced in Chapter 12, *Diagnostic and Tuning Tools*. This chapter shows in greater detail how to use the tools with an existing database.

Because many sites are still running ORACLE Version 6, this chapter describes performance for both Version 6 and Version 7 databases.

Although performance tuning is a joint effort, the database administrator does have the primary responsibility for overall database performance. We have high hopes for DBAs and their ability to make a difference. Our goal, in this book and in the systems we tune, is to achieve as close as possible to the ideally performing ORACLE system. For that reason, our recommendations are often more stringent than ORACLE's own. Here's one example. The *ORACLE RDBMS Performance Tuning Guide* makes this recommendation: "If your hit ratio is low (less than 60% or 70%) you may want to increase the number of database cache buffers to improve performance." We consider 90% an achievable goal at almost all ORACLE sites. We recommend that if your system has ample memory and a hit ratio of 70% or less, you should define the DB_BLOCK_- BUFFERS parameter to make better use of memory and get better performance. We feel that even a performance improvement of 5% will pay off by reducing, by tens or even hundreds of thousands of I/Os, the demands during times of peak usage on your system. Throughput, morale, and perhaps your organization's finances will all benefit.

Using the SQL*DBA MONITOR Facility

Many of the examples presented in this chapter show the use of the SQL*DBA MONITOR facility to allow you to monitor activity and performance in your system by looking at the views of a variety of system performance tables that are held in memory. The way you use this facility depends on your particular platform, but its function is consistent across platforms. It provides a way for you to view the various performance tables maintained by the system. For example, to look at the table containing information about the read and write activity on the database files in the system, you might type the following for Version 6 under VMS:

```
SQLDBA> MON FILES
```

On a Macintosh system, you would invoke the Files function from the MONITOR menu. Either way, ORACLE will display information on requests for reads and writes, response times, and other information. For a complete list of MONITOR functions, see the section in Chapter 12 called "MONITOR: Monitoring System Activity Tables."

Tuning Memory

You have a lot of control over the use of memory in an ORACLE system, and it is up to you to monitor its use and make sure programs are using memory as efficiently as they can. Memory access is vastly faster than disk access, so the more you are able to keep information in memory, rather than having ORACLE seek it on disk, the better your response time and your overall system performance will be. If you are moving from Version 6 to Version 7, this tuning information may be particularly helpful. Version 7 provides some enhancements that give you as much as a 50% performance improvement over their untuned Version 6 counterparts.

This section describes the following tunable areas of memory and makes recommendations for tuning each of them.

For both Version 6 and Version 7:

- Buffer cache
- Log buffer

For Version 6:

- Dictionary cache
- Context areas

For Version 7:

- Shared buffer pool (contains library cache, dictionary cache, and session information)
- Private SQL and PL/SQL areas

System-specific Monitoring and Tuning Tools

In addition to the ORACLE memory monitoring and tuning tools described in this section, there are a number of operating system facilities that you and your system administrator can use to improve memory usage. ORACLE facilities cannot provide you with such system-specific information as the available memory on your machine, the amount of memory currently free on your machine, and the amount of memory being used by non-ORACLE applications. You must become familiar with the operating system commands and utilities that allow you to do memory monitoring. These differ from system to system. Under VMS, for example, you'll issue the command MON SYS or SH MEM. Under UNIX, you'll use *vmstat* or *sar -M*. Consult your operating system documentation for the facilities available in your own system.

Tuning the Dictionary Cache (Version 6 Only)

The ORACLE data dictionary is a set of tables and views that contain information about the database files, tablespaces, rollback segments, tables, indexes, and other objects that make up your database, along with storage allocations for these objects. In Version 6, the dictionary is stored in a separate area of the SGA called the data dictionary cache (DC).

Dictionary tuning is extremely important, and you should do this tuning before you tune any of the other memory components. Chapter 14, *Tuning the Data Dictionary*, describes in detail how you detect performance problems that are caused by poor dictionary memory management, and how you can correct these problems by resetting the parameters that control dictionary memory allocation. (These are the INIT.ORA parameters that begin with a DC_ prefix. For example, DC_TABLES allocates memory in the dictionary for information about the tables in your system.)

Tuning Context Areas (Version 6 Only)

In Version 6, the PGA contains a context area for each user process. In this area, the process holds information it needs to be able to process an SQL statement. The time required to parse an SQL statement is sometimes significant. If you tune your context areas carefully, you can reduce this time quite a bit by making sure statements are retained in memory after they are parsed the first time; this avoids the need to have to parse them again—a major time drain. There is a trade-off, of course. Retaining the statement in memory saves parsing time, but it does require additional memory. If you can spare the memory, you'll realize substantial performance gains. We have seen situations in which response times were cut in half when statements were cached in memory.

Sometimes, the term "cursor" is used synonymously with "context area." When a user runs a transaction, he or she may need many cursors for parsing. Parameters you can set to tune the context areas are the following:

OPEN_CURSORS	Maximum number of context areas a single process can open at any one time
CONTEXT_AREA	Initial size of the context area that will hold the cursor
CONTEXT_INCR	Incremental size of the context area

On virtual memory machines, you'll find that you can specify a large number of OPEN_ CURSORS. If your machine has limited memory, however, make sure your cursors are closed as soon as possible.

How can you tell how much parsing is being performed on your statements? One good way is to trace what happens during parsing and execution of your query. You can do this by running the SQL_TRACE utility (to create the trace file) and then the TKPROF utility (to produce readable output from the trace file). Below is an example of TKPROF output. Here, you can see the number of times a statement is parsed (in the intersection of "Parse" and "Count"), as well as the CPU ("cpu") and elapsed ("elap") times necessary to parse. Your goal in tuning the context area is to reduce the parsing time to an absolute minimum. If you have enough memory available in your system, you should have no problem minimizing parsing. (See Chapter 12 for a description of SQL_TRACE and TKPROF including a discussion of a problem you may notice in Version 6 TKPROF output.)

	Count	cpu	elap	phys	cr	cur	rows
Parse:	1	4	14	0	5	0	
Execute:	4	2	12	0	12	0	0
Fetch:	4	0	8	2	12	0	4

In addition to setting the appropriate INIT.ORA parameters, you can control the parsing of SQL statements by using certain product-dependent facilities. If you are using one of the ORACLE precompiler languages, set the following variables either in the program or on the precompiler command line:

HOLD_CURSORS   Holds cursors open

RELEASE_CURSORS   Releases cursors after use

MAXOPENCURSORS   Maximum number of cursors that can be held open simultaneously

If you are using the ORACLE Call Interface (OCI), use OOPEN to establish a cursor and context area, and OSQL3 to parse the SQL statement into a context area.

If you are using SQL*Forms, you will have to program intelligently to avoid using too many cursors. (See Chapter 9, *Tuning SQL*Forms*, for suggestions.)

Tuning the Shared Pool (Version 7)

In Version 7, the SGA contains a shared buffer pool that holds the following:

- Library cache, which contains shared SQL and PL/SQL statements
- Dictionary cache, which stores data dictionary information
- Some session information (only if you have a multi-threaded server architecture)

Remember that in Version 6, to tune the shared area you have to set all of the data dictionary parameters (those beginning with "DC") to tune the dictionary cache, and the CONTEXT_AREA and CONTEXT_INCR parameters to tune the context areas. To tune this pool in Version 7, you need to set only one INIT.ORA parameter, SHARED_POOL_SIZE.

This section describes each of these components and suggests how to monitor the shared buffer pool to make sure you have allocated enough space for this area.

Tuning the library cache (Version 7)

The library cache (sometimes called the shared SQL area) included in the shared buffer pool in Version 7 is similar to the context areas discussed for Version 6. The difference is that in Version 7, SQL statements reside in a shared area, so each user process does not need to allocate its own context area.

How can you get the best performance out of the library cache area? There is only a certain amount of memory in the library cache. If no more room is available in the cache for new entries, old statements are removed from the cache to make room. Then, if the statement removed from the cache is needed again, ORACLE will have to parse it again before putting it back into the shared area. This will consume CPU and I/O resources. To avoid this, be sure the value of SHARED_POOL_SIZE is large enough.

How can you figure out the optimal size for the library cache? One good way is to monitor your system to find out how often ORACLE is looking for statements in the cache that have been removed because of inadequate memory. There are several ways to find this out. You can use SQL*DBA to look at the MONITOR displays, you can run a query against the V$LIBRARYCACHE table, or you can examine the V$SQLAREA table.

NOTE

If you wish to observe the free space in the shared pool part of the SGA, you can perform this query:

```
SELECT * FROM V$SGASTAT
    WHERE NAME = 'free memory';
```

Looking at the monitor displays

There are two SQL*DBA MONITOR displays that provide information about the shared SQL area: SQLAREA and LIBRARYCACHE:

SQLDBA> MON SQLAREA

The display looks similar to this:

```
 File   Edit   Session   Instance   Storage   Log   Backup   Security   Monitor   Help
+-------------------------------- Output --------------------------------+
|-------------------- ORACLE Shared Memory SQL Area ---------------------|
|                                                                        |
|Statement Filter: %%                                                    |
|                                                                        |
|                                        Version Sharable --Per User Memory-- |
|SQL Statement Text                       Count   Memory Persistent  Runtime |
|------------------------------------------------------------------------|
| COMMIT                                     1     1968       408      208 |
| DELETE FROM REPORT_QUEUE WHERE REQST_NU    1     4546       432     4920 |
| insert into report_queue  (  REQST_NUM,    1    12084       420     9692 |
|COMMIT                                      1     2002       408      208 |
|DELETE  FROM report_queue WHERE   reqst_    1     4819       503     5236 |
|DELETE FROM REPORT_QUEUE WHERE REQST_NUM    1     4583       499     4920 |
|DELETE REPORT_QUEUE WHERE ROWID=:0001       1     4761       483     4464 |
|INSERT  INTO  report_queue_hist SELECT      1    21375       582    13980 |
|INSERT INTO ALL_TRANSACTIONS_AUDX ( Audt    1     6293       420     9124 |
|INSERT INTO MENU_GROUPS( MENU_CODE,GROUP    1     8354       515    10444 |
|------------------------------------------------------------------------|
|                                        (Restart)  (Hide)   (Quit) |
|------------------------------------------------------------------------|
|                                                                        |
+------------------------------------------------------------------------+
```

This example was taken from an actual Version 7 quality assurance database. Note the combining of upper and lower case in SQL statements, which is not a good idea. Remember that, unless SQL statements are absolutely identical, the parser will not know that they can be shared. Note also that the COMMIT command is stored twice because the first occurrence has a space in front of it. This display highlights the need to introduce site standards so you'll be able to share as many statements as possible.

Now, consider the LIBRARYCACHE display:

SQLDBA> MON LIBRARYCACHE

The display looks similar to this:

```
 File  Edit  Session  Instance  Storage  Log  Backup  Security  Monitor  Help
+-----------------------------------------------------------------------------+
+----------------------- ORACLE Library Cache Monitor -----------------------+
|                                                                             |
|Name Space Filter: %%                                                        |
|                                                                             |
|              ---------Gets-------- ---------Pins--------                     |
|Name Space    Requests  Hits Ratio Requests  Hits Ratio Reloads Invaldtns    |
|---------------------------------------------------------------------------- |
|BODY                 0     0     1        0     0     1       0          0 |
|CLUSTER             22     7   .32       15     5   .33       0          0 |
|INDEX               23     0     0       24     1   .04       0          0 |
|OBJECT               0     0     1        0     0     1       0          0 |
|PIPE                 0     0     1        0     0     1       0          0 |
|SQL AREA          3428  3181   .93    23484 22939   .98      43          6 |
|TABLE/PROCEDURE   1345  1016   .76     2499  2182   .87       5          0 |
|TRIGGER              0     0     1        0     0     1       0          0 |
|                                                                             |
|                                                                             |
|--------------------------------------------------------------------------- |
|                                              (Restart)  (Hide)  (Quit) |
+-----------------------------------------------------------------------------+
|                                                                             |
+-----------------------------------------------------------------------------+
```

Notice the 43 reloads against the SQL area. This is 43 more than we would like to see. Consider enlarging your SHARED_POOL_SIZE, but not by a large percentage. Also, see what you can do to make the wording of the statements more consistent.

Looking at the V$LIBRARYCACHE table

The V$LIBRARYCACHE table contains a column called RELOADS whose value gives you valuable tuning information. If the sum of this column is greater than zero, ORACLE has been forced to reparse a statement, or reload a statement that has been removed because of a lack of memory (even though it might still be required by a process). You can issue a query against the table, for example:

```
SELECT SUM(RELOADS) FROM V$LIBRARYCACHE;
```

If RELOADS is too large, increase the SHARED_POOL_SIZE parameter. You may also need to increase the OPEN_CURSORS parameter, which specifies the maximum number of cursors allowed for each session. In addition to setting these parameters that are under your control, you will need to enlist the support of others in your organization by adhering to application standards. There are several rules about consistency that will help performance a great deal:

- SQL statements can be shared in the cache only if they are identical. "Identical" means just that. There must be no variation. For example, if one letter is uppercase in one statement, it must be uppercase in the other.

- Encourage developers to make use of shared procedures. (Such procedures also have the advantage of being stored in parsed form.)

- Encourage developers to use bind variables whenever possible. For example, use this statement:

```
SELECT ACCT_NAME, ACCT_LIMIT FROM ACCOUNT WHERE ACCT_NO = :ACCNO;
```

instead of these:

```
select acct_name, acct_limit from account where acct_no = 10301;

select acct_name, acct_limit FROM account WHERE acct_no = :accno;

SELECT ACCT_NAME, ACCT_LIMIT
    FROM ACCOUNT
    WHERE ACCT_NO = :ACCNO;
```

Another parameter that you should be aware of is the CURSOR_SPACE_FOR_TIME parameter. This parameter causes statements to be deallocated from the shared SQL area only when the program cursors requiring the statements are closed. This provides some performance improvements of execution calls. We recommend that you set it to TRUE if you have enough memory to store all of the SQL statements you are currently using in the library cache. You must be careful that the library cache is large enough to store all required statements because if it is not, and CURSOR_SPACE_FOR_TIME is set to TRUE, an error will occur.

Looking at the V$SQLAREA table

You can also examine the V$SQLAREA table to observe which statements are currently stored in your shared SQL area. If you want to identify which statements are being used against the ACCOUNT table, for example, issue the statement:

```
SELECT SQL_TEXT FROM V$SQLAREA
    WHERE UPPER(SQL_TEXT) LIKE '%ACCOUNT%';
```

Tuning the dictionary cache (Version 7)

As we've mentioned, Version 6 dictionary tuning involves setting a number of individual INIT.ORA parameters. In Version 7, because the dictionary cache is part of the overall shared buffer pool, dictionary tuning is more integrated into general database tuning. You need to set only one parameter, SHARED_POOL_SIZE, to control the amount of space allocated for this entire area.

Conceptually, tuning the Version 7 dictionary cache is similar to Version 6 tuning. You need to monitor the number of times ORACLE tried but failed to find items in the dictionary. This process is described in Chapter 14, along with Version 6 tuning information.

Tuning session data (Version 7)

If you are using ORACLE's multi-threaded server, you may need to allocate a larger-than-usual SHARED_POOL_SIZE. This is because for such systems the shared pool stores the user process's private SQL area and sort areas.

To gauge how much larger to make your shared pool size to accommodate session data access, query the V$SESSTAT table as follows:

```
SELECT SUM(VALUE) FROM V$SESSTAT
    WHERE NAME = 'session memory'
```

The result indicates the memory currently allocated to all sessions. You can use this figure to increase the shared pool size if you are planning to use the multi-threaded server. (For a discussion of this feature, see Appendix A, *Planning for Version 7.*)

Tuning the Buffer Cache (Version 6 and Version 7)

The buffer cache is an area in memory that stores copies of database blocks for tables, indexes, rollback segments, and clusters. Each buffer holds a single ORACLE data block. The buffer cache significantly reduces disk I/O and improves performance. By simply increasing one INIT.ORA parameter, DB_BLOCK_BUFFERS, you can often realize 50% performance improvements for long-running update jobs, and between 5% and 20% improvements for online transaction processing systems. In general, the larger the buffer cache, the faster ORACLE runs on most systems. This is obviously not the case if enormous tables are being serially scanned on a continual basis, but it is true for the more common online transactions.

In DB_BLOCK_BUFFERS you specify the number of ORACLE database blocks that will fit in the buffer cache. To make this change take effect, you must shut down the database or database instance and then restart it.

ORACLE recommends that you gauge the performance of the buffer cache by looking at the hit ratio—how often the data being retrieved is available in memory (rather than having to be retrieved from disk). We find, however, that the hit ratio is only one part of the performance story. Some of the sites we have tuned have improved long-running jobs by as much as 50% reduction in runtime with a hit ratio improvement of less than 10%; for online transaction processing, they have realized a 15% improvement in response times with the hit ratio improving by less that 1%. There are a number of other ways to test the effectiveness of the buffer cache.

NOTE

For Version 6, always increase the buffer cache only after you have tuned the dictionary cache and the context areas. For Version 7, increase the buffer cache only after you have tuned the shared pool size.

Remember that you must have at least 5% free memory on your machine. If you have closer to 10%, ask yourself if you would benefit from adding this memory to your buffer cache. The answer is almost always yes.

One site we worked at had a buffer cache of four megabytes. (The DBA claimed that an expert told him that was the optimum size.) The site was a large one, with several hundred megabytes of free memory, that was experiencing response time problems across all systems, particularly with one particular large overnight update run. After a heated debate, the DBA finally agreed to increase the buffer cache to 40 megabytes, but made no other changes to the database. The overnight processing time immediately dropped from eight hours to four hours.

When DBAs increase the buffer cache to 20 megabytes, we observe marked improvements in response time. The amount of improvement beyond 20 megabytes is less, but is still substantial. We tend to see the greatest improvements in large overnight batch update jobs, and these jobs continue to improve beyond 20 megabytes. One site allocated one gigabyte for its buffer cache! Every site is different. Our advice is to keep an open mind about what size is right for your site. Test and then decide.

There are several ways to test how effective the current hit ratio of the buffer cache is; these are described below.

- Use the SQL*DBA MONITOR I/O function.

- Set INIT.ORA parameters on a test basis, and assess the results.

- Look at the SQL_TRACE and TKPROF output for information.

- Look at the snapshot created by running the BSTAT and ESTAT scripts.

Looking at SQL*DBA MONITOR I/O

Look at the MONITOR IO display and observe the current hit ratio. This is the rate at which ORACLE finds the data blocks it needs already in memory. It is computed by:

```
(logical reads - physical reads)  /  (logical reads)
```

The closer the hit ratio approaches 1.00, the better your system will perform. If you have already tuned your dictionary cache, you still have free memory, and the hit ratio is below .95, try increasing the value of DB_BUFFER_BLOCKS. Make sure that you always have at least 5% free memory.

```
SQLDBA> CONNECT INTERNAL
SQLDBA> MON IO


                ORACLE System I/O Distribution Monitor   Tue Oct 20  20:00:46
-------------Interval-------------              -----------Cumulative-----------
% Logical   % Physical  % Logical              % Logical   % Physical  % Logical
   Reads       Reads      Writes                  Reads       Reads      Writes
0      100  0      100  0      100  PID(SNO)   0      100  0      100  0      100
----------  ----------  ----------  --------   ----------  ----------  ----------
                                     2(1)
                                     3(1)
                                     4(1)
                                     5(1)
                                     6(1)
                                     7(1)
                                     8(1)
----------  ----------  ----------             ----------  ----------  ----------
        0           0           0  Totals             0           0           0
     0.00                          Hit Ratio                               0.00
```

You may need to buy more memory if the following conditions are true:

- Your ratio is below 50%.

- You have already tuned your dictionary cache and your application.

- Your response times are bad.

- You have no free memory.

In fact, this situation sounds pretty grim; buy that memory today!

Testing INIT.ORA parameters for the effect of increasing buffer cache

Sometimes, the best way to figure out whether the buffer cache needs to be increased or decreased is to try it out on a test basis. With this method, you make changes to the INIT.ORA parameters and then assess the results. When you use the approach we describe below in production, make sure to turn it off as soon as you have gathered your results. Do not leave this function activated as an ongoing check on your production database. The function will continue to degrade your response times by about 20%.

Even if enlarging certain parameters shows only marginal increases, these may equate to significant improvements in response times. Even a 5% improvement may make a big difference in your system. Be sure to monitor during periods of peak usage, not over the course of an entire day. Daily figures that average times of high and low activity may give you unrealistic results. If you change your buffer cache to suit these results, your performance may suffer significantly.

To measure the effect of increasing the buffer cache, set the INIT.ORA parameter, DB_BLOCK_LRU_EXTENDED_STATISTICS (specified in ORACLE blocks), to the value that you are considering as an increase to the buffer cache. Shut down the database instance and then restart it. Statistics will be placed in the SYS.X$KCBRBH table. You can query this table to see the effect of increasing the buffer cache. For example, to see the effect of increasing the cache in chunks of 250, perform the following query:

```
SELECT 250 * TRUNC(INDX / 250) +1 || 'to' ||250 * (TRUNC(INDX / 250) +1)
INTERVAL,
    SUM(COUNT) CACHE_HITS
    FROM SYS.X$KCBRBH
    GROUP BY TRUNC(INDX / 250);
```

To test a different interval, change 250 to the next increment you want to test. You'll see output in the following format:

Interval	Cache_Hits
1 to 250	21000
251 to 500	15000
501 to 750	10000
751 to 1000	3500

This shows that, if 250 cache blocks were added to DB_BLOCK_BUFFERS, there would be 21,000 additional cache hits over and above the current DB_BLOCK_BUFFERS setting. If an additional 250 blocks were added, there would be 21,000 + 15,000 cache hits, or a total of 36,000.

Testing INIT.ORA parameters for the effect of decreasing buffer cache

To measure the effect of decreasing the buffer cache, set the INIT.ORA parameter DB_BLOCK_LRU_STATISTICS to TRUE. Shut down the database instance and then restart it. Statistics are placed in the SYS.X$KCBCBH table. You can query this table to see the effect of decreasing the cache.

```
SELECT 250 * TRUNC(INDX / 250) +1 || 'to' || 250 * (TRUNC(INDX / 250) +1)
INTERVAL,
    SUM(COUNT) CACHE_HITS
    FROM SYS.X$KCBCBH
    WHERE INDX > 0
    GROUP BY TRUNC(INDX / 250);
```

The output produced will be in the format:

```
    Interval          Cache_Hits
    _____      _____
    1 to 250            1021000
    251 to 500          115000
    501 to 750          50000
    751 to 1000         9500
```

If memory is scarce, you can reduce the DB_BLOCK_BUFFERS parameter by 250, which will increase your disk I/O but probably provide better response times by lessening the CPU-intensive paging and swapping operations caused by the lack of memory. If memory is not scarce, do not decrease the parameter. The 9500 hits in cache eliminate disk I/O which may occur during peak usage times and increase user response times.

Using TKPROF to test timing

You can use the SQL_TRACE and TKPROF tracing facilities to find out what is going on during your queries and whether you should change the size of the buffer cache.

Start by adjusting the parameters in the INIT.ORA file as follows:

```
    SQL_TRACE          TRUE
    TIMED_STATISTICS   TRUE
```

As you adjust your buffer cache, you can create a number of directories to store your trace output files. If you enlarge your DB_BLOCK_BUFFERS from 1250 to 4000, you may have two directories, one called */bmark/1250* and another called */bmark/4000,* to assist you with finding your trace files.

The first time through, set these parameters:

```
    DB_BLOCK_BUFFERS   1250
    USER_DUMP_DEST     /bmark/1250
```

Then shut your database down and restart it with these parameters:

```
DB_BLOCK_BUFFERS        4000
USER_DUMP_DEST          /bmark/4000
```

Make sure that all of your comparisons take place when the machine is fully dedicated to your test.

You must observe the total times at the bottom of your output files to check both the total elapsed and CPU times, as well as the physical database reads. Listed below are sample times from a site's online transaction processing program. This is a real-life example where the buffer cache was increased from four megabytes to 16 megabytes.

For four megabytes:

```
Overall Totals For All Statements
```

	count	cpu	elap	phys	cr	cur	rows
Parse:	38	360	1520	66	155	0	
Execute:	38	197	700	69	70	184	10
Fetch:	101	100	230	46	57	0	90

For 16 megabytes:

```
Overall Totals For All Statements
```

	count	cpu	elap	phys	cr	cur	rows
Parse:	38	280	1180	66	155	0	
Execute:	38	161	470	57	70	184	10
Fetch:	101	78	197	31	57	0	90

For online transaction processing tests, ask your QA staff to test a typical mix of transactions, to mimic as closely as you can the work of actual production users. (As we've mentioned elsewhere, you can use the RUNFORMS and RUNMENU echo functions to record a user's key strokes and then replay the keystrokes.)

For longer-running jobs, simply use scripts that will be used in production.

Using BSTAT/ESTAT for testing

You can use ORACLE's BSTAT and ESTAT scripts (or their Version 7 equivalents, *UTLB-STAT.sql* and *UTLESTAT.sql*) to take a snapshot of program activity, including buffer cache activity. Chapter 12 shows a detailed listing of BSTAT/ESTAT output and details a number of performance tests you can run on it.

The following example extracts some statistics from BTAT/ESTAT output and shows the effects of different figures as the buffer cache is enlarged. In this particular example of an actual system we tuned, the buffer cache was increased from 4 megabytes to 16 megabytes. The long-running job's elapsed time improved by 50% and the online trans-action processing test improved by 12%. We also observed a big reduction in message latch counts in the latch monitor output from BSTAT/ESTAT. It went from 48,000 gets with a four-megabyte buffer cache to 15,000 with a 16-megabyte buffer cache.

Run Type	-- OLTP --		---- Batch Update --	
Buffer Cache Size	4MB	16MB	4MB	16MB
background timeouts	15.51	10.01	115.5	168.5
buffer busy waits	.59	.14	1	0
busy wait time	1.7	.29	.3	0
free buffer inspected	.24	.03	508.5	1
free buffer requested	62.25	58.2	2195	1777.5
free buffer scans	62.25	58.2	2195	1777.5
parse count	43.64	40.53	97.5	80.5
parse time cpu	17.01	13.98	90	67
parse time elapsed	89.01	71.51	643	260.5
physical reads	6.83	5.74	1381	963.5
physical writes	5.74	4.83	1063.5	757
recursive calls	293.16	185.68	2878	1901

Looking at the V$SYSSTAT table

The V$SYSSTAT table contains a variety of performance statistics, including buffer cache statistics. If you are using Version 7, you can query this table, as described in Chapter 12 in the section called "Looking at the V$SYSSTAT Table."

Sharing Executable Images

Some platforms allow you to install the ORACLE product executables as shared execut-able images. Products like SQL*Forms may be installed once in memory and shared by all users. This feature can save enormous amounts of memory, but unfortunately it is not available on all platforms. For example, on a VMS system, suppose you have 50 concurrent ORACLE users running RUNFORM (*iap30*). If the RUNFORM executable isn't installed in memory, more than 50 megabytes of memory will be required. Each user will have his or her own copy of RUNFORM residing in memory. If you install RUNFORM as a shared executable, you'll save most of this memory. On VMS, to install the shared executable, you run the utility, *@ORA_INSTALL:ORA_INSUTL.* Check to see if your system supports image sharing and make sure users take advantage of this facility.

Tuning Disk I/O

ORACLE provides many ways for you to monitor the use of disk and the number of disk accesses in your system. Because disk access is so much slower than memory access, your focus must be on ways to reduce the amount of disk I/O required. You can do this by allocating large enough areas in memory and by assigning large enough disk space allocations for tables, indexes, and other objects. In this way, you can avoid the problems of disk fragmentation and disk chaining.

Make sure when you monitor disk activity that you sample at the times of day when your system experiences peak usage. You should also be sure to monitor disk activity for long-running overnight batch jobs, which often are poor at sharing the disk load.

System Monitoring and Tuning Tools for Disk I/O

In addition to the ORACLE tools for disk monitoring and tuning, your own operating system provides facilities that you and your system administrator can use to improve disk I/O usage. ORACLE facilities cannot provide you with information on disk I/O speeds, seek operations, available channels, data transfer rates, and spread across disk devices. You must become familiar with the operating system commands and utilities that allow you to monitor disk access on your machine. These differ from system to system. Under VMS, for example, you'll issue the command *MON DISK*. Under UNIX, you'll run *iostat* in the form:

        iostat *drives interval count*

where:

drives   Drives to be monitored

interval   Interval in seconds

count   Number of samples taken

Consult your operating system documentation for the facilities available in your own system.

Using the MONITOR Function to Monitor Disk Activity

You can display information about disk activity for the ORACLE database files in your system by invoking the SQL*DBA MONITOR facility as follows:

        SQLDBA> CONNECT INTERNAL
        SQLDBA> MON FILES

The following example displays I/O activity for all of the database files for a given instance in Version 6. Unfortunately, I/O performed by non-ORACLE activity is *not* displayed. The column "Batch Size blks/W" is the number of data blocks written to each database file for a single write. The total I/O rate for a given data file is the "Request Rate Reads" + "Request Rate Writes" which are both expressed in I/O per second.

```
              ORACLE File I/O Monitor          Tue Oct 20  20:02:02

             Reqst Rate   Batch Size   Response Time   Total Blocks
File Name    Reads Writes blks/R blks/W ms/Read ms/Write Read    Written
/disk1/systemPROD 1.20 0.10  1.00   1.00   0.00    0.00    108     4
/disk2/data1PROD  5.60 0.07  3.20   1.60   0.00    0.00    1222    3134
/disk3/data2PROD  7.30 0.15  5.20   3.60   0.00    0.00    12972   3172
/disk4/index1PROD 4.60 0.00  3.20   1.60   0.00    0.00    4323    312
/disk5/index2PROD 5.60 0.00  3.20   1.60   0.00    0.00    5456    1212
/disk6/temp1PROD  1.40 1.07  1.20   0.60   0.00    0.00    12000   3120
/disk7/userPROD   0.60 0.00  0.20   0.60   0.00    0.00    128     31
/disk8/rback1PROD 5.60 0.07  1.20   0.80   0.00    0.00    1526    1428
/disk9/rback2PROD 5.60 0.07  2.20   1.60   0.00    0.00    123     312
```

In the system shown in the monitor, each database file is on a separate disk device. If the I/O rate for a given disk is continually close to its recommended maximum I/O, select one of the following approaches:

1. Break the tablespace down into two data files. Place each on a separate disk device.

2. Place the entire data file on a faster device.

3. If you have memory available, reduce disk I/O by enlarging the buffer cache.

4. If more than one tablespace is sharing a physical disk drive, physically place high-activity tablespaces between the less frequently accessed tablespaces. This can significantly reduce disk seek times.

The next example shows the same output for Version 7.

```
 File  Edit  Session  Instance  Storage  Log  Backup  Security  Monitor  Help
 +----------------------------------------------------------------------------+
 +----------------------------------------------------------------------------+
 |                                                                            |
 | Data File Filter: %%                                                       |
 |                                                                            |
 |                     Request Rate     Batch Size      Response Time|
 |Data File            Reads/s Writes/s blks/rd blks/wt   ms/rd   ms/w|
 |----------------------------------------------------------------------------|
 |oracle7\dat\ora_dbs.sys      0       0        0       0         0    |
 |oracle7\dat\ora_dbs.dev      0       0        0       0         0    |
 |oracle7\dat\ora_idx.dev      0       0        0       0         0    |
 |oracle7\dat\ora_rbk.dev      0       0        0       0         0    |
 |oracle7\dat\ora_tmp.dev      0       0        0       0         0    |
 |oracle7\dat\ora_aud.dev      0       0        0       0         0    |
 |                                                                            |
 |----------------------------------------------------------------------------|
 |                                      (Restart)  (Hide)  (Quit) |
 +----------------------------------------------------------------------------+
 |                                                                            |
 +----------------------------------------------------------------------------+
```

Looking at Disk I/Os per Disk File

Version 7 provides a file-monitoring table that you can query to find out the number of disk I/Os per disk file. The output from this query will show you which files are the most active. However, it does not show you if any disk is exceeding its maximum I/Os per second at any given point in time. If you combine all of the I/Os on data files on a per-disk basis, you can identify the data files most likely to cause a disk bottleneck. You must spread your database differently if you are experiencing disk bottlenecks.

Perform the following query:

```
SELECT NAME, PHYSRDS, PHYSWRTS
    FROM V$DATAFILE DF, V$FILESTAT FS
    WHERE DF.FILE# = FS.FILE#;
```

Name	Physrds	Physwrts
oracle7\dat\ora_dbs.sys	17882	3235
oracle7\dat\ora_dbs.dev	139	99
oracle7\dat\ora_idx.dev	191	100
oracle7\dat\ora_rbk.dev	1992	2929
oracle7\dat\ora_tmp.dev	0	0
oracle7\dat\ora_aud.dev	1010	199

In this sample, one file has a large number of I/Os. There is, however, no indication that a disk bottleneck is occurring. But the output does indicate that one data file (the system data file) is overworked compared with the other data files. We can assume from this information that the system tablespace contains more than just data dictionary information. Don't let this happen in a production database. Further investigation is definitely required.

NOTE

The same information can be obtained by the Version 6 tables V$DBFILE and V$FILESTAT.

Reducing Disk I/O by Increasing the Sort Area

A sort area in memory is used to sort records before they are written out to disk. In both Version 6 and Version 7, increasing the size of this area by increasing the value of the INIT.ORA parameter, SORT_AREA_SIZE, lets you sort more efficiently. To allow a new value for SORT_AREA_SIZE to take effect, you must shut down the database and then restart it.

Most online sorting queries request sorts of only a handful of records at a time, so unless the size of your sort area is unusually small, the whole operation can usually be done in memory. But, In large batch jobs the size of the sort area becomes an issue.

If the data being sorted does not fit in memory, ORACLE must sort it in small runs. As each run is completed, ORACLE stores the data in temporary segments on disk. After all of the runs have completed, ORACLE merges the data to produce the sorted data. Of course, this is less efficient than doing the entire sort in memory.

In general, try to allocate as much space in memory as possible for SORT_AREA_SIZE. However, because SORT_AREA_SIZE is allocated per user, increasing this parameter can exhaust memory very quickly if a large number of users are logged on. You also need to make sure that the temporary segments to which the sort operation will write its output (if it runs out of memory) are large enough.

To find out whether sorting is affecting performance in your system, monitor the sorting disk activity in your system and then adjust accordingly. How can you monitor sorting activity? One good way is to define a separate tablespace for temporary tables. By watching the I/O rate on the temporary tablespaces, you can detect how frequently the sort process failed to perform the entire sort in memory. You can monitor the V$STAT-NAME and V$STATISTIC table (in Version 6) or the V$SYSSTAT table (in Version 7) to observe memory and disk activity. (For information on special considerations when running overnight and other long jobs, see Chapter 15, *Tuning Long-running Jobs*.

Here is an example of querying the V$SYSSTAT table:

```
SELECT NAME, VALUE FROM V$SYSSTAT
    WHERE NAME IN ('sorts(memory)', sorts(disk)');
```

Name	Value
sorts(memory)	1291
sorts(disk)	2

The figures in this example raise little cause for concern.

The "sorts(memory)" statistic shows the total number of sort operations that could be performed completely within the sort buffer in memory, without using the temporary tablespace segments. The "sorts(disk)" statistic shows the number of sort operations that could not be performed in memory. (Note that this number does not represent the total number of times a temporary table extent was written by a sort process.) Out of a total of 1293 sorts, only two required disk usage.

You may not always realize that your program statements invoke a sort. Sorting is performed by the following statements:

- CREATE INDEX
- DISTINCT
- GROUP BY
- ORDER BY
- INTERSECT
- MINUS
- UNION
- Unindexed table joins
- Some correlated subqueries

If your monitoring shows that you have a sorting problem, follow these suggestions:

1. Before you incur any sort overhead, ask a basic question: Is this sort really necessary? Has an index been inadvertently overlooked? Can a SQL statement be structured more efficiently.

2. Increase the value of the SORT_AREA_SIZE parameter. Because this increase applies to all user processes, this is likely to consume a lot of memory. Make sure you don't increase the value of SORT_AREA_SIZE to the point where you have little free memory. The maximum allowable value is system-dependent.

3. When you create your files, make sure that you specify large enough table extents (in the INITIAL and NEXT parameters on the CREATE statement) to hold each sort operation in a single extent. Make your temporary segments a minimum of SORT_AREA_SIZE + 1 block.

4. A less likely, but possible, alternative, is to let users who require larger sorts, such as those who regularly run reports, use a temporary tablespace with larger INITIAL and NEXT default tablespace storage parameters. This will help reduce the degree of dynamic extension. For example, during daily online transaction processing hours, set your default settings to:

```
ALTER TABLESPACE TEMP_TSPACE DEFAULT STORAGE
    (INITIAL 260K  NEXT 260K  PCTINCREASE 0);
```

   For overnight processing, you might set the default storage to:

```
ALTER TABLESPACE TEMP_TSPACE DEFAULT STORAGE
    (INITIAL 5M  NEXT 5M  PCTINCREASE 0);
```

5. To achieve minor improvements in response times, you might also consider setting your INITIAL and NEXT extent sizes to one block plus a multiple of the sort area size. Assuming that you have a DB_BLOCK_SIZE of 4K and a SORT_AREA_SIZE of 64K, you may consider any of the following sizes or a higher size, depending on your requirements:

```
4K  +  (1 * 64K)  =   68K
4K  +  (2 * 64K)  =  130K
4K  +  (3* 64K)   =  196K
4K  +  (4 * 64K)  =  260K
```

6. Make sure to use the Version 7 parameter, SORT_AREA_RETAINED_SIZE. ORACLE will restore the sort area available to user processes to the size specified in this parameter if it believes the sort area data will not be referenced in the near future. This will save memory. If memory is tight, we highly recommend that you take advantage of this feature by setting your SORT_AREA_RETAINED_SIZE to half the SORT_AREA_SIZE. For example, you might set:

```
SORT_AREA_SIZE           = 131072   (128K)
SORT_AREA_RETAINED_SIZE  = 65536     (64K)
```

Reducing Dynamic Extension

In Chapter 11, we introduced the problem of dynamic extension, in which additional extents allocated for a table or an index are on areas of the disk that are not contiguous with the initial allocation. The result of dynamic extension is usually poor performance because disk access is less efficient. This section describes how you monitor for dynamic extension and tune your system to avoid this problem.

There are a few cases in which dynamic extension may be acceptable. Having many extents may be desirable when your tables are striped or when rollback segments have many transactions sharing them. If your database is badly fragmented, and the free storage consists of many small extents, you may need to use many small extents until you are able to perform a database reorganization.

Detecting dynamic extension

To monitor dynamic extension using Version 6, identify the recursive calls from the SQL*DBA MONITOR STAT function. Make sure that you have tuned the dictionary cache before you check the display; otherwise, you may be confused by the fact that some dictionary cache problems also manifest themselves as recursive calls.

```
SQLDBA> CONNECT INTERNAL
SQLDBA> MON STAT 0 0 3
```

The following output indicates that recursive calls are occurring and that they are particularly bad because they are exceeding the user calls.

```
                        ORACLE Statistics Monitor      Tue Oct 20  20:02:02
            ORACLE PID: 0      Session #: 0    User Name: SYSTEM STATISTICS
```

Statistic	Cur	Tot	Statistic	Cur	Tot	Statistic	Cur	Tot
logons	0	418	phys write	0.00	0	dbw buf sc	0.00	0
cur logons	0	8	db blk chg	0.00	0	dbw chckpo	0.00	0
cum opn cu	0	11392	chg wrt tm	0.00	0	cns frcout	0.00	0
cur opn cu	0	23	cons chang	0.00	0	rdo entrie	0.00	0
usr commit	0.00	0	wrt cmp wa	0.00	0	rdo size	0.00	0
usr rollba	0.00	0	wrt wat tm	0.00	0	rdo ent li	0.00	0
user calls	**0.40**	4	buf bsy wa	0.00	0	rdo bf alo	0.00	0
recur call	**2.00**	0	bsy wat tm	0.00	0	rdo sml cp	0.00	0
msgs sent	0.00	0	rdo syn wr	0.00	0	rdo wastag	0.00	0
msgs recei	0.00	0	rdo syn tm	0.00	0	rdo wrt la	0.00	0
bkgr tmout	0.60	6	dbw ex wai	0.00	0	rdo writes	0.00	0
enq timout	0.00	0	ex deadlok	0.00	0	rdo blk wr	0.00	0
enq waits	0.00	0	fre bf req	0.00	0	rdo wrt tm	0.00	0
enq deadlk	0.00	0	fre bf sca	0.00	0	rdo swi wa	0.00	0
enq reques	0.20	3	fre bf ins	0.00	0	rdo chk al	0.00	0
enq conver	0.00	0	fre bf wai	0.00	0	rdo spa re	0.00	0
enq releas	0.20	3	fre wai tm	0.00	0	rdo spa wa	0.00	0
db blk get	0.00	0	dbw timeou	0.20	3	rdo swi in	0.00	0
consis get	0.00	0	dbw fre ne	0.00	0			
phys reads	0.00	0	dbw fre lo	0.00	0			

If the dictionary cache has been tuned, you know the dictionary calls are not to blame, and you must now turn to the database to identify which segments are causing the dynamic extension. Keep in mind that the segments should ideally be contained within a single extent.

If you are running Version 7, you can also check for recursive calls by querying the V$SYSSTAT table with the following query:

```
SELECT NAME
    VALUE FROM V$SYSSTAT
    WHERE NAME = 'recursive calls';
```

Name	Value
recursive calls	1203

To determine how many of your recursive calls are caused by dynamic extension under Version 7 is more complicated than under Version 6. Under Version 6, dictionary cache misses were the only other cause (aside from dynamic extension) for recursive calls. Under Version 7, there are several possibilities:

* Misses on dictionary cache

* Firing of database triggers

- Execution of DDL statements such as ALTER INDEX, and CREATE INDEX

- Execution of SQL statements within stored procedures, functions, packages, and anonymous PL/SQL blocks

- Enforcement of referential integrity constraints

Here is a simple script you can use for either Version 6 or Version 7 to report on all segments exceeding two extents:

```
TTITLE   'REPORT SHOWING ALL SEGMENTS WITH > 2 EXTENTS'

COLUMN TABLESPACE_NAME        FORMAT A22
COLUMN SEGMENT_NAME           FORMAT A22
COLUMN SEGMENT_TYPE           FORMAT A8

SELECT     TABLESPACE_NAME,
           SEGMENT_NAME,
           SEGMENT_TYPE,
           COUNT(*)
           FROM DBA_EXTENTS
           GROUP BY    TABLESPACE_NAME,
                       SEGMENT_NAME,
                       SEGMENT_TYPE
           HAVING COUNT(*) > 2;
```

You may wish to exclude the rollback segments by including WHERE SEGMENT TYPE != 'ROLLBACK'.

Rebuilding your segment into a single extent may require a database reorganization. There may not be a single extent large enough to create it. To inquire about available extent sizes, perform the following query:

```
SELECT TABLESPACE_NAME, BYTES
    FROM DBA_FREE_SPACE
    WHERE TABLESPACE_NAME = UPPER('&tspace')
    ORDER BY BYTES DESC;
```

where *tspace* is the name of the tablespace the segment resides in. If you are unable to place the segment into a single extent, the next best thing would be to place the segment into two extents or perhaps rebuild the segment into one extent in a different tablespace.

NOTE

When you rebuild your tables and indexes, you may use more space than the original size. The original amount of free space in each block has to be re-established. The way around this problem is to create the table or index with a lower value for the PCTFREE parameter, and then alter the table's PCTFREE definition to the appropriate size after the table has been created. (See the discussion of PCTFREE and other parameters in Chapter 11.)

To place the data from tables into one contiguous extent, follow these steps; note that if your table contains LONG columns, you must export and import.

1. Export the table.
2. Drop the table.
3. Create the table with the appropriate size.
4. Import the table.

Or, if you have sufficient space in your database:

1. Rename the table to TABLE_COPY.
2. Create the table with the new storage definition as SELECT * FROM TABLE_COPY.
3. Drop the table TABLE_COPY.
4. Recreate the indexes.

To place indexes into one contiguous extent:

1. Drop the index.
2. Create the index with the appropriate size.

Dynamic extension on temporary segments

DBAs often forget temporary segments when they are doing tuning. But, by avoiding dynamic extension on temporary segments, you'll realize performance improvements of as much as 50% on large index creation and lengthy sort jobs.

If your temporary tables are the cause of the dynamic extension, the solution is to alter the default TABLESPACE STORAGE parameters on your temporary tables' tablespace. If only certain users are causing the dynamic extension, you have the alternative of placing the users into a second temporary tablespace that has a larger INITIAL extent in its default storage clause. If you cannot determine which users are causing the dynamic extension, you can increase the INITIAL or NEXT extent if space permits. As a rule of thumb, in many of these situations an INITIAL extent of 256K + 1 block and a NEXT extent of 256K + 1 block appear to solve the problem.

Chained rows

Disk chaining occurs when a row is updated in an ORACLE block and the amount of free space in the block is not adequate to store all of the row's data. Another block is required to store the remainder of the row. Chaining can cause serious performance problems.

If a table has chaining problems, you can rebuild the table, specifying a larger value for the PCTFREE parameter. (See Chapter 11 for a discussion of this parameter.) If the bulk of the rows currently in the table have already been updated to their full lengths, there will be a lot of space wasted. The free space will be reserved for rows that will not expand any further. To eliminate this waste, you can create the table with a smaller PCTFREE parameter, load the existing data, and then run the ALTER command on the table with a larger PCTFREE.

To detect chaining under Version 6, perform the following query:

```
SELECT SUBSTR(ROWID, 1, 8)||SUBSTR(ROWID, 15, 4) BLCK,
    SUM (NVL(VSIZE(ACC_NO) + 1, 0)
       +(NVL(VSIZE(ACC_DESC) + 1, 0)
       +(NVL(VSIZE(ACC_TYPE) + 1, 0)
       +(NVL(VSIZE(ACC_LIMIT) + 1, 0)
       +(NVL(VSIZE(ACC_COST_ELEMENT) + 1, 0) + 5)
          FROM ACCOUNT
          GROUP BY SUBST(ROWID,1,8)||SUBSTR(ROWID,15,4)
          HAVING
    SUM (NVL(VSIZE(ACC_NO) + 1, 0)
       +(NVL(VSIZE(ACC_DESC) + 1, 0)
       +(NVL(VSIZE(ACC_TYPE) + 1, 0)
       +(NVL(VSIZE(ACC_LIMIT) + 1, 0)
       +(NVL(VSIZE(ACC_COST_ELEMENT) + 1, 0) + 5) > 4096 - 100;
```

NOTE

Assume that 4096 is the value of DB_BLOCK_SIZE on your machine.

In the query above, we are trying to establish if the ACCOUNTS table has blocks containing rows with a combined length of longer than the block size. Rows may have initially been placed into the block, but have been expanded by an UPDATE statement. They cannot now fit completely in the block, so part of the row must be placed into a different block.

Any blocks listed in this query are blocks that contain chained rows. If there are only one or two blocks with chaining problems on a very large table, the likelihood of the chained rows being accessed may be slim, and is probably not worth rebuilding. You can observe which rows are in the chained block by performing the following query.

```
SELECT * FROM ACCOUNT
    WHERE SUBSTR(ROWID,1,8) || SUBSTR(ROWID,15,4) = '000007230004';
```

where '000007230004' is the block and file combination returned from your chaining query. Here is an explanation of what is going on in this statement:

- SUBSTR(ROWID,1, 8) is the block in which the row resides

- SUBSTR(ROWID, 15, 4) is the file in which the row resides

- One byte has been added for each NOT NULL column

- Five rows have been added for each block

- 100 bytes are required for the block header

- In the example above, the block size is 4096

- The table is the ACCOUNT table which has the columns ACC_NO, ACC_DESC, ACC_TYPE, ACC_LIMIT and ACC_COST_ELEMENT

If the rows are heavily used, you may consider issuing the following:

```
CREATE TABLE CHAINED_TEMP AS
SELECT * FROM ACCOUNT
    WHERE SUBSTR(ROWID,1, 8)||SUBSTR(ROWID,15, 4) = '000007230004';

DELETE FROM ACCOUNT
    WHERE SUBSTR(ROWID,1, 8)||SUBSTR(ROWID,15, 4) = '000007230004';

INSERT INTO ACCOUNT
SELECT * FROM CHAINED_TEMP;
```

When you are convinced everything has worked properly, you can drop the temporary table.

```
DROP TABLE CHAINED_TEMP;
```

Version 7 handles chaining a little differently from Version 6. If a block is updated and the row no longer fits into the original block in which the row was inserted, ORACLE tries to place the entire row into a new block. This is called "migrating a row." If there is insufficient free space in any block to hold the entire row, the row will be stored in multiple blocks (i.e., chained). Rows can also be inserted and will experience chaining if there is insufficient space in any blocks to store the entire row. This will be most common when you are handling rows containing a long column.

Version 7 offers a handy command that lists all of the chained rows in any selected table. To run the query, you must have created a table named CHAINED_ROWS. First, issue the ANALYZE command to collect the necessary statistics:

```
ANALYZE TABLE ACCOUNT LIST CHAINED_ROWS;
```

Then, query the CHAINED_ROWS table to see a full listing of all chained rows, as shown below. (Chapter 12 describes ANALYZE in greater detail and describes a script you can use to examine chained rows.)

```
SELECT * FROM CHAINED_ROWS
    WHERE TABLE_NAME = 'ACCOUNT';
```

```
Owner_name    Table_Name    Cluster_Name    Head_Rowid                        Timestamp
---------------------------------------------------------------------------------------
GURRY         ACCOUNT                       00000723.0012.0004                30-SEP-93
GURRY         ACCOUNT                       00000723.0007.0004                30-SEP-93
    CREATE TABLE CHAINED_TEMP AS
    SELECT * FROM ACCOUNT
        WHERE ROWID IN (SELECT HEAD_ROWID  FROM CHAINED_ROWS
        WHERE TABLE_NAME = 'ACCOUNT');
    DELETE FROM ACCOUNT
        WHERE ROWID IN (SELECT HEAD_ROWID  FROM CHAINED_ROWS
        WHERE TABLE_NAME = 'ACCOUNT');
    INSERT INTO ACCOUNT
    SELECT * FROM CHAINED_TEMP;
```

When you are convinced everything has worked properly, you can drop the temporary table:

```
DROP TABLE CHAINED_TEMP;
```

Now, clean out the CHAINED_ROWS table:

```
DELETE FROM CHAINED_ROWS
    WHERE TABLE_NAME = 'ACCOUNT';
```

Avoiding Contention

Contention occurs when one or more of your user processes vies with another process for use of an ORACLE or system resource. This section describes contention in both Version 6 and Version 7 environments.

Tuning the Database Writer

The database writer (DBWR) process handles all writes to the database. This process maintains two lists of buffers. The dirty list holds modified buffers not yet written to disk. The least-recently-used (LRU) list holds free buffers in use or pinned buffers waiting on multiblock buffering before writing dirty buffers that have not yet moved to the dirty list. You must be sure that free buffers are available in the buffer cache as needed.

When a user process requires a block that is currently in the cache, it moves it to the most-recently-used end of the LRU list. If the block is not in the cache, a search begins at the least-recently-used end of the LRU list and searches until it finds a free buffer or until the DB_BLOCK_MAX_SCAN_CNT buffers have been scanned. If your user process finds dirty buffers, it moves them to the dirty list. The DBWR writes dirty buffers to disk under the following circumstances:

- A user process finds that there are DB_BLOCK_WRITE_BATCH / 2 buffers in the dirty list.

- A user process scans DB_BLOCK_MAX_SCAN_CNT buffers but doesn't find a free one.

- A time-out occurs (time-outs occur every three seconds).

- A checkpoint occurs, and LGWR gives DBWR a list of buffers to write.

One way to monitor the effectiveness of your DBWR process is to display SQL*DBA MONITOR output for the "dbwr free needed" statistic. Make sure this statistic never rises above zero.

```
SQLDBA> CONNECT INTERNAL
SQLDBA> MON STAT 0 0 3
```

			ORACLE Statistics Monitor			Tue Oct 20	20:02:02	
	ORACLE PID: 0		Session #: 0	User Name: SYSTEM STATISTICS				
Statistic	Cur	Tot	Statistic	Cur	Tot	Statistic	Cur	Tot
logons	0	418	phys write	0.00	0	dbw buf sc	0.00	0
cur logons	0	8	db blk chg	0.00	0	dbw chckpo	0.00	0
cum opn cu	0	11392	chg wrt tm	0.00	0	cns frcout	0.00	0
cur opn cu	0	23	cons chang	0.00	0	rdo entrie	0.00	0
usr commit	0.00	0	wrt cmp wa	0.00	0	rdo size	0.00	0
usr rollba	0.00	0	wrt wat tm	0.00	0	rdo ent li	0.00	0
user calls	0.40	4	buf bsy wa	0.00	0	rdo bf alo	0.00	0
recur call	0.00	0	bsy wat tm	0.00	0	rdo sml cp	0.00	0
msgs sent	0.00	0	rdo syn wr	0.00	0	rdo wastag	0.00	0
msgs recei	0.00	0	rdo syn tm	0.00	0	rdo wrt la	0.00	0
bkgr tmout	0.60	6	dbw ex wai	0.00	0	rdo writes	0.00	0
enq timout	0.00	0	ex deadlok	0.00	0	rdo blk wr	0.00	0
enq waits	0.00	0	fre bf req	0.00	0	rdo wrt tm	0.00	0
enq deadlk	0.00	0	fre bf sca	0.00	0	rdo swi wa	0.00	0
enq reques	0.20	3	fre bf ins	0.00	0	rdo chk al	0.00	0
enq conver	0.00	0	fre bf wai	0.00	0	rdo spa re	0.00	0
enq releas	0.20	3	fre wai tm	0.00	0	rdo spa wa	0.00	0
db blk get	0.00	0	dbw timeou	0.20	3	rdo swi in	0.00	0
consis get	0.00	0	**dbw fre ne**	**0.00**	0			
phys reads	0.00	0	dbw fre lo	0.00	0			

If the "dbw fre ne" statistic does rise above zero, there is a DBWR contention problem that must be remedied immediately. To reduce DBWR contention, some implementations of ORACLE allow the ability to increase the number of database writer processes. To do this, you must increase the INIT.ORA parameter, DB_WRITERS. Do not set this parameter higher than three times the number of disk drives that hold database files that are being written to. Regardless of whether there is DBWR contention, using additional DB_WRITERS processes can improve performance, and we recommend that you take advantage of this parameter.

Another parameter that can be modified to reduce DBWR contention is the INIT.ORA parameter, DB_BLOCK_WRITE_BATCH. By increasing the value of this parameter, you reduce the frequency with which the user process signals the DBWR to write, and you increase the number of blocks that the DBWR attempts to write. With a higher value, the DBWR will be able to better utilize the operating system facilities, writing to different disks in parallel, and writing adjacent blocks in a single I/O.

Another way to monitor the DBWR process is to run the BSTAT/ESTAT scripts and examine the output. See Chapter 12 for a discussion of performance tests you can run with these scripts.

Tuning Rollback Segments

Rollback segments are used by all kinds of transactions for rollback, transaction, read consistency, and recovery. Tuning problems can occur when transactions experience contention for rollback segments. To examine contention, run the SQL*DBA MONITOR STATISTICS command and look at the following statistics:

```
db blk get
consis get
buf bsy wa
```

For example:

```
SQLDBA> CONNECT INTERNAL
SQLDBA> MON STAT 0 0 3
```

If the result of the following is greater than 10%, you have rollback contention:

```
buf bsy wa / (db blk get + consis get)
```

```
                            ORACLE Statistics Monitor          Tue Oct 20  20:02:02
            ORACLE PID: 0       Session #: 0     User Name: SYSTEM STATISTICS
Statistic       Cur     Tot Statistic      Cur     Tot Statistic      Cur     Tot
----------  -------  ------- ----------  -------  ------- ----------  -------  -------
logons            0      418 phys write     0.00        0 dbw buf sc     0.00        0
cur logons        0        8 db blk chg     0.00        0 dbw chckpo     0.00        0
cum opn cu        0    11392 chg wrt tm     0.00        0 cns frcout     0.00        0
cur opn cu        0       23 cons chang     0.00        0 rdo entrie     0.00        0
usr commit     0.00        0 wrt cmp wa     0.00        0 rdo size       0.00        0
usr rollba     0.00        0 wrt wat tm     0.00        0 rdo ent li     0.00        0
user calls     0.40        4 **buf bsy wa**    **0.00**        0 rdo bf alo     0.00        0
recur call     0.00        0 bsy wat tm     0.00        0 rdo sml cp     0.00        0
```

msgs sent	0.00	0	rdo syn wr	0.00	0	rdo wastag	0.00	0
msgs recei	0.00	0	rdo syn tm	0.00	0	rdo wrt la	0.00	0
bkgr tmout	0.60	6	dbw ex wai	0.00	0	rdo writes	0.00	0
enq timout	0.00	0	ex deadlok	0.00	0	rdo blk wr	0.00	0
enq waits	0.00	0	fre bf req	0.00	0	rdo wrt tm	0.00	0
enq deadlk	0.00	0	fre bf sca	0.00	0	rdo swi wa	0.00	0
enq reques	0.20	3	fre bf ins	0.00	0	rdo chk al	0.00	0
enq conver	0.00	0	fre bf wai	0.00	0	rdo spa re	0.00	0
enq releas	0.20	3	fre wai tm	0.00	0	rdo spa wa	0.00	0
db blk get	**0.00**	0	dbw timeou	0.20	3	rdo swi in	0.00	0
consis get	**0.00**	0	dbw fre ne	0.00	0			
phys reads	0.00	0	dbw fre lo	0.00	0			

A better way of detecting rollback segment contention is to perform the following query on the V$WAITSTAT table in Version 6.

```
SELECT CLASS, SUM(COUNT) CONTENTION_RATE
    FROM V$WAITSTAT
    WHERE OPERATION = 'buffer busy waits'
    AND CLASS IN ('undo segment header','undo blocks')
    GROUP BY CLASS;
```

or, for Version 7 (and note that later releases of Version 6 have the same columns and require the same statement as Version 7):

```
SELECT CLASS, COUNT FROM V$WAITSTAT
    WHERE CLASS IN ('system undo header', 'system undo block',
    'undo header', 'undo block');
```

The system rollback segment is created when the database is created. An instance always requires a system rollback in addition to any other rollback segments you may have created. The first two classes, 'system undo header' and 'system undo block,' refer to the system rollback segment only, which is used for special system transactions.

Regardless of which version of ORACLE you are using, the following rules apply:

Waits. If you have any waits, you have rollback contention. To eliminate rollback contention, consider adding more rollback segments. As a rule of thumb, you should have four users per rollback up to 200 users, but should have no more than 50 rollbacks for a site that has a mixture of transaction sizes. If your site has many small updates to the database, you may consider having one rollback segment per transaction, with each rollback segment between 10K and 64K in size.

Large updates. Transactions performing large updates perform better with larger rollbacks because of the minimizing of dynamic extension. If you are using Version 6.0.33 or later, take advantage of the statement:

```
SET TRANSACTION USE ROLLBACK SEGMENT
```

Long-running jobs. Long-running overnight-style jobs use very large rollback segments. It is common to swap rollback segments from small to large for overnight processing, and back to small for daily processing.

Monitoring and Tuning Redo Log Files

As discussed earlier, the role of the redo logs is to protect your database against losing a disk, having the processor suddenly go off the air, or suffering any other kind of system failure. The system writes heavily to the redo logs. They contain all of the changes made to your tables, as well as information on checkpoint and other administrative information that can be used to recover your database.

There are performance implications of redo logs in both Version 6 and Version 7. One important issue is the frequency of checkpoints. When frequent checkpoints occur, they can have a marked effect on system performance while the checkpoint is going on. A somewhat less pressing issue is the effect on performance of redo log buffer latch contention. This section describes the INIT.ORA parameters you can set to make the writing of redo log files as efficient as possible.

LOG_CHECKPOINT_INTERVAL. Number of new redo log file blocks needed to trigger a checkpoint. (These are operating system blocks, not ORACLE blocks.) This parameter controls the frequency of checkpoints, which has a major impact on performance. Checkpoints occur regardless of archiving method. Each checkpoint forces all modified database buffers to be written to the database; old log files don't need to be kept for instance recovery. Because database processing overheads are incurred each time a checkpoint is written, we recommend that you perform checkpoints only as each log file fills. You can cause this to happen by setting LOG_CHECKPOINT_INTERVAL larger than the size of the redo log file size. All of your redo logs should be set to the same size.

Forcing checkpoints within your redo log files reduces the time taken to do instance recovery, because the amount of work needed to roll forward is not as large. The same effect can be achieved by having very small redo log files, automatically forcing checkpoints every time each one fills. The ongoing performance of the database is a more important consideration than the time taken to perform a recovery of your database. We have found that three redo logs of five megabytes each works well for most sites.

CHECKPOINT_PROCESS. Enables the CKPT process, a new Version 7 process. When a checkpoint occurs, it forces the redo log writer process (LGWR) to update each data file in your database with the latest checkpoint information. This writing momentarily stops the LGWR process from performing its primary role of writing log entries to the redo logs. Setting CHECKPOINT_PROCESS to TRUE causes CKPT to handle the updating of the data files and prevents the LGWR process from being held up while it performs this task.

LOG_CHECKPOINT_TIMEOUT. Specifies the frequency, in seconds, with which checkpoints will occur. We recommend that you leave this parameter, available only in Version 7, at its default value of 0. That value forces the LOG_CHECKPOINT_INTERVAL parameter to be the deciding factor on the frequency of checkpoints.

LOG_BUFFER. Number of physical bytes allocated to the redo log buffer in the SGA. Whenever a database buffer block is modified, the redo information is also written to the redo buffer pool. Only the modified data is written by the LGWR to the redo buffer, not the entire database block. Whenever a commit occurs, only the changes within the redo buffer need to be written to disk. The actual database blocks can be written by the DBWR at a later time.

If the redo log buffer is too small, LGWR will have to write to disk too frequently. If many processes are accessing the log buffer, they will be forced to wait for the write to complete; the result is redo log contention.

You can reduce log file disk I/O overheads and redo log contention by increasing the value of the LOG_BUFFER parameter to at least 64K on a busy database. We have done benchmarks showing that heavily used applications that have a lot of database modifications will have their response times improved 5% to 15% by enlarging the LOG_BUFFER to one megabyte. Overnight jobs that perform heavy updates may also improve by increasing LOG_BUFFER even more.

WARNING

Do *not* enlarge your log buffer to the point where you have little free memory available on your machine.

LOG_IO_SIZE. Number of physical blocks to write at any one time. Leave this Version 6 parameter at its default value.

LOG_ALLOCATION. Number of blocks of the redo log files that are allocated to an instance (Version 6 only). As each allocation fills, another is allocated until the total redo log file is full. To reduce frequent file extension, set this parameter to be greater than the maximum redo log file. If you do this, then each time a log switch occurs, the entire redo log file can be initialized during one contiguous allocation.

The background process LGWR is activated only if a commit is processed, the redo log buffer is full, or the SGA dirty data buffer blocks need to be flushed.

To optimize redo log file disk I/O, do the following:

1. Separate redo log files from database data files.
2. Place redo files on faster disks.

3. Increase the LOG_BUFFER parameter, as discussed above; in the next section we tell you how you can determine whether you need to increase this parameter.

Monitoring for redo buffer space contention

To figure out if there is contention for redo buffer space in your system, you can issue the SQL*DBA MONITOR command in Version 6:

```
SQLDBA> CONNECT INTERNAL
SQLDBA> MON STAT 0 0 3
```

The "redo log space wait" parameter indicates the number of times a process could not find space in the redo log buffer. This is caused because the LGWR process is not able to write to the redo logs fast enough to clear the log buffer for new entries to be written. This should not happen in an efficient system; if it does, increase your log buffer.

```
                        ORACLE Statistics Monitor       Tue Oct 20  20:02:02
            ORACLE PID: 0      Session #: 0   User Name: SYSTEM STATISTICS
Statistic      Cur     Tot Statistic     Cur     Tot Statistic     Cur     Tot
---------- ------- ------- ---------- ------- ------- ---------- ------- -------
logons           0     418 phys write  0.00       0 dbw buf sc   0.00       0
cur logons       0       8 db blk chg  0.00       0 dbw chckpo   0.00       0
cum opn cu       0   11392 chg wrt tm  0.00       0 cns frcout   0.00       0
cur opn cu       0      23 cons chang  0.00       0 rdo entrie   0.00       0
usr commit    0.00       0 wrt cmp wa  0.00       0 rdo size     0.00       0
usr rollba    0.00       0 wrt wat tm  0.00       0 rdo ent li   0.00       0
user calls    0.40       4 buf bsy wa  0.00       0 rdo bf alo   0.00       0
recur call    0.00       0 bsy wat tm  0.00       0 rdo sml cp   0.00       0
msgs sent     0.00       0 rdo syn wr  0.00       0 rdo wastag   0.00       0
msgs recei    0.00       0 rdo syn tm  0.00       0 rdo wrt la   0.00       0
bkgr tmout    0.60       6 dbw ex wai  0.00       0 rdo writes   0.00       0
enq timout    0.00       0 ex deadlok  0.00       0 rdo blk wr   0.00       0
enq waits     0.00       0 fre bf req  0.00       0 rdo wrt tm   0.00       0
enq deadlk    0.00       0 fre bf sca  0.00       0 rdo swi wa   0.00       0
enq reques    0.20       3 fre bf ins  0.00       0 rdo chk al   0.00       0
enq conver    0.00       0 fre bf wai  0.00       0 rdo spa re   0.00       0
enq releas    0.20       3 fre wai tm  0.00       0 rdo spa wa   0.00       0
db blk get    0.00       0 dbw timeou  0.20       3 rdo swi in   0.00       0
consis get    0.00       0 dbw fre ne  0.00       0
phys reads    0.00       0 dbw fre lo  0.00       0
```

In Version 7, perform the following query against the V$WAITSTAT table to see whether there is a redo log space wait:

```
SELECT NAME, VALUE FROM V$SYSSTAT
    WHERE NAME = 'redo log space waittime';
```

Ideally, the output from this query should be zero. If it is greater than zero, increase the INIT.ORA parameter, LOG_BUFFER, to force fewer but larger writes to the redo logs. This will reduce the likelihood of redo log buffer contention.

Monitoring for redo log latch contention

A system that performs many updates can often experience contention for redo log buffer latches; this can cause degradation of your system response times. As a process performs database changes, it allocates space in your redo log buffer using the redo allocation latch. If the amount of the redo data to be copied is greater than the value of the LOG_SMALL_ENTRY_MAX_SIZE parameter, the redo allocation latch is released and the data is copied using a redo copy latch. If the process is unable to obtain a latch, redo latch contention is occurring. The process waits a short amount of time and requests the latch again.

In Version 6, issue a SQL*DBA MONITOR command as follows. If the calculation:

```
Timeouts / Total (Willing-to-Wait-Requests)
```

is greater than zero, follow the guidelines we present below. If the result is greater than 3%, you have unacceptable latch contention in your system.

```
SQLDBA> CONNECT INTERNAL
SQLDBA> MON LATCH
```

		ORACLE Latch Monitor		Tue Oct 20	20:00:56	
	Holder	----Willing-to-Wait-Requests---			--No-Wait-Requests--	
Latch Name	PID	Total	Timeouts	Immediates	Total	Successes
process allocation	1	1216	0	1216	0	0
session allocation		156767	0	156767	0	0
messages		91104	3	91101	0	0
enqueues		116829	6	116824	0	0
cache buffers chains		2096577	5	2096572	536769	536750
cache buffers lru ch		71740	13	71727	905506	905468
cache buffer handles		6445	0	6445	0	0
multiblock read obje		13302	0	13302	0	0
system commit number		22356	0	22356	0	0
archive control		0	0	0	0	0
redo allocation		**27170**	**0**	**27170**	**0**	**0**
redo copy		**0**	**0**	**0**	**1786**	**1786**
dml/ddl allocation		35347	0	35347	0	0
transaction allocati		1404	0	1404	0	0
undo global data		1038	0	1038	0	0
sequence cache		2168	0	2168	0	0
row cache objects		320276	4	320273	0	0

In Version 7, issue a query against the V$LATCH table as follows:

```
SELECT NAME, GETS, MISSES, IMMEDIATE_GETS, IMMEDIATE_MISSES
    FROM V$LATCH L, V$LATCHNAME LN
    WHERE LN.NAME IN ('redo allocation', 'redo copy')
        AND L.LATCH# = LN.LATCH#;
```

Name	Gets	Misses	Immediate Gets	Immediate Misses
redo allocation	172872	172	0	0
redo copy	0	0	12810	3

If the number of misses or immediate misses is not zero, there is contention in your system. ORACLE recommends that if the ratio of misses to gets, or the ratio of immediate misses to immediate gets, is greater that 1%, you should act to reduce latch contention. We recommend that you eliminate any latch contention at all.

To reduce contention on your redo allocation latch, decrease the LOG_SMALL_MAX_ SIZE parameter to force more copies to use the copy latches. It will decrease the number and size of redo copies made using the redo allocation latch.

To reduce contention of redo copy latches, increase the parameter LOG_SIMULTA- NEOUS_COPIES to increase the number of latches available (if you are using a multi- CPU computer). Do not set the parameter any higher than three times the number of CPUs available to your instance. In addition, increase the LOG_ENTRY_PREBUILD_ THRESHOLD to force processes to build more entries before copying them. This will force user processes to pre-build all entries smaller than the size specified by this param- eter before requesting a latch. The parameter is specified in bytes. The default is to not pre-build any entries.

Reducing Multi-threaded Server Process Contention (Version 7 Only)

The multi-threaded server available in Version 7 is an option that greatly reduces the overheads that exist for user processes. To get the full advantage from the multi- threaded server architecture, you must reduce contention for the dispatcher processes and shared server processes. (Appendix A, *Planning for Version 7,* contains a summary of how the multi-threaded server architecture works.)

Contention for dispatcher processes is indicated by a high busy rate of dispatcher processes or an increase in the wait time for responses from the dispatcher processes. To find out if there is contention in your system, ORACLE recommends that you issue the following query against the V$DISPATCHER table:

```
SELECT NETWORK, SUM(BUSY) / (SUM(BUSY) + SUM(IDLE)) "BUSY RATE"
    FROM V$DISPATCHER
    GROUP BY NETWORK;
```

```
Network           Busy Rate
------------------------------------------
tcp               .320000978
```

The figures in this output indicate that in your TCP/IP network you are experiencing a 32% busy rate. If you are busy more than 50% of the time, ORACLE recommends that you add dispatcher processes. You achieve this by enlarging the number of dispatchers in the INIT.ORA parameter, MTS_DISPATCHERS. For example, to increase the value from two to four TCP/IP dispatchers, specify:

```
MTS_DISPATCHERS = TCP, 4
```

You can also increase the number of dispatchers for your instance by adjusting the value of MTS_DISPATCHERS in the ALTER SYSTEM command. Make sure that if you do this you don't exceed the value specified in the INIT.ORA parameter.

To test the response times of the dispatcher process queues, perform the following query:

```
SELECT NETWORK, DECODE (SUM(TOTALQ), 0 , "NO RESPONSES",
    SUM(WAIT)/SUM(TOTALQ) || '  100THS SECS') "AVERAGE WAIT "
    FROM V$QUEUE Q, V$DISPATCHER D
    WHERE Q.TYPE = 'dispatcher'
        AND Q.PADDR = D.PADDR
        GROUP BY NETWORK;


NETWORK                        AVERAGE WAIT
------------------------------------------
TCP                   .219287726 100THS SECS
```

ORACLE recommends that if your wait time increases, you should consider adding dispatcher processes. We suggest that you add dispatcher processes to see if the wait times come down. The lower the wait times the better.

To determine contention for shared server processes, perform the following query:

```
SELECT DECODE( TOTALQ, 0, 'NO REQUESTS'
                WAIT/TOTALQ ||'  100THS SECS') "AVERAGE WAIT"
    FROM V$QUEUE
    WHERE TYPE='common';


AVERAGE WAIT
------------------------------------------
.072727622   100THS SECS
```

The wait time for a shared server request is .07. If this time is increasing in your system, see if you can solve the problem by increasing the number of shared servers. You can do this by increasing the values of the INIT.ORA parameters, MTS_SERVERS and MTS_MAX_SERVERS. You can also adjust these values dynamically with the SQL*DBA MONITOR QUEUE facility.

Reducing Locking Problems

Locking can be extremely destructive to the performance of ORACLE applications. Locking creates a situation where a process has to wait for another process to free the resource before the process lock can proceed. You must make sure that locking situations in your system don't hinder the performance of users as they access data.

Fortunately, locking problems are scarce in Version 6 and 7 of ORACLE, compared with Version 5. To avoid most locking problems in Versions 6 and 7, enable the Transaction Processing Option (TPO), which allows you to use row-level locking. Make sure you set the INIT.ORA parameter, ROW_LOCKING, to ALWAYS, in all database instances. (See Chapter 10, *Selecting a Locking Strategy*, for details.)

We have found the single biggest cause of locking problems is when a user leaves his or her screen in the middle of an update and goes for lunch without committing the changes. You must train your users to commit all transactions and exit the screen back to the menu whenever they are going to leave their terminals for any period of time.

ORACLE provides several tools that can help you monitor the locks in your system:

- The SQL*DBA MONITOR function, LOCK
- For Version 6, the *BLOCKING.sql* script, followed by the *LOCKTREE.sql* script
- For Version 7, the *CATBLOCK.sql* script, followed by the *UTLLOCK.sql* script

We find the MONITOR display a little difficult to use. If you have hundreds or even thousands of transactions running against many tables on your system, it is particularly difficult to pick up who is locking whom out. It also doesn't allow you to look at a row being locked and readily determine which table it belongs to. In most cases, we find that the scripts provide a more effective way to get this information.

*Using SQL*DBA MONITOR to look at locks*

This section shows how you can use the SQL*DBA MONITOR function to investigate locking problems.

```
SQLDBA> CONNECT INTERNAL
SQLDBA> MON LOCK ALL

                ORACLE Lock Monitor       Mon Nov 23  18:30:45
                    UPPER case = owner  lower case = waiter
    16 Resources 10  Processes     S=share X=exclusive L=row-S R=row-X C=S/row-X
=====================--2-3-4-5-6-7-8---0-1-------5---------+------------------
TD.....316.......0            S
TD.....3c2.......0        S
TD.....3d0.......0        S
TD.....3d4.......0        S
TD.....69e.......0
```

```
TD.....6ae.......0        S
TD.....6c9.......0        S
TD.....6d8......0         S
TD.....6d9.......0        S
TD.....6f9.......0        S
TD.....87f.......0                  S
TD.....8a7.......0                  S
TM.....69e.......0              L
TM.....87f.......0        R
TX...50072.....3ac        X
```

A common lock, but not a well-documented one, is:

```
RW.c000120.......d   C   xN
```

Note the C lock. This indicates that the process with the C lock against a row will be the next process to lock the row. If another process needs to lock the same row, it will get an xN lock against the row.

You will see these abbreviations in the output:

RT   Locks; specifies the redo log buffer lock that is being held by the log writer.

RW   Enqueues; indicates a process waiting for a row lock. See the discussion below.

TD   DDL locks. This also shows the object ID in hexadecimal. You can now use the SQL*DBA MONITOR TABLES display to obtain the object name.

TM   Data lock on a table. This also shows the object ID. You can now use the SQL*DBA MONITOR TABLES to translate this ID.

TS   Locks on temporary segments.

TX   Transaction locks that indicate a process holding a row lock.

The RW output shows the ROWID in the following form:

```
RW, file#, block#, row# and tab#.
```

For example:

```
RW.c000120.......d
```

In this example:

A string consisting of all dots (.) is equivalent to 0 .

.c is the file number in hex, that is 12 decimal. What you do now is system-dependent; for example, for UNIX, you must divide by 4, resulting in 3; for VMS, you must divide by 1, resulting in 12.

`000120`   is the block number in hex, 288 decimal

The first two dots in the string (. .) are the table number in the cluster if the table is part of a cluster

The next five dots in the string, followed by "d" (. . . . .d) is the slot number in the block = 13.

If you enjoy complex queries, here is a nice way of working out the table that the row belongs to. You will need the decimal value for the block; in the case of the example, 288 and the file number following the conversion for your operating system.

```
SELECT A.NAME, A.OWNER#
    FROM SYS.OBJ$ A, SYS.TAB$ B, SYS.UET$ C
    WHERE C.FILE#=3
    AND 288 BETWEEN C.BLOCK# AND
            (C.BLOCK#+C.LENGTH-1)
    AND C.SEGFILE# = B.FILE#
    AND C.SEGBLOCK# = B.BLOCK#
    AND B.OBJ# = A.OBJ#;
```

When you have found your table, you can find the row in the table being locked by doing the following; assume in this case that the table locked was the ACCOUNT table.

```
SELECT * FROM ACCOUNT
    WHERE ROWID =  '00000120.000d.0003;
```

Looking at locking problems with scripts

As an alternative to the MONITOR LOCKS facility, you can run, from SQL*Plus, scripts provided by ORACLE Corporation to monitor the database locks in your system. In Version 6, you run *BLOCKING.sql*, followed by *LOCKTREE.sql*. In Version 7, you run *CATBLOCK.sql*, followed by *UTLLOCKT.sql*. See the description of these scripts in Chapter 12.

14

Tuning the Data Dictionary

Tuning the ORACLE data dictionary is a simple process and a necessary one. A badly tuned dictionary can degrade overall performance by as much as 50% and nearly bring your system to its knees. The dictionary tuning you do can pay you back with significant and almost immediate improvements in performance. For best results, tune your dictionary before you tune your buffer cache, as described in Chapter 13, *Monitoring and Tuning an Existing Database*. A good deal of the discussion in Chapter 13 applies to both the dictionary and the rest of the data in your database.

Because many sites are still running ORACLE Version 6, this chapter describes performance for both Version 6 and Version 7 databases. Dictionary tuning is different for the two versions. As earlier chapters have explained, the dictionary occupies a separate area of SGA memory in Version 6, but is part of a shared buffer pool in Version 7. In Version 6, you must tune a number of distinct INIT.ORA dictionary parameters (the set beginning with the prefix, DC_; for example, DC_FILES and DC_TABLESPACES). In Version 7, you simply tune the SHARED_POOL_SIZE parameter as part of tuning your overall database. ORACLE then works out its own dictionary sizing.

Because the data dictionary is accessed by the RDBMS on such a regular basis as it parses SQL statements, it makes sense for ORACLE to store as much of the dictionary as possible in memory so it can be retrieved as quickly as possible. If you are having performance problems caused by inadequate dictionary cache and if your system has any free memory, you *must* increase the values of the dictionary-related parameters. The larger the area of memory used for your dictionary, the more likely ORACLE will be to find dictionary items in memory, rather than on disk. By reducing the need for more time-consuming disk access, you'll boost system performance.

Version 6 Dictionary Tuning

This section describes how you tune your data dictionary for a Version 6 database.

Dictionary Cache

In Version 6, the dictionary is stored in a separate area of memory called the data dictionary cache (DC) within the System Global Area (SGA), as shown in Figure 14-1.

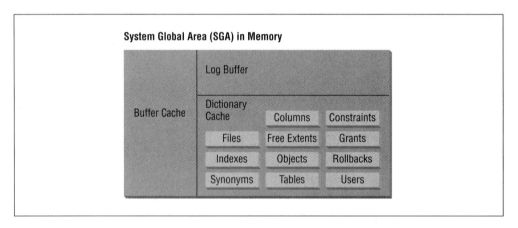

Figure 14-1: Data dictionary's use of memory (Version 6)

The more memory you are able to allocate to the dictionary cache, the more efficient your processing will be. If there is plenty of free memory in your system, increase the size of the dictionary cache as much as necessary. On most machines, of course, you don't have this luxury. If your machine is short on memory and subject to a lot of paging and swapping, you'll have to closely monitor the dictionary cache and adjust the necessary DC parameters so they give you the best performance possible within your memory constraints.

When ORACLE starts up, some data dictionary items are placed into dictionary cache as part of the startup procedure, and the others remain on disk. When a particular item that is not already in memory is requested via a SELECT statement, a logon, or a number of other operations, the system obtains the value from disk and brings it into the dictionary cache. It resides there as long as there is room for it. If a user requests a table called LOCATION, for example, that is not in the cache, the system brings it in from disk. If another user needs the same table, ORACLE will find LOCATION already in memory the next time.

If the dictionary cache fills up (i.e., exceeds the space you have allocated for it) and requests are made for items that are not already in memory, the system figures out which values to drop and which to keep using the least-recently-used (LRU) algorithm. This means that values most recently accessed are kept in memory. Suppose you have specified a value of 50 for the DC_SYNONYMS parameter (see the discussion of these parameters in the next section). If the DC_SYNONYMS area is full (i.e., it already contains 50 synonyms) and you need a 51st, the system figures out which of the 50 existing synonyms has been used least recently. It replaces that value with the new (51st) value. If a program later needs the synonym that was eliminated, the system will have to find it on disk, a much slower process than finding it in memory. If this process occurs frequently, you will have chronic problems with response time in your system.

The section below called "Monitoring Dictionary Problems" explains how you can tell how often the system is able to find the items it needs in memory. If ORACLE needs to access the items from disk an excessive amount, you'll need to increase the size of your dictionary's memory area.

Setting DC Parameters

To tune your dictionary cache in Version 6, you set the DC parameters in your INIT.ORA file. In the list below we show each DC parameter, its default value and valid range, and suggestions for values to assign. Note, however, that sites vary a great deal, and you will have to consider carefully the performance and memory needs of your own system before assigning values.

WARNING

Don't run out of memory! Make sure your system still has free memory after you increase the size of dictionary cache. We can't stress enough how important it is to avoid excessive paging and swapping, which is caused by insufficient memory. Make sure that you don't reduce the DC parameters below the defaults shown in this section. The ORACLE script, SQL.bsq, which creates the initial data dictionary and its views, requires at least the default sizes to execute.

DC_COLUMN_GRANTS
    Default: 50
    Values: 1 - unlimited
    Version: Version 6 only

    Number of columns that have grants against them; note that you do not specify the total number of grants against columns. For a typical medium-sized system, set this parameter to 150 or more; for a larger system, set it to 500 or more.

DC_COLUMNS
>   Default: 300
>   Values: 150 - unlimited
>   Version: Version 6 only

>   Number of items in the column descriptions cache (the number of table columns referenced by all concurrent users at any given time). You will ordinarily have to increase this value for a new database; never reduce it below the default. For a typical medium-sized system, set this parameter to 1000 or more; for a larger system, set it to 4000 or more.

DC_CONSTRAINT_DEFS
>   Default: 200
>   Values: 1 - unlimited
>   Version: Version 6 only

>   Number of constraint definitions in the constraints cache. Unless the application has a great many constraints, leave the value at the default setting. Many sites set this value too low because they believe their system has no constraints defined. Remember, "NOT NULL" definitions on columns, as well as normal referential integrity rules, are classified as constraints.

DC_CONSTRAINTS
>   Default: 150
>   Values: 1 - unlimited
>   Version: Version 6 only

>   Number of total constaints. The default is adequate for a typical medium-sized system, but you will have to increase it for larger systems or an unusual number of constraints. (See the note about NULL in the parameter above.)

DC_FILES
>   Default: 25
>   Values: 1 - unlimited
>   Version: Version 6 only

>   Number of file descriptions in the file descriptions cache. Allow one for each data file. For a typical medium-sized system, set this parameter to 12; for a larger system, set it to 20.

DC_FREE_EXTENTS
>   Default: 50
>   Values: 5 - unlimited
>   Version: Version 6 only

Number of entries in the free extent descriptions cache (NEXT extents of free space). For a typical medium-sized system, set this parameter to 150; for a larger system, set it to 750. You might want to increase this parameter to 1000 while you are creating your database.

DC_INDEXES
Default: 50
Values: 20 - unlimited
Version: Version 6 only

Number of entries in the index descriptions cache. You will typically increase this value if you are loading new applications as part of database creation. For a typical medium-sized system, set this parameter to 150; for a larger system, set it to 750. You may need an even larger number.

DC_OBJECT_IDS
Default: 50
Values: 1 - unlimited
Version: Version 6 only

Number of object IDs in cache. You will typically decrease this value to 10. There is currently only a small set number of database objects.

DC_OBJECTS
Default: 100
Values: 50 - unlimited
Version: Version 6 only

Number of descriptions of tables, indexes, clusters, sequences, views, and synonyms in cache. You will almost always need to increase the value of this parameter. For a typical medium-sized system, set this parameter to 400; for a larger system, set it to 1500.

DC_ROLLBACK_SEGMENTS
Default: 25
Values: 2 - unlimited
Version: Version 6 only

Number of rollback segments stored in cache. For a typical medium-sized system, set this parameter to 25; for a larger system, set it to 150.

DC_SEGMENTS
Default: 50
Values: 50 - unlimited
Version: Version 6 only

Number of entries in the segment description cache for tables, indexes, clusters, and rollback segments in use at any one time. You will usually need to increase this value. For a typical medium-sized system, set this parameter to 150; for a larger system, set it to 600.

DC_SEQUENCE_GRANTS
Default: 20
Values: 2 - unlimited
Version: Version 6 only

Number of grants on sequences that are placed in cache. If your application uses sequences extensively, you will need to increase this parameter. For a typical medium-sized system, set this parameter to 50; for a larger system, set it to 150.

DC_SEQUENCES
Default: 20
Values: 2 - unlimited
Version: Version 6 only

Number of sequences stored in cache. You will usually need to increase this parameter. For a typical medium-sized system, set this parameter to 50; for a larger system, set it to 100.

DC_SYNONYMS
Default: 50
Values: 3 - unlimited
Version: Version 6 only

Number of synonyms stored in cache. You will usually need to increase this parameter. For a typical medium-sized system, set this parameter to 300; for a larger system, set it to 2000.

DC_TABLE_GRANTS
Default: 50
Values: 2 - unlimited
Version: Version 6 only

Number of tables that have grants against them; note that you do not specify the total number of grants against columns. You will typically need to increase this value. For a typical medium-sized system, set this parameter to 150; for a larger system, set it to 600.

DC_TABLES
Default: 100
Values: 30 - unlimited
Version: Version 6 only

Number of distinct tables referenced by all users at any one time. You will typically need to increase this parameter. For a typical medium-sized system, set this parameter to 250; for a larger system, set it to 750.

DC_TABLESPACE_QUOTAS
>   Default: 25
>   Values: 1 - unlimited
>   Version: Version 6 only

Number of entries in the tablespace that stores individual users' quotas for tablespaces. If you are applying quotas to your users, you will need to increase this parameter. For a typical medium-sized system, set this parameter to 100; for a larger system, set it to 600.

DC_TABLESPACES
>   Default: 25
>   Values: 2-unlimited
>   Version: Version 6 only

Number of online tablespaces. You should ordinarily decrease this parameter; the default is too high for most databases. For a typical medium-sized system, set this parameter to 10; for a larger system, set it to 20.

DC_USED_EXTENTS
>   Default: 50
>   Values: 50 - unlimited
>   Version: Version 6 only

Number of used extents in cache. For a typical medium-sized system, set this parameter to 200; for a larger system, set it to 750.

DC_USERNAMES
>   Default: 50
>   Values: 1 - unlimited
>   Version: Version 6 only

Number of distinct usernames logged on at any one time. The best value is system-dependent. For a typical medium-sized system, you might want to set this parameter to 100; for a larger system, set it to 750.

DC_USERS
>   Default: 50
>   Values: 1 - unlimited
>   Version: Version 6 only

The number of physical users logged on at any one time. The best value is system-dependent. For a typical medium-sized system, you might want to set this parameter to 150; for a larger system, set it to 750.

Table 14-1 shows the memory needs for the DC parameters. Use these figures as a guide, not as an absolute measure. These figures are fairly consistent, but not identical, across ORACLE platforms. (These particular figures were obtained from an ORACLE system running Version 6.0.33 on a Novell server system.)

Table 14-1: Dictionary Memory Requirements

Parameter	Memory Used, in Bytes	Default Memory
DC_COLUMNS	80	24000
DC_COLUMN_GRANTS	61	3050
DC_CONSTRAINTS	132	19800
DC_CONSTRAINT_DEFS	79	15800
DC_FILES	106	2650
DC_FREE_EXTENTS	110	5500
DC_INDEXES	61	3050
DC_OBJECTS	147	14700
DC_OBJECT_IDS	132	6600
DC_ROLLBACK_SEGMENTS	154	3850
DC_SEGMENTS	137	6850
DC_SEQUENCES	213	4260
DC_SEQUENCE_GRANTS	34	680
DC_SYNONYMS	194	9700
DC_TABLES	155	15500
DC_TABLESPACES	267	6675
DC_TABLESPACE_QUOTAS	112	2800
DC_TABLE_GRANTS	34	1700
DC_USED_EXTENTS	122	6100
DC_USERNAMES	128	6400
DC_USERS	171	8550
Total	2629	168215

If you are fortunate enough to have plenty of memory to store the entire dictionary cache in the SGA, you'll avoid the need to monitor the DC parameters on a continual basis. You can find out exactly how much memory you need to store the entire dictionary in cache in your own system by counting the number of rows in the system tables shown in Table 14-2.

Table 14-2: Files Containing Memory Requirements for Dictionary Parameters

Parameter	Derived From
DC_COLUMNS	SYS.COL$
DC_COLUMN_GRANTS	SYS.COLAUTH$
DC_CONSTRAINTS	SYS.CON$
DC_CONSTRAINT_DEFS	SYS.CDEF$
DC_FILES	SYS.FILE$
DC_FREE_EXTENTS	SYS.FET$
DC_INDEXES	SYS.IND$
DC_OBJECTS	SYS.OBJ$
DC_OBJECT_IDS	Set to the value 7
DC_ROLLBACK_SEGMENTS	SYS.UNDO$
DC_SEGMENTS	SYS.SEG$
DC_SEQUENCES	SYS.SEQ$
DC_SEQUENCE_GRANTS	SYS.TABAUTH$
DC_SYNONYMS	SYS.SYN$
DC_TABLES	SYS.TAB$
DC_TABLESPACES	SYS.TS$
DC_TABLESPACE_QUOTAS	SYS.TSQ$
DC_TABLE_GRANTS	SYS.TABAUTH$
DC_USED_EXTENTS	SYS.UET$
DC_USERNAMES	SYS.USER$
DC_USERS	SYS.USER$

Version 7 Dictionary Tuning

Dictionary tuning is simpler with Version 7 because you set only one parameter to assign memory space for the dictionary and for the other parts of the shared buffer pool. The INIT.ORA parameter, SHARED_POOL_SIZE, must be large enough to accommodate the data dictionary, the shared context area (for SQL and PL/SQL statements), and some session information (if you are running the multi-threaded server architecture). Chapter 13 describes these other uses of the shared buffer pool.

As a rule of thumb, we recommend that you set a value of about one megabyte for a small ORACLE system; about 3.5 megabytes (the default) for a small- to medium-sized system; and about 10 megabytes for a medium- to large-sized system.

The next section describes ways you can monitor the use of shared memory in your system and assess whether you need to increase the initial value you have specified for the SHARED_POOL_SIZE parameter.

Monitoring Dictionary Performance Problems

Most sites do not have the luxury of allocating enough memory to store the entire dictionary cache in memory. At these sites you run the risk that the memory shortage will cause performance problems. This section describes several ways in which you can identify such performance problems before they cause major slowdowns in your system. Use all of these methods to help figure out the optimum DC parameter values (in Version 6) or SHARED_POOL_SIZE parameter value (in Version 7) to use in your system.

Most of the techniques described in this section apply to both Version 6 and Version 7. Where a feature applies to only one of the versions, we tell you.

Using the MONITOR Function

You can use the SQL*DBA MONITOR function to find out how many recursive calls ORACLE is performing. Recursive calls occur when the system needs to read from disk, rather than finding the item it is looking for in memory. ORACLE keeps track of how many times it must perform a recursive call. Some of these calls indicate dictionary problems (i.e., the dictionary item was not in cache, but had to be retrieved from disk). Others indicate that ORACLE has had to do dynamic extension on tables, indexes, clusters, or rollback segments. (Dynamic extension is discussed in Chapter 13.)

Run SQL*DBA with the MONITOR STATISTICS function to check the "recur call" statistic. Recursive calls with values that regularly exceed zero may indicate that the dictionary cache is too small. Take a look at the V$ROWCACHE table, described in the next section, for more information.

```
SQLDBA> CONNECT INTERNAL
SQLDBA> MON ST 0 0 3

          ORACLE PID: 0     Session #: 0    User Name: SYSTEM STATISTICS
```

Statistic	Cur	Tot	Statistic	Cur	Tot	Statistic	Cur	Tot
logons	0	418	phys write	0.00	0	dbw buf sc	0.00	0
cur logons	0	8	db blk chg	0.00	0	dbw chckpo	0.00	0
cum opn cu	0	11392	chg wrt tm	0.00	0	cns frcout	0.00	0
cur opn cu	0	23	cons chang	0.00	0	rdo entrie	0.00	0
usr commit	0.00	0	wrt cmp wa	0.00	0	rdo size	0.00	0

usr rollba	0.00	0	wrt wat tm	0.00	0	rdo ent li	0.00	0
user calls	0.40	4	buf bsy wa	0.00	0	rdo bf alo	0.00	0
recur call	**2.00**	0	bsy wat tm	0.00	0	rdo sml cp	0.00	0
msgs sent	0.00	0	rdo syn wr	0.00	0	rdo wastag	0.00	0
msgs recei	0.00	0	rdo syn tm	0.00	0	rdo wrt la	0.00	0
bkgr tmout	0.60	6	dbw ex wai	0.00	0	rdo writes	0.00	0
enq timout	0.00	0	ex deadlok	0.00	0	rdo blk wr	0.00	0
enq waits	0.00	0	fre bf req	0.00	0	rdo wrt tm	0.00	0
enq deadlk	0.00	0	fre bf sca	0.00	0	rdo swi wa	0.00	0
enq reques	0.20	3	fre bf ins	0.00	0	rdo chk al	0.00	0
enq conver	0.00	0	fre bf wai	0.00	0	rdo spa re	0.00	0
enq releas	0.20	3	fre wai tm	0.00	0	rdo spa wa	0.00	0
db blk get	0.00	0	dbw timeou	0.20	3	rdo swi in	0.00	0
consis get	0.00	0	dbw fre ne	0.00	0			
phys reads	0.00	0	dbw fre lo	0.00	0			

Running BSTAT/ESTAT

In Version 6 you can run BSTAT/ESTAT to look at the dictionary cache parameters and find out how often the system is able to find the items it needs in memory.

```
SQLDBA> set charwidth 20;
SQLDBA> set numwidth 8;
SQLDBA> rem GET_MISS and SCAN_MISS should be very low compared to requests.
SQLDBA> rem CUR_USAGE is the number of entries being used in the cache.
SQLDBA> select * from stats$kqrst;
```

NAME	GET_REQS	GET_MISS	SCAN_REQ	SCAN_MISS	MOD_REQS	CUR_USAGE
dc_free_extent	16	8	8	0	8	12
dc_used_extents	8	8	0	0	8	12
dc_segments	24	8	0	0	24	1
dc_tablespaces	277	0	0	0	0	2
dc_tablespaces	8	0	0	0	8	1
dc_tablespace_quotas	0	0	0	0	0	0
dc_files	0	0	0	0	0	0
dc_users	1743	1	0	0	0	7
dc_rollback_segments	456	0	0	0	0	7
dc_objects	4728	39	0	0	16	203
dc_constraints	2	1	0	0	2	3
dc_object_ids	465	0	0	0	0	8
dc_tables	5902	11	0	0	8	4
dc_synonyms	1555	5	0	0	0	57
dc_sequences	92	2	0	0	5	4
dc_usernames	1687	4	0	0	0	11
dc_columns	16089	76	658	3	43	73
dc_table_grants	3047	20	0	0	0	96
dc_column_grants	0	0	0	0	0	0

```
dc_indexes             3647    1      2697    3        0        98
dc_constraint_defs     0       0      0       0        1        2
dc_sequence_grants     34      4      0       0        0        6
22 rows selected.
```

Investigating the SYS.V$ROWCACHE Table

You'll get a lot of information about dictionary use by examining the SYS.V$ROW-CACHE view table on a regular basis. This table contains details on dictionary cache activity. The system records in this table each dictionary cache parameter, with its activity since the database was last started. Remember, the longer the database has been running, the more useful the statistics in SYS.V$ROWCACHE will be. The table contains statistics on all dictionary usage since your database instance started running.

The SYS.V$ROWCACHE table contains the following columns; note that both Version 6 and Version 7 use this table.

Table 14-3: SYS.V$ROWCACHE Table

Column	Description
PARAMETER	This DC parameter (e.g., DC_TABLES, DC_USERS). The DC parameters are used internally by Version 7, even though you do not need to set them explicitly.
COUNT	The value assigned to the parameter (for Version 6, this is the value in the INIT.ORA file). For example, if DC_TABLES is set to 750, then 750 values can fit in the dictionary, and COUNT = 750. If a value is not specified, the default value is displayed in COUNT.
GETS	The number of requests for the corresponding dictionary cache item.
GETMISSES	The number of times the required value could not be found in the dictionary cache in memory and had to be obtained from disk. See the discussion below.
USAGE	The number of cache entries that contain data. If the cache is full, USAGE equals COUNT.

To figure out which DC parameters need to be increased, run the following type of query:

```
SELECT parameter, COUNT, GETMISSES,
    USAGE FROM V$ROWCACHE
    WHERE GETMISSES > COUNT
    OR USAGE = COUNT;
```

The following output from this query shows COUNT and GETMISSES for three DC parameters:

```
DC_TABLES       50      176
DC_COLUMNS     100     1982
DC_SYNONYMS    100      350
```

Look at the output and figure out which values you need to increase. (Remember, for Version 6 you will increase specific DC parameters; for Version 7 you will increase the size of the overall shared buffer pool.) This output tells you that DC_TABLES has been set to too small a value, and you need to increase it. Only 50 slots have been allocated for table storage in the dictionary cache.

A lot of people are confused about what GETMISSES means. Not every GETMISSES count represents a problem. After ORACLE starts up, each time a SELECT is issued the desired item is brought in from disk, and GETMISSES is incremented; there is no way to keep these GETMISSES counts from occurring. In the example, there have already been 176 requests from disk; the first 50 of these were necessary to load the initial values into cache, but the remaining 126 were the result of having inadequate space in the cache.

When ORACLE starts up, all USAGE figures should equal the GETMISSES. However, you will note that some objects actually have lower GETMISSES. This is because at startup, ORACLE loads (creates) pseudo-tables into the cache. Because these tables are not read from a physical disk, they do not register a GETMISSES. These "pseudo-reads" are listed below.

PARAMETER	GETMISSES	USAGE
DC_COLUMNS	37	216
DC_INDEXES	222	
DC_OBJECTS	6	47
DC_ROLLBACK	9	10
DC_TABLEs	5	6

For Version 6, COUNT corresponds directly to the value of a DC parameter. If COUNT is greater than USAGE and also greater than·GETMISSES, reduce the value of the parameter corresponding to that COUNT to either USAGE or GETMISSES, whichever is higher. For example, in the following, you can, in theory, reduce COUNT to 171.

PARAMETERS	COUNT	GETS	GETMISSES	USAGE
DC_TABLES	300	3000	150	171

It is not wise to set parameters so close to the line. To avoid further performance problems, we advise setting the parameter corresponding to COUNT to a number slightly higher than the minimal setting (ideally about 10% more than this setting); for example:

```
171 + 10% = 190
```

NOTE

In situations where you need to set dictionary cache parameters so tightly, be sure to monitor the V$ROWCACHE on a daily basis.

If GETMISSES is higher than COUNT, set COUNT to GETMISSES. Or, if you are concerned about memory use, increase COUNT by a number which is approximately 25% of the difference between COUNT and GETMISSES. After you've done this, check the values the next day. At this point, if COUNT is greater than GETMISSES and USAGE (which we would expect it to be), set COUNT to the higher of USAGE or GETMISSES (or, ideally about 10% higher). For example:

On day 1, display the current values, as follows:

PARAMETER	COUNT	GETS	GETMISSES	USAGE
DC_TABLE	300	13000	450	300

On day 2, set COUNT to 450 and observe V$ROWCACHE.

PARAMETER	COUNT	GETS	GETMISSES	USAGE
DC_TABLES	450	14007	375	396

On day 3, set COUNT to USAGE (i.e., higher than GETMISSES) with a margin for growth. The example below illustrates a tightly-tuned DC_TABLES parameter:

PARAMETER	COUNT	GETS	GETMISSES	USAGE
DC_TABLES	400	14031	374	395

You may have read complex descriptions of mathematical formulas, hit-and-miss ratios, and other algorithms to achieve ideal tuning of dictionary cache. Our advice is to keep things simple. If GETMISSES exceeds COUNT for any of your DC parameters, you increase COUNT. By definition, USAGE may not exceed COUNT. If USAGE equals COUNT and/or GETMISSES exceeds COUNT, increase the value of the corresponding DC parameter.

NOTE

Dictionary usage statistics are informative only after a prolonged period of time. The longer the database has been running and the more widespread the activity, the more accurate the figures will be. Shortly after a database has been started, the dictionary cache values will still be loading into cache for the first time, and GETMISSES will always occur when this is happening. Withhold judgment unti you have enough information to make an informed choice about what to do next.

Looking at TKPROF Output

There are two tell-tale signs of dictionary cache problems you might note in TKPROF output. If the amount of time it takes to parse is consistently as high as or higher than the time it takes to fetch and execute a statement, there may be dictionary cache problems. Investigate the V$ROWCACHE statistics for more information.

In the following example, there is a dictionary cache problem:

	Count	cpu	elap	phys	cr	cur	rows
Parse:	1	4	14	0	15	0	
Execute:	4	2	12	0	12	0	0
Fetch:	4	0	8	2	12	0	4

Here are the statistics after increasing the DC parameters:

	Count	cpu	elap	phys	cr	cur	rows
Parse:	1	4	2	0	15	0	
Execute:	4	2	12	0	12	0	0
Fetch:	4	0	8	2	12	0	4

Another indicator of a possible dictionary cache problem is finding that your TKPROF output contains statements that access dictionary tables. The following shows an example of output that may indicate a problem with the dictionary cache:

```
SELECT COL#, SEGCOL$, TYPE#, LENGTH, NVL(PRECISION,0),
    DECODE(TYPE#,2,NVL(SCALE,-128),0), NULL$OFFSET,
    FIXEDSTORAGE, NVL(DEFLENGTH,0)
    FROM  COL$
    WHERE OBJ#  = :1
    AND NAME    = :2
```

TKPROF output can reveal a lot about system operation. At one site we tuned, TKPROF output showed a total elapsed response time of 11 seconds. This was broken down into 5.9 seconds parse time and 6.1 seconds for executing and fetching. Although the system was heavily used, an elapsed time of 11 seconds was consistent. When we looked further, we found that many calls were being made to system dictionary tables (e.g.,

TAB$, SEG$). By setting the DC parameters to values that allowed more of the dictionary to be stored in memory, we were able to reduce the response times more than 5
seconds to just under 6 seconds elapsed, and to reduce the parsing time to 0.4 seconds.
See Chapter 12, *Diagnostic and Tuning Tools*, for additional information about
TKPROF, including a problem you may notice in Version 6 output.

NOTE

Don't forget to shut down and restart your database, or the new parameters
won't take effect

Running the UTLBSTAT.sql and UTLESTAT.sql Scripts (Version 7)

A good way to gauge the effectiveness of the dictionary cache in Version 7 is to run two
ORACLE-supplied scripts: *UTLBSTAT.sql* after the databse has been running for a while,
and *UTLESTAT.sql* some time later (perhaps 30 minutes). This delay allows the cache
entries to be loaded into memory from disk for the first time.

These particular scripts produce a very long listing. The part of it that is relevant to the
dictionary cache is shown below:

```
SELECT * FROM STATS$DC
       WHERE GET_REQS != 0 OR SCAN_REQS != 0 OR MOD_REQS != 0
```

NAME	GET_REQS	GET_MISS	SCAN_REQ	SCAN_MIS	MOD_REQS	COUNT	CUR_USAG
dc_segments	23	0	0	0	0	59	49
dc_users	19	0	0	0	0	19	15
dc_user_grants	8	0	0	0	0	32	12
dc_objects	129	1	0	0	0	325	320
dc_tables	644	0	0	0	0	123	117
dc_columns	1387	0	53	0	0	1344	1332
dc_table_grants	589	1	0	0	0	303	258
dc_indexes	58	0	33	0	0	106	82
dc_constraint_d	1	0	7	0	0	152	117
dc_synonyms	36	0	0	0	0	46	43
dc_usernames	42	0	0	0	0	30	13
dc_sequences	2	0	0	0	0	12	4
dc_database_lin	4	0	0	0	0	8	7

```
13 rows selected.
```

The figures in the sample output above indicate that there has been only one miss
against the DC_TABLE_GRANTS table and the DC_OBJECTS table. It appears that the
value of the SHARED_POOL_SIZE parameter is set large enough.

Chapter 12 describes these scripts and a variety of other monitoring and tuning tools.

VI

Tuning for System Administrators

Part VI describes what ORACLE system administrators need to know about tuning ORACLE products. Because ORACLE runs on so many hardware and software platforms, this discussion can't address them all. You'll have to work with your own operating system and vendor to get the most out of your overall system. This part does provide you with some system-specific performance guidelines. It also covers some of the main tuning jobs of the system administrator: dealing with long-running jobs, client-server tuning issues, and capacity planning.

15

Tuning Long-running Jobs

In Chapter 3, *Planning and Managing the Tuning Process*, we introduced the special performance problems of long-running jobs—batch jobs that may run for many hours, usually overnight. Performance tuning so often focuses on short interactive jobs, ignoring these behemoths that labor unnoticed overnight. This chapter describes special considerations for such jobs. The suggestions here supplement those in the rest of the book. Remember that most tuning—for example, tuning of SQL statements, is identical for batch and interactive jobs. Before you carry out any of these tuning suggestions, be sure that you have tuned your database and your SQL statements, as described in earlier chapters.

The tuning of long-running jobs is one that the system administrator and the DBA will have to coordinate. Although many of the recommendations in this chapter involve DBA tuning operations, those requiring interaction with backup, recovery, and a number of other jobs will need to be coordinated with the system administrator.

Improving Sort Performance

We mention in earlier chapters how important your tuning of memory areas and temporary segments are for performance. Because large batch jobs so often sort many thousands of records, the tuning of sorting areas is critical for such jobs. The section in

Chapter 13, *Monitoring and Tuning an Existing Database*, called "Reducing Disk I/O by Increasing the Sort Area" describes in detail how you monitor the efficiency of sort operations and how you tune your system to improve sort performance. We summarize this information briefly here and tell you specifically what you can do to improve sort performance for long-running jobs.

By setting the INIT.ORA parameter, SORT_AREA_SIZE, you specify the size of the sort area in memory. ORACLE tries to perform the entire sort or sort/merge operation in this area of memory. If the area fills up, the system writes data out to temporary segments. To keep sorting from degrading performance, especially for long-running jobs, you need to set the sizes of SORT_AREA_SIZE and the temporary segments to the largest sizes you can. (The section below called "Resizing Temporary Tables" describes how you change the size of the temporary tables for long-running jobs.) The section in Chapter 13 mentioned in the previous paragraph describes how you can monitor system tables to observe memory and disk activity and determine how much activity is in memory and how much involves much slower disk access.

If you determine that sorting is slowing down processing in your system (a far greater risk with long-running jobs), follow these tuning steps:

1. Before you incur any sort overhead, ask a basic question: Is this sort really necessary? Has an index been inadvertently overlooked? Can an SQL statement be structured more efficiently?

2. Increase the value of the SORT_AREA_SIZE parameter. The maximum allowable value is system-dependent. If you are increasing this value only for this particular job, comment out the original parameter assignment so you can easily reinstate it:

    ```
    ### SORT_AREA_SIZE = 65536
    SORT_AREA_SIZE = 5120000
    ```

3. Another option is to increase the value of the SORT_AREA_RETAINED_SIZE parameter (Version 7 only). ORACLE will restore the sort area available to user processes to the size specified in this parameter if it believes the sort area data will not be referenced in the near future.

4. Shut down the database:

    SQLDBA> SHUTDOWN IMMEDIATE

5. Restart the database.

6. If necessary, assign different or larger default INITIAL and NEXT extents for the temporary tablespaces for the temporary segments written by the sort. (See the next section for details.)

7. Run the long-running job.

8. After you have run the overnight job, change the parameter settings and tablespace storage allocations back to their daily values, and then stop and restart the database over again.

Resizing Temporary Tables

Long-running jobs often need to write data out to temporary segments on disk. For example, if you are sorting more data than can fit in your sort area in memory (specified in SORT_AREA_SIZE), ORACLE will write data out to temporary segments. If you put your temporary segments in a separate tablespace, you can monitor disk and memory activity in this tablespace and determine whether its size needs to be increased.

The use of temporary segments is particularly important for long-running jobs because the job may fail if it cannot acquire a temporary segment. Such a failure might be the result of finding the tablespace (temporarily) full, or having the process reach its maximum number of temporary tablespace extents. The larger you make the INITIAL and NEXT allocations for the tablespace, the larger the temporary extents will be and the less likely the process will fail due to maximum allowable extents being exceeded.

By increasing the size of the temporary extents, and thus reducing the number of temporary extents needed, you also reduce the CPU requirements of a long-running job. Tablespace expansion is very expensive in terms of CPU time. The internal overheads involved in searching the free list and allocating extents has a severe impact on long-running jobs.

Because the requirements of a long-running job are often very different from those of an interactive job, you may want to define two distinct sets of tablespace allocation information, one for daily processing and one for overnight processing. (This approach is similar to the one we describe for SORT_AREA_SIZE in the previous section.) You assign much larger INITIAL and NEXT values for the tablespaces used overnight.

If you determine that temporary tablespace size is slowing down processing of your long-running job, follow these tuning steps:

1. Make sure that the temporary tablespace used by temporary segments is separate from the tablespaces used for application data, rollback data, and the system. For example:

```
ALTER USER OPS$SCOTT
    DEFAULT TABLESPACE USER_TSPACE
    TEMPORARY TABLESPACE TEMP_TSPACE;
```

2. Change the DEFAULT STORAGE parameter on the temporary tablespace:

```
ALTER TABLESPACE TEMP_TSPACE
    DEFAULT STORAGE (INITIAL      10M
```

```
                            NEXT          10M
                            PCTINCREASE   0);
```

3. Run the long-running job.

4. Change the DEFAULT STORAGE parameter back to its daily setting:

```
    ALTER TABLESPACE TEMP_TSPACE
         DEFAULT STORAGE (INITIAL      100K
                          NEXT         100K
                          PCTINCREASE  0);
```

Enlarging the Buffer Cache

When you are running long-running jobs, there will typically be many fewer user processes logged onto the system. This means that more memory is available for a larger buffer cache area in the SGA. The buffer cache holds database data for tables, indexes, rollback segments, and clusters. It also reduces application I/O. The larger the buffer cache, the more application data can be cached in memory, and the faster long-running jobs will execute. By holding more data in memory, you avoid expensive disk I/O that can adversely affect performance. And, once data is stored in memory, it becomes accessible to other processes, alleviating the need to read it again from the database.

If you are able to increase the buffer cache for your system, perform the following steps:

1. Increase the value of the DB_BLOCK_BUFFERS parameter. The maximum allowable value is system-dependent. If you are increasing this value only for this particular job, comment out the original parameter assignment so you can easily reinstate it:

    ```
    ### DB_BLOCK_BUFFERS = 7500
    DB_BLOCK_BUFFER = 25000
    ```

2. Shut down the database:

    SQLDBA> SHUTDOWN IMMEDIATE

3. Restart the database.

4. Run the long-running job.

5. After you have run the overnight job, change the parameter settings back to their daily values, and stop and restart the database once again.

Choosing Rollback Segments

Like tables, rollback segments may run out of space during processing and need to request additional extents. The process of dynamic extension that occurs can have a serious impact on performance, particularly on the performance of long-running jobs. RDBMS Version 6.0.33 introduced the ability to assign a transaction to an individual roll-back segment. By assigning larger rollback segments to long-running jobs, you can improve performance.

If your application rollback tablespace is not large enough to hold both the small and large rollbacks simultaneously, you can assign alternative rollback segments for daily and overnight processing. You drop all of the smaller rollback segments used for high-transaction daily usage, and replace them with a smaller number of larger rollback segments for overnight processing. When the overnight jobs are completed, you can then drop the larger rollback segments and reinstate the smaller segments. You assign a particular rollback segment to a transaction with the statement:

```
SET TRANSACTION USE ROLLBACK SEGMENT segment
```

To be effective, this statement must be the first DML statement (of any kind) after a successful connect, DDL, commit, or rollback statement. You must issue this statement after each subsequent commit or rollback. Figure 11-12 in Chapter 11, *Tuning a New Database*, illustrates how the alternative assignment of rollback segments works.

To completely replace your smaller daily rollback segments with larger overnight roll-backs, perform the following steps:

1. Create the larger rollback segments:

    ```
    CREATE ROLLBACK SEGMENT LARGE_ROLB1
    TABLESPACE ROLLBACK_TSPACE
    STORAGE (INITIAL 5M NEXT 5M);

    CREATE ROLLBACK SEGMENT LARGE_ROLB2
    TABLESPACE ROLLBACK_TSPACE
    STORAGE (INITIAL 5M NEXT 5M);
    ```

2. Set the INIT.ORA parameter, ROLLBACK_SEGMENTS, to activate the larger roll-backs. Comment out the original parameter assignment so you can easily reinstate it:

    ```
    ### ROLLBACK_SEGMENTS = (SMALL_ROLLB1, SMALL_ROLLB2)
    ROLLBACK_SEGMENTS = (LARGE_ROLLB1, LARGE_ROLLB2)
    ```

3. Shut down the database:

    ```
    SQLDBA> SHUTDOWN IMMEDIATE
    ```

4. Restart the database.

5. If the rollback tablespace is not large enough to accommodate both types of roll-back segments, drop the smaller rollback segments:

    ```
    DROP ROLLBACK SMALL_ROLLB1;
    DROP ROLLBACK SMALL_ROLLB2;
    ```

6. Run the long-running job.

7. After you have run the overnight job, change the parameter settings back to their daily values, add back the daily rollback segments, if necessary, and stop and restart the database once again.

Sizing Tables and Indexes

The accuracy with which you assign table and index sizes can contribute a great deal to the performance of long-running jobs. If a table or index fits in one large contiguous extent, ORACLE can read the entire thing with a single multi-block read. If the table or index consists of many small extents, scattered all over the disk (as the result of dynamic extension), the many disk accesses will slow down overall processing. Chapter 11 describes in detail the process of creating tables and indexes and assigning their sizes.

We include below an example of how poor table sizing damaged the performance of a typical, long-running job.

We created a simple table:

```
ACCTS (ACC_NO   NUMBER(6),
       ACC_DESC  CHAR(6));
```

To populate the ACC_DESC column, we inserted 8000 rows in the table, using the statements:

```
INSERT INTO ACCTS VALUES ( NULL, 'ACDESC' );
INSERT INTO ACCTS SELECT * FROM ACCTS;
```

We performed the second INSERT statement until a single insert placed 4000 rows, resulting in a total of 8000 rows. Next, we updated the table:

```
UPDATE ACCTS SET
ACC_NO = ROWNUM;
```

Then, on a UNIX machine with a single user, we dropped the table and recreated it, using various storage parameters.

Run 1

We first assigned the following STORAGE parameters to the ACCTS table:

```
(INITIAL 20K NEXT 20K PCTINCREASE 0 PCTFREE 70 PCTUSED 30)
```

Here is how long it took to insert, update, and drop:

Insert the last 4000 rows	:	3.62 seconds
Update the 8000 rows	:	27.42 seconds
Drop the table	:	1 min, 31.17 seconds

In this case, there is no chaining because PCTFREE is adequate. The time needed to insert is relatively high because of the number of extents needed (because INITIAL and NEXT are not well-sized). A large amount of time is needed to drop the table because of the high PCTFREE area left on all blocks, and the large number of extents in the table.

Run 2

Now, suppose we assign the following STORAGE parameters to the ACCTS table:

```
(INITIAL 20K  NEXT 20K  PCTINCREASE 0  PCTFREE 10  PCTUSED 90)
```

Here is how long it took to insert, update, and drop:

Insert the last 4000 rows	:	.92 seconds
Update the 8000 rows	:	52.82 seconds
Drop the table	:	25.73 seconds

INSERT: Because we set a low value for PCTFREE value, the time to insert the rows has been reduced because fewer extents are being created.

UPDATE: The time to perform the update is double the previous run because of extensive record chaining. This resulted from the expansion of each record and less free block space.

DROP: The time to drop the table is less than the previous run because there are fewer extents.

Run 3

Now, suppose we assign the following STORAGE parameters to the ACCTS table:

```
(INITIAL 500K  NEXT 500K  PCTINCREASE 0  PCTFREE 70  PCTUSED 30)
```

Here is how long it took to insert, update, and drop:

Insert the last 4000 rows	:	.76 seconds
Update the 8000 rows	:	27.24 seconds
Drop the table	:	5.29 seconds

This is the best result by far. There has been no chaining, so the number of extents is minimized. The insert is five times faster than Run 1, the update is twice as fast as Run 2, and the table drop is 18 times faster than Run 1.

Run 4

Now, suppose we assign the following STORAGE parameters to the ACCTS table:

```
(INITIAL 500K  NEXT 500K  PCTINCREASE 0  PCTFREE 10  PCTUSED 90)
```

Here is how long it took to insert, update, and drop:

Insert the last 4000 rows	:	.47 seconds
Update the 8000 rows	:	46.47 seconds
Drop the table	:	5.31 seconds

Inserts and drops are very fast because of the low value of PCTFREE (more records per block) and the minimizing of extents through larger INITIAL and NEXT settings. Updating, however, is slower because of the low PCTFREE value and the effect of record chaining.

Be sure you understand the negative effects of dynamic extension and row chaining (described more in the next section), and the impact different storage parameters will have on your performance. As we have shown, proper sizing can have a major effect on how quickly your long-running jobs are able to operate.

Detecting and Avoiding Chained Rows

When you create a data row in an ORACLE block, you must always traverse through that particular block to read the row's data header. Remember, parts of the row may exist in any available block of the table. Unlike Version 5, Version 6 and Version 7 do not allocate a block dedicated to storing chained pieces. Instead of reserving an unused block, Versions 6 and 7 put chained pieces into other, partially used blocks. Therefore, any block may contain some whole rows, plus some partial rows from other rows; these partial rows may have their headers in other blocks.

How can you minimize the chaining of rows with this scheme? In Version 6, you can run a query against the V$STATNAME and V$SYSSTAT tables to monitor the number of chained rows. In the output from the following query, the "table fetch continued row" shows the current number of rows chained since the last startup.

```
SELECT  SUBSTR(ST.NAME,1,40),SY.VALUE, SY.STATISTIC#
    FROM  V$STATNAME ST, V$SYSSTAT SY
    WHERE  ST.STATISTIC#  =  SY.STATISTIC#
    AND  ST.NAME  =  'table fetch continued row';
```

Now, issue the following query to display the results:

```
SELECT COUNT(*) FROM table;
```

Now, repeat the first query and compare the results. The variation indicates the number of chained rows.

In earlier releases of Version 6, this method handles rows only if they are larger than an ORACLE block. If your rows are physically smaller than an ORACLE block, run the following query instead. It shows the approximate total cumulative length of all rows within the block. Note that in this output one byte is added for each column that is not null, five bytes are added for each row in the block, and approximately 100 bytes are added for each block header.

```
SELECT  SUBSTR(ROWID, 1, 8)  BLK,
    SUM  (  NVL( VSIZE( COL1 ) + 1, 0)
       +   NVL( VSIZE( COL2 ) + 1, 0)
       +   NVL( VSIZE( COL3 ) + 1, 0)
       +   NVL( VSIZE( COL4 ) + 1, 0)  + 5)
    FROM  BAD_TABLE
    GROUP
    BY SUBSTR(ROWID, 1, 8)
    HAVING
    SUM  (  NVL( VSIZE( COL1 ) + 1, 0)
       +   NVL( VSIZE( COL2 ) + 1, 0)
       +   NVL( VSIZE( COL3 ) + 1, 0)
       +   NVL( VSIZE( COL4 ) + 1, 0)  + 5) > 'BLOCK_SIZE' - 100
```

In Version 7, you can use the ANALYZE command to examine chained rows. By issuing ANALYZE in the form:

```
ANALYZE TABLE . . . LIST CHAINED ROWS
```

you tell ORACLE to write all chained row references into the system table, CHAINED_ROWS, which is created via the SQL script, *UTLCHAIN.sql.* (You can specify your own table via the INTO clause.)

Setting the Array Size

You can specify the ARRAYSIZE parameter, through a number of different ORACLE tools, to control the number of rows that can be returned from disk in a single network transfer. If you set ARRAYSIZE correctly, multiple SELECT, INSERT, and UPDATE operations can be performed in a single access. This improves performance substantially, particularly for long-running jobs.

NOTE

Increasing the value of ARRAYSIZE has a major impact on client-server performance. Our benchmarks indicate that increasing ARRAYSIZE when you are running in a unitary environment has little or no effect on performance.

In Chapter 16, *Tuning in the Client-server Environment*, the section entitled "Tuning ARRAYSIZE" describes how you can increase ARRAYSIZE, or its equivalent parameter, in a number of ORACLE tools, including SQL*Forms, SQL*Plus, and the precompilers. The impact on long-running jobs is the greatest for EXPORT and IMPORT jobs, which are described below in "Tuning EXPORT and IMPORT Utilities." If possible, try to avoid executing these utilities across network nodes. If it is absolutely necessary, you can improve response time by setting the BUFFER parameter to an appropriate size. If the row length is 100, and BUFFER is 65,536, the effective array size is approximately 655. Most sites set their buffers on exports and imports to at least 64K. Some UNIX sites set buffers as high as one megabyte. The maximum value is operating system-dependent.

Running Jobs in Parallel

Overnight jobs are often run in single stream. That is, one phase of the overnight job stream must complete successfully before the next phase can begin. This approach may be necessary for certain parts of the overnight process; for example, you might need to run an extract of the database before you can do reporting, or you may need to run backups before you execute certain overnight reports. However, many of your processes may be able to be run in parallel. Doing so will considerably improve performance.

The number of jobs that can be submitted in parallel will vary from site to site. Although, in general, running jobs in parallel improves performance, if you submit too many jobs simultaneously, the overall elapsed time may actually be greater than running jobs in a single stream. The CPU-intensive nature of some jobs and the fact that they may be fighting for the same resources (software and hardware) determines the outcome.

We recommend that you never run more than four jobs in parallel. Carefully monitor the timings for these jobs to optimize overnight processing at your site. Try to run the jobs in a way that will spread resource demands (I/O, CPU, logical data) evenly across the system.

Creating Overnight Extract Tables

Most sites run reports against fully normalized databases. However, as more and more overnight reports are scheduled, many involving complex multiple-table joins and full-table scans, the system may become increasingly overburdened during overnight processing.

You'll frequently find that the reports users produce tend to involve data from the same set of core tables and the same table joins. Rather than having to perform the same database retrieval operations over and over again, you can create a single, highly denormalized extract file from the database, and let users run their reports against this extract file instead. (Most sites will need several such extract tables.) By doing this, you can realize enormous improvements in performance. Complex, multi-table joins need to be performed only once, and performance can be improved still more by creating indexes against the extract tables. Make sure, though, to create these indexes after creating the extract table.

The most common method for producing extract tables is to populate the tables by running an automated process overnight, when performance needs may not be quite so pressing. Once the tables are created, programs that need this data can access the extract tables, instead of the full database. If users typically use GUI interfaces for their reporting, you'll realize even greater performance gains.

The performance gains of using extract tables can be significant. Some overnight reporting runs we've tuned have saved several hours of processing. Queries of extract tables, rather than the database itself, are much faster as well.

SQL*Reportwriter gives you an efficient way to create extract files in which many tables are joined together. You can create an operating system flat file from SQL*Reportwriter, and then use SQL*Loader to load the table into the extract tables.

Creating Indexes After Inserts

When you are inserting large numbers of rows into a table, you'll find that dropping the indexes before you perform the insert is considerably faster than inserting into a table with all of its indexes intact. When you are running long-running jobs, this approach is particularly beneficial. As a rule of thumb, we recommend that if the insert will increase the number of rows by 10% or more, consider dropping the indexes temporarily. If the number of rows is significant, the performance gains can be major. However, if the insert will increase the number of rows in a table by less than 10%, it is better to leave the indexes in place. In this case, the amount of time taken to rebuild the index for all of the rows exceeds the amount of extra time to update the indexes as rows are inserted into the table.

Consider the following example. A table called TRANSACTION has zero rows in it. A conversion will insert 8192 rows into the table, which has one 2-column index. With the index in place, inserting these rows takes 67.8 seconds elapsed time. Now, try inserting rows into the table without the index, and then creating the index after the insertion has completed:

```
Insertion       :     13.1   seconds
Index creation :     26     seconds
Net savings     :     28.7   seconds
```

To increase performance still more, specify an appropriate STORAGE clause on the CREATE INDEX. By specifying the following clause, the total index creation takes only 14.3 seconds:

```
CREATE   INDEX  TRANS_IDX1 ON TRANSACTION
         CATEGORY, TRANS_DATE)
         STORAGE (INITIAL 200K  NEXT 100K);
```

When you create indexes on large tables, make sure that you use the temporary tablespace for the sorting of rows. Make sure that the STORAGE allocation has been assigned correctly (via the DEFAULT STORAGE parameters) for the temporary tablespace. In addition, make sure that there is enough overall free space to fit the index into the temporary tablespace and the index's destination tablespace.

Using PL/SQL to Speed up Updates

If you are performing a parent/child update, a common activity in long-running jobs, you can improve performance quite a bit by using PL/SQL, described in Chapter 8, *Tuning PL/SQL.*

Consider the following example. A table called ACCOUNT_TOTALS is updated from various other systems every night to reflect the accounts' current expenditures against budget. Unfortunately, the system is not an integrated one, with data loaded into a transaction (child) table, and changes then made against the ACCOUNT_TOTALS table. There are about 10,000 rows in the ACCOUNT_TOTALS table, and about 200 rows in the TRANSACTION table. Using SQL, you'd do the daily update as follows:

```
UPDATE   ACCOUNT_TOTALS   A
   SET   CURRENT_EXP = CURRENT_EXP + ( SELECT  DAILY_EXP
                                       FROM    TRANSACTION T
                                       WHERE   T.ACC_NO = A.ACC_NO )
   WHERE   EXISTS ( SELECT 'X'
                    FROM    TRANSACTION T
                    WHERE   T.ACC_NO = A.ACC_NO  );
```

This type of update takes several minutes. Now, suppose you use PL/SQL to achieve the same result:

```
DECLARE
    CURSOR READ_TRAN  IS
    SELECT ACC_NO, DAILY_EXP
    FROM TRANSACTION;
    .
    .
    .
    ACC_NO_STORE   NUMBER (6);
    DAILY_EXP_STORE    NUMBER (9,2);
```

```
BEGIN
    OPEN READ_TRAN;
    LOOP;
        FETCH READ_TRAN INTO  ACC_NO_STORE, DAILY_EXP_STORE;
        EXIT WHEN READ_TRAN%NOTFOUND;
        .
        .
        .
        UPDATE ACCOUNT_TOTALS A
        SET  CURRENT_EXP  =  CURRENT_EXP +  DAILY_EXP_STORE
        WHERE  ACC_NO  =  ACC_NO_STORE ;
    END LOOP;
END;
```

This form of the update takes seconds.

PL/SQL isn't always faster. Beware of daily transaction files that update more than 10% to 15% of the rows in the master table. With the PL/SQL method, more physical reads will be required against the ACCOUNT_TOTALS table using indexes than would be required with a full-table scan using SQL.

Minimizing the Number of Updates

One mistake programmers make is to scan through entire tables to update one column. In long-running jobs, such processing can be particularly costly. Consider a table, called ACCOUNT, that has three columns:

```
ACC_NO     NUMBER(6)
ACC_DESC   CHAR(80)
CATEGORY   CHAR(10)
```

You must update two columns, ACC_DESC and CATEGORY.

Programmer A codes the following statements:

```
UPDATE ACCOUNT
SET ACC_DESC = 'CONSULTING SERVICES' ;
UPDATE ACCOUNT
SET CATEGORY = 'INCOME' ;
```

Programmer B decides to place both updates in the same statement, which is much more efficient:

```
UPDATE ACCOUNT
SET ACC_DESC = 'CONSULTING SERVICES',
    CATEGORY = 'INCOME';
```

You can realize similar savings when two columns are updated by selecting from another table. Some developers are not aware that they can update more than one column using a single SET clause. The following statement is very efficient:

```
UPDATE ACCOUNT   A
SET   ( ACC_DESC,
        CATEGORY ) = ( SELECT  ACC_DESC,
                               CATEGORY
                       FROM  INPUT_TABLE   I
                       WHERE   A.ACC_NO  =  I.ACC_NO )
            WHERE EXISTS  ( SELECT  'X'
                           FROM INPUT_TABLE   I
                           WHERE   A.ACC_NO = I.ACC_NO );
```

For best performance, use the above statement rather than the ones below:

```
UPDATE ACCOUNT
SET  ACCOUNT_DESC  = ( SELECT ACC_DESC
                       FROM INPUT_TABLE I
                       WHERE   A.ACC_NO = I.ACC_NO  )
         WHERE EXISTS  ( SELECT  'X'
                         FROM INPUT_TABLE I
                         WHERE A.ACC_NO = I.ACC_NO  ) ;
UPDATE ACCOUNT
SET  CATEGORY  =     ( SELECT CATEGORY
                       FROM INPUT_TABLE I
                       WHERE A.ACC_NO = I.ACC_NO  )
          WHERE EXISTS ( SELECT 'X'
                         FROM INPUT_TABLE I
                         WHERE A.ACC_NO = I.ACC_NO  ) ;
UPDATE ACCOUNT
SET  ACCOUNT_DESC = ( SELECT ACC_DESC
                      FROM INPUT_TABLE I
                      WHERE A.ACC_NO = I.ACC_NO  ),
        CATEGORY = ( SELECT CATEGORY
                     FROM INPUT_TABLE I
                     WHERE A.ACC_NO = I.ACC_NO  )
         WHERE EXISTS ( SELECT 'X'
                        FROM INPUT_TABLE I
                        WHERE A.ACC_NO = I.ACC_NO  ) ;
```

Tuning Data Propagation Across Databases

Some sites that have distributed databases take the extract table approach a step further. They have a central database for reporting, and they propagate a regional database from this central database that their interactive "line" systems use for normal business operations. This way, creating reports from the large central database doesn't slow down processing for interactive users. The propagation of data from the large central database is handled by an overnight job that creates denormalized extract tables. These extract tables may use multiple indexes to achieve even greater efficiency.

The most efficient way to propagate data is to include an UPDATE_DATE column indexed on all columns in the regional database. To propagate the data across to the reporting database, you use this indexed column to obtain the rows from tables updated since the last propagation. Data can then be put into the appropriate extract tables in the central reporting database. Because Pro*C and the other precompilers offer excellent array processing capabilities, you might want to use such tools. (For a discussion of setting ARRAYSIZE through these tools, see Chapter 16.)

Follow these guidelines for data propagation:

- Do not use MINUS across the network

- Do not use JOIN across the network

- Propagate only the required columns from the regional databases

- Store an UPDATE_DATE column and, optionally, an UPDATED_BY column as well, in all tables and indexes

Tuning Audit Jobs

Many applications perform nightly data integrity checks of the system in order to revalidate logical integrity references (business rules) and denormalized data. In Version 7, which supports the inclusion of data integrity rules built into the application design, such integrity checks may not be needed.

If you are not using Version 7, or have not adopted its database-level referential integrity features, you should audit on a fairly regular basis. This is all the more important if your application data is updated from many sources (e.g., SQL*Forms, SQL*Plus, Pro*C, etc.). The sooner a referential error is identified, the easier it will be to correct.

One common auditing function involves checking tables that contain denormalized running totals against their individual source entries (contained in a detail table). You might also audit to check for business rule "referential integrity," checking against a number of related tables to make sure certain data is in valid locations, etc. Often, the MINUS command is used for such auditing. Consider the following examples:

```
SELECT    ACCOUNT_NAME, FIN_YEAR, TOTAL_EXPEND
FROM      ACCT_FIN_YR
MINUS
SELECT    ACCOUNT_NAME,FIN_YEAR,SUM(AMOUNT)
FROM      POSTING
WHERE     TYPE = 'EXPEND'
```

```
GROUP BY ACCOUNT_NAME,FIN_YEAR;

SELECT    LOCATION_ID, PROJECT_NAME
FROM      PROJECT
WHERE     LOCATION_ID IN ( SELECT LOCATION_ID
                           FROM   PROJECT
                           MINUS
                           SELECT LOCATION_ID
                           FROM   LOCATION);
```

Tuning EXPORT and IMPORT Utilities

The ORACLE utilities, EXPORT and IMPORT, are used for backup and recovery. These functions are usually the last functions you think about when you are developing and tuning a new application. When we review tuning plans with clients, we usually don't even see EXPORT and IMPORT on the list of items to be tuned. And yet, these utilities can fail. A major job of the system administrator and the DBA is to prevent failures (e.g., media, software, incomplete application backup, or simply inadequate backup timing) and to minimize the damage that occurs if failures do occur.

Tuning EXPORT

The EXPORT utility, the most common tool for an ORACLE database backup, produces a flat ASCII file that can be transported from one hardware platform to another. EXPORT backups are compatible for all ORACLE platforms. There are a number of ways to tune EXPORT.

By placing export files on a different disk from the one used for the data that is being exported (database files), you can read and write faster, and you minimize disk contention. You can also improve performance by dividing large exports into several smaller exports that run in parallel. This can result in excellent performance if all of the individual exports are over tablespaces or user tables located on different physical disks, and if each outputs to a different physical disk.

Another good way to improve performance is to export only the information that is necessary for recovery. If indexes are never imported during recovery, don't export them. If user profiles, roles, and security never change after the initial setup, export these tables once, store the dump file in a separate location, and back up only day-to-day data when you do an EXPORT.

If at all possible, export disk-to-disk, rather than disk-to-tape. If a system does have enough spare capacity, write dump files to disk and copy them to tape when the backup is complete. Tape copying does not affect system performance as much as disk copying does.

EXPORT functions do allow you to perform incremental or cumulative exports, but we have not found these functions to be very useful. They seem to be a good idea in theory, but not in practice. Unfortunately, the larger tables of a database tend to be the most volatile. If you're going to have to back up 90% of the database, you might just as well perform a full backup, which is likely to be more useful. Having a full backup provides the added benefit that recovery will require only a single file. Otherwise, you may find yourself having to deal with a whole week's worth of files.

Split the physical database into logical sections to help speed up exports. At one site we worked at, the application was for a financial lending institution, consisting of more than 30,000 active loans, and a loan history table of more than 4,000,000 records. Every action against a loan was written to the history file. Because the history table was added to every day, this ruled out the option of performing incremental or cumulative exports. Once the history was generated, it could never be modified or deleted. By splitting the history table into two pieces, one for the current month's records and one for the remainder of the time, it became possible to back up only the active part of the database. For historic queries, a simple view could join the two tables. Splitting the table in this way reduced the length of the overnight export by two-thirds (from 200 megabytes to 70 megabytes in size). As part of this job, we developed a special monthly procedure that rolls the current month's history into the second, larger table. Then, an EXPORT procedure exports the entire application. This procedure is shown in Figure 15-1.

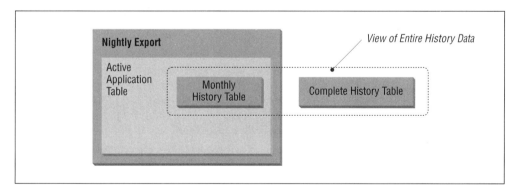

Figure 15-1: Monthly export

Set the EXPORT parameter, BUFFER, to as large a value as possible. A size of 64K is usual; two megabytes is not uncommon. The maximum value of BUFFER is operating system-dependent. Be sure you set this value to at least as large as the largest table column value. If a long field contains 64K of data and the BUFFER size is 32K, the field will be truncated (lost forever!).

By building an update indicator into the application, you can allow exports to be done online while online users are still querying the system. This indicator is set to TRUE when an export begins and to FALSE when it completes. If the flag is set, you need to be sure to restrict application screens and reports that potentially perform updates (e.g., CALL_QUERY, rather than CALL). The system can continue processing (in Query mode), even though an overnight export has continued into the next day's processing. Note that if you want your application to adopt this function, you must build it into the application right from the start.

NOTE

When you are migrating from one database to the next, be sure that you use compatible versions of EXPORT and IMPORT. Although database versions may differ, the EXPORT and IMPORT versions should be the same.

The physical timing of your database exports can be just as important as the backup itself. If an application backup is several days old, it may be as useless as the current (damaged) database. Individual application requirements usually determine how frequently you do your backups. Although your organization may allow exports to be done during business hours, this is often impractical. In addition to the fact that exports slow down processing for other users, they are frequently impractical for another reason. If interactive users are modifying data during the export, a constant recovery point (snapshot) cannot be achieved. One way around this problem is to take particular tablespaces offline so they can be exported safely. Make sure, though, that each tablespace is recoverable on its own. A collection of different tablespaces, each exported at a different time, may be just as useless as a backup performed in the middle of peak activity.

Overnight processes can also govern the timing of the backup procedure. At one site we tuned, the overnight processing routine was the major update module of the application. Exports were always performed immediately prior to the overnight routine (end of day). The DBA assumed that an application recovery (one not caused by hardware failure) would be justified only if the overnight process ran amok (for example, 20,000 employes, all receiving a 50% pay raise). On the other hand, errors entered online could always be reversed online. With this approach, if hardware failures were encountered, the application could be restored to the last backup, the overnight process rerun, and the day's transactions reapplied either manually or through archive logs.

You need to study each possible failure scenario for your own site and determine the reasonable recovery options. ORACLE's automatic archiving routines are the only way to guarantee application recovery back to the point of disaster. (For example, log files handle instance recovery caused by power failure, etc.) Archive files allow applications to be rolled forward from the last system backup. Archiving does come at a cost. Benchmarks have shown that overheads can be up to 5% of overall system performance. Archive file swapping can cause larger overheads as each file is copied to a secondary disk. The application can actually come to an absolute halt if previous archive files are waiting to be copied to tape.

The use of mirrored disks is a popular alternative to transaction archiving. If a single disk crash occurs, the disk can simply be replaced. You will still have to do regular system exports, but you can avoid export-to-export archiving. The chance of two head crashes occurring at one time, on corresponding disks, is many times more remote than a single head crash coupled with a recovery tape failure. Mirror disks usually represent substantial performance improvement and zero overhead. Disks are written simultaneously, without any overhead beyond a single disk write. In fact, disk reads are actually improved. Smart controllers choose which mirrored disk is the most efficient to read from, thus reducing disk head movement and wait times.

Tuning Imports

The ORACLE utility, IMPORT, recovers a database. The success of a data import depends not only on its operation, but also on its timeliness. The quicker you can restore database activity, the less application downtime your users will experience, and the fewer complaints you'll hear.

To improve the performance of the IMPORT utility, place import files on a different disk from the one used for the database files. This allows you to read and write faster, and it minimizes disk contention. Divide large imports into several smaller imports that run in parallel. This can result in excellent performance if all of the individual imports are over tablespaces or user tables located on different physical disks, and if each outputs to a different physical disk.

Import only the information that is necessary for immediate system access. If an export file contains all of the essential information for recovery, plus a number of very large, non-critical files, restore only the mandatory files in your first pass. (For many applications, this does mean all tables.) Tables can be skipped by creating dummy table definitions with incompatible columns. Create such definitions with very small INITIAL extents because these definitions will be dropped after the import. When the import encounters such a table, it simply reports an ORACLE error and continues on. The non-critical tables can be imported again, at a later time. For example:

```
CREATE TABLE EMP_HISTORY
    (DUMMY CHAR(1))
    STORAGE (INITIAL 1K  NEXT 1K);
```

Before you import any file, size and create all files first. Make sure that each table will fit into a single table extent; always factor future table growth into the INITIAL extent. Generate indexes after you restore tables and load data. Assign a large temporary tablespace, with a very large INITIAL extent, and allocate a large value for the memory sort area (specified in SORT_AREA_SIZE) to speed up index generation.

If at all possible, import directly from disk, rather than tape-to-disk. It is preferable to keep the dump file on disk, if your system has the capacity. Restoring from tape to disk, or importing from tape, are both time-consuming. Remember that if you compress files, you can usually hold several dump files on disk. To allow ORACLE dump files to be compatible across all platforms, ORACLE makes them extremely verbose. Our tests show that simple, platform-specific compression utilities will reduce the size of exports to less than 25% of the original size. A simple compression could allow two or three export files to be retained on disk, rather than having to be exported to tape.

Make sure that you maintain log files of your exports and check them regularly. The export logs are the best way of detecting internal database corruption of application tables. Image backups do not detect or correct data file corruption; they only repeat it. You want to be sure that your entire production database hasn't turned into vaporware! Even a simple 10-line C program to test a dump file's size can be of value. Such a program might check that the dump file is approximately the right size—perhaps 100 megabytes plus or minus 10%. If the dump file varies from this expected size, the program can send an automatic mail message to the DBA.

Run IMPORT with the following option to reveal the physical size of each table and index, if compressed to a single extent:

```
IMP indexfile = ABC.LST ROWS = n  FILE = EXP_SYS_DMP
```

This output file is actually an SQL file for every table and index to be generated into a single initial extent. Be aware, though, that no actual export is performed.

By default, IMPORT commits only after restoring all of the records of each table. This is possible only for small tables. Very large tables will not fit into the available rollback segments. To import large tables, set the COMMIT option within the IMPORT parameter file. This is the only way to import very large tables. For example, you can specify:

```
IMP PARFILE = \usr\dump\import.par
```

where *import.par* contains:

```
COMMIT   = Y
FROMUSER = OPS$SMITH
TOUSER   = OPS$JONES
```

16

Tuning in the Client-server Environment

The topic of client-server computing is the subject of many books, and we're not going to try to write another one here. The aim of this chapter is simply to summarize the specific ways in which client-server computing affects performance, and the specific ways in which you can tune your client-server environment to get the best possible performance out of your applications.

ORACLE has invested enormous resources in making client-server computing an effective and financially rewarding equipment choice. The trend in the industry is towards downsizing. Many large organizations that relied in the past on mainframe computing are now discovering how much money they can save by downsizing to a client-server configuration. The section below called "Client-server: A Case Study" describes the cost savings one such organization realized.

Advances in computing and networking have made client-server solutions, even for the largest systems, a reality. The advance in powerful, inexpensive microcomputers (even laptops) that deliver enormous processing power at a fraction of the cost of a mainframe, new networking facilities, and recent advances in chip technology (e.g., pentium 80586) and parallel processing all play a role in making client-server computing a viable solution to the most demanding application needs. When I was at university, my lecturer jokingly described the difference between a PC, a minicomputer, and a mainframe this way: "A PC is small enough to be transported by car, a mini can be transported in the back of a van, and a mainframe needs a semi-trailer, a large crane, and very careful movers." These words have finally rung true. Other than price, physical machine size rather than CPU capacity may be the only way we distinguish types of computers in the future.

Despite the major benefits of client-server, we are not recommending that you rush, willy-nilly, out to buy a database server, file servers, and a truckload of PC workstations to replace your existing hardware—without a lot of planning, that is. If your existing applications have been developed with a "mainframe mentality," downsizing the application, unchanged, is unlikely to achieve significant performance improvements. Client-server environments have just as many bad features as good ones. What you need to do, if you are serious about exploring the benefits of client-server configurations, is to learn how to exploit their good points while avoiding the bad ones. Tuning for client-server, which we focus on in this chapter, is vital if you are going to take advantage of this technology.

What is Client-server?

The term, "client-server," can be defined with varying degrees of rigor and a multitude of interpretations. For purposes of this book, we define it as "two or more distinct computers working together. One computer (the server) performs the job of coordinating access to the ORACLE database; the other computer (the client) serves the application users." In most environments, there are multiple client computers. To run applications in a client-server environment, a processor must be able to communicate between the server computer and the client computer(s), usually via a network.

Historically, ORACLE has run in a unitary environment. In such an environment, the application user processes communicate with the database within the boundaries of the same physical computer. All processes (database and user) share the same memory, disk, and CPU resources. User terminals are typically dumb ones, incapable of functioning on their own. Each terminal is physically cabled to the central computer. A unitary environment is shown in Figure 16-1.

By contrast, ORACLE client-server applications run on many CPUs, with the ORACLE database and the application user process(es) communicating from different computers. Resources are not shared between the client and server. Instead, messages (usually called packets) are sent and received. Client processes act on their own, not as the result of concurrent operator requests. The typical mode of operation involves the database process looping idly on the database server, waiting to service client requests. Most application overhead is incurred at the client machine by the initiating client only, and does not impact other clients.

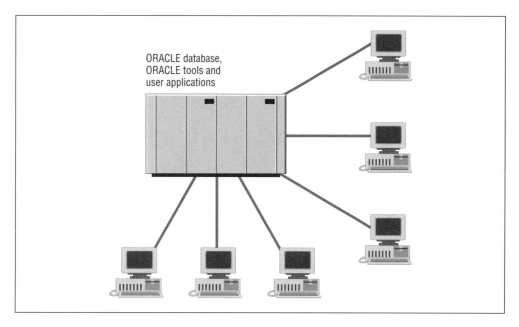

Figure 16-1: Running ORACLE in a unitary environment

There are many workable configurations of client-server networks. An organization's application needs, number of connected users, software requirements, and budget all play a part in dictating the right choice for a client-server implementation. Figure 16-2 shows one possible configuration—a Novell network utilizing a token ring configuration. In this environment, each operator has a PC on his or her desk acting as a client machine. (In addition to running ORACLE applications, these PCs can also be used to perform other, more traditional desktop functions, such as word processing.) The ORACLE database (kernel and tablespace data files) resides on the database server, and all other components (ORACLE tools, third-party software, and user files) reside on the file server. In this particular configuration, client PCs do not need local hard disks. Instead, network drivers are loaded via a floppy boot disk, and all other software, including ORACLE tools, is retrieved over the network from a common file server disk.

Figure 16-3 demonstrates a different type of client-server configuration. In this example, a UNIX client-server application consisting of several client servers is connected to a common database. Each server caters to a group of individual terminals (database connections), with each workstation reduced to a simple, dumb terminal emulator. No processing is performed for (or offloaded to) the user workstations.

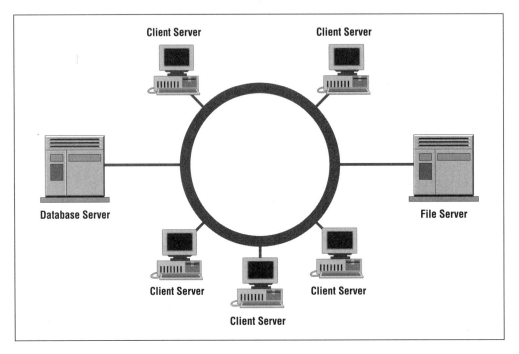

Figure 16-2: Client-server environment (Novell token ring network)

Network Topology

In a client-server environment, processes communicate with one another via a network. When you are tuning an ORACLE database, you will need to provide for network communications. Remember, operators do not interact directly with the database server (the back-end processes), but rather with the client (the front-end process). The physical arrangement of client and server nodes is called network topology. The choice of network arrangement, client and server node location, and overall network length can all affect application performance. Networks commonly make use of message routers and node bridges to build large environments that are often complicated, but nevertheless efficient.

For a token ring network such as the one demonstrated in Figure 16-2, the length of the physical network is likely to be a performance issue. The speed with which the token (packets) is passed around a network is constant (typically 4 to 16 megabits). The larger the ring, the farther the token will need to travel, and the longer it will take to reach its destination. If a great many terminals are added to the ring, obviously the ring becomes longer, and the more times each packet has to be inspected by a terminal (checking packet header destination information) before it can reach its ultimate destination.

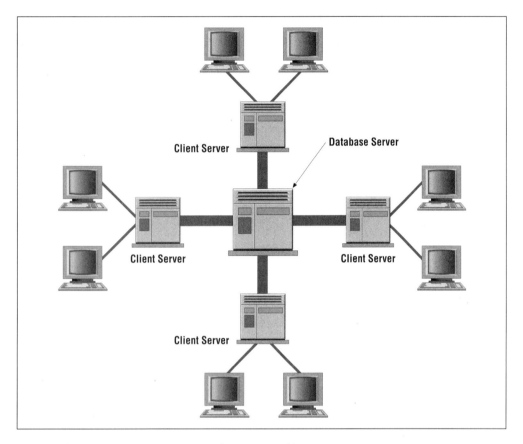

Figure 16-3: Client-server environment (UNIX network)

On the other hand, the UNIX network identified in Figure 16-3 can support many varied topology arrangements. When you have a choice, make it carefully because application performance can be adversely affected by topology selection. Some of the more common network topologies are described briefly below.

Star Topology

In a star or radial topology shown in Figure 16-4, all nodes are joined at a single point. These networks are common in situations where all control is located at a central node, and communication between nodes and remote stations is processed via that node. This relieves outlying nodes of control function overheads.

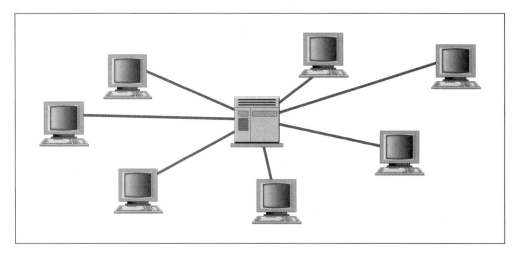

Figure 16-4: Star topology

Ring Networks

Ring networks are a very popular type of network topology. In a ring network, shown in Figure 16-5, all nodes are connected via point-to-point links, making up an unbroken loop. Network messages travel around the ring. Each node recognizes its own messages by looking for a specific message header, and passes other messages further around the ring. Ring networks are less complex than star or hybrid networks because they do not require routers.

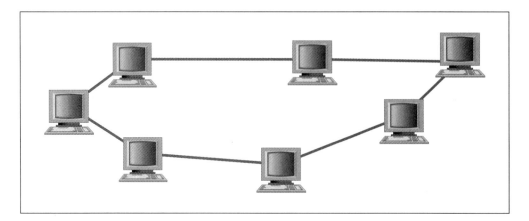

Figure 16-5: Ring topology

Bus Networks

Bus topologies, shown in Figure 16-6, function in a way that is similar to star and ring networks. All nodes are fully connected via a single physical channel and cable taps. Bus networks are frequently used for distributing control in local area networks. As with ring networks, each message must carry a node identifier. But unlike ring networks, messages do not have to be retransmitted, relieving each node of network control overheads.

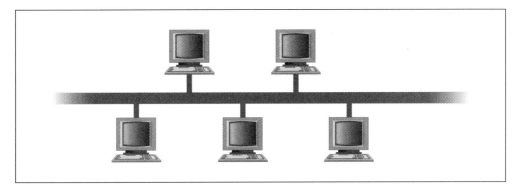

Figure 16-6: Bus topology

Hybrid Topologies

Unconstrained, hybrid network configurations, shown in Figure 16-7, are random in form. The number of connections is usually determined by budget. Because line costs are high, in such networks only physical connections that are actually needed are cabled.

Client-server: A Case Study

Although in general computer costs are dropping, mainframe applications are still very expensive, especially compared with the cost of running such applications on distributed systems. Far too often, organizations that have bought mainframe systems in the past continue to run and upgrade those systems, rather than taking the time to look into client-server computing and performance tuning. Time and time again, we see tens or even hundreds of millions of dollars being wasted on unnecessary hardware purchases and upgrades. And it gets worse. Every new hardware resource carries with it the ongoing legacy of larger maintenance contracts and costlier software licences.

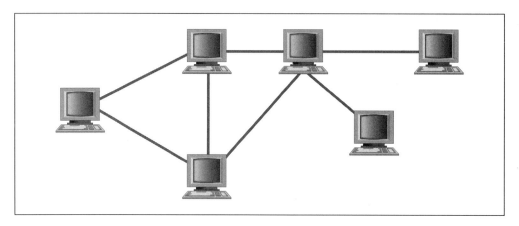

Figure 16-7: Hybrid topology

Because some organizations have invested so much money in huge, single-host configurations, they are sometimes hesitant to rock the boat. And yet, client-server computing can often offload as much as two-thirds of the processor overhead from a host computer. In Chapter 1 we mentioned a particularly expensive system that we had occasion to downsize and tune during early 1993. This system was owned by a large financial organization and serviced 80 online users. Here is what the organization was spending to keep its system running; notice we're not even talking about the initial purchase price here:

Mainframe:

Annual running costs

- IBM mainframe

- System software

  100 user licenses

  Operating system compilers

$2,500,000.00 outgoings (conservative)
(Australian dollars)

Operation costs

- Operations

- Backup / tape drives

- Air conditioning

- Special power requirements

We replaced this system with a Novell-based client-server configuration (with the topology shown in Figure 16-2). The list below shows the required purchase price and maintenance fees:

Client-server	Initial Cost	Maintenance Fees
Hardware Database server (64 users)	$39,000.00	$3,900.00
• Compaq 486 33-Mhz		
• 64-megabyte memory (up to 128 megabytes)		
• 3-gigabyte disk		
• 2 disk controllers		
• 1 EISA network card		
File server	$10,000.00	$1,000.00
• Compaq 486 25-Mhz		
• 16-megabyte memory		
• 1-gigabyte disk		
• 1 controller		
• 1 EISA network card		
Client servers (60 Units x $1870)	$112,200.00	—
• "XYZ" 386 33-Mhz		
• No hard disk		
• SVGA color monitor		
• 4-megabyte memory		
• Network card		
Novell 100 user license	$10,795.00	—
ORACLE server licenses (64 users)	$53,000.00	$17,000.00
ORACLE tools (64 users)	$27,000.00	$9,000.00
Operation costs		
• Operations	• —	
• Air conditioning	• —	
• Special power requirements	• —	
• 5-gigabyte Exabyte tape drive	$7,500.00	

Client-server	Initial Cost	Maintenance Fees
Total	$259,495.00	$30,900.00

Other:

- Sub 2-second response times
- 24-hour online query access
- 16-megabyte ORACLE SGA
- Overnight processing (less than three hours, including application export)

Database server upgrade	486 DX 66-Mhz	$5,500.00
	Extra 32-MB mem.	$5,000.00

You don't have to be Einstein to grasp the huge savings that were achieved at this site.

What were the people costs? We had to convert the system from COBOL to ORACLE RDBMS and SQL*Forms. This cost approximately $1.2 million (Australian) in staff training, staff salaries, and contractor wages. The project took 14 months from initial database specification to application launch. The IBM mainframe was shut down two months after launching the new system. Considering all of the development expenses, new hardware, and ongoing maintenance, the costs were fully recouped seven months after the launch of the new system. The annual costs of running the system after that date dropped from $2,500,000 to $31,000.

The new system meets the needs of system users. It provides response times of under two seconds, even though it processes a large history table containing more than four million records. Users also have the added bonus of cheap,,off-the-shelf, third-party software packages—for example, Lotus, Excel, Microsoft Windows, and various word processors.

The system described above was a total replacement. It is also possible to replace equipment more gradually. Several years ago we worked on a VAX memory upgrade costing more than $120,000 for an additional 32 megabytes of memory. For as little as $10,500, the system database server could triple its processing power and increase its memory by 32 megabytes.

Once you have downsized, you have the potential to replace pieces of the configuration, without doing a complete overhaul. Because most of the client processing is performed at client workstations, you can selectively improve the response times of your most troublesome users—perhaps those loud, complaining managers. By upgrading a PC workstation to a 486 25-Mhz or even a 486 33-Mhz machine, you can cut response times in half for that client. In benchmarks, we've found that this type of configuration incurs more than 80% of online application overhead at the client worksta-tions, not at the database or file server end.

Where Should You Put the Network Hardware?

When you are considering where to locate your physical hardware in a client-server environment, make sure you are familiar with how ORACLE will be interacting between the client and server processors. ORACLE uses SQL*Net to communicate across the network. SQL calls are requested at the client machine and passed back and forth to the database processor. This conversation can generate over a thousand packets from a single form of medium complexity.

If your company has its application client-server(s) and database server physically located at different sites, the distance this "process-to-process communication" has to travel could result in a response delay of as much as 20 seconds. You will find that a SQL*Forms program that performed adequately in a unitary environment (where all communication was within the single computer) may suddenly see its response times raised well above the required standards for your site.

The best way of improving client-server performance is to reduce the number of packets being transferred across the network. For applications that have been devel-oped for a unitary environment, you'll have to do a substantial amount of programming. Before you undertake what might be a tedious rewrite, you can realize immediate performance improvements simply by locating the database and client servers as physi-cally close together as possible. This approach may sound simplistic, but it is remarkably effective because it allows you to put higher-speed lines between the processors.

Your ability to make this particular improvement obviously depends on your choice of network topology. The token ring topology shown in Figure 16-2 cannot benefit from this practice. Because each client server is actually a user workstation, it must be located on the user's desk. This type of network is appropriate only for a company operating in one building or in a close group of buildings.

The UNIX client-server configuration described in Figure 16-3, on the other hand, can achieve large performance gains from hardware location. Each workstation acts as a simple terminal emulator to each client processor. The communication between the workstation and the client is minimal. The communication between the client and the database server, however, is major. You can achieve huge savings by reducing the phys-ical distance between the many thousands of packets that must travel back and forth from database to client servers, at the expense of the few packets that move between the client server and the operator terminal. Figure 16-8 demonstrates how an Australia-wide network could be configured.

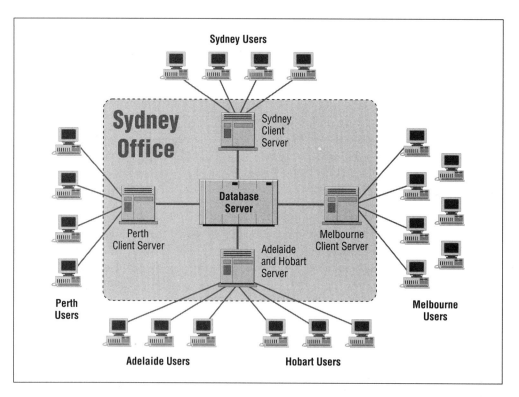

Figure 16-8: Wide-area network

Client-server Performance Issues

This section describes a variety of performance issues for client-server configurations.

Reducing ORACLE Network Traffic

Reducing the number of packets transferred (trips) across the network is key to making a client-server configuration run efficiently. The speed and efficiency of the network is the gating factor to a high-performance system. In a unitary environment, processes cross-communicate via a physical memory board. Messages do not need to be shuffled from one machine to the next. Many networks have very impressive performance, but no matter what you do, you'll never be able to match the process-to-process performance of a unitary machine.

In numerous tests, we have concluded that the number of packets transmitted across a network is actually more important than the size of each packet. Both small and large packets take roughly the same amount of time passing between machines. But sending a large number of packets can wreak havoc on your system's response times.

Consider the simple SQL query below:

```
SELECT EMP_NO, EMP_NAME
    FROM EMP
    WHERE EMP_DEPT = :BLK.EMP_DEPT
```

This query generates a surprising number of network round-trips every time it is executed:

1. Open the cursor

2. Parse the statement (check its syntax)

3. Bind the variables

4. Describe (are the fields numbers, characters, dates, etc.?)

5. Execute the statement (search the database)

6. Fetch the rows (the number of rows per fetch depends on ARRAYSIZE)

7. Close the cursor

When this sample SQL statement was executed directly on a database server, it took 0.34 seconds. When it was executed on a client-server network between Melbourne and Sydney, it took about 3.5 seconds for the packet transfer.

Consider the huge savings you can realize if you can cut down on the number of transfers needed. Transferring a packet across a TCP/IP network from Melbourne to Sydney (approximately 550 miles) can be accomplished at the rate of 120 packets per second. If the ARRAYSIZE you have specified is 1 (see the following section for information about this parameter), 20 fetches are required to return 20 rows, and 26 packets need to be transferred. If ARRAYSIZE is 20, however, only one fetch and seven packets are required.

It does not take long for the number of packets to build up to a point where they have a significant impact on performance. Some SQL*Forms programs generate more than 1000 packets. Not only do client stations need to wait for packets to be sent and received from the database server, the packets themselves begin to wait for a time slot on the network itself.

Tuning ARRAYSIZE

You can specify the ARRAYSIZE parameter to control the number of rows that can be returned from disk in a single network transfer. If you set ARRAYSIZE correctly, you can substantially reduce the number of network packets. An adequate value for this parameter allows multiple SELECT, INSERT, and UPDATE operations to be performed in a single database server access.

To figure out how many packets need to be transferred for a particular SQL statement or set of statements (for example, the series of network round-trips described in the previous section), divide the number of required fetches by the ARRAYSIZE in effect for your current database interface tool.

NOTE

Our benchmarks indicate that increasing ARRAYSIZE when you are running in a unitary environment has little or no effect on performance.

You can increase ARRAYSIZE, or its equivalent parameter, in a number of ORACLE tools:

SQL*Forms. Uses array processing by default.

Precompiler 3GL languages (e.g., Pro*C). Support array processing implicitly. For example:

```
EXEC SQL
INSERT INTO EMP ( EMP_NO, EMP_NAME)
    VALUES ( :BLK.EMP_NO,:BLK.EMP_NAME );
```

If the values are part of an array of 200, 200 rows will be inserted with the one execution of the statement. Array selects, updates, and deletes are also supported.

ORACLE Call Interface (OCI). Uses the OFEN parameter to specify the number of rows to be returned via each OEXN fetch. This is equivalent to ARRAYSIZE.

SQL*Plus. You can set ARRAYSIZE in the SET command. The default is 20. If you set it to 200 or more, you will improve performance over the network. (MAXDATA must be large enough to contain that many rows.)

EXPORT and IMPORT. Try to avoid executing these utilities across network nodes. If it is absolutely necessary, you can improve response time by setting the BUFFER parameter to an appropriate size. If the row length is 100, and BUFFER is 32,768, the effective array size is approximately 327. Most sites set their buffers on exports and imports to at least 32K. Some UNIX sites set buffers as high as one megabyte. The maximum value is operating system-dependent.

SQL*Loader. Set the ROWS parameter to allocate a buffer or array size. The actual buffer size is set by multiplying the size of each row by the value you specify for the parameter. Set this value as high as possible for your site. The maximum is system-dependent.

Tuning PL/SQL

PL/SQL's block structure makes its network performance very efficient. Each PL/SQL block can contain many individual SQL statements (SELECT, UPDATE, DELETE, and INSERT). Each block is passed to the kernel at the database server end in a single network transmission. The statements in the block are executed as a unit at the database end, and the results are returned on completion of the entire block. Overall network traffic can be reduced by as much as a thousand times. Note that this functionality is applicable to all ORACLE tools that use PL/SQL (except SQL*Forms, which has its own version of PL/SQL linked directly into its own executable). See Figure 16-10 for a comparison of SQL and PL/SQL operations.

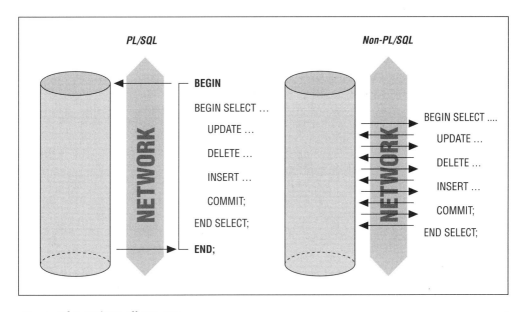

Figure 16-9: PL/SQL efficiencies

You can save additional network traffic by limiting the number of local field bindings within the PL/SQL block. Initialize each bind variable into a temporary PL/SQL-defined variable once, and reference that temporary variable for the remainder of the procedure.

The reduction of network traffic via PL/SQL has a particular impact on SQL*Forms. RUNFORM *(iap)* has its own copy of PL/SQL linked into it, and it can be used to perform functions that would otherwise have to be done by the database kernel. You can also use PL/SQL to avoid all table accesses of the form:

```
SELECT . . . FROM DUAL
```

You can also manipulate numbers and strings, and can add and subtract dates, locally via PL/SQL.

All of the ORACLE tools support PL/SQL procedures, and can use these procedures to improve their response times substantially.

Choosing Explicit SELECT Statements

You can also reduce the number of network trips for SQL SELECT statements by using explicit, rather than implicit, cursors. Implicit cursors must perform a second fetch for every SELECT statement. If an application were to perform 100 implicit database selects within a single session, then the program would incur 100 extra database fetches and 100 extra network trips. See the section in Chapter 8 called, "Using Explicit and Implicit Cursors in PL/SQL" for examples of the two types of cursors.

Combining SELECT Statements

Another simple way to reduce network traffic is to combine several unrelated SQL statements, as we have suggested in Chapter 7, *Tuning SQL*.

The following statements were executed on a unitary ORACLE database and then on a client-server database between Sydney and Melbourne. This simple exercise indicates that the time taken to traverse the network from client to database server is approximately 0.45 seconds. By simply combining both statements into one, we are able to improve the elapsed time on the client-server by more than 33%. In this first example the following elapsed times result:

Unitary machine: *.54 seconds*

Client-server configuration: *1.45 seconds*

```
DECLARE
    CURSOR  C1 (E_NO  NUMBER)  IS
    SELECT  EMP_NAME, SALARY, GRADE
        FROM  EMP
        WHERE  EMP_NO = E_NO;
BEGIN
    OPEN  C1  (342);
    FETCH C1  INTO  ..., ..., ...;

    OPEN  C1  (291);
    FETCH  C1 INTO ..., ..., ...;
    CLOSE  C1;
END;
```

In this next example the following elapsed times result:

Unitary machine: *.51 seconds*

Client-server configuration: *.99 seconds*

```
SELECT  A.EMP_NAME, A.SALARY, A.GRADE,
        B.EMP_NAME, B.SALARY, B.GRADE
    FROM    EMP   A,
            EMP   B
    WHERE  A.EMP_NO  =  0342
    AND    B.EMP_NO  =  0291 ;
```

SQL*Forms Base Table Views

When there is a substantial distance between the client and the database servers, you can improve performance by using views as SQL*Forms base tables.

SQL*Forms applications commonly perform two or three post-change triggers, as well as a post-query trigger, after every successful row fetch. These triggers are often used to look up foreign key descriptions, and other such operations. Multi-row forms may perform as many as 60 triggers (3 x 20 rows per screen) for every EXEQRY macro. This, in turn, means 60 database calls, every one across the network.

If you have set the SQL*Forms SET parameter, ARRAYSIZE, to 20, then by creating a view over the "base table" table and the three "lookup" tables, you can reduce the number of network calls from 61 to 1. If the form is a maintenance-type form, you'll have to incorporate special updating logic into the form to simulate base table updating. (See the discussion of this approach in Chapter 9, *Tuning SQL*Forms.*)

Look again at the client-server application between Melbourne and Sydney. The creation of the view has reduced the elapsed time from more than 20 seconds to less than 2.5 seconds. The unitary elapsed times show that the overhead of the view is actually less than the combined overheads of navigating and executing the 60 post-change triggers. The elapsed time of the client-server environment has actually been improved by tenfold. In this first example the following elapsed times result:

Unitary machine: *1.74 seconds*

Client-server configuration   *22.50 seconds*

```
BASE TABLE   EMP
DATABASE FIELDS EMP_NO
                    EMP_NAME
                    EMP_DEPT    FK
                    MGR_EMP_NO  FK
                    EMP_CAT     FK
```

```
POST-CHANGE      LOOKUP DEPT DESCRIPTION
                 LOOPUP MANAGER NAME
                 LOOKUP CATEGORY DESCRIPTION
```

In this next example the elapsed time for the client-server configuration has dropped dramatically:

Unitary machine: *1.61 seconds*

Client-server configuration   *2.35 seconds*

```
CREATE VIEW  EMP_VIEW AS

SELECT  E.EMP_NO, E.EMP_NAME, E.EMP_DEPT,
    E.MGR_EMP_NO, E.EMP_CAT, D.DEPT_DESC,
    M.EMP_NAME MGR_NAME,  C.CAT_DESC
    FROM   CATEGORY    C,
           DEPARTMENT  D,
           EMP   M,
           EMP   E
    WHERE E.EMP_NO      >  0
    AND    E.EMP_DEPT   =  D.DEPT_CODE   (+)
    AND    E.MGR_EMP_NO =  M.EMP_NO   (+)
    AND    E.EMP_CAT    =  C.CAT_CODE   (+)


BASE TABLE  EMP_VIEW
DATABASE FIELDS  EMP_NO
                 EMP_NAME
                 EMP_DEPT
                 DEPT_DESC
                 MGR_EMP_NO
                 MGR_NAME
                 EMP_CAT
                 CAT_DESC
```

Client-server Issues for Version 7

This section mentions the new features of Version 7 that you can exploit to get the best performance out of your client-server configuration. The discussion below does not describe how to use these features, but simply mentions the client-server implications of them. For more information about these features, see Appendix A, *Planning for ORACLE7*, and for complete information, consult your standard ORACLE documentation for Version 7.

Stored Database Triggers and Procedures

The stored triggers and procedures available in Version 7 are stored within the database and are triggered automatically by the RDBMS kernel itself. Triggers and procedures are stored in parsed form. After the initial reference, they are kept in the database cache so they can be shared by all users (not only the originating user). This feature substantially reduces the amount of network traffic and improves overall client-server performance.

Distributed Databases

With distributed database processing, an organization's database can be strategically divided among multiple physical databases located on distinct database servers. From the user's point of view, however, there is a single logical database. For example, assume that a company's accounting department is in Melbourne and the manufacturing department is in Sydney, as illustrated in Figure 16-10. These two divisions have two distinct application modules, with very little data crossover. By intelligently placing the database servers in the two cities, and adding a super-fast data communications link between the two, you can actually improve network and application performance.

Version 6 supported distributed database queries. Version 7 now supports distributed updates as well. With the two-phase commit feature, automatic and transparent updates guarantee that commits or rollbacks issued against a distributed database transaction are always performed as a single unit. Global database integrity is always maintained.

Automatic Table Replication/Snapshots

Under Version 7, an automatic, asynchronous table replication feature allows read-only copies of an updatable master table. (Version 7.1 promises update capability of all replicated database nodes.) These replications can be refreshed at intervals defined by a user. A table snapshot can replicate a single table, a subset of a table, or a complex query join. You can refresh a table for either the entire master table data or only the most recent changes.

To improve performance in a client-server configuration, make sure that you perform replication during off-peak network hours. Then, during high-peak hours, users do not have to drag tables or table subsets across the network. Doing this will improve your performance. However, remember that this practice does lead to the possibility that a client may be using some obsolete data, so you may not want to do this for all of your tables. Choose the tables to be replicated carefully.

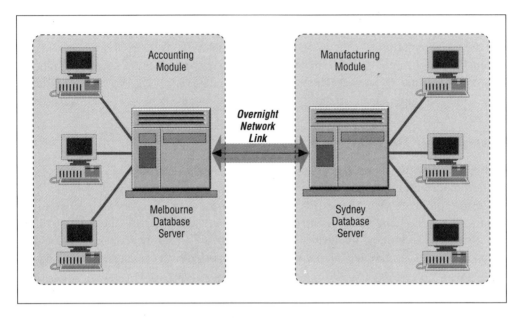

Figure 16-10: Distributed database processing

Running Long-running Jobs at the Server End

Running overnight reports and performing exports, imports, and other long-running batch jobs at the database server end will improve overall response time in a client-server configuration. By eliminating the transfer of packets across the network and restricting the larger jobs to one machine, you can improve performance by a factor of ten. In fact, if you restrict your work in this way, you will get performance equal to what you would achieve by executing long-running procedures in a unitary environment.

On the Novell client-server configuration shown in Figure 16-2 (a 16 megabit, token-ring network), we dramatically improved the performance of the database backup procedure (the EXPORT utility). The nightly database export of the financial system was 250 megabytes. When the export was run from a client workstation (with a DOS executable), it took more than five hours to run. When we performed it at the database server end (with a network-loaded module) it took only 40 minutes to run.

WARNING

Never store database exports on the database server disks on which your physical database files reside. If you lose that disk, you will lose both the database and the export files (and probably your job!).

Tuning Precompilers For Client-server

Sometimes, to get better performance out of critical areas of an application, developers may resort to developing these critical modules using a precompiler such as Pro*C or Pro*COBOL. We say "resort to," because using these precompilers is, for most programmers, more difficult than using the usual ORACLE tools. For large, overnight processing jobs, or complex and time-critical update routines (e.g., user exits), using the precompilers may prove necessary. They give you more detailed, low-level cursor and data control, and this can substantially improve performance.

You need to be aware of certain special considerations when you are using the precompilers in a client-server environment.

Arrays. Always use arrays if you are fetching, updating, deleting, or inserting more than one row in one operation for the same table. Pro*C allows the dynamic allocation and deallocation of memory to hold the array data. This allows the program to use and release memory resources as required. You might consider using a large array size; even one over 200 is not unreasonable.

Dynamic SQL. Use dynamic SQL features to limit the number of rows returned and to determine which indexes the optimizer will use. The precompilers support this facility. We were once asked to look at a Pro*C program which was performing very poorly. It turned out that the driving SELECT statement had no WHERE clause at all. There was no array processing. All rows had to be fetched from the database, one at a time; those not needed were then pruned via a series of IF clauses. By incorporating the IF clauses into the driving SQL statement and introducing array processing, we were able to reduce the elapsed time of the routine from four hours to 25 minutes.

Parameters. If the same statements are used repeatedly within the program, set these parameters to minimize parsing:

```
HOLD_CURSOR      YES
RELEASE_CURSOR   NO
```

Do the reverse if cursors are referenced only once for the life of the program (in the initialization section). Set the following parameters to release unrequired cursor resources:

```
HOLD_CURSOR      NO
RELEASE_CURSOR   YES
```

PL/SQL cursors. Use PL/SQL explicit cursors whenever you need to perform multiple SELECTs, INSERTs, DELETEs, and UPDATEs.

No syntax checking. To speed up the precompiling function in the client-server environment you can set the CHECK_SQL parameter to NO. No statement syntax checking will be performed against the database. (Setting this parameter should be a last resort; do it only if absolutely necessary to speed up program compilation times.) Note that you will have to set CHECK_SQL to NO if your precompiler program physically connects to more than one ORACLE database. This may happen on overnight data cross-loads between separate applications. A precompiler program can be compiled (syntaxed) against only one of the two databases at a time. If this option is not disabled, any references to tables in the other database will be reported as errors during compilation (i.e., "UNDEFINED TABLES REFERENCED").

Tuning the Network Itself

Several network equipment choices will have a major impact on client-server performance. There are a number of choices to consider when determining what network will best meet your organization's needs:

- Media bandwidth. For example, Ethernet is 10 MBits/second and Async is only .0096 MBits/second).

- Communications protocol. Different protocols differ markedly in their performance. TCP/IP, DECnet, and APPC are known to be top performers; sync is known to lag behind.

- Physical protocol latency issues.

- Communication bus speeds at both the server and client ends.

Against these physical choices you will have to balance the expected workload in your system—for example, the mix of work and whether the application will be performing mostly interactive jobs or many long-running jobs.

A communications protocol (common language) is required at both the client and server ends for the machines to communicate. The SQL*Net communications package (described in the next section) simply inherits all of the characteristics of its underlying network and communications protocol. If the network and communications protocol are built for speed, SQL*Net will perform accordingly.

Enlarging Packet Size

Most communication protocols allow you to adjust network packet sizes. Larger packet sizes require fewer overall packets and therefore less overall overhead. ORACLE recommends that if the protocol allows you to choose, you select a minimum of at least 1024 bytes.

Reducing Network Delays

In VTAM-based protocols, which have a built-in delay, you can improve performance by setting the DELAY parameter to 0.0. Doing this does require more CPU. You will have to assess your own system's CPU capacity and decide whether to set this parameter.

Tuning SQL*Net

SQL*Net is the ORACLE communications package that allows users to access information residing on different databases stored on different machines. It runs across a variety of communications protocols, and it supports client-server applications as well as distributed databases. SQL*Net can be used on a local ORACLE database (shown in Figure 16-1) or in a client-server environment (shown in Figure 16-2 and Figure 16-3). When the client is accessing a database on a remote computer, SQL*Net handles the actual connection.

Because many sites are still running SQL*Net Version 1, the following discussion mentions particular client-server performance issues for both Version 1 and Version 2. However, be aware that, although ORACLE is currently supporting both versions for all protocol types, Version 1 will eventually be dropped. For some RDBMS Version 7 features (e.g., multi-threaded server), you need to be using SQL*Net Version 2, so we advise you to upgrade to Version 2 as soon as possible.

Tuning SQL*Net Version 1

To improve the performance of SQL*Net over your network, follow the suggestions for the particular product you are using:

SQL*Net Asynch:

- Increase the packet size to the maximum allowable
- Use raw mode instead of line mode
- Reduce timeouts and increase retries in your connection scripts

SQL*Net for DECnet:

- Increase buffers to the maximum allowable

SQL*Net for TCP/IP:

- Use as large a buffer size as possible (by default, the TCP/IP buffer size is set to its maximum of 4096)

- Use out-of-band breaks; this is not the default for Version 1. Out-of-band breaks can improve performance by as much as 50% when applied to TWO_TASK; for example, in the following, the final "O" requests out-of-band breaks:

  ```
  TWO_TASK=t:machine:dbase:,,,O )
  ```

  This parameter reduces the regularity of interrupt checks by the RDBMS. In testing, we created a table with 30 rows called XX with a single column and performed the following query with out-of-band breaks turned on.

  Before you can turn on out-of-band breaks, you must enable them. Start ORASRV as follows:

  ```
  ORASRV O
  SELECT COUNT (*) FROM XX, XX, XX, XX; Response time = 8 seconds.
  ```

  We performed the same query with out-of-band breaks turned off:

  ```
  SELECT COUNT (*) FROM XX, XX, XX, XX; Response time = 29 seconds
  ```

For SQL*Net ACCP/LU6.2:

- Set PACING high to minimize APPC handshaking
- Set RU size higher for better performance

For SQL*Net for PC LANs:

- Increase the Netware parameter, MINIMUM PACKET RECEIVE BUFFERS, from the default of 10 to a minimum of 100
- Prespawn shadows processes to allow faster connections.

Tuning SQL*Net Version 2

SQL*Net Version 2 provides client-server applications with more functions and makes them run more efficiently. All of the Version 1 recommendations apply to Version 2 as well. In addition, there are several new features that affect client-server operations.

Of particular importance is the Multiprotocol Interchange feature. This feature allows two different ORACLE client-server protocol networks to cross-communicate so they can function logically as a single network. In this way, SQL*Net Version 2 offers network transparency and protocol independence.

Version 2 features that affect client-server performance are:

Multiprotocol Interchange. Through this feature, heterogeneous networking supports communication across networks, using multiple protocols.

Fastpath. This internal feature helps minimize data read and write times.

Configuration control files. These files can be generated automatically. They files contain generic database connection descriptors (TNS connect descriptors) that are constant across all platforms and all protocols.

Diagnostics. Improved diagnostics, including extensive logging and tracing facilities, have been built into Version 2.

Multi-threaded server. Version 2 supports the ORACLE Version 7 multi-threaded server. For a brief description of this feature, see Appendix A, *Planning for Version 7.*

Simultaneous version support. Version 2 supports both SQL*Net Version 1 and SQL*Net Version 2 clients simultaneously. Note, however, that SQL*Net Version 1 cannot use the Multiprotocol Interchange, nor communicate outside the one community.

UPIALL. UPIALL is supported for all ORACLE tools via SQL*Net Version 2. UPIALL requires only two network trips per SQL statement: one for opening a statement and one for closing the statement, compared with the many packets currently being passed across the network for the one SELECT.

One difference between SQL*Net Version 1 and Version 2 is important to security. There is always a possibility that unauthorized users will gain access to a client-server network via remote logins (e.g., OPS$ usercodes). ORACLE recommends against your use of operating system logins to remote databases. This does not imply that you should avoid using OPS$ usercodes within your database, but do avoid using them across the network, from one database to another. In Version 1, proxy logins are enabled by default. In RDBMS Version 7, operating system logins are disabled by default (although ORACLE does say that security problems are much less likely to occur because of enhancements in OS login security).

Client-server: Adapting it in the Real World

In this section we describe a few real-world projects we've performed in which we have overcome weaknesses in client-server or exploited the strengths of the technology. Don't view these as suggestions for everybody. They represent solutions to particular problems, not overall strategies. But they should give you some ideas about how you might get the best performance out of your own client-server configuration.

Using a Dedicated Report Server

In the Novell client-server configuration (presented in Figure 16-2) all of the client work-stations were no-frills IBM clones, each with four megabytes of memory, no hard disk, and the standard DOS operating system. We got excellent performance (less than two seconds of response time) out of this configuration. However, there were occasional problems. Whenever an operator requested a report, the application would break out of the SQL*Forms environment (by spawning to a DOS subprocess) and begin the report. In general, this operation functioned well, although it did have some problems.

DOS is a single-tasking operating system. When a report was executing, the operator's workstation was dedicated to that report. No other online processing could be performed. When the report was completed, control returned to the SQL*Forms and life was restored. Some reports were quite large and involved considerable processing. Each client workstation was only a workstation, not a workhorse. As a result, some reports took more than 30 minutes to complete. Network traffic and client CPU size adversely affected performance. Some reports could not be executed within the 4-megabyte bounds of the client workstations. The large amounts of resources required by the subprocess were not available. Remember, we had to spawn from SQL*Forms before the report could even begin processing.

What was the solution?

It did not make sense, financially or logistically, to upgrade 80 workstations just to allow some of the operators to get access to a particular reporting function. Instead, we added one extra client workstation to the network. This client was an OS/2 client server, especially beefed up to act as the application report scheduler. The machine was actually a Compaq 486 25 with 16 megabytes of memory. OS/2 provided an efficient multi-tasking operating system that could function on the existing Novell token ring network, using the SPX/IPX protocol. All of the client workstations had indirect access to this new client. Whenever a report was requested, a single row was added to the report queuing table. We wrote a Pro*C scheduler to wake up every minute, check the report queue, and execute up to ten simultaneous reports. Each user's default printer was recorded on the system, and the reports were automatically directed back to the initiator. Reports magically emerged from printers only minutes after their request, rather than thrashing away for twenty minutes, locking up the initiating machine.

The report scheduling approach also presented the added bonus of flexibility. We could monitor operations to find out if the reporting load was becoming too much even for the upgraded configuration. If so, we could simply add a second report-scheduling machine. Another advantage was software; if reporting tools change or are upgraded (SQL*Reportwriter 2.0 is very, very hungry), we could simply upgrade one or two machines, not 80 client workstations.

The OS/2 report scheduler became so successful that we expanded its functionality to include update routines and overnight scheduling.

Every application has a handful of complex update/validation routines that perform large amounts of work. These routines often have to read, validate, modify, and audit (before and after images) many rows of the database. In our application we wrote these routines in Pro*C and linked them into the scheduler. Now, rather than having a client commit function take 10 to 20 seconds to run (and keep everything else from running), the application simply writes a request record to the 'transaction queue." In less than a minute, the scheduler process wakes up and executes the update routine. The initiating client could optionally be informed of the outcome of the routine via automatically-generated electronic mail.

We also added an overnight reporting queue to the application. The scheduler switches to night mode at a predetermined time and automatically commences overnight processing. The scheduler runs many reports and directs them to the proper places. When users come to work the next day, the reports are waiting for them. Gone is the need for a high-speed printer and an operator to separate and disperse the application overnight reporting.

Local Cache

Every client has its own processor and memory. ORACLE provides extensive caching facilities on the server database itself (via the SGA, PGA, and in Version 7, the shared buffer pool), but provides no caching facilities at the client workstation. However, at several sites we have used local memory on client machines to load static data programmatically into a local cache that can be refreshed at regular intervals. Future validation and reference of this data is performed via the client machine cache, and not the database.

At one particular site, we were able to compress more than 1500 static code-table records into less than 30K of memory via a SQL*Forms user exit (a very minor overhead for a major benefit). We were able to reduce the elapsed time for a single, multi-record SQL*Forms query from 14.7 seconds to 2.3 seconds using local cache. This particular case involved fetching 20 rows, with three post-change triggers executed per row. The result was that 60 distinct statements had to be transmitted across the network, parsed, executed, and returned—very wasteful because the local cache already has the data within the RUNFORM working storage area.

This approach offers several advantages and disadvantages. Advantages are:

- Reads static data from the database only once.

- Loads data selectively into each user's cache, allowing implementation, for example, of complex security systems without suffering any of the ongoing overheads. Multiple table joins are performed once and the summary data loaded into the cache. Each user loads only his or her own view of the world.

- Avoids RDBMS overheads because it performs no SQL parsing or index searching. ORACLE's SGA can be better utilized by other, more dynamic, core table data.

- Reduces network traffic. This is the biggest performance advantage. All data is held locally, and does not have to be continually transmitted via the network.

- Allows local data to be stored more efficiently than in the database. We are able to use a smart compression algorithm (avoiding repetitive primary key and index overheads).

There are some disadvantages as well. The data must be static and unlikely to be changed or deleted. And, when each user logs onto the system, the local cache must be initialized (loaded). This can take several seconds.

The following PL/SQL procedural code is for SQL*Forms applications only and demonstrates how to build generic libraries to retrieve data from the cache.

Assume that all application code tables are held in one physical database table and that a standard library procedure accesses it. (See the discussion of code tables in Chapter 7 and the discussion of library procedures in Chapter 9.) The procedural functionality varies according to the operator's global variable, GLOBAL.CACHE_ACCESS. You can program particular users to always access the database directly, and others to use only their local data cache.

```
    TABLE : CODE_TABLE      CODE_TYPE    CHAR(20)
                            CODE_CODE    CHAR(20)
                            CODE_DESC    CHAR(60)


    GLOBAL.CACHE_ACCESS     'Y' :  ONLY SEARCH LOCAL CACHE
                            'N' :  ONLY SEARCH DATABASE.
                            'X' :  SEARCH LOCAL CACHE, IF NOT FOUND,
                                       SEARCH DATABASE.


  TRIGGER PRE-FORM :  USER_EXIT ('LCACHE LOAD');              Loads local cache


  TRIGGER KEY-F10  :  USER_EXIT ('LCACHE LOAD');              Reloads local cache


  PROCEDURE LOOKUP_CODE (TYP IN        CHAR,
                         CDE IN        CHAR,
                         DSC IN OUT    CHAR ) IS
      DECLARE
      CURSOR CT IS SELECT    CODE_DESC
                   FROM   CODE_TABLE
                   WHERE CODE_TYPE = TYP
                   AND    CODE_CODE = CDE;
      BEGIN

          IF  :GLOBAL.CACHE_ACCESS = 'Y'
          OR  :GLOBAL.CACHE_ACCESS = 'X' THEN
```

```
        USER_EXIT ('LCACHE ' || TYP ||' '|| CDE);

        IF   :GLOBAL.LCACHE_DESC IS NULL
        AND :GLOBAL.CACHE_ACCESS = 'Y' THEN
            MESSAGE ('INVALID CODE ENTERED  . . . ');
            RAISE FORM_TRIGGER_FAILURE;
        ELSE
        DSC := :GLOBAL.LCACHE_DESC;
        END IF;
        ERASE ('GLOBAL.LCACHE_DESC');
    END IF;

    IF :GLOBAL.CACHE_ACCESS = 'N'
    OR ( :GLOBAL.CACHE_ACCESS = 'X' AND DSC IS NULL  ) THEN

        OPEN  CT;
        FETCH CT INTO DSC;

        IF CT%NOTFOUND THEN
            CLOSE CT;
            MESSAGE ('INVALID CODE ENTERED ...');
            RAISE FORM_TRIGGER_FAILURE;
        END IF;

        CLOSE CT;
    END IF;
END;
```

17

Capacity Planning

Accurate capacity planning can save your organization a great deal of money. If you incorrectly evaluate your equipment needs and buy a machine that is too large, you will have spent more money than you need to on hardware. On the other hand, if you underestimate your workload requirements and buy a machine that is too small, you will not be able to satisfy the throughput and response times of your users. And, if you don't plan for growth in the future, you may not end up with a machine that you'll be able to upgrade as you need more memory, disk devices, and processors.

It's easy to make a mistake. Some organizations buy equipment too early, before the applications that are going to run on the machines have been coded. The problem with this approach is that, if more modern, cost-effective hardware appears on the market, you may not be able to take advantage of it. Many organizations play it too safe. They tend to overestimate their requirements because they fear cutting it too close, and they end up with more equipment than they need—and perhaps more than they can really afford. Other organizations don't plan ahead, and end up with too little processor, memory, or disk power a year or two down the road.

What's the right way to go about capacity planning? The following list contains our general advice. Later in this chapter are several checklists showing specifically how you gather the information you need to make an informed decision about your system resources.

- Take advantage of ORACLE's portability. You can develop an application on a smaller and cheaper machine, and then use the same code to run on a larger machine once you've decided exactly which configuration you need.

- Forget about transaction rates and definitions, and concentrate on setting up a service agreement that will specify the required response times at your site. (See the discussion of tuning service agreements in Chapter 3, *Planning and Managing the Tuning Process.*)

- Put your effort into ensuring that every program will run within the required response times. You should buy a machine that is big enough for a tuned application, not an untuned one.

- Borrow a machine from your hardware vendor to use in your capacity planning. This is an excellent way to put the system you're considering buying through its paces. If your vendor won't agree, you may want to consider alternative sources.

- Ask for advice from other sites that have configurations similar to the one you're planning. Other sites' use of memory, disk, CPU, and workload mix can help you assess your own requirements.

- Plan your capacity planning exercise carefully. Follow the checklists we provide, and don't skimp on testing and documentation.

- Consider the use of client-server computing. You can realize enormous financial savings, as we show in Chapter 16, *Tuning in the Client-server Environment.*

What Do You Need to Test?

To do an accurate capacity planning exercise, you basically tune your system, from start to finish, putting all of the components of the system through their paces, keeping track of what you've done, and assessing how well your results mesh with your present and future requirements.

What does it mean to have a well-tuned system? We explore this question in Chapter 2, *What Causes Performance Problems?* To summarize, a tuned system is one in which:

- As close as possible to 100% of your memory is used.

- Your disk load is spread evenly across devices, and all of your disks are operating marginally within their recommended maximum I/O rates.

- As close as possible to 100% of your CPU is used during peak periods, with no user programs waiting for the CPU.

- Network traffic is only marginally below the maximum recommended, with no collisions.

- There is an insignificant amount of paging and swapping going on.

- User throughput and response times meet the standards established for your organization.

See the illustrations of untuned and perfectly tuned systems (Figure 2-2 and Figure 2-3) in Chapter 2.

This section briefly summarizes some of the main performance goals of the different components of your system. Earlier chapters describe all of these components in much more detail.

Memory

In general, the more memory you have in your system, and the more memory you can devote to ORACLE and its databases, the better your performance will be. Chapter 2 introduces the use of memory and its bottlenecks in the ORACLE system. Chapter 11, *Tuning a New Database*, and Chapter 13, *Monitoring and Tuning an Existing Database*, describe in detail what the memory structures and requirements are.

Tune all of the ORACLE areas of memory as best you can, and be prepared to shift memory assignments to meet changing needs. See the diagrams in Chapter 11 of overall memory, the System Global Area (SGA), the shared buffer pool, and other special areas. Make sure you don't use up all your memory. A good goal is 5% free memory.

Disk I/O

The main goal for disk use in your system is to spread the load evenly across the different disk devices so no disk is running at or exceeding its maximum recommended I/Os per second. You'll usually find that it is better to have many medium-sized disks (500 megabytes), rather than several large disks (one gigabyte), because the more disks you have, the more options you will have for sharing and balancing the load.

Remember, disk access is much slower than memory access. If you have not allocated enough memory for data dictionary items, database blocks, and other objects to remain in memory, ORACLE will have to go fetch them from disk, which slows down processing.

Make sure you define tables and other objects with the right sizes for both initial allocations and later expansion so you avoid problems of disk fragmentation and chaining.

CPU

CPU is the most costly resource in your system, so make sure you size it correctly. Your main goal is to prevent CPU contention, a condition in which processes are waiting for the CPU. Often, CPU problems are actually caused by memory and disk problems. When there is not enough room in memory for needed data and ORACLE objects, like data dictionary items, the CPU is forced to page and swap processes.

CPU MIPS (millions of instructions per second) can be a valuable guide in comparing machines and determining a machine's ability to meet your throughput needs. Although MIPS are not consistent across vendor boundaries, they usually are consistent within one vendor's product lines. Here is an example of how we use a MIPS rating to help in capacity planning. Figure 17-1 illustrates that, as we add users to a machine, there is no decrease in the throughput per user until the sixth user is added; then, throughput degrades rapidly.

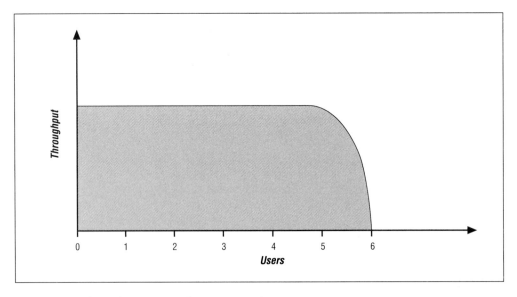

Figure 17-1: Throughput per user for one CPU MIP

Network

Make sure your network is fast enough to meet your needs, and that your equipment is positioned strategically. For example, if you are in San Francisco, and the bulk of your messages go to Los Angeles, your packets should not all be routed through New York. There are many special issues for client-server computing, described in Chapter 16.

Database

The way you tune your database will have an enormous impact on performance. An untuned database will eat up expensive hardware resources unnecessarily. Remember that your normalization (and sometimes denormalization) of data, your choice of indexes, your selection of primary and other types of keys, and other such choices will have a lot to do with how much equipment you will need, and how little you can get by with. Chapters 5, 11, and 13 discuss in detail the tuning issues for your database.

Capacity Planning Checklist

If you're going to end up with accurate information about your configuration needs, you must have a thorough and well-documented capacity plan. Without a thorough plan, you could easily overlook a critical part of the capacity planning exercise. The result will be that you will have to repeat the exercise or, far worse, your organization will buy equipment that is oversized or undersized for your configuration. For example, suppose you don't properly set your INIT.ORA parameters for the size of the configuration on which you're testing. Your testing results might lead you to conclude (erroneously) that the capacity of the machine is far less than it actually is.

This section summarizes the steps you need to follow to do a thorough capacity planning. Be sure to complete each step before moving on to the next one.

Step 1: Obtaining Background Information

Before you run anything on the computer, you need to collect some background information. Too often, system administrators are so eager to run transaction benchmarks that they don't correctly identify what they're benchmarking. Make sure you understand who your users are, how many there are, where they are located, and what they are doing. You also need to do some research into determining the most cost-effective hardware vendors. Finally, you need to have obtained access to a machine that you can use to perform a thorough benchmark. (If you are testing in a client-server environment, make sure you have access to all of the machines you need to test.)

Follow these steps:

1. Put one person in charge of controlling this capacity planning checklist, and assign every task to a particular, accountable person. Make sure every step is completed. As each step is completed, the person controlling the checklist must place a checkmark against the item and place the information into a folder for future reference. Do not proceed past any point until all necessary information has been obtained.

2. Obtain the expected number of total users at all client sites.

3. Obtain the number of concurrent users at all client sites. If users will be allowed to log onto the system more than once, note this fact; treat each logon as a separate user for purposes of calculating memory requirements.

4. Categorize users of the application into roles, and specify their expected activities. For example:

```
Sydney:
      Management inquiries    2
      Account control        12
      Transaction entry      80
      Phone queries          30

  .   Melbourne:
      Management inquiries    2
      Account control        10
      Transaction entry      60
      Phone queries          25
```

5. Determine the usage pattern of each of the programs; for example:

```
      Financial Transaction Entry (AF100FR)   40%
      Account Entry (AF120FR)                 25%
      Account Balance Inquiry (AF110FR)       10%
      Budget Inquiry (AF200FR)                10%
      Budget Maintenance (AF210FR)            10%
      Other programs                           5%
```

This information will be used later to test the application realistically in a multi-user environment.

6. Obtain information on expected peaks and troughs of activity at your site, and remember that there might be month-to-month, as well as hour-to-hour, variation. You can develop a graph like the one shown in Figure 17-2 for both daily and overnight processing. Remember when you are performing this capacity planning that you must be able to cope with the maximum load, not the average load.

7. Determine a workload that will give a true indication of the expected activity on your system. You must determine the maximum workload that you expect to have on your machine. (This is determined by the combination of the most resource-hungry programs and the maximum number of users.)

8. Predict the future growth of your workload and users on your system. We recommend that you specify the anticipated figures for 3 months, 6 months, 9 months, 12 months, 18 months, 2 years, and 3 years in the future.

9. Obtain a full list of operating system parameters on your machine. (If you are running client-server, get this list for both the application server and the database server.) These will differ from system to system. On Sun UNIX machines, the MAXUSERS configuration variable determines the sizes of many important parameters. There are also many parameters that you can set to determine the UNIX file buffer areas in memory; these allow you to specify the amount of memory available

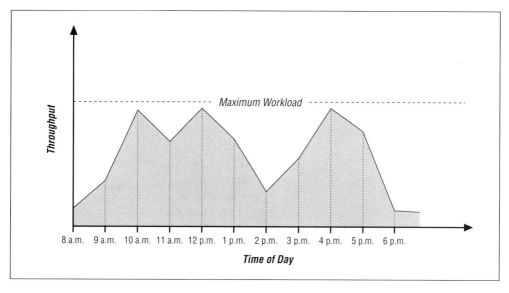

Figure 17-2: Sample throughput for capacity planning

to different applications which will vary the amount of memory available to other applications. Under VMS, obtain the working set quotas. If these quotas are set too low, excessive paging, and overuse of the CPU, may result.

10. Document the version of every tool you are using; for example:

```
ORACLE RDBMS
SQL*Plus
SQL*Net
SQL*Forms
PRO*COBOL
PRO*C
SQL*Reportwriter
PL/SQL
SQL*Loader
Other products
Operating system
```

(Do this for both client and server if you are running in a client-server environment.) Because newer releases of some of these products provide performance improvements, you need to make sure you are using the most up-to-date software. For example, SQL*Forms Version 3.0.16.8 offers significant improvements over previous versions by reducing both memory usage and the number of packets transferred in the client-server environment.

11. Obtain the size of swap space on both the application server and the database server. The swap space is an often-overlooked file on disk that must be kept contiguous and large enough to assist with performance.

12. Obtain the configuration details of the application, and the network and hardware configuration you are using for your capacity planning exercise. If you are benchmarking on an existing hardware configuration at your site, you will usually already have a diagram that you use for other reasons.

```
Machine name
Number of disks
Size of disks
Maximum I/Os per second
Memory size
CPU MIPS rating
```

See the diagram in Figure 17-3 for a way to document these.

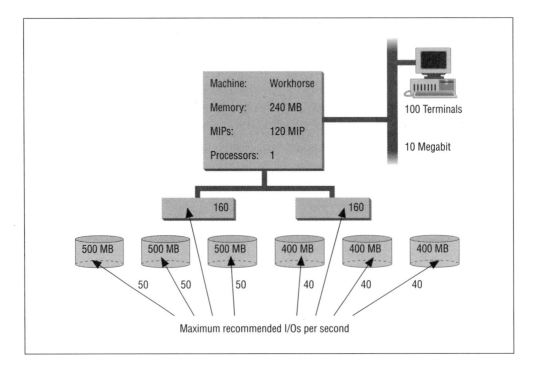

Figure 17-3: Typical configuration diagram

13. Obtain a network configuration diagram showing line speeds. This is particularly useful when you are running client-server.

14. Most applications have a test plan for the quality assurance of their systems. Obtain the plan for later use in the single-user application tuning exercise. This will assist in entering realistic values into the various programs and will ensure that you have performed a thorough response time test against all parts of the program.

15. Document the performance monitoring commands relevant to your operating system. These commands allow you to monitor disk I/O, CPU activity, memory usage, paging, swapping, and if applicable, the network activity. They are system-dependent. (See Chapter 18, *Tuning for Specific Systems*, for a summary of common commands used in VMS and UNIX systems.)

Step 2: Structuring the Database and SGA

The purpose of this step is to ensure that your database structure is tuned, Read Chapter 11 thoroughly for information about how to structure the original database and the SGA. Read Chapter 13, *Monitoring and Tuning an Existing Database*, for how to change these values over time. Follow these steps:

1. If the application is to run on UNIX machines, ensure that raw devices are being used for all tablespaces and redo logs. If another system is being used, make sure that the database files are contiguous on disk. This may require that you defragment the disk.

2. Place heavily used tablespaces onto the same disk device as lightly used tablespaces, or separate different tablespaces onto different disks. Keep in mind that no disk should be running at or exceeding its maximum recommended I/O-per-second rate.

3. Use many medium-sized disks rather than fewer large disks. In this context, a medium-sized disk is 500 megabyte and a large disk is one gigabyte or greater. Choose medium-sized disks because the maximum I/O rates on both are usually the same, and the medium-sized disks allow better load sharing across disks.

4. Ensure that all tables and indexes have been pre-sized to minimize the number of extents. You must rebuild any table or index consisting of more than three extents.

5. Try to place the entire dictionary cache in memory to avoid any possibility of recursive calls. If this is not possible, consult Chapter 14, *Tuning the Data Dictionary*, for suggestions.

6. If you are using Version 7, make sure that you have set a proper value for SHARED_POOL_SIZE.

7. Set the DB_BLOCK_BUFFER parameter to fit as much of the tables, indexes, clusters, and rollback segments as possible in memory

8. Make sure you have placed as many terminals on the network as necessary to perform a realistic benchmark. Ideally, have the same number of terminals available as you will have users logged onto your system during peak usage times.

9. Check that all of the indexes that were in the development environment exist in your benchmark environment. To check this, you can produce an index listing. Run the following script in both the development and the benchmark environments:

```
COLUMN TABLE_NAME          FORMAT A22
COLUMN INDEX_NAME          FORMAT A22
COLUMN COLUMN_NAME         FORMAT A22
COLUMN COLUMN_POSITION     FORMAT A99
COLUMN UNIQUENESS          FORMAT A6

BREAK ON TABLE_NAME ON INDEX_NAME ON UNIQUENESS

SELECT UIC.TABLE_NAME,
       DECODE(UI.UNIQUENESS, 'UNIQUE','UNIQUE','') UNIQUENESS,
       UIC.INDEX_NAME, UIC.COLUMN_NAME, UIC.COLUMN_POSITION
       FROM USER_IND_COLUMNS UIC,USER_INDEXES UI
   WHERE UI.TABLE_NAME=UIC.TABLE_NAME
   AND UI.INDEX_NAME=UIC.INDEX_NAME
   ORDER BY TABLE_NAME, INDEX_NAME, COLUMN_POSITION;
```

10. Set a sufficient number of rollback segments, and size them appropriately for this system.

11. Set an appropriate value for FREE_LIST_PROC (Version 6) or FREELISTS (Version 7) before you create tables with a high insertion ratio.

12. Make the INITRANS parameter large enough if you have multiple transactions updating the same physical block of a table.

13. Set the following INIT.ORA parameters (and any others relevant to your situation) to the correct values for this system:

```
DB_WRITERS
LOG_BUFFER
LOG_CHECKPOINT_INTERVAL
DB_FILE_MULTIBLOCK_READ_BLOCK
DB_BLOCK_WRITE_BATCH
SORT_AREA_SIZE
DML_LOCKS
DDL_LOCKS
ENQUEUE_RESOURCES
```

Step 3: Tuning the Application in Single-User Mode

Once your database has been tuned, the next step is tuning your application. The purpose of this tuning is to perform all transactions within the required response times for your site. If you don't do a thorough job of tuning the application, then your capacity planning will inevitably result in the purchase of an oversized and more expensive configuration in an attempt to provide better response and compensate for poor tuning. Remember, it takes only one inefficient program to cause poor performance in your entire system.

1. Turn the SQL trace facility on by setting the following INIT.ORA parameters:

   ```
   SQL_TRACE          TRUE
   TIMED_STATISTICS   TRUE
   USER_DUMP_DEST     desired destination
   ```

2. Check all programs individually using the QA test plan. Run all parts of the program to make testing as similar as it will be in production.

3. Prepare a document detailing all programs that are to be tested. If you skip even one program, a perverse law states that the very program you skip will bring your system to its knees.

4. Go through each program and record response times using a stop watch. The reason for using a stop watch is that the results must reflect the end user's perspective. Behind-the-scenes measurements often don't take into account problems like network collisions that seriously slow down end user response time. Remember, for most sites, response times must meet the standard specified. (Often, the maximum allowable response time is about 2.5 seconds for an online transaction processing system.)

5. Record the amount of memory, CPU, disk I/Os, and network activity against each program. If you are running client-server, you must get the readings from both the client and the server end.

NOTE

If you are running a UNIX database server, the size of the process at the server end contains more than just the shadow process. It also contains the text of the ORACLE executable, which must not be included in your memory sizing. Use the *ps* command with the appropriate option to determine the process size, and use the *size* command on the ORACLE executable to determine the amount by which to reduce the shadow process.

6. After each program has been completed, run TKPROF against the trace file produced by the SQL trace facility. This file is located in the directory specified in the USER_DUMP_DEST parameter. See Chapter 12 for information about inter-

preting this output. One particularly useful piece of output is "Full Table Scans." Another is the number of SQL statements that take longer than 0.4 seconds CPU. These values will help you determine if the correct index and driving tables are being used.

7. Remove the trace file after it has been displayed. Rename the output file from the specified trace file name to *program_name.lis*, where *program_name* is the name of the program being tested. You will need to log in again to the application to create a new trace file for the next program.

8. Document each program that is not performing up to the necessary response time standards. Use the format shown in Figure 17-4.

Program Response Time Report			
Menu Name	Program Name	Description / Function	Response
Accounts Account Maint	ACU100FR	Account Maintenance and Inquiry Screen Query List of Values on Acct Type List of Values on Cost Element Commit the New Account	 1.2 seconds 0.5 seconds 3.5 seconds ◄ 1.8 seconds

This list of values requires attention because it exceeds 2.5 seconds.

Figure 17-4: Program response time report

9. Add indexes or adjust the offending statements as required and retest the program. Continue this process until you are satisfied that all response time problems have been remedied. Be sure to document any new index and program changes to make sure the changes are enforced when the application goes to production.

Here is an example of how you might proceed. In the previous example, one list of values program took 3.5 seconds to run. This slow performance is likely to be because indexes are missing or are not being used. The most common cause of ORACLE's not using an index is finding an improper ORDER BY clause (one that does not include all of the key fields in the index). You can fix such problems by including a dummy WHERE clause in the statement or adding an appropriate index. See Chapter 7, *Tuning SQL*, for information about SQL statement tuning.

10. If certain functions cause poor performance (for example, deleting hundreds of rows of data in an online transaction), you will need to find a smarter way to perform the function, or explain to the users at your site the tradeoffs between function and performance. (Actually, such problems should have been resolved at the time of application design.)

11. Adjust the response time columns in the Program Response Time Report after tuning.

12. To help with future tuning exercises, prepare a report on the outcome of the application tuning stage. Document the reasons why various changes were made to the application. This report will show all response times shown on the Program Response Time Report that exceed those specified in the service agreement.

13. If all participants in your site's capacity planning exercise are convinced that the application has been acceptably tuned, proceed to the multi-user application test.

Step 4: Tuning the Application in Multi-user Mode

The next stage of the capacity planning exercise requires you to test the application in a multi-user environment whose transaction mix is as close to production as possible. There will probably be at least two iterations of this test, with each new run making adjustments for performance.

1. Run the *BSTAT.sql* script (in Version 6) or the *UTLBSTAT.sql* script (in Version 7) to begin taking a snapshot of activity in your system. You will leave this script running for the duration of the test:

    SQLDBA> @BSTAT

    (See Chapter 12 for a discussion of these tools.)

2. Organize your users so they perform realistic tasks that simulate real production conditions. Make sure they represent an accurate mix of user roles and programs. Plan ahead of time what each user's workload will be. Pay attention to the mix of queries and updates. If real production conditions include 90% queries and 10% updates, make sure that the benchmark contains a similar load. Your goal is to place your application under the maximum amount of stress it will suffer when it is running in production.

3. Have your users log in and start work, according to the plan. Give them stop watches to use in their work. Tell them to document all functions that exceed the expected response times.

4. Every two minutes, run SQL*DBA MONITOR with the options shown below. (Make sure you don't use the same file name for each output!). The MON names below are for a VMS system; replace if necessary with your own Monitor function.

MON P	Monitor processes
MON ST 0 0 3	Monitor various statistics
MON I/O	Monitor the hit ratio of data in memory
MON F	Monitor the I/O distribution between database files
MON R	Monitor rollback segments
MON T	Monitor table usage
MON L	Monitor locks

5. Every two minutes, run the operating system commands available for your system to check the CPU, memory, and disk use at the database and server ends. Get 20 seconds worth of statistics each time. This information returns the average I/O per user, average memory per user (at client and server ends, for client-server), and the average MIPS per user. For example, if you are running UNIX on a Sun, use the commands:

vmstat 5	CPU and memory usage
ps -aux	Individual process details
netstat -i	Network statistics
iostat -i	I/O statistics

For UTS, you would issue:

sar -m	Memory usage
sar -C	CPU usage
sar -d	Disk usage
sar -y	Terminal activity

6. When the test is complete, run the *ESTAT.sql* script (in Version 6) or the *UTLESTAT.sql* script (in Version 7) to stop the job and display its output.

7. Make any adjustments that will improve performance in your own particular system. The next section provides some suggestions for doing this.

Step 5: Fixing the Bottlenecks You Discover

Depending on the bottlenecks you discover in the system you are tuning, you may need to do some additional tuning. This step is very much a site-dependent one. You may have a major problem with recursive calls to the database, whereas another site may have no problem at all. On the other hand, that site may be experiencing packet delays in its client-server environment, whereas you may not have to worry about network performance because you are running in a unitary environment. Here are some guidelines for identifying bottlenecks and doing additional tuning. Chapter 13 describes all of these tuning operations in detail.

Memory. If your memory usage is 100%, and if paging and swapping are occurring at an excessive rate, you have a memory bottleneck. Decrease the size of the SGA by reducing the size of the buffer cache, the log buffer, or the dictionary cache. (Remember, in Version 7 the dictionary cache is part of the shared buffer pool.) However, never reduce the dictionary cache to the point where it causes excessive cache misses. If you must choose, choose to reduce the buffer cache before reducing the dictionary cache.

You can also reduce memory for an individual process by reducing the size of the sort buffer (specified by the SORT_AREA_SIZE parameter) or the context area (specified by OPEN_CURSORS, CONTEXT_AREA, and CONTEXT_INCR in Version 6). Remember, in Version 7, the context area is replaced by the library cache, which is part of the shared buffer pool in the SGA; the entire shared buffer pool is controlled by the SHARED_ POOL_SIZE parameter. You may also need to enlarge the swap area as well.

Disk I/O. If one or more disks are exceeding the recommended maximum I/Os per second, you have a disk bottleneck. Try to transfer tablespaces to alternative disks to reduce the load on the overworked disk. Combine heavily used tablespaces with those that are less frequently used.

CPU. If paging and swapping are causing excessive CPU activity, you have a CPU bottleneck. Most such bottlenecks are the result of memory or I/O bottlenecks. If not, you will probably need a faster CPU.

Network. If you are experiencing packet delays in a client-server environment, you have a network bottleneck. You may be able to change your application program code to eliminate this problem by reducing the number of required disk accesses. You may also be able to move your client and server machines closer together physically (ideally in the same building).

Recursive calls. Reduce your recursive calls to the database (they should be close to zero). Recursive calls often occur when data dictionary items have to be brought in from disk instead of being accessible in memory; usually the reason is that the dictionary cache parameters are set too low (DC_ parameters for Version 6, SHARED_POOL_SIZE for Version 7). Because disk I/O is so much slower than memory access, recursive calls adversely affect response times.

Hit ratio. The hit ratio is the ratio of finding rollback, table, index, and cluster data in memory rather than having to perform I/Os from disk to retrieve the data. The hit ratio should be as high as possible. Anything above 90% is very good.

Redo latch contention. Reduce your redo latch contention. This contention occurs because a transaction has to wait for a latch to copy its changed data to the redo buffer. In the context of the capacity planning exercise, this contention is normally caused by two users simultaneously requesting the same rows from a table. One user will have to wait for the other user to complete work on these rows before beginning modifications.

Rollback extension and contention. Reduce your rollback extension and contention. Rollback extension occurs when a transaction making a lot of changes has to extend its size because the current rollback is not large enough to contain all of the rollback data. Rollback contention occurs when there aren't enough rollback segments, and some of the transactions requesting rollbacks are being forced to wait for a rollback segment to become available.

Chaining and dynamic extension. Eliminate chaining and dynamic extension. These occur when tables, indexes, temporary segments, and rollback segments grow in size, and the current extents assigned are not large enough to store the extra information. This extension can degrade performance significantly.

Excessive I/O. Eliminate excessive I/O on particular data files. Excessive I/O will inevitably lead to a bottleneck on one of your disks.

When you are satisfied that you can't tune any more, and your system is still experiencing a memory, disk, CPU, or network bottleneck, start taking users off the machine, one at a time, until the bottleneck disappears. You will then know exactly how many users your machine can support with its current configuration. (Make sure before you remove users that your memory is being used to cache as much data as possible, and the disk load is spread across disks as evenly as possible.)

If you are using less memory, disk, CPU, and/or networking than is available, try adding users until you deliberately cause a bottleneck. This way, you'll know how far you can push your system, and where its weak points might be.

Step 6: Reporting the Results of the Exercise

The final step is to report on the results of the capacity planning exercise. Don't sell your efforts short by failing to carry through by writing a thorough report to corporate management. Document your findings and recommendations in a professional report that can be distributed to the management at your site. The precise contents and format of this report will differ for different sites, but here are some general recommendations for what you need to include:

Management summary. This should not exceed three pages. It includes all of your recommendations and associated costs. Include detailed information in appendices. Use graphical information wherever possible.

Aims. Major aims of the benchmark, including:

- Identify and repair bottlenecks

- Fix any application programs not meeting required response times

- Establish hardware/software configurations required for your sites

- Fine tune the ORACLE RDBMS

- Allow staff to see applications working under realistic conditions

Other. Anything not being included in the study (e.g., your report might not address the issue of overnight reporting).

Tuning plan. Details of the tuning plan:

- Tuning of the application in single-user mode.

- Report indicating all programs, and functions within programs, with timings.

- Load test in the expected environment (e.g., client-server). Mention the number of users who participated and the throughput they generated. Highlight at what point response times and throughput began to degrade after all tuning was performed.

Results. List the results of the benchmark:

- Average I/O generated per user (e.g., 500 I/Os per minute).

- Average memory per user (at both client and server ends for client-server configuration). Typical use is two megabytes per user.

- Average MIPS used per user; for example, 0.3 MIPS per user. (MIPS ratings vary from one vendor to the next, but are normally consistent within vendors.)

- Network traffic generated by average user; for example, 150 packets per minute.

- Any ORACLE or operating system actions you must perform to make the application perform optimally; for example, in a UNIX system, you might need to use raw devices and decrease your UNIX file buffer cache from 20% to 5% of the machine's memory.

Using the sample figures above, and assuming you have 150 concurrent users logging on to your application at the time of peak usage, typical ORACLE hardware requirements for an online transaction processing system might look like this:

```
150 * 500 I/Os per minute = 7500 I/Os per minute or 125 I/Os per second
150 * 2 MB per user = 300 MB + SGA (typically 50 MB) = 350 MB memory
150 * 0.3 MIPS = 45 MIPS
```

Recommendations. List your recommendations:

- Size of the configuration that is required to run your application.

- Any adjustments that could be made to improve the performance. For example, try having more memory on the client (application server) and less on the database server.

- Any adjustments that were found to improve throughput (e.g., enlarging the swap space).

Supporting evidence. This will involve detailing what happens if the configuration varies from the one that you recommend.

Environment. Show full details of the environment in which you worked. Ideally this includes diagrams of your hardware configuration.

Programs. Show full details of all your programs and their subfunctions. Show how they were tested to show they performed within the response time guidelines. Attach the Program Response Time Report (Figure 17-4).

Database. Show a list of the database configuration, rows per table, extents per object, and INIT.ORA parameters.

Adjustments. Show a list of all adjustments made and the reasons why they were made. For example, increasing the buffer cache from four megabytes to 40 megabytes improved response times by 33% with an improvement in the hit rate of 10%.

18

Tuning for Specific Systems

The performance tuning information in this book applies, in virtually all cases, to all versions of ORACLE, whether it's running on an IBM mainframe, a DEC minicomputer, a Sun workstation, or an Apple Macintosh. Most of the advice is equally applicable to MVS, VMS, UNIX, and DOS. Nevertheless, there are system-specific performance issues related to your own particular configuration of hardware and software and the way that ORACLE interacts with your system resources. In general, the details of operating system tuning are beyond the scope of this book. You'll find some helpful information in the platform-specific *ORACLE Installation and User's Guide* that comes with your version of the system. Your operating system documentation is the best source of information about the specifics of tuning general system resources. This chapter supplements those sources by providing hints for UNIX and VMS, two of the most popular operating system platforms for ORACLE. In future editions of this book, we hope to expand this coverage to several additional operating systems.

UNIX-specific Tuning

This section contains several hints for getting the best performance out of ORACLE running on a UNIX platform.

Writing to Raw Devices

You can improve performance quite a bit by setting up your database files and redo logs as raw devices. By doing this, you avoid having to go through the UNIX buffer. Instead, ORACLE writes directly from the System Global Area (SGA) buffer area to disk. You reduce CPU activity substantially, avoiding paging within memory between the

UNIX buffer cache and the SGA. This approach also avoids the need to incur UNIX read ahead overhead and UNIX file system overhead.

We have found that on systems dedicated to ORACLE, the size of the UNIX buffer area can be reduced from approximately 15% of memory to approximately 5% of memory. With the memory you save, you can support more users, increase the sort area size, or perhaps even release the memory to another computer. By writing to raw devices in this way, we have seen overall performance increase as much as 50%.

To write to raw devices, issue a CREATE DATABASE statement in the following form:

```
CREATE        DATABASE ACCOUNTS
CONTROLFILE   REUSE
DATAFILE      '/dev/raw1'  25M   REUSE,
LOGFILE       '/dev/raw2'  5M    REUSE,
              '/dev/raw3'  5M    REUSE,
              '/dev/raw4'  5M    REUSE;

CREATE        TABLESPACE ACCOUNT_DATA
DATAFILE      '/dev/raw5'  500M
DEFAULT       STORAGE  (  INITIAL      4K
                          NEXT         10K
                          MAXEXTENTS   110
                          PCTINCREASE  0   );
```

The UNIX buffer cache and the ORACLE buffer cache can be independently tuned. Note that some machines do not allow the UNIX buffer cache to be tuned at all. For example, the SunOS dynamically adjusts the UNIX buffer cache. Some versions of UNIX, such as DYNIX on Sequents, provide an option to allow you to bypass the UNIX buffer cache and avoid the need for raw devices. It is important that you read your *ORACLE Installation and User's Guide* for more information on how to best configure your own system.

You can figure out which UNIX parameters need tuning by looking for the letters "BUF." For example, on a Digital Equipment Corporation system running ULTRIX, the parameters you need to tune are NBUF and BUFFPAGES. NBUF is the number of buffer headers that controls the number of buffers that can exist and BUFFPAGES sets the size of the buffer cache in 1K pages.

We recommend that because raw devices can be a little tricky to set up and administer, only sites with full-time experienced DBAs and system administrators utilize raw devices.

Latches

The ORACLE RDBMS is composed of many source code modules. Approximately 100 of these are system-specific modules designed to handle operations such as memory allocation, process creation, and disk I/O. One important module of this kind is the one that acquires and handles latches. Latches are used to protect data structures inside the SGA (such as the hash table) and provide quick access to the database buffers.

A process that needs to access the hash table must first acquire and own the latch associated with the hash table. Under UNIX, the latch is associated with a byte of shared memory in the SGA. A process requiring the latch must first test the latch to see if it is available. If it is available, the process obtains it. If it is not available, the process establishes a method of queuing for the latch. UNIX has several methods of queuing, described in the following sections. The method you'll use depends on whether the version of UNIX being used is System V- or Berkeley-based, and whether the system uses a single CPU or multiple CPUs.

Spin locks

The spin lock method of latching is used on multiple-CPU systems. Multiple processes operate simultaneously with one process per CPU. A latch is held for a brief moment (milliseconds). Chances are, if a latch is required, a process running on any of a number of CPUs will soon be freed. By repeatedly retrying the latch (i.e., spinning on the latch), the waiting process is likely to be able to avoid using more costly operating system queuing facilities. The number of times the process will spin on the latch before relinquishing the CPU is determined by the INIT.ORA parameter, SPIN_COUNT.

On single-CPU systems, spin locks are not applicable. If a process finds that a latch is busy, it must relinquish the CPU so the process holding the latch can run. On Berkeley-based systems, the process will sleep for a predetermined timeout period before trying again.

Semaphore based queues

System V UNIX systems use semaphore-based queues. If a process cannot acquire a latch, it joins a queue of processes waiting for the latch. This is done by updating a data structure in the SGA, indicating that it is waiting for a specific latch, and then sleeping on its semaphore. The process relinquishes the CPU, allowing another process to run. When the running process has completed, the waiting process's semaphore is incremented, which causes it to awaken and attempt to retry the latch again. This method minimizes operating system overhead.

Concurrent Disk Writes

In some versions of UNIX, parallel disk I/O may not be a standard feature, and this can cause performance problems. ORACLE compensates for this by providing the ability to perform multiple database writes. You invoke this facility through the DB_WRITERS parameter in the INIT.ORA file. If you set this parameter to 4, ORACLE creates the following processes:

```
ORA_DB01_PROD
ORA_DB02_PROD
ORA_DB03_PROD
ORA_DB04_PROD
```

At checkpoint time, the master database writer determines which blocks in the database buffer cache need to be written to disk. The master then divides the work and notifies each slave database writer about the blocks for which it is responsible. Because these are done in parallel, you reduce performance bottlenecks.

When you set DB_WRITERS, set it to a value between 1 and twice the number of disks containing your data files. Many sites set the DB_WRITERS equal to the number of disks containing data files. If you are using DB_WRITERS, set the DB_BLOCK_WRITE_BATCH parameter to at least twice the number of DB_WRITERS.

If your version of UNIX offers asynchronous I/O (i.e., multiple database writes without the need for additional database writers), we strongly recommend that you set either the ASYNC_WRITE or ASYNC_IO parameter (depending on your UNIX version) to TRUE. This will allow parallel disk writes and will improve performance up to 20%.

Non-standard UNIX Functionality

Many machines running UNIX have unique characteristics. You must be aware of what these characteristics are to get the most out of your machine. For example, extensive graphical performance monitoring tools are available on Sun computers and UTS (stats command). In the SunOS system, adjusting the MAXUSERS parameter affects the number of processes able to operate, the number of files allowed to be open simultaneously, and many other kernel table parameters. (See the Sun manuals for details.) Other machines offer dynamic tuning of operating system parameters; for example, DYNIX on Sequent machines offers a VMTUNE command. The list goes on. Check with your own system vendor for complete information.

Smart Ways to Export Under UNIX

Space is at a premium on many machines. There are several ways that you can save space. For example, under UNIX you can export directly to a compressed file by using named pipes, as shown below:

```
$mknod gl_export.dmp p
$cat gl_export.dmp | compress > gl_export.dmp.Z &
$exp gl/gl file=gl_export buffer=131072
```

You can also export to tape, which sometimes requires a symbolic link pointing to the tape device:

```
$ln -s /dev/rst0 tape.dmp
$exp gl/gl file=tape buffer=131072
```

UNIX Commands to Monitor Performance

This section briefly looks at some of the commands that can be used to identify performance bottlenecks. Almost all machines that run UNIX have additional commands that can be used to monitor your system (for example, the *stats* command in the UTS environment). You must gather information on the commands relevant to your site.

Remember that you can issue the *man* command to display the syntax of the commands on your system; for example, *man vmstat.*

Identifying disk bottlenecks

As we have mentioned elsewhere in this book, you can improve performance by spreading the load across disk drives as evenly as possible. Each disk drive has recommended maximum I/Os per second. It is important that every disk drive operate within the recommended maximum.

iostat is a BSD UNIX command that allows you to identify the average number of transfers per second. In the simple example below, there is only one disk being displayed, the system disk "dk0". The column to observe is the "tps" column, which is the average number of disk transfers per second since the last interval.

The format of the *iostat* command is

iostat *drives interval count*

For example, this command produces the following output:

```
iostat 5 5
```

tty				dk0			id002				cpu	
tin	tout	bps	tps	msps	bps	tps	msps	us	ni	sy	id
2	125	4	1	0.0	4	0	18.5	1	0	2	97
0	0	0	0	0.0	0	0	0.0	2	0	0	98
0	0	0	0	0.0	0	0	0.0	0	0	0	100
0	0	0	0	0.0	3	0	43.3	0	0	0	99
0	0	0	0	0.0	0	0	0.0	0	0	01	00

System V machines use the *sar* -d command. The important column to observe is the "r+w/s" column, which show the reads and writes per second (on average) since the last interval, as follows.

```
sar -d

mel01      vic01 5.     1a-910507c   0419f    MIS-4/03        07/12/93

17:53:53  device     %busy    avque     r+w/s    blks/s    avwait    avserv

17:53:58  sdisk04      5       3.1        3        12        43.5      20.8
          sdisk14      2       2.8        1         2        37.5      20.5
          sdisk24      9       1.5        4        25        12.2      23.0

17:54:03  sdisk04      4       1.2        1         8         6.1      29.0
          sdisk14      2       1.3        1         5         6.0      17.4
          sdisk24      1       1.1        1         2         1.0      18.7

17:54:08
17:54:13
17:54:18  sdisk14      1       1.0        0         2         1.5      31.5
          sdisk24      1       1.0        0         2         1.0      24.5

Average   sdisk04      2       2.3        1         4        30.4      23.7
          sdisk14      1       1.7        1         2        15.0      20.5
          sdisk24      2       1.4        1         6        10.0      22.6
```

Identifying memory bottlenecks

Memory bottlenecks occur when you are short on memory, and excessive paging and swapping is occurring. Paging and swapping can dramatically degrade your system's response times. Paging occurs when part of a process is either shuffled within memory or paged to disk. Swapping occurs when an entire process is removed from disk. Paging and swapping both use CPU, although swapping represents a bigger drain on your system if it becomes excessive. Swapping is of no concern if the process being swapped is a dormant process. Paging of the non-active part of a process is also not a major concern; only part of an active process is usually required in memory at any point in time to allow the process to proceed with its execution. But, a major performance drain occurs when an active process is swapped out of memory or an active part of a process is paged from memory.

The usual cause of swapping and paging problems is insufficient memory to cope with the workload. To detect the amount of free memory on your computer use the *vmstat* command under Berkeley UNIX or XENIX to look at overall system performance. The following example reports on five sets of statistics with five-second intervals.

```
vmstat 5 5

 procs     memory               page                   disk          faults    cpu
 r b w avm fre    re at  pi po  fr  de sr d0 d1 i0 i1   in   sy  cs us sy id

 0 0 0   0 55340  0  3  11  0   1   0  0  0  0  2  0   52 162  75  1  2 97
 0 0 0   0 55300  0  0   0  0   0   0  0  0  0  1  0 1096 248 104  2  1 97
 1 0 0   0 55176  0  0   0  0   0  16  0  0  0  1  0 1234 389 210  2  2 95
 1 0 0   0 54932  0  1   0  0   0   0  0  0  0  2  0 1241 384 211  3  1 95
 0 0 0   0 54684  0  0  16  0   0   0  0  0  0  3  0 1236 421 215  3  3 94
```

The values that are of particular interest are "memory fre," which is the free memory in kilobytes; "page po," which is the number of 1K pages that have been paged out, and "cpu sys," which is the percentage of CPU being used by system activity such as swapping and paging. There is an abundance of free memory on our sample machine (54 megabytes is the minimum amount of free memory recorded). There is little chance of excessive paging and swapping under these circumstances.

For System V sites, you would issue:

```
sar  -r

00:00:01     Freemem   Freeswp
02:00:00     12010     65636
04:00:00     10100     65636
06:00:00     14120     65636
08:00:00     16786     65636
10:00:00     12632     65636
```

The "Freemem" column in this example is the number of free memory in pages on your system. In the example above, the minimum memory available (on our example system, a Pyramid with 2K pages) is 20 megabytes. Excessive paging and swapping will not occur with this much free memory.

You can also observe the amount of swapping by using the *sar* -w command. Ensure that "swpot/s" (swap outs per second during the interval) and "bswot/s" (the number block swapped out per second) remain at 0.

```
sar -w

vic    vic    systemV  2.1.3   5995    07/12/93

16:57:50    cpu#   swpin/s   bswin/s   swpot/s   bswot/s   pswch/s
            rawch/s canch/s   outch/s   rcvin/s   xmtin/s   mdmin/s
16:57:55      0    0.00       0.0       0.00       0.0       667
              2    0.00       0.0       0.00       0.0       398
16:58:00      0    0.00       0.0       0.00       0.0       613
              2    0.00       0.0       0.00       0.0       331
16:58:05      0    0.00       0.0       0.00       0.0       505
```

	2	0.00	0.0	0.00	0.0	295
16:58:10	0	0.00	0.0	0.00	0.0	567
	2	0.00	0.0	0.00	0.0	351
16:58:15	0	0.00	0.0	0.00	0.0	579
	2	0.00	0.0	0.00	0.0	324
Average	0	0.00	0.0	0.00	0.0	586
	2	0.00	0.0	0.00	0.0	340

Identifying CPU bottlenecks

Under Berkeley UNIX you can pinpoint CPU bottlenecks via the *vmstat* command (to observe overall system performance, similar to the *iostat* command described above), and *ps* -aux (to observe the percentage of CPU being consumed by each process).

```
vmstat   5 5
```

```
 procs     memory            page             disk       faults      cpu
 r b w avm   fre   re at  pi  po  fr  de   sr d0 d1 i0 i1   in  sy   cs us sy id
 0 0 0   0 55340    0  3  11   0   1   0    0  0  0  2  0   52 162   75  1  2 97
 0 0 0   0 55300    0  0   0   0   0   0    0  0  0  1  0 1096 248  104  2  1 97
 1 0 0   0 55176    0  0   0   0   0  16    0  0  0  1  0 1234 389  210  2  2 95
 1 0 0   0 54932    0  1   0   0   0   0    0  0  0  2  0 1241 384  211  3  1 95
 0 0 0   0 54684    0  0  16   0   0   0    0  0  0  3  0 1236 421  215  3  3 94
```

The three columns of particular interest are "us" (the percentage of CPU used by users), "sy" (the percentage of CPU used by system resources), which should be significantly less than the "us" reading, and "id" (the percentage of time that the CPU was idle).

```
ps -aux
```

```
USER        PID   %CPU %MEM   SZ  RSS TT STAT START   TIME COMMAND

oracle    15343   0.0  0.9  304 1128 ?  S    01:32   1:12 ora_smon_DEV6
oracle    15340   0.0  0.5  192  636 ?  S    01:32   0:02 ora_pmon_DEV6
oraclev7    444   0.0  0.9  212 1084 ?  S    Jul 11  0:11 ora_pmon_DEV7
oraclev7    445   0.0  1.2  208 1408 ?  S    Jul 11  0:19 ora_dbwr_DEV7
oraclev7    446   0.0  1.0  208 1192 ?  S    Jul 11  0:17 ora_lgwr_DEV7
oraclev7    447   0.0  0.0  344    0 ?  IW   Jul 11  1:18 ora_smon_DEV7
oraclev7    448   0.0  0.0  228    0 ?  IW   Jul 11  0:05 ora_reco_DEV7
peter     21810   0.0  0.0 1192    0 p4 IW   16:44   0:26 sqlforms30 -c vt100
peter     22346   0.0  0.0  444    0 p2 IW   17:43   0:02 runmenu50 PERS
oracle    15342   0.0  0.9  248 1096 ?  S    01:32   0:11 ora_lgwr_DEV6
oracle    15341   0.0  3.2  328 3892 ?  S    01:32   0:12 ora_dbwr_DEV6
mark      22757   0.0  0.4  288  536 p0 R    18:44   0:00 ps -aux
oracle    22347   0.0  0.0  528    0 ?  IW   17:43   0:01 oracleS T:I,,5
root       8040   0.0  0.0  104    0 ?  IW   Jul 12  0:12 orasrv
awanker   21032   0.0  0.0  272    0 q2 IW   15:12   0:04 sqlplus
oracle    21811   0.0  0.0  344    0 ?  IW   16:44   0:31 oracleS T:I,,5
```

This display shows the ORACLE processes only. The relevant column to observe in this case is the "%CPU". Any process using an unusually large "%CPU" should be checked. Notice also the memory percentage is displayed ("%MEM") and the virtual memory required for the data and stack segments of the processes ("SZ").

Under System V you can use the *sar*-u command to observe overall system activity.

```
sar -u

vic01     vic101 5.    1a-910507c      0419f      MIS-4/03        07/12/93

17:54:18        %usr      %sys      %wio      %idle
17:54:23         8         5         5         81
17:54:28         9         2         1         89
17:54:33        11         4         8         78
17:54:39         7         4         4         85
17:54:44         1         2         2         95

Average          7         4         4         86
```

The columns in this display are the percentage of CPU allocated to user processes (%usr), system functions (%sys), waiting for I/O (%wio), and the percentage idle (%idle).

You can use the *ps* -ef command to see a display of the amount of CPU time each process has used. The column to observe is the "TIME" column, which is the amount of CPU in minutes and seconds.

ps -ef

```
UID       PID   PPID   C    STIME     TTY     TIME   COMMAND

oracle    189   1      0    Jul 11    ?       0:20   ora_db07_PERS
pers017   3049  8987   0    16:01:09  ttyp017 0:00   sqlplus
oracle    7680  1      0    Jul  7    ?       1:44   orasrv O opsoff
daemon    4858  7680   81   17:25:17  ?       5:53   oraclePERS T:I,,5
pers124   8069  8068   0    18:55:44  ?       0:00   oraclePERS P:4096,5,8,
pers172   8211  8210   0    18:56:54  ?       0:00   oraclePERS P:4096,4,7,
pers918   8092  8070   0    18:55:55  ?       0:00   sqlplus
oracle    171   1      0    Jul 11    ?       22:51  ora_pmon_PERS
oracle    15793 15791  0    Jul 12    ?       0:00   oraclePERS P:4096,4,7,
daemon    1235  7680   0    06:01:08  ?       0:00   oraclePERS T:I,,5
oracle    186   1      0    Jul 11    ?       0:18   ora_db06_PERS
oracle    174   1      0    Jul 11    ?       2:52   ora_arch_PERS
pers118   15909 15905  0    Jul 12    ttyp048 0:00   sqlplus
pers987   28882 28878  0    18:32:58  ?       0:00   oraclePERS P:4096,4,7,
daemon    12854 7680   0    07:00:11  ?       0:00   oraclePERS T:I,,5
oracle    183   1      0    Jul 11    ?       0:19   ora_db03_PERS
oracle    185   1      0    Jul 11    ?       0:19   ora_db05_PERS
oracle    184   1      0    Jul 11    ?       0:19   ora_db04_PERS
```

```
oracle    178    1      0    Jul 11      ?    1:27  ora_smon_PERS
pers662   14917 14913  0    17:52:37    ?    0:06  oraclePERS P:4096,4,7,
daemon    7772  7680   81   17:38:26    ?    5:50  oraclePERS T:I,,5
oracle    181    1      0    Jul 11      ?    0:20  ora_db02_PERS
oracle    172    1      0    Jul 11      ?    1:46  ora_dbwr_PERS
persadm   8093  8092   27   18:55:56    ?    0:04  oraclePERS P:4096,3,6,
oracle    16692 16691  0    Jul 12      ?    0:07  oraclePERS P:4096,4,7,
oracle    191    1      0    Jul 11      ?    0:18  ora_db08_PERS
oracle    179    1      0    Jul 11      ?    0:22  ora_db01_PERS
mgurry    8741  8444   44   18:58:09  ttyp00a  0:00  ps -ef
oracle    177    1      0    Jul 11      ?    1:41  ora_lgwr_PERS
pers771   449    445    0    08:57:58  ttyp00a  0:00  sqlplus -s
pesr142   8385  8381   0    17:39:54  ttyp010  0:00  sqlplus -s
pers181   28878 274    0    18:32:57  ttyp012  0:00  sqlplus
pers185   8068  8033   0    18:55:39  ttyp016  0:00  runmenu50 PERSADM -m f TNE
pers615   8210  18257  0    18:56:54  ttyp007  0:00  sqlplus
```

Notice in the display that the PERS database instance has both client-server (oraclePERS T:I,5) users running TWO_TASK and users logged on in unitary fashion (oraclePERS P:4096,4,7,). The largest user of CPU is ORACLE's detached process "ora_pmon_PERS". This usually indicates that the database instance has been up for a lengthy period. If one of the processes has an excessive amount of CPU (e.g., 10 minutes) and is increasing rapidly, it should be investigated.

Identifying network bottlenecks

As mentioned in Chapter 16, *Tuning in the Client-server Environment*, you must try to minimize the number of packets that your applications transfer across your networks. You must also be aware that bad packets can be passed across the network. Data corruption leads to performance problems because when an error is detected, your system requests the packet to be sent again. Corrupt packets are usually associated with an overloaded network. To see if your network is overloaded, use the *netstat* -i command. There will be several columns listed including "Ierrs" and "Oerrs," which represent the number of input errors and number of output errors respectively. Both of these values should ideally be zero. (Issue *man netstat* for a full explanation of *netstat* on your system).

When you are running client-server, knowledgable users will periodically ask you, "Is our network down?" Novice users will ask, "Why is the machine so slow?" There are several problems that may have occurred; the most common are:

- The database server machine is down
- The database instance is down
- SQL*Net (*orasrv*) is down

To test if the database machine or network is down, issue the command:

```
ping machine_name
```

where *machine_name* is the database server machine your users log onto. If the message "HOST IS ALIVE" is returned instantly, you have no problem with the machine being up and your network is functioning correctly. It will pay to run *ping* several times to ensure that the time taken to return is minimal. If there is an irregular delay in the message being returned, you probably have an intermittent network problem which must be cured.

If the machine and network are running, you must now test if the database instance is running. To do this, try logging onto your database server machine using SQL*Plus with your ORACLE_SID set to your database instance ID. (Be sure that you do not have TWO_TASK set). If this is not the problem, it must be the SQL*Net process *orasrv* which is causing the problem. Set TWO_TASK and try logging onto the instance (on the database server machine) using SQL*Plus to confirm that *orasrv* is the problem. See your *ORACLE Installation and User's Guide* for details on how to cure this problem.

Keeping all ORACLE Processes at the Same Priority

You must never adjust the priority of any of the ORACLE processes, including optional processes such as additional database writers. ORACLE itself is finely tuned and assumes that all of its processes will be able to communicate at the same priority.

Enlarging Your System Global Area

We have visited sites where the DBA has claimed that they can't enlarge their SGA beyond a small size because their machine won't allow it. This may occasionally be the case, but very often this problem is caused because the SHMMAX parameter has not been set large enough. SHMMAX specifies the maximum single shared segment size. If it is not set large enough, starting ORACLE with too large an SGA will fail.

Check the SHMMNI and SHMSEG parameters as well. All are documented in your *ORACLE Installation and User's Guide.*

VMS-specific Tuning

This section contains several hints for getting the best performance out of ORACLE running on a VMS platform.

VMS Tuning Parameters

Several VMS operating system parameters have an impact on ORACLE tuning:

BALSETCNT
: Maximum number of working sets in memory. If this is set too low, swapping can occur and will seriously degrade performance.

MAXPROCESSCNT
: Maximum number of processes currently in memory.

SRP
: Number of preallocated small request packets. In the SH MEM command, the free level should always be greater than 100. Use the SH MEM command to make sure the free level is at least 50.

IRP
: Number of preallocated I/O large request packets. Use the SH MEM command to make sure the level is at least 25.

NPAGEDYN
: Size of the non-paged dynamic pool in bytes. Use the SH MEM POOLFULL command to make sure that NPAGEDYN is never less than 100000 during peak times. If it is, increase the value.

PAGEDYN
: Size of the paged dynamic pool in bytes. Use the SH MEM POOL-FULL command to make sure that PAGEDYN is never less than 200000.

MPW_HILIMIT
: Upper limit of modified page list. This is a SYSGEN parameter that you must set to 15% of the total physical memory size. The default is 500 pages.

MPW_IOLIMIT
: Lower limit of modified page list. This is a SYSGEN parameter that you must set to half MPW_HILIMIT.

MPW_WAITLIMIT
: Number of pages of the modified page list that will cause a process to wait until the next time the modified page writer writes the modified page list. This parameter must be set to the same value as MPW_HILIMIT.

MPW_THRESH
: Lower bound of pages that must exist on the modified page list before the swapper writes this list to the free page list.

VMS Tools to Identify Bottlenecks

We find the VAX/VMS operating system a pleasure to tune because of the vast array of tools that it offers and the comprehensive set of tuning manuals that Digital Equipment Corporation provides. This section simply introduces the basic commands we would use to tune a VMS/ORACLE site. We strongly recommend that you get more information from the VAX/VMS manuals and consider using such performance tools as the VAX Performance Advisor (VPA) and the VAX Software Performance Monitor (SPM).

Identifying disk I/O bottlenecks

As mentioned throughout this book, the primary goals of disk I/O tuning are to balance the load of I/O across devices, to have sufficient disks and controllers to allow load sharing, and to have disks that process data fast enough to satisfy our needs. To identify a disk I/O bottleneck, check first to see if there are any outstanding requests for I/O waiting in the disk queue. To determine this, use the command:

```
MON DISK / ITEM = QUEUE
```

The average queue length should be no greater than 0.2. You can also use the MON DISK command to observe the I/O rates per second to determine if the I/O rates for each disk device are approaching the maximum number of I/Os per disk device. Use the command:

```
MON DISK / ITEM = ALL
```

If a disk is approaching its maximum load capacity, which is usually 40 I/Os per second, you should seriously consider spreading the load. Consult Chapter 13, *Monitoring and Tuning an Existing Database*, for advice.

You can also determine whether extraordinary activity is occurring by looking at the individual processes consuming most I/O activity. It is possible that you will find out that last night's backups are still running! At several sites we've worked at, we've found that the root of performance problems is a developer investigating problems on the production machine.

To find out the heavy users of I/O and the ones succeeding in obtaining I/O, issue the command:

```
MON PROC / TOPDIO
```

If you discover that the disk that contains your page and swap files is a problem, and you suspect excessive paging and swapping, you can confirm this by using the MON IO command and observe the "Page Read IO rate" and the "Page Write IO rate" in the output for paging and the "Inswap" rate for swapping. To help solve this problem, read the following section.

Identifying memory bottlenecks

Memory bottlenecks are almost always the result of excessive paging and swapping. The ideal situation is to have no paging and swapping activity at all; this option is usually too expensive because it requires the purchase of too much memory. VMS categorizes its paging into soft page faulting (within memory) or hard page faulting (to disk). Soft page faulting is preferable to hard page faulting because shuffling a process to memory is faster than moving it out to disk. Swapping occurs when an entire process is removed from memory and placed on disk. This is acceptable when a process is dormant but creates a performance problem when the process is active when swapped.

VMS differs from UNIX in that individual working sets (memory allocations) can be set on a per-user basis. We have found that categorizing your users into types and applying an appropriate working set quota for each user type can result in very efficient use of memory. For example, users who run complex forms will be assigned a larger working set quota than those who run simpler, smaller forms. You should have a large working set assigned to the user who runs overnight reports, so you have the ability to assign a larger SORT_AREA_SIZE and avoid excessive working set increments and decrements, and their associated CPU activity.

NOTE

> VMS working set quotas are also assigned to the SYSTEM and ORACLE user. Never reduce the working sets for these users unless you are absolutely certain that it is necessary. You must be in desperate need of memory and have reduced all other users' working sets before considering decreasing the working sets for these users.

The factor that determines if either hard page faulting or soft page faulting occurs is the size of the page cache. (See the parameters MPW_LOLIMIT, MPW_THRESH, FREE-GOAL, and FREELIM.) If hard page faulting is excessive, consider increasing these parameters, as described in the previous section. If you have a lot of inactive users on your system, consider reducing the BALSETCNT parameter, which is the maximum number of working sets kept in memory. This will cause the swapping of dormant processes and provide more memory.

To determine which users are experiencing paging problems, run these commands:

MON PROC / TOPFAULT

> Determines which processes are paging excessively. A well-managed site will be adjusting individual working sets frequently.

SHOW PROC / CONT

> Determines how much memory each process is using and what it is doing. Make sure that a resource-consuming activity is not running during prime production time (not one of those developers again!)

SHOW SYS of MON PROC

> Checks the memory being used by all processes.

Identifying CPU bottlenecks

CPU bottlenecks occur when there are processes waiting for CPU. CPU problems are commonly associated with memory and disk I/O problems. CPU bottlenecks can also occur when some user processes have been assigned higher priorities and are getting unfair use of the CPU. In addition to using the memory commands described in the previous section, use these commands:

MON STATES

The count returned should be as close to zero as possible and should never exceed 4. If any processes are experiencing CPU contention, they will appear with a state of COM or COMO.

MON PROC / TOPCPU

If MON STATES shows any processes waiting for CPU, this command allows you to perform further investigation.

SHOW PROC / CONT

Views the current and base priorities.

NOTE

The higher the priority, the more CPU time slice a process will receive. Do *not* adjust the priorities of any of the ORACLE processes. ORACLE is finely tuned and depends on certain processes having identical priorities.

Other Tuning Hints

Here is an assortment of hints to make your ORACLE system run more efficiently under VMS:

Page and swap files. Make sure page and swap files are on a separate disk from the one that holds the ORACLE database. The page and swap files must be contiguous. The page file is allocated dynamically, so it is important that the contiguous space on disk is available to it. The swap file must be at least greater than or equal to the value of (MAXPROCESSCNT * AVERAGE_WSQUOTA). To check if a file is contiguous under VMS, use the following command

```
dump / header / block (count : 0) file name
```

Types of transactions. Be aware of the types of transactions your users run. There may be a chance that you can decrease the users' working set quotas, which will allow you to free up memory for a larger SGA.

Contiguous disk space. Always defragment your disk before you create database files. This guarantees that the files will be created contiguously on disk. In addition, make sure that all programs are copied throughout the development life cycle (via the COPY/-CONTIG option) to ensure programs are stored contiguously on disk and minimize the number of I/Os when the program is required to be loaded into memory.

Shared executables. Ensure that all ORACLE executables (for example SQL*Menu, SQL*Forms, SQL*Reportwriter, SQL*Plus, etc.) are stored as shared executables. The potential for memory savings is enormous. Having SQL*Plus installed as a shared executable means a saving of more than one megabyte per SQL*Plus user. Doing the same with SQL*Forms saves nearly two megabytes per user. Sharing executables in this way helps the whole system by freeing up memory that will allow the configuration to support more users or increase the size of the SGA. You will also find that sharing executables reduces hard page faults.

SGAPAD. Ensure that the SGAPAD parameter is set large enough to store a large SGA. This parameter reserves contiguous shared memory. The larger the buffer cache, the faster ORACLE runs. If you can increase DB_BLOCK_BUFFERS without having to relink this parameter, you'll have more flexibility in tuning.

VII

Appendices

Part VII includes summary information. Appendix A is a summary of the features in ORACLE RDBMS Version 7 that have an impact on performance. Appendix B lists the most common performance questions, their answers, and references to the sections of the book where you can get more information. Appendix C provides summary information about tuning the ORACLE Financials product. Appendix D lists the dynamic performance tables you can access via a number of utilities and scripts described in this book.

Planning for ORACLE7

ORACLE7 (Version 7 of the ORACLE system) contains many new features and changes to existing features. In addition to describing these features in the relevant sections of this book, we have summarized them in this appendix so you will be able to refer to a single source when planning for or migrating to ORACLE7. To keep your applications running efficiently, and to take advantage of new performance features available in ORACLE7, you'll have to learn how to use ORACLE7 to best advantage.

ORACLE7 moves certain areas of responsibility for overall application performance from the developer to the DBA. These include performing physical application design and enforcing day-to-day business rules via stored procedures, triggers, and constraints. Although ORACLE7 provides features for everyone, the DBA has a special responsibility to plan carefully for the upgrade to ORACLE7 well in advance. You'll need to examine all new features carefully to make sure you, in fact, want to use them. If your Version 6 applications are well-tuned, you may find that in some cases, the performance improvements in ORACLE7 may not justify the overhead of having to convert software and upgrade all programs to the new release.

In this appendix, we describe briefly the following major enhancements in ORACLE7. The features that have a major impact on performance are described in greater detail elsewhere in this book.

- Cost-based optimizer
- Shared SQL context area
- Multi-threaded server
- Hash clusters
- Multiplexed redo logs
- Rollback segment changes
- TRUNCATE command
- Declarative data integrity constraints
- DELETE CASCADE function
- Stored procedures, functions, triggers, and packages
- Database security
- Distributed databases
- Table replication and snapshots
- New arithmetic functions
- UNION ALL extension

We also suggest ways to prepare for, perform, and monitor your conversion from Version 6 to ORACLE7.

Cost-based Optimizer

ORACLE7 (Version 7) provides a cost-based optimizer that is more intelligent than the rule-based optimizer supported by Version 6. The optimizer determines the most efficient retrieval path for a database access. The new optimizer can eliminate the performance problems posed by poorly written, long-running SQL statements.

How do the two optimizers differ? The rule-based optimizer determines a retrieval path by applying a set of preprogrammed rules. Does an index exist? Is the index unique? Is it over a single or composite table column? The optimizer asks these and many other questions. The cost-based optimizer, on the other hand, uses physical table characteristics to perform the access path calculations. Table volumes, index key spread, and other characteristics are all examined. In addition to the performance improvements available in the new optimizer, it provides greater flexibility because the cost-based algorithm can adapt to changes in data over time, whereas the rule-based algorithm cannot.

ORACLE gathers statistics for each table, computes the cost of each possible retrieval path, and chooses the path with the least overhead. The new ANALYZE command is responsible for collecting statistics for such table characteristics as table size, column selectivity and spread, and degree of data physically clustered around index values. If statistics are not available for a table referenced in an SQL statement, the system estimates these statistics based on such data dictionary information as table extents.

The overhead associated with collecting statistics can be substantial, especially for large tables. Don't issue ANALYZE as a matter of course, but use it regularly for key tables. The more dynamic the table, the more frequently you should collect statistics.

It is possible to use the cost-based optimizer without issuing an ANALYZE command. If the table is part of a multi-table SQL statement where at least one of the tables has been ANALYZEd (and no /*+RULE*/ hint has been included), then ORACLE uses the cost-based optimizer. If no statistics are available for a table, the optimizer tries to make an educated guess about the best retrieval path to use. If it cannot even guess, based on dictionary and other information, it will use the rule-based optimizer instead.

Some organizations have carefully tuned their statements to get the most out of the Version 6 optimizer. These sites are not likely to get better performance out of the cost-based optimizer at first. You can override the use of the cost-based optimizer, and choose the rule-based optimizer for your SQL statements, by setting the INIT.ORA parameter, OPTIMIZER_MODE, to RULE (the default is CHOOSE).

There are a number of advantages, and a few disadvantages as well, to using the cost-based optimizer available in Version 7. Advantages are:

Performance. On the average, the cost-based optimizer selects an execution plan that is at least as good as, if not better than, the plan selected by the Version 6 rule-based optimizer. The actual amount of improvement depends on how carefully you have tuned your Version 6 SQL statements. The Version 7 optimizer out-performs the Version 6 optimizer most significantly on large queries that perform multiple table joins.

No manual tuning. With the cost-based optimizer, you don't need to do manual tuning of your SQL statements. The result is increased productivity for developers who no longer need to labor over their SELECT statements.

Switch between optimizers. Developers can use the embedded SQL statement comments described in the previous section to switch between the cost-based optimizer and the rule-based optimizer. In this way you can preserve your already well-tuned queries while getting good performance out of untuned ones while you experiment further.

Use of optimization hints. The in-line hints (described in the next section) also give you a way to spell out the desired execution plan explicitly to get the best performance.

Users have reported a few disadvantages to using the new optimizer:

Ignores Version 6 tuning. The cost-based optimizer can inadvertently alter, from Version 6 to Version 7, the way a well-tuned SQL statement accesses the database. If you are not vigilant, and you fail to include a RULE hint in the SQL statement, the Version 7 optimizer will make its own choice about an execution plan.

Needs refreshed statistics. To get the best performance out of the cost-based optimizer, you must keep refreshing the statistics gathered by the ANALYZE command. This can add a lot of overhead. If tables become too active, you may do better to use estimated, not computed, statistics. (See the discussion of ANALYZE below.)

Overhead. The cost-based optimizer incurs a substantial amount of overhead in calculating the best execution plan. You need to consider whether the benefits of the performance improvements outweigh the increased overhead. The biggest overhead is incurred by SQL statements involving the largest number of tables; of course, you'll also realize the biggest performance gains by speeding up these table retrievals. Note that the shared SQL facility (described in the section called "Shared SQL Context Area") helps reduce the internal optimizer overhead.

Inserting Optimization Hints in SQL Statements

With Version 7, you can manually tune individual SQL statements, overriding the optimizer's decisions for that statement by including your own optimization hints within the SQL statement. By including hints as comments within the SQL statement, you force the statement to follow your retrieval path, rather than the one worked out by the optimizer. In the following example, by including /*+ RULE */ inside the SELECT statement, you tell SELECT to use the Version 6 rule-based optimizer, rather than the Version 7 cost-based optimizer.

```
SELECT
    FROM EMP, DEPT /*+  RULE   */
    WHERE . . .
```

Other hints are listed in the section in Chapter 7 called "Manually Tuning SQL Statements."

ANALYZE Command

The ANALYZE command allows you to validate and compute statistics for an index, table, or cluster. If you are going to use the Version 7 cost-based optimizer, you must generally issue the ANALYZE command. ANALYZE is important to performance tuning, but it also helps in validating object structures and in managing space in your system.

For a description of the options available through the ANALYZE statement and a list of the statistics produced by ANALYZE, see the section in Chapter 14 called "ANALYZE: Validating and Computing Statistics."

Shared SQL Context Area

In Version 7, ORACLE has allotted a portion of the System Global Area (SGA) of memory to a shared SQL context area. This area contains previously referenced SQL statements in their parsed and optimized form. Once the context area is full, statements are swapped in and out automatically using a last-referenced, first-out algorithm. The physical number of SQL statements that can fit in the context area depends on the size allocated for the area. The size of the context area is governed by the INIT.ORA parameter, SHARED_POOL_SIZE.

In Version 6, cursor details are stored within each user's individual Program Global Area (PGA). Multiple copies of the same SQL statements might simultaneously reside in many user PGAs, all incurring the same overheads. By contrast, Version 7 combines all of these duplicated user process cursors into the global context area in the SGA. In Version 7, a sophisticated string comparison algorithm within the database kernel quickly determines whether a cursor is already residing within the cache in its parsed form. Very little extra overhead is incurred if the SQL statement is not in the cache and has to be parsed anyway.

The availability of the shared context area in the Version 7 SGA improves the performance of SQL statements in a number of ways:

Saves overall application memory. As we've mentioned, combining SQL statements in the shared context area, rather than maintaining individual statements in individual users' PGAs, saves memory.

Saves repetitive SQL parsing overhead. Version 6 allows processes to reuse cursors from their own PGA. This means if a process performs the same function many times, the SQL statement will be parsed only once. Version 7 improves parsing efficiency still more. Because each statement's cursor information is in the shared context area, after the initial reference to the statement, all processes can then share it. The statement is parsed only once per application, rather than once per user process.

Includes internal recursive SQL statements. This point is very significant for application performance. Throughout this book, we have emphasized the significance of storing the ORACLE data dictionary within the SGA cache. Recursive database calls continue to occur whenever a table or index extension is triggered. Data dictionary scanning (to validate SQL statements), index scanning (to calculate execution path), and recursive database calls all benefit from the shared context area.

Used by both 3GL and 4GL applications. The shared context area improves performance for all ORACLE database tools. All front-end software used to access the database must communicate via SQL statements.

Includes both static and dynamic SQL statements. All precompiler and OCI programs can take advantage of the performance improvements gained from the shared SQL area. Each statement is stored and compared once it is sent (as a whole unit) to the RDBMS kernel. Once final construction of a dynamic statement has completed, it must be identical to a previously stored statement to be shared.

Used by stored procedures, functions, and triggers. The parsed forms of these PL/SQL macros are actually stored within the SGA once they have been initially referenced. These macros are then available to all other processes.

Is implemented transparently. Perhaps the most significant advantage of the SGA is that we get it for free. By upgrading to Version 7, all existing applications use the shared area by default. You need not perform any specific analysis or conversion.

In determining whether a SQL statement is already in the shared context area, the ORACLE RDBMS kernel performs an exact string comparison to find out whether two statements are equivalent. To be shared, the SQL statements must be identical. Carriage returns, spaces, and case (upper vs. lower) all affect the comparison. The section in Chapter 7 called "Sharing SQL Statements" describes this string comparison in some detail.

You can find out which statements are currently being cached within the shared context area in the SGA via the system view table, V$SQLAREA. This function is typically performed by the DBA. At present, there is no way of detecting which process is referencing a statement within the shared context area.

Multi-threaded Server

Multi-threaded dispatchers reduce the large memory overheads that exist for every process connected to the ORACLE RDBMS. You must have SQL*Net Version 2 to be able to use this feature, shown in Figure A-1.

Our tests have shown that each user connection to an ORACLE database requires approximately 300K of memory from the database server. This requirement usually grows to around 500K for active users. When 100 active users simultaneously connect to the database, nearly 50 megabytes of memory are required just to connect active users, and more for the SGA and data buffer cache. Dispatchers lower this memory connection overhead.

Multiple clients connect to an individual dispatcher process via a network-monitoring process called a listener. The listener process participates only in the initial connection task. Once a user has been successfully assigned a dispatcher process, the listener has no further communication with the user. Each dispatcher process submits requests to a shared server process via a request queue in the SGA. Server processes reply to database requests via the same request queue. The dispatcher process then returns the response to the originating client.

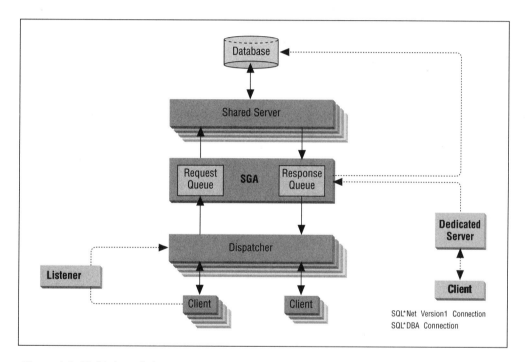

Figure A-1: Multi-threaded server

ORACLE automatically balances the shared server and dispatcher processes. You can control the way ORACLE does this balancing by specifying the correct values for these new INIT.ORA parameters:

MTS_DISPATCHERS
>   Number and type of dispatchers to create when the database is first started

MTS_MAX_DISPATCHERS
>   Maximum number of simultaneous dispatcher processes allowed

MTS_MAX_SERVERS
>   Maximum number of simultaneous shared server processes allowed

The SQL statement text, parsed data, and execution path are all stored within the SGA. The stack space (internal working storage) is held within the PGA. The stack space is the working storage memory needed by the shared server process to communicate.

User session data consists of information about the user and his or her connection. This data includes the user's actual ORACLE username. If multi-threaded servers are not being used, this information remains within the PGA. If multi-threaded servers are being used, the user session information is held within the SGA. This is necessary because any one of the shared servers can execute any client request, and the shared server must know the initiating username.

The availability of the multi-threaded server in Version 7 provides several advantages:

Reduces system memory overheads. Fewer processes are actually directly connected to the database. Only the shared servers need to be physically connected. This increases the maximum number of simultaneous user connections allowed per node.

Uses a single dispatcher. Once a user process has been allocated a dispatcher process (by the listener), that one dispatcher is used for the duration of the user process. Users do not float between dispatcher processes.

Performs automatic load balancing. ORACLE automatically balances the number of shared server and dispatcher processes, governed by the current length of the request queue. When the number of processes is reduced, memory is saved. When extra processes are started during application peak periods, client wait-times are also reduced. You can control this balancing by setting the appropriate INIT.ORA parameters (the MTS parameters listed above).

Allows manual load balancing. The DBA can manually override the number of servers and dispatcher process numbers by means of the ALTER SYSTEM command. Remember that you don't need to shut down the database to allow modified INIT.ORA parameters to take effect.

Allows simultaneous access to the queues. Even though there is only one request and one response queue (in the SGA) servicing all dispatcher processes, several processes can simultaneously read from and write to different entries of the queue. This prevents bottlenecks in the request and response queues.

Is implemented transparently. By upgrading to Version 7 and SQL*Net Version 2, all existing applications use the multi-threaded server by default. You need not perform any specific analysis or conversion.

Can use dedicated servers. If dedicated servers are allocated to particular user processes, these servers can access the database directly and avoid using the dispatcher and shared server. This may be an advantage for critical processes with large data loads.

Supports SQL*Net Version 1 connections. Although SQL*Net Version 2 is required to use the multi-threaded server, a process accessing the database via SQL*Net Version 1 can be connected via a dedicated server process.

Hash Clusters

Version 7 supports a new database structure called hash clusters. Hash clusters use a hashing function instead of an index to locate rows within a table. The cluster key can be an ORACLE-generated or a user-supplied value. In certain circumstances, hashed clusters can be significantly more efficient than standard indexes.

Instead of randomly storing rows in arbitrary table blocks and using indexes to locate them, hash cluster rows are stored according to their key values. Each row's location is directly (or indirectly) derived from its key value. The physical disk block is calculated from the table's initial disk offset plus the hashed key times the row length.

Figure A-2 shows a table that is estimated to have 100 rows maximum. Space is preallocated for the 100 rows, and a hashing algorithm positions each row in an individual location.

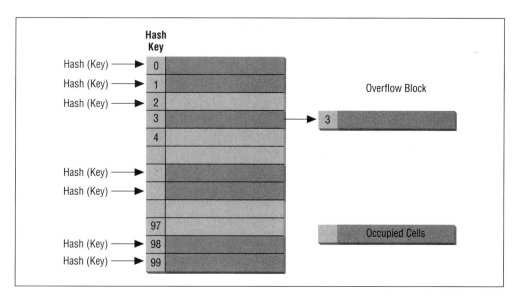

Figure A-2: Use of hashed clusters

The availability of hash clusters in Version 7 provides a number of advantages:

Reduces CPU and I/O overheads. Indexes need to be tree-walked to locate the leaf node of the index. The hashing algorithm provides the exact cluster block containing the required record.

Avoids indexing the primary key. Row entries are located by hashing the primary key, not by reading an index structure.

Offers special performance for equality predicate key lookups. Consider the following example:

```
SELECT . . .
    FROM EMP
    WHERE EMP_NO = 123;          Equality predicate
```

Note that full table scans and range checking are not as well suited to hash clusters.

Although hash clusters provide many advantages, they present some drawbacks to performance as well:

Preallocates space. Hash cluster space is preallocated at creation time. All space is allocated, even when the table has no data.

Does not allow increase. Cluster keys cannot be increased in size after the initial creation of the cluster.

May cause block chaining. Poor cluster keys can cause extensive block chaining. This chaining can actually overshadow all of the advantages of the hash cluster.

Limits the number of keys. You must be able to calculate the approximate number of distinct hash keys held within the table. You specify this number in the HASHKEYS clause of the CREATE HASH CLUSTER statement. This number caps the absolute number of distinct keys allowed.

Limits the number of records. You must also be able to calculate the approximate number of records per hash key. You specify the amount of space per cluster block in the SIZE clause of the CREATE HASH CLUSTER statement. This size limits the total number of rows that can be stored for any single hash key.

Multiplexed Redo Logs

Version 7 allows multiple redo log files to be written concurrently. The collection of identical redo files is known as a group. This Version 7 feature works exactly the way the concurrent control files feature works in Version 6.

The redo log files are extremely important in protecting the integrity of your application. Multiplexed redo files help the DBA guard against disk failure. We advise you to adopt them as quickly as you can after upgrading an application to Version 7. With this feature, you need to archive only one log file to allow up-to-the-minute recovery. It is not unreasonable, however, to archive all log files.

Each log file within a group:

- Must be identical in size

- Must be for the same log sequence number

- Should be on different disks

- Should have identical or similar names

You create multiplexed redo logs through the CREATE DATABASE statement as follows:

```
CREATE DATABASE   . . .
    LOGFILE GROUP 1 ( 'DISK:A\ORA1.LOG',
                      'DISK:B\ORA1.LOG',
                      'DISK:C\ORA1.LOG') SIZE 100K,
    LOGFILE GROUP 2 ( 'DISK:A\ORA2.LOG',
                      'DISK:B\ORA2.LOG',
                      'DISK:C\ORA2.LOG') SIZE 100K,
    LOGFILE GROUP 3 ( 'DISK:A\ORA3.LOG',
                      'DISK:B\ORA3.LOG',
                      'DISK:C\ORA3.LOG') SIZE 100K
```

If a disk failure does occur while writing to a redo log file, but the log writer (LGWR) successfully writes at least one of the log file group members, the LGWR ignores the corrupted file(s) and continues on. Once a log switch is performed, the excluded log files(s) are brought back online. All redo log file failures are written by the LGWR to the trace/alert file history.

Under Version 7, system instance recovery has not changed. Parallel server log files have been altered only slightly; log files are not dynamically allocated per instance. This means that there are no more log allocation chunks.

Rollback Segment Changes

Version 7 RDBMS allows rollback segments to be altered from online to offline and back again. Each rollback segment now defaults only to the settings in the INIT.ORA parameters when the system is first started. For example, you can specify:

```
ALTER [PUBLIC] ROLLBACK SEGMENT RB1 ONLINE;
```

You can now drop, recreate, and bring rollback segments back online without having to shut down the database. However, the only way to change a segment type (from public to private, and vice versa) is by dropping and recreating it. If a rollback segment is taken offline while being used by an active transaction, it waits for the transaction to be completed (committed or rolled backed). No other transaction can access it during this wait. Once the transaction is complete, the rollback segment status is set from IN_USE to AVAILABLE.

Setting Rollback Segment Sizes

Applications can individually specify which rollback segment a transaction is to use. This option is very useful for long-running updating jobs. By allocating larger rollback segments to long-running jobs, you can help to avoid getting a "SNAPSHOT TOO OLD" error. For example:

```
SET TRANSACTION USE ROLLBACK SEGMENT RB1;
```

To be effective, the SET TRANSACTION statement must be the first DML statement of any kind encountered after a successful user connect, DDL statement, commit, or rollback. To keep the statement continually in effect, you must execute it after each subsequent commit/rollback.

Unfortunately, ORACLE does not yet allow rollback segments (or rollback groups) to be allocated to particular users or roles, although this feature may be available in the future. Such a feature would allow applications to make use of the SET TRANSACTION feature without having to perform all of the necessary maintenance.

NOTE

This statement has actually been supported since Version 6.0.33, but many Version 6 users are not aware that it exists.

Setting an Optimal Size for a Rollback Segment

Version 7 allows a rollback to shrink back to its optimal size. For example, after a long-running update transaction has caused several rollback extensions, this feature automatically deallocates inactive extensions until the total rollback size approximately equals the specified optimal rollback size. ORACLE deallocates the oldest extents first, therefore minimizing the effect on consistent reads.

This feature can deallocate only entire extents, not pieces. Also, because of all the variables involved (INITIAL extent size, NEXT extent size, and PCTINCREASE factor of the rollback STORAGE clause), rollback segments will shrink to approximately their optimal size, not to the precise size specified.

Here is an example of specifying an optimal size; PUBLIC is optional.

```
CREATE PUBLIC ROLLBACK SEGMENT RB1
        TABLESPACE  RB_TS
        STORAGE (OPTIMAL 50K . . .);
```

With Version 7.0.12 and after, you can use the OPTIMAL clause to shrink the system roll-back segment. Prior to Version 7.0.12, the system rollback segment could not use this operation. Note that the system rollback segment does not include the shrink option by default. You will need to either modify the *SQL.BSQ* initialization file before creating a new database, or ALTER the rollback segment afterwards.

Planning for Rollback Overhead

If you set the optimal rollback segment size too small, unnecessary overhead can occur. As we've shown earlier, extent allocations (table, rollback segment, or temporary) incur large system overheads. This fact is highlighted by the importance placed on setting initial table extent sizes correctly. If a rollback segment's optimal size is set too small, it will continually allocate and then deallocate rollback extents, over and over again.

Rollback segments can have extents automatically released, via the OPTIMAL option, even though they still have segments with active transactions preventing them from being compressed all the way back to their optimal size.

You will need to analyze carefully the purpose of each rollback segment and the optimal size for it. Remember, the fact that transactions can now nominate particular rollback segments does away with much of the guess-work. If rollback segments are defined with varying NEXT extent sizes, the actual rollback tablespace can become very fragmented. Even though large portions of the tablespace are technically available, the shrinking exercise may further fragment the rollback tablespace.

TRUNCATE Command

The new TRUNCATE command is the quickest way for you to delete all rows from a table or cluster without dropping the actual structure. TRUNCATE provides a lot of power and efficiency, but it can be very dangerous too.

```
TRUNCATE    [TABLE] . . . [DROP]      STORAGE;
            [CLUSTER]     [REUSE]
```

The TRUNCATE command commits all changes (deletes) immediately and cannot be rolled back. The effect is the same as dropping the table and then recreating it.

The DROP STORAGE clause is the default and actually shrinks the table/cluster extents back to the MINEXTENTS value. Although this action incurs more resource overheads, it helps in overall performance by releasing the extents for other database objects. If you specify REUSE STORAGE instead, TRUNCATE simply erases all rows while retaining the currently allocated extents.

The TRUNCATE command provides a number of advantages:

Deletes rows efficiently. TRUNCATE is the most efficient way to delete all rows from a table. Resource overheads are not dependent on the size of a table. Tables containing one million rows can be truncated just as quickly as tables with ten rows. All of the tables' extent headers are simply marked as empty. Table and index extents do not have to be inserted into the free extents queue. Associated indexes do not have to be dropped.

Does not flag all dependent views and procedures for recompilation. If a table is dropped and recreated, all dependent objects need to be recompiled, and associated cursors are flushed from the shared SQL area.

Does not drop associated indexes. This saves having to recreate all indexes after reinstating the table.

Preserves table privileges, grants, and referential constraints. Because attributes remain defined, TRUNCATE is more efficient overall than dropping and recreating the table. You do not have to regenerate all the associated table attributes, and you don't run the risk of forgetting some of them.

Removes clusters automatically. If you specify TRUNCATE CLUSTER, the command removes all rows from all tables that are members the cluster.

TRUNCATE presents some disadvantages as well:

Results in immediate action. TRUNCATE does not require a user confirmation via a COMMIT action. TRUNCATE actions are immediate.

Does not provide rollback. TRUNCATE actions cannot be aborted or recovered. If a table is truncated by accident, the data has to be imported again. If you don't have a current backup, you're out of luck. There is no recovery because no detailed redo log and no detailed archive file is written. This saves processor and I/O overheads, but prevents recovery.

Does not provide selective features. TRUNCATE has the same effect as deleting all rows via DELETE (but it operates much faster). However, with TRUNCATE, you can't partially truncate a table, and you can't specify a WHERE clause to allow selective deletion.

Does not fire database triggers. Any associated stored table triggers will not be executed. This includes table-level and record-level triggers.

Does not truncate single tables in a cluster. The entire cluster has to be truncated. If all rows need to be removed from a table within a cluster, all the records have to be conventionally deleted from the table.

Does not truncate hash clusters. All hash cluster rows must be deleted.

Requires disabling of referential constraints. Before you truncate a table with a referenced key (foreign key constraint), you must disable the referential constraint.

Declarative Data Integrity Constraints

Declarative data integrity gives you a powerful way to guarantee that data within the database will always adhere to a particular set of internal business rules. By defining integrity rules within the actual database, you can guarantee that the rules remain true, regardless of the data input and updating methods you use. Regardless of whether you are using SQL*Forms, SQL*Plus, PRO*C, PRO*COBOL, IMPORT, EXPORT, SRW, RPT, or any other product that can access an ORACLE database (including third-party products), declarative data integrity forces them all to conform to a single set of database constraints. Through Version 7, you can also enforce data integrity constraints via stored database procedures and triggers, or declaratively using table definition constraints.

Integrity constraints offer a number of benefits:

They are self-documenting. All business rules and primary and foreign key checks are stored directly in the data dictionary. These constraints explicitly record all verification logic applied to each table or row.

They offer absolute integrity. No matter what tool is used to update rows within a table, all rows are subjected to the same strict rules. No ad hoc program or interface routine can inadvertently corrupt database integrity.

They improve performance. Because each constraint is defined internally within the ORACLE data dictionary itself, integrity checks are often implemented below the SQL level. Checks are performed as part of the table update, not as a secondary update or database call. This behavior reaps the greatest performance benefits in client-server environments. Network traffic is reduced, because all checks are identified internally within a single database visit.

They optimize integrity checks. Checks are performed only if the column is actually modified. The database retains a copy of the column before it is updated and detects where any change is actually taking place. Only the affected integrity checks are performed.

The most common types of rules you might specify as database constraints are listed below and are described in the sections that follow.

Entity (table) integrity constraints. These are the major table integrity constraints you can specify:

- Non-null column constraints

- Default column values on insert

- Column uniqueness checks

- Common table WHERE clause conditions

Examples of these constraints are shown in the following CREATE TABLE statement:

```
CREATE TABLE EMP    (EMP_NO      NUMBER (6,0)     UNIQUE NOT NULL,
                     EMP_NAME    VARCHAR2 (30)    NOT NULL,
                     SEX         VARCHAR2  (1),
                     HIRE_DATE   DATE             DEFAULT  SYSDATE)
                     CHECK (SEX IN ('M', 'F'))
                     CONSTRAINT  EMP_PK  PRIMARY KEY ( EMP_NO )
```

Referential integrity constraints. Referential integrity constraints enforce a primary key/foreign key relationship between tables. These checks include single table, self dependencies, and master/detail table dependencies. For example:

```
CREATE TABLE EMP    (EMP_NO        NUMBER (6,0)
                     .
                     .
                     .
                     MGR_EMP       NUMBER (6,0)     CONSTRAINT EMP_MGR
                                                    REFERENCES EMP,
                     . . . )
            CONSTRAINT   EMP_PK
                         PRIMARY KEY  ( EMP_NO )
            CONSTRAINT   EMP_SALARY_TYPE
                         FOREIGN KEY ( DEPT, GRP )
                         REFERENCES   SALARY_GROUPS
```

General business rules. Complex business rules can be enclosed within the actual database table definition. These rules are always enforced, no matter what product is used to manipulate rows within the table. Business rules can be globally modified. By declaring all rules in one area, they can be readily modified and immediately enforced without having to identify, modify, and recompile all application programs. For example:

```
CREATE   TABLE   EMP ( . . . )
                     CHECK     (COLUMN3, COLUMN4 IS UNIQUE)
                     CHECK     (COLUMN3  >=  '01-JUL-93' )
                     CHECK     (COLUMN6 IN ('A', 'C', 'X'))
```

If you are creating a table, you can name the constraints you associate with it. If you do not specify a name, the system allocates a constraint name. Each constraint name must be unique to its owner. Automatically-generated system constraints are of the form *SYS_Cnnnn*. We recommend that you always assign explicit names. The name you assign is the name you will use to enable and disable a constraint. The name will also appear in error messages when constraints are violated. They are also used as documentation within the data dictionary.

You define in-line constraints directly against an individual column, and such a constraint can be dependent only on that particular column. You define out-of-line constraints, on the other hand, outside the table definition. Such constraints are used for composite key constraints. Note that you can define in-line constraints as out-of-line constraints, but not vice versa. For example, this is an in-line constraint:

```
CREATE TABLE   . . .
     (COLUMN1 CHAR(10) NOT NULL);
```

This is an out-of-line constraint:

```
CREATE TABLE   . . .
     (COLUMN1  CHAR(10))
     CHECK  (COLUMN1 IS NOT NULL);
```

CHECK Constraints

The CHECK CONSTRAINT extension to the CREATE TABLE statement may be used as a common WHERE clause that is applied against all rows. For example:

```
CREATE TABLE  . . .
     ( column1  . . .,
       column2  . . .,
       column3  . . .  )
CONSTRAINT CHK_SEX
     CHECK    ( COLUMN1 IN ( 'M', 'F', 'O') )
     CHECK    ( COLUMN2 >= COLUMN3 ) ;
```

CHECK constraints can:

- Reference more than one column at a time

- Compare columns to constants

- Compare columns against other columns

- Use SQL syntax

CHECK constraints cannot:

- Include subqueries

- Include SYSDATE or USER

DEFAULT Constraints

Although the DEFAULT constraint does not meet the strict definition of a constraint, it operates in the same way. The DEFAULT clause sets columns to a predetermined value when a new row is inserted. For example:

```
CREATE TABLE ......
     ( column1 . . .,
       column2 . . .DEFAULT  SYSDATE,
       column3 . . .DEFAULT  99999,
       column4 . . .DEFAULT  TRAN_REFN.NEXTVAL );
```

Default clauses are applied only during row inserts. They are not applied if the column is created with an explicit null value, or when an existing row has the column set back to null. Note the following about the DEFAULT constraint:

- Default values cannot be expressions or include functions.

- Default values can reserve column space within a row. This tends to be effective when the column is commonly inserted with a null value, and is later updated to a non-null value. This helps to prevent row chaining and is more accurate than the guessing games that are sometimes performed with the PCTFREE and PCTUSED table attributes. (See Chapter 11, *Tuning a New Database*.)

- Defaults are not enforced if the column is generated from a second column which is null. This is equivalent to inserting the column with an actual value. For example:

```
INSERT INTO   xxx_table   (column1, column2, column3)
SELECT        column1, column2, column3
      FROM    yyy_table;
```

UNIQUE Constraints

The UNIQUE constraint works basically the same way it did in Version 6. The one difference is that it may also be included within an out-of-line constraint clause, thus allowing composite keys to have their uniqueness validated. For example:

```
CREATE TABLE . . .
     ( column1 CHAR (10),
       column2 CHAR (10),
       column3 NUMBER )
CHECK ( column1, column2 UNIQUE);
```

The UNIQUE constraint actually creates a unique index over the relevant column(s). The index adopts the constraint name (user-defined or system-defined) as the index name. Note the following about UNIQUE constraints:

- The index may be dropped from the database if it is not required. This is not advisable because if this happens the unique constraint will not be enforced. The existence of a unique index is used to actually enforce the constraint.

- When you are defining UNIQUE constraints, don't forget to also include the associated index definition via the USING INDEX clause. If no STORAGE or TABLESPACE clause is included, undesirable results may occur when the default settings are adopted. For example:

```
CREATE TABLE . . .
    ( column1  CHAR (10),
      column2  CHAR (10),
      column3  NUMBER
CONSTRAINT  CST_ABC  UNIQUE ( column1, column2)
            USING INDEX PCTFREE 10   TABLESPACE TS_DATA
                STORAGE  ( INITIAL 1M  NEXT 250K  PCTINCREASE 0 )
```

- Drop and then recreate the index if the STORAGE and/or TABLESPACE definitions need to be altered from their original settings.

- If the unique constraint needs to be (temporarily) removed, disable it rather than deleting the physical index.

Primary Key Constraints

A primary key constraint is included within the CREATE TABLE definition to indicate a single column or group of columns as the table's primary key. Each table may have only one primary key constraint. Primary key definitions cause a unique index to be automatically generated over the key. As with the UNIQUE constraint, make sure the index is not dropped. The index is the only mechanism for guaranteeing the constraint. Remember to include the USING INDEX to define index parameters properly, rather than relying on the default options.

Defining a primary key constraint for a single column is in fact identical to defining the field as UNIQUE and NOT NULL. For example:

```
CREATE TABLE . . .
    ( column1  . . .CONSTRAINT TAB_PK PRIMARY KEY,
      column2  . . .,
      column3  . . .) ;
CREATE TABLE . . .
    ( column1  . . .,
      column2  . . .,
      column3  . . .)
CONSTRAINT TAB_PK
    PRIMARY KEY ( column1, column2 );
    USING INDEX PCTFREE 10   TABLESPACE TS_DATA
        STORAGE ( INITIAL 1M  NEXT 250K  PCTINCREASE 0 )
```

Foreign Key Constraints

Foreign key constraints can now be defined directly within the table definition. These constraints may be for single columns or composite foreign keys. Foreign keys can be declared only over previously declared primary keys.

Foreign keys, by definition, may only be null or a member of the foreign key group. There is no limit to the number of foreign key constraints allowed per table. Each constraint guarantees data integrity between primary and foreign keys, no matter what product is used to update the tables. For example:

```
CREATE TABLE. . .
     ( column1 . . . CONSTRAINT TAB_FK REFERENCES TAB,
       column2  . . .,
       column3  . . .) ;
CREATE TABLE . . .
     ( column1  . . .,
       column2  . . .,
       column3  . . . )
CONSTRAINT TAB_FK
          FOREIGN KEY ( column1, column2 ) REFERENCES TAB;
```

NOTE

Because a table may only have one primary key definition, foreign key constraints need only identify the table name they are referencing, rather than table and column(s) name, or constraint name.

Integrity Constraint Warnings

Here are some things to watch out for when you use integrity constraints.

Foreign key constraints. Foreign key constraints will cause a SHARE LOCK and FULL TABLE SCAN on the parent table, if the child table does not have an index on the foreign key column(s). This is the case for INSERT, UPDATE, and DELETE statements on the child table. There is some suggestion that this problem might be corrected in future Version 7 releases.

Normalized database and full table only. Referential integrity cannot be enforced over part of a table. You cannot attach a WHERE condition to a primary or foreign key. You can use referential integrity automatically only in a truly normalized database. Denormalized tables cannot use declarative data integrity.

One database. Declarative data integrity can enforce integrity constraints only within one database. Integrity rules may not be specified for remote databases.

Large inserts. When you are performing large table inserts (e.g., initial data takeup), you may need to disable foreign key constraints to improve performance times. Once the table has been loaded, constraints can then be enabled. If violations occur, constraint exceptions will automatically be directed to an exceptions table. For example:

```
ALTER TABLE tab      DISABLE PRIMARY KEY;
ALTER TABLE tab      DISABLE CONSTRAINT Tab_FK;

PERFORM DATA TAKEUP  .....

ALTER TABLE tab      ENABLE PRIMARY Key;
ALTER TABLE tab      ENABLE CONSTRAINT Tab_FK
                     EXCEPTIONS INTO excep_tab;
```

The EXCEP_TAB table must be defined as:

```
TABLE EXCEP_TAB (ROW_ID       ROWID,
                 CONSTRAINTS  VARCHAR2 (30),
                 OWNER        VARCHAR2 (30),
                 TABLE_OWNER  VARCHAR2 (30) );
```

Deleting rows. Performance problems may occur if you are deleting rows from a table that has one or more foreign key constraint references. As a rule of thumb, all primary key tables with more than about 250 rows should have unique indexes. This is not always true for foreign key references.

In this example, assume that a key application table has many foreign key constraints; 10 to 15 constraints is not unusual for certain core tables. It is unreasonable to assume that all of these foreign keys will be indexed. For example:

```
TABLE EMPLOYEE_MASTER.
    EMP_NUM         PRIMARY KEY      INDEXED
    COMPANY_CODE    FOREIGN KEY      INDEXED
    REPORT_GRP      FOREIGN KEY
    DEPT_CODE       FOREIGN KEY      INDEXED

    CREDIT_RATING   FOREIGN KEY
    SALARY_GRADE    FOREIGN KEY
    ADDRESS_LINE1
    ADDRESS_LINE2
    ADDRESS_LINE3
    POST_CODE       FOREIGN KEY
```

Assume that the EMPLOYEE_MASTER table has many thousands of records. In practice, only particular foreign keys will be indexed. Other foreign keys are declared only for the automatic enforcement of referential integrity, not for online data queries and/or report sequencing. If a record from the CREDIT_RATING table is deleted, for example, referential integrity has to be upheld. All foreign keys need to be cross-referenced and validated. If the foreign key is referenced in another table, a suitable error will be reported. Unfortunately, this integrity violation check could mean the serial search of several different tables, each containing many hundreds of thousands of records.

A simple solution for this particular example would be to ban all deletes from those particular foreign key tables. This approach is crude and not very effective. A better alternatively is for the DBA to disable constraints while deletion takes place. The DELETE function would still need to be removed from the online application, and the action left to the care of the DBA.

DELETE CASCADE Function

Version 7 also provides referential integrity during deletion. If you enable this feature by specifying ON DELETE CASCADE in the CREATE TABLE statement, then when a master row is deleted, all detail rows are deleted as well. For example, you can specify:

```
CREATE TABLE . . .
    ( column1 . . .CONSTRAINT  TAB_FK  REFERENCES TAB
                    ON DELETE CASCADE,
      column2 . . .,
      column3 . . . );
CREATE TABLE . . .
```

DELETE CASCADE presents some of the same potential for performance problems described for foreign key referential integrity. Each time a row is deleted from the parent table, the system needs to do a search (possibly a serial search) of the detail table to identify and delete all detailed rows.

In some cases, the DELETE CASCADE function can actually cause further cascading. If the detail table also has a detail (dependent) table, the DELETE will cascade further. This could turn a simple deletion function into a huge update, as shown in Figure A-3.

Stored Procedures, Functions, Packages, and Triggers

Version 7 supports a powerful set of stored entities: procedures, functions, packages, and triggers.

Procedures and Functions

Stored procedures and functions are simply a collection of SQL and PL/SQL statements held as a single compiled unit within the database. They can also be retained within the special shared SQL context area to be shared by all users. Procedures and functions can

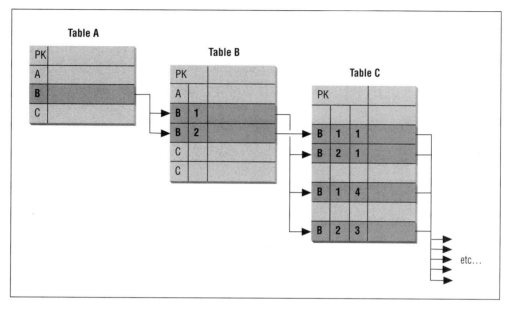

Figure A-3: Problem with DELETE CASCADE

call each other, including themselves, and can be called from all ORACLE products that are compatible with Version 7. The main difference between procedures and functions is that functions act as user-defined verbs and return a value. Chapter 9, *Tuning SQL*Forms*, describes the differences in greater detail.

ORACLE automatically tracks all procedure and function entity dependencies. Whenever the dependent tables for a procedure or function are altered, they are automatically flagged as needing recompilation. The next time the procedure is referenced, it is recompiled before actually being executed.

Stored procedures and functions are best suited for the following:

- Common global enforcement of business rules and functionality. These routines are available to all ORACLE tools.

- Storing batch update routines. Large complex update routines can be held directly within the database.

- Enforcing modifications on a table. These can be performed in a particular manner and/or sequence. Stored procedures and functions can be called by stored triggers.

When procedures and functions are created (or altered), the PL/SQL kernel first compiles the source text and retains the following information in the database:

- Original source text

- Execution parse tree

- Pseudo execution code

- All dependency information (both direct and indirect)

- Any syntax errors

Figure A-4 demonstrates how ORACLE tracks object dependencies. Before executing a stored procedure or trigger, the system compares all dependency time-stamps to the procedure time-stamp and recompose the procedure if necessary.

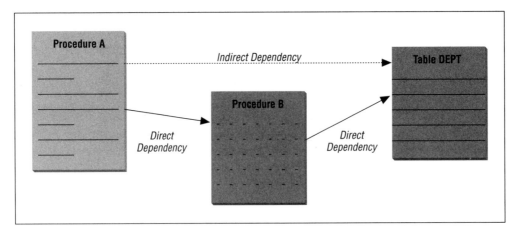

Figure A-4: Tracking object dependencies with stored procedures and functions

You can review information about procedures, functions, and packages by examining data dictionary views and tables as follows:

USER_DEPENDENCIES   Procedure, function, and package dependencies

USER_ERRORS   Procedure, function, and package compilation errors

USER_SOURCE   Procedure, function, and package text

Stored procedures and functions offer a number of advantages:

Automatically recompile source text. Every time a dependency is altered, source text is recompiled automatically. This keeps you from having to do a complete system recompilation, which until now has been necessary when you modify a common in-line library.

Offer additional security. Text is executed under the security domain of the owner, not that of the calling user. Common procedures can now programmatically control access to database objects to which a user does not have privileges.

Provide additional data integrity. Stored procedures and functions provide an additional level of data integrity by forcing related activities to execute together, every time.

Reduce database calls. By reducing the number of database calls required, the use of stored procedures and functions reduces network traffic and increases performance. Performance is improved because procedures and functions are stored in parsed form and are shared from the cache after they have been referenced the first time.

Make instant system-wide changes. By changing a single stored procedure or trigger you can make immediate changes throughout the system.

Realize productivity gains. Because you can now develop a centralized bank of common functions, all of the applications in your system can access them and reduce the need to develop their own procedures.

Save memory. Because of the availability of the shared SQL context area, only one copy of the code is required for all application users, regardless of which interface program is being run.

SQL*Forms Version 3 provides system libraries, a facility that is similar to the Version 7 stored procedures and functions. The SQL*Forms facility is much less efficient than the new Version 7 facility. System libraries are pseudo-libraries that incur larger overheads than stored procedures and functions. Every time a form is generated, each library must be (unnecessarily) parsed and recompiled. The system libraries used for a form are physically included within each and every *.FRM* file. The SQL*Forms libraries are not necessarily shared within the shared SQL context area. If an SQL*Forms library has been copied rather than referenced, it cannot be automatically updated via a system-wide modification. There is no way for the DBA to force a programmer to reference a library rather than copy it, so there is no easy way to improve performance.

Packages

Packages are database objects that are used to group related stored procedures. Packages have the added advantage of being able to define public and/or private package cursors and variables for each user referencing the package. These objects retain their value and cursor context for the entire user session.

Packages can group procedures and functions that are public, private, or a combination of public and private. Public procedures must be defined as part of the package header definition and may be referenced (called) as an individual entity (stored procedure) or from within the owning package.

Packages containing private procedures and functions are useful for hiding certain sections of code. For example, you might include in an application such sensitive procedures as password generators or auditing check-digit calculators. By including them in a package, you allow limited, controlled access to them. The package handles the logic of allowing this code to be referenced only by those privileged to use them.

Packages consisting only of public procedures and functions, shown in Figure A-5, ease the security burden on the DBA. By granting access to a package, you indirectly grant access to the public procedures and functions enclosed in that package. You can divide applications logically into separate modules, and can include all relevant procedures and functions in each module. For example, you can include all ACCOUNTS_PAYABLE procedures in a single package (all public references) and can grant access to that package (via GRANT EXECUTE) to those particular users who are authorized to use the procedures.

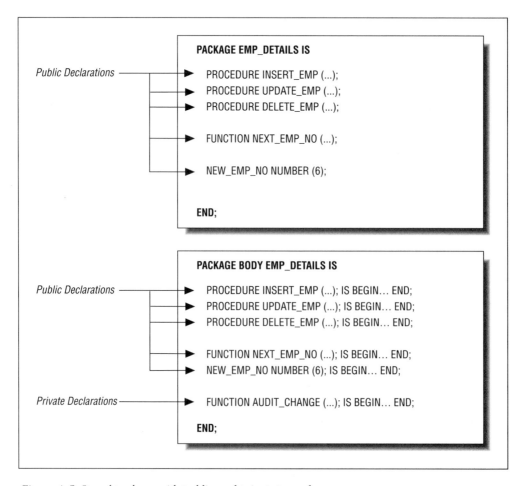

Figure A-5: Stored package with public and private procedures

Stored packages offer a number of advantages:

Physically group related procedures and functions. These are physically stored in the database together.

Provide variables. They support the use of globally accessible variables.

Simplify security. You need to grant the EXECUTE privilege only to the package, not to individual constructs within it.

Reduce dependencies. Packages reduce the number of procedure and function dependencies. Dependencies need to be stored only at the package level.

Reduce disk I/O. The entire package (all procedures) is loaded into memory on the first call of a package. When the first step of a business process is performed, all necessary procedures and functions for successive steps are also loaded. This reduces overall disk I/O requirements.

There are also a few disadvantages to using stored packages:

Retain local variables. Packages can retain local variables from one execution of the package to the next. This can lead to numerous problems when the package is automatically (re)compiled as the result of a data dictionary change to a dependent object. All variables are automatically initialized on each new compilation. This spasmodic initialization is impossible to detect programmatically and can lead to undesirable behavior. To retain data throughout a user's session, be sure to use RDBMS global variables.

Retain local information. Package variables can be used only to retain local information across procedures within a single package. Package variables cannot be shared across packages. Once again, use global variables.

Triggers

Stored triggers, shown in Figure A-6, are effectively the same as user-defined PL/SQL triggers; they are associated with a specific table and are automatically triggered by a set event. Do not confuse stored triggers with SQL*Forms triggers.

Stored triggers can be fired only by the following DML table events:

- INSERT of row
- DELETE of row
- UPDATE of row
- UPDATE of column(s)

You can set triggers to fire before and after each DML statement, or before and after each individual row update. You can also set triggers to fire for an individual column update. Row-level triggers can even be extended to include a WHERE clause that logically restricts which rows qualify to execute the trigger.

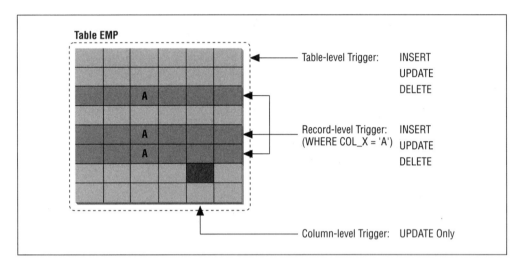

Figure A-6: Stored triggers

The memory, productivity, and performance benefits of stored triggers are similar to those described for stored procedures. The potential power of the stored trigger facility is enormous. It lets you automatically audit value-based table changes, regardless of the updating tool you are using. It also lets you apply security restrictions on updating, ranging from time of day to user privileges.

But stored triggers do pose a few possible dangers. Don't let these warnings deter you from using such a valuable feature. Just realize that you need to plan carefully before you use them.

Raise errors. Stored triggers can raise ORACLE errors, just as any SQL statement would. If an error is raised, the initiating SQL statement will also fail. You must provide for error handling.

Maximum triggers. Each table has a maximum of 12 triggers.

Cascading trigger loops. Cascading trigger loops can occur when one table update causes a trigger to fire, which in turn updates another table, tripping a second stored trigger which updates the original table.

Restricted SELECT access. A trigger cannot SELECT from or change a row within the originating (triggering) table, other than the current row (via the :NEW.column and :OLD.column facility). This is known as a mutating table. It makes sense to prevent same-table-updates from a stored trigger, but restricted SELECT access can become a problem with recursive tables.

Limited updating. Stored triggers cannot update columns which are marked for explicit update via the initial triggering SQL statement. These fields can be identified by the clause:

```
IF UPDATING ('column') . . .
```

Automatic firing. Low-level stored triggers are automatically fired regardless of the number of rows affected. If 5,000 rows are updated within a table, 5,000 row-level updated triggers will also be fired. Under these circumstances, it may be more efficient to disable the trigger(s) before performing the update.

Stored Triggers and Stored Procedures

Stored triggers and stored procedures offer many similar performance improvements:

- Both can include PL/SQL blocks.

- Both use shared SQL cache areas.

- Both have automatic dependency tracking, and recompilation on dependency change.

However, stored triggers differ from stored procedures in several ways as well:

- Triggers are fired automatically. They trigger by database events, rather than procedurally.

- Triggers are attached to database tables.

- Triggers do not support COMMIT, ROLLBACK, or SAVEPOINT statements.

- Triggers have access to both before (:OLD.column) and after (:NEW.column) images of each column or the row.

- Triggers have access to extra Boolean variables that can be used to programmatically identify the trigger type. For example:

```
IF INSERTING . . .
IF UPDATING . . .
IF DELETING . . .
```

- Triggers are able to programmatically identify which columns are to being updated. For example:

```
IF UPDATING ('column') . . .
IF INSERTING ('column') . . .
```

Database Security

Version 7 improves system security by providing several new features. These features offer performance improvements by reducing the need to do extensive system administration and to build custom security features into your programs.

Role-based Security

Role-based security, available in Version 7, allows different user roles to have distinct sets of data access rights and system privileges. The use of roles improves application security and significantly reduces the overhead associated with system administration for large applications. You should establish roles at the time of system installation and should specify passwords for roles at that time. You can grant and revoke access to roles for specific users. You can establish a default role for new application users. You can even achieve hierarchical security by granting roles to other roles under certain circumstances.

Version 6 offered a number of system privileges. Version 7 defines five pseudo-roles that group those earlier privileges together in a way that simplifies the assignment of default privileges to users. Default roles are listed in Table A-1.

Table A-1: Version 7 Roles and Privileges

Role	Privilege
Connect	CREATE SESSION
	ALTER SESSION
	CREATE SYNONYM
	CREATE VIEW
Resource	CREATE TABLE
	CREATE INDEX
	CREATE CLUSTER
	CREATE SEQUENCE
	CREATE DATABASE LINK
DBA	System privileges with ADMIN option
EXP_FULL_DATABASE	SELECT any table
	Back up any table
	UPDATE access to SYS.INCVID,
	SYS.INCFIL, and SYS.INCEXP
IMP_FULL_DATABASE	Become user
	Write down

Resource profile limits

Under Version 7, a user can be allowed a set of resources, as shown in Table A-2. Collectively, these resources are known as a resource profile. An individual user can have a particular profile or can adopt a default profile. You can enforce profiles at the session level or at the individual statement level. There are two types of profiles:

Session-level profiles. These limit the resources per connection (session). Once a limit is reached, the ORACLE connection is automatically aborted.

SQL statement profiles. These limit the total resources available to an individual database access. If limits are exceeded, the offending statement is aborted and rolled back. Supported profile resources are:

Profiles provide unlimited resource control over application access. They can also be used to help identify troublesome programs. Profiles can also help identify untuned SQL statements in development and QA databases.

Table A-2: Version 7 Resources

Resource	Description
SESSIONS_PER_USER	Total concurrent sessions per username
CPU_PER_SESSION	Maximum CPU per session
CPU_PER_CALL	Maximum CPU per call
CONNECT_TIME	Maximum continuous connect time per session
IDLE_TIME	Maximum allowable idle time before user is disconnected
LOGICAL_READS_PER_SESSION	Maximum database blocks read per session
LOGICAL_READS_PER_CALL	Maximum database blocks read per database call
PRIVATE_SGA	Maximum number of bytes of private space within SGA
COMPOSITE_LIMIT	Maximum weighted sum of: CPU_PER_SESSION, CONNECT_TIME, LOGICAL_READS_PER_SESSION, and PRIVATE_SGA

Distributed Database

Version 7 supports full distributed database processes, whereas Version 6 supports only distributed queries. This feature provides a number of very substantial benefits:

Data access. You can easily access and modify data on multiple databases. All Version 7 databases now support remote updating.

Autonomy. Each site can control its own databases, while still making these databases globally available. Hardware used at a particular site is not important. The SQL*Net and Multiprotocol Interchange facilities remove all hardware and software incompatibilities.

Global concurrency. Changes can be easily propagated to all databases as a single update with the Version 7 two-phase commit feature. Changes no longer have to be cross-updated via nightly Pro*C or other routines, thus helping to ensure point-in-time global data concurrency.

Location transparency. It no longer matters where the physical database resides. SQL*Net links all ORACLE databases. SQL*Net Version 2 improves network performance and reduces the problems of physical location.

Two-phase Commits

Version 7 supports distributed database updates via a two-phase commit feature. Each distributed database update has an initial prepare phase, followed by a commit phase.

The two-phase commit provides automatic, transparent updates that guarantee that all databases updated via a single distributed transaction either commit or roll back as a single unit. The effect is that global database integrity is always maintained. If a failure does occur on any updated node, all nodes work together to coordinate the global transaction rollback.

Transactions that perform cross-database updates are more susceptible to failure than single database commits. These statements are exposed to network and remote database failure. If a distributed update does fail, and nodes have already been updated before the failure, those nodes continue to hold resources via IN-DOUBT distributed transaction locks. These locks remain in place until one of the following occurs:

- The offending network problem is rectified and transaction recovery completes (or rolls back).

- The offending database is corrected and transaction recovery completes (or rolls back).

- The DBA forces a commit or rollback of all IN-DOUBT database locks.

Table Replication and Snapshots

The Version 7 table replication feature allows you to create multiple read-only copies of an updatable master table. Table replication is asynchronous and can be automatically refreshed at user-defined intervals. Version 7.1 will support multiple replication updating. That is, all distributed copies of the one master table can be updated with ORACLE automatically propagating the changes. An error log is maintained for all conflicting updates caused by distributed updating of the same data by different operators.

With the CREATE SNAPSHOT statement you can take a snapshot of an individual table, a subset of a table, or a complex query join (via a view). You can refresh all of the master table data or only the most recent changes.

A snapshot log is an internal ORACLE table containing all of the ROWIDs of the rows modified since the last snapshot or refresh. Snapshot logs are used with simple snapshots for fast refresh operations. In such operations only the modified rows are refreshed. Once changes have been propagated, the modified rows are erased from the snapshot log. Note that you cannot refresh a table via a snapshot log if you are performing a multiple table join.

Figure A-7 illustrates a typical example of when you might do complete and simple refreshing.

How do snapshots differ from user-defined table triggers?

- Snapshots are less vulnerable to network failure. They are refreshed less frequently and do not have to traverse the network every time a row within the table is updated.

- Snapshots do not need to be individually coded and maintained each time the table is recreated.

- Snapshots can improve network performance by performing all modifications in a single network trip. By contrast, with user-defined table triggers, one network access is required for each row modification.

- Snapshots need to update only the local master table. Triggers, on the other hand, must synchronously update all replicated tables per modification. This will slow master table updates.

- Triggers do not have the refresh time lag that replicated tables do. Data is always current.

- Triggers expose each master table update to network failures. A remote network failure, for example, causes a simple local update to fail.

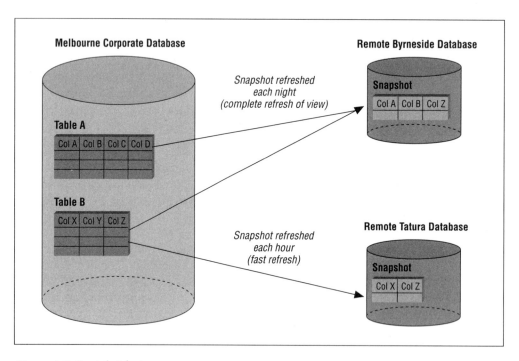

Figure A-7: Snapshot feature

New Arithmetic Functions

ORACLE has introduced the following SQL functions in Version 7:

COS	Cosine
COSH	Hyperbolic cosine
EXP	Exponential
LN	Natural logarithm
LOG	Logarithm
POWER	Raise power
SIN	Sine
SINH	Hyperbolic sine
SQRT	Square root
TAN	Tangent
TANH	Hyperbolic tangent

UNION ALL Extension

A new extension to the UNION statement, UNION ALL, preserves record duplicates that would otherwise be filtered out. This was a cumbersome process in Version 6. The SQL statement had to (unnecessarily) include the column ROWID within the SELECT list to guarantee row uniqueness, as in the following example:

```
Select  Emp_Name,  ROWID
    From Emp@DB1
    UNION
Select  Emp_Name,  ROWID
    From Emp@DB2
```

In Version 7, you can use UNION ALL, as shown below:

```
Select Emp_Name
    From  Emp@DB1
    UNION  ALL
Select Emp_Name
    From Emp@DB2
```

Migrating to ORACLE7

Because ORACLE has modified the internal structure of several database data files in Version 7, you will need to do a database upgrade when migrating from Version 6. The following database files have been altered in structure:

- Data dictionary
- Database control files
- Database files headers
- Rollback segments

ORACLE provides two methods for upgrading to Version 7. With the first method, you export and import between database versions. With the second method, you use a special migration utility.

WARNING

Before you attempt to upgrade using either method, take at least one full database backup (export). Never upgrade your production database before first practicing the migration procedure and thoroughly testing the new software on your development environment. Never delete the Version 6 database software until you are sure the upgrade is successful. You never know when you may need to revert back!

Migrating Using IMPORT and EXPORT

One way to migrate to Version 7 is to use the ORACLE utilities, IMPORT and EXPORT, as follows:

1. Run EXPORT to export all data from the Version 6 database.

2. Install ORACLE Version 7.

3. Run IMPORT to import data directly into the new Version 7 database.

The advantage of running IMPORT and EXPORT is that this approach allows you to perform database housekeeping after the EXPORT and before the IMPORT. For example, you can alter table sizes, clean up database fragmentation, restructure rollback segments, introduce hash clusters, and build referential integrity into the database.

The disadvantage is the time it takes to complete the upgrade. On the other hand, such a substantial software upgrade should not be rushed. You will be spending a lot of time planning for how to take best advantage of the new version, so the actual time of running these utilities should not be a major factor.

Migrating with MIGRATE

ORACLE provides a MIGRATE utility in Version 7 that effectively converts the database from Version 6 to Version 7. Do the following:

1. Run the MIGRATE utility against the Version 6 database. This utility:

    — Creates a temporary user named MIGRATE_6_TO_7

    — Creates a Version 7 data dictionary within the new user

    — Creates Version 7 control file(s)

    — Alters bootstrap segments

    — Converts CHAR to VARCHAR2

    — Alters tablespace headers

2. Update the INIT.ORA file. (See Chapter 11, *Tuning a New Database*, for suggested values for the parameters in this file.)

3. Install the ORACLE Version 7 software.

4. Open the Version 7 database on the existing database.

    **** **NO TURNING BACK** ****

5. Execute the statement: ALTER DATABASE CONVERT.

6. Execute the statement: DROP USER MIGRATE_6_TO_7.

Plan ahead! Your system tablespace must have enough free space to hold both the Version 6 and the Version 7 data dictionaries simultaneously.

Be sure you shut down the Version 6 database cleanly (no unapplied redo entries) before you run the MIGRATE utility.

Preparing for ORACLE7

There is a lot you can do to prepare for using the new Version 7 facilities before the conversion actually takes place. We suggest you become familiar with all of the new features and work on preparing the data described below:

Stored procedures. Code SQL*Forms system (reference) libraries with the goal of transposing them directly into stored procedures. Make sure the libraries are self-contained (compilable) to enable them to communicate with the form only via procedure parameters. Remember that stored procedures, functions, and triggers cannot reference local SQL*Forms variables (e.g., :BLK.FIELD) or system variables (e.g., :SYSTEM.CURSOR_VALUE).

Shared cursor cache. Modularize as much as possible of your application via Version 6 procedures, triggers, and functions. By avoiding the use of unique cursors, you will improve the chances that your cursors can be shared and thus can remain resident within the Version 7 shared cache. Remember, every cursor you plan to share must be coded identically.

Rollback optimal size. Before Version 7 migration begins, you can do benchmark testing to determine the optimal sizes for your rollback segments and to match particular update tasks to individual rollback segments. Remember that the SET TRANSACTION USER ROLLBACK SEGMENT is actually available in all releases after Version 6.0.33, although many ORACLE users are not aware of it. You can begin using this feature right now.

Cost-based optimizer. If you have painstakingly tuned SQL statements to use the rule-based optimizer, you will not want to upgrade to the new cost-based optimizer right away. Include the /* + RULE */ comment string in these statements. This will prevent the Version 7 optimizer from executing the statement in a different way. Remember that any statements that do not contain this comment string will default to the use of the cost-based optimizer algorithm and may, in fact, use a retrieval path that is different from the Version 6 path in accessing the database.

After the Conversion

As we've mentioned, you will want to study and assess some of the Version 7 features (such as the cost-based optimizer) before you begin to use them. You can use most features, however, immediately after you complete your database conversion and back up the database. Why not take advantage of the major performance gains offered by Version 7 as soon as possible? Features you can use without any particular preparation are listed below:

Shared SQL area. To use the shared SQL area, developers must make sure their SQL statements are coded according to rigid standards. To take advantage of the fact that an identical statement is already in the shared area (and thus avoid a disk access), the two statements must truly be identical (case and all).

Multiplexed redo logs. Redo log files are critical for database instance recovery. To allow your system to recover from a database failure in the best possible way, disperse redo logs across several physical disks. Having these logs available is equivalent to having control files across many disks.

Restricting rollback segments. Set rollback segments for any long-running update jobs, particularly overnight processes. The SET feature is critical to the performance of such jobs. The overhead of having to perform rollback segment extensions can affect the performance of a SQL statement more than the actual statement itself.

Shrink rollback segments. Set the OPTIMAL rollback size for each rollback segment. This allows the database to shrink back rollback segment extents to a manageable number. This helps prevent jobs from failing when they are unable to obtain an extra rollback segment because all space has been consumed by another rollback segment.

TRUNCATE command. Use TRUNCATE to delete all records from a table before repopulating it. Overnight jobs that generate extract tables for reporting procedures are good candidates for TRUNCATE.

ANALYZE command. Generate statistics for the handful of key application tables via ANALYZE. Use of this command will allow the cost-based optimizer to make more informed decisions. Be sure to refresh ANALYZE statistics regularly for dynamic tables.

Multi-threaded server. If your machine is memory-bound, you can save a substantial amount of memory and you can improve overall performance by controlling all user connections via multi-thread dispatchers. This feature requires SQL*Net Version 2.

Resource profiles. You can put system-wide statement-level resource profiles in place to identify runaway SQL statements. This feature is useful in two ways. Within the production environment, it prevents poorly programmed statements from adversely affecting other users. Within the development database, it helps identify poorly programmed statements.

Stored procedures. Remove as many SQL*Forms system (referenced) libraries as possible from the *.INP* files and insert them directly into the physical database. This feature reduces network traffic and immediately improves overall application performance.

One particular Version 7 feature is not easy to implement right away: declarative data integrity. If your application is complete, or almost complete, when you convert to Version 7, you may decide that taking advantage of the declarative data integrity feature is not worth the effort of applying this feature to your data retrospectively. For example, if most of your user interface screens have already been developed with business and integrity rules enforced for them, you'll basically be replicating your data editing efforts when adding integrity constraints. You'll have to decide if this effort is worth it.

For some applications, the benefits offered by the new integrity constraints do outweigh the cost of having to reenter all of these constraints. For example, for character mode applications that use SQL*Forms as the main user interface to the database, declarative data constraints are a blessing in disguise. Often, integrity checks are validated only at the time of user input (via POST-CHANGE, POST-FIELD, ON-VALIDATE-FIELD, KEY-NXTFLD, etc., triggers), not at the time the record is committed. From the operator's view, this situation is more palatable, because each relevant error message is displayed only when a violation occurs. But this approach is not an altogether sound one. During the period between initial data entry/validation and record commit, many things can change in your database. For example, other processes can delete foreign keys out from under you, resulting in the addition of invalid or corrupted foreign key references. Validation really ought to be done again at commit time.

Although executing field validation information again (to take advantage of the declarative data integrity feature) is repetitive, it offers a fail-safe feature in cases like this one where validation has not been performed at commit time.

ORACLE7 Conversion Anomalies

One of the most annoying things associated with a software upgrade is discovering that existing features have been dropped or changed in small ways, or that they suddenly don't work at all. Usually, such occurrences aren't bugs in the new version but the consequences of features that never actually worked correctly or completely in the previous release. In the following list we mention some of the small annoyances we've noted in Version 7. This is not an exhaustive list, but simply a personal compilation. We would be very grateful if readers could let us know what anomalies they find in Version

7 as well, so we can expand this list in the next edition of this book, and help other readers avoid pitfalls in the new release.

MAXEXTENTS limit. Under Version 7, when you created an object, you could specify as large a value for MAXEXTENTS as you wished. When we created SQL statements under Version 6, we typically set the default MAXEXTENTS to 999999 and then decreased this value as required for particular object definitions. All of our Version 7 automatic table generations now fail. Why?

In Version 6, there was an implicit physical limit: the size of an ORACLE block. Therefore, a database with 2K ORACLE blocks would be limited to 121 extents per object; a database with 4K blocks would be limited to 249 extents per object. With Version 7, this physical limit has turned into a logical limit. You must specify a value for MAXEXTENTS that is within the valid range for your block size.

VARCHAR2. To conform to ANSI standards, ORACLE has modified the storage type for character fields. In Version 6, alphanumeric columns contained in tables are defined and displayed as CHAR. However, within the ORACLE7 data dictionary, they are actually held as type VARCHAR2. If you are comparing the application data dictionary and ORACLE's physical dictionary for object definition discrepancies, you will see that every alphanumeric column is reported as different.

VALIDATE INDEX. In Version 7, the VALIDATE INDEX command has been replaced with the ANALYZE command (along with a number of new features offered by ANALYZE, as described in the section in Chapter 13 called "Chained Blocks").

GRANT RESOURCE. In Version 7, the GRANT RESOURCE command is no longer supported. In Version 6, you could specify a GRANT RESOURCE command in the form:

```
GRANT RESOURCE (10 M) ON TS_DATE TO OP$SMITH;
```

In Version 7, you can achieve the same result by specifying:

```
ALTER USER OPS$SMITH QUOTA 10 M ON TS_DATE
```

SQL*DBA database startup. In Version 7, the DBA must be connected to the database before he or she can issue the STARTUP command. In Version 6, the database could be started without being connected. In Version 6 you simply type:

```
SQLDBA STARTUP
```

In Version 7, automatically loading the RDBMS via a machine bootup routine is not quite so simple. You will need to write a special startup script and issue the following command:

```
SQLDBA @ . . . \ . . . \STARTUP.SQL
```

where STARTUP.SQL contains the commands:

```
1>  CONNECT INTERNAL
2>  STARTUP
```

OPS$ usercodes. In Version 7, you can specify a new INIT.ORA parameter that allows sites to choose their own operating system usercode prefixes. For example, you can specify:

```
OS_AUTHENT_PREFIX = OPS$
```

The default is OS_AUTHEN_PREFIX = OPS$ (the Version 6 alternative). The problem with this feature is that it means Version 7 databases can no longer recognize an OS usercode by its prefix. To get around this problem, you must create all OS usercodes as:

```
CREATE USER OPS$SMITH IDENTIFIED EXTERNALLY;
```

In this way (not including a password), Version 7 realizes that the usercode is actually an OS connection user. This is something of a nuisance in applications in which the DBA created all users with the same (secret) password—a password the users did not know about. By logging in as any application user, the DBA could trace the steps a user performed when he or she encountered a problem with the database. Because users are not created with particular passwords in Version 7 (just with the EXTERNALLY clause), this DBA trick is no longer possible.

Remote database access via OPS$. Because of the dangers associated with using default operating system connections (e.g., OPS$SMITH) across client-server and distributed databases, you no longer can use remote database access via OPS$ usercodes by default. It is still possible to use this feature, though, if you set the INIT.ORA parameter, REMOTE_OS_AUTHENT, to TRUE.

Remote database links. Version 7 extends the database naming options to include a database domain. You can specify this domain in the INIT.ORA parameter, DB_DOMAIN. It helps to generate unique database references across large networks. Your database link definitions will have this name suffixed to it, as in:

```
CREATE [PUBLIC] DATABASE LINK PRD . . .
```

where the link name is actually stored as PRD.*domain* (where *domain* is the value of DB_DOMAIN). Earlier releases of Version 7 had problems communicating with Version 6 databases via these extended database links. ORACLE provides a work-around for this problem by disabling database naming. You can do this by setting the INIT.ORA parameter, GLOBAL_NAMES, to FALSE.

B

Hot Tuning Tips

This appendix contains the performance questions we are asked most frequently, along with brief answers and pointers to other sections in the book where you can get more information. (If no specific section reference is given, skim the whole chapter for information in this area.) The appendix is divided by role: planners and managers; designers and analysts; programmers; database administrators; and system administrators. In a few cases, the same question is asked from the perspective of several different roles because the advice for each role may be somewhat different.

Questions from Planners and Managers

Manager: Our organization's computer staff has asked for a larger computer. How can I be sure that there really is a need for a larger machine?

This is a commonly asked question and a very sensible one. If you buy too large a configuration, it will cost your organization many millions of dollars. If you buy too small a configuration, it may severely disrupt your organization's day-to-day workload. Make sure your computer staff is able to answer these questions before you seriously consider buying a larger computer:

- **Has your application been completely tuned in single-user mode? Is every response time within the standard specified in your service agreement?** There can be no exceptions to the rule. Do not proceed past this point until your application is totally tuned!

- What is your average amount of memory per user, the expected disk I/Os per user, and the average CPU MIPS per user in the current configuration? You must know what you are using now before you can assess statistics for any new equipment or applications you'll be considering.

- What is the expected growth rate in users at your site? You'll usually need to plan for growth, but in some organizations the number of users will actually be expected to drop over time. Make sure you have correct projections for your own organization.

- What resources are causing the most performance problems in your system? Is the machine short of memory? Is it experiencing CPU wait times? Is it I/O bound? Is it experiencing network bottlenecks? Make sure you get solid answers from your DBA and system administrator.

References: Chapter 17, *Performing Capacity Planning*

Manager: What size machine do I need?

One of the advantages of ORACLE is that applications can be developed on a small computer and run in production on a much larger computer. After you have cost-justified a computer purchase, seek information from other sites that are running similar sizes and types of applications. This is particularly necessary when you are buying a package written in ORACLE. When you are ready to buy a computer for an application you have developed in-house, you can get a more accurate idea of how big a configuration you need by running some of the programs on the type of computer you are thinking of buying. It is essential that individual programs be tuned prior to the test.

Ideally, collect statistics on the average I/O, CPU MIPS, memory usage, and network usage per user. Combine this information with the expected number of users and make some allowance for unanticipated activity on the system (perhaps 15%). This will give you a reasonably accurate formula for a realistic configuration.

References: Chapter 17, *Performing Capacity Planning*

Manager: My production users keep complaining that response times are poor. My computer staff denies it. Is there a way in ORACLE to determine response times from an end-user perspective?

Your computer staff will provide you with all types of performance figures, but they will probably be disjointed, for example, the time taken for the SQL statement against the database, the network response times for a predefined request. Production users are sometimes prone to overreact to response time problems, particularly when a system is slow. You need a means of having an independent function log into the application and run as a production user would run.

The online forms programming tool, SQL*Forms, provides a function that allows the recording of keystrokes to simulate an interactive online user. Some sites use this facility effectively to record response time variations. It may also provide proof that response times are within the requirements specified in your organization's tuning service agreement. It works like this: You record the time of day just prior to running the recorded function; then, you run various inquiry forms using the recorded keystrokes; finally, after exiting the programs you again record the time of day. If your site is running a client-server configuration, make sure you run the same script from the various client machines. This is necessary because of the possible variable response times that may exist at the various client machines. The limitation of this approach is that only a subset of the functions can be performed.

References: ORACLE's SQL*Forms manuals

Manager: How can I increase the chances that my application will perform well?

Like any other construction, if sound foundations are not in place for ORACLE applications, the construction is doomed to failure. Here is a summary list of key performance hints that will help you plan and manage your ORACLE system to get the best performance out of it.

- If possible, make sure your development staff consists of people who have worked on highly-tuned ORACLE applications in the past. There is no substitute for experience.

- Identify and correct potential problems early in the development life cycle. If poor decisions are made during analysis and design, fixing the problem later on will take a lot longer and cost a lot more money.

- Make sure you have solid standards (for software selection, version control, modular programming, system libraries, and other such topics) in place at all stages of the development life cycle.

- Put in place a tuning service agreement that includes strict response time requirements. If you are buying a canned package, make sure that package also meets your standards for response time.

- Do not allow developers and quality assurers to work on the same machine as production users.

- Remember that, like one bad apple in the barrel, one ORACLE program, or even one SQL statement, that performs very poorly has the potential to degrade the performance of all of the functions in the system. Worse still, if you put an untuned application on a machine that was previously running tuned applications, the untuned application will degrade the performance of all of the applications on the machine.

- Make sure that programs are developed and maintained in a modular fashion. This will decrease development time and memory requirements, and it will make the application easier to maintain.

- Make sure to log inactive users off the system after a specified period of time. Also, monitor those users who repeatedly log on two or three times, making sure there is a genuine need for their behavior.

- Code applications to best suit the particular configuration you are running. For example, make sure that your staff members are aware of the additional coding considerations for tuning client-server.

- Do not allow users to submit untuned ad hoc queries that will compete with online transaction processing users on your system. Set up a procedure to review and tune all such ad hoc queries before they are run.

- Don't size your configuration too small; this may cause organization-wide poor response if an unanticipated workload appears on your machine.

- Check with other sites for their experiences with configurations similar to the one your site intends to use.

References: Chapter 1, *Introduction to ORACLE Performance Tuning*
               Chapter 2, *What Causes Performance Problems*
               Chapter 3, *Planning and Managing the Tuning Process*
               Chapter 4, *Defining System Standards*
               Chapter 16, *Tuning in the Client-server Environment*
                   "What is Client-server?"
                   "Client-server Performance Issues"

Manager: Does ORACLE Version 7 offer any performance advantages over Version 6?

When ORACLE Version 6 was introduced, users found that the new version offered tremendous improvements in performance. Version 7 offers even better performance, as well as many tools that allow you to tune your system still further. Version 6 put a lot of tuning responsibility in the hands of the programmer; Version 7 extends the ability of the DBA to tune the database for performance. With both Version 6 and Version 7, the ability of the data model to perform is still a crucial step in development and is key to performance.

The most remarkable improvements in Version 7 performance are at sites where programmers did not know how to optimize their programs for performance. This is because the cost-based optimizer available in Version 7 relieves much of the burden on the programmer to figure out how SQL statements can best access the database.

Version 7 also greatly improves performance in client-server environments. When combined with SQL*Net Version 2.0, Version 7 substantially reduces the number of packets that need to be transferred across the network, which results in a corresponding increase in performance.

Here is a summary of the major new Version 7 features that have an impact on performance:

Cost-based optimizer. In Version 6, a rule-based optimizer applies a predefined set of rules, precedence operations, and indexes to figure out the most efficient execution plan, or retrieval path. This path is the set of physical steps needed to access the database for a retrieval or update. In Version 7, a more sophisticated and intelligent optimizer looks at statistics collected about the characteristics of your actual data, and makes a decision based on the comparative costs of alternative access paths. As we mentioned above, use of the cost-based optimizer significantly improves performance, especially for untuned SQL statements. As discussed in Chapter 7, *Tuning SQL*, you may still need to do some manual tuning of complex statements.

Shared SQL area. In Version 6, all individual user processes have individual areas. In Version 7, there is a SQL area that can be shared by users. In addition to using less memory, the shared SQL area may use less CPU because statements need to be parsed only once if they remain in the shared area.

Multi-threaded server. This server lessens the burden each user system process places on the ORACLE system. The server creates less system overhead, increases the maximum user connections possible for a given configuration, and automates load balancing.

Hash clusters. Up until now, hash clusters have been available only to high-performance hierarchical databases. They provide very fast access to data by performing a computation on the key field(s) of a table to obtain an address to access the desired location in the database directly.

Rollback size adjustment. Rollback size can now be adjusted without having to shut down the database. By allowing larger rollback segments to be created for overnight processing, this feature has the effect of speeding up large update operations. An optimal SIZE clause allows a rollback segment to shrink back to its original size, enabling the DBA to control more closely the space in the database.

TRUNCATE command. This command allows all rows to be deleted from a table significantly faster than with the Version 6 DELETE command. The command is equivalent to dropping and recreating a table.

Database integrity constraints. These constraints can now be stored in the database. Because integrity checking code no longer needs to be included in programs, this reduces the size of programs and the amount of memory required per program. It also reduces network traffic. Because all checks are stored within the database and can be performed within one database visit, fewer packets need to be transferred between the client and the server machine. Integrity checks are also optimized because they are performed only when the column is modified.

Stored procedures, functions, and packages. These are simply a collection of PL/SQL and SQL statements that are stored as a single compiled unit within the actual database. Having them available in the database means fewer database calls across the network. All procedures and functions are stored in a parsed form and are shared among users, thus reducing the size of the programs and their memory requirements. The SQL is shared, regardless of which interface package is being used to access it.

Resource profile limits. These limits prevent user processes from running away with system resources and inhibiting the response times of other users. The major limitations that can be applied are concurrent sessions per username, maximum CPU per session, maximum CPU per SQL call, maximum continuous connect time per session, maximum idle time before a user is disconnected, maximum database blocks read per session and per database call, and maximum size of the private SGA.

Distributed database. Version 6 provides a distributed query feature that allows you to retrieve data that is distributed on various machines. In Version 7, you can update that data as well, via a two-phase commit function. This facility can bolster performance when the majority of local data is required locally and there is a need to reduce network traffic.

Table replication or snapshots. These allow read-only copies of single tables, subsets of tables, or complex query joins. The copies have the potential to provide a source for GUI and ad hoc reporting users. Snapshots can improve performance by reducing the amount of network traffic because they maintain these tables at the database end for all changes made.

References: Appendix A, *Planning for Version 7*

Questions from Analysts and Designers

Designer: I have problems making overnight jobs perform. Are there ways I can improve their responsiveness?

From a design perspective there are many ways to improve the responsiveness of overnight jobs. This book assumes that the design specification is detailed enough to determine the language used in development and a pseudo-English description of what each statement should do. The designer will also have a large say in the physical tables used by the programs. Overnight jobs normally include data loads to and from other applications as well as overnight reports. The following checklist summarizes special considerations for the design of overnight jobs:

- If you are transferring data from an application, make sure each table that is to have data taken from it has a column that stores the date modified. This will make it more efficient to transfer the day's changes using an index on the date-modified column.

- If data load tables have to be created for any temporary tables, make sure the table and any indexes created on the table are correctly sized. Create the indexes after the rows have been placed into the tables. Following this advice causes your application to run significantly faster. It is also much faster to drop and recreate tables instead of deleting from a table.

- Be aware that PL/SQL offers advantages in performing updates.

- Make sure there aren't multiple UPDATE statements against the same table. There are ways of updating many columns with a single statement.

- If data is being transferred into an application and the application being transferred from is also an ORACLE system, don't join tables or perform MINUS operations across the network. Transfer data into this application and do all joins and MINUS operations from within the a single database.

- Do not use NOT IN in your programs. Use NOT EXISTS instead.

- Create an extract file or a number of extract files for overnight reports. These extract files can then be used by all of the reports, instead of requiring each individual report to traverse through many tables in the database over and over again. Make sure that the extract tables are correctly sized.

- Be aware of the power and speed of the MINUS command when you are performing audit checks of tables that store running totals against tables storing individual transactions (e.g., financial year totals for a region against individual transactions for a region).

References: Chapter 15, *Tuning Long-running Jobs*

Designer: A request has been made for users at my site to be able to run reports during peak usage times. Benchmarks have shown that they will run too long and adversely affect the interactive users. What can be done?

To achieve acceptable response times for reports run during prime production times, consider the following:

- You may need to provide redundancy, particularly to store running totals.

- If the users will run several reports against the same set of data, create a temporary extract table for the users' selection criteria; this table can then be reused for subsequent reports. Doing this avoids the expensive task of traversing repeatedly through many database tables.

- If the data as of last night is satisfactory for any reports, product a set of multi-indexed redundant tables and run the reports against them. Ideally there should be no more than three extract files.

- Make sure that each report has been extensively tuned in the development and quality assurance environments before it is placed into production. An untuned report will have a very damaging effect on a site's response times.

- If any reports run for longer than two minutes, ask the question: Must this report be run during prime usage times? Ideally, no online report should run for longer than 45 seconds. This often appears out of reach, but given sufficient effort, redundant storage of data can usually help you meet this goal.

References: Chapter 5, *Designing Your Data Model For Performance*
                "Denormalizing a Database"
                Chapter 15, *Tuning Long-running Jobs*
                "Creating Overnight Extract Tables"

Designer: Our database is fully normalized but response times are bad. How can this be?

A fully normalized database is usually not able to provide satisfactory performance for complex queries within an application. You might need to consider denormalizing some of the data. Don't denormalize just for the sake of doing so. A good designer knows what the requirements of the data model are, and what future user requirements of the user will be. If you are considering denormalizing, first make sure your data model is fully normalized. Then, check each step to see if the system resource to maintain the redundancy outweighs the improved query speed benefits achieved by storing the redundant data. Situations that are candidates for denormalization is listed below:

- A fixed number of children, for example, 12 months of the year.

- The most recent data in a parent, for example, the last date a transaction was made against an account.

- Static data such as MALE or FEMALE; you can hard-code such data.

- Running totals, such as financial year totals for a given account.

- Reference (domain lookup) tables; you can combine these into one domain table.

Some relational theory dictates that surrogate keys must be created for all tables in case the natural key fields are required to be changed. If carried to its logical conclusion, this theory also dictates that the surrogate key will be transferred to all child tables. The problem is that most queries are made using natural keys rather than surrogate keys. If the natural keys are not likely to change, or rarely change, the natural keys should be transferred to all child tables.

Keys should be stored below the immediate child of the owning table to the child of the child in any case; for example, the account ID may be transferred to the transaction and the transaction description table.

References: Chapter 5, *Designing Your Data Model For Performance*
                  Chapter 6, *Defining Indexes*

Designer: I don't have experience with a relational database. The programmers, who are very experienced with ORACLE, keep telling me my data model is not suited to a relational database and performance will suffer. How can I check this?

If the data model you have created is perfectly normalized, there is a possibility that you may need to perform some denormalization to achieve acceptable performance. This is not unique to relational databases. Even high-speed hierarchical databases like IMS are full of redundancy.

It is important that the designer listens to the programmers for their reasoning on why response times may be caused by the data model. It is also important that the programmers are given the opportunity to provide feedback. The earlier these types of problems are determined, the better. If they are not found early, a lot of code may have to be reworked after the data model is changed.

Program reviews are essential to ensuring that the data model is adequate. They should be attended by the designer, the programmer who will write the program, and the DBA. Performance is one of the aspects that should be included in the review.

Here is one rule of thumb: if the programmer has to join more than five tables for any one query in an interactive program, there is a good chance that the data model is inadequate. This is often caused by the over-use of surrogate keys, while database searches are made by natural keys.

References: Chapter 5, *Designing Your Data Model For Performance*
                  Chapter 6, *Defining Indexes*

Designer: When and what do I index? How many indexes should I have on each table, and how do I know when I have too many indexes?

Some sites have rigid rules for the maximum number of indexes per table (usually five or six). Such a rule should be taken as a guideline, not as an absolute. If a table is not very volatile, there may need to be many more than six indexes on a table required to satisfy all search criteria.

The bottom line is that your response times must be within those specified within the tuning service agreement for your organization. If a seventh index is added to a table and causes a response time reduction from 45 seconds to one second, and the modifications to the table have their response times increase from two seconds to 2.5 seconds, the users are likely to be happy to have the seventh index added.

Redundant extract tables are often created overnight for use by overnight reports and GUI users. These tables tend to contain many columns and are often accessed from many different angles. There is nothing wrong with having many indexes on these types of tables, because they will not be modified after their creation.

References: Chapter 6, *Defining Indexes*

Designer: When it is a good time not to index?

In general, don't apply an index in the following circumstances:

- If the columns in the index already apply on the same columns in the same order; for example, if ACCOUNT NAME & ACCOUNT CATEGORY is a concatenated index already existing, an index in ACCOUNT NAME is a superfluous index.

- When a table is better accessed using full-table scans, because every time the table is queried more than 15% of the rows are returned.

- When columns are very long; indexes on long columns are not allowed and should not be contemplated.

- When it may speed up one program at the expense of slowing down several other programs. It is a good time not to index until this type of problem is fully resolved.

References: Chapter 6, *Defining Indexes*

Designer: How far should I denormalize?

You should not denormalize any more than is required to meet the response times specified by your site's service agreement. An astute designer will be aware of the parts of the data model that are likely to result in unsatisfactory performance. There are no hard and fast rules that can be followed. Judge each data model on its own merits.

Suppose that an inquiry screen is intended to display financial year running totals for an account from a financial transaction table. The maximum number of transactions that any account may have is 300. You'll need to perform 300 reads from the index, plus an additional 300 from the table, totaling 600 physical reads. Assume your site has a mini-computer that is able to perform 50 I/Os per second; 600 physical reads will take twelve seconds. This is a case in which specifying a redundant table that stores an account's financial year totals could greatly improve performance.

Of course, there are other considerations, such as how many rows are stored in the buffer cache. All the same, the type of calculation we've done above does give an early warning that a redundant table might be required.

References: Chapter 5, *Designing Your Data Model For Performance*

Designer: Is it preferable to have a few large programs in an application or many smaller programs?

The ideal way to develop an ORACLE application is in a modular fashion. Code each function of the application (e.g., maintain account details) once in a separate form; do not repeat the same function many times. For example, don't include account detail updating functionality inside many forms. Users may sometimes dictate that such specific modularization is not the way they would like to use the system, so you may have to balance different needs. There are ways to call modules to provide all combinations of functionality requirements.

Keep your online programs small and concise, and make sure each performs a specific function. This approach will save development time because the same code will not have to be recoded over and over. It will also make the system more maintainable. From a performance perspective, smaller forms use less memory, thus making more memory available to add additional users or increase the size of tunable parameters such as the block buffer or the log buffer. This helps improve the overall responsiveness of the system.

References: Chapter 4, *Defining System Standards*

Designer: Our managers are very keen on taking advantage of the GUI interfaces that are able to access the ORACLE production database on an ad hoc basis. What design issues should I consider?

The number of ad hoc GUI users accessing ORACLE database is expected to grow significantly during the 1990s. It is important that you design the data model to cope with growth in this area. Ad hoc GUI users tend to want to retrieve data from the data model as quickly as possible, without having to understand the intricacies of a complex data model. The ideal way to present data to this type of user is usually in the form of a wide, denormalized table resembling a spreadsheet.

The best time to create this type of table is overnight. However, if this is unsuitable to the users at your site, you could create it in a fashion similar to the online reporting users described earlier. Consider the following:

- You may need additional redundancy, particularly to store running totals.

- If users will require several extracts against the same set of data, create a redundant spreadsheet table using the user's selection criteria, and then reuse it for subsequent GUI downloads. This avoids the expensive task of traversing through many database tables.

- Tune each type of extract extensively in the development and quality assurance environments prior to being allowed into production. An untuned extract will have a very damaging effect on a site's response times.

- If any extract runs for longer than two minutes, ask the question: Must this extract be run during prime usage times? Ideally, no online extract should run for longer than 45 seconds. This goal may seem out of reach, but if you try hard enough to implement redundant storage of data, you can usually achieve response times within this limit.

References: Chapter 5, *Designing Your Data Model For Performance*
                 "Denormalizing Your Database"
                 Chapter 15, *Tuning Long-running Jobs*
                 "Creating Overnight Extract Tables"

Questions from Programmers

Programmer: How do I structure a SQL statement for performance?

There are many factors to consider when structuring a statement for performance. You must understand the ORACLE optimizer, the benefit of indexes and how they are best used, the effect of positioning table names in the FROM clause, and the order of the conditions in the WHERE clause. Pay attention to this checklist:

- Be sure to tune SQL statements thoroughly to return data in the least amount of time.

- Use a WHERE clause if at all possible to assist with index usage. For example:

```
SELECT . . .
   FROM DEPT WHERE EMP_NO > 0
```

will use an index, with EMP_NO as its leading column, and will return rows in EMP_NO order.

- Never do a calculation on an indexed column if you intend to use the index to assist with response times. For example, don't specify:

  ```
  WHERE SALARY * 12 > 50000
  ```

- Never specify IS NULL or IS NOT NULL on index columns.

- If more than 25% of the rows in a table are going to be returned, use a full-table scan rather than an index.

- Avoid using NOT in any WHERE condition.

- Use UNION instead of OR.

- Avoid the use of HAVING; in general, use WHERE predicates instead.

- Minimize the number of times a table is queried and maximize the number of columns updated with a single SQL statement.

- Use table aliases to prefix all column names.

- Use DECODE to minimize the number of times a table has to be selected.

- If two indexes are of equal ranking in the WHERE clause, ORACLE will use the index of the column specified higher in the WHERE clause (i.e., the indexes will be applied top-down). (This applies to Version 6.0.33 and later.)

- If two or more indexes are of equal ranking, you can force a particular index to be used. Concatenate the following characters to the columns whose indexes you *don't* want to use: concatenate a | |" to character columns or a +0 to numeric columns.

- Do not mix data types because it may prevent use of the index, for example, an index won't be used in the following:

  ```
  WHERE EMP_NAME = 123
  ```

- Use joins in preference to subqueries.

- The ordering of the table names in the FROM clause determines the driving table. If you are using the rule-based optimizer, if the clause is ordered correctly it can significantly reduce the number of physical reads required to satisfy the query. ORACLE initially scans and sorts the table specified *last* in the FROM clause using any available indexes. ORACLE then reads the second table, which is positioned *second to last* in the FROM clause and merges its data with the data returned from the table specified last. Therefore, make sure that the table specified last in the FROM clause will return the fewest rows based on its WHERE conditions. This is not always the table that has the fewest rows in it.

References: Chapter 7, *Tuning SQL*

Programmer: How do I tell how much elapsed time each statement uses in an overnight SQL procedure?

It is good practice to run all long-running SQL procedures with the following settings:

SET TIMING ON Shows the elapsed time needed for the SQL statement to complete, in the form **real: 1.2866**

SET TIME ON Shows the time of day next to the SQL prompt; for example:

    17:13:26 SQL>

DOC Provides documentation entered by the programmer to indicate each step run in the procedure; for example:

    17:15:32 DOC>
    17:15:32 DOC> Running the load of the transaction table
    17:15:32 DOC>

Programmer: How do I investigate a problem with a SQL statement?

Assuming that you have identified the particular SQL statement causing the problem, extract it from the program code and investigate it as a single item. SQL statements (non-dynamic) will perform identically, whether they are executed as a single unit or contained within a complex routine.

You will need to isolate all bind variables and replace them within the statement with their corresponding constant values. SQL*Plus is the best utility to begin using for statement investigation. Set statement timing on and repetitively execute the statement to check that it is actually slow. Many statements you originally think are slow actually turn out to be part of slow programs or the result of slowness in other SQL statements.

Enable SQL_TRACE to identify which indexes (if any) are being used. Before you proceed, make sure you know all available indexes and have an idea of all desirable indexes. Use TKPROF to interpret the trace output.

The actual execution plan of a single SQL statement can be detailed via the EXPLAIN PLAN utility. This utility not only indicates which indexes are being used, but also shows the sequence of the index execution and the internal data sorts and sort/merges that are performed.

Never be afraid to experiment. Every statement has many, many alternatives. Only one alternative can possibly be the most efficient. Try all the alternatives. Replace NOT IN clauses with NOT EXISTS clauses. Try using table joins rather than subqueries. Always break statements down to their lowest levels. Extract each subquery or UNION portion from the statement and test it on its own.

You should also identify data volumes via SQL*Plus. A statement may, in fact, be efficient, but may be acting over many thousands of records. If this is the case, you will need to revisit the application program and possibly redesign it. Try to break down the functionality into smaller actions. Use of array processing can improve SQL using large volumes of data.

Investigate any SQL statement using an ORDER BY, a GROUP BY, or a HAVING to make sure that the grouping or ordering is actually required. Many statements consume large amounts of system resources performing unnecessary table sorting, not realizing that the rows can be returned in the desired sequence via an index.

Be careful of type casting problems. Index paths will be used when testing SQL statements with constants, but may not be used when a bind variable is of an incorrect type.

After you have tuned an individual statement, replace the new SQL back into the originating routine and test for the problem again. Remember too that badly performing SQL can also be due to locking contention.

References:	Chapter 7, *Tuning SQL*
	Chapter 8, *Tuning PL/SQL*
	Chapter 9, *Tuning SQL*Forms*
	Chapter 10, *Selecting A Locking Strategy*
	Chapter 12, *Diagnostic and Tuning Tools*
	Chapter 16, *Tuning in the Client-server Environment*

*Programmer: Some of my lists of values in SQL*Forms program take forever despite the fact that the function has an index. Why?*

The default list of values functionality of SQL*Forms does have some dangerous properties. If a small number of rows (less than about 250) exist in the table or are or selected via the list of values WHERE clause the list of values routine is very powerful. It generates a very nice pop-up window from a handful of keystrokes.

However, a list of values routine which selects large (greater than 250) numbers of records is not so attractive. The very nature of the list of values macro is to return (fetch) all eligible rows before the first is displayed. The availability of an index will obviously improve performance, but cannot overcome the time taken to fetch 10,000 rows. This functionality is directly opposite to the way a base table query performs. Base table queries fetch only the number of rows indicated by the ARRAYSIZE option.

Never use a list of values macro for large tables. The only real alternative is to code a SQL*Forms pop-up form to replace the default list of values functionality. This is a common practice, but creates problems when you try to access the pop-up screen when entering query conditions (query mode). Chapter 9, *Tuning SQL*Forms*, describes a special list of values definition that helps you work around this problem.

Be sure to check all list of values functions that have an ORDER BY clause. An ORDER BY clause can accidently cause the records to be sorted before the rows can be returned. This can happen even with the existence of an index.

References: Chapter 7, *Tuning SQL*
                         "Using WHERE Instead of ORDER BY"
                   Chapter 9, *Tuning SQL*Forms*
                         "Tuning The List of Values Function"
                         "Using Unqualified ORDER BY Clauses"

Programmer: My base table query in my SQL*Forms program runs very slowly. What can the problem be?

A poorly performing base table query can devastate an application. Many, many things can cause a base table to execute slowly. Before you do anything else, extract the individual base table SQL statement from the form and tune and test it on its own.

Check the base table ORDER BY clause. Our experiences have shown that nine out of ten times the poor performance of base tables is due to the ORDER BY clause causing an internal sort rather than utilizing the intended index.

If the statement makes use of dynamic SQL, include debug messages to display the field containing the SQL text. The generated SQL is not always what was intended, and may conflict with other parts of the SQL, causing the wrong index to be used.

Execute the form in debug mode (i.e., RUNFORM ... -D) to check what triggers are executing as part of the query. A Post-Query, Post-Change or even a Post-Record trigger may be causing the poor performance. It does not have to be the actual base table query.

Check that the base table query has not been triggered via the command EXECUTE_ QUERY (ALL_RECORDS). This option of the macro causes all the eligible records to be fetched before the first record is displayed.

References: Chapter 7, *Tuning SQL*
                         "Using WHERE Instead of ORDER BY"
                   Chapter 9, *Tuning SQL*Forms*
                         "Tuning Base Tables"
                         "Viewing Dynamic Base Table Queries"
                         "Protecting Against Risky Macros"
                         "Using Unqualified ORDER BY Clauses"

Programmer: Our site has decided to go with Version 7. Can our SQL*Forms Version 3 application run under Version 7? What changes are recommended to improve performance?

From our experiences, all applications developed using SQL*Forms Version 3 for RDBMS Version 6 will execute as intended when run against RDBMS Version 7. This includes user exits, SQL*Plus scripts, SQL*Reportwriter programs, and Pro*C programs. Existing applications do not need to be modified when the database is upgraded. A Version 6 database can also access a Version 7 database via SQL*Net Version 1 without modification.

New versions of the tools have been released to support Version 7 functionality. This allows RUNFORM to access stored procedures and triggers, truncate tables etc. Existing Version 6 applications will also function normally when utilizing these upgraded executables. This permits new functionality to be introduced gradually into an existing application as time permits.

If application tools are upgraded, (i.e., SQL*Forms Version 4 etc.), the application programs will need to be revisited.

Performance improvements available from RDBMS Version 7 that can be immediately introduced include the following:

Shared SQL area	This feature is available and is used by default.
Multiplexed redo logs	Disperse redo logs across differing physical disks.
TRUNCATE table	Truncate table data when deleting all rows.
Resource profiles	Set up resource profiles to detect and prevent long-running jobs from running wild. You can abort sleeping "bombshell" SQL before the statement takes over the machine.
Stored procedures	Create stored procedures and triggers to replace existing PL/SQL libraries.
References:	Chapter 9, *Tuning SQL*Forms* Appendix A, *Planning for Version 7*

Programmer: Sometimes my SQL*Forms base table query runs fast; other times it runs slowly. How can this be?

Many SQL statements appear to work efficiently. When you investigate them using TKPROF and EXPLAIN PLAN, you find that the statement is executing as intended. So why do statements sometimes run slowly?

The first place to begin is to check what other jobs are running at the time the SQL is performing badly. The problem could actually be some other process, completely unrelated. When an ORACLE task needs a resource, it simply takes it! However, if the machine is not CPU- and/or I/O-bound then this is not the problem.

Check the Monitor Locks display to see if another process has any resources locked, required by the waiting SQL process.

The most common reason for this problem is the uneven data spread of the table. Indexes are worth their weight in gold if they limit the number of records needed to be searched. Suppose the EMP table has an EMP_STATUS field which records an employee's employment status (Active or Resigned). When querying all "active" employees, the SQL must process 25,000 rows. When querying "resigned" employees, the SQL has only 250 rows to process. This problem is magnified when the offending SQL also has an ORDER BY clause. Sorting 20 records can be performed in memory (within the buffer allocated by the SORT_AREA_SIZE parameter), but enormous sorts must write temporary segments to the temporary tablespace. If this situation begins to cause a real problem, try to make your indexes more precise.

References: Chapter 7, *Tuning SQL*
                Chapter 9, *Tuning SQL*Forms*
                    "Tuning Base Tables"
                Chapter 10, *Selecting a Locking Strategy*

Programmer: Is it possible to perform dynamic queries against the database?

Dynamic SQL is a very powerful programming facility. Dynamic SQL statements can be individually shaped to suit individual situations. Each SQL statement can be formed to utilize the best possible indexes, removing repetitive AND/OR conditions not always required at all times.

All Pro* tools, ORACLE Call Interface (OCI), and SQL*Plus facilities support dynamic SQL, some better than others. SQL*Forms indirectly allows dynamic SQL. Only the base table query has the ability to use dynamic SQL. You can achieve enormous resource savings by using dynamic SQL. The WHERE clause can be altered. Even the ORDER BY clause can be added or altered. Dynamic SQL does increase the complexity of forms development and maintenance.

References: Chapter 9, *Tuning SQL*Forms*
                    "Performing Pseudo-Dynamic Base Table Queries"

Programmer: The form ran well in the test environment but is giving poor response in production. How is this happening?

Many things can cause this situation and you must investigate all of them. The most common problems are listed below.

- Indexes available within the development environment have not been generated or are different from the production environment. Extra indexes can even alter the performance of a SQL statement. The driving index is governed by the optimizer ranking, but may not always be the best choice.

- Data volume variances between the two environments is always an area of concern. The development database has only a few hundred records per table. What was supposed to be a tuned, efficient program may turn out to have never been tuned. When applied against production data volumes, response times begin to reflect the inadequacy of the development environment.

- Table and row locking contention always affect application performance. Most often during the development life cycle, programs are developed and tuned as stand-alone modules. When they are executed as part of the entire application, locking practices begin to conflict and damage response times.

- Poor response times can actually be due to a poorly tuned or configured production environment. The production machine may actually have memory shortages, disk I/O overloads, or abnormally high swapping. Prior to the migration of the last program, the machine was coping acceptably. One more program could actually have sent it over the limit.

- Different environment configurations can produce surprising results. Just because both environments are using ORACLE does not mean they will perform identically. If the target environment is a client-server environment, do not use a unitary development machine. If the physical distance between the two machines (client and server) is many hundreds of miles apart, allow for this during the development cycle.

References: Chapter 7, *Tuning SQL*
                    "Using Indexes to Improve Performance"
               Chapter 10, *Selecting a Locking Strategy*
               Chapter 16, *Tuning in the Client-server Environment*

Programmer: I am fine-tuning a form using TKPROF. I have noticed that the number of fetches on the tables is consistently twice the number of rows fetched. Why is this so?

The reason for this problem is very straightforward. Every time the ORACLE RDBMS performs a SELECT operation, it must execute a second database fetch to ascertain if any more rows exist. If another row is located, an ORACLE error is raised. The functionality is necessary to conform to ANSI standards.

It is easy to avoid this overhead. Use explicit cursors; you do this by specifying DECLARE, OPEN, FETCH, and CLOSE for all SELECT cursors. Do not use implicit, inline SELECT statements.

References: Chapter 8, *Tuning PL/SQL*
                   "Using Explicit and Implicit Cursors in PL/SQL"

Programmer: How can I find out what indexes exist in a particular environment?

Environment indexes are vital to the performance of an application. Be sure to document all indexes extensively and distribute them to your development staff. To review which indexes currently exist, use the ORACLE views USER_IND_COLUMNS and USER_INDEXES. See Chapter 17 for an example of the actual SELECT statement you use to query (join) these tables.

References: Chapter 17, *Performing Capacity Planning*
                   "Step 2: Structuring the Database and SGA"

Programmer: We are converting from a large non-ORACLE application to an ORACLE application. Loading the data into the new system takes four days. How can I reduce this time lag?

Most data take-on tasks are performed via SQL*Loader. This utility is very fast and very effective. To speed up load times, increase the ROWS parameter to as large a value as possible. This parameter in effect increases the ARRAYSIZE or number of rows inserted per commit.

You can also achieve overall improvements by executing many simultaneous loads, provided that the loaded tables reside on different disks. Source data and the target database should also be positioned on different disks.

Do not load data into tables with prebuilt indexes. Generate indexes after the table is fully populated. Do not perform data loads over the network. If you are utilizing client-server architecture, perform all loads as a process on the database machine. If you are loading data into a Version 7 database, ensure that all referential integrity constraints and table triggers have been disabled.

References: Chapter 16, *Tuning in the Client-server Environment*
                   "Tuning ARRAYSIZE"

Programmer: We have trouble getting our overnight reports completed within the required time frame. What can I do?

Many areas of the overnight process can be improved, but programmers often neglect them. So much effort is put into refining online, interactive response times, but many fewer people seem to be concerned if the nightly routine takes two hours or eight hours. However, when overnight processing cannot complete during the overnight and encroaches onto the next day, all application users suffer. Chapter 15 describes the various areas of overnight processing you can tune.

The first areas to address are SORT_AREA_SIZE, the ORACLE buffer cache, temporary tablespace sizing, rollback segment allocation, rollback segment size, SQL array sizes, temporary extract tables, exploiting PL/SQL updating, breaking up the EXPORT, and tuning the EXPORT.

References: Chapter 15, *Tuning Long-running Jobs*

Programmer: My SQL is running very slowly. How can I tell if it is using an index?

The easiest way of identifying index usage is via the EXPLAIN PLAN facility. This utility can be run system wide or as part of an individual connect session for a single SQL statement. You can use EXPLAIN PLAN stand-alone through SQL*Plus via the EXPLAIN PLAN verb, or as a command line option of the TKPROF facility.

References: Chapter 12, *Diagnostic and Tuning Tools*
                "SQL_TRACE: Writing a Trace File"
                "TKPROF: Interpreting the TRACE File"
                "EXPLAIN PLAN: Explaining the Optimizer"

Programmer: My database query is using indexes but is still slow. How can this be?

Just because an index is being used does not always mean the statement is efficient. Each index may be only one of many paths into the database. You must investigate if any other (more efficient) index paths exist over the tables in question. What percentage of the table is being read? Would a full-table scan be more efficient? Is the statement a multi-table join? Are the tables and indexes in question fragmented with many extents? Is the overall application memory CPU or I/O bound? Does the index in question have a poor data spread? Is the correct index being used? Is the SQL driving table incorrect? If the SQL statement is a DML statement (UPDATE, INSERT, DELETE), are other processes locking resources that you require? Is your application running over a client-server environment and the statement clogging up network traffic? Is the SORT_AREA_SIZE too small?

One of the most common reasons for this problem is the ORDER BY clause. Even though the index is retrieving rows in the fastest possible manner, an ORDER BY clause can also cause all rows fetched to be sorted before the first can be displayed. If more than 100 records are fetched, the ORDER BY will affect performance. If more than 1000 records are fetched, the ORDER BY will seriously degrade performance.

In summary, you cannot assume that indexes will solve all your problems. Remember that SQL is the backbone of the database, not the indexes. Only by reading and applying all of the advice in this book can you completely answer the question.

References: Chapter 7, *Tuning SQL*
                     "How does The Optimizer Work?"
                     "Selecting the Most Efficient TABLE Sequence"
                     "Selecting the most Efficient WHERE Sequence"
                     "Which is faster: Indexed Retrieval or a Full-table Scan"
                     "Explicitly Disabling an Index"
                     "Using WHERE Instead of ORDER BY"
                     Chapter 15, *Tuning Long-running Jobs*
                     "Improving SORT Performance"
                     "Setting the Array Size"
                     "Creating Overnight Extract Tables"
                     Chapter 16, *Tuning in the Client-server Environment*
                     "Tuning ARRAYSIZE"

Programmer: I have developed a report that uses an index but still takes 45 minutes. An entire table is being reported upon. Can this be sped up?

This problem is common and can take some investigation to solve. Other than addressing the underlying (driving) SQL statements (see the prior question), the most usual approach is to look at the amount of disk I/O and associated head movement that is needed as a result of the non-contiguous sequence in which the rows are read via the index. When large portions of a table are being read, it can be more efficient to perform a full-table scan of the entire table.

References: Chapter 7, *Tuning SQL*
                     "Which is faster: Indexed Retrieval or a Full-table Scan"

Programmer: We had a complex query that was very slow and we replaced it with a view. The view is performing just as slowly. How can this be?

Views can be used to speed up SQL*Forms performance over distant networks under certain circumstances. However, views do not solve general performance problems.

Many programmers (and analysts) mistakenly believe that a view will cure the inadequacies of the underlying application design or of a poorly structured SQL statement. Views are simply shorthand representations of the underlying SQL. They can never be faster than their base SQL, and in fact, incur slightly more overheads. Views are not magical snapshots of complex multi-table joins, nor are they automatically populated extract tables. Views of views will in fact cause even worse statement performance.

If your SQL statement is not performing the way it should, tune the statement; do not hide the poor performance in a database view.

References: Chapter 7, *Tuning SQL*
                   Chapter 16, *Tuning in the Client-server Environment*
                       "SQL*Forms Base Table Views"

Programmer: I have a report that queries a large financial transaction table many times, totaling amounts for different types of transactions. This requires repeatedly reading through the table. Is there a better way?

This problem is a common one and can be handled in a number of ways. Pay the most attention to your individual SQL statement(s). Assuming that the SQL has been tuned, what else can be done? A report should never have to traverse the same table more than once. Make use of the DECODE verb to satisfy many selection criteria in a single table access. Depending on the reporting tool, you may also be able to use array processing (by setting ARRAYSIZE) to reduce network and database traffic.

Fetch only records of interest. Let the database do the work (via the various WHERE clauses), not the report logic! If the report is fetching a large percentage of the table rows, also investigate whether you might be able to disable table indexes altogether and use a full-table scan. This will reduce I/O overheads and may improve overall performance.

References: Chapter 7, *Tuning SQL*
                       "Using DECODE"

Programmer: A large table update is taking too long. How can I speed it up?

Most programmers prefer to perform updates via one or more simple UPDATE statements. Even though this may be more attractive to code and clearer to read, the overall effect can be less efficient. If UPDATEs incorporate more than one subquery clause over the same table, they can often be combined into one subquery, reducing extensive I/O. This feature is commonly overlooked by many inexperienced programmers.

If you have larger updates, make use of array processing (ARRAYSIZE) whenever possible. This reduces overall network and database overheads.

PL/SQL is another powerful way to improve large UPDATE statement performance. Again, if the statement has a subquery clause, you can make improvements by setting up an outer driving loop (i.e., LOOP ... END LOOP) and performing the actual update multiple times inside the loop.

Large update routines should also consider locking strategies. These updates will prevent other processes from updating the same information. If you have processes that run for many minutes or more over core application tables during the day, you should consider batching the update into smaller, less restrictive units.

References: Chapter 10, *Selecting a Locking Strategy*
                            "Using Pseudo-code to Lock Large Tables"
                     Chapter 15, *Tuning Long-running Jobs*
                            "Setting the Array Size"
                            "Using PL/SQL to Speed up Updates"
                            "Minimizing the Number of Updates"

Programmer: *A large insert into a table is taking too long. How can I speed it up?*

All of the arguments for the previous question (large table updates) also apply to large table inserts. There are also several other ways to improve insert performance.

If possible, drop indexes over the table prior to inserting (importing) the new records and then recreate them afterwards. This will give better overall insert performance.

For Version 7 databases, disable all table integrity rules and stored triggers before loading the data and then re-enable them on completion. All exception violations will be reported via an exception table.

References: Chapter 10, *Selecting a Locking Strategy*
                            "Using Pseudo-code to Lock a Large Table"
                     Chapter 15, *Tuning Long-running Jobs*
                            "Setting the Array Size"
                            "Creating Indexes After Inserts"
                            "Using PL/SQL to Speed up Updates"
                            "Minimizing the Number of Updates"
                     Appendix A, *Planning for Version 7*

Programmer: *One table in our application takes much longer than other tables to query data, despite the fact that the index is very specific. What causes this and how can I speed it up?*

The most common reason for this problem is table and/or index fragmentation. If the table or the index is held in many extents, dispersed over the disk or a number of disks, performance will be affected. Ask your DBA to check your observations.

Other possible reasons for this problem may be row chaining within the table or poor index selectivity. If the indexed columns do not have an even spread over the table, the index can actually reduce performance.

Applications should never have both the table and its associated index(es) located on the same physical disk. This will cause the table to perform slower than other tables when reading via the index path.

You should also alert the system administrator to check the performance of the disk on which the table is located. Possibly, the disk is not as fast as other application disks (not all disks operate at the same speed), or the disk is exceeding its recommended I/O rates due to contention from other poorly tuned applications sharing the same disk.

Another possibility is a faulty disk. Normally, when devices encounter I/O errors, they perform a number of retries before giving up. This could also explain the problem.

References: Chapter 12, *Diagnostic and Tuning Tools*
                  "ANALYZE: Validating and Computing Statistics"
                  "Tuning I/O Spread"
                  "ONEIDXS.sql: Testing an Individual Index"
                  "Identifying Database Extents"
            Chapter 18, *Tuning for Specific Systems*

Programmer: I have the indexed column in the WHERE clause, but the index is not being used. Why?

Indexes can be used only if at least the leading part of the index is referenced within the WHERE clause. Some indexes will actually be omitted from the execution path if other, more precise indexes exist over the same table (i.e., a UNIQUE index will override a non-unique index). If two indexes over a single table are both referenced via range predicates in the WHERE clause only one will be utilized, the other discarded.

The other more common reason is that the programmer has inadvertently incorporated the indexed columns within an SQL function. This could be via a complex DECODE or a simple date conversion macro.

References: Chapter 7, *Tuning SQL*
                  "Combining Indexes"
                  "Explicitly Disabling an Index"
                  "Automatically Suppressing Indexes"
                  "Beware of the WHEREs"

Questions from Database Administrators

DBA: I've just been appointed DBA at my site. I've been told that there are severe performance problems with production users. What do I do?

We have observed that between 80% and 90% of all performance problems are caused by a poor database design or programs that are not coded efficiently. This leaves only 10% to 20% that can be gained by working on the database structure and parameters. If the application is correctly tuned, that 10% to 20% can be significant, however. The following steps will provide a structured path that you can follow to tune your site.

Gather information on any programs that are causing poor response times. Make *no* exceptions to this rule. You must thoroughly tune any poorly responding programs, then place them back into production with the response times rechecked. You must also repair locking problems.

Monitor the response times of users at all sites to establish if the response problems are widespread or are confined to one site. Document information on each site's configuration, including the memory size, MIP rating of the CPU, recommended disk speeds, and network speeds. Also investigate usage patterns on a per-site basis. Do users log onto the system once or many times? What are the peak usage times? How many users are there? What is the typical memory, I/O, CPU, and network usage per user?

Next, investigate the operating system monitor utilities.

If any disks are operating above their recommended I/O levels, is it possible to spread the disk load across other disks? If there is free memory remaining on the machine, disk I/O load can be transferred from the disks to memory. This can be achieved by enlarging the DB_BLOCK_BUFFER area, which will store tables, indexes, clusters, and rollback segments in memory. Dictionary cache (DC_) parameters can store ORACLE dictionary information in memory (Version 6 only). Disk writes can also be reduced by increasing the amount of modified data buffered before writes are made to the redo log files. This is achieved by increasing the LOG_BUFFER parameter. Eliminating database fragmentation and chaining will also improve I/O problems.

If there is a good deal of paging and swapping of processes caused by inadequate memory on the machine, ORACLE's share of memory must be reduced by decreasing the values of the DB_BLOCK_BUFFER, the LOG_BUFFER, and (for Version 6) the dictionary cache (DC_) parameters. It is possible at some sites that these changes can be made without adversely affecting ORACLE's performance. Per-ORACLE user memory usage can also be reduced, by decreasing the SORT_AREA_SIZE and/or the CONTEXT_ AREA and CONTEXT_INCR parameters.

If there are regularly many processes waiting for the CPU, you can sometimes transfer the load from the CPU to disk by reducing the size of the DB_BLOCK_BUFFER parameter. This should provide your site with better overall response. However, it will reduce the likelihood of data being found in memory, and the reduced disk speed may slow down certain transactions.

If the network is causing the bottleneck, try to reduce the number of packets being passed across the network. This may require some recoding of programs. Version 7 offers significant benefits over Version 6 in reducing network traffic. Locating the hardware appropriately (e.g., putting the client and server computers close together) can also improve responsiveness by sending the packets a lesser distance and making higher-speed lines a more cost-effective alternative. The number of packets transferred from the client machine to the user screen is minuscule compared to the large number of packets transferred from the server to the client processors.

Another way to improve responsiveness is to ensure that none of the dictionary cache parameters are too low (for Version 6 only). These parameters store the various components of the ORACLE data dictionary in cache. If they are set too low, the chances of the dictionary item being found in cache are reduced, and a disk I/O may be required to obtain it. Dictionary cache problems can have a significant negative effect on response times.

References: Chapter 3, *Planning and Managing the Tuning Process*
"Managing the Workload in Your System"
Chapter 11, *Tuning a New Database*
Chapter 12, *Diagnostic and Tuning Tools*
Chapter 13, *Monitoring and Tuning an Existing Database*
Chapter 14, *Tuning the Data Dictionary*
Chapter 16, *Tuning in the Client-server Environment*
Chapter 17, *Performing Capacity Planning*
Chapter 18, *Tuning For Specific Systems*

DBA: *How can I best use memory to improve response times? How can I monitor memory usage?*

Memory speed is at least several thousand times faster than disk access. If ORACLE can be made to access more information from memory as opposed to disk, performance can be improved dramatically. Be careful not to use too much memory. If free memory is low, there is a high probability that paging and swapping will be excessive, which is much more damaging than the advantage of storing more information in memory. If many processes are waiting for CPU in certain situations, ORACLE's usage of memory can be transferred from memory to disk by decreasing the parameters that affect ORACLE's memory usage. This is an unusual situation, however.

It is essential that the ORACLE dictionary cache be tuned effectively, because of the potentially large increase in response times offered by good tuning. This area is easily tuned, and if settings are correct, it uses little memory relative to the DB_BLOCK_ BUFFER.

If there is spare memory on the computer, ORACLE systems can normally be sped up by increasing the DB_BLOCK_BUFFER parameter. This will store more data from tables, indexes, clusters, and rollback segments in memory. This data is useful only if it is queried by many users. If many updates are occurring on a system, you can enlarge the LOG_BUFFER to write changed data to the redo logs less often, but in larger chunks. This will result in reducing the number of I/Os. Individual ORACLE users can obtain improved sort times by enlarging the SORT_AREA_SIZE parameter. This is particularly useful for overnight processing when sorted, long-running reports are produced.

If there is not enough memory on a machine, too much paging and swapping of processes occurs, as the operating system attempts to give all processes a fair share of memory. ORACLE's share of memory must be reduced in these circumstances by reducing the DB_BLOCK_BUFFER, the LOG_BUFFER and (for Version 6 only) dictionary cache (DC_) parameters. It is possible at some sites that these changes can be made without adversely affecting ORACLE's performance. Per-ORACLE user memory usage can also be reduced, by decreasing the SORT_AREA_SIZE and/or the CONTEXT_ AREA and CONTEXT_INCR parameters.

To monitor memory usage, you must become familiar with the relevant operating system memory monitoring commands, including the total memory available, free memory, and the paging and swapping rates. Work closely with the system administrator to monitor any memory problems, especially on machines that also run non-ORACLE systems. You and the system administrator must keep each other informed of any proposed changes to memory usage, including adjusting parameters or plans for changes in the expected number of users.

From the ORACLE database perspective, you can monitor the effectiveness of the dictionary cache by querying the V$ROWCACHE table, the SQL*DBA recursive calls statistic, or the BSTAT/ESTAT output. The effectiveness of the buffer cache is detected by the hit ratio in the SQL*DBA MON IO option, or the hit ratio in the BSTAT/ESTAT report. The closer the hit ratio is to 100, the more effective the use of buffer cache will be. Increase the cache until the hit ratio stops increasing, given that there is free memory and no consistent CPU waits. You can also set the DB_BLOCK_LRU_EXTENDED_STATISTICS parameter to monitor the effects of increasing the buffer, and can set DB_BLOCK_LRU_ STATISTICS to monitor the effect of decreasing the cache. Observe the LOG_BUFFER effectiveness by the MON STAT SQL*DBA statistic "rdo spa wa" (redo space wait). This value should remain zero.

References: Chapter 3, *Planning and Managing the Tuning Process*
       "Managing the Workload in Your System"
    Chapter 12, *Diagnostic and Tuning Tools*
       "BSTAT, ESTAT, UTLBSTAT.sql, and UTLESTAT.sql"
    Chapter 13, *Monitoring and Tuning an Existing Database*
       "Tuning Memory"
       "Tuning the Dictionary Cache"
       "Tuning Buffer Cache"
       "Sharing of Executable Images"
       "Reducing Disk I/O by Increasing the Sort Area"
       "Monitoring and Tuning Redo Log Files"

Chapter 14, *Tuning the Data Dictionary*
Chapter 16, *Tuning in the Client-server Environment*
Chapter 17, *Performing Capacity Planning*
Chapter 18, *Tuning For Specific Systems*

DBA: ***Creating an index on a large table takes hours, and often crashes because of extent problems. Can I speed this up?***

Creating an index requires a sort, which can be sped up by using memory instead of disk. This can be achieved by enlarging the SORT_AREA_SIZE parameter. As each sort area size is filled in memory, the sorted entries will be written to disk and merged with those entries already written. This sorting is done in temporary segments.

Always place temporary segments into their own tablespace, so the default temporary segment sizing can be altered. This is achieved by having users assigned a tablespace that contains no tables, indexes, or clusters as their default temporary tablespace. Temporary segments have initial and next extent allocation assigned using the default INITIAL and NEXT extent specifications of the temporary tablespace. A typical daily default setting is INITIAL extent 256K and NEXT extent 256K. Always set PCTINCREASE to 0 and PCTFREE to 0. To create a large index, the temporary segment will need its INITIAL and NEXT extents to allow large sorts to occur without exceeding the maximum number of extents. Ideally, the INITIAL extent should be large enough to fit the entire index into one extent. The NEXT extent must be large enough to ensure that even if you miscalculated in the index size, you still won't blow the MAXEXTENTS setting.

The index will eventually be stored on disk. If the space the index is going to use is scattered across the disk in a discontiguous fashion, its performance can only be reduced, both on creation and eventually when accessed. The size of the index must also be assigned, preferably with the entire index fitting into one extent. Always set PCTINCREASE to 0.

It is important to size an index correctly when it is created. Ensure that the index sizing is for the expected number of entries in 12 months time, not the entries at the time of index creation.

References: Chapter 11, *Tuning a New Database*
"Creating the Tablespaces"
Chapter 13, *Tuning an Existing Database*
"Tuning Memory"
Chapter 15, *Tuning Long-running Jobs*
"Resizing Temporary Tables"

DBA: *Even though a statement is using an index, it is still running too slowly.*
                  Is there a way of checking how well an index is structured?

Index usage alone is not always sufficient to make a database query perform well. The index must also be specific enough to allow the values being checked to be found without reading too many rows from the index. Consider the following example. An index is placed on the ACCOUNT_ID column in the ACCOUNT transaction table. Each account can have as many as 10,000 transactions against it for a given financial year. If the query is made against the transaction table for a specific transaction date and ACCOUNT_ID, the whole 10,000 index rows may have to be searched. A more suitable concatenated index should be created on ACCOUNT_ID and TRANSACTION_DATE.

If multiple indexes exist, the question must be asked: is it the most specific index? The ordering of the index columns can be important. The data must be retrieved from the index with as few physical reads to the database as possible. If all of the columns required by the SQL statement can be stored in the index, and the ORDER BY clause on the SQL statement is in the same order as the columns in the index, this will assist performance by avoiding the need to read the columns from the table.

In Version 6, or if the rule-based optimizer is used in Version 7, the sequence of table names in the FROM clause can also have a significant effect on performance by indicating which table will be used as the driving table in the query. This is an issue when the rankings of the indexes available for both tables have the same ranking; for example, a single-column index that is non-unique.

Another problem that may cause problems is if the index contains many extents and is scattered widely across the disk. This problem can be avoided by sizing the index correctly at the time it is created. Ideally, the entire index must be stored in the initial extent.

The balancing of the index tree could also be a factor in terms of the depth of the tree. We have not seen an unbalanced tree with more than four levels, which means that the ORACLE index depth optimizing algorithm works effectively. We have observed that indexes can grow consistently in size, even when more rows are being deleted from an index than are inserted.

References: Chapter 7, *Tuning SQL*
                   "Selecting the Most Efficient Table Name Sequence"
                   "Selecting the Most Efficient WHERE Clause Sequence"
                   "Using Indexes to Improve Performance"
                   Chapter 11, *Creating a New Database*
                   "Creating Indexes"
                   "Creating Users"

DBA: *Dropping a table takes an excessive amount of time. What can I do to speed it up?*

If there are many extents contained within a table, the used extents dictionary table must flag each used extent as now being free. If the table contained several indexes that are also scattered across many extents, the extents that were being utilized will also have to be flagged as free. This drop function will be sped up if tables and indexes are sized correctly when they are created. This minimizes the number of extents that the table or index occupies.

References: Chapter 15, *Tuning Long-running Jobs*
                "Sizing Tables and Indexes"

DBA: *Deleting rows from a tables takes forever. What can I do?*

Deleting all the rows from a table is usually significantly slower than dropping a table. This is because work has to be done to flag free space in every one of the blocks that contained a row. If the table has indexes, the entries in the index are marked for deletion. This is a very resource-consuming process. A trick that some sites perform is to update a row as deleted by setting a DELETED_DATE column to the date the row was deleted, and to perform the actual deletions on a periodical basis outside prime usage times.

Rollback and redo log activity will add to the lengthy delays.

Version 7 offers a new command that will overcome this problem. The TRUNCATE command deletes rows from a table, but its performance is similar to the much faster operation of dropping and recreating the table and its indexes. This function does not cause rollback activity and does not write any detailed redo information.

References: Chapter 15, *Tuning Long-running Jobs*
                "Sizing Tables and Indexes"
                Appendix A, *Planning for Version 7*
                "TRUNCATE Command"

DBA: *The import takes too long. What can I do?*

The import facility is normally used to perform a database reorganization or to recover a database. It is typically performed over a weekend. Any DBA who has worked at a medium- to large-sized site has felt the extra pressure over the reorganization weekend. What if the database is not rebuilt by Monday morning when the production users arrive for work? The faster the import can be made to run, the more time will be available to rerun the import if something goes wrong. ORACLE imports take considerably longer than exports, mainly because indexes are created as part of the import, with only the

INDEX statement, not the index entries, being exported. Typical time differences are three hours for the export and 12 hours for a full import.

To avoid the need for reruns, it is important that you realize the biggest causes of import failure. If a table or index has large initial or next extents, ensure that the appropriate sized extents are available prior to running the import. Many DBAs reorganize one tablespace at a time. They will drop and then recreate the tablespace, and then import the tables, indexes, and clusters that exist in that tablespace. If you overlook indexes that reside in other tablespaces placed on tables in the tablespace being reorganized, problems can occur. Make sure that these indexes are also created.

The buffer size chosen as part of the import can have an effect on the time taken by the import. With a larger buffer size, the system writes larger chunks of data less often than when there is a smaller buffer size. Another factor that may decrease the time taken is to drop all of the indexes and create them after the table has been imported into. This will speed up the import significantly. Enlarge the sort area size to ensure that much of the sorting required for the index is done in memory.

Export files could also contain several tables each. This will allow multiple imports to be performed at the same time. Another factor that speeds up imports is to lower the PCTFREE parameter on tables, perform the import, and then correct the PCTFREE to its correct value on the table using the ALTER TABLE statement. If you are running client-server, you should run the import with the export file situated on the database server. This will eliminate potential network delays.

References: Chapter 11, *Tuning a New Database*
                         "Creating Tables and Indexes"
                 Chapter13, *Monitoring and Tuning an Existing Database*
                         "Detecting Dynamic Extension"
                 Chapter 15, *Tuning Long-running Jobs*
                         "Creating Indexes after Inserts"
                         "Tuning EXPORT and IMPORT"
                 Chapter 16, *Tuning in the Client-server Environment*
                         "Running Long-running Jobs at the Server End"

DBA: *The export takes too long. What can I do?*

An export that takes too long will intrude into the window of time available to run other overnight jobs. Exports are an essential part of any backup strategy because they allow individual tables to be restored and also highlight any table corruption. There are several ways to speed up an export, including increasing the buffer size. Increasing the buffer size allows larger chunks of data to be written less often than when there is a smaller buffer size.

The export can also be broken up into several jobs, with each exporting several tables. The jobs can be run in parallel. Many DBAs export tables and indexes on a per-tablespace basis. Perhaps several tables require only weekly, rather than nightly, export; for example, historical or summary tables may fall into this category. Some redundant tables may not require exporting because they can be recreated from other tables. If you are running client-server, make sure that the export process is initiated and the export file written to the same machine as the one on which the database resides.

If tables contain many extents, this can also slow down exports. The export facility will be forced to scan discontiguous sets of data, scattered across the disk. The system must access the table header before obtaining each additional extent. If a table is stored contiguously on disk within one extent, a large section of the extent can be read with one multi-block read.

References: Chapter 11, *Tuning a New Database*
      "Creating Tables"
      "Creating Indexes"
     Chapter 13, *Tuning an Existing Database*
      "Detecting Dynamic Extension"
     Chapter 15, *Tuning Long-running Jobs*
      "Tuning EXPORT and IMPORT"
     Chapter 16, *Tuning in the Client-server Environment*
      "Running Long-running Jobs at the Server End"

DBA: *Our overnight data loads from other applications are taking far too long. What can I do?*

Overnight data loads are a common occurrence at a lot of ORACLE sites. Circumstances will vary from site to site, but regardless of the exact situation, you should attempt to minimize the amount of data being transferred from the other application. In every application, make sure that you include a DATE_CHANGED column and a WHO_CHANGED column against every table. Each night, transfer only the data that has changed across applications.

If the system having its data transferred is another ORACLE-based system, it is more efficient to transfer the day's changes across to the system being updated, into a temporary table, and then do any necessary comparisons in the single database, rather than performing comparisons across a network.

You must appropriately size any temporary tables created and their associated indexes so they fit within one extent. Ideally, place the temporary load tables onto different disks from those that contain the tables that are to be updated or added to. It is more efficient to drop and recreate the temporary table than to delete from it. It is also faster to insert the data into the load tables, and create the indexes afterwards. If you are using Version 7, take advantage of the TRUNCATE command.

Choosing the appropriate columns to index on the temporary load tables is just as critical as for the application tables. These should also be sized to minimize extents. Attempt to store all temporary tables and indexes in one extent. You can do this by setting the INITIAL storage parameter large enough to store all of the data in the table. If fragmentation of the database doesn't allow the table or index to be stored in one extent, try to use as few extents as possible, making the NEXT storage parameter as large as the largest free extent.

Always try to minimize the number of updates against each table. You can use a single UPDATE statement to update many columns in a single table. Take advantage of PL/SQL for updates to minimize the number of rows read for update in the production tables.

If you are running client-server, perform all overnight processing at the database server end.

If you are using SQL*Loader, make sure the ROWS parameter has been set large enough to reduce the number of array inserts into the database.

When you are running overnight jobs, there will be tend to be fewer users logged onto a machine, and therefore more free memory than during prime usage times. This will allow you to enlarge the DB_BLOCK_BUFFER, LOG_BUFFER, and SORT_AREA_SIZE parameters. Increasing the parameters will usually improve performance, for the reasons described in the references below. Temporary tablespace default parameters may be increased to improve sort/merge operations, including index creation. Larger rollback segments may replace the smaller daily rollbacks at sites to improve the responsiveness of updates. Make sure that all of the changes you make for overnight processing are adjusted back to their daily sizes when you complete the overnight jobs.

References: Chapter 11, *Tuning a New Database*
                 "Creating Tables"
                 "Creating Indexes"
              Chapter 15, *Tuning Long-running Jobs*
              Chapter 16, *Tuning in the Client-server Environment*
                 "Running Long-running Jobs at the Server End"

DBA: *We've gone client-server. The system ran fine when it was running on one machine, but now it's slow. What can the problem be?*

Client-server adds a new dimension to tuning an application: the need for one processor to communicate with another across a network.

You must try to reduce the number of packets being transferred between processors. This is achieved by setting the relevant ARRAYSIZE parameter effectively in the product being used, tuning any relevant parameters in the communications protocol, taking advantage of DECODEs, UNIONs, and views in SQL*Forms, and applying features such as local cache.

The closer you can locate processors together, the less distance the packets will need to travel. The amount of processor-to-processor network traffic is significantly larger than the traffic from the application client (server) to the user's terminal. You can have an application server (client) that services Sydney users, for example, and an application server that services Melbourne users located in the same computer room. This will considerably reduce the distance the bulk of the network traffic has to travel. The network traffic from the application servers (clients) to the terminal is usually quite light in comparison.

If possible, you should attempt to run all long-running jobs at the database server end. These jobs will include overnight reports, overnight updates, and daily reporting functions. The daily reports requested can be placed into a table, with a job running continuously at the database (server) end, which will interrogate the table and use its contents to submit the appropriate program with any supplied parameters.

Version 7 has many features that will improve client-server computing performance, including a multi-threaded server (which increases the maximum number of possible user connections and performs automatic load balancing) and the storing of integrity constraints, stored procedures, functions, and packages (which will considerably reduce the number of packets transferred across the network).

SQL*NET Version 2 has an internal feature called fastpath, that will minimize read and write times.

References: Chapter 16, *Tuning in the Client-server Environment*
                   Appendix A, *Planning for Version 7*
                       "Multi-Threaded Server"
                       "Declarative Data Integrity Constraints"
                       "Stored Procedures, Functions, Packages, and Triggers"

DBA: *The application ran fast in tests but grinds to a halt in production. What can the problem be?*

There are many possible causes for sudden increased response time in production. Are the indexes the same in both environments? Is the amount of data in production considerably larger? Is the distribution of data different in test and production? For example, a table in the test environment may have the same number of rows for all categories, whereas in production one category may have 95% of the entries, with the other 50 categories having only a handful of rows each.

You need to ask various questions about the operating system. How many users are logged on? Is there any free memory? Is excessive paging or swapping occurring? Is the disk I/O correctly balanced? Are there any network bottlenecks? Is the test environment running in the same type of configuration as the production environment?

It is not good practice to run the test environment in unitary (with the database users and the database on the one machine) and production in client-server or any other differing combination. Use the test environment as a response testing ground; be sure it uses the same type of configuration as production.

There are also DBA issues to consider. Has the database been structured for an even I/O spread? Is memory being used effectively to store data, indexes, rollbacks, and dictionary information? (The dictionary is a concern in Version 6 only.) Are the database segments fragmented or chaining and in need of repair?

DBA: Can creating views help overcome performance problems?

There is a misconception by some people that views are able to provide better performance than running the query that created the view. Some DBMSes create duplicate data when a view is created. ORACLE and other relational database management systems can achieve the same effect by maintaining redundant tables.

In ORACLE, a view will perform identically to the SQL statement used to create the view. There will be only a small overhead to parse the view. It is critical that you tune the statement used to create the view like any other SQL statement.

Views can provide certain performance benefits in a client-server environment. This is achieved by reducing the number of packets transferred across the network by avoiding Post-Query triggers in SQL*Forms inquiries. Another advantage of views is that they offer a means of applying security by showing specific users only the columns they need to see, and they save programmers from having to recode complex SELECT statements.

Do not use views of views, except where they are absolutely necessary. Views of views are extremely hard to administer, maintain, and tune.

References: Chapter 9, *Tuning SQL*Forms*
                            "Base Table View Updating"
                       Chapter 11, *Creating a New Database*
                            "Creating Views"
                       Chapter 16, Tuning in the Client-server Environment
                            "SQL*Forms Base Table Views"

DBA: **Is there a way of killing long-running jobs in ORACLE?**

Version 6 of ORACLE relies on the operating system to kill long-running jobs. SQL*DBA MON PROC can be used to determine the identifier of the offending process.

Version 7 offers a large advantage in being able to prevent jobs from exceeding the amount of CPU used or exceeding disk I/Os. If jobs do exceed the limits specified, they are cancelled automatically. Version 7 also offers an option in SQL*DBA to kill any unwanted user process.

References: Appendix A, *Planning for Version 7*
         "Resource Profile Limits"

DBA: **What performance advantages does SQL*Net Version 2 have over SQL*Net Version 1?**

SQL*Net Version 2 provides significant performance benefits over Version 1 by passing fewer packets across the network using a feature called fastpath.

Another major advantage of SQL*Net Version 2 is the multi-threaded server, which significantly increases the maximum number of connections and performs load balancing. automatically. The maximum number of users can be increased because a single dispatcher process controls many clients via a network monitoring process which differs from SQL*Net Version 1 (in which each user process has the full SQL*Net over-head). SQL*Net Version 2 demands many fewer system resources to handle the same number of users.

SQL*Net Version 2 offers UPIALL in all tools. This reduces the number of packets required to be passed across the network by having one pass open a statement and one close the statement, compared to SQL*Net Version 1 which requires many packets to be passed for each individual SQL statement.

References: Chapter 16, *Tuning in the Client-server Environment*
         "Tuning SQL*Net"
        Appendix A, *Planning for Version 7*
         "Multi-Threaded Server"

DBA: **A developer has a slow-running function but indicates that indexes are being used and response times are fine. What can the problem be?**

There are two main reasons why the figures may be low. First, the TKPROF output file is being run against a different user from the one that the initial run was processed against. If this is the case, the columns in the indexes may be different or in a different order from those in the environment that actually produced the inadequate response times. The amount of data or the spread of data in the table may also differ significantly from one environment to the other.

Another possibility is that the program being monitored has a column specified as numeric, and the database has an indexed character column. If this is true, the index will not be used. TKPROF will always assume that the column type provided will be as it is in the database against which TKPROF is being run.

References: Chapter 7, *Tuning SQL*
                             "SQL Performance Hints"
                             "Problems when Converting Index Column Types"
                    Chapter 12, *Diagnostic and Tuning Tools*
                             "SQL_TRACE: Writing a Trace File"
                             "TKPROF: Interpreting the Trace File"
                             "EXPLAIN PLAN: Explaining the Optimizer"

DBA: *The system response has been deteriorating over time. What are the possible causes?*

This is a common situation. There are a number of possible causes.

Indexes may be inappropriate or non-existent. Indexes may not exist because the application designers did not envision the selection criteria that the users will utilize. With only a small amount of data, a full-table scan might have been as fast or faster than an indexed SELECT. As the number of rows in the database has grown, however, the missing index causes a dramatic degradation in response time.

Indexes may have been added to speed up a new program, which may cause existing programs to operate less efficiently. This may be the result of a new index ranking higher in the optimizer's ranking conditions than the index that provides the program with efficient performance, or may result from the order of the WHERE clause causing the new index to be utilized.

Another common cause of performance degradation is database fragmentation, in which database segments span many extents. Chaining could also be a problem, but it is more likely to be picked up during the system test stage if the appropriate monitoring is performed.

External influences also affect many applications over time. New untuned or partially tuned applications often find their way onto a machine known for its good response times. This inevitably results in two systems performing badly rather than the one poorly tuned application.

Uncontrolled ad hoc queries against the production database by production users can also cause overall poor performance if the SQL queries are not optimally structured. Developers may also log into a production database to check problems. It is essential for the DBA to be aware of all ad hoc activity to ensure that it is either done at times other than those of heavy usage or to be absolutely sure that the activity will not adversely affect performance if it must run during prime time. If you are running Version 7 you can apply resource limits on users.

There may also be many more users than there have been in the past, causing memory on the machine to be fully utilized, and paging and swapping to occur. Perhaps the degradation is caused by poor I/O distribution across disks. Other possibilities include inadequate use of memory to store database or dictionary information, or contention in writing to the tables, rollback segments, or redo logs.

Additional database checks that should be made if there is sufficient free memory on your machine are listed below:

- Ensure that the block buffer which stores table data, indexes, clusters, and rollback segments is large enough to provide a high hit rate. This guarantees that as much information can be found in memory (as opposed to disk) as possible.

- Make the dictionary cache large enough to ensure that ORACLE database information is stored in memory. In Version 6, this involves individually setting dictionary cache parameters; in Version 7, you need only tune the dictionary cache buffer pool. An inadequately sized dictionary cache can cause severe response delays. Correctly sizing the dictionary cache uses a small amount of memory relative to the buffer cache. You *must* be sure to size the dictionary cache correctly.

- Enlarge the redo log buffer to reduce frequent I/Os to the redo logs if there is excessive I/O on the disk that contains the redo logs.

Contention problems that may be occurring and have to be investigated include the following:

- Redo log contention has a relatively small effect on database performance, but ORACLE provides the tools to monitor it. Each minor improvement that can be made to the database may add up to a major improvement when combined with many other small improvements. Use the SQL*DBA MON ST screen to examine "rdo spa wa" (redo log space wait,) the number of times a user is waiting for space in the redo log buffer.

- The redo log buffer latches can have multiple users trying to access them, and contention may occur. This problem is detected by viewing the SQL*DBA MON LA screen and inspecting the "redo allocation" and "redo copy latches" to ensure that the time-outs do not exceed 5% of the total willing to wait requests.

- Rollback segment contention can occur with contention for data buffers in the buffer cache area of the SGA or buffer contention due to rollback segment contention. Ensure that the block buffer section of the SGA is large enough to avoid contention. Also ensure that dynamic extension of rollbacks is not occurring for transactions that are modifying large amounts of data. If your application has many online transaction processing users, with only small amounts of data being modified, keep all of your rollback segments small to improve their chance of being kept in the buffer cache. If your site is performing many large updates, ensure that the large update transactions are assigned larger rollback segments.

- Table and row contention can also occur where one user process is forced to wait for another user process to release the lock before proceeding. Code your application to minimize the chances of locking problems occurring.

References: Chapter 3, *Planning and Managing the Tuning Process*
                 Chapter 7, *Tuning SQL*
                     "SQL Performance Hints"
                     "Selecting the Most Efficient WHERE Clause Sequence"
                     "Using Indexes to Improve Performance"
                 Chapter 13, *Monitoring and Tuning an Existing Database*
                 Chapter 14, *Tuning the Data Dictionary*
                 Chapter 15, *Tuning Long-running Jobs*
                     "Sizing Tables and Indexes"

DBA: *Our systems administrator has informed me that our system is I/O bound. What can I do?*

It is important to understand what I/O bound means. Simply put, it means that one or more disks are exceeding their recommend I/O usage, creating a bottleneck. Typical disks on a minicomputer have recommended maximum I/O rates of between 30 to 60 I/Os per second, depending on the hardware. Excessive disk I/Os can dramatically degrade application response times.

When a database is initially created, there are steps that can be taken to ensure that the disk load spread is evenly balanced across disks, and to ensure that the cause of the excessive disk I/O can be more accurately pinpointed. A summary of the rules follows:

- Locate redo log files on a disk other than the disk holding the database files.
- Split tables and indexes into separate tablespaces.
- Separate tables commonly used together onto separate disks. Try to combine infrequently used tables with frequently used tables.
- Have a separate temporary tablespace.
- Place users into their own tablespace.
- Store the ORACLE products in a products tablespace.
- Store only the ORACLE system tables in the system tablespace.

- Do not store any part of the ORACLE database on the operating system disk; in particular, keep away from the operating system disk where paging and swapping takes place.

- Allocate many medium-sized tablespaces instead of fewer large tablespaces.

- Spread your disk I/O across as many disk drives and disk controllers as possible.

- Be aware of your machine-specific disk characteristics such as the advantages of raw devices on many UNIX systems.

Badly tuned application programs or a data model that is unable to provide adequate performance are the principal causes of systems becoming I/O bound. Make sure that programs are responding within the required site standard response times. If the response times are sufficiently tight (e.g., 95% of online responses within 2.5 seconds elapsed and no longer than 10 seconds elapsed for any online response), the likelihood of the application causing the system to be I/O bound is reduced significantly.

Many sites may require reporting of small batch updates during prime usage times. These jobs must also have their response times monitored closely. An appropriate maximum run time for such jobs at a typical site would be 95% of them running within 30 seconds elapsed with no job exceeding two minutes.

If the application has been tuned appropriately and the system is still I/O bound, you should investigate other sources of the problem. If one disk has become I/O bound, there will probably be a way of spreading the load by relocating tables and indexes into different tablespaces on alternative disks. A table and its indexes should be separated. Heavily used tables and lightly used tables should be placed onto the same disks, with no one disk having too many heavily used tables on it.

A database reorganization can help if there is more than one extent on table and index segments. After the reorganization, fewer I/Os will be needed to access data than from a table or index that exists in one extent.

Indexing problems can also cause excessive I/Os. Make sure that no indexes have been accidentally dropped or not recreated after a database reorganization. Ensure also that a new index that has been added to assist a new program is not adversely affecting other programs which may now be using the new index rather than a more optimally tuned index.

If free memory is available, you can store data, indexes, rollbacks, clusters, and the ORACLE data dictionary (Version 6 only) in memory. Doing this speeds up response times considerably for a tuned application. This is achieved by transferring the load from I/O to memory, which is several thousand times faster. If sorts or groupings and totaling are common in the application, and there is sufficient memory, you can enlarge the SORT_AREA_SIZE parameter to force more sorting in memory rather than on disk. You can also enlarge the log buffer to reduce the number of writes to the redo logs.

References: Chapter 3, *Planning and Managing the Tuning Process*
                         "Understanding the Effect of Workload on Performance"
                  Chapter 5, *Designing your Data Model for Performance*
                  Chapter 6, *Defining Indexes*
                         "Using Indexes to Improve Performance"
                  Chapter 7, *Tuning SQL*
                         "SQL Performance Hints"
                         "Using Indexes to Improve Performance"
                  Chapter 11, *Tuning a New Database*
                         "Creating the Database"
                         "Creating Tables"
                         "Creating Indexes"
                         "Creating Users"
                  Chapter 12, *Diagnostic and Tuning Tools*
                         "BSTAT, ESTAT, UTLBSTAT.sql, and UTLESTAT.sql"
                  Chapter 13, *Monitoring and Tuning an Existing Database*
                         "Tuning Disk I/O"
                  Chapter 18, *Tuning for Specific Systems*
                         "Writing to Raw Devices"

DBA: *One disk is always on or above its maximum recommended I/Os per second. What can I do?*

Make sure that the application has been thoroughly tuned. Even a single badly tuned program that is not utilizing indexes correctly or has an incorrect driving table can cause overall poor response times and an overworked disk. Do not run long-running batch jobs during prime production times, when the system contains many interactive users. Excessive I/Os may also occur when an index is missing. If the application is tuned correctly, there are certain measures that you can take to spread the disk load.

An inappropriate database structure can cause excessive I/Os across disks. Be sure to separate redo logs from database files onto separate disk drives. If possible, split tables from their indexes, and split commonly used tables onto different drives. Do not store any database files on the same disk as the operating system files. Even when you follow these basic rules, unbalanced disk loading can still occur.

The usual way to spread the disk load is to relocate tables and indexes into different tablespaces across disks. A database reorganization can help if there is more than one extent on table and index segments that exist on this disk. This will mean that more I/Os will be needed to access data than from a table or index that exists in one extent.

Excessive disk I/Os may also occur when there are many sorts taking place with an inadequate sort area size, and many users have their default temporary tablespace on a single disk. Enlarge the sort area size to alleviate the problem, or assign temporary tablespaces assigned for users to alternative tablespaces across several disks.

If the disk containing the redo logs is experiencing excessive I/Os, increase the log buffer size if there is sufficient memory available. This will cause the redo logs to be written to less frequently.

If the operating system disk is experiencing excessive I/O, the usual cause is excessive paging and swapping. If this is the case, you will need to decrease ORACLE's slice of memory, normally by reducing the DB_BLOCK_BUFFER size or in some cases the LOG_BUFFER or the SORT_AREA_SIZE.

If the disk containing the system tablespace that is experiencing problems has excessive I/Os, the probable cause is that you are storing more than just the system tablespaces in the tablespace. Other segments should be moved away from the system tablespace. Another possible cause is that the dictionary cache is too small. If this is the case, the cache parameters (note that in Version 7 there is only one parameter) must be enlarged.

External influences also affect many applications. New untuned or partially tuned applications often find their way onto a machine known for its good response times. They may share the same disks as your application. You must be familiar with the operating system disk monitoring commands to detect this cause. Solving this problem may be a simple case of subtracting your application's disk I/Os from the overall system I/Os.

Uncontrolled ad hoc queries against the production database often attack individual large tables, and this can cause overall poor performance. It is essential that you be aware of all ad hoc activity, to ensure that no part of the database is adversely affected. If you are using Version 7, you will be able to apply resource limits on the user.

Make sure you take advantage of any offerings the hardware vendor provides to enhance performance. For example, use raw devices if they are available, and take advantage of any disk caching ability your computer may have. You must work closely with the system administration staff to do this.

References: Chapter 3, *Planning and Managing the Tuning Process*
                        "Understanding the Effect of Workload on Performance"
                 Chapter 5, *Designing your Data Model for Performance*
                 Chapter 6, *Defining Indexes*
                        "Using Indexes to Improve Performance"
                 Chapter 7, *Tuning SQL*
                        "SQL Performance Hints"
                        "Using Indexes to Improve Performance"

Chapter 11, *Tuning a New Database*
  "Disk I/O Checklist"
  "Creating the Database"
  "Creating Tables"
  "Creating Indexes"
  "Creating Users"
Chapter 12, *Diagnostic and Tuning Tools*
  "BSTAT, ESTAT, UTLBSTAT.sql, and UTLESTAT.sql"
Chapter 13, *Monitoring and Tuning an Existing Database*
  "Tuning Disk I/O"
Chapter 18, *Tuning for Specific Systems*
  "Writing to Raw Devices"

DBA: We keep running out of memory and swapping occurs. What can I do?

Excessive swapping is probably the most damaging factor in a machine's performance. Simply put, swapping occurs when an entire process is moved from memory to disk. Excessive swapping is known as thrashing. This occurs when 100% of the CPU is spent continuously moving processes in and out of memory. Swapping of dormant processes is quite acceptable. Problems occur when memory is not large enough to store all active processes. It is essential that you work with the system administrator to ensure that there is always free memory. As a rule of thumb, there must be at least 5% of memory free at all times, including peak activity times.

There are many ways to reduce memory usage, but as we have mentioned already, you must be careful not to squeeze free memory so tightly that overall performance begins to diminish. Memory prices are coming down considerably. This does not mean that memory usage should become reckless. The decreased memory usage will cause an increased I/O usage. Keep in mind that I/O is many, many thousand times slower than memory processing. After any changes are made to memory usage, the responsiveness of the system should be checked. Don't compare the response times to those when the system is in a swapping state. Compare them to the response times just prior to all of the memory being used.

One simple solution to the memory problem is to limit users to one login each. At some sites, users may be logged on three or four times. At others, users are logged in all day although they use the system only briefly. We have observed sites where people arrive at work, log onto the ORACLE system, quickly check one inquiry screen, and do not use the application for the rest of the day. When a user is logged on, he or she uses memory. Consider logging users off the system after a period of inactivity. You might also investigate rotating shifts if these are possible at your site; for example, shift 1 works 7 a.m. to 3 p.m. and shift 2 works 3 p.m. to 11 p.m.

Some operating systems allow the sharing of executables in memory; for example, under VMS, iap30 (runform) can be stored once and shared by many users. If it is not installed as a shared executable, each user will have his or her own copy of iap30, each consisting of 2 megabytes. This will quickly use all of the memory. Any executables that are not being used on a production machine can be removed from memory if they have been installed. Typical examples would be the iad30 (SQL*Forms executable) and sqlrep.

Another way to reduce memory usage is to reduce the size of the SGA. The areas that can be reduced are the dictionary cache (reduce this only if it is oversized), the log buffer (do not reduce it to the extent of causing contention for redo logs or excessive I/Os to the disks containing the redo logs), and the block buffer size (do not reduce it to a point where excessive I/Os occur and the system response times rise above those set by the site's response time standard).

The amount of memory per ORACLE user can also be adjusted. by reducing the sort area size which sets the amount of memory per user for sorting. Other parameters assigned on a per-user basis are the CONTEXT_SIZE and CONTEXT_INCR parameters, which are used to store SQL statements. Although these parameters can be reduced, it is not advisable to decrease either of them by more than 50% of the default ORACLE settings.

References: Chapter 3, *Planning and Managing the Tuning Process*
        "Understanding the Effect of Workload on Performance"
        Chapter 12, *Diagnostic and Tuning Tools*
        "BSTAT, ESTAT, UTLBTAT.sql, and UTLESTAT.sql"
        Chapter 13, *Monitoring and Tuning an Existing Database*
        "Tuning Memory"
        Chapter 14, *Tuning the Data Dictionary*
        Chapter 18, *Tuning for Specific Systems*
        "VMS-specific Tuning"

DBA: *How large a value should I set the DB_BLOCK_BUFFERS parameter to?*

The DB_BLOCK_BUFFERS parameter sets the amount of memory ORACLE will use to store tables, indexes, clusters, and rollbacks. This area is called the buffer cache, which is held in the SGA. Be careful that you do not enlarge the parameter to the point where there is less than 5% free memory during peak usage time. If all the memory on the machine is used, the performance is likely to grind to a halt through excessive paging and swapping.

Our experience has shown that enlarging the parameter continuously to the point where the hit rate of finding data in memory approaches 100% will improve the performance of ORACLE at most sites. This is because memory access is many, many thousand times faster than disk access. If the hit rate of finding data, indexes, or roll-backs in memory improves even by only 5%, this may mean a significant reduction in I/Os during peak usage times of a system. If there is an abundance of free memory on a system, the dictionary cache and log buffer are tuned, and the hit ratios continue to increase when the parameter is increased, you should use the memory to enlarge the DB_BLOCK_BUFFERS. *However, it is critical that you leave free memory on your system at all times.*

There is an obvious exception to the rule. This occurs when the data is unlikely to be found in cache because large table scans are being performed on a continual basis from tables too large to fit into the buffer area. CPU will be consumed searching the cache, with little likelihood of the required data being found, and disk I/O will be required regardless.

Some sites take advantage of the fact that fewer users log onto the system at night, and, consequently, there is more free memory available at such times. Each night, they shut their instance down, increase the DB_BLOCK_BUFFERS parameter upwards, run the long-running overnight jobs, and then shut the instance down again, adjust the parameter to it's daily setting, and restart the instance.

References: Chapter 3, *Planning and Managing the Tuning Process*
                 "Understanding the Effect of Workload on Performance"
                 Chapter 12, *Diagnostic and Tuning Tools*
                 "BSTAT, ESTAT, UTLBSTAT.sql, and UTLESTAT.sql"
                 Chapter 13, *Monitoring and Tuning an Existing Database*
                 "Tuning Memory"
                 Chapter 15, *Tuning Long-running Jobs*
                 "Enlarging the Buffer Cache"

DBA: *We've had a user waiting for 30 minutes for a response. The user is not using an excessive amount of disk I/O or CPU. What can the problem be?*

The most likely cause is a locking problem. Often, a program performs well during testing as a single unit, but when many users operate many programs in a system test, locking problems occur. This system test is critical to detect any locking problems, as is a sound locking strategy for developers.

A common cause of locking problems is when users are updating information in an application and go to lunch, leaving the uncommitted transaction sitting on the screen. It is essential to train users not to leave uncommitted transactions for an excessive amount of time.

Another cause of this situation occurs when an overnight job locks a table, or rows in a table, that have failed to complete before the online users log onto the system and commence their day's work using online updates. A third cause occurs when an ad hoc update of the database is applied by a developer to the database during online usage times.

References: Chapter 10, *Selecting a Locking Strategy*

DBA: *How do I know when my tables and indexes need to be reorganized? How is this best achieved?*

Ideally, tables and indexes should be sized to fit within a single extent. If a table or index has more than five extents, rebuild it to fit into one extent. The exception to the rule is when a table has been created utilizing the striping facility.

You should also rebuild tables when chaining occurs on many of the rows within the table. This occurs when a row expands and can't fit within a single physical block. The problem is caused by too small a PCTFREE being specified for a table. Indexes are also subject to chaining if the columns in the index have increased in length.

Make sure that all tables and indexes are sized to allow for expected growth over the next 12 months. Never size an index or table for its current number of rows. When resizing tables, don't forget to recreate the indexes on the table.

The IMPORT utility has an INDEXFILE=*filename* option which is particularly useful for rebuilding tables and indexes. This option must be run without importing the data (ROWS=*n*) to create a file containing all index and table creation scripts. Edit the file (adding the expected growth rate onto the initial extent), create the table, import the rows from the export file, and then apply the indexes for a table or simply drop and recreate the index using the INDEXFILE definition for an index.

Another situation in which tables and indexes may have to be rebuilt is the case in which the DBA requires free space in the database to create a new table or index and the tables or indexes are oversized. To determine the used blocks in a table, obtain the distinct blocks, and, for an index, use the VALIDATE INDEX statement to interrogate the INDEX_STATS view. Both methods are documented in this book.

References: Chapter 6, *Defining Indexes*
                         "Using Indexes to Improve Performance"
                   Chapter 8, *Tuning a New Database*
                         "Creating Tables"
                         "Creating Indexes"
                   Chapter 15, *Tuning Long-running Jobs*
                         "Sizing Tables and Indexes
                         "Creating Indexes after Inserts"

*DBA :   My site has a program that has been running for more than 30 minutes.
             How can I monitor the program to see which statements have caused the
             largest response delays? It appears the program may be stuck on one
             particular statement.*

Set the following parameters in the INIT.ORA file:

```
SQL_TRACE           TRUE
TIMED_STATISTICS    TRUE
```

Alternatively, include the statement ALTER SESSION SET SQL_TRACE TRUE at the start
of the program. Then, you will be able to run the TKPROF utility against the trace file
created by the program to determine the timings for each statement. Some developers
have the misconception that TKPROF has to run against a completed program's trace
file and will take the same amount of time that the program took to run. This is not the
case. The program can still be running when you run TKPROF, and the TKPROF output
will take only a few moments.

If you cannot run TKPROF, you can use SQL*DBA to run MON TAB to establish the
tables being used and then find the relevant statement from the program. This is obviously difficult if many statements use the same tables. If the statement can be identified,
you can run the EXPLAIN PLAN utility against the statement, or you can enable
SQL_TRACE and then run TKPROF against the trace file after the statement has been
running for a few minutes to determine how the statement is accessing the database.

If the program that is running is a SQL*Plus program running interactively, the current
statement can be listed using the / command in SQL*Plus. Once again, use TKPROF or
EXPLAIN PLAN to determine the access path of the statement.

Another method is to run the EXPLAIN PLAN utility against all of the statements, and
search through the output to find any full-table scans, uses of incorrect indexes, or uses
of an inappropriate driving table.

References: Chapter 7, *Tuning SQL*
                 Chapter 12, *Diagnostic and Tuning Tools*
                     "SQL_TRACE: Writing a Trace File"
                     "TKPROF: Interpreting the TRACE File"
                     "EXPLAIN PLAN: Explaining the Optimizer"

*DBA: When I use the SQL*DBA MONITOR screens, I see several hundred figures.
             Which are the important figures that can be used for tuning and how do
             I interpret them?*

A summary of the parameters that are most relevant to the tuning process are listed
below. Detailed information on how to repair the problems is described in this book.

SQL*DBA> MON STAT 0 0 3

recursive calls	Should be as close to zero as possible. If it is greater than zero, either the dictionary cache does not contain a required entry and a disk read has taken place on the system tables, or dynamic extension is occurring. Either needs repairing.
dbw fre ne	Indicates DBWR contention. This value should never exceed zero. If it does, this problem must be prepared.
buf bsy wa	Compare with "db blk get" and "consi get" using ("buf bsy wa" / "db blk get" + "consi get"). If the result is greater than 10%, you have rollback contention.
rdo spa wa	Should never rise above zero. If it does, a process cannot find space in the redo log buffer.
fre buf ins	If excessive, the DBWR is not functioning well and too many buffers are being skipped to find a free buffer.
fre bf wai	The number of times a free buffer was not available. The lower the value the better.

SQLDBA> MON IO

Processes may be viewed to identify the biggest I/O user processes.

hit ratio	This parameter indicates the ration of table, index, cluster and rollback blocks found in memory. The closer to 1.00, the better the performance.

$$\texttt{Hit Ratio} = \frac{(\texttt{cumulative logical reads} - \texttt{physical reads})}{\texttt{cumulative logical reads}}$$

SQLDBA> MON LA

Make sure no latch has timeouts (more than 5% of total willing to wait).

SQLDBA>MON FILE

Make sure no file has excessive I/Os with disk exceeding maximum I/Os

SQLDBA>MON IO ALL

Make sure there are no waiters (lower case) in the Lock display screen

References:	Chapter 13, *Monitoring and Tuning an Existing Database*
	Appendix D, *Dynamic Performance Tables*

DBA: *When I am monitoring statistics it is very tedious to go through three screens all the time. Is there a better way?*

SQL*DBA allows three columns to be displayed on the screen at once. In the command MON STATS 0 0 3, the first zero is the first process in the range to monitor, the second zero indicates the last process in the range to monitor, and the 3 indicates the number of columns to display across the screen.

References: Chapter 13, *Monitoring and Tuning an Existing Database*
                 See examples in text

DBA: *Our backups are taking too long. What can I do to speed them up?*

Every site has a certain fixed amount of time in which to perform such tasks as backups. Backups are critical; never give preference to running long-running batch jobs or reports. There is always a way of speeding up backups.

We believe that you must have archiving turned on for all jobs (except when overnight data loads are being run), with periodic image copies of the database files including tablespaces, redo logs, and control files. Back up the archive files nightly. You must also run exports nightly against a database to indicate any internal database corruption and to allow individual table recovery.

If archiving is turned on, you may shut your database down weekly to back up all database files, and just back up the archive files nightly. Hot backups allow tablespaces to be backed up without having to shut down the database. This form of backup can be run with little effect on overnight processing.

If there is sufficient time overnight to perform a full image copy of your database with the database shut down, this will provide the fastest recovery. If possible, run disk-to-disk-image copies of all of the database files. As soon as this process has completed, you can begin the overnight reporting and batch jobs with tape backups taken of the image copies of the database on disk.

Remember that if a database is shut down you can enlarge rollback segments when you restart. You can also enlarge the block buffer, the log buffer, and the sort area size to take advantage of having fewer users on the system and more available memory. The default INITIAL and NEXT storage allocations on the temporary tables may also be enlarged. The resulting changes may cause all other jobs to run faster and make the window of time to run the backups significantly larger. Don't forget to change the parameters back for the daily processing.

Exports may be run at the same time that overnight reports are running because the tables are not being updated. Separate export runs may be made on a per-tablespace basis. Multiple exports will run faster than one long export job. Some tables may not require exporting, such as redundant tables, or historical tables.

References: Chapter 15, *Tuning Long-running Jobs*
                "Tuning EXPORT"

DBA: ***We've achieved good response times for our application. What should I monitor to be sure that we can maintain these response times?***

Follow these guidelines:

- Make sure your machine has free memory at all times and is not experiencing excessive paging and swapping.

- Make sure that the I/O load is balanced across all disks and controllers.

- Make sure that the number of users waiting for CPU is never excessive

- Make sure that you consider performance when making all changes made to the network.

- Collect regular response time feedback from production users and, if the response times are unacceptable, investigate the cause.

- Be aware of the numbers of users being added to your system and gauge what effect they will have on performance.

- If any part of the database is reorganized, always check to make sure that all expected indexes are resident.

- If any changes are made to the application, including table structure, program changes, or index changes, make sure they are thoroughly tested for performance to meet the levels specified in your site's tuning service agreement.

- Make sure you consider performance in making all changes to the database structure, for example, adding a tablespace.

- Make sure to monitor closely all ad hoc usage of the system.

- Be aware of any other applications running on your machine.

- Make sure that the data dictionary is cached adequately.

- Make sure that the hit rate of finding data, indexes, and rollbacks in memory is tuned as high as possible.

- Make sure that there is no segment in the database with excessive extents (dynamic extension). This includes tables (including temporary), indexes, and rollbacks.

- Make sure that the number of processes waiting for locks is minimized.

- Avoid all redo log and rollback contention in your database.

- Make sure that memory is being used adequately to assist sorting, especially of overnight jobs.

DBA: *What is chaining and how can I tell if it is having a negative impact on my users' response times?*

UPDATE statements cause chaining when a row expands beyond one physical database block. When each database block is created, it is given an area of free space; the size of this space is determined by the PCTFREE parameter in the STORAGE clause of the table or index that is being created. When a row in the block expands, ORACLE attempts to store the row's information in the same physical block. If the PCTFREE is too low, however, the row's data will be spread across several blocks, and this can seriously degrade performance.

Chaining will definitely affect the performance of users. You must monitor for chaining by running programs to check chaining against tables on a regular basis, perhaps about twice a month.

DBA: *Response times have been degrading over time. Can this be caused by database fragmentation? How can I tell if the database is badly fragmented?*

Database fragmentation can adversely affect response times because extra physical reads are required for a fragmented database. Database fragmentation includes both database segments that have many extents, and also the physical files on disk that make up a database.

Try to keep the number of extents to no greater than five. Our tests have shown that any more than five can start to have a severe effect on the segments' access times.

Ensure that all database files, including data files and redo logs, are contiguous on disk. If raw devices are available, use them. Check to make sure there is enough contiguous space on the disk prior to creating the database file. The machines that experience discontiguous database files tend to be lower-end machines that have every imaginable piece of software on them as well as the ORACLE database.

References: Chapter 3, *Planning and Managing the Tuning Process*
       "Understanding the Effect of Workload on Performance"
    Chapter 11, *Tuning a New Database*
       "Disk I/O Checklist"
       "Creating Tables"
       "Creating Indexes"
       "Creating Users"
    Chapter 12, *Diagnostic and Tuning Tools*
       "BSTAT, ESTAT, UTLBSTAT.sql, and UTLESTAT.sql"
    Chapter 13, *Monitoring and Tuning an Existing Database*
       "Tuning Disk I/O"
    Chapter 15, *Tuning Long-running Jobs*
       "Sizing Tables and Indexes"
    Chapter 18, *Tuning for Specific Systems*
       "Writing to Raw Devices"

DBA: *Is fragmentation on rollback segments bad?*

Having multiple extents for a rollback segment is not a bad thing because one rollback segment handles many transactions at a single time, with each transaction requiring its separate extent within the rollback segment. One transaction may dynamically extend to many extents within the one rollback segment however, and this can affect performance.

It pays to keep all extents the same size for a rollback segment, making the INITIAL and NEXT storage allocations the same size and setting the PCTINCREASE to zero. This will allow other transactions to reuse extents used by prior transactions.

Most sites have many online transaction processing users and a few longer-running update jobs. If your site has a mixed transaction size, you may have a couple of larger rollback segments, and many small rollback segments. Make sure that the size of the small rollback segments is a multiple of the larger rollback segments.

Versions 6.0.33 and later provide the SET TRANSATION USE ROLLBACK *SEGMENT roll-back_segment* command. You can issue this command for all long-running jobs to minimize dynamic extension of the rollback. Other users will have a good chance of being assigned one of many smaller rollbacks, which may be as small as 10K in size, and this will increase the chance of the rollback being held in buffer cache.

In Version 6, the size of rollbacks can become unwieldy, especially where long-running jobs use different rollbacks from one night to the next, making all rollback segments large. Overnight processing tends to involve many large modifications to tables. Many sites shut their database down, and restart with new larger rollback segments, then restart the database with smaller rollback segments for the next day's processing.

Version 7 offers a shrink-back facility to control the size of rollbacks. The rollbacks will shrink back to the size specified after completing the transaction that enlarged the roll-back.

References: Chapter 11, *Tuning a New Database*
                 "Creating Rollback Segments"
                 Chapter 13, *Monitoring and Tuning an Existing Database*
                 "Tuning Rollback Segments"
                 Chapter 15, *Tuning Long-running Jobs*
                 "Choosing Rollback Segments"

DBA: *I've noticed that larger update jobs perform better if they are able to use larger rollback segments. Is there a way to force a job to use a larger rollback?*

In Version 6.0.33 and later, use the SET TRANSACTION USE ROLLBACK SEGMENT *roll-back_segment* command mentioned above. Take advantage of this command by setting all larger transactions that will perform many data modifications to larger rollback segments. This will reduce dynamic extension and can speed up response times considerably.

References: Chapter 15, *Tuning Long-running Jobs*
                 "Choosing Rollback Segments"

DBA: *My site has a procedure that uses the SET TRANSACTION USE ROLLBACK SEGMENT* rollback_segment *statement to force the procedure to use a large rollback segment. The statement works well for some of the statements, but uses other rollback segments for other statements. This has a harmful effect on our run time. What can the cause be?*

Your procedure must contain a COMMIT or ROLLBACK statement, or you must be changing SQL jobs, which forces an implicit COMMIT. As soon as a ROLLBACK or COMMIT statement is processed, each new statement will be allocated a new rollback segment. Ensure that each statement has the SET TRANSACTION USE ROLLBACK SEGMENT *rollback_segment* command in it, or remove the COMMIT and ROLLBACK statements from your script. Make sure autocommit is not set on.

References: Chapter 11, *Tuning a New Database*
                "How Many Rollback Segments?"

DBA: *How do I know when the redo logs are correctly tuned?*

You can tune certain aspects of redo logs, as summarized below:

- There may be excessive I/Os being performed on the disks containing the redo logs. This problem is cured by enlarging the log buffer; this causes the system to write larger amounts of redo data less often. Our tests have indicated improvements of around 7% by enlarging the log buffer to one megabyte on medium-sized applications. You should also ensure that the LOG_CHECKPOINT_INTERVAL parameter is not set to a figure smaller than your redo logs. Each time a checkpoint occurs, a write is made to the database files. Set the LOG_CHECKPOINT_INTERVAL equal to or larger than the size of the redo logs. Make all redo logs the same size. Ensure that the redo logs are not too small, because this will also cause continual writes to redo log files. Redo log file sizes of five megabytes operate well at most sites.

- There may be contention of processes waiting to find free buffer space to place redo information into the redo log buffer. Once again, this can be cured by enlarging the log buffer.

- There may be contention occurring for the redo allocation latch, which allocates space in the redo log buffer. This problem is cured on multi-processor systems by decreasing the parameter LOG_SMALL_ENTRY_MAX_SIZE to force the larger copy latch to be used. You should also increase LOG_SIMULTANEOUS_COPIES to twice as many as the number of CPUs. For multi-processor systems, you can also increase the LOG_ENTRY_PREBUILD_THRESHOLD parameter to build more entries prior to writing them to the log buffer.

References: Chapter 11, *Tuning a New Database*
                     "INIT.ORA Parameter Summary"
                     "Creating the Database"
                     Chapter 13, *Monitoring and Tuning An Existing Database*
                     "Avoiding Contention"

DBA: *You mention an INIT.ORA parameter _OPTIMIZER_UNDO_CHANGES.*
             *This parameter is not documented and is not listed in my SQL*DBA*
             SHOW PARAMETERS output. How do I get a list of all parameters?

Run this query to see the ORACLE "hidden parameters:"

```
SELECT KSPPINM FROM X$KSPPI
WHERE SUBSTR (KSPPINM, 1, 1) = '_';

_LOG_CHECKPOINT_RECOVERY_CHECK
_DISABLE_LOGGING
_DB_NO_MOUNT_LOCK
_OFFLINE_ROLLBACK_SEGMENTS
_CORRUPTED_ROLLBACK_SEGMENTS
_USE_ROW_ENQUEUES
_REUSE_INDEX_LOOP
_REPLICATION
_OPTIMIZER_UNDO_CHANGES
_NO_SYNC
```

References: Chapter 11, *Tuning a New Database*
                     "INIT.ORA Parameter Summary"

DBA: *Is it possible to get a full list of all the available V$ performance*
             monitoring tables?

Run this query:

```
SELECT * FROM X$KQFVI;

ADDR       INDX       KQFTANAM
--------   ----------  ------------------------------
00171670          0   V$WAITSTAT
001716A8          1   V$ROWCACHE
001716E0          2   V$PROCESS
00171718          3   V$BGPROCESS
00171750          4   V$SESSION
00171788          5   V$TRANSACTION
001717C0          6   V$LATCH
001717F8          7   V$LATCHNAME
00171830          8   V$LATCHHOLDER
00171868          9   V$RESOURCE
001718A0         10   V$_LOCK1
001718D8         11   V$_LOCK
```

```
00171910          12 V$LOCK
00171948          13 V$SESSTAT
00171980          14 V$SYSSTAT
001719B8          15 V$STATNAME
001719F0          16 V$ACCESS
00171A28          17 V$DBFILE
00171A60          18 V$FILESTAT
00171A98          19 V$LOGFILE
00171AD0          20 V$ROLLNAME
00171B08          21 V$ROLLSTAT
00171B40          22 V$SGA
00171B78          23 V$PARAMETER
00171BB0          24 V$LOADCSTAT
00171BE8          25 V$LOADTSTAT
```

DBA: *Is there a way I can structure a database particularly for performance?*

If you structure your database correctly from the outset, you will get excellent initial performance. You will also facilitate the close monitoring of the database to pinpoint which part of the database needs attention, and you will minimize the effects of any new requirements from the database, such as a new application being added to it. Follow these guidelines:

- Locate redo log files on a disk other than the disk holding the database files. Redo logs of between five and ten megabytes perform well at most sites.

- Split tables and indexes into separate tablespaces.

- Separate tables commonly used together onto separate disks. Try to combine infrequently used tables from frequently used tables.

- Have a separate temporary tablespace.

- Place users into their own tablespace.

- Store the ORACLE products in a products tablespace.

- Store only the ORACLE system tables in the system tablespace.

- Create tablespaces on a per-application basis. Tables and indexes shared by many applications are best placed into common tablespaces.

- Do not store any part of the ORACLE database on the operating system disk; in particular, keep away from the operating system disk where paging and swapping takes place.

- Allocate many medium-sized tablespaces instead of fewer large tablespaces.

- Spread your disk I/O across as many disk drives and disk controllers as possible.

- Be aware of your machine-specific disk characteristics such as the advantages of raw devices on many UNIX systems.

- Ensure that care is taken in sizing every part of the database to allow for growth. There should be enough free space in your database to rebuild the largest table in your application

References: Chapter 11, *Tuning a New Database*

Questions from System Administrators

SA: **The overnight backups are taking too long. What options are available to speed them up?**

ORACLE offers you several ways to back up your system. If you are running with archiving enabled, you have the option of performing hot backups, that is, backing up to tape without shutting your database down. You must ensure that your archives are backed up to tape. If you don't have the time to perform a full image database copy nightly, hot backups may be a good alternative for you. If you use hot backups, we recommend that you take a full consistent database backup, with the database shut down periodically--at least twice a month.

We recommend that all sites take an export of their database nightly. If you are running client-server, make sure that all exporting takes place at the database server end, not across the network. Consider having a larger BUFFER parameter for the export, having multiple exports running (with each exporting a different set of tables), and exporting from disk to disk, which is considerable faster than exporting to tape.

References: Chapter 15, *Tuning Long-running Jobs*
                  "Tuning EXPORT"

SA: **Our CPU is overworked coping with the ORACLE users. What can I do?**

One of the most common causes of an overworked CPU is a lack of memory on your machine. First, find out if this is the case by issuing the appropriate command for your operating system. ORACLE has several parameters that can be tuned to minimize the use of memory. The parameter that should usually be reduced first is the DB_BLOCK_ BUFFER parameter, followed by the LOG_BUFFER and then DC_ dictionary cache parameters (in Version 6) or SHARED_POOL_SIZE in (Version 7). The SORT_AREA_ SIZE (and SORT_AREA_RETAINED_SIZE in Version 7), indicating the amount of memory reserved for each user process to sort in memory, is also an important parameter to tune.

If you have free memory, investigate which processes are using the most CPU resources. From our experience, these processes tend to be those from untuned programs or poor design either of the database or the program. They may also quite often be run by developers who shouldn't even be on the machine at the time.

References: Chapter 2, *What Causes Performance Problems?*
                Chapter 18, *Tuning For Specific Systems*

SA: ***We have excessive paging and swapping. What can be done to ORACLE to alleviate this problem?***

You must reduce your memory usage immediately by reducing ORACLE's memory usage. Consider reducing DB_BLOCK_BUFFER, LOG_BUFFER, SORT_AREA_SIZE, and DC_ parameters (SHARED_POOL_SIZE in Version 7) in the order listed here.

There are many machine-specific ways of reducing memory usage. If you are running UNIX, consider reducing the UNIX buffer cache if you are using raw devices. If you are running VMS, make sure that all ORACLE executables have been installed as shared.

References: Chapter 2, *What Causes Performance Problems?*
                    "Memory Problems and Tuning"
                Chapter 11, *Tuning a New Database*
                    "Tuning Memory"
                Chapter 13, *Monitoring and Tuning an Existing Database*
                    "Tuning Memory"
                Chapter 18, *Tuning For Specific Systems*

SA: ***The ORACLE application is I/O bound. What can be done?***

Your disk I/O must be spread evenly across disk devices and controllers. If one disk exceeds its maximum I/Os per second, and if users requests are forced to wait in a queue for their reads or writes to occur, your users response times will suffer accordingly. Follow this checklist to avoid excessive disk I/Os:

* Keep developers and QA staff off your production machines

* Separate redo log files and database files onto separate disk drives

* Do not store any part of the database on the operating system disk

* Split tables and indexes into separate tablespaces on different disks

* Split tables that are commonly used into separate tablespaces on different disks

* Avoid arbitrary site standards (we have found these at some sites), such as allowing only the system tablespace to reside on a specified disk.

* Size your tables, indexes, rollbacks, and temporary segments correctly to avoid dynamic extension and chaining

* Make effective use of memory by storing as much data in memory buffers as possible, and allow sorting to take place in memory instead of disk wherever possible.

References: Chapter 11, *Tuning a New Database*
                  "Tuning Disk I/O"
                Chapter 13, *Monitoring and Tuning an Existing Database*
                  "Tuning Disk I/O"

SA: *We have a UNIX-based network which has many machines attached. Monitoring the network and ORACLE database is giving me a real headache. Are there any tools on the market that provide online monitoring of distributed systems?*

We are aware of three excellent products that revolutionize the monitoring of distributed systems. Patrol, from Patrol Software, was developed under the guidance of Martin Picard, the former Director of Networking products at ORACLE; Ecosphere was developed by Ecosystems; and DB-Vision, which has a very good reputation, was developed by Aston Brooke Software, Inc. All of these products allow system administrators to monitor and manage remote workstations and applications, including ORACLE. All have attractive graphical front ends that make the job of administering a distributed network featuring an ORACLE database a pleasure. These products are state-of-the-art; we are certain that, as time goes on, more and more products will be developed in this area.

C

Tuning ORACLE Financials

We are grateful to Stuart Worthington, formerly of ORACLE and now Senior DBA for British Petroleum European Centre of Expertise—Accounting, for writing this appendix.

Introduction to ORACLE Financials Tuning

ORACLE Financials is an accounting package available from ORACLE that includes modules for general ledger, accounts payable, accounts receivable, fixed assets, purchasing, inventory, and other accounting functions. ORACLE Financials is a best-selling package that has matured into a stable and well-supported product. There have been some criticisms of performance and other characteristics of the early releases of the package, but Releases 9 and 10 are quite robust, and they offer vastly improved documentation and quality control. By tuning ORACLE Financials as described in this appendix, you can get even better performance out of the product.

Our first recommendation is that if your site is experiencing performance problems and running Release 8 or earlier, you upgrade to Release 9.3 or later.

Getting the most out of your hardware for a Financials database is very different from tuning an in-house application. Unless your site is writing a substantial amount of custom code, you will not be able to change any of the database design. Also, because you do not have access to most of the source code, you will not have many options to change the programs themselves. In addition, we recommend that you do not make too many changes to the indexes because the ORACLE developers have written their code with particular indexes in mind. By changing indexes, you might fall into the trap of making one particular program run faster, only to find that some other program (one you may never have heard of) that previously took an hour now needs to be killed after twelve hours!

You also won't be able to do as much with SQL*Trace as you would be able to do with other applications. In fact, the only way you'll be able to set it at all for some programs is at the database level. But, if you do this, you'll find that all your user processes write trace files to the same disk, and you'll run into the problem of identifying which ones you're interested in. In fact, if you don't have the source code, you may not be able to do much with the trace file anyway.

Are you discouraged yet? Although there are a number of aspects of ORACLE Financials that you can't tune, there are still many other areas where your tuning can make a big difference in overall performance. Note too that many of our recommendations apply as well to other products that use the Application Object Library (AOL, formerly known as Application Foundation). These products include ORACLE*Alert, ORACLE*Personnel, and ORACLE*Payroll.

Installing ORACLE Financials

If your ORACLE Financials database has not yet been installed, you have a lot of decisions to make. If you are not experienced with Financials, we recommend that you consider engaging the services of ORACLE Professional Services to help with your installation. The consultant assigned to you will typically have installed and upgraded several versions at many different sites, and this person will be able to save you a lot of time. You will probably learn much more by participating in a joint installation than by doing it yourself the hard way. With luck, you will have the luxury of being able to install the database and applications for a long testing and evaluation period, knowing that you will be able to completely rebuild your database before going live. Without careful planning, you might have to do this anyway.

First, and most obviously, try an "RYM"—Read Your Manual. Although the installation manual is dauntingly thick, it is thick for a reason. There is a lot you need to know. You won't normally be expected to know much about the applications themselves, but you will have to know a lot about how they fit together from a DBA's perspective. It is not unreasonable for a DBA who is experienced with ORACLE but new to Financials to spend a week or even two weeks reading through the documentation before even creating the database.

Pay particular attention to the appendix in the manual describing how to size your database. Financials is very disk-hungry, and many installations fail because unwary DBAs assume that Financials is just another application and that a 500-megabyte partition will be more than enough. It won't be. Even just installing Accounts Payable requires the installation of executables for six other dependent products, plus ORACLE*Alert and the Application Object Library (which are always required). This initial installation uses 250 megabytes of disk by itself. Add to that 180 megabytes for a demonstration database, and more for some rollback segments and a temporary tablespace. Even if you haven't already run out of space, you will do so as soon as your users start writing output files and log files.

Take the time to figure out how much space you'll need for executables, add at least an approximate database sizing, and then add a generous comfort factor. Don't forget that you'll need to upgrade one day, and may need to keep two versions of either ORACLE or Financials on-line. Disk space really isn't that expensive these days, especially when you take into account how much of your time and therefore your organization's money you'll save. Our recommendation: go for the extra gigabyte! Be similarly generous when choosing your "sizing factor." Although any value from zero to 999% is possible, we would never recommend less than 50% for any instance that you plan to keep for longer than a month.

If you are an experienced DBA using Release 9 or later and you want more flexibility than simply using the sizing factor, you might consider modifying the Object Description Files (ODFs). Under UNIX, these are stored under *$MOD_TOP/install/odf*, where *$MOD_TOP* represents the top module of any directory (e.g., *$FND_TOP* or *$GL_TOP*). The ODFs store the table definitions and sizings and provide a convenient method of presizing your tables and indexes. The tables are grouped together according to function. You can also use the *odfgen* and *odfcmp* utilities to check that what exists in the database matches what should be there. In a UNIX installation, *odfgen* and *odfcmp* are stored under *$APPL_TOP/install*.

Some ODFs you might find of particular interest are:

$GL_TOP/install/odf/glje.odf	GL journal entries tables
$GL_TOP/install/odf/glbal.odf	GL balances table
$GL_TOP/install/odf/glaccflx.odf	GL code combinations table
$AR_TOP/install/odf/artrx.odf	AR payment schedules and transactions tables
$RA_TOP/install/odf/rainv.od	RA invoicing and transactions tables
$FA_TOP/install/odf/fadeprn.odf	FA depreciation tables

Database-Level Tuning

The Release 9 installation manual lists "certain parameters that affect the performance of ORACLE Applications products," along with recommended values for these parameters. Unfortunately, the values shown are not appropriate for the size of the database discussed in the manual and would not allow all of the "60 simultaneous ORACLE users" mentioned in the manual to connect, even if there were no concurrent processing going on.

We recommend the following parameter settings as a starting point for a Financials database running Accounts Payable, General Ledger, and Fixed Assets and supporting 20 concurrent users:

```
4 x 5-megabyte log files

4 rollback segments, each of which is at least 20 megabytes,
    with total rollback space available of at least 100 megabytes

DC_COLUMNS = 4000           #V6 Only
DC_COLUMN_GRANTS = 10       #V6 Only
DC_INDEXES = 600            #V6 Only
DC_OBJECTS = 1000           #V6 Only
DC_SEQUENCES = 40           #V6 Only
DC_SEQUENCES_GRANTS = 40    #V6 Only
DC_SYNONYMS = 300           #V6 Only
DC_TABLES = 400             #V6 Only
DC_TABLE_GRANTS = 800       #V6 Only

OPEN_CURSORS = 255
ROW_CACHE_ENQUEUES = 2500

DB_BLOCK_BUFFERS = 2000
DDL_LOCKS = 2000
PROCESSES = 60

NLS_SORT = FALSE
_OPTIMIZER_UNDO_CHANGES = TRUE     # 6.0.33.2 and above only
```

The _OPTIMIZER_UNDO_CHANGES parameter is an interesting one. ORACLE made an important change to the optimizer in Version 6.0.31 of the kernel, as they explain in The README document.

> "For increased performance, additional subqueries are now transformed into joins by the optimizer. Queries with an 'IN subquery' such as:
>
> ```
> SELECT col_list FROM t1 WHERE col2 IN (SELECT col2 FROM t2)
> ```
>
> are now transformed into the form:

```
SELECT col_list FROM t1, t2 WHERE t1.col2 = t2.col2
```

when t2.col2 is known to be unique. The EXPLAIN command indicates the new execution plan" (From *$ORACLE_HOME/rdbms/doc/vms_readme.doc*).

This change in the optimizer had the unforeseen effect of making some areas of Financials run more slowly. Although the new optimizer indeed results in increased performance for many queries and for most applications, it causes problems for certain long-running queries in Financials. These queries had been manually optimized by using subqueries to force a certain execution plan.

To allow an application to ignore the new optimizer and use its own execution plan, you can now (in Version 6.0.33.2 and later) set the parameter, _OPTIMIZER_UNDO_ CHANGES to TRUE. Always set this parameter to TRUE for a Financials database. Don't forget your test or development instances, especially when your site is creating its own custom code. Otherwise, your developers and testers might be working with the wrong version of the optimizer. Remember to set this parameter before making any changes to the indexes; your change might have unforeseen consequences. (Note that _OPTIMIZER_UNDO_CHANGES is a "hidden parameter." See the section called "INIT.ORA Parameter Summary" in Chapter 11, *Tuning a New Database,* for a discussion of such parameters.)

Concurrent Request Processing

One of the most powerful features of the Application Object Library is its support of concurrent processing. This feature gives the system administrator many ways to fine-tune daily processing. Too many sites use default processing of a set number of concurrent managers which handle all programs for all users from the time when the database comes up to the time when it shuts down again. Some sites set up processing with enough managers so that nothing ever has to wait in the queue before being processed. However, this approach defeats one of the main purposes of having concurrent processing, which is to prevent long-running updates and reports from interfering with users' interactive processing.

At sites that have too many concurrent managers, the reasoning seems to be that they never want to have to wait for a quick job to hang around in the queue. For example, if someone is waiting for a rush check, and all six concurrent managers are running FSGs, then the easy solution is to have 10 managers running, so that no matter how many FSGs are running, checks can be printed any time. This approach solves one problem, but creates another: you may end up with several large, non-urgent jobs running right in the middle of the morning when all of your data entry clerks are working flat out getting processing ready for the end of the quarter.

Here is another possible reason for taking this approach. Consider the case in which a senior manager needs some reports in a hurry for the Board of Directors. She doesn't get them in time, because the concurrent queue is too busy processing journal reversals and trial balances. After she's chewed out the system administrator (because the only concurrent request she cared about kept getting leap-frogged by everyone else's work), she insists that the number of concurrent managers be doubled to make absolutely sure this situation never happens again. Even though most of these extra managers will never be needed, they will still cause a small drain on the system because each requires at least one extra process and ORACLE connection.

Some sites don't have enough concurrent managers. The system is so busy in the morning that the concurrent managers have been cut to a minimum. Unfortunately, this means that over lunch and in the evening, only a fraction of the CPU power, memory, and disk capacity that cost so much money is being utilized. The effect is that your Finance department staff, for example, gets frustrated, because the jobs they submit one day are still pending the next morning.

What's the solution? You could suggest a hardware upgrade, or you could take a more economical approach: use the power of the concurrent managers to make your machine resources work more effectively. Be sure to read thoroughly the section on concurrent managers in your system administrator documentation to find out how the situations we describe above should be handled. Here are some brief suggestions:

One good approach is to classify programs according to different request types, so that you might define one queue for the short fast jobs that have to run right away, and another queue for your long-running reports. Your long reports queue might not even get started up till late afternoon, but will concurrently run enough large jobs to keep your machine fully utilized right through the night, when the clerks have gone home. Overnight response time isn't especially important. What you care about in this case is throughput. You might find that if you have three times as many jobs running, you'll get twice as much done overnight. This approach is a particularly important one for multi-CPU machines, where you should aim for between one and three jobs running on each processor.

Are you still worried about that manager who chewed you out? Use the \ Navigate Profile Levels screen to set her "Concurrent:Request Priority" higher so that now she leap-frogs other people in the concurrent request queue. If she is your boss's boss, you might want to consider giving her own personal queue.

There are many different approaches to concurrent processing tuning. For instance, you could set default priorities at the application or responsibility level. You could grant a responsible user the system administrator responsibility so he or she can change the priorities of jobs after they have been submitted. You could permit a different number of concurrent requests to run every hour of the day. You could educate users to put jobs on hold or request a start time in the afternoon. If you have a program that makes the lights go dim, you can use the \ Navigate Concurrent Programs screen to make it incompatible with itself, so that it can never be running more than once at a time. When required, you can reset the number of concurrent managers manually through the \ Navigate Concurrent Managers Define screen, and then reset the managers using the \ Navigate Concurrent Control screen.

Most sites do not need this much flexibility in handling concurrent requests, but even for a small Financials instance (e.g., 10 concurrent users), you should, at a minimum, think about having separate queues for quick urgent jobs and long slow jobs, and you should set up work shifts so that more of the long jobs can run at night, and more of the quick jobs can run during the day.

If you want to monitor your concurrent queues more closely, take a look at the wealth of information stored in the FND_CONCURRENT_REQUESTS table, normally owned by ORACLE user APPLSYS. This table holds all the information in the \ Navigate Concurrent Requests screen and more. You can use this to answer questions such as the following:

How many jobs were in the queue at a given time and either running or scheduled to run? Run this query:

```
SELECT COUNT(*)
    FROM FND_CONCURRENT_REQUEST
    WHERE REQUEST_DATE < TO_DATE
        ('&&WHEN','DD-MON-YY HH24:MI')
    AND REQUESTED_START_DATE < TO_DATE
        ('&&WHEN','DD-MON-YY HH24:MI')
    AND ACTUAL_COMPLETION_DATE > TO_DATE
        ('&&WHEN','DD-MON-YY HH24:MI');
```

How many jobs today had to wait ten minutes or longer to run? Run this query:

```
SELECT COUNT(*)
    FROM FND_CONCURRENT_REQUESTS
    WHERE ACTUAL_START_DATE-GREATEST
        (REQUEST_DATE,REQUESTED_START_DATE) > 10/(24*60*60)
        AND REQUEST_DATE > TRUNC(SYSDATE);
```

How many jobs this week have taken longer than an hour to run? Run this query:

```
SELECT COUNT(*)
    FROM FND_CONCURRENT_REQUESTS
    WHERE NVL(ACTUAL_COMPLETION_DATE,SYSDATE) -
        ACTUAL_START_DATE > 1/24
        AND REQUEST_DATE > TRUNC(SYSDATE,'DAY');
```

It is worthwhile making a copy of this table that will never get purged so that you can look back at how long a particular job normally takes when it is run with a certain set of parameters. This can be very useful when planning quarter-end. Don't be tempted not to purge at all though. The concurrent requests screen will start to slow down. Because this is the screen that users use most and query most, you have to store the data you need somewhere else.

Try to work with your accounting staff. They will be able to tell you about priorities and experiences: when they are running the big jobs, which jobs can be killed and which are critical, which screens are slow, and which jobs seem to be taking longer and longer.

One problem you might encounter when using machines with 80386 processors is that memory "leaks" can cause the resident set size of the FNDLIBR processes to grow ever larger. You can reclaim some of this memory by reducing the number of concurrent managers, resetting them, setting the number of concurrent managers back to normal, then resetting again.

Another problem you might run into on some platforms (e.g., ULTRIX) is that because the concurrent managers are started in the background, they are also run at a lower priority. Because ORACLE performs best when all user processes and background processes are running at the same priority, you can edit *$FNT_TOP/bin/batchmgr* so that the concurrent managers are started up with the normal priority using *nohup* and *nice -0.*

A final problem you might encounter is that when concurrent jobs are terminated through the Concurrent Requests screen, there is a problem with some versions of UNIX and some releases of the kernel: stray shadow processes may be left running. When a process is running normally, there is a user process running *rpt* (SQL*Report) or *runrep* (SQL*Reportwriter), for example, and there is an ORACLE background process. Both of these process IDs can be found through the SQL*DBA Monitor Users screen. Occasionally the user process is killed, but the ORACLE background process does not die. This problem seems to happen more with CPU-intensive programs, especially custom code. The stray process can cause problems for two reasons. First, it can hold locks, which then cause problems for other users. Second, the process can run wild, using up as much CPU as it can find. If you notice this happening, you should kill the ORACLE background process manually through UNIX. You will be able to see your action reflected in the SQL*DBA Monitor Processes screen after a few seconds delay. It is possible to create a *cron* job, which automatically kills unmatched ORACLE background processes.

Archiving and Purging

The Financials systems require more housecleaning in the form of archiving and purging than most applications. In release 9 and above, you can do this via menus by running a report, although most sites prefer to have this done automatically every night. There's no need to write your own purge script. Use the one ORACLE provides in the script *$FND_TOP/sql/FNDCPDRQ.sql*. This will clear the three tables that are the biggest problem. We recommend that you run it daily. Sites that are running auditing will periodically want to purge from the following:

```
FND_LOGINS,
FND_LOGIN_RESPONSIBILITIES
FND_LOGIN_RESP_FORMS
```

If you want to check, or change your level of Auditing, go to the \ Navigate Profile Levels screen and query the site profile options "Audit Trail:Activate" and "Sign-On:Audit Level". Remember that every change to every table is audited at row-level anyway, so you might wish to turn off this profile option, especially for test instances. Auditing can be set at the Site, Application, Responsibility, or User levels. The level of auditing will determine how much you can see through the \ Navigate Security Monitor screen.

All accounting applications are disk-hungry, and ORACLE Financials is no exception. You will come to know, if you don't already, the tables that, like a variant on that bunny in the battery ads, just keep on growing and growing. The biggest tables we've ever worked with in our BP German production database are the following:

Table	Rows	Size (including indexes)
GL_JE_LINES	3,900,000	1120 megabytes
GL_JE_HEADERS	200,000	85 megabytes
GL_BALANCES	3,250,000	678 megabytes
AP_PAYMENT_SCHEDULES	490,000	41 megabytes
FA_DEPRN_SUMMARY	2,100,000	360 megabytes (oldest data 19 months)
FA_DEPRN_DETAIL	2,000,000	390 megabytes
RA_CUSTOMER_TRX	420,000	555 megabytes (only 3 months on-line)
RA_CUSTOMER_TRX_LINES	1,800,000	1376 megabytes (archived monthly)

We've heard of other sites that have even larger tables. Talk with your accounting staff about how many months of past data are really required. If, like many accountants, they never want to purge anything, then calculate how many extra disks they'll need to pay for per year, and let them work out a compromise!

The table that is most likely to cause a problem is GL_BALANCES, because this table doesn't grow at a constant rate per month, but grows irregularly, particularly when new budgets are being created. Don't plan on taking any vacation for at least the first two quarter-ends after going live. Remember, your users have deadlines too.

When you are archiving such large tables you'll need to plan especially carefully.

First, remember that your bottleneck is likely to be the archiver, so either use "ping-ponging" so your log files switch disks, or (if you feel lucky), temporarily turn off archiving altogether.

Consider the following example. A medium-sized site running unattended overnight backups might move its Friday night backup to Sunday night. This allows the DBA to shut down the database, start it up in *noarchivelog* mode, run the purges, then start up the database in *archivelog* mode in time for the Sunday night backup. You should be able to recover users' work from a disk crash on Friday afternoon, or Monday afternoon. Be careful though. If Sunday night's backup isn't 100% reliable, you are vulnerable until your next backup. A safer alternative for sites that normally run archiving to disk is to archive to tape temporarily. That way, the archiver runs faster and is less likely to run out of space.

While we're on the subject of backups, we'd like to recommend that most production Financials sites run "hot" backups. Sites that run cold backups every night are squandering machine resources. Although Financials will automatically restart any jobs in the concurrent queue after a database restart, these jobs will typically have to be killed when the clerks start logging on. Properly managed, your hardware can do just as much work at 11 p.m. as at 11 a.m.

After a large purge, you should consider rebuilding your tables or at least your indexes. The same advice applies to tables which get purged more regularly. You will often be surprised at just how much space you can save by rebuilding tables and indexes. We were able to save 120 megabytes by rebuilding the indexes alone on GL_INTERFACE at one site in Switzerland, and 13 megabytes just by rebuilding FND_DUAL at another.

The GL Optimizer

The GL optimizer mimics a cost-based optimizer for version 6 of the kernel. It stores information about the selectivity of each of your segment values and creates indexes where appropriate. You should run the GL optimizer at least once a period or after creating a large number of segment values, defining a new chart of accounts, or changing summary templates.

When your Accounting Flexfield structure is set up through the \ Navigate Setup Financials Flexfields Key Segments screen, pay attention to the Indexed field in the segment zone. If this part of the implementation is being done in-house, we recommend that you index all segments except for those with six or fewer values. You can use the *ONEIDXS. sql* script under *$ORACLE_HOME/rdbms/admin* to measure the selectivity of all your segments. See *$ORACLE_HOME/rdbms/doc/idxstat.doc* for details.

The GL optimizer is designed primarily to make FSGs run faster. We recommend that for validation of flex-fields, you also create a non-unique concatenated index on the account segment followed by all the other segments in flex-field order.

NOTE

No indexes will be created until you run the GL optimizer through the \ Navigate Setup System Optimize screen. Also, be aware that this approach will not drop any indexes, so you might want to make sure that you don't have redundant indexes still defined.

Using Trace in ORACLE Applications Forms

Follow these instructions to turn on the trace facility in any AOL form. Note that trace will not be turned on for any concurrent jobs submitted by that form.

1. Sign on to AOL using the "Application Developer" responsibility.

2. Go to the \ Navigate **Menu** Define screen and query up the "OTHER" screen for application "Application Object Library"

3. Add the following menu entries:

```
  Sequence   ------------------ Action --------------------
  Prompt     Description   Type        Application   Name    Arguments
4 TraceOn    Trace on      User Exit   Application   TRACE   ON
5 TraceOff   Trace off     User Exit   Application   TRACE   OFF
```

4. When you log out and log back in, your menus are recompiled, and you can now turn trace on or off via \ Other TraceOn or \ Other TraceOff. Being able to turn tracing on and off in an on-line way gives you the capability to isolate any problems. For instance, if you have a long delay with a particular QuickPick, you could turn Trace on just before you move to the field in question, and turn it off again after you have moved to the next field.

If you are still using release 8, the process is a little more complicated:

1. Go to the \ Navigate **Menu** Subroutine screen, and for the application you are interested in (e.g., ORACLE Inventory), add the following macros:

Macro Name	Description
FORCESQL "ALTER SESSION SET SQL_TRACE TRUE"	Enable trace
FORCESQL "ALTER SESSION SET SQL_TRACE FALSE"	Disable trace

2. Go to the \ Navigate **Menu** Define screen. Query application "Application Foundation" and menu name "OTHER".

3. Go to the next zone and add the subroutines you have just created as menu options for your particular application.

4. Exit and re-enter Financials to allow your menus to be recompiled.

Dynamic Performance Tables

Dynamic performance tables are tables in which ORACLE stores system statistics. Part V of this book describes how the DBA can access these tables to get information on system activity that may be helpful in tuning the database and other aspects of the system. The sections below list the columns and public synonyms for all Version 6 and Version 7 tables that you can access via queries, as well as the tables that are accessed automatically by various functions available from the SQL*DBA MONITOR facility (described in Chapter 12, *Diagnostic and Tuning Tools*).

WARNING

The V$ tables are prone to frequent change. If you are using some of the later releases of Version 6, you may find that your layout resembles the ORACLE7 table layout. We have made every attempt to make the table descriptions as accurate and up to date as possible, and we will continue to review the layouts with each new release of this book.

Version 6 Dynamic Performance Tables

V$ACCESS—Describes the owners of tables.

PID	NUMBER	Process identifier
TABLE#	NUMBER	Table object identifier
OWNER	NUMBER	Identifier of table owner
OWNERNAME	CHAR(30)	Name of table owner
TABLENAME	CHAR(30)	Table name

V$BGPROCESS—Describes the background processes.

PADDR	RAW(4)	Address of the process state object
NAME	CHAR(5)	Name of this background process
DESCRIPTION	CHAR(64)	Description of the background process

V$DBFILE—Information about each database file in the database.

| FILE# | NUMBER | File identifier number |
| NAME | CHAR(255) | Filename |

V$FILESTAT—Information about file read/write statistics.

PHYWRTS	NUMBER	Number of physical writes done
PHYRDS	NUMBER	Number of physical reads done
PHYBLKWRT	NUMBER	Number of physical blocks written
PHYBLKRD	NUMBER	Number of physical blocks read
READTIM	NUMBER	Time spent doing reads if the parameter TIMED_STATISTICS is TRUE; 0 if FALSE
WRITETIM	NUMBER	Time spent doing writes if the parameter TIMED_STATISTICS is TRUE; 0 if FALSE

V$LATCH—Information about each type of latch. (The rows of this table and the rows of V$LATCHNAME correspond one-to-one.)

ADDR	RAW(4)	Address of latch object
LATCH#	NUMBER	Latch number
LEVEL#	NUMBER	Latch level
WAITS	NUMBER	Number of times wanted with wait
IMMEDIATES	NUMBER	Number of immediate successes when wanted wait
TIMEOUTS	NUMBER	Number of timeouts when wanted wait
NOWAITS	NUMBER	Number of times wanted without wait
SUCCESSES	NUMBER	Number of successes when wanted no wait

V$LATCHHOLDER—Information about the current latch holders.

| PID | NUMBER | Identifier of process holding the latch |
| LADDR | RAW(4) | Latch address |

V$LATCHNAME—The decoded latch names for the latches shown in table V$LATCH. (The rows of this table and the rows of V$LATCH correspond one-to-one.)

| LATCH# | NUMBER | Latch number |
| NAME | CHAR(64) | Latch name |

V$LOCK—Addresses of locks, resources, and processes holding the locks.

LADDR	RAW(4)	Address of lock
PADDR	RAW(4)	Address of process who acquired the lock
RADDR	RAW(4)	Address of resource for this lock
LMODE	NUMBER(38)	Lock mode held
REQUEST	NUMBER(38)	Lock mode requested

V$LOCK—Information about locks.

ADDR	RAW(4)	Address of lock
PID	NUMBER	Identifier of process holding the lock
TYPE	CHAR(2)	Resource type
ID1	NUMBER	Resource identifier #1
ID2	NUMBER	Resource identifier #2
LMODE	NUMBER(38)	Lock mode held
REQUEST	NUMBER(38)	Lock mode requested

V$LOGFILE—Information about redo log files.

FILE#	NUMBER	Redo log file identifier number
NAME	CHAR(255)	Redo log filename

V$PARAMETER—Information about current parameter values.

NUM	NUMBER	Parameter number
NAME	CHAR(64)	Parameter name
TYPE	NUMBER	Parameter type
VALUE	CHAR(50)	Parameter value

V$PROCESS—Information about currently active processes.

ADDR	RAW(4)	Address of process state object
PID	NUMBER	ORACLE process identifier
SPID	CHAR(9)	Operating system process identifier
USERNAME	CHAR(13)	Operating system process user name
SERIAL#	NUMBER	Process serial number
TERMINAL	CHAR(8)	Operating system terminal identifier
PROGRAM	CHAR(64)	Program in progress
BACKGROUND	CHAR(40)	1 for a background process; null for a normal process

| LATCHWAIT | CHAR(8) | Address of latch waiting for; null if non (raw) |
| LOCKWAIT | CHAR(40) | Address of lock waiting for; null if non (raw) |

V$RESOURCE—Information about resources.

ADDR	RAW(4)	Address of resource object
TYPE	CHAR(2)	Resource type
ID1	NUMBER	Resource identifier #1
ID2	NUMBER	Resource identifier #2

V$ROLLNAME—Names of rollback segments. (Although this table has no join key with V$ROLLSTAT, the rows of the two tables correspond one-to-one.)

| USN | NUMBER | Rollback ("undo") segment number |
| NAME NOT NULL | CHAR(30) | Rollback segment name |

V$ROLLSTAT—Rollback segment statistics. (Although this table has no join key with V$ROLLNAME, the rows of the two tables correspond one-to-one.)

EXTENTS	NUMBER	Number of rollback extents
RSSIZE	NUMBER	Size in bytes of rollback segment
WRITES	NUMBER	Number of bytes written to rollback segment
XACTS	NUMBER	Number of active transactions
GETS	NUMBER	Number of header gets
WAITS	NUMBER	Number of header waits

V$ROWCACHE—Statistics for data dictionary activity: each row contains statistics for one data dictionary cache.

CACHE#	NUMBER	Row cache ID number
TYPE	CHAR(11)	Parent or subordinate row cache type
SUBORDINATE#	NUMBER	Subordinate set number
PARAMETER	CHAR(32)	Name of the INIT.ORA parameter that determines the number of entries in the data dictionary cache
COUNT	NUMBER	Total number of entries in the cache (cache size)
USAGE	NUMBER	Number of cache entries that contain valid data
FIXED	NUMBER	Number of fixed entries in the cache

GETS	NUMBER	Total number of requests for Information on the data object
GETMISSES	NUMBER	Number of data requests resulting in cache misses
SCANS	NUMBER	Number of scan requests
SCANMISSES	NUMBER	Number of times a scan failed to find the data in the cache
SCANCOMPLETES	NUMBER	For a list of subordinate entries, the number of times the list was scanned completely
MODIFICATIONS	NUMBER	Number of inserts, updates, and deletions
FLUSHES	NUMBER	Number of times flushed to disk

V$SESSION—Session information for each current session.

SID	NUMBER	Session identifier
PADDR	RAW(4)	Address of parent process state object
SESSION#	NUMBER	User session number
USER#	NUMBER	ORACLE user identifier
USERNAME	CHAR(30)	ORACLE user name
COMMAND	NUMBER	Command in progress
TADDR	CHAR(8)	Address of transaction state object

V$SESSTAT—For each current session, the current statistics values.

SID	NUMBER	Session identifier
STATISTIC#	NUMBER	Statistic number (identifier)
VALUE	NUMBER	Statistic value

V$SGA—Information about the System Global Area.

NAME	CHAR(20)	Component name
VALUE	NUMBER	Value

V$STATNAME—Decoded statistic names for the statistics shown in the tables V$SESSTAT and V$SYSSTAT.

STATISTIC#	NUMBER	Statistic number
NAME	CHAR(64)	Statistic name
CLASS	NUMBER	Statistic class

V$SYSSTAT—The current system-wide value for each statistic in table V$SESSTAT.

STATISTIC#	NUMBER	Statistic number
VALUE	NUMBER	Statistic value

V$TRANSACTION—Information about transactions.

ADDR	RAW(4)	Address of transaction state object
SCNBASE	NUMBER	First part of the system commit number invalid if inactive
SCNWRAP	NUMBER	Second part of the system commit number invalid if inactive
XIDUSN	NUMBER	Rollback ("undo") segment number; invalid if inactive
XIDSLOT	NUMBER	Slot number; invalid if inactive
XIDSQN	NUMBER	Sequence number; invalid if inactive
UBADBA	NUMBER	Database block address for rollback data; invalid if inactive
UBASQN	NUMBER	Sequence number for rollback data; invalid if inactive
UBAREC	NUMBER	Record number for rollback data; invalid if inactive

V$WAITSTAT—Block contention statistics.

OPERATION	CHAR(20)	Type of operation causing the contention
CLASS	CHAR(19)	Class of block subject to contention
RANGE	CHAR(9)	Range of waiting time, in milliseconds
COUNT	NUMBER	Number of waits by this OPERATION for this CLASS of clock lasting for this RANGE of time
TIME	NUMBER	Sum of all wait times for all the waits by this OPERATION for this CLASS of block lasting for this RANGE of time

Version 7 Dynamic Performance Tables

V$ACCESS—Describes the owners of objects.

SID	VARCHAR2	Session number that is accessing an object
OWNER	VARCHAR2	Owner of the object
OBJECT	VARCHAR2	Name of the object
OB_TYP	VARCHAR2	Type identifier for the object

V$ARCHIVE—Information on archive logs for each thread in the database system. (Each row provides information for one thread.)

GROUP#	NUMBER	Logfile group number
THREAD#	NUMBER	Logfile thread number
SEQUENCE#	NUMBER	Logfile sequence number
CURRENT	VARCHAR2	Archive log currently in use
FIRST_CHANGE#	NUMBER	First SCN stored in the current log

V$BACKUP—Backup status of all on-line data files.

FILE#	NUMBER	File identifier
STATUS	VARCHAR2	File status: NOT ACTIVE, ACTIVE (backup in progress), OFFLINE NORMAL, or description of an error
CHANGE#	NUMBER	System change number when backup started
TIME	NUMBER	Time the backup started

V$BGPROCESS—Describes the background processes.

PADDR	RAW(4)	Address of the process state object
NAME	VARCHAR2	Name of this background process
DESCRIPTION	VARCHAR2	Description of the background process
ERROR	NUMBER	Error encountered

V$CIRCUIT—Information about virtual circuits (user connections to the database through dispatchers and servers).

CIRCUIT	RAW(4)	Circuit address
DISPATCHER	RAW(4)	Current dispatcher process address
SERVER	RAW(4)	Current server process address
WAITER	RAW(4)	Address of server process that is waiting for the (currently busy) circuit to become available
SADDR	RAW(4)	Address of session bound to the circuit
STATUS	VARCHAR2	Status of the circuit: BREAK (currently interrupted), EOF (about to be removed), OUTBOUND (an outward link to a remote database), NORMAL (normal circuit into the local database)
QUEUE	VARCHAR2	Queue the circuit is currently on: COMMON (on the common queue, waiting

		to be picked up by a server process), DISPATCHER (waiting for the dispatcher), SERVER (currently being served), OUTBOUND (waiting to establish an outbound connection, NONE (idle circuit)
MESSAGE0	NUMBER	Size in bytes of the messages in the first message buffer
MESSAGE1	NUMBER	Size in bytes of the messages in the second message buffer
MESSAGES	NUMBER	Total number of messages that have gone through this circuit
BYTES	NUMBER	Total number of bytes that have gone through this circuit
BREAKS	NUMBER	Total number of breaks (interruptions) for this circuit

V$DATABASE—Database information from the control file.

NAME	VARCHAR2	Name of the database
CREATED	VARCHAR2	Creation data
LOG_MODE	VARCHAR2	Archive log mode: NOARCHIVELOG or ARCHIVELOG
CHECKPOINT_ CHANGE#	NUMBER	Last SCN checkpointed
ARCHIVE_CHANGE#	NUMBER	Last SCN archived

V$DATAFILE—Data file information from the control file.

FILE#	NUMBER	File identification number
STATUS	VARCHAR2	Type of file (system or user) and its status. Values: OFFLINE, SYSOFF, ONLINE, SYSTEM, RECOVER
CHECKPOINT_CHANGE#	NUMBER	SCN at last checkpoint
BYTES	NUMBER	Size in bytes
NAME	VARCHAR2	Name of the file

V$DBFILE—All data files making up the database. This view is retained for historical compatibility. Use of V$DATAFILE is recommended instead.

FILE#	NUMBER	File identifier
NAME	VARCHAR2	Name of file

V$DB_OBJECT_CACHE—Shows database objects that are cached in the library cache. Objects include tables, indexes, clusters, synonym definitions, PL/SQL procedures and packages, and triggers.

OWNER	VARCHAR2	Owner of the object
NAME	VARCHAR2	Name of the object
DB_LINK	VARCHAR2	Database link name, if any
NAMESPACE	VARCHAR2	Library cache namespace of the object: INDEX, TABLE, CLUSTER, VIEW, SET, SYNONYM, SEQUENCE, PROCEDURE, FUNCTION, PACKAGE, PACKAGE BODY, TRIGGER, CLASS, OBJECT, USER, DBLINK
SHARABLE_MEM	NUMBER	Amount of sharable memory in the shared pool consumed by the object
LOADS	NUMBER	Number of times the object has been loaded. This count also increases when an object has been invalidated
EXECUTIONS	NUMBER	Total number of times this object has been executed
LOCKS	NUMBER	Number of users currently locking this object
PINS	NUMBER	Number of users currently pinning this object

V$DISPATCHER—Information on the dispatcher processes.

NAME	VARCHAR2	Name of the dispatcher process
NETWORK	VARCHAR2	Network protocol supported by this dispatcher; for example, TCP or DECNET.
PADDR	RAW(4)	Process address
STATUS	VARCHAR2	Dispatcher status: WAIT (idle), SEND (sending a message), RECEIVE (receiving a message), CONNECT (establishing a connection), DISCONNECT (handling a disconnect request), BREAK (handling a break), OUTBOUND (establishing an outbound connection)
ACCEPT	VARCHAR2	Whether this dispatcher is accepting new connections: YES, NO
MESSAGES	NUMBER	Number of messages processed by this dispatcher

BYTES	NUMBER	Size in bytes of messages processed by this dispatcher
BREAKS	NUMBER	Number of breaks occurring in this connection
OWNED	NUMBER	Number of circuits owned by this dispatcher
CREATED	NUMBER	Number of circuits created by this dispatcher
IDLE	NUMBER	Total idle time for this dispatcher, in hundredths of a second
BUSY	NUMBER	Total busy time for this dispatcher, in hundredths of a second

V$ENABLEDPRIVS—Which privileges are enabled.

| PRIV_NUMBER | NUMBER | Numeric identifier of enabled privileges |

V$FILESTAT—Information about file read/write statistics.

FILE#	NUMBER	Number of the file
PHYRDS	NUMBER	Number of physical reads done
PHYWRTS	NUMBER	Number of physical writes done
PHYBLKRD	NUMBER	Number of physical blocks read
PHYBLKWRT	NUMBER	Number of physical blocks written
READTIM	NUMBER	Time spent doing reads if the parameter TIMED_STATISTICS is TRUE; 0 if FALSE
WRITETIM	NUMBER	Time spent doing writes if the parameter TIMED_STATISTICS is TRUE; 0 if FALSE

V$FIXED_TABLE—Shows all fixed tables, views, and derived tables in the database.

NAME	VARCHAR2	Name of the object
OBJECT_ID	NUMBER	Identifier of the fixed object
TYPE	VARCHAR2	Object type: TABLE, VIEW

V$INSTANCE—State of the current instance.

| KEY | VARCHAR2 | Name of state variable, from the table below |
| VALUE | NUMBER | Value of state variable |

Instance State Variable	Value
RESTRICTED MODE	0 (False), 1 (True)
SHUTDOWN PENDING	0 (False), 1 (True)
STARTUP TIME-JULIAN	Start time and date in Julian format
STARTUP TIME-SECONDS	Number of seconds since midnight on the startup date

V$LATCH—Information about each type of latch. (The rows of this table and the rows of V$LATCHNAME correspond one-to-one.)

ADDR	RAW(4)	Address of latch object
LATCH#	NUMBER	Latch number
LEVEL#	NUMBER	Latch level
GETS	NUMBER	Number of times obtained with wait
MISSES	NUMBER	Number of times obtained with wait but failed first try
SLEEPS	NUMBER	Number of times slept when wanted wait
IMMEDIATE_GETS	NUMBER	Number of times obtained with no wait
IMMEDIATE_MISSES	NUMBER	Number of times failed to get with no wait

V$LATCHHOLDER—Information about the current latch holders.

PID	NUMBER	Identifier of process holding the latch
LADDR	RAW(4)	Latch address

V$LATCHNAME—The decoded latch names for the latches shown in table V$LATCH. The rows of this table and the rows of V$LATCH correspond one-to-one.)

LATCH#	NUMBER	Latch number
NAME	VARCHAR2	Latch name

V$LIBRARYCACHE—Statistics on library cache management.

NAMESPACE	VARCHAR2	Library cache namespace: SQL AREA, TABLE/PROCEDURE, BODY, TRIGGER, INDEX, CLUSTER, OBJECT, PIPE
GETHITS	NUMBER	Number of times the handles are already allocated in the cache. If the handle is not already allocated, it is a miss. The handle is then allocated and inserted into the cache.
GETHITRATIO	NUMBER	Number of GETHITS divided by GETS. Values close to 1 indicate that most of the handles the system has tried to get are cached.
PINS	NUMBER	Number of times the system issues pin requests for objects in the cache in order to access them
PINHITS	NUMBER	Number of times that objects the system is pinning and accessing are already allocated and initialized in the cache. Otherwise, it is

a miss, and the system has to allocate it in the cache and initialize it with data queried from the database or generate the data.

PINHITRATIO	NUMBER	Number of PINHITS divided by number of PINS. Values close to 1 indicate that most of the objects the system has tried to pin and access have been cached
RELOADS	NUMBER	Number of times that library objects have to be reinitialized and reloaded with data because they have been aged out or invalidated
INVALIDATIONS	NUMBER	Number of times that no-persistent library objects (like shared SQL areas) have been invalidated

V$LICENSE—Information about license limits.

SESSIONS_MAX	NUMBER	Maximum number of concurrent user sessions allowed for the instance
SESSIONS_ WARNING	NUMBER	Warning limit for concurrent user sessions for the instance
SESSION_CURRENT	NUMBER	Current number of concurrent user sessions
SESSION_ HIGHWATER	NUMBER	Highest number of concurrent user sessions since the instance started
USERS_MAX	NUMBER	Maximum number of named users allowed for the database

V$LOADCSTAT—SQL*Loader statistics compiled during the execution of a direct load. These statistics apply to the whole load. Any select against this table results in "no rows returned" since you cannot load data and do a query at the same time.

READ	NUMBER	Number of records read
REJECTED	NUMBER	Number of records rejected
TDISCARD	NUMBER	Total number of discards during the load
NDISCARD	NUMBER	Number of discards from the current file
SAVEDATA	NUMBER	Whether or not save data points are used

V$LOADTSTAT—SQL* Loader statistics compiled during the execution of a direct load. These statistics apply to the current table. Any select against this table results in "no rows returned" since you cannot load data and do a query at the same time.

LOADED	NUMBER	Number of records loaded
REJECTED	NUMBER	Number of records rejected

FAILWHEN	NUMBER	Number of records that failed to meet any WHEN clause
ALLNULL	NUMBER	Number of records that were completed
LEFT2SKIP	NUMBER	Number of records yet to skip during a continued load

V$LOCK—Information about locks and resources. Does not include DDL locks.

ADDR	RAW(4)	Address of lock state object
KADDR	RAW(4)	Address of lock
SID	NUMBER	Identifier of process holding the lock
TYPE	VARCHAR2	Resource type (see following table)
ID1	NUMBER	Resource identifier #1
ID2	NUMBER	Resource identifier #2
LMODE	NUMBER	Lock mode held: 1 (null), 2 (row share), 3 (row exclusive), 4 (share), 5 (share row exclusive), 6 (exclusive)
REQUEST	NUMBER	Lock mode requested (same values as LMODE)

The following locks are obtained by user applications. Any process which is blocking others is likely to be holding one of these locks:

User Lock Type	Description
RW	Row wait enqueue lock
TM	DML enqueue lock
TX	Transaction enqueue lock
UL	User supplied lock

The following system locks are held for extremely short periods of time:

System Lock Type	Description
BL	Buffer hash table instance lock
CF	Cross-instance function invocation instance lock
CI	Control file schema global enqueue lock
CS	Control file schema global enqueue lock
DF	Data file instance lock
DM	Mount/startup db primary/secondary instance lock
DR	Distributed recovery process lock
DX	Distributed transaction entry lock
FI	SGA open-file information lock
FS	File set lock

System Lock Type	Description
IR	Instance recovery serialization global enqueue lock
IV	Library cache invalidation instance lock
LA..LP	Library cache lock instance lock (A..P=namespace)
LS	Log start/log switch enqueue lock
MB	Master buffer hash table instance lock
MM	Mount definition global enqueue lock
MR	Media recovery lock
PA..PZ	Library cache pin instance lock (A..Z=namespace)
QA..QZ	Row cache instance lock (A..Z=cache)
RE	USE_ROW_ENQUEUES enforcement lock
RT	Redo thread global enqueue lock
SC	System commit number instance lock
SH	System commit number high water mark enqueue lock
SN	Sequence number instance lock
SQ	Sequence number enqueue lock
ST	Space transaction enqueue lock
SV	Sequence number value lock
TA	Generic enqueue lock
TD	DDL enqueue lock
TE	Extend-segment enqueue lock
TS	Temporary segment enqueue lock (ID2=0)
TT	Temporary table enqueue lock
UN	User name lock
WL	Being-written redo log instance lock
WS	Write-atomic-log-switch global enqueue lock

V$LOG—Log file information from control file.

GROUP#	NUMBER	Log group number
THREAD#	NUMBER	Log thread number
SEQUENCE#	NUMBER	Log sequence number
BYTES	NUMBER	Size of the log in bytes
MEMBERS	NUMBER	Number of members in the log group
ARCHIVED	VARCHAR2	Archived status: TRUE, FALSE
FIRST_CHANGE#	NUMBER	Lowest SCN in the log
FIRST_TIME	VARCHAR2	Time of first SCN in the log

V$LOGFILE—Information about redo log files.

GROUP#	NUMBER	Redo log group identifier number
STATUS	VARCHAR2	Status of this log member: INVALID (file is inaccessible), STALE (file's contents are incomplete), DELETED (file is no longer used), or blank (file is in use)
MEMBER	VARCHAR2	Redo log member name

V$LOGHIST—Log history information from the control file. This view is retained for historical compatibility. Use of V$LOG_HISTORY is recommended instead.

THREAD#	NUMBER	Log thread number
SEQUENCE#	NUIMBER	Log sequence number
FIRST_CHANGE#	NUMBER	Lowest SCN in the log
FIRST_TIME	VARCHAR2	TIME OF FIRST SCN in the log
SWITCH_CHANGE#	NUMBER	SCN at which the log switch occurred; one more than highest SCN in the log

V$LOG_HISTORY—Archived log names for all logs in the log history.

THREAD#	NUMBER	Thread number of the archived log
SEQUENCE#	NUMBER	Sequence number of the archived log
TIME	NUMBER	Time of first entry (lowest SCN) in the log
LOG_CHANGE#	NUMBER	Lowest SCN in the log
HIGH_CHANGE#	NUMBER	Highest SCN in the log
ARCHIVE_NAME	VARCHAR2	Name of file when archived, using the naming convention specified by the LOG_ARCHIVE_FORMAT initialization parameter

V$NLS_PARAMETERS—Current values of NLS parameters.

NAME	VARCHAR2	Parameter name: NLS_LANGUAGE, NLS_SORT, NLS_TERRITORY, NLS_CHARACTERSET, NLS_CURRENCY, NLS_ISO_CURRENCY, NLS_NUMERIC_CHARACTERS, NLS_FORMAT, NLS_DATA_LANGUAGE
VALUE	VARCHAR2	NLS parameter value

V$OPEN_CURSOR—Cursors that each user session currently has opened and parsed.

SADDR	RAW	Session address
USER_NAME	VARCHAR2	User that is logged into the session

ADDRESS	RAW	Used with HASH_VALUE to uniquely identify the SQL statement being executed in the session
HASH_VALUE	NUMBER	Used with ADDRESS to uniquely identify the SQL statement being executed in the session
SQL_TEXT	VARCHAR2	First 60 characters of the SQL statement that is parsed into the open cursor

V$PARAMETER—Information about current parameter values.

NUM	NUMBER	Parameter number
NAME	VARCHAR2	Parameter name
TYPE	NUMBER	Parameter type
VALUE	VARCHAR2	Parameter value
ISDEFAULT	VARCHAR2	Default value in use: TRUE, FALSE

V$PROCESS—Information about currently active processes.

ADDR	RAW(4)	Address of process state object
PID	NUMBER	ORACLE process identifier
SPID	VARCHAR2	Operating system process identifier
USERNAME	VARCHAR2	Operating system process username. Any two-task user coming across the network has "–T" appended to the username.
SERIAL#	NUMBER	Process serial number
TERMINAL	VARCHAR2	Operating system terminal identifier
PROGRAM	VARCHAR2	Program in progress
BACKGROUND	VARCHAR2	1 for a background process; null for a normal process
LATCHWAIT	VARCHAR2	Address of latch waiting for; null if none

V$QUEUE—Information on the multi-thread message queues.

PADDR	RAW(4)	Address of the process that owns the queue
TYPE	VARCHAR2	Type of queue: COMMON (processed by servers), OUTBOUND (used by remote servers), DISPATCHER.
QUEUE	NUMBER	Number of items in the queue
WAIT	NUMBER	Total time that all items in this queue have waited. Divide by TOTALQ for average wait per item.

| TOTALQ | NUMBER | Total number of items that have ever been in the queue |

**V$RECOVERY_LOG**—Archived logs needed to complete media recovery. This information is derived from the log history (V$LOG_HISTORY). The amount of information available is limited by the setting of the MAX_LOG_HISTORY intialization parameter.

THREAD#	NUMBER	Thread number of the archived log
SEQUENCE#	NUMBER	Sequence number of the archived log
TIME	NUMBER	Time of first entry (lowest SCN) in the log
ARCHIVE_NAME	VARCHAR2	Name of the file when it is archived, using the naming convention specified by the LOG_ARCHIVE_FORMAT initialization parameter

V$RECOVER_FILE—Status of files needing media recovery.

FILE#	NUMBER	File identifier number
ONLINE	VARCHAR2	Online status: ONLINE, OFFLINE
ERROR	VARCHAR2	Why the file needs to be recovered: NULL if reason unknown, or OFFLINE NORMAL if recovery not needed
CHANGE#	NUMBER	SCN where recovery must start
TIME	VARCHAR2	Time of SCN where recovery must start

V$REQDIST—Histogram of request times, divided into 12 buckets, or ranges of time. The time ranges grow exponentially as a function of the bucket number. BUCKET NUMBER Bucket number: 0.11; maximum time for each bucket is $(4*2^N)/100$ seconds

| COUNT | NUMBER | Count of requests whose total time to complete (excluding wait time) falls in this range. |

V$RESOURCE—Information about resources.

ADDR	RAW(4)	Address of resource object
TYPE	VARCHAR2	Resource type
ID1	NUMBER	Resource identifier #1
ID2	NUMBER	Resource identifier #2

V$ROLLNAME—Names of all online rollback segments.

USN	NUMBER	Rollback ("undo") segment number
NAME	VARCHAR2	Rollback segment name

V$ROLLSTAT—Statistics for all online rollback segments.

USN	NUMBER	Rollback segment number
EXTENTS	NUMBER	Number of rollback extents
RSSIZE	NUMBER	Size in bytes of rollback segment
WRITES	NUMBER	Number of bytes written to rollback segment
XACTS	NUMBER	Number of active transactions
GETS	NUMBER	Number of header gets
WAITS	NUMBER	Number of header waits
OPTSIZE	NUMBER	Optimal size of rollback segment
HWMSIZE	NUMBER	High water mark of rollback segment
SHRINKS	NUMBER	Number of times rollback segment shrank, eliminating one or more additional extents each time
WRAPS	NUMBER	Number of times rollback segment wraps from one extent to another
EXTENDS	NUMBER	Number of times rollback segment was extended to have a new extent
AVESHRINK	NUMBER	Total size of freed extents divided by number of shrinks
AVEACTIVE	NUMBER	Current average size of active extents, where "active" extents have uncommitted transaction data
STATUS	VARCHAR2	ONLINE if the segment is online, or PENDING OFFLINE if the segment is going offline but some active (distributed) transactions are using the rollback segment. When the transactions complete, the segment goes offline.

V$ROWCACHE—Statistics for data dictionary activity. (Each row contains statistics for one data dictionary cache.)

CACHE#	NUMBER	Row cache ID number
TYPE	VARCHAR2	Parent or subordinate row cache type

SUBORDINATE#	NUMBER	Subordinate set number
PARAMETER	VARCHAR2	Name of the INIT.ORA parameter that we can view (by selecting from this table), but cannot change (e.g., XC_TABLES). In Version 7, change SHARED_POOL_SIZE, which automatically adjusts the dictionary cache parameters.
COUNT	NUMBER	Total number of entries in the cache
USAGE	NUMBER	Number of cache entries that contain valid data
FIXED	NUMBER	Number of fixed entries in the cache
GETS	NUMBER	Total number of requests for information on the data object
GETMISSES	NUMBER	Number of data requests resulting in cache misses
SCANS	NUMBER	Number of scan requests
SCANMISSES	NUMBER	Number of times a scan failed to find the data in the cache
SCANCOMPLETES	NUMBER	For a list of subordinate entries, the number of times the list was scanned completely
MODIFICATIONS	NUMBER	Number of inserts, updates, and deletions
FLUSHES	NUMBER	Number of times flushed to disk

V$SECONDARY—A Trusted ORACLE view that lists secondary mounted databases. For details, see the *Trusted ORACLE7 Server Administrator's Guide*.

V$SESSION—Session information for each current session.

SADDR	RAW(4)	Session address
SID	NUMBER	Session identifier
SERIAL#	NUMBER	Session serial number. Used to uniquely identify a session's objects. Guarantees that session-level commands are applied to the correct session objects in the event that the session ends and another
AUDSID	NUMBER	Auditing session ID
PADDR	RAW(4)	Address of the process that owns this session
USER#	NUMBER	ORACLE user identifier
USERNAME	VARCHAR2	ORACLE user name

COMMAND	NUMBER	Command in progress; see the table on the next page
TADDR	VARCHAR2	Address of transaction state object
LOCKWAIT	VARCHAR2	Address of lock waiting for; null if none
STATUS	VARCHAR2	Status of the session: ACTIVE, INACTIVE, KILLED
SERVER	VARCHAR2	Server type: DEDICATED, SHARED, PSEUDO, NONE
SCHEMA#	NUMBER	Schema user identifier
SCHEMANAME	VARCHAR2	Schema user name
OSUSER	VARCHAR2	Operating system client user name
PROCESS	VARCHAR2	Operating system client process ID
MACHINE	VARCHAR2	Operating system machine name
TERMINAL	VARCHAR2	Operating system terminal name
PROGRAM	VARCHAR2	Operating system program name
TYPE	VARCHAR2	Session type
SQL_ADDRESS	RAW	Used with SQL_HASH_VALUE to identify the SQl statement that is currently being executed
SQL_HASH_VALUE	NUMBER	Used with SQL_ADDRESS to identify the SQL statement that is currently being executed; numbers are listed below.

Command Number	Command
1	CREATE TABLE
2	INSERT
3	SELECT
4	CREATE CLUSTER
5	ALTER CLUSTER
6	UPDATE
7	DELETE
8	DROP
9	CREATE INDEX
10	DROP INDEX
11	ALTER INDEX
12	DROP TABLE
13	—

Command Number	Command
14	—
15	ALTER TABLE
16	—
17	GRANT
18	REVOKE
19	CREATE SYNONYM
20	DROP SYNONYM
21	CREATE VIEW
22	DROP VIEW
23	—
24	—
25	—
26	LOCK TABLE
27	NO OPERATION
28	RENAME
29	COMMENT
30	AUDIT
31	NOAUDIT
32	CREATE EXTERNAL DATABASE
33	DROP EXTERNAL DATABASE
34	CREATE DATABASE
35	ALTER DATABASE
36	CREATE ROLLBACK SEGMENT
37	ALTER ROLLBACK SEGMENT
38	DROP ROLLBACK SEGMENT
39	CREATE TABLESPACE
40	ALTER TABLESPACE
41	DROP TABLESPACE
42	ALTER SESSION
43	ALTER USER
44	COMMIT
45	ROLLBACK
46	SAVEPOINT

V$SESSION_WAIT—Lists the resources or events that active sessions are waiting for.

SID	NUMBER	Session identifier
SWQ#	NUMBER	Sequence number that uniquely identifies this wait. Incremented for each wait.
EVENT	VARCHAR2	Resource or event the session is waiting for
P1TEXT	VARCHAR2	Description of first additional parameter
P1	VARCHAR2	First additional parameter
P2TEXT	VARCHAR2	Description of second parameter
P2	VARCHAR2	Second additional parameter
P3TEXT	VARCHAR2	Description of third parameter
P3	VARCHAR2	Third additional parameter
WAIT_TIME	NUMBER	A non-zero value is the session's last wait time. A zero value means that the session is currently waiting.

V$SESSTAT—For each current session, the current statistics values.

SID	NUMBER	Session identifier
STATISTIC#	NUMBER	Statistic number (identifier)
VALUE	NUMBER	Statistic value

V$SESS_IO—I/O statistics for each user session.

SID	NUMBER	Session identifier
BLOCK_GETS	NUMBER	Block gets for this session
CONSISTENT_GETS	NUMBER	Consistent gets for this session
PHYSICAL_READS	NUMBER	Physical reads for this session
BLOCK_CHANGES	NUMBER	Block changes for this session
CONSISTENT_ CHANGES#	NUMBER	Consistent changes for this session

V$SGA—Summary information on the System Global Area.

NAME	VARCHAR2	SGA component group
VALUE	NUMBER	Memory size in bytes

V$SGASTAT—Detailed information on the System Global Area.

NAME	VARCHAR2	SGA component name
BYTES	NUMBER	Memory size in bytes

V$SHARED_SERVER—Information on the shared server processes.

NAME	VARCHAR2	Name of the server
PADDR	RAW(4)	Server's process address
STATUS	VARCHAR2	Server status: EXEC (executing SQL), WAIT (ENQ) (waiting for a lock), WAIT (SEND) (waiting to send data to user), WAIT (COMMON) (idle; waiting for a user request), WAIT (RESET) (waiting for a circuit to reset after a break), QUIT (terminating)
MESSAGES	NUMBER	Number of messages processed
BYTES	NUMBER	Total number of bytes in all messages
BREAKS	NUMBER	Number of breaks
CIRCUIT	RAW(4)	Address of circuit currently being serviced
IDLE	NUMBER	Total idle time in hundredths of a second
BUSY	NUMBER	Total busy time in hundredths of a second
REQUESTS	NUMBER	Total number of requests taken from the common queue in this server's lifetime

V$SQLAREA—Statistics on the shared cursor cache. Each row has statistics on one shared cursor.

SQL_TEXT	VARCHAR2	Text of the SQL statement requiring the cursor, or the PL/SQL anonymous code
SHARABLE_MEM	NUMBER	Amount of memory in bytes that is sharable between users
PERSISTENT_MEM	NUMBER	Amount of per-user memory in bytes that persists for the life of the cursor
RUNTIME_MEM	NUMBER	Amount of pre-user memory, in bytes, that is needed only during execution
SORTS	NUMBER	Number of sorts performed by the SQL statement.
VERSION_COUNT	NUMBER	Number of different versions of this cursor. The same SQL text might be used by different users, each on their own version of a table (for example, "SELECT* from EMP" by SCOTT and JONES, when they each have their own version of EMP). In

		that case, multiple versions of the cursor would exist.
LOADED_VERSIONS	NUMBER	Versions of the cursor that are currently fully loaded, with no parts aged out
OPEN_VERSIONS	NUMBER	Number of versions that some user has an open cursor on.
USERS_OPENING	NUMBER	Number of users that currently have this SQL statement parsed in an open cursor
EXECUTIONS	NUMBER	Total number of times this SQL statement has been executed
USERS_EXECUTING	NUMBER	Number of users that are currently executing this cursor
LOADS	NUMBER	Number of times the cursor has been loaded after the body of the cursor has been aged out of the cache while the text of the SQL statement remained in it, or after the cursor is invalidated
FIRST_LOAD_TIME	VARCHAR2	Loaded into the SGA
INVALIDATIONS	NUMBER	Number of times the contents of the cursor have been invalidated. For example: because tables referenced in the cursor are dropped, validated, or indexed
PARSE_CALLS	NUMBER	Number of times users executed a parse call for this cursor
DISK_READS	NUMBER	Number of disk blocks read by this cursor and all cursors caused to be executed by this cursor
BUFFER_GETS	NUMBER	Number of buffers gotten (in any mode) by this cursor and all cursors caused to be executed by this cursor
ADDRESS	RAW	Used together with HASH_VALUE to select the full text of the SQL statement from V$SQLTEXT
HASH_VALUE	NUMBER	Used together with ADDRESS to select the full text of the SQL statement from V$SQL-TEXT

V$SQLTEXT—The text of SQL statements belonging to shared SQL cursors in the SGA.

ADDRESS	RAW	Used with HASH_VALUE to uniquely identify a cached cursor
HASH_VALUE	NUMBER	Used with ADDRESS to uniquely identify a cached cursor
PIECE	NUMBER	Number used to order the pieces of SQL text
SQL_TEXT	VARCHAR2	A column containing one piece of the SQL text

V$STATNAME—Decoded statistic names for the statistics shown in the V$SESSTAT table.

STATISTIC#	NUMBER	Statistic number
NAME	VARCHAR2	Statistic name
CLASS	NUMBER	Statistic class: 1 (User), 2 (Redo), 4 (Enqueue), 8 (Cache)

V$SYSLABEL—A Trusted ORACLE view that lists system labels. For details, see the *Trusted ORACLE7 Server Administrator's Guide*.

V$SYSSTAT—The current system-wide value for each statistic in table V$SESSTAT.

STATISTIC#	NUMBER	Statistic number
NAME	VARCHAR2	Statistic name
CLASS	NUMBER	Statistic class: 1 (User), 2 (Redo), 4 (Enqueue), 8 (Cache)
VALUE	NUMBER	Statistic value

V$THREAD—Thread information from the control file.

THREAD#	NUMBER	Thread number
STATUS	VARCHAR2	Thread status: OPEN, CLOSED
ENABLED	VARCHAR2	Enabled status: DISABLED, (enabled) PRIVATE, or (enabled) PUBLIC
GROUPS	NUMBER	Number of log groups assigned to this thread
INSTANCE	VARCHAR2	Instance name, if available
OPEN_TIME	VARCHAR2	Last time the thread was opened
CURRENT_GROUP#	NUMBER	Current log group
SEQUENCE#	NUMBER	Sequence number of current log

CHECKPOINT_ CHANGE#	NUMBER	SCN at last checkpoint
CHECKPOINT_TIME	VARCHAR2	Time of last checkpoint

V$TIMER—The current time in hundredths of seconds.

HSECS	NUMBER	Time in hundredths of a second

V$TRANSACTION—Information about transactions.

ADDR	RAW(4)	Address of transaction state object
SCNBASE	NUMBER	First part of the system change number; invalid if inactive
SCNWRAP	NUMBER	Second part of the system change number; invalid if inactive
XIDUSN	NUMBER	Rollback (undo) segment number; invalid if inactive
XIDSLOT	NUMBER	Slot number; invalid if inactive
XIDSQN	NUMBER	Sequence number; invalid if inactive
UBADBA	NUMBER	Database block address for rollback data; invalid if inactive
UBASQN	NUMBER	Sequence number for rollback data; invalid if inactive
UBAREC	NUMBER	Record number for rollback data; invalid if inactive

V$TYPE_SIZE—Sizes of various database components for use in estimating data block capacity.

COMPONENT	VARCHAR2	Component name, such as segment or buffer header
TYPE	VARCHAR2	Component type
DESCRIPTION	VARCHAR2	Description of component
SIZE	NUMBER	Size of component

V$VERSION—Version numbers of core library components in the ORACLE Server. There is one row for each component.

BANNER	VARCHAR2	Component name and version number

V$WAITSTAT—Block contention statistics. This table is updated only when timed statistics are enabled.

CLASS	VARCHAR2	Class of block subject to contention

COUNT	NUMBER	Number of waits by this OPERATION for this CLASS of block
TIME	NUMBER	Sum of all wait times for all the waits by this OPERATION for this CLASS of block

Version 6 Tables Accessed by MONITOR Functions

MONITOR Function	Table
FILES	V$DBFILE
	V$FILESTAT
IO	V$PROCESS
	V$SESSION
	V$SESSTAT
	V$SYSSTAT
LATCH	V$LATCHNAME
	V$LATCH
LOCK	V$LOCK
	V$PROCESS
	V$SESSION
PROCESSES	V$PROCESS
	V$SESSION
ROLLBACK	V$ROLLNAME
SEGMENTS	V$ROLLSTAT
STATISTICS	V$STATNAME
	V$PROCESS
	V$SYSSTAT
TABLE	V$ACCESS
USER	V$PROCESS
	V$SESSION
	V$LATCH
	V$LATCHNAME

Version 7 Tables Accessed by MONITOR Functions

MONITOR Function	Table
FILE IO	V$DBFILE
	V$FILESTAT
LATCH	V$LATCH
	V$LATCHHOLDER
	V$LATCHNAME
LIBRARYCACHE	V$LIBRARYCACHE
LOCK	V$LOCK
	V$SESSION
PROCESSES	V$PROCESS
ROLLBACK	V$ROLLNAME
SEGMENTS	V$ROLLSTAT
SESSION	V$PROCESS
	V$SESSION
SQLAREA	V$SQLAREA
STATISTICS	V$SYSSTAT
	V$SESSTAT
SYSTEM IO	V$PROCESS
	V$SESSTAT
TABLE	V$ACCESS
SESSION	V$PROCESS
	V$SESSION
	V$LATCH
	V$LATCHNAME

Multi-threaded options (available only if you are running the multi-threaded server):

MONITOR Function	Table
CIRCUIT	V$CIRCUIT
	V$DISPATCHER
	V$SESSION
	V$SHARED_SERVER
DISPATCHER	V$DISPATCHER
	V$QUEUE
SHARED SERVER	V$SHARED_SERVER

Index

About the Authors

Peter Corrigan runs a small consulting company in Australia called Gauntlet Computers and works as a senior database administrator and project leader developing ORACLE applications and tuning systems. His speciality areas include client-server architecture and application downsizing, and he is the co-developer of the Rainbow Financial package, sold internationally. He is a frequent speaker on the topic of tuning and programming at the ORACLE Asia Pacific user group conferences and the Victoria ORACLE user's group.

As a database administrator on a financial IMS project about eight years ago, **Mark Gurry** was asked to investigate his company's database direction for the next five years. The number of users was up to 950, the cost of maintaining the mainframes was huge, and he'd heard about relational databases and downsizing. After much investigation, he chose ORACLE, and has stuck with the system ever since. He has worked as Manager of Computing and Network Services, senior database administrator, senior ORACLE technical support, and other jobs. He now has a small consulting company called New Age Consultants. Mark has worked for many large organizations and is currently working for Telecom Australia, the largest computer site in Australia and one of the largest in the world. He has also spoken on tuning at ORACLE user group meetings and has given internal tuning courses at several of his larger client sites. He has been a senior team member on award-winning systems that have been developed using ORACLE.

Colophon

Our look is the result of reader comments, our own experimentation, and feedback from distribution channels.

Distinctive covers complement our distinctive approach to technical topics, breathing personality and life into potentially dry subjects. UNIX and its attendant programs can be unruly beasts. Nutshell Handbooks help you tame them.

The animal featured on the cover of *ORACLE Performance Tuning* is the honeybee, appreciated worldwide as a pollinator of crops and producer of honey. Honeybees are highly social creatures. A single hive or colony usually contains one queen (the only fertile female), fifty- to sixty-thousand workers (all sterile females), and a few hundred drones (the only males). Workers are responsible for locating and collecting the pollen, nectar, water, and resin necessary to the hive. When a worker locates such a source, she returns to the hive and performs a beedance. This dance communicates precise instructions—both distance and direction—enabling other workers to make a beeline to the booty. It takes about ten million such worker-trips to gather enough nectar to make one pound of honey. Workers also build and maintain the hive, and feed the colony.

There is no biological difference among female bees at birth. Queens are simply given larger cells in which to develop, and are allowed to continue their privileged diet of "royal jelly" long after the other developing bees are cut off from the delicacy. Royal jelly is a secretion generated from the glands of young workers. Worker larvae are nourished by it during their first six days of existence, drones receive it for eight days, while the queen gets it until she is fully grown. The first thing a new queen will do upon emerging from her cell is deliver a death sting to all the other larval queens. (The previous queen will have vacated the hive with a small entourage a few days before.) After a week or two, the new queen will mate with a few drones (who die immediately after copulation). The rest of the drones are then put out of the hive to starve. The queen returns to the hive and begins her job of laying over a thousand eggs a day.

Honeybees are native to Europe, Africa, and the Middle East. In Ancient Greece, honeybees were associated with a famous oracle. The regular god of prophecy was Apollo, who presided over the greatest of Greek oracles, at Delphi. Apollo gave his tricky brother, Hermes, a piece of the action on a smaller shrine farther down the slopes of the same mountain, Mt. Parnassus, where the prophecy was given by three honeybee-maidens, all sisters. Apollo gave them the ability to speak the truth, which they willingly did if they were fed honey and honeycombs; if not, they buzzed and buzzed and told only lies.

Edie Freedman designed this cover and the entire UNIX bestiary that appears on other Nutshell Handbooks. The beasts themselves are adapted from 19th-century engravings from the Dover Pictorial Archive. The cover layout was produced with Quark XPress 3.1 using the ITC Garamond font.

The inside layout was formatted in FrameMaker 3.1 by Mike Sierra and Lar Kaufman using ITC Garamond Light and ITC Garamond Book fonts, and was designed by Edie Freedman. The figures were created in Aldus Freehand 3.1 by Chris Reilley and Michelle Willey. The colophon was written by Michael Kalantarian and Lenny Muellner.

Programming

UNIX, C and MULTI-PLATFORM

Books from O'Reilly & Associates, Inc.

Fall/Winter 1994-95

Fortran/Scientific Computing

Migrating to Fortran 90

By James F. Kerrigan
1st Edition November 1993
389 pages, ISBN 1-56592-049-X

Many Fortran programmers do not know where to start with Fortran 90. What is new about the language? How can it help them? How does a programmer with old habits learn new strategies?

This book is a practical guide to Fortran 90 for the current Fortran programmer. It provides a complete overview of the new features that Fortran 90 has brought to the Fortran standard, with examples and suggestions for use. The book discusses older ways of solving problems—both in FORTRAN 77 and in common tricks or extensions—and contrasts them with the new ways provided by Fortran 90.

The book has a practical focus, with the goal of getting the current Fortran programmer up to speed quickly. Two dozen examples of full programs are interspersed within the text, which includes over 4,000 lines of working code.

Topics include array sections, modules, file handling, allocatable arrays and pointers, and numeric precision. Two dozen examples of full programs are interspersed within the text, which includes over 4,000 lines of working code.

"This is a book that all Fortran programmers eager to take advantage of the excellent feature of Fortran 90 will want to have on their desk." —*FORTRAN Journal*

High Performance Computing

By Kevin Dowd
1st Edition June 1993
398 pages, ISBN 1-56592-032-5

High Performance Computing makes sense of the newest generation of workstations for application programmers and purchasing managers. It covers everything, from the basics of modern workstation architecture, to structuring benchmarks, to squeezing more performance out of critical applications. It also explains what a good compiler can do— and what you have to do yourself. The book closes with a look at the high-performance future: parallel computers and the more "garden variety" shared memory processors that are appearing on people's desktops.

UNIX for FORTRAN Programmers

By Mike Loukides
1st Edition August 1990
264 pages, ISBN 0-937175-51-X

This handbook lowers the UNIX entry barrier by providing the serious scientific programmer with an introduction to the UNIX operating system and its tools. It familiarizes readers with the most important tools so they can be productive as quickly as possible. Assumes some knowledge of FORTRAN, none of UNIX or C.

C Programming Libraries

POSIX.4

By Bill Gallmeister
1st Edition Winter 1994-95 (est.)
400 pages (est.), ISBN 1-56592-074-0

A general introduction to real-time programming and real-time issues, this book covers the POSIX.4 standard and how to use it to solve "real-world" problems. If you're at all interested in real-time applications—which include just about everything from telemetry to transation processing—this book is for you. An essential reference.

POSIX Programmer's Guide

By Donald Lewine
1st Edition April 1991
640 pages, ISBN 0-937175-73-0

Most UNIX systems today are POSIX compliant because the Federal government requires it for its purchases. Given the manufacturer's documentation, however, it can be difficult to distinguish system-specific features from those features defined by POSIX. The *POSIX Programmer's Guide*, intended as an explanation of the POSIX standard and as a reference for the POSIX.1 programming library, helps you write more portable programs.

"If you are an intermediate to advanced C programmer and are interested in having your programs compile first time on anything from a Sun to a VMS system to an MSDOS system, then this book must be thoroughly recommended."
—*Sun UK User*

Understanding and Using COFF

By Gintaras R. Gircys
1st Edition November 1988
196 pages, ISBN 0-937175-31-5

COFF—Common Object File Format—is the formal definition for the structure of machine code files in the UNIX System V environment. All machine code files are COFF files. This handbook explains COFF data structure and its manipulation.

Using C on the UNIX System

By Dave Curry
1st Edition January 1989
250 pages, ISBN 0-937175-23-4

This is the book for intermediate to experienced C programmers who want to become UNIX system programmers. It explains system calls and special library routines available on the UNIX system. It is impossible to write UNIX utilities of any sophistication without understanding the material in this book.

"A gem of a book.... The author's aim is to provide a guide to system programming, and he succeeds admirably. His balance is steady between System V and BSD-based systems, so readers come away knowing both." —*SUN Expert*

Practical C Programming

By Steve Oualline
2nd Edition January 1993
396 pages, ISBN 1-56592-035-X

C programming is more than just getting the syntax right. Style and debugging also play a tremendous part in creating programs that run well. *Practical C Programming* teaches you not only the mechanics of programming, but also how to create programs that are easy to read, maintain, and debug. There are lots of introductory C books, but this is the Nutshell Handbook®! In this edition, programs conform to ANSI C.

"This book is exactly what it states—a practical book in C programming. It is also an excellent addition to any C programmer's library." —Betty Zinkarun, *Books & Bytes*

Programming with curses

By John Strang
1st Edition 1986
76 pages, ISBN 0-937175-02-1

Curses is a UNIX library of functions for controlling a terminal's display screen from a C program. This handbook helps you make use of the curses library. Describes the original Berkeley version of curses.

C Programming Tools

Software Portability with imake

By Paul DuBois
1st Edition July 1993
390 pages, ISBN 1-56592-055-4

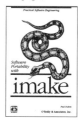

imake is a utility that works with *make* to enable code to be compiled and installed on different UNIX machines. *imake* makes possible the wide portability of the X Window System code and is widely considered an X tool, but it's also useful for any software project that needs to be ported to many UNIX systems.

This Nutshell Handbook®—the only book available on *imake*—is ideal for X and UNIX programmers who want their software to be portable. The book is divided into two sections. The first section is a general explanation of *imake*, X configuration files, and how to write and debug an *Imakefile*. The second section describes how to write configuration files and presents a configuration file architecture that allows development of coexisting sets of configuration files. Several sample sets of configuration files are described and are available free over the Net.

Managing Projects with make

By Andrew Oram & Steve Talbott
2nd Edition October 1991
152 pages, ISBN 0-937175-90-0

make is one of UNIX's greatest contributions to software development, and this book is the clearest description of *make* ever written. It describes all the basic features of *make* and provides guidelines on meeting the needs of large, modern projects. Also contains a description of free products that contain major enhancements to *make*.

"I use *make* very frequently in my day to day work and thought I knew everything that I needed to know about it. After reading this book I realized that I was wrong!"
—Rob Henley, Siemens-Nixdorf

"If you can't pick up your system's *yp Makefile*, read every line, and make sense of it, you need this book."
—*Root Journal*

Checking C Programs with lint

By Ian F. Darwin
1st Edition October 1988
84 pages, ISBN 0-937175-30-7

The *lint* program checker has proven time and again to be one of the best tools for finding portability problems and certain types of coding errors in C programs. *lint* verifies a program or program segments against standard libraries, checks the code for common portability errors, and tests the programming against some tried and true guidelines. *Linting* your code is a necessary (though not sufficient) step in writing clean, portable, effective programs. This book introduces you to *lint*, guides you through running it on your programs, and helps you interpret *lint's* output.

"I can say without reservation that this book is a must for the system programmer or anyone else programming in C."
—*Root Journal*

lex & yacc

By John Levine, Tony Mason & Doug Brown
2nd Edition October 1992
366 pages, ISBN 1-56592-000-7

Shows programmers how to use two UNIX utilities, *lex* and *yacc*, in program development. The second edition contains completely revised tutorial sections for novice users and reference sections for advanced users. This edition is twice the size of the first, has an expanded index, and now covers Bison and Flex.

Power Programming with RPC

By John Bloomer
1st Edition February 1992
522 pages, ISBN 0-937175-77-3

RPC, or remote procedure calling, is the ability to distribute the execution of functions on remote computers. Written from a programmer's perspective, this book shows what you can do with RPCs, like Sun RPC, the de facto standard on UNIX systems. It covers related programming topics for Sun and other UNIX systems and teaches through examples.

Multi-Platform Programming

Guide to Writing DCE Applications

By John Shirley, Wei Hu & David Magid
2nd Edition May 1994
462 pages, ISBN 1-56592-045-7

 A hands-on programming guide to OSF's Distributed Computing Environment (DCE) for first-time DCE application programmers. This book is designed to help new DCE users make the transition from conventional, nondistributed applications programming to distributed DCE programming. In addition to basic RPC (remote procedure calls), this edition covers object UUIDs and basic security (authentication and authorization). Also includes practical programming examples.

"This book will be useful as a ready reference by the side of the novice DCE programmer." —*;login*

Distributing Applications Across DCE and Windows NT

By Ward Rosenberry & Jim Teague
1st Edition November 1993
302 pages, ISBN 1-56592-047-3

 This book links together two exciting technologies in distributed computing by showing how to develop an application that simultaneously runs on DCE and Microsoft systems through remote procedure calls (RPC). Covers the writing of portable applications and the complete differences between RPC support in the two environments.

Understanding DCE

By Ward Rosenberry, David Kenney & Gerry Fisher
1st Edition October 1992
266 pages, ISBN 1-56592-005-8

 A technical and conceptual overview of OSF's Distributed Computing Environment (DCE) for programmers, technical managers, and marketing and sales people. Unlike many O'Reilly & Associates books, *Understanding DCE* has no hands-on programming elements. Instead, the book focuses on how DCE can be used to accomplish typical programming tasks and provides explanations to help the reader understand all the parts of DCE.

Encyclopedia of Graphics File Formats

By James D. Murray & William vanRyper
1st Edition July 1994
928 pages (CD-ROM included), ISBN 1-56592-058-9

 The computer graphics world is a veritable alphabet soup of acronyms; BMP, DXF, EPS, GIF, MPEG, PCX, PIC, RTF, TGA, RIFF, and TIFF are only a few of the many different formats in which graphics images can be stored. The *Encyclopedia of Graphics File Formats* is the definitive work on file formats— the book that will become a classic for graphics programmers and everyone else who deals with the low-level technical details of graphics files. It includes technical information on nearly 100 file formats, as well as chapters on graphics and file format basics, bitmap and vector files, metafiles, scene description, animation and multimedia formats, and file compression methods.

Best of all, this book comes with a CD-ROM that collects many hard-to-find resources. We've assembled original vendor file format specification documents, along with test images and code examples, and a variety of software packages for MS-DOS, Windows, OS/2, UNIX, and the Macintosh that will let you convert, view, and manipulate graphics files and images.

Multi-Platform Code Management

By Kevin Jameson
1st Edition August 1994
354 pages (two diskettes included), ISBN 1-56592-059-7

 For any programmer or team struggling with builds and maintenance, this book—and its accompanying software (available for fifteen platforms, including MS-DOS and various UNIX systems)—can save dozens of errors and hours of effort. A "one-stop-shopping" solution for code management problems, it shows you how to structure a large project and keep your files and builds under control over many releases and platforms. The building blocks are simple: common-sense strategies, public-domain tools that you can obtain on a variety of systems, and special utilities developed by the author. The book also includes two diskettes that provide a complete system for managing source files and builds.

Understanding Japanese Information Processing

By Ken Lunde
1st Edition September 1993
470 pages, ISBN 1-56592-043-0

Understanding Japanese Information Processing provides detailed information on all aspects of handling Japanese text on computer systems. It brings all of the relevant information together in a single book and covers everything from the origins of modern-day Japanese to the latest information on specific emerging computer encoding standards. Appendices provide additional reference material, such as a code conversion table, character set tables, mapping tables, an extensive list of software sources, a glossary, and more.

"A programmer interested in writing a computer program which will handle the Japanese language will find the book indispensable." —*Multilingual Computing*

"Ken Lunde's book is an essential reference for everyone developing or adapting software for handling Japanese text. It is a goldmine of useful and relevant information on fonts, encoding systems and standards."
—Professor Jim Breen, Monash University, Australia

Business

Building a Successful Software Business

By Dave Radin
1st Edition April 1994
394 pages, ISBN 1-56592-064-3

This handbook is for the new software entrepreneur and the old hand alike. If you're thinking of starting a company around a program you've written—and there's no better time than the present—this book will guide you toward success. If you're an old hand in the software industry, it will help you sharpen your skills or will provide a refresher course. It covers the basics of product planning, marketing, customer support, finance, and operations.

"A marvelous guide through the complexities of marketing high-tech products. Its range of topics, and Radin's insights, make the book valuable to the novice marketeer as well as the seasoned veteran. It is the Swiss Army Knife of high-tech marketing." —Jerry Keane, Universal Analytics Inc.

ORACLE Performance Tuning

By Peter Corrigan & Mark Gurry
1st Edition September 1993
642 pages, ISBN 1-56592-048-1

The ORACLE relational database management system is the most popular database system in use today. Organizations, ranging from government agencies to small businesses, from large financial institutions to universities, use ORACLE on computers as diverse as mainframes, minicomputers, work-stations, PCs, and Macintoshes.

ORACLE offers tremendous power and flexibility, but at some cost. Demands for fast response, particularly in online transaction processing systems, make performance a major issue. With more organizations downsizing and adopting client-server and distributed database approaches, performance tuning has become all the more vital.

Whether you're a manager, a designer, a programmer, or an administrator, there's a lot you can do on your own to dramatically increase the performance of your existing ORACLE system. Whether you are running RDBMS Version 6 or Version 7, you may find that this book can save you the cost of a new machine; at the very least, it will save you a lot of headaches.

"This book is one of the best books on ORACLE that I have ever read.... [It] discloses many Oracle Tips that DBA's and Developers have locked in their brains and in their planners.... I recommend this book for any person who works with ORACLE, from managers to developers. In fact, I have to keep [it] under lock and key, because of the popularity of it."
—Mike Gangler

O'Reilly & Associates—
GLOBAL NETWORK NAVIGATOR™

The Global Network Navigator (GNN)™ is a unique kind of information service that makes the Internet easy and enjoyable to use. We organize access to the vast information resources of the Internet so that you can find what you want. We also help you understand the Internet and the many ways you can explore it.

In GNN you'll find:

Navigating the Net with GNN

 The *Whole Internet Catalog* contains a descriptive listing of the most useful Net resources and services with live links to those resources.

 The *GNN Business Pages* are where you'll learn about companies who have established a presence on the Internet and use its worldwide reach to help educate consumers.

 The *Internet Help Desk* helps folks who are new to the Net orient themselves and gets them started on the road to Internet exploration.

News

 NetNews is a weekly publication that reports on the news of the Internet, with weekly feature articles that focus on Internet trends and special events. The Sports, Weather, and Comix Pages round out the news.

Special Interest Publications

 Whether you're planning a trip or are just interested in reading about the journeys of others, you'll find that the *Travelers' Center* contains a rich collection of feature articles and ongoing columns about travel. In the *Travelers' Center*, you can link to many helpful and informative travel-related Internet resources.

The *Personal Finance Center* is the place to go for information about money management and investment on the Internet. Whether you're an old pro at playing the market or are thinking about investing for the first time, you'll read articles and discover Internet resources that will help you to think of the Internet as a personal finance information tool.

All in all, GNN helps you get more value for the time you spend on the Internet.

 The Best of the Web

GNN received "Honorable Mention" for **"Best Overall Site," "Best Entertainment Service,"** and **"Most Important Service Concept."**

The *GNN NetNews* received "Honorable Mention" for **"Best Document Design."**

Subscribe Today

GNN is available over the Internet as a subscription service. To get complete information about subscribing to GNN, send email to **info@gnn.com**. If you have access to a World Wide Web browser such as Mosaic or Lynx, you can use the following URL to register online: `http://gnn.com/`

If you use a browser that does not support online forms, you can retrieve an email version of the registration form automatically by sending email to **form@gnn.com**. Fill this form out and send it back to us by email, and we will confirm your registration.

O'Reilly on the Net—
ONLINE PROGRAM GUIDE

O'Reilly & Associates offers extensive information through our online resources. If you've got Internet access, we invite you to come and explore our little neck-of-the-woods.

Online Resource Center

Most comprehensive among our online offerings is the O'Reilly Resource Center. Here, you'll find detailed information and descriptions on all O'Reilly products: titles, prices, tables of contents, indexes, author bios, software contents, reviews... you can even view images of the products themselves. We also supply helpful ordering information: how to contact us, how to order online, distributors and bookstores world wide, discounts, upgrades, etc. In addition, we provide informative literature in the field: articles, interviews, and bibliographies that help you stay informed and abreast.

 The Best of the Web

The *O'Reilly Resource Center* was voted "**Best Commercial Site**" by users participating in "Best of the Web '94."

To access ORA's Online Resource Center:

Point your Web browser (e.g., `mosaic` or `lynx`) to:

`http://gnn.com/ora/`

For the plaintext version, `telnet` or `gopher` to:

`gopher.ora.com`

(telnet login: `gopher`)

FTP

The example files and programs in many of our books are available electronically via FTP.

To obtain example files and programs from O'Reilly texts:

`ftp` to:

`ftp.ora.com`

or

`ftp.uu.net`

`cd published/oreilly`

Ora-news

An easy way to stay informed of the latest projects and products from O'Reilly & Associates is to subscribe to "ora-news," our electronic news service. Subscribers receive email as soon as the information breaks.

To subscribe to "ora-news":

Send email to:
listproc@online.ora.com

and put the following information on the first line of your message (not in "Subject"):
subscribe ora-news "your name" **of** "your company"

For example:
subscribe ora-news Jim Dandy of Mighty Fine Enterprises

Email

Many customer services are provided via email. Here's a few of the most popular and useful.

nuts@ora.com
> For general questions and information.

bookquestions@ora.com
> For technical questions, or corrections, concerning book contents.

order@ora.com
> To order books online and for ordering questions.

catalog@ora.com
> To receive a free copy of our magazine/catalog, "ora.com" (please include a postal address).

Snailmail and phones

O'Reilly & Associates, Inc.
103A Morris Street, Sebastopol, CA 95472
Inquiries: **707-829-0515, 800-998-9938**
Credit card orders: **800-889-8969** (Weekdays 6a.m.- 6p.m. PST)
FAX: **707-829-0104**

O'Reilly & Associates—
LISTING OF TITLES

INTERNET

!%@:: A Directory of Electronic Mail
   Addressing & Networks
Connecting to the Internet: An O'Reilly Buyer's Guide
Internet In A Box
The Mosaic Handbook for Microsoft Windows
The Mosaic Handbook for the Macintosh
The Mosaic Handbook for the X Window System
Smileys
The Whole Internet User's Guide & Catalog

SYSTEM ADMINISTRATION

Computer Security Basics
DNS and BIND
Essential System Administration
Linux Network Administrator's Guide (Winter '94/95 est.)
Managing Internet Information Services
Managing NFS and NIS
Managing UUCP and Usenet
sendmail
Practical UNIX Security
PGP: Pretty Good Privacy (Winter '94/95 est.)
System Performance Tuning
TCP/IP Network Administration
termcap & terminfo
X Window System Administrator's Guide: Volume 8
The X Companion CD for R6 (Winter '94/95 est.)

USING UNIX AND X

BASICS

Learning GNU Emacs
Learning the Korn Shell
Learning the UNIX Operating System
Learning the vi Editor
MH & xmh: Email for Users & Programmers
SCO UNIX in a Nutshell
The USENET Handbook (Winter '94/95 est.)
Using UUCP and Usenet
UNIX in a Nutshell: System V Edition
The X Window System in a Nutshell
X Window System User's Guide: Volume 3
X Window System User's Guide, Motif Ed.: Vol. 3M
X User Tools (with CD-ROM)

ADVANCED

Exploring Expect (Winter 94/95 est.)
The Frame Handbook
Learning Perl
Making TeX Work
Programming perl
sed & awk
UNIX Power Tools (with CD-ROM)

PROGRAMMING UNIX, C, AND MULTI-PLATFORM

FORTRAN/SCIENTIFIC COMPUTING

High Performance Computing
Migrating to Fortran 90
UNIX for FORTRAN Programmers

C PROGRAMMING LIBRARIES

Practical C Programming
POSIX Programmer's Guide
POSIX.4: Programming for the Real World
   (Winter '94/95 est.)
Programming with curses
Understanding and Using COFF
Using C on the UNIX System

C PROGRAMMING TOOLS

Checking C Programs with lint
lex & yacc
Managing Projects with make
Power Programming with RPC
Software Portability with imake

MULTI-PLATFORM PROGRAMMING

Encyclopedia of Graphics File Formats
Distributing Applications Across DCE and
   Windows NT
Guide to Writing DCE Applications
Multi-Platform Code Management
ORACLE Performance Tuning
Understanding DCE
Understanding Japanese Information Processing

BERKELEY 4.4 SOFTWARE DISTRIBUTION

4.4BSD System Manager's Manual
4.4BSD User's Reference Manual
4.4BSD User's Supplementary Documents
4.4BSD Programmer's Reference Manual
4.4BSD Programmer's Supplementary Documents
4.4BSD-Lite CD Companion
4.4BSD-Lite CD Companion: International Version

X PROGRAMMING

Motif Programming Manual: Volume 6A
Motif Reference Manual: Volume 6B
Motif Tools
PEXlib Programming Manual
PEXlib Reference Manual
PHIGS Programming Manual (soft or hard cover)
PHIGS Reference Manual
Programmer's Supplement for Release 6 (Winter '94/95 est.)
Xlib Programming Manual: Volume 1
Xlib Reference Manual: Volume 2
X Protocol Reference Manual, R5: Volume 0
X Protocol Reference Manual, R6: Volume 0
   (Winter '94/95 est.)
X Toolkit Intrinsics Programming Manual: Vol. 4
X Toolkit Intrinsics Programming Manual,
   Motif Edition: Volume 4M
X Toolkit Intrinsics Reference Manual: Volume 5
XView Programming Manual: Volume 7A
XView Reference Manual: Volume 7B

THE X RESOURCE

A QUARTERLY WORKING JOURNAL FOR X PROGRAMMERS

The X Resource: Issues 0 through 13
   (Issue 13 available 1/95)

BUSINESS/CAREER

Building a Successful Software Business
Love Your Job!

TRAVEL

Travelers' Tales Thailand
Travelers' Tales Mexico
Travelers' Tales India (Winter '94/95 est.)

AUDIOTAPES

INTERNET TALK RADIO'S "GEEK OF THE WEEK" INTERVIEWS

The Future of the Internet Protocol, 4 hours
Global Network Operations, 2 hours
Mobile IP Networking, 1 hour
Networked Information and
   Online Libraries, 1 hour
Security and Networks, 1 hour
European Networking, 1 hour

NOTABLE SPEECHES OF THE INFORMATION AGE

John Perry Barlow, 1.5 hours

O'Reilly & Associates—
INTERNATIONAL DISTRIBUTORS

Customers outside North America can now order O'Reilly & Associates books through the following distributors. They offer our international customers faster order processing, more bookstores, increased representation at tradeshows worldwide, and the high-quality, responsive service our customers have come to expect.

EUROPE, MIDDLE EAST, AND AFRICA

(except Germany, Switzerland, and Austria)

INQUIRIES

International Thomson Publishing Europe
Berkshire House
168-173 High Holborn
London WC1V 7AA
United Kingdom
Telephone: 44-71-497-1422
Fax: 44-71-497-1426
Email: ora.orders@itpuk.co.uk

ORDERS

International Thomson Publishing Services, Ltd.
Cheriton House, North Way
Andover, Hampshire SP10 5BE
United Kingdom
Telephone: 44-264-342-832 (UK orders)
Telephone: 44-264-342-806 (outside UK)
Fax: 44-264-364418 (UK orders)
Fax: 44-264-342761 (outside UK)

GERMANY, SWITZERLAND, AND AUSTRIA

International Thomson Publishing GmbH
O'Reilly-International Thomson Verlag
Attn: Mr. G. Miske
Königswinterer Strasse 418
53227 Bonn
Germany
Telephone: 49-228-970240
Fax: 49-228-441342
Email: anfragen@orade.ora.com

THE AMERICAS, JAPAN, AND OCEANIA

O'Reilly & Associates, Inc.
103A Morris Street
Sebastopol, CA 95472 U.S.A.
Telephone: 707-829-0515
Telephone: 800-998-9938 (U.S. & Canada)
Fax: 707-829-0104
Email: order@ora.com

ASIA

(except Japan)

INQUIRIES

International Thomson Publishing Asia
221 Henderson Road
#05 10 Henderson Building
Singapore 0315
Telephone: 65-272-6496
Fax: 65-272-6498

ORDERS

Telephone: 65-268-7867
Fax: 65-268-6727

AUSTRALIA

WoodsLane Pty. Ltd.
Unit 8, 101 Darley Street (P.O. Box 935)
Mona Vale NSW 2103
Australia
Telephone: 61-2-979-5944
Fax: 61-2-997-3348
Email: woods@tmx.mhs.oz.au

NEW ZEALAND

WoodsLane New Zealand Ltd.
21 Cooks Street (P.O. Box 575)
Wanganui, New Zealand
Telephone: 64-6-347-6543
Fax: 64-6-345-4840
Email: woods@tmx.mhs.oz.au

Here's a page we encourage readers to tear out...

O'REILLY WOULD LIKE TO HEAR FROM YOU

Which book did this card come from?

_____

Where did you buy this book?
　❏ Bookstore　　❏ Direct from O'Reilly
　❏ Bundled with hardware/software　　❏ Class/seminar

Your job description:　❏ SysAdmin　❏ Programmer

　❏ Other_____

What computer system do you use?　❏ UNIX
　❏ MAC　❏ DOS(PC)　❏ Other_____

Name _____ Company/Organization Name _____

Address _____

City _____ State _____ Zip/Postal Code _____ Country _____

Telephone _____ Internet or other email address (specify network) _____

Nineteenth century wood engraving
of the horned owl from the O'Reilly
& Associates Nutshell Handbook®
Learning the UNIX Operating System

POST CARD

O'Reilly & Associates, Inc., 103A Morris Street, Sebastopol, CA 95472-9902

BUSINESS REPLY MAIL
FIRST CLASS MAIL   PERMIT NO. 80   SEBASTOPOL, CA

Postage will be paid by addressee

O'Reilly & Associates, Inc.
103A Morris Street
Sebastopol, CA 95472-9902